Principles of
Microeconomics

second canadian edition

ROBERT H. FRANK
Cornell University

BEN S. BERNANKE
Princeton University

LARS OSBERG
Dalhousie University

MELVIN L. CROSS
Dalhousie University

BRIAN K. MacLEAN
Laurentian University

McGraw-Hill Ryerson

Toronto Montréal Boston Burr Ridge, IL Dubuque, IA Madison, WI New York San Francisco
St. Louis Bangkok Bogotá Caracas Kuala Lumpur Lisbon London Madrid Mexico City
Milan New Delhi Santiago Seoul Singapore Sydney Taipei

The McGraw·Hill Companies

Mc
Graw
Hill **McGraw-Hill
Ryerson**

Principles of Microeconomics
Second Canadian Edition

ISBN-13: 987-0-07-088915-6
ISBN-10: 0-07-088915-5

3 4 5 6 7 8 9 10   TCP   0 9 8

Printed and bound in Canada

Vice President, Editorial and Media Technology: Pat Ferrier
Executive Sponsoring Editor: Lynn Fisher
Economics Editor: Ron Doleman
Developmental Editor: Daphne Scriabin
Senior Marketing Manager: Kelly Smyth
Senior Supervising Editor: Margaret Henderson
Copy Editor: Gillian Scobie
Production Coordinator: Paula Brown
Composition: Bookman Typesetting Company
Cover Design: Dianna Little
Printer: Transcontinental Printing Group

Statistics Canada information is used with permission of the Ministry of Industry, as Minister responsible for Statistics Canada. Information on the availability of the wider range of data from Statistics Canada can be obtained from Statistics Canada's Regional Offices, its World Wide Web site at http://statcan.ca, and its toll-free access number 1-800-263-1136.

Library and Archives Canada Cataloguing in Publication

Principles of microeconomics / Robert H. Frank ... [et al.]. — 2nd Canadian ed.

Includes bibliographical references and index.
ISBN 0-07-088915-5

1. Microeconomics—Textbooks.   I. Frank, Robert H.

HB172.P75 2004   338.5   C2004-905767-7

About the Authors

 **Robert H. Frank** received his B.S. from Georgia Tech in 1966, then taught math and science for two years as a Peace Corps Volunteer in rural Nepal. He received his M.A. in statistics and his Ph.D. in economics in 1972 from The University of California at Berkeley. He is the Goldwin Smith Professor of Economics at Cornell University, where he has taught since 1972 and where he currently holds a joint appointment in the department of economics and the Johnson Graduate School of Management. During leaves of absence from Cornell he served as chief economist for the Civil Aeronautics Board (1978–1980), a Fellow at the Center for Advanced Study in the Behavioral Sciences (1992–93), and Professor of American Civilization at l'École des Hautes Études en Sciences Sociales in Paris (2000–01).

Professor Frank is the author of a best-selling intermediate economics textbook—*Microeconomics and Behavior*, Fourth Edition (Irwin/McGraw-Hill, 2000). He has published on a variety of subjects, including price and wage discrimination, public utility pricing, the measurement of unemployment spell lengths, and the distributional consequences of direct foreign investment. His research has focused on rivalry and cooperation in economic and social behavior.

 **Lars Osberg** is currently the McCulloch Professor of Economics at Dalhousie University. He was born and raised in Ottawa, Ontario. As an undergraduate, he attended Queen's University, Kingston and the London School of Economics and Political Science, graduating from Queen's in 1968. From 1968 to 1970 he served as a CUSO volunteer, working primarily with the Tanzania Sisal Corporation in Tanga, Tanzania. He received his Ph.D. in Economics from Yale University in 1975.

His first book was *Economic Inequality in Canada* (1981), which has been followed by nine others, most recently *The Unemployment Crisis: All for Naught* (1996) (with Brian MacLean), *Hard Money, Hard Times* (1998) (with P. Fortin) and *The Economic Implications of Social Cohesion* (Editor) 2003. He is also the author of numerous refereed articles, book chapters, reviews, reports and miscellaneous publications. His major fields of research interest have been the measurement and determinants of poverty and economic well being, with particular emphasis in recent years on social policy and the implications of changing patterns of working time. Among other professional responsibilities, he was president of the Canadian Economics Association in 1999/2000 and is now Review Editor for the *Review of Income and Wealth*.

 **Ben S. Bernanke** received his B.A. in economics from Harvard University in 1975 and his Ph.D. in economics from MIT in 1979. He taught at the Stanford Graduate School of Business from 1979 to 1985 and moved to Princeton University in 1985, where he is the Howard Harrison and Gabrielle Snyder Beck Professor of Economics and Public Affairs, and currently Chairman of the Economics Department. He has consulted for the Board of Governors of the European Central Bank and other central banks, and he serves on a U.S. State Department Committee that advises the Israeli government on economic policy. He is a Fellow of the Econometrics Society and a Research Associate for the National Bureau of Economic Research. He has been a visiting scholar at the Federal Reserve System in Boston, Philadelphia, and New York, and he is currently an advisor to the Federal Reserve Bank of New York.

Professor Bernanke's intermediate textbook, with Andrew Abel, *Macroeconomics*, Third Edition (Addison-Wesley, 1998) is a best seller in its field.

 **Melvin L. Cross** received an Associate of Arts degree from Dawson Community College in 1968, a B.A. from the University of Montana in 1970, an M.A. from Simon Fraser University in 1972, and a Ph.D. in economics from Texas A&M University in 1976. He is an Associate Professor in the Department of Economics at Dalhousie University, which he joined in 1975. He also holds an adjunct appointment in the School of Resource and Environmental Studies and was an Associate Fellow in the Foundation Year Program of the University of King's College from 1991 to 2002. In 1994–95, he was a Visiting Adjunct Associate Professor at Queen's University and in 2002 he was a Visiting Lecturer at the University of Sydney. His teaching and research interests are in the economics of natural and environmental resources and the history of economic thought. He has taught principles of economics throughout his career. He is an author or co-author of articles in the *Canadian Journal of Fisheries and Aquatic Science*, *Canadian Public Policy*, *History of Political Economy*, *Marine Resource Economics*, and other journals.

 **Brian K. MacLean** is Professor and Chair of Economics at Laurentian University in Sudbury, Ontario, where he has been Director of the Institute of Northern Ontario Research and Development and the organizer of an annual economic policy conference series. He speaks Japanese as a second language and has been a visiting professor at Hokkaido University in Sapporo, Japan, and at Saitama University, just outside of Tokyo. He has edited *Out of Control? Canada in an Unstable Financial World* (Lorimer, 1999), co-edited *The Unemployment Crisis: All for Naught?* (McGill-Queen's, 1996) and has published in the *Cambridge Journal of Economics*, *Review of Income and Wealth*, *Canadian Business Economics*, and other journals. His keen interest in economic policy issues is reflected in these publications and also in the monthly economics columns he has written for the *National Post* for two years.

Dedication

For Ellen R. H. F.

For Anna B. S. B.

For Molly L. S. O.

For Carmelita, Anna, Nathan, and Thomas M. L. C.

For Kathleen and Vera, in memory of Ken B. K. M.

Brief Contents

Contents

Preface

Feedback from users of the First Edition supports our conviction that there is a different, and better, way to introduce beginning students to economics. In its bare bones, the philosophy of this text rests on two pillars: (1) the development and repeated application of a set of core economic principles and (2) an active, student-centred approach to learning.

THE FIRST PILLAR: REPEATED USE OF CORE PRINCIPLES

The best way to teach introductory economics—or to introduce virtually any subject, for that matter—is to expose students to repeated applications of a short list of the core ideas of the discipline. Of course, if we asked a thousand economists to provide their own versions, we would get a thousand different lists. But we suspect that almost all the lists would start from much the same basic problem, that of scarcity, and would use much the same basic principle, that of comparing costs and benefits.

> **The Scarcity Problem:** Although we have boundless needs and wants, the resources available to us are limited. So having more of one good thing usually means having less of another.

> **The Cost–Benefit Principle:** An individual (or a firm or a society) will be better off taking an action if, and only if, the extra benefits from taking the action are greater than the extra costs.

From this basic starting point, five other important principles follow:

> **The Principle of Relevant Costs:** In considering whether to produce or consume more of a good, what matters is the cost of one more unit (marginal cost).

> **The Principle of Comparative Advantage:** Total output is largest when each person (or each country) concentrates on the activities for which his or her opportunity cost is lowest.

> **The Principle of Increasing Opportunity Cost:** In expanding the production of any good, first employ those resources with the lowest opportunity cost. Only when all of the lowest cost resources are employed does it make economic sense to use resources that have higher opportunity costs.

> **The Efficiency Principle:** Economic efficiency occurs when total economic surplus is maximized. Efficiency is an important social goal because, when the economic pie grows larger, everyone can potentially have a larger slice.

> **The Equilibrium Principle:** A market in equilibrium leaves no incentives no unexploited opportunities for individuals but may not exploit all gains achievable through collective action.

Our point is not that this is the best short list, but that the introductory course will be taught most effectively if it begins with a well-articulated short list of some principles, illustrating and applying each principle in many different contexts.

THE SECOND PILLAR: ACTIVE LEARNING

Our second guiding principle has been that active learning by students—"student-centred" learning, in the jargon—is an essential part of an effective learning process. By "learning" we do not mean being able to answer a test question the next day. By the time they reach university, many students have become quite good at quick memorization—and at forgetting "useless stuff" equally rapidly. Even the brightest students never fully internalize a concept unless they actually use it repeatedly. We think it is useful for instructors to ask themselves: "What do I want my students to retain from this course, five, ten, or twenty years from now?" Our reading of research in education is that long-term retention depends on students both seeing the value of a concept and *actively* using it. So, throughout the book we use a number of devices to foster active learning.

1. **Worked Examples.** New ideas and concepts are not simply asserted, as in most books. Instead, they are introduced by means of simple examples, usually numerical, which are developed step by step in the text. These examples display the reasoning process used to reach the economic conclusion or insight, and they provide a model for the student to apply when working exercises and problems.

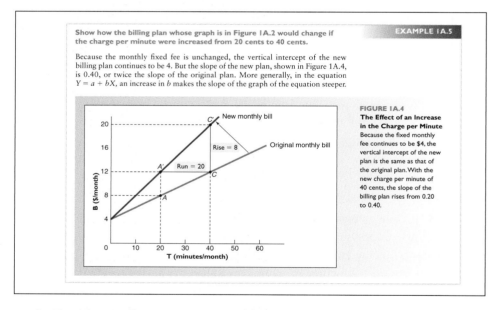

EXAMPLE 1A.5

Show how the billing plan whose graph is in Figure 1A.2 would change if the charge per minute were increased from 20 cents to 40 cents.

Because the monthly fixed fee is unchanged, the vertical intercept of the new billing plan continues to be 4. But the slope of the new plan, shown in Figure 1A.4, is 0.40, or twice the slope of the original plan. More generally, in the equation $Y = a + bX$, an increase in b makes the slope of the graph of the equation steeper.

FIGURE 1A.4
The Effect of an Increase in the Charge per Minute
Because the fixed monthly fee continues to be $4, the vertical intercept of the new plan is the same as that of the original plan. With the new charge per minute of 40 cents, the slope of the billing plan rises from 0.20 to 0.40.

2. **Exercises.** Following many examples, and indeed throughout each chapter, we pose exercises in the running text that challenge the student to test and extend his or her understanding of the ideas being discussed. Answers to these exercises are provided at the end of the chapter, allowing immediate feedback.

Ground beef with high fat content is another example of an inferior good. For health reasons, most people prefer grades of meat with low fat content, and when they do buy high-fat meats it is usually a sign of budgetary pressure. When people in this situation receive higher incomes, they usually switch quickly to leaner grades of meat.

EXERCISE 3.2

Normal and inferior goods were defined in terms of how their demand curves are affected by an increase in income. How will a *decrease* in income affect the demand for a normal good? an inferior good?

Preferences, or tastes, are another important factor that determines whether a given good will meet the cost–benefit test. Steven Spielberg's films *Jurassic Park* and *The Lost World* appeared to kindle a powerful, if previously latent, preference among children for toy dinosaurs. In the wake of these films, the demand for such toys shifted sharply to the right. And the same children who couldn't find enough dinosaur toys suddenly seemed to lose interest in toy designs involving horses and other pres-

3. **Anecdotes and Illustrations.** Active learning is more likely to take place when students are engaged and motivated. We begin every chapter with an anecdote that motivates the discussion, and we illustrate the ideas with memorable cartoons, photographs, and original line drawings. Most important, we have striven to minimize jargon and engage the student with direct, friendly writing. (For examples, see pages 2, 189, and 304.)

4. **Recap Boxes and Summaries.** To keep students focused on the forest as well as the trees, at strategic points in each chapter we have provided "recap boxes." Recaps summarize the main ideas of the previous section. The recap boxes are also reiterated by bulleted end-of-chapter summaries, which are designed to review the most important concepts presented in the chapter.

If the Petro Canada station on Quinpool Road raised its gasoline prices by 1 cent/litre, would all its customers shop elsewhere?

> **RECAP   COMPARATIVE ADVANTAGE AND INTERNATIONAL TRADE**
>
> Nations, like individuals, can benefit from exchange, even though one trading partner may be more productive than the other in absolute terms. The greater the difference between domestic opportunity costs and world opportunity costs, the more a nation can potentially benefit from exchange with other nations. But expansions of exchange do not guarantee that each individual citizen will do better. Unskilled workers in high-wage countries may be hurt in the short run by the reduction of barriers to trade with low-wage nations. International trade may also raise issues about the distribution of benefits between trading partners, national sovereignty, and the extent to which an existing pattern of comparative advantage might change over time.

5. **Core Principles Icon.** Throughout the book, whenever one of the core principles is discussed, a small icon appears in the margin. Each core principle is thereby reinforced many times.

> **MARGINAL REVENUE FOR THE MONOPOLIST**
>
>
> COST–BENEFIT
>
> The logic of profit maximization is precisely the same for the monopolist as for the perfectly competitive firm. In both cases, the firm increases output as long as the benefit of doing so exceeds the cost. The calculation of marginal cost is also precisely the same for the monopolist as for the perfectly competitive firm. *The only significant difference between the two cases concerns the calculation of marginal revenue.*
>
> As we saw in Chapter 5, marginal revenue for a competitive firm is simply the market price. If that price is $6, then the marginal benefit of selling an extra unit

6. **Review Questions and Problems.** Questions for review at the end of each chapter encourage the student to test his or her understanding of the main ideas of the chapter. End-of-chapter problems are carefully crafted to help students internalize and extend core concepts.

ECONOMIC NATURALISM

Economics is all around us, every day. Economics is fascinating because of its power to explain. As part of the active-learning approach, we encourage students to become "economic naturalists," who employ basic economic principles to understand and explain what they see around them in the "laboratory of life." Studying biology enables people to observe and marvel at many details of the natural environment that would otherwise have escaped notice. For the naturalist, a walk in a quiet wood becomes an adventure. In much the same way, studying economics can enable students to see the world in which they live and work in a new light. Throughout the text, Economic Naturalist examples show students the relevance of economics to their world—how economics can help them to understand (and perhaps improve) the world they live in. For example:

1. Why do some countries have more problems with littering than others?
2. Why do many movie theatres offer discount tickets to students?
3. Why does a house with a view cost more in Vancouver than in Prince Rupert?
4. Why does Céline Dion earn millions more than singers of only slightly lesser ability?

3.1   ECONOMIC NATURALIST

Why has the consumption of French fries increased substantially during the last 25 years?

Commercial techniques for peeling, cutting, cooking, and storing French fries are much more sophisticated now than they were 25 years ago. Today, raw potatoes are processed into French fries in a few large plants, frozen, and shipped to restaurants and consumers. Once in restaurants and homes, French fries are easily cooked. In the United States, consumption of potatoes has increased by about 30 percent since 1977, most of it because Americans are eating more French fries and potato chips.[3]

In Figure 3.9, the curves labelled S and D depict the supply and demand curves for French fries during the late 1970s. The curve S' represents the supply curve today. The increase in supply is the result of technological improvements in the production of French fries. As the graph shows, the equilibrium quantity of French fries has increased, and the price has decreased.

5. How does comparative advantage arise and why might countries *not* take advantage of it?
6. Why does London, England, impose a tax of £5 on every vehicle that enters the central business district during business hours?

Once students realize that they can pose and answer such questions on their own, they often are hooked. The excitement of discovery provides its own motivation. A student who tastes this excitement is much more likely to use economics long after completing an introductory course. We cannot claim that every student who uses our text will continuously improve his understanding of economics throughout the rest of his life. However, we do believe that our book will help an instructor come closer to this ideal, and even modest progress toward the ideal is a worthy objective. Our students will journey deep into the twenty-first century. What an instructor accomplishes in the classroom may prove to be the most enduring part of her professional legacy.

WHAT IS NEW AND IMPROVED IN THIS EDITION

All of the chapters in *Principles of Microeconomics* have been extensively revised. In some places, clarity is improved by cutting: we have reduced the text by about thirty pages and the number of chapters from sixteen to fifteen. However, we have also added important topics.

CHAPTER 1 THINKING LIKE AN ECONOMIST

Chapter 1 merges Chapters 1 and 2 of the First Canadian Edition. The opening discussions of opportunity cost and economic models have been streamlined, but the chapter retains the discussion of pitfalls to economic reasoning that was the subject of the old Chapter 2. Since many students are rightly concerned with environmental issues, Chapter 1 contains a new Economic Naturalist case on littering—specifically, the problem of discarded beer cans and abandoned cars. We develop the idea that littering is influenced by the opportunity costs facing people, which in turn are influenced by public policy (sometimes sub-optimally). The new Chapter 1 is about 40 percent shorter than the combined length of Chapters 1 and 2 in the First Canadian Edition.

CHAPTER 2 COMPARATIVE ADVANTAGE: THE BASIS FOR EXCHANGE

A new introductory example stresses that the gains from trade depend on comparative advantage, not absolute advantage. We develop the theme of potential surplus from trade at both the micro and macro levels—and we note the potential importance of dynamic comparative advantage for international trade.

CHAPTER 3 SUPPLY AND DEMAND: AN INTRODUCTION

Supply and Demand are central concepts in economics but they are often introduced using examples that are confined entirely to the sphere of microeconomics. In this revision, we develop an example of supply and demand in such a market (hamburgers in downtown Toronto)—but we also show how supply and demand can explain foreign exchange rates. Our treatment of foreign-exchange rates builds naturally on the previous chapter's discussion of comparative advantage and international trade, and it provides students with an early introduction to the importance of international trade for the Canadian economy. As well, a new Economic Naturalist case (based on the fast-food industry and the changing technology of producing French fries) explains how advances in technology can shift the supply curve.

CHAPTER 4 DEMAND: THE BENEFIT SIDE OF THE MARKET

The price elasticity of demand is a crucial conceptual tool for analyzing markets, but markets are not all the same—so this chapter now includes empirical estimates of price elasticity of demand for ten goods and services. A new table then summarizes the effect of a price change on total expenditure for different price elasticities of demand. The chapter also includes a new discussion of the income and substitution effects—and a new Economic Naturalist on complementary goods (why do some bars give away peanuts but charge more for their beer?).

CHAPTER 5 PERFECTLY COMPETITIVE SUPPLY: THE COST SIDE OF THE MARKET

Throughout the text a number of recurring examples provide continuity. Picking up on the problem of beer can litter in Chapter 1, we discuss in Chapter 5 the profit-maximization problem facing bottle producers. A thorough revision has improved the display of key tables and graphs, and we now discuss the price elasticity of supply in this chapter instead of jointly with the price elasticity of demand.

CHAPTER 6 EFFICIENCY AND EXCHANGE

The central message of this chapter is the efficiency argument for voluntary exchange. We have clarified the discussion of the loss in economic surplus from price controls, and we use the example of rent controls to show how both the redistributional impact and the magnitude of the loss in surplus arising from controls depend on the elasticity of demand and supply. In our discussion of the deadweight loss from taxation, a new Economic Naturalist case (Gandhi's march to the sea in 1930 to protest the excise tax on salt) provides an illustration of the incidence of a tax (and its political implications). Denmark's excise tax on automobiles provides a modern day Economic Naturalist case that illustrates the incidence of a tax and its environmental impact.

CHAPTER 7 THE QUEST FOR PROFIT AND THE INVISIBLE HAND

As in other chapters, the presentation has been clarified and streamlined. The chapter now includes an expanded discussion of economies of scale and long-run equilibrium.

CHAPTER 8 MONOPOLY AND OTHER FORMS OF IMPERFECT COMPETITION

Chapter 8 now includes new graphical analyses of monopolistic competition, price discrimination, and the impact of a shift of marginal cost on a monopolist's price and quantity. A new Economic Naturalist case uses monopolistic competition to analyze the differentiation of single malt Scotches. Another new case explores how, in the past, drug companies could segment their Canadian and

American markets, while now, the appearance of Internet pharmacies has reduced their ability to price discriminate. The chapter also includes a new discussion of network economies and updates the discussion of fixed cost and market share in the market for video game consoles.

CHAPTER 9 THINKING STRATEGICALLY

Game theory has had a revolutionary impact on many aspects of economics—we do not think it should be treated as a minor issue, under the general heading of "imperfect competition." We have rewritten this chapter extensively, updating examples and clarifying the role of norms of behaviour as devices that coordinate behaviour in game solutions.

CHAPTER 10 EXTERNALITIES AND PROPERTY RIGHTS

The new Chapter 10 emphasizes much more clearly the reciprocal nature of externalities and links externalities more tightly with opportunity costs. The chapter also includes a new example concerning the external costs that might arise from production of genetically modified barley. A new Economic Naturalist case discusses the tax of £5 that London imposes on every vehicle that enters the central business district during business hours, thereby showing how prices can be used to deal with congestion externalities.

CHAPTER 11 THE ECONOMICS OF INFORMATION

Abandoned cars were discussed as an environmental problem in Chapter 1, but how can one be sure, when buying a used car, that it will not prove to be a lemon? Chapter 11 now starts with the problem faced by every purchaser of a used car. It shows how that problem illustrates two central issues in the economics of information: what is the optimal amount of information to acquire? When information is inherently asymmetric, how is economic behaviour affected? The chapter analyzes both issues and develops their implications for adverse selection and market structure in a variety of markets.

CHAPTER 12 LABOUR MARKETS

Students are vitally interested in how wages are determined. This chapter shows how the concepts of human capital and marginal productivity can partially explain wage differentials—and an Economic Naturalist (and a short appendix) shows students how to calculate the net present value of their own university education. Building on the analysis of imperfect information in Chapter 11, this chapter also develops the ideas of observationally equivalent workers and statistical discrimination.

CHAPTER 13 THE ECONOMICS OF PUBLIC POLICY

The section on regulation of a natural monopoly includes a new graphical analysis, which compares monopoly, cost-plus, and subsidized marginal cost pricing. The chapter builds on the discussion of externalities in Chapter 10 to analyze effluent charges as a pollution abatement strategy, and it uses the implications of asymmetric information developed in Chapter 11 to analyze health care policy. It also discusses the pricing of public services and the dilemmas surrounding the taxation or regulation of addictive commodities.

CHAPTER 14 PUBLIC GOODS AND TAXATION

All statistics have been updated and the discussion of public goods, publicly supplied private goods, and the regulation of externalities has been clarified.

CHAPTER 15 INCOME DISTRIBUTION

All statistics have been updated and a new discussion of the distribution of wealth included. There are new, clearer presentations of how to measure the intensity of poverty, of the criteria of distributional equity, and of alternative anti-poverty policies.

EVIDENCE MATTERS

Getting students to appreciate the power of economic theory and the importance of a few simple economic principles is a crucial goal of an introductory course, but economics would be a very simple (and dull) subject if all markets could be analyzed in terms of the intersection of two straight lines—a supply curve sloping up at 45 degrees and a demand curve sloping down at 45 degrees. If that were all there was to it, there would be hardly any point in having upper level courses in economics, since all markets would be the same. If all markets were the same, all problems of economic policy could be similarly solved, from the comfort of an armchair—by anybody who had taken the one all-purpose economics course that universities (or high schools) would teach.

However, practising economists know that much of the intellectual fascination of economics comes from the variety of contexts in which economic principles are useful as well as the interplay of theory and data. As instructors, we think that it is a big mistake in an introductory text not to let students in on this interplay, in part because many students (particularly the smarter ones) are turned off by the unrealism of a "one size fits all" approach. Hence, we return continually to the theme that "evidence matters." For example, we now present in Chapter 4 empirical estimates of the price elasticity of demand for a variety of commodities and we show in Chapter 6 how the costs of rent controls in lost economic surplus depend crucially on the elasticity of demand and supply. Chapters 12 and 15 similarly note how the costs and benefits of minimum wage legislation depend crucially on the empirical magnitude of the disemployment effects of minimum wages. Only data can tell us if any effects are large or small. A key refrain running through the text is to respect the empirical evidence.

THOROUGHLY MODERN MICRO

Pedagogy is extremely important because a text that does not communicate effectively is pointless. But the decision about *what* to teach is at least as important as the decision of *how* to teach it. Because we believe that a central concern of economics is efficiency, we have devoted extensive space to the concept of economic surplus. Introduced in Chapter 1 and applied repeatedly in Chapters 2 to 5, this concept is developed more fully in Chapter 6 than in any leading introductory text. Throughout the book, the concept of economic surplus underlies our ongoing argument in support of economic efficiency as an important social goal. We stress that maximizing economic surplus aids the achievement of *all* goals, both public and private. We also note that if society is to preserve the institutions that enable economic surplus to be maximized, some agreement about the equity of the distribution of economic returns is essential.

Our book also emphasizes, from start to finish, the implications of economic theory for individual decision making. Chapter 1, for example, starts by discussing three widespread and important pitfalls: the tendency to ignore opportunity costs, the tendency not to ignore sunk costs, and the tendency to confuse average and marginal costs and benefits. Chapter 15 concludes by noting how the effectiveness of minimum wages as an anti-poverty policy depends partly on the wage elasticity of demand for labour. Throughout the book, we call students' attention to situations in which economic theory can help them analyze individual and social choices.

An introductory course in economics should help two types of students: those who will never take another economics course should be able to understand the world around them; and continuing students should be prepared for some of the ideas they will encounter in more advanced courses. We are troubled that many people receive postsecondary degrees without ever having been exposed to ideas like the prisoner's dilemma or the tragedy of the commons. These and other simple applications of game theory have enormous power to explain events in the world. They are also ideal vehicles for illustrating several of the core ideas of economics—ideas that are hugely important in modern courses in microeconomic theory, industrial organization, international trade, etc.

In Chapter 9, we introduce students to the principles of games and strategic behaviour in a highly intuitive way that does not rely on formal mathematics. We develop a limited number of simple principles that have proved entirely accessible to first-year students. In our experience, students are delighted to learn that these few principles can explain, among other things, why urban highways are too crowded, why whales have been hunted to near extinction, why North Atlantic fisheries are near collapse, why the ozone layer is in danger, and why the National Hockey League has a helmet rule. Similarly, Chapter 11 develops some of the key issues in the economics of information. These ideas have had an enormous influence on other areas of economics (e.g., macro, labour, public finance, and development). In Chapter 12 we show how these ideas help to explain discrimination in the labour market, and in Chapter 13 we illustrate their importance for understanding Canada's current debates on public policy in health care.

ORGANIZATION OF TOPICS

Principles of Microeconomics is divided into four parts. Part 1, which also appears in *Principles of Macroeconomics,* is composed of three chapters. Parts 2–4 are composed of four chapters each. Many Canadian examples are used to illustrate microeconomic principles and policies, and some are noted here.

Part 1 introduces students to the most basic ideas of economics, including the core principles that are used throughout the book. Chapter 1 focuses on the ideas of scarcity, tradeoffs, costs, and benefits, including the fundamental notion that the desirability of any action depends on its marginal costs and benefits. Opportunity cost is introduced with a discussion of the appropriate size of a class in principles of economics, which provides an opportunity to discuss how Canadian universities have responded to the scarcity of resources they face. As mentioned earlier, Chapter 1 also examines some common pitfalls for decision-makers, such as the sunk cost fallacy. Following Chapter 1 is a brief appendix that reviews the basic mathematical tools—working with equations, graphs, and tables—students will need for the course. Chapter 2 introduces the ideas of specialization and gains from trade. Finally, Chapter 3 provides an introductory overview of the tools of supply-and-demand analysis—and we emphasize the generality of these tools by showing how they apply both to markets limited to the microeconomic sphere (like the market for hamburgers in Toronto) and to markets that have macroeconomic implications (like markets for foreign exchange). The development of Canada's pulp-and-paper industry, the basis of one of our Economic Naturalist cases, is used to illustrate the principle of dynamic comparative advantage.

Part 2 explores in detail the concepts of demand, supply, economic surplus, and efficiency in the context of pure competition. Building on the introduction to supply and demand in Chapter 3, Chapter 4 shows how demand curves illustrate how people spend their limited income in rational ways. This chapter also discusses price elasticity of demand and its uses. Chapter 5 turns to the sellers' side of the market, showing how upward-sloping supply curves follow from profit-maximizing decisions by producers. Chapter 6 develops the concept of economic surplus and explains Adam Smith's crucial insight: when demand and supply curves fully reflect social benefits and costs, competitive markets maximize economic surplus. Finally, Chapter 7 clarifies how the quest for profit can drive competitive firms to provide a socially efficient allocation of resources. As well, the discussion of price controls includes an analysis of the National Energy Program of 1980, which was the Trudeau government's response to the oil price shocks of the 1970s.

In our revision of this text, we have paid close attention to the excellent comments/critiques of a panel of referees and early users. Since most Canadian courses in principles of microeconomics develop short-run and long-run cost curves, Chapter 5 includes a section that shows how the law of diminishing marginal returns shapes the graphs of short-run marginal and average costs, and how average fixed cost decreases as output increases. Chapter 7 provides a discussion of how, in a perfectly competitive market, entry and exit cause firms to operate at minimum long-run average cost. Graphs of long-run average cost are included. Some instructors may prefer to de-emphasize cost curves in order to reinforce basic applications of opportunity cost. Chapters 5 and 7 are designed so those instructors who prefer to concentrate on other topics can omit detailed treatments of cost curves.

Part 3 studies markets that depart from the ideal of pure competition. Chapter 8 examines the implications of monopolistic, oligopolistic, and monopolistically competitive markets. When only a few producers exist in a market—and in many other noncompetitive situations—behaviour often takes on a strategic component, so Chapter 9 introduces some elementary tools of game theory, demonstrating their applicability to a variety of economic situations. Chapter 10 considers the effects of externalities. We show that elementary game theory—including the ideas of the prisoner's dilemma, the arms race, and the tragedy of the commons—is quite useful for analyzing many situations with externalities. Chapter 11 examines incomplete and asymmetric information. The examples of the "lemons" problem in the used-car market, and statistical discrimination between young males and females in the market for automobile insurance provide clear evidence of the relevance of economics to issues that our target audience is likely to have experienced.

Finally, Part 4, on applied economics and public policy, uses the tools that have been developed in parts 1 through 3 to approach some issues of applied economics and economic policy. In addition, it explores a number of Canadian issues. For example, about 70 percent of employed Canadian women work in nursing and related health occupations, teaching, clerical, administrative, sales, and service positions. Chapter 12 tackles differentials in pay using the tools developed earlier—human capital investment, marginal productivity, imperfect information, and positional externalities—and includes a discussion of occupational segregation and Canadian policies that attempt to deal with it. Chapter 13 shows how economic principles can be used to design economic policies that mitigate the effects of market imperfections, including competition policy as well as policies about health care and the environment. The discussion of public policy includes a comparison of the Canadian and American health care systems. Although many introductory texts gloss over the distinctions between federal, provincial, and municipal governments, Canada is a federal state, with a relatively high degree of decentralization (compared to other federal states); examples in Part 4 present this reality. Chapter 14 discusses public goods and taxation, as well as broader issues concerning the government's role in the economy. It also notes that total program spending by the provinces now greatly exceeds that of the federal government, and we examine the reasons why this pattern has emerged. Chapter 15 considers the benefits and pitfalls of government policies to redistribute income and reduce poverty. As well, we note Canada's success in reducing poverty among senior citizens and we examine the complexities of designing adequate policies for children and for Canadians of working age. In all these chapters we emphasize the importance of differences between markets and how such differences imply that no one public policy can solve all social problems.

TECHNOLOGY SOLUTIONS

ONLINE LEARNING CENTRE

More and more students are studying online. That is why we offer an Online Learning Centre (OLC) that follows *Principles of Microeconomics* chapter by chapter. You don't have to build or maintain anything and it's ready to go the moment you and your students type in the URL:

www.mcgrawhill.ca/college/frankbernanke

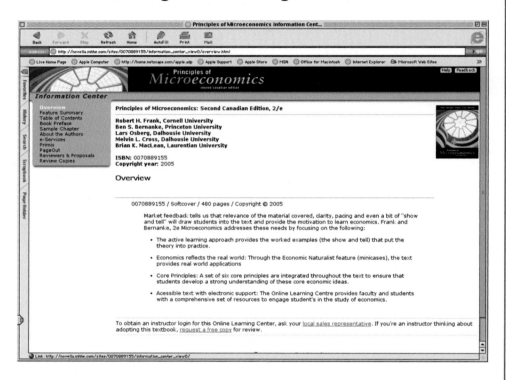

As your students study, they can refer to the OLC Web site for such benefits as:

- Cyber Lectures
- CBC Video Segments
- Video Cases
- Data Update Links
- Internet Application Questions
- Chapter Outlines
- Glossary and Key Terms
- Chapter Summary
- Practice Activities
- Separate Pre- and Post-tests
- Interactive Graphing Exercises
- Economic Naturalist Exercises
- Sample Exam Questions
- Internet Resource Sites
- Concept Maps
- Study to Go

Remember, the *Principles of Microeconomics* OLC content is flexible enough to use with any course management platform currently available. If your department or school is already using a platform, we can help. For information on our course management services, contact your *i*-Learning Sales Specialist or see "Superior Service" on page xxix.

CLASSROOM PERFORMANCE SYSTEM (CPS)

Bring interactivity into the classroom or lecture hall.

CPS by eInstruction is a student response system using wireless connectivity. It gives instructors and students immediate feedback from the entire class. The response pads are remotes that are easy to use and engage students.

- CPS helps you to increase **student preparation, interactivity, and active learning** so you can receive immediate feedback and know what students understand.
- CPS allows you to administer quizzes and tests, and provide **immediate grading**.
- With CPS, you can create lecture questions that can be multiple choice, true/false, and subjective. You can even create questions on the fly as well as conduct group activities.
- CPS not only allows you to **evaluate classroom attendance, activity, and grading** for your course as a whole, but CPS Online allows you to provide students with an immediate study guide. All results and scores can easily be imported into Excel and can be used with various classroom management systems.

CPS-ready content is available for use with Frank & Bernanke *Principles of Microeconomics*. Please contact your *i*-Learning Sales Specialist for more information on how you can integrate CPS into your microeconomics classroom.

MOBILE LEARNING

Study To Go   The businesses and companies of today want their new employees to be adept in all aspects of the changing business environment. They are quick to tell us they want graduates with the skills of tomorrow . . . today. From laptops to cell phones to PDAs, the new medium is mobility.

As a leader in technology and innovation, McGraw-Hill Ryerson has developed material providing students with optimum flexibility for use anytime, anywhere they need to study—whether with a laptop, PDA, or tablet. These innovations provide instructors with a number of exciting ways to integrate technology into the learning process.

With **Study To Go** we have introduced wireless activities as a part of our Online Learning Centre. Now, whether you are waiting in line, riding on transit, or just filling some spare time, homework and practice are just a click away.

McGraw-Hill's **Study To Go**

COURSE MANAGEMENT

PageOut McGraw-Hill Ryerson's course management system, PageOut, is the easiest way to create a Web site for your microeconomics course. There is no need for HTML coding, graphic design, or a thick how-to book. Just fill in a series of boxes in plain English and click on one of our professional designs. In no time, your course is online!

For the integrated instructor, we offer *Principles of Microeconomics* content for complete online courses. Whatever your needs, you can customize the *Principles of Microeconomics* Online Learning Centre content and author your own online course materials. It is entirely up to you. You can offer online discussion and message boards that will complement your office hours, and reduce the lines outside your door.

Content cartridges are also available for course management systems, such as **WebCT** and **Blackboard**. Ask your *i*-Learning Sales Specialist for details.

GradeSummit GradeSummit is a self-assessment, diagnostic service helping students make the most efficient use of their study time. This Internet service provides many ways for students to analyze what they know and do not know to quickly discover those subject areas where study time will help most. GradeSummit reveals subject strengths and weaknesses and provides feedback and direction, which enables students to focus their study time.

The ability to create automatically graded quizzes provides a vehicle to you, the instructor, to make accountable homework assignments.

GradeSummit's diagnostic reports yield valuable data about student understanding of the course material. With as little as an hour per term, you can create graded homework assignments, use a variety of reporting features, download homework scores to use with your existing grade book, and know you have given your students a service they will thank you for. Try it today at *www.gradesummit.com,* or for more information, contact us at info@gradesummit.com.

SUPERIOR SERVICE

SUPERIOR SERVICE

Service takes on a whole new meaning with McGraw-Hill Ryerson and *Principles of Microeconomics*. More than just bringing you the textbook, we have consistently raised the bar in terms of innovation and educational research–both in economics and in education in general. These investments in learning and the education community have helped us to understand the needs of students and educators across the country, and allowed us to foster the growth of truly innovative, integrated learning.

INTEGRATED LEARNING

Your Integrated Learning Sales Specialist is a McGraw-Hill Ryerson representative who has the experience, product knowledge, training, and support to help you assess and integrate any of our products, technology, and services into your course for optimum teaching and learning performance. Whether it's using our test bank software, helping your students improve their grades, or putting your entire course online, your *i*-Learning Sales Specialist is there to help you do it. Contact your *i*-Learning Sales Specialist today to learn how to maximize all of McGraw-Hill Ryerson's resources!

i-LEARNING ADVANTAGE

McGraw-Hill Ryerson offers a unique *i*-Service package designed for Canadian faculty. Our mission is to equip providers of higher education with superior tools and resources required for excellence in teaching. For additional information, visit *www.mcgrawhill.ca/highereducation/eservices*.

TEACHING, TECHNOLOGY & LEARNING CONFERENCE SERIES

The educational environment has changed tremendously in recent years, and McGraw-Hill Ryerson continues to be committed to helping you acquire the skills you need to succeed in this new milieu. Our innovative Teaching, Technology & Learning Conference Series brings faculty together from across Canada with 3M Teaching Excellence award winners to share teaching and learning best practices in a collaborative and stimulating environment. Pre-conference workshops on general topics, such as teaching large classes and technology integration, will also be offered. We will also work with you at your own institution to customize workshops that best suit the needs of your faculty.

RESEARCH REPORTS INTO MOBILE LEARNING AND STUDENT SUCCESS

These landmark reports, undertaken in conjunction with academic and private sector advisory boards, are the result of research studies into the challenges professors face in helping students succeed and the opportunities that new technology presents to impact teaching and learning.

COMPREHESIVE TEACHING AND LEARNING PACKAGE

We believe that an ancillary package is most useful if each element in it is part of a well-considered whole. Each member of this book's development team is committed to the quality and cohesiveness of the supplementary package.

FOR THE INSTRUCTOR

The Instructor's Online Learning Centre The OLC at **www.mcgraw hill.ca/college/frankbernanke** includes a password-protected Web site for Instructors. The site offers downloadable supplements and PageOut, the McGraw-Hill Ryerson course Web site development centre.

Instructor's CD-ROM This CD-ROM contains all of the necessary Instructor Supplements, including:

Instructor's Manual Adapted by Teresa Cyrus of Dalhousie University, this manual is extremely useful for all teachers, but especially for those new to the job. It offers suggestions for using the Study Guides, the Test Bank, and the Economic Naturalist cases. It supplies sample syllabi with assignments, sample exams, and supplemental material. For each chapter, it provides an overview, an outline, teaching objectives, additional Economic Naturalist discussion questions, answers to textbook questions and problems, homework assignments with answers, and sample quizzes with answers.

Computerized Test Banks The test banks (micro and macro), ensure maximum flexibility in test preparation, including the reconfiguring of graphing exercises. The Micro Test Bank is prepared by Chandan Shirvaikar of Red Deer College and the Macro Test Bank by Akhter Faroque of Laurentian University. Collectively, the test banks contain more than 5000 multiple-choice questions categorized by Learning Objective; Learning Level (knowledge, comprehension, application, analysis); Type (graph, calculation, word problem); and Source (textbook, Study Guide, Web, unique).

PowerPoint Slides Adapted by Lars Osberg, Dalhousie University, this package contains dynamic slides of the important illustrations in the textbook, along with detailed, chapter-by-chapter reviews of the important ideas presented in the text. Carefully prepared concept maps relate the different topics in each of the micro and macro texts.

CBC Video Cases Accompanying the texts is a series of video segments drawn from CBC broadcasts of *Undercurrents*, *The National*, *Current Affairs*, and *Venture*. These videos have been chosen to aid students in relating real-world economic issues to the text, and to illuminate key ideas and concepts presented in the text. A set of instructor notes, developed by Kevin Richter, Douglas College, accompanies the segments available at the Instructor's Online Learning Centre. The video segments will be available in a VHS format for use in class and through video streaming on the Online Learning Centre and are accessible by both instructors and students.

ECONX: Online Experiments in Economics   Developed at Carnegie Mellon University's Open Learning Initiative, EconX is an innovative collection of online microeconomic experiments and related workbooks that can be used in any principles of microeconomics course. EconX is completely Web based, and students and instructors only need access to the Internet and a Web browser to use it. EconX can be used to supplement a traditional course with minimal effort. Most of the work of administering the experiments and doing the grading is taken care of for you by the software. EconX brings economics alive for students, who will enjoy learning about and testing the economic theory. Students are active participants attempting to make deals with other traders, and the workbook (all online) guides them through the analysis and the economic theory needed to understand the experiment. For information on seeing a demo, please contact your local *i*-Learning Sales Specialist.

FOR THE STUDENT

Study Guide   Prepared by David Sabiston (Mount Royal College), the Study Guide [ISBN 007-0951071] provides the following elements: chapter overview, chapter review, knowledge and skills table, and self-test, (key terms with fill-in-the blanks, multiple choice questions, and short answer problems) with answers.

Student Online Learning Centre   Prepared by Sigrid Ewender (Kwantlen University College), this electronic learning aid at **www.mcgrawhill.ca/college/ frankbernanke** is robust enough for any distance-education program. It includes cyber-lectures, quizzes, practice activities, separate pre- and post-tests, interactive graphing exercises, Economic Naturalist exercises, sample exam questions with answers, understanding questions, Internet questions, Internet resource sites, Study To Go, a Math Tutor, EconGraph Toolkit, concepts maps, key terms, chapter outlines, chapter summaries, data update links, CBC Videos and Cases, a searchable glossary and much more!

ACKNOWLEDGEMENTS

Our thanks first and foremost go to Ron Doleman, our Editor. From the outset of the project, Ron has encouraged our distinctive vision and has been constantly available to share his broad experience, most notably with the introductory economics textbook market. The entire team at McGraw-Hill Ryerson deserves credit for keeping the project moving in a timely fashion. But Daphne Scriabin, our Development Editor, deserves special mention for guiding the manuscript through two revisions with patience and tact. We thank Pat Ferrier, Vice President of Editorial & Media Technology, and Lynn Fisher, Executive Sponsoring Editor, for making this textbook a priority project and supporting design innovations. We also thank Gillian Scobie for her close and accurate copyediting. We are grateful to Margaret Henderson for transforming the final manuscript into a handsome book and to Kelly Smyth for promoting it with such enthusiasm. And we are grateful for the outstanding work of the McGraw-Hill Ryerson production team: Coordinator Paula Brown, designer Sharon Lucas. We would also like to thank Lynn Lethbridge for her outstanding work as research assistant.

Finally, we would like to express our sincere thanks to David Cape (Ryerson University) for the close reading and perceptive comments provided in his technical reviews of the manuscript. We also thank the following teachers and colleagues, whose thorough reviews and thoughtful suggestions led to innumerable substantive improvements:

Shari Corrigan, Camosun College
Philippe Cyrenne, University of Winnipeg
Yolina Denchev, University of Victoria
Ida Ferrara, York University
Michael Hare, University of Toronto
Barrie Hebb, St. Mary's University
Muhammed N. Islam, Concordia University
Cheryl Jenkins, John Abbott College
Alan Kwan, Alliance University College
Gordon Lee, University of Alberta
Frank Millerd, Wilfrid Laurier University
Marc Prud'Homme, University of Ottawa
Marianne Vigneault, Bishop's University

Introduction

Economics is a *way of thinking* about the world. Over many years economists have developed some simple principles and tools that are useful for understanding a wide range of situations, from the relatively simple economic decisions that individuals make every day to the workings of highly complex markets, such as international financial markets. A major objective of this book is to help you learn these principles and tools and how to apply them to a variety of issues.

The three chapters of Part I introduce the problem of scarcity and develop six core principles that will be used throughout the book. Chapter 1 presents scarcity—the unavoidable fact that although our needs and wants are limitless, the resources available to satisfy them are limited—as the fundamental economic problem. Without scarcity, the discipline of economics would have no reason to exist. The chapter shows that deciding whether to take an action by comparing the cost and benefit that the action provides is a useful approach for dealing with the inevitable trade-offs that scarcity creates and identifies several pitfalls that plague many decision makers. Chapter 2 goes beyond individual decision making to consider trade among both individuals and countries. An important reason for trade is that it permits people (or countries) to specialize in the production of particular goods and services, which in turn enhances productivity and raises standards of living. Finally, Chapter 3 presents an overview of the concepts of supply and demand, perhaps the most basic and familiar tools of economists.

Chapter 1

THINKING LIKE AN ECONOMIST

How many students are in your introductory economics class? Some classes have just 20 or so. Others average 35, 100, or 200 students. At some large universities, introductory economics classes may have as many as 2000 students. What size is best?

If cost were no object, the best size for an introductory economics course—or any other course, for that matter—might be only a single student. Everything could be tailored to your own background and ability, allowing you to cover the material at just the right pace. The tutorial format would also promote close communication and personal trust between you and your professor. And your grade would depend more heavily on what you actually learned than on the vagaries of multiple-choice exams. We may even suppose, for the sake of discussion, that studies by educational psychologists prove definitively that students learn best in the tutorial format.

Why then, have many Canadian universities reduced the number of introductory economics classes they offer while increasing the number of students per class? The simple reason is that costs *do* matter. They matter not just to the university administrators who must build classrooms and pay faculty salaries but also to *you*. The direct cost of providing you with your own personal introductory economics course—most notably, the professor's salary and the expense of providing a classroom in which to meet—might easily top $20 000. *Someone* has to pay these costs. Since Canadian universities receive part of their revenue from governments and part from students' fees, the cost would be covered by higher tuition payments and higher tax payments. Of course, you are well aware that although class sizes have increased, students' fees have also increased. At the same time, governments have reduced their funding of colleges and universities. Without fee increases, class sizes would have become even larger.

With a larger class size, of course, the cost per student goes down. For example, in a class of 300 students, the cost of an introductory economics course might be as little as $100 per student. However, there is a trade-off. Although few students like large classes, they are significantly more affordable.

In choosing what size introductory economics course to offer, university administrators confront a classic economic trade-off. In making the class larger, they increase the student–faculty ratio; but at the same time, they reduce costs per student and hence the tuition students must pay.

■ 1.1 ECONOMICS: STUDYING CHOICE IN A WORLD OF SCARCITY

If we could always have whatever we wanted, for free, right now, we would never have to choose—all we would ever have to say is "more please," and we would get it. Unfortunately, the real world is not like that. Most things have a cost, in time or money or other resources, and we have a limited amount of these available. Scarcity means that we have to make choices. More of one good means choosing less of another. **Economics** is the study of how people make choices under conditions of scarcity and of the results of those choices for society.

In the class-size example just discussed, a motivated economics student might definitely prefer to be in a class of 20 rather than a class of 100, everything else being equal. But other things, of course, are not equal. Students can enjoy the benefits of having smaller classes, but only at the price of having less money for other activities. The student's choice inevitably will come down to the relative importance of competing activities.

That such trade-offs are widespread and important is the core problem of economics. We call it the **scarcity problem**, because the simple fact of scarcity makes trade-offs necessary. Another name for the scarcity problem might be the "no-free-lunch" idea (which comes from the observation that even a lunch that is given to you takes time to eat—time you could have spent doing other useful things). Without the scarcity problem, the subject of economics would have no reason to exist.

The Scarcity Problem: Although we have boundless needs and wants, the resources available to us are limited. Scarcity means that we have to make choices—having more of one good thing usually means having less of another.

Inherent in the idea of a trade-off is the fact that choice involves compromise between competing interests. Cost–benefit analysis is based on the disarmingly simple principle that an action should be taken if, and only if, its benefits exceed its costs. We call this statement the **cost–benefit principle**. It is one of the core principles of economics:

The Cost–Benefit Principle: An individual (or a firm or a society) will be better off taking an action if, and only if, the extra benefits from taking the action are greater than the extra costs.

The cost–benefit principle sounds simple, but to apply it we need some way to measure the relevant costs and benefits—a task that is often difficult in practice. If we make a few simplifying assumptions, however, we can see how the analysis might work. On the cost side, suppose that the only relevant expenses are the professor's salary and the cost of a classroom big enough to hold the class. Imagine that the professor is paid $20 000 per course and that classroom space can be obtained at a cost of $30 per student per semester. Suppose further that the university charges tuition for the course equal to the direct costs of providing it and that the university has only two classroom sizes, so classes of 20 and 100 are the only alternatives. At the current class size of 100 students, the total cost is $23 000—$20 000 for the professor plus $100($30) = $3000 for the classroom—which means that tuition is $230 per student. But if there were just 20 students in the class, the total cost would be $20 000 + 20($30) = $20 600—so tuition would be $1030 per student.

Are small classes "better" than large ones?

economics the study of how people make choices under conditions of scarcity and of the results of those choices for society

COST–BENEFIT

The cost of reducing class size from 100 to 20 is simply the difference between the two tuition figures just calculated, namely, $1030 − $230 = $800 per student. Will administrators switch to the smaller class size? If they apply the cost–benefit principle, they will realize that *the reduction in class size makes sense only if the value to students of attending the smaller class is at least $800 greater than the value of attending the larger class.*

Would you (or your parents, if they are paying your tuition) be willing to part with an extra $800 for a smaller economics class? If not, and if other students feel the same way, then maintaining the larger class size makes sense. But if you and others would be willing to pay the extra tuition, then reducing the class size to 20 makes good economic sense.

Notice that the "best" class size, from an economic point of view, may not be the same as the "best" size from the point of view of an educational psychologist. The difference arises because the economic definition of "best" takes into account both the benefits *and* the costs of different class sizes. The psychologist ignores costs and looks only at the learning benefits of different class sizes.

In practice, of course, different people will feel differently about the value of smaller classes. People with high incomes, for example, tend to be willing to pay more for the advantage, which helps to explain why the average class size is smaller, and tuition higher, at those private schools whose students come predominantly from high-income families.

The cost–benefit framework for thinking about the class-size problem also suggests a possible reason for the gradual increase in average class size that has been taking place in Canadian colleges and universities. Between 1990–91 and 1998–99, public operating grants to Canadian universities decreased by about 25 percent. This reduction is part of a pattern of reduced expenditures that enabled the federal government to move from large deficits in the early 1990s to large surpluses by the end of the decade. To address the shortfall, Canadian colleges and universities have increased class sizes and raised fees. By 2003–04, after adjusting for inflation, fees were about twice what they had been ten years earlier. Students today borrow more to finance their education than did students in the past.[1]

Students are paying higher fees to attend larger classes. The size of classes could be reduced if a sufficient number of students paid even higher fees, or if governments increased their funding of universities. However, universities believe that students are not willing to pay even higher fees. Governments believe that taxpayers are not willing to pay more taxes to increase the funding of postsecondary education. Apparently, an insufficient number of people are willing to bear the cost of smaller classes; thus, class sizes have increased. The increase in class size follows from a governmental position concerning deficits, not from market behaviour.

Notice that we have used the cost–benefit principle to find a plausible explanation of why class sizes have increased. You may believe that a policy that eliminated federal deficits is appropriate. But you may also believe it would have been fairer to reduce the deficit by raising taxes, rather than by cutting spending—in particular, you may think that it was not fair to remove deficits by including measures that raised students' debt, especially if you have borrowed to finance your education. The cost–benefit principle helps to explain cause and effect; however, it is not helpful in determining whether a policy is distributionally fair.

---

[1] "Students Pay More for Less," *CAUT ACPPU Bulletin*, 48(6), p. 1, June 2001 and "Students in for a Rough Ride," *CAUT ACPPU Bulletin*, 50(7), p. A9, Sept. 2003. Students' fees are an important source of revenue and their increase has enabled many universities to prevent services from being cut even further. However, notice that if fees rise by 100 percent, a university's revenue will rise by far less than 100 percent. Suppose that 25 cents of every dollar of a university's revenue comes from students' fees, which is typical. The university raises fees by 100 percent: $1.00 \times \$0.25 = \$0.25$. Thus, a 100 percent increase in students' fees increases the university's revenue by 25 percent.

■ 1.2 APPLYING THE COST–BENEFIT PRINCIPLE

In studying choice under scarcity, it is often useful to begin with the premise that people are **rational**, which means they have well-defined goals and try to fulfill them as best they can. The cost–benefit principle illustrated in the class-size example is a fundamental tool for the study of how rational people make choices.

rational person someone with well-defined goals who tries to fulfill those goals as best as he or she can

As in the class-size example, often the only real difficulty in applying the cost–benefit rule is coming up with reasonable measures of all the relevant benefits and costs. Only in rare instances will exact dollar measures be conveniently available. But the cost–benefit framework can lend structure to your thinking even when no relevant market data are available.

To illustrate how we proceed in such cases, the following example asks you to decide whether to perform an action whose cost and benefits are described only in vague, qualitative terms.

EXAMPLE 1.1

Will you be better off if you walk downtown to save $10 on a $25 computer game?

Imagine you are about to buy a $25 computer game at the nearby campus store when a friend tells you that the same game is on sale at a downtown store for only $15. If the downtown store is a 30-minute walk away, will you buy the game?

COST–BENEFIT

The cost-benefit principle tells us that you will buy it downtown if the benefit of doing so exceeds the cost. The benefit of taking any action is the dollar value of everything you gain by taking it. Here, the benefit of buying downtown is exactly $10, since that is the amount you will save on the purchase price of the game. The cost of taking any action is the dollar value of everything you give up by taking it. Here, the cost of buying downtown is the dollar value you assign to the time and trouble it takes to make the trip. But how do we estimate that dollar value?

One way is to perform the following hypothetical action. Imagine that a stranger has offered to pay you to do an errand that involves the same walk downtown (perhaps to drop off a letter for her at the post office). If she offered you a payment of, say, $1000, would you accept? If so, we know that your cost of walking downtown and back must be less than $1000. Now imagine her offer being reduced in small increments until you finally refuse the last offer. For example, if you would agree to walk downtown and back for $9.00 but not for $8.99, then your perceived cost of making the trip is $9.00. In this case, you will be better off if you buy the game downtown, because the $10 you save (your benefit) is greater than your $9.00 cost of making the trip.

On the other hand, suppose that your cost of making the trip is greater than $10. In that case, the cost–benefit principle tells you to buy the game from the nearby campus store.

ECONOMIC SURPLUS

Suppose again that in Example 1.1 your "cost" of making the trip downtown was $9. Compared to the alternative of buying the game at the campus store, buying it downtown resulted in an **economic surplus** of $1, the difference between the benefit of making the trip and its cost. In general, your goal as an economic decision maker is to choose those actions that generate the largest possible economic surplus. This means taking all actions that yield a positive total economic surplus, which is just another way of restating the cost-benefit principle.

economic surplus the benefit of taking any action minus its cost

ECONOMIC SURPLUS

Note that the fact that your best choice was to buy the game downtown does not imply that you *enjoy* making the trip, any more than choosing a large class means that you prefer large classes to small ones. It simply means that the trip is less unpleasant than the prospect of paying $10 extra for the game. Once again, you've faced a trade-off—in this case, the choice between a cheaper game and the free time gained by avoiding the trip.

OPPORTUNITY COST

opportunity cost the value of the next-best alternative that must be foregone in order to undertake the activity

Of course your mental action could have produced a different outcome. Suppose, for example, that the time required for the trip is the only time you have left to study for a difficult test the next day. Or suppose you are watching one of your favourite movies on cable, or that you are tired and would love a short nap. In such cases, we say that the **opportunity cost** of making the trip—that is, the value of what you must sacrifice to walk downtown and back—is high, and you are more likely to decide against making the trip.

In this example, if watching the last hour of the cable TV movie is the most valuable opportunity that conflicts with the trip downtown, the opportunity cost of making the trip is the dollar value you place on pursuing that opportunity—that is, the largest amount you'd be willing to pay to avoid missing the end of the movie. Note that the opportunity cost of making the trip is not the combined value of *all* possible activities you could have pursued, but only the value of your *best* alternative—the one you would have chosen had you not made the trip.

Throughout the text we will pose exercises like the one that follows. You will find that pausing to answer them will help you to master key concepts in economics. Because doing these exercises is not very costly (indeed, many students report that they are actually fun), the cost–benefit principle indicates that it is well worth your while to do them.

OPPORTUNITY COST

EXERCISE I.I

You would again save $10 by buying the game downtown rather than at the campus store, but your cost of making the trip is now $12, not $9. How much economic surplus would you get from buying the game downtown? Where does the cost–benefit principle tell you to buy it?

EXAMPLE I.2

What is the opportunity cost of selling flowers on the sidewalk?

Suppose that you are a flower seller, with a stock of cut roses that will wilt by tomorrow morning. If you do not sell them tonight, their value tomorrow will be zero. You can think of two possible places to sell your flowers—on the sidewalk outside your home or downtown in upscale romantic restaurants where you can embarrass people into buying flowers for their dates. However, to get into these restaurants, you have to pay off the headwaiter ($30) and it will cost you $10 in extra time and bus fares to travel downtown. Suppose that you expect to sell them all in about an hour wherever you are and expect to be able to get about $50 for your flowers if you go downtown. You do not have anything else to do during the time you will spend selling flowers. What would be the opportunity cost of selling them on the sidewalk? What is the least revenue from sidewalk sales that would make selling on the sidewalk your best choice?

By selling on the sidewalk, you give up the surplus that you could get by selling downtown. If you had sold the flowers downtown you would have gotten a net return of $10 ($50 revenue minus $30 payoff minus $10 in extra travel costs). So the opportunity cost of selling the flowers on the sidewalk is $10. You are better off selling on the sidewalk only if you expect to make more than $10 at that location. (Notice that this and the next example do not specify how you got the flowers. Whether you grew them yourself, bought them in the marketplace, or received them as a gift, *it does not matter*. The important thing is that the flowers will wilt by tomorrow and be valueless—hence the opportunity cost of the flowers themselves is zero.)

Suppose that you think you could sell your flowers for $8 on the sidewalk. What would be the opportunity cost of selling them downtown?

If you sell your flowers downtown, you forego $8 in revenue obtained from selling flowers on the sidewalk, and you incur $30 in payoff costs and $10 in transportation expenses. Therefore, the total value of everything you give up in order to sell downtown is $48. Your surplus from sales downtown net of all opportunity costs is $2.

THE ROLE OF ECONOMIC MODELS

Economists often use abstract models of how an idealized rational individual would choose among competing alternatives. A computer model of a complex phenomenon like climate change, which must ignore many details and includes only the major forces at work, is also an example of an abstract model (a simplified description that captures the essential elements of a situation and allows us to analyze them in a logical way.)

Noneconomists are sometimes harshly critical of the economist's cost–benefit model on the grounds that people in the real world never conduct complex mental calculations before making simple decisions. But this criticism betrays a fundamental misunderstanding of how abstract models can help to explain and predict human behaviour. Economists know perfectly well that people do not conduct hypothetical mental actions when they make simple decisions. All the cost–benefit principle really says is that a rational decision is one that is explicitly or implicitly based on a weighing of costs and benefits.

Most of us make sensible decisions most of the time, without being consciously aware that we are weighing costs and benefits, just as most people ride a bike without being consciously aware of what keeps them from falling. Through trial and error, we gradually learn what kinds of choices tend to work best in different contexts, just as bicycle riders internalize the relevant laws of physics, usually without being consciously aware of them.

Even so, learning the explicit principles of cost–benefit analysis can help us make better decisions, just as knowing about physics can help make us better bicycle riders. Athletes who compete in bicycle races pay careful attention to gearing, the size of the bicycle's frame relative to their bodies, air pressure in the tires, and so on. Knowledge of the relevant physical principles can be very useful.

Finally, economic models are examples of positive economics. **Positive economics** has two dimensions. First, it offers cause-and-effect explanations of economic relationships. Ideally, positive economics is value free. Second, positive economics has an empirical dimension. In principle, data can be used to confirm or refute propositions, or hypotheses, that emerge from positive economics. Data also can be used to measure the magnitude of effects that emerge from cause-and-effect relationships. Thus, we can predict that if resources available to colleges and universities are reduced, class sizes will increase. We can use data to determine whether class sizes do, in fact, increase. If they do, data can be used to determine by how much they increase. An example of positive economics occurs when the cost–benefit principle is used *to explain* why class sizes have increased. In contrast, **normative economics** reflects subjective value judgments and is based on ethical positions. Whether larger classes and higher fees are unfair to students is a normative issue.

positive economics economic analysis that offers cause-and-effect explanations of economic relationships; the propositions, or hypotheses, that emerge from positive economics can, in principle, be confirmed or refuted by data; in principle, data can also be used to measure the magnitude of effects predicted by positive economics

normative economics economic statements that reflect subjective value judgments and are based on ethical positions

RATIONALITY AND IMPERFECT DECISION MAKERS

Imagine you are confronted with the question "Will I be better off if I perform some action?" and "perform some action" could mean anything from "eat another cookie" to "choose Simon Fraser University over the University of British Columbia." The cost–benefit principle says that if the benefits of the action exceed its costs, then performing the action will make you better off. However, if the benefits are less than the costs, then performing the action will make you worse off. If its benefits and costs happen to be equal, then it does not matter whether you perform the action or not.

Rational people will apply the cost–benefit principle most of the time, although probably in an intuitive and approximate way, rather than through explicit and precise calculation. To the extent that people are rational, their tendency to compare costs and benefits will help economists to predict their likely behaviour. For example, we can predict that students from wealthy families are more likely than others to attend private foreign universities that offer smaller classes.

RECAP   **COST–BENEFIT ANALYSIS**

Scarcity is a basic fact of economic life. Because of it, having more of one good often means having less of another (the scarcity problem). Economics is devoted to studying how we can make intelligent choices in a world of scarcity. In fact, without scarcity, there would be no reason for the subject of economics to exist.

The cost–benefit principle holds that an individual (or a firm or a society) is better off taking an action if, and only if, the extra benefit from taking the action is greater than the extra cost. The benefit of taking any action minus the cost of taking the action is called the *economic surplus* from that action. Thus, the cost–benefit principle suggests that we take only those actions that create additional economic surplus.

Applying the cost–benefit principle requires measurement. The benefit of an action is the most *you would be willing to pay* someone to perform it. The cost of an action is the value of the next-best alternative that you must forego to perform the action.

COST–
BENEFIT

■ 1.3 THREE COMMON PITFALLS

The cost–benefit principle suggests that an introductory economics course should emphasize a short list of those principles with the greatest power to predict and explain behaviour. But it also suggests that among those principles, we should focus especially on those that are most difficult to master. As we explore the cost–benefit approach in greater detail, we will emphasize the errors people commonly make when trying to implement it. People tend to ignore certain costs that they ought to take into account, for example, and sometimes they are influenced by costs that are irrelevant to the decision at hand. Three of the most commonly encountered pitfalls concern opportunity costs, sunk costs, and the difference between average and marginal cost.

■ 1.4 PITFALL 1: IGNORING OPPORTUNITY COSTS

Sherlock Holmes, Arthur Conan Doyle's legendary detective, was successful because he saw details that most others overlooked. In *Silver Blaze*, Holmes is called on to investigate the theft of an expensive racehorse from its stable. A Scotland Yard inspector assigned to the case asks Holmes whether some particular aspect of the crime required further study. "Yes," Holmes replies, and describes

Opportunity costs are like dogs that fail to bark in the night.

"the curious incident of the dog in the nighttime." "The dog did nothing in the nighttime," responds the puzzled inspector. But as Holmes realized, that was precisely the problem. The watchdog's failure to bark when Silver Blaze was stolen meant that the watchdog knew the thief. This clue substantially reduced the number of suspects and eventually led to the thief's apprehension.

Just as we often don't notice when a dog fails to bark, many of us tend to overlook the implicit value of activities that fail to happen. As we have seen, however, intelligent decisions require taking the value of foregone opportunities properly into account. What *is not* stated may be as important as what *is* explicitly stated.

RECOGNIZING THE RELEVANT ALTERNATIVE

EXAMPLE 1.4

Will you be better off if you use your frequent-flyer coupon to fly to Vancouver for winter break?

With winter break only a week away, you are still undecided about whether to fly to Vancouver, then go to Whistler with a group of classmates at the University of Alberta. The round-trip airfare from Edmonton to Vancouver is $500. All other relevant costs for the vacation while at Whistler will total exactly $1000. The maximum you are willing to pay for the vacation is $1350. You could get to Whistler by paying $500 to fly from Edmonton to Vancouver, or by using a frequent-flyer coupon to pay for the flight. Your only alternative use for your frequent-flyer coupon is for your plane trip to Ottawa the weekend after winter break to attend your brother's wedding. (Your coupon expires shortly thereafter.) If the Edmonton–Ottawa round-trip airfare is $400, will you be better off if you use your frequent-flyer coupon to fly to Vancouver for winter break?

COST–
BENEFIT

The *cost–benefit* criterion tells you to go to Vancouver if the benefits of the trip exceed its costs. If not for the complication of the frequent-flyer coupon, solving this problem would be a straightforward matter of comparing the maximum price you would pay for the week at Whistler (your benefit from the trip) to the sum of all relevant costs. And since your airfare and other costs would sum to $1500, or $150 more than your reservation price for the trip, you would be better off not going.

But what about the possibility of using your frequent-flyer coupon to make the trip? Using it for that purpose might make the flight to Vancouver seem free, suggesting you would reap an economic surplus of $350 by making the trip. But doing so would also mean you would have to pay $400 for your airfare to Ottawa. So the opportunity cost of using your coupon to fly to Vancouver is really $400. If you use it for that purpose, the cost of the trip still exceeds its benefit and it still fails the cost–benefit test. In cases like these, you are much more likely to decide sensibly if you ask yourself, "Will I be better off if I use my frequent-flyer coupon for this trip or save it for an upcoming trip?"

We cannot emphasize strongly enough that the key to using the concept of opportunity cost correctly lies in recognizing precisely what taking a given action prevents us from doing. To illustrate, suppose we modify Example 1.4 slightly, as follows:

EXAMPLE 1.5

Same as Example 1.4, except that now your frequent-flyer coupon expires in a week, so your only chance to use it will be for the flight to Vancouver. Will you be better off if you use your coupon?

Since you now have no alternative use for your coupon, the opportunity cost of using it to pay for the flight to Vancouver is zero. That means your economic surplus from the trip will be $1350 − $1000 = $350 > 0$, so the cost–benefit principle tells you to use your coupon and go to Whistler.

THE TIME VALUE OF MONEY

We saw that taking an action now can mean being unable to take some other action in the future. To take the value of future opportunities properly into account, we often need to be able to weigh future costs and benefits against those we incur or receive in the present. As the next example illustrates, having to pay someone a dollar one year from now is not the same as having to pay someone a dollar today.

EXAMPLE 1.6

Same as Example 1.4, except that instead of flying to Ottawa your best alternative use for your frequent-flyer coupon is to use it for a flight you expect to take 1 year from now, for which the airfare is $363. If your savings account pays 10 percent interest per year, does the cost–benefit principle tell you to fly to Vancouver, then go to Whistler?

How does this new information alter the opportunity cost of using your coupon to fly to Vancouver? Using it now means having to pay $363 for your flight one year from now. The opportunity cost of using the coupon now might therefore seem to be exactly $363. But this way of thinking about the coupon misses an important aspect of opportunity cost.

The question you must ask yourself is "How much am I willing to pay *today* to avoid making an airfare payment of $363 *one year from now?* To answer this question, ask, "How much would I have to put in my savings account today, at 10 percent annual interest, to have $363 one year from now?" The answer is $330, since that amount will earn $33 in interest (10 percent of $330) over the next year, for a total of $363.

Your economic surplus from the trip to Whistler is therefore $1350 − $1000 − $330 = $20. Therefore, the cost–benefit principle tells you to take the trip to Whistler.

EXERCISE 1.2

Would your answer to Example 1.6 have been different if the annual interest rate had been 2 percent instead of 10 percent? (*Hint:* Would a deposit of $350 in your account today earn enough money to pay for your $363 air ticket one year from now?)

Example 1.4 and Exercise 1.2 drive home the point that the opportunity cost of a dollar spent today is not the same as the opportunity cost of a dollar spent one year from now. In general, the opportunity cost of resources that are expended in the future will be lower than the opportunity cost of resources that are expended in the present. The reason involves the **time value of money**—the fact that money deposited in an interest-bearing account today will grow in value over time. Indeed, the very fact that banks and other borrowers pay interest is a consequence of the opportunity cost concept.

As simple as the concept of opportunity cost is, it is one of the most important in economics. The art in applying the concept correctly lies in being able to recognize the most valuable alternative to a given activity. And though the concept is simple, its application can be subtle. For example, if we must choose between spending a dollar today or spending a dollar tomorrow, time itself will influence opportunity cost through the time value of money.

time value of money the fact that a given dollar amount today is equivalent to a larger dollar amount in the future, because the money can be invested in an interest-bearing account in the meantime

1.5 PITFALL 2: FAILURE TO IGNORE SUNK COSTS

The opportunity cost pitfall is one in which people ignore opportunity costs. In another common pitfall, the reverse is true: People are influenced by costs that really are not opportunity costs. *The only costs that are relevant to a decision about whether to take an action are those that we can avoid by not taking the action.* As a practical matter, however, many decision makers appear to be influenced by **sunk costs**—costs that are beyond recovery at the moment a decision is made. For example, money spent on a nontransferable, nonrefundable airline ticket is a sunk cost.

> *sunk cost* a cost that is beyond recovery at the moment a decision must be made

Because sunk costs must be borne *whether or not an action is taken,* they are irrelevant to the decision of whether to take the action. The sunk cost pitfall (the mistake of being influenced by sunk costs) is illustrated clearly in the following examples.

EXAMPLE 1.7

Will you drive through a snowstorm to get to a hockey game?

You and your friend Joe have identical tastes. At 2 P.M. you log on to Ticketmaster and buy a $30 nonrefundable ticket to a hockey game to be played that night in Ottawa, 70 km north of your home in Smiths Falls. Joe plans to attend the same game, but he plans to buy his ticket at the game. Tickets sold at the game cost only $25, because they don't carry a Ticketmaster surcharge. (Many people nonetheless pay the higher price at Ticketmaster, to be sure of getting good seats.) At 4 P.M. an unexpected snowstorm begins, making the prospect of the drive to Ottawa much less attractive than before. If both you and Joe are rational, is one of you more likely to attend the game than the other?

Since you have already bought your ticket, the $30 you spent on it is a sunk cost. It is money you cannot recover, whether or not you go to the game. In deciding whether to see the game, then, the cost–benefit principle tells you to compare the benefit of seeing the game (as measured, the largest dollar amount you would be willing to pay to see it) to only those *additional* costs you must incur to see the game (the opportunity cost of your time, whatever cost you assign to driving through the snowstorm, etc.). However, whether you attend the game or not, you will never see the $30 you paid for your ticket again. Therefore, it is a sunk cost, not an opportunity cost and you should ignore the $30 when applying the cost–benefit principle.

Joe, too, must weigh the opportunity cost of his time and the hassle of the drive in deciding whether to attend the game. But he must also weigh the $25 he will have to spend for his ticket. At the moment of deciding, therefore, the remaining costs Joe must incur to see the game are $25 higher than the remaining costs for you. And since you both have identical tastes—that is, since your respective benefits of attending the game are exactly the same—Joe is less likely to make the trip. You might think the cost of seeing the game is higher for you, since your ticket cost $30, whereas Joe's will cost only $25. But at the moment of deciding whether to make the drive, the $25 is a relevant cost for Joe, whereas your $30 is a sunk cost, and hence an irrelevant one for you.

Now suppose we change the structure of Example 1.7 slightly.

EXAMPLE 1.8

Same as Example 1.7, except now a friend gives Joe a free ticket to the game at 2 P.M. Is one of you more likely to attend the game than the other?

This time neither of you faces any additional ticket expenses at the moment you must decide whether to drive through the snowstorm. Since your respective costs and benefits are the same, your decisions about whether to make the trip will be the same if you both apply the cost–benefit principle.

According to the cost–benefit criterion, the decision to attend the game does not depend on whether someone bought a ticket or was given one. Yet people often seem to decide differently in the two cases. In particular, people who paid cash for a ticket often feel a need to use it, "to avoid wasting $30." People who get a free ticket seem to feel much more comfortable with the notion of staying home.

Such differences in judgment cannot be the result of economic reasoning. A rational economic decision maker weighs the benefit of seeing the game against only the *additional* costs he must incur to see it—in this example, the opportunity cost of time, the psychological cost, and the physical risk of driving through the snowstorm. How a person came to possess a ticket has no bearing on either the relevant benefits or the relevant costs.

RECAP	THE PITFALL OF NOT IGNORING SUNK COSTS

When deciding whether to perform an action, it is important to ignore sunk costs—those costs that cannot be avoided even if the action is not taken. Even though a ticket to a concert may have cost you $100, if you have already bought it and cannot sell it to anyone else, the $100 is a sunk cost. If your decision to attend the concert is based entirely on the cost–benefit principle, sunk cost will be irrelevant.

■ 1.6 PITFALL 3: FAILURE TO UNDERSTAND THE AVERAGE–MARGINAL DISTINCTION

marginal cost the increase in total cost that results from carrying out one additional unit of an activity.

marginal benefit the increase in total benefit that results from carrying out one more unit of an activity.

average cost total cost of undertaking n units of an activity divided by n

average benefit total benefit of undertaking n units of an activity divided by n

As we have seen, economic decisions take proper account of opportunity costs. Because sunk costs are not opportunity costs, sunk costs are irrelevant to economic decisions and are not counted when the cost–benefit principle is applied. Further, accurate application of the cost–benefit principle is not possible if marginal costs and benefits are confused with average costs and benefits.

Often we are confronted with the choice of whether or not to engage in an activity (for example, whether or not to attend a hockey game). But in many situations, the issue is not whether to pursue the activity, but whether or not to increase it. The cost–benefit framework emphasizes that the only relevant costs and benefits in deciding whether to increase an activity are *marginal* costs and benefits. Economists define the **marginal cost** of an activity as the increase in total cost that results from carrying out one additional unit of the activity. Similarly, the **marginal benefit** of an activity is the increase in total benefit that results from carrying out one more unit of the activity. In many contexts, however, people seem more inclined to compare **average costs** and **average benefits**—total cost or benefit per unit of activity.

As Example 1.9 makes clear, increasing the level of an activity may not be justified, even though its average benefit at the current level is significantly greater than its average cost.

EXAMPLE 1.9	

Does the cost–benefit principle tell NASA to expand the space shuttle program from four launches per year to five?

Professor Kösten Banifoot, a prominent supporter of the NASA space shuttle program, has estimated that the gains from the program are currently $24 billion per year (an average of $6 billion per launch) and that its costs are currently $20 billion per year (an average of $5 billion per launch). True or false: If these estimates are correct, the cost–benefit principle tells NASA to expand the program. (Canadian astronauts have flown on the space shuttle, and Canada supplies components to NASA. Expansion of the space shuttle program would provide additional opportunities for Canadian science and technology.)

To decide whether an additional launch makes sense, we need to compare the cost of adding that launch with the benefit of adding it. The *average* benefit and *average* cost per launch for all shuttles launched thus far simply are not useful in deciding whether to expand the program. Of course, the average cost of the launches undertaken so far *might* be the same as the cost of adding another launch. But it also might be either higher or lower than the marginal cost of a launch. The same statement holds true regarding average and marginal benefits.

Suppose, for example, that the benefit of an additional launch is in fact the same as the average benefit per launch thus far, namely, $6 billion. Should NASA add another launch? Not if the cost of adding the fifth launch would be more than $6 billion. Suppose the relationship between the number of shuttles launched and the total cost of the program is as described in Table 1.1.

TABLE 1.1
How Total Cost Varies with the Number of Launches

Number of launches per year	Total costs per year ($billions)
1	6
2	8
3	12
4	20
5	30

At the current level of four launches per year, the average cost is $20 billion/4 = $5 billion per launch. But adding a fifth launch would raise costs from $20 billion to $30 billion, so the marginal cost of the fifth launch is $10 billion. If the benefit of an additional launch is constant at $6 billion, the cost–benefit principle does not justify increasing the number of launches. Indeed, the fourth launch itself would not be justified, since it cost $8 billion and produced only $6 billion in additional benefits. Based on the numbers shown in the table, which are completely consistent with Professor Banifoot's data on average costs and benefits, the optimal number of launches would be only three per year.

FIXED AND VARIABLE COSTS

Sometimes the failure to distinguish between average and marginal costs arises from a failure to distinguish between **fixed costs**—costs that we incur now but which do not vary with the level of an activity—and **variable costs**—costs that do vary with the level of activity.

fixed cost a cost that does not vary with the level of an activity

For example, the membership fee you pay to join most health clubs is the same whether you visit the club four times a week or only once a month. This fee is a fixed cost. Once you have paid it, it is *usually* also a sunk cost—but not always. Some health clubs offer an introductory period in which a membership may be cancelled with a full refund. In such cases the membership fee is a fixed cost but not a sunk cost.

variable cost a cost that varies with the level of activity

Many health clubs also have tennis or racquetball courts for which they charge hourly court fees. Because these charges depend on the number of hours you play, they are variable costs. If you've already become a member and use the cost–benefit principle to decide how many times a week to play racquetball, you will ignore the membership fee but take into account the hourly court fee.

How is a fixed cost different from a sunk cost? Since a sunk cost is one that is irretrievably committed, it cannot vary with the level of an activity. *All sunk costs are therefore also fixed costs. But not all fixed costs are sunk costs* (as in the example of a refundable membership fee).

As the next example makes clear, the ability to distinguish between fixed and variable costs is an important component of sound business decisions.

| EXAMPLE 1.10 | **If Commercial Airlines cancels its 10:00 A.M. flight will its profits increase?** |

In an effort to improve profitability, managers of a passenger airline have considered cancelling flights on the least heavily travelled routes. The typical aircraft in the airline's fleet makes 1000 flights a year and generates the following yearly costs:

Annual interest on money borrowed to buy plane	$ 400 000
Annual interest on money borrowed to buy other equipment	400 000
Fuel	400 000
Flight crew salaries	500 000
Maintenance labour	300 000
Total	$2 000 000

Flight crew salaries and maintenance labour are constant amounts for each flight. One flight that may be dropped currently uses an aircraft that makes 1000 flights a year, at an average cost of $2000 per flight. An average of 30 passengers travel on this flight at a ticket price of $60 each, for total ticket revenue of $1800 per flight. Since this flight's revenue is less than its cost, the managers cancel the flight. Is their decision a good one?

The decision is faulty because the managers have failed to distinguish between fixed and variable costs. The labour and fuel expenses they have listed are variable, but interest expenses are fixed. Because labour and fuel expenses total only $1200 per flight—much less than the flight's $1800 ticket revenue—the flight should not be cancelled.

Needless to say, Commercial Airlines could not hope to remain in business if the ticket revenue from *each* of its flights fell short of the average cost of operating that flight. But the criterion for deciding whether any *particular* flight makes sense is to compare its ticket revenues only to those extra costs generated by that flight.

Failure to appreciate the importance of the average–marginal distinction is an important source of error, not just within the world of business but in academia, government—indeed, virtually every sphere of professional and personal life. And a little bit of knowledge can sometimes be a dangerous thing. For example, tennis star Andre Agassi appears to know what a fixed cost is but seems confused about the extent to which such costs matter in deciding how to use his $12 million jet aircraft. "There are certain fixed costs when you own a plane," he explained during a break in the action at a recent tournament, "so the more you fly it the more economic sense it makes." Agassi then said, "The first flight after I bought it, I took some friends to Palm Springs for lunch." Taking the plane on such trips does indeed reduce the average fixed cost per flight. In the same vein, if you purchase a car for $10 000, you can reduce fixed cost per kilometre by driving the car back and forth between two interchanges on the Trans-Canada Highway. Divide $10 000 by 20 000 kilometres, and you will get a smaller number than if you divide by 10 000 kilometres. The more you drive, the lower will be fixed cost per kilometre. To make frivolous flights solely to reduce the average fixed cost per flight makes no more sense than driving aimlessly on the highway so that you can divide the purchase price of your car by a greater number of kilometres.

The conclusion that some costs, especially marginal costs and opportunity costs, are important, while others, like sunk costs and average costs, are irrelevant to economic decisions is implicit in our original statement of the *cost–benefit principle* (taking an action if, and only if, the extra benefits of taking it exceed the extra costs). Yet, the pitfalls of (1) ignoring opportunity costs, (2) considering sunk costs, and (3) confusing average with marginal cost are so important that we enumerate them separately. As a result, a core principle worthy of repeated emphasis emerges:

COST–
BENEFIT

The Principle of Relevant Costs: In considering whether to produce or consume more of a good, what matters is the cost of one more unit (marginal cost).

RELEVANT
COSTS

RECAP	THREE IMPORTANT PITFALLS

1. **The pitfall of ignoring opportunity costs.** When performing a cost–benefit analysis of an action, it is important to account for the full opportunity cost of the action. The opportunity cost of an action is the value of the next best alternative that is foregone by taking the action.

   In calculating opportunity cost, it is important to consider the time value of money. Because money can be invested in an interest-bearing account, a dollar paid or received in the future is worth less than a dollar paid or received today.

2. **The pitfall of not ignoring sunk costs.** When deciding whether to perform an action, it is important to ignore sunk costs—costs that cannot be avoided even if the action is not taken. Even though a ticket to a game may have cost $30, if you have already bought it and cannot sell it to anyone else, the $30 is a sunk cost. If your decision to attend the game is based entirely on the cost–benefit principle, you will ignore the sunk cost.

3. **The pitfall of using average instead of marginal costs and benefits.** Decision makers often have ready information about the total cost and benefit of an activity, and from these it is easy to calculate the activity's average cost and benefit. A common mistake is to conclude that an activity should be increased if its average benefit exceeds its average cost. The cost–benefit principle tells you to increase the level of an activity if, and only if, the *marginal* benefit of doing so exceeds the *marginal* cost.

■ 1.7 ECONOMICS: MICRO AND MACRO

By convention, we use the term **microeconomics** to describe the study of individual choices and of group behaviour in individual markets. **Macroeconomics,** by contrast, is the study of the performance of national economies and of the policies that governments use to try to affect that performance. Macroeconomics tries to understand the determinants of such things as the national unemployment rate, the overall price level, and the total value of national output.

We focus in this chapter and the next on issues that confront the individual decision maker. Further on, we will consider economic models of groups of individuals, such as all buyers or all sellers in a specific market. Later still we will turn to broader economic issues and measures.

No matter which of these levels is our focus, however, our thinking will be shaped by the fact that although economic needs and wants are effectively unlimited, the material and human resources that can be used to satisfy them are finite. Clear thinking about economic problems must therefore always take into account the idea of trade-offs—the idea that having more of one good thing usually means

microeconomics the study of individual choice under scarcity and its implications for the behaviour of prices and quantities in individual markets

macroeconomics the study of the performance of national economies and the policies that governments use to try to improve that performance

having less of another. Our economy and our society are shaped to a substantial degree by the choices people make when faced with trade-offs.

◼ 1.8 THE APPROACH OF THIS TEXT

Choosing the number of students to register in each class is just one of many important decisions in planning an introductory economics course. Another decision, to which the *scarcity problem* applies just as strongly, concerns which of many different topics to include on the course syllabus. There is a virtually inexhaustible set of topics and issues that might be covered in an introductory course but only limited time in which to cover them. There is no free lunch. Covering some topics inevitably means omitting others. Therefore, our strategy is to focus on a short list of core ideas. We promote the understanding of these ideas by returning to each of them repeatedly, in many different contexts.

◼ 1.9 ECONOMIC NATURALISM

With the rudiments of the cost–benefit framework under your belt, you are now in a position to become an "economic naturalist," someone who uses insights from economics to help make sense of observations from everyday life. People who have studied biology are able to observe and marvel at many details of nature that would otherwise escape their notice. For example, while the novice may see only trees on a walk in the woods in early April, the biology student notices many different species of trees and understands why some are already into leaf while others still lie dormant. Likewise, the novice may notice that in some animal species, males are much larger and more impressive in appearance than females, but the biology student knows that that pattern occurs only in species in which males take several mates. Natural selection favours larger males because their greater size helps them to prevail in the often bloody contests among males for access to females. By contrast, males tend to be roughly the same size as females in monogamous species, in which there is much less fighting for mates.

In similar fashion, learning a few simple economic principles enables us to see the mundane details of ordinary human existence in a new light. Whereas the uninitiated often fail even to notice these details, the economic naturalist not only sees them but becomes actively engaged in the attempt to understand them by using positive economics. Let's consider two examples of questions that economic naturalists might pose for themselves.

 1.1   ECONOMIC NATURALIST

Why are some places littered with beer cans and wrecked cars while others are not?

Arriving in the U.K. from Nova Scotia in the summer of 2001, a visiting economic naturalist was surprised to see how much the back alleys of British towns were littered with discarded beer cans and how many abandoned cars could be seen at the side of English roads.

Why did the U.K. have these problems of littering when Nova Scotia (and other Canadian provinces) did not?

The beer can litter problem has an easy explanation—in the U.K. there was no system of deposits on beverage containers, so they were often thrown away after they were emptied, and aluminium cans accumulated at the roadside and in back alleys. Although aluminium can be recycled,

scrap yards did not pay enough, per can, to make it worthwhile for people to collect them. By contrast, in Nova Scotia (and other Canadian provinces) consumers pay a deposit on beverage containers—even if they do not bother to return their empties, the cans and bottles they discard in public places are collected and turned in for the refund. Although the deposit on each container is not large, it is enough of a reward to motivate street people and kids to collect them. Although collecting discarded cans is, on an hourly basis, a poorly paid "job," it still pays more than the opportunity costs of their time. The deposit system means that discarded bottles and cans have, effectively, a market value.

It turns out that the same idea of market value explains the problem of abandoned cars in the U.K. Typically, auto wrecking yards in Canada are willing to pay a few dollars for old cars because the steel has value as scrap iron and there are often usable parts, even on an old heap. Driving (or towing) an old car to the scrap yard may be a sad event, but there are at least a few dollars to be had in recompense. However, this wasn't true in the U.K. in 2001. Because there had been a decline in the price of scrap iron, and because the British government had introduced an environmental charge for disposal of tires and car batteries, disposing of old cars cost money—if done legally. Since the low scrap iron price meant that the value of the steel and parts in a car was now less than the environmental charge for disposal, old cars became a liability rather than a small asset. Faced with this liability, some drivers in the U.K. just took off the plates and walked away from their cars

(which were usually soon stripped of anything valuable and vandalized). The visiting economic naturalist observed several cars abandoned outside the front gate of an auto wrecking yard—the yard owners wanted to be paid to accept the vehicles, but the car owners did not want to actually pay to dispose of their cars. Since they could just park their cars and leave—they did.

Although littering is neither legally nor ethically defensible, it is influenced by the basic cost–benefit economic principle—so public policy to reduce litter has to try to ensure that the benefits to individuals of reducing litter exceeds their costs. In the U.K. case, government policy did not even try to influence that cost–benefit calculation to make it worthwhile to avoid beer can littering, and the new environmental charges on automobiles backfired by increasing the private benefits of littering—thereby creating a new (and worse) environmental problem.

1.2 ECONOMIC NATURALIST

Why do many hardware manufacturers include more than $1000 worth of free software with a computer selling for only slightly more than that?

The software industry is different from many others in the sense that its customers care a great deal about product compatibility. When you and your classmates are working on a project together, for example, your task will be much simpler if you all use the same word-processing program. Likewise, an executive's life will be easier at tax time if her financial software is the same as her accountant's.

The implication is that the benefit of owning and using any given software program increases with the number of other people who use that same product. This unusual relationship gives the producers of the most popular programs an enormous advantage and often makes it hard for new programs to break into the market, creating a *barrier to entry.*

Recognizing this pattern, the Intuit Corporation offered computer makers free copies of *Quicken,* its personal finan-

cial-management software. Computer makers, for their part, were only too happy to include the program, since it made their new computers more attractive to buyers. *Quicken* soon became the standard for personal financial-management programs. By giving away copies of the program, Intuit "primed the pump," creating an enormous demand for upgrades of *Quicken* and for more advanced versions of related software. Thus *TurboTax* and *Macintax,* Intuit's personal income tax software, have become the standards for tax-preparation programs.

Inspired by this success story, other software developers have jumped onto the bandwagon. Most hardware now comes bundled with a host of free software programs. Some software developers are even rumoured to *pay* computer makers to include their programs!

The free-software example illustrates a case in which the *benefit* of a product depends on the number of other people who own that product.

■ SUMMARY

- **1.1** Economics is the study of how people make choices under conditions of scarcity and of the results of those choices for society. Without scarcity, there would be no reason for the subject of economics to exist. Economic analysis of human behaviour begins with the assumption that people are rational—that they have well-defined goals and try to achieve them as best they can. In trying to achieve their goals, people normally face trade-offs: Because material and human resources are limited, having more of one good thing usually means making do with less of some other good thing.

- **1.2** Our focus in this chapter was on how rational people make choices between alternative courses of action. Our basic tool for analyzing these decisions is cost–benefit analysis. The cost–benefit principle says that a person will be better off by taking an action if, and only if, the benefit of that action is greater than its cost. The benefit of an action is measured as the largest dollar amount the person would be willing to pay to take the action. The cost of an action is measured as the dollar value of everything the person must give up to take the action.

- **1.2** Often the question is not whether to pursue an activity but rather how many units of it to pursue. In these cases, the rational actor pursues additional units as long as the marginal benefit of the activity (the benefit from pursuing an additional unit of it) exceeds its marginal cost (the cost of pursuing an additional unit of it).

- **1.4** Three common pitfalls can undermine economic decisions. The first involves the mistake of failing to consider

opportunity costs. The opportunity cost of an activity is the value of the next-best alternative that must be forgone to engage in that activity. If people make the mistake of ignoring the value of forgone alternatives, they are much more likely to make erroneous decisions. We are less likely to make this mistake if we translate questions such as "Should I use my one frequent-flyer coupon on the next flight I take?" into "Will I be better off if I use my one frequent-flyer coupon on the next flight, or wait and use it on another flight?"

- **1.5** The second pitfall involves the tendency not to ignore sunk costs. A sunk cost is a cost that is already irretrievably committed at the moment a decision must be made. In deciding whether to drive through a snowstorm to see a hockey game, the amount you have already paid for your ticket is irrelevant. In deciding whether to pursue an activity, the *only* costs and benefits that matter are the ones that will change with your pursuit of that activity. All other costs and benefits are irrelevant.

- **1.6** The third and final pitfall is the tendency to confuse average and marginal costs and benefits. In deciding whether to increase the number of space shuttle flights, comparing the average cost of current shuttle flights with their average benefit is not instructive. Instead, we must compare the cost of an additional shuttle flight with the benefit of an additional shuttle flight. Such a comparison will often yield different results from a comparison of average costs and benefits.

■ CORE

The Scarcity Problem (See definition page 3)
Without the scarcity problem, there would be no reason for the subject of economics to exist.

The Cost–Benefit Principle
An individual (or a firm or a society) will be better off by taking an action if, and only if, the extra benefits from taking the action are greater than the extra costs.

The Principle of Relevant Costs
In considering whether to produce or consume more of a good, what matters is the cost of one more unit (marginal cost).

■ KEY TERMS

average cost (12)	marginal benefit (12)	positive economics (7)
average benefit (12)	marginal cost (12)	rational person (5)
economics (3)	microeconomics (15)	sunk cost (11)
economic surplus (5)	normative economics (7)	time value of money (10)
fixed cost (13)	opportunity cost (6)	variable cost (13)
macroeconomics (15)		

REVIEW QUESTIONS

1. A friend of yours on the tennis team says, "Private tennis lessons are definitely better than group lessons." Explain what you think your friend means by this statement. Then use the cost–benefit principle to explain why private lessons are not necessarily the best choice for everyone.

2. One of the two bicycle shops near campus is having a sale on new mountain bikes. Sam nonetheless decides to buy his new bike from the other shop, paying $30 more in the process. Describe an example of conditions under which his decision might nonetheless be considered rational.

3. True or false: Your willingness to drive downtown to save $30 on a new appliance should depend on what fraction of the total selling price $30 is. Explain.

4. Why might someone who is trying to decide whether to see a movie be more likely to focus on the $9 ticket price than on the $20 she would fail to earn by not babysitting?

5. Many people think of their air travel as being free when they use frequent-flyer coupons. Explain why these people are likely to make wasteful travel decisions.

6. Why is a lottery ticket that pays you $10 million now worth more than a lottery ticket that pays you $1 million each year for the next 10 years?

7. Is the nonrefundable tuition payment you made to your university this semester a sunk cost? Is it a fixed cost? How would your answers differ if your university were to offer a full tuition refund to any student who dropped out of school during the first two months of the semester?

PROBLEMS

1. The maximum price you would pay for having a freshly washed car when you go out to dinner is $6. The smallest amount for which you would be willing to wash someone else's car is $3.50. You are going out to dinner this evening, and your car is dirty. How much economic surplus would you receive from washing it?

2. To earn extra money in the summer, you grow tomatoes and sell them at the farmers' market for 30 cents per kilogram. By adding compost to your garden, you can increase your yield as shown in the following table. If compost costs 50 cents per kilogram and your goal is to make as much money as possible, how many kilograms of compost will you add?

Kilograms of compost	Kilograms of tomatoes
0	100.0
1	120.0
2	125.0
3	128.0
4	130.0
5	131.0
6	131.5

3. For each long distance call anywhere in Canada, a new phone service will charge users 30 cents per minute for the first 2 minutes and 2 cents per minute for additional minutes in each call. Tom's current phone service charges 10 cents per minute for all calls, and his calls are never shorter than 7 minutes. If Tom's dorm switches to the new phone service, what will happen to the average length of his calls?

4. The meal plan at university A lets students eat as much as they like for a fixed fee of $500 per semester. The average student there eats 125 kg of food per semester. University B charges $500 for a book of meal tickets that entitles the student to eat 125 kg of food per semester. If the student eats more than 125 kg, he or she pays extra; if the student eats less, he or she gets a refund. If students are rational, at which university will average food consumption be higher? Explain briefly.

5. Residents of your city are charged a fixed weekly fee of $6 for garbage collection. They are allowed to put out as many cans as they wish. The average household disposes of three cans of garbage per week under this plan. Now suppose that your city changes to a "tag" system. Each can of refuse to be collected must have a tag affixed to it. The tags cost $2 each and are not reusable. What effect do you think the introduction of the tag system will have on the number of bags of garbage collected in your city? Explain briefly.

6. Once a week, Smith purchases a six-pack of cola and puts it in his refrigerator for his two children. He invariably discovers that all six cans are gone on the first day. Jones also purchases a six-pack of cola once a week for his two children, but unlike Smith, he tells them that each may drink no more than three cans. Explain briefly why the cola lasts much longer at Jones's house than at Smith's.

7. Tom is a mushroom farmer. He invests all his spare cash in additional mushrooms, which grow on otherwise useless land behind his barn. The mushrooms double in weight during their first year, after which time they are harvested and sold at a constant price per kilogram. Tom's friend Dushan asks Tom for a loan of $200, which he promises to repay after 1 year. How much interest will Dushan have to pay Tom for Tom to be no worse off than if he had not made the loan? Explain briefly.

8. When John increased his computer's random-access memory by 64 megabytes, the total benefit he received from using the computer went up $55. John purchased the additional memory at a cost of $0.75 per megabyte, for a total cost of $48.
   a. How much economic surplus did John receive from the additional memory? Explain briefly.
   b. True or false: Because the total benefit of the additional memory was larger than its total cost, John should have added more than 64 megabytes of memory. Explain briefly.

9. A shirt company spends $1000 per week on rent for its factory. Each shirt made at the factory requires $2 worth of cloth and $6 worth of labour and energy. If the factory produces 2000 shirts per week:
   a. What is the average cost of a shirt?
   b. What is the marginal cost of a shirt?

   If the factory produces 3000 shirts per week:
   c. What is the average cost of a shirt?
   d. What is the marginal cost of a shirt?

10. You have won a prize in a provincial lottery. In exchange for your lottery ticket, the provincial government will send you a cheque for $424 one year from now. If bank deposits pay interest at the rate of 6 percent a year, and you already have several thousand dollars in your account, what is the lowest price at which you would be willing to sell your lottery ticket today?

11. A group has chartered a bus trip to Niagara Falls. The driver's fee is $95, the bus rental $500, and the fuel charge $75. The driver's fee is nonrefundable, but the bus rental may be cancelled a week in advance at a charge of $100. At $25 a ticket, how many people must buy tickets a week before so that cancelling the trip definitely will not pay?

12. Sam bought a Trek bicycle for $800 instead of a Cannondale for $1000. Now he finds out that another bike store in town is selling the Cannondale for $800. Mikkel, Sam's friend, offers him $600 for his Trek. If Sam is a rational consumer, should he sell Mikkel his Trek and buy the Cannondale?

13. Courtney planned to travel from Ottawa to Toronto to see Shania Twain in a free Canada Day concert, and had already purchased her $50 round-trip bus ticket (nonrefundable, nontransferable) when she found out that the Tragically Hip was giving a show at the same time in Ottawa for $50. Had she known about the Tragically Hip's show before she bought her bus ticket, she would have chosen to see the Tragically Hip in her hometown. If she is a rational person and her friend Sally offers to give her one of several extra tickets she has for the Tragically Hip's show, what should she do?

14. Mandy and Tomas, who live in Calgary, have identical tastes. They both plan to attend a concert by Alanis Morisette at the Stampede Grounds. The tickets cost $20. Mandy has bought her ticket by phone using her credit card, but Tomas, who doesn't have a credit card, plans to buy his ticket at the door. On the same evening the University of Calgary announces a surprise free fireworks display on campus. If Mandy had known about the fireworks display in advance, she would not have bought the concert ticket. True or false: Assuming Mandy and Tomas are rational and that Mandy cannot resell her ticket, it follows that Mandy will go to the concert, while Tomas will go to the fireworks display. Explain briefly.

■ ANSWERS TO IN-CHAPTER EXERCISES

1.1 The benefit of buying the game downtown is again $10 but the cost is now $12, so your economic surplus from buying it downtown would be $10 − $12 = −$2. Since your economic surplus from making the trip would be negative, you are better off if you buy at the campus store.

1.2 Example 1.4 tells you that if the opportunity cost of the round-trip flight from Edmonton to Vancouver is zero, your economic surplus for the winter vacation will be $350. However, in this case your frequent-flyer coupon has an opportunity cost. Using the frequent-flyer coupon for the trip to Vancouver means having to pay $363 for your airfare one year from now. How much would you be willing to spend today to avoid paying $363 one year from now? Suppose you deposit $350 in your account today at 2 percent interest. By the end of the year, your deposit would be worth $357 (the original $350 plus $7 interest). Because that amount is not enough to pay for your $363 air ticket, the opportunity cost of using the frequent-flyer coupon now must be *more* than $350. Therefore, the cost of the trip to Vancouver is greater than its $1350 benefit, and the cost–benefit principle tells you not to go to Vancouver.

WORKING WITH EQUATIONS, GRAPHS, AND TABLES

Although many of the examples and most of the end-of-chapter problems in this book are quantitative, none require mathematical skills beyond basic high-school algebra and geometry. In this brief appendix we review some of the skills you will need for dealing with these examples and problems.

The ability to translate simple verbal descriptions into the relevant equations or graphs is important. You will also need to translate tabular information into equations or graphs, and sometimes you will need to translate graphical information into a table or equation. The following examples illustrate all the tools you will need.

1A.1 USING A VERBAL DESCRIPTION TO CONSTRUCT AN EQUATION

We begin with an example that shows how to construct a long-distance telephone billing equation from a verbal description of the billing plan.

Your long-distance telephone plan charges you $5/month plus 10 cents/ minute for long-distance calls. Write an equation that describes your monthly telephone bill.

An **equation** is a simple mathematical expression that describes the relationship between two or more **variables,** or quantities, that are free to assume different values in some range. The most common type of equation we'll work with contains two types of variables: **dependent variables** and **independent variables.** In this example, the dependent variable is the dollar amount of your monthly telephone bill, and the independent variable is the variable on which your bill depends, namely, the volume of long-distance calls you make during the month. Your bill also depends on the $5 monthly fee and the 10 cents/minute charge. But in this example, those amounts are **constants,** not variables. A constant, also called a **parameter,** is a quantity in an equation that is fixed in value, not free to vary. As the terms suggest, the dependent variable describes an outcome that depends on the value taken by the independent variable.

Once you have identified the dependent variable and the independent variable, choose simple symbols to represent them. In algebra courses, X is typically used to represent the independent variable and Y the dependent variable. Many people find it easier to remember what the variables stand for, however, if they choose symbols that are linked in some straightforward way to the quantities that the variables represent. Thus, in this example, we might use B to represent your monthly *bill* in dollars and T to represent the total *time* in minutes you spent during the month on long-distance calls.

Having identified the relevant variables and chosen symbols to represent them, you are now in a position to write the equation that links them:

$$B = 5.00 + 0.10T, \qquad (1A.1)$$

where B is your monthly long-distance bill in dollars and T is your monthly total long-distance calling time in minutes. The fixed monthly fee (5.00) and the charge per minute (0.10) are parameters in this equation. Note the importance of being clear about the units of measure. Because B represents the monthly bill in dollars, we must also express the fixed monthly fee and the per-minute charge in dollars, which is why the latter number appears in equation 1A.1 as 0.10 rather than 10. Equation 1A.1 follows the normal convention in which the dependent variable appears by itself on the left-hand side while the independent variable or variables and constants appear on the right-hand side.

Once we have the equation for the monthly bill, we can use it to calculate how much you will owe as a function of your monthly volume of long-distance calls. For example, if you make 32 minutes of calls, you can calculate your monthly bill by simply substituting 32 minutes for T in equation 1A.1:

$$B = 5.00 + 0.10(32) = 8.20. \qquad (1A.2)$$

Your monthly bill when you make 32 minutes of calls is thus equal to $8.20.

equation a mathematical expression that describes the relationship between two or more variables

variable a quantity that is free to take a range of different values

dependent variable a variable in an equation whose value is *determined by* the value taken by another variable in the equation

independent variable a variable in an equation whose value *determines* the value taken by another variable in the equation

constant (or parameter) a quantity that is fixed in value

EXERCISE 1A.1

Under the monthly billing plan described in Example 1A.1, how much would you owe for a month during which you made 45 minutes of long-distance calls?

■ 1A.2 GRAPHING THE EQUATION OF A STRAIGHT LINE

The next example shows how to portray the billing plan described in Example 1A.1 as a graph.

EXAMPLE 1A.2

Construct a graph that portrays the monthly long-distance telephone billing plan described in Example 1A.1, putting your telephone charges, in dollars per month, on the vertical axis, and your total volume of calls, in minutes per month, on the horizontal axis.

The first step in responding to this instruction is the one we just took, namely, to translate the verbal description of the billing plan into an equation. When graphing an equation, the normal convention is to use the vertical axis to represent the dependent variable and the horizontal axis to represent the independent variable. In Figure 1A.1, we therefore put B on the vertical axis and T on the horizontal axis. One way to construct the graph shown in the figure is to begin by plotting the monthly bill values that correspond to several different total amounts of long-distance calls. For example, someone who makes 10 minutes of calls during the month would have a bill of $B = 5.00 + 0.10(10) = \$6.00$. Thus, in Figure 1A.1 the value of 10 minutes/month on the horizontal axis corresponds to a bill of $6/month on the vertical axis (point A). Someone who makes 30 minutes of long-distance calls during the month will have a monthly bill of $B = 5.00 + 0.10(30) = \$8.00$, so the value of 30 minutes/month on the horizontal axis corresponds to $8/month on the vertical axis (point C). Similarly, someone who makes 70 minutes of long-distance calls during the month will have a monthly bill of $B = 5.00 + 0.10(70) = \$12.00$, so the value of 70 minutes on the horizontal axis corresponds to $12 on the vertical axis (point D). The line joining these points is the graph of the monthly billing equation 1A.1.

FIGURE 1A.1
The Monthly Telephone Bill in Example 1A.1
The graph of the equation $B = 5.00 + 0.10T$ is the straight line shown. Its vertical intercept is 5.00, and its slope is 0.10.

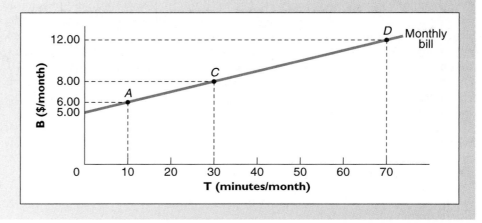

vertical intercept in a straight line, the value taken by the dependent variable when the independent variable equals zero

As shown in Figure 1A.1, the graph of the equation $B = 5.00 + 0.10T$ is a straight line. The parameter 5.00 is the **vertical intercept** of the line—the value of B when $T = 0$, or the point at which the line intersects the vertical axis. The parameter 0.10 is the **slope** of the line, which is the ratio of the **rise** of the line to the corresponding **run.** The ratio rise/run is simply the vertical distance between any two points on the line divided by the horizontal distance between those points. For example, if we choose points A and C in Figure 1A.1, the rise is $8.00 - 6.00 = 2.00$ and the corresponding run is $30.00 - 10.00 = 20.00$, so rise/run = $2.00/20.00 = 0.10$. More generally, for the graph of any equation $Y = a + bX$, the parameter a is the vertical intercept and the parameter b is the slope.

slope in a straight line, the ratio of the vertical distance the straight line travels between any two points *(rise)* to the corresponding horizontal distance *(run)*

1A.3 DERIVING THE EQUATION OF A STRAIGHT LINE FROM ITS GRAPH

The next example shows how to derive the equation for a straight line from a graph of the line.

EXAMPLE 1A.3

Figure 1A.2 shows the graph of the monthly billing plan for a new long-distance plan. What is the equation for this graph? How much is the fixed monthly fee under this plan? How much is the charge per minute?

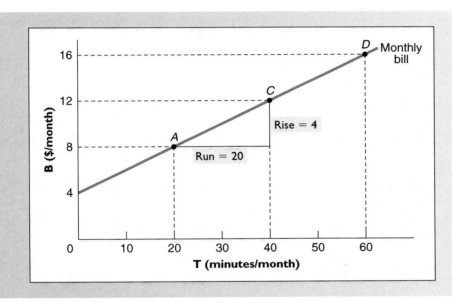

FIGURE 1A.2
Another Monthly Long-Distance Plan
The vertical distance between points A and C is $12.00 - 8.00 = 4.00$ units, and the horizontal distance between points A and C is $40.00 - 20.00 = 20.00$, so the slope of the line is $4.00/20.00 = 1.00/5.00 = 0.20$. The vertical intercept (the value of B when $T = 0$) is 4.00. So the equation for the billing plan shown is $B = 4.00 + 0.20T$.

The slope of the line shown is the rise between any two points divided by the corresponding run. For points A and C, rise = $12.00 - 8.00 = 4.00$, and run = $40.00 - 20.00 = 20.00$, so the slope equals rise/run = $4.00/20.00 = 1.00/5.00 = 0.20$. And since the horizontal intercept of the line is 4.00, its equation must be given by

$$B = 4.00 + 0.20T. \qquad (1A.3)$$

Under this plan, the fixed monthly fee is the value of the bill when $T = 0$, which is \$4. The charge per minute is the slope of the billing line, 0.20, or 20 cents/minute.

EXERCISE 1A.2

Write the equation for the billing plan shown in the accompanying graph on the next page. How much is its fixed monthly fee? its charge per minute?

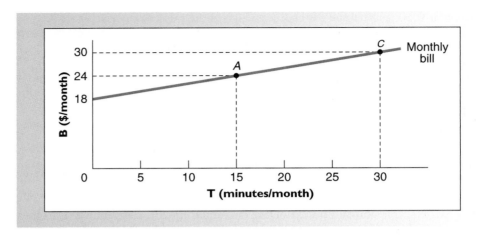

1A.4 CHANGES IN THE VERTICAL INTERCEPT AND SLOPE

Examples 1A.4 and 1A.5 and Exercises 1A.3 and 1A.4 provide practice in seeing how a line shifts with a change in its vertical intercept or slope.

EXAMPLE 1A.4

Show how the billing plan whose graph is in Figure 1A.2 of Example 1A.3 would change if the monthly fixed fee were increased from $4 to $8.

An increase in the monthly fixed fee from $4 to $8 would increase the vertical intercept of the billing plan by $4 but would leave its slope unchanged. An increase in the fixed fee thus leads to a parallel upward shift in the billing plan by $4, as shown in Figure 1A.3. For any given number of minutes of long-distance calls, the monthly charge on the new bill will be $4 higher than on the old bill. Thus 20 minutes of calls per month cost $8 under the original plan (point A) but $12 under the new plan (point A′). And 40 minutes costs $12 under the original plan (point C), $16 under the new plan (point C′); and 60 minutes costs $16 under the original plan (point D), $20 under the new plan (point D′).

FIGURE 1A.3

The Effect of an Increase in the Vertical Intercept

An increase in the vertical intercept of a straight line produces an upward parallel shift in the line.

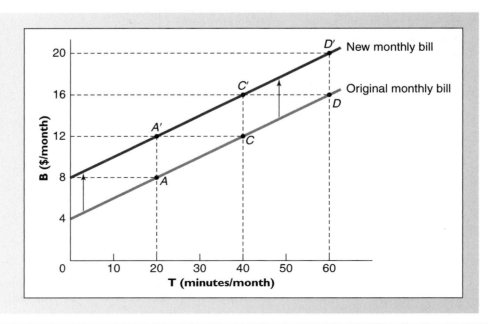

EXERCISE 1A.3

Show how the billing plan whose graph is in Figure 1A.2 would change if the monthly fixed fee were reduced from $4 to $2.

EXAMPLE 1A.5

Show how the billing plan whose graph is in Figure 1A.2 would change if the charge per minute were increased from 20 cents to 40 cents.

Because the monthly fixed fee is unchanged, the vertical intercept of the new billing plan continues to be 4. But the slope of the new plan, shown in Figure 1A.4, is 0.40, or twice the slope of the original plan. More generally, in the equation $Y = a + bX$, an increase in b makes the slope of the graph of the equation steeper.

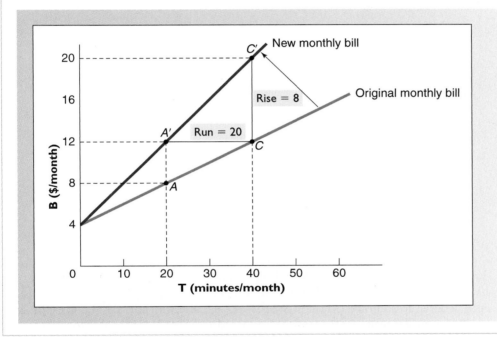

FIGURE 1A.4

The Effect of an Increase in the Charge per Minute Because the fixed monthly fee continues to be $4, the vertical intercept of the new plan is the same as that of the original plan. With the new charge per minute of 40 cents, the slope of the billing plan rises from 0.20 to 0.40.

EXERCISE 1A.4

Show how the billing plan whose graph is in Figure 1A.2 would change if the charge per minute were reduced from 20 cents to 10 cents.

Exercise 1A.4 illustrates the general rule that in an equation $Y = a + bX$, a reduction in b makes the slope of the graph of the equation less steep.

■ 1A.5 CONSTRUCTING EQUATIONS AND GRAPHS FROM TABLES

Example 1A.6 and Exercise 1A.5 show how to transform tabular information into an equation or graph.

EXAMPLE 1A.6

Table 1A.1 shows four points from a monthly long-distance telephone billing equation. If all points on this billing equation lie on a straight line, find the vertical intercept of the equation and graph it. What is the monthly fixed fee? What is the charge per minute? Calculate the total bill for a month with 1 hour of long-distance calls.

TABLE IA.I
Points on a Long-Distance Billing Plan

Long-distance bill ($/month)	Total long-distance calls (minutes/month)
10.50	10
11.00	20
11.50	30
12.00	40

FIGURE IA.5

Plotting the Monthly Billing Equation from a Sample of Points

Point *A* is taken from row 2, Table IA.I, and point *C* from row 4. The monthly billing plan is the straight line that passes through these points.

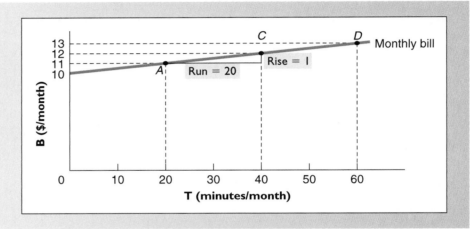

One approach to this problem is simply to plot any two points from the table on a graph. Since we are told that the billing equation is a straight line, that line must be the one that passes through any two of its points. Thus, in Figure 1A.5 we use *A* to denote the point from Table 1A.1 for which a monthly bill of $11 corresponds to 20 minutes/month of calls (second row) and *C* to denote the point for which a monthly bill of $12 corresponds to 40 minutes/month of calls (fourth row). The straight line passing through these points is the graph of the billing equation.

Unless you have a steady hand, however, or use extremely large graph paper, the method of extending a line between two points on the billing plan is unlikely to be very accurate. An alternative approach is to calculate the equation for the billing plan directly. Since the equation is a straight line, we know that it takes the general form $B = f + sT$, where f is the fixed monthly fee and s is the slope. Our goal is to calculate the vertical intercept f and the slope s. From the same two points we plotted earlier, A and C, we can calculate the slope of the billing plan as s = rise/run = 1/20 = 0.05.

So all that remains is to calculate f, the fixed monthly fee. At point C on the billing plan, the total monthly bill is $12 for 40 minutes, so we can substitute $B = 12$, $s = 0.05$, and $T = 40$ into the general equation $B = f + sT$ to obtain

$$12 = f + 0.05(40), \tag{1A.4}$$

or

$$12 = f + 2, \tag{1A.5}$$

which solves for $f = 10$. So the monthly billing equation must be

$$B = 10 + 0.05T. \qquad\qquad (1A.6)$$

For this billing equation, the fixed fee is \$10/month, the calling charge is 5 cents/minute (\$0.05/minute), and the total bill for a month with 1 hour of long-distance calls is $B = 10 + 0.05(60) = \$13$, just as shown in Figure 1A.5.

The following table shows four points from a monthly long-distance telephone billing plan.

Long-distance bill ($/month)	Total long-distance calls (minutes/month)
20.00	10
30.00	20
40.00	30
50.00	40

If all points on this billing plan lie on a straight line, find the vertical intercept of the corresponding equation without graphing it. What is the monthly fixed fee? What is the charge per minute? How much would the charges be for 1 hour of long-distance calls per month?

■ KEY TERMS

constant (23)
dependent variable (23)
equation (23)
independent variable (23)

parameter (23)
rise (25)
run (25)

slope (25)
variable (23)
vertical intercept (24)

■ ANSWERS TO APPENDIX EXERCISES

1A.1 To calculate your monthly bill for 45 minutes of calls, substitute 45 minutes for T in equation 1A.1 to get $B = 5.00 + 0.10(45) = \$9.50$.

1A.2 Calculating the slope using points A and C, we have rise $= 30.00 - 24.00 = 6.00$ and run $= 30.00 - 15.00 = 15.00$, so rise/run $= 6.00/15.00 = 2.00/5.00 = 0.40$. And since the horizontal intercept of the line is 18, its equation is $B = 18.00 + 0.40T$. Under this plan, the fixed monthly fee is \$18, and the charge per minute is the slope of the billing line, 0.40, or 40 cents/minute.

1A.3 A $2 reduction in the monthly fixed fee would produce a downward parallel shift in the billing plan by $2.

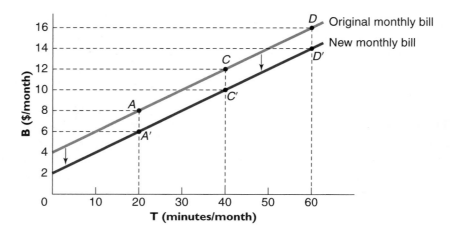

1A.4 With an unchanged monthly fixed fee, the vertical intercept of the new billing plan continues to be 4. The slope of the new plan is 0.10, half the slope of the original plan.

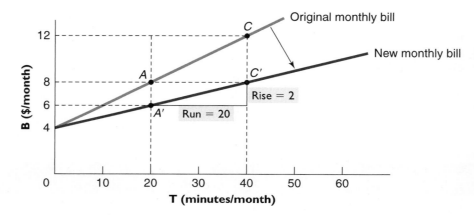

1A.5 Let the billing equation be $B = f + sT$, where f is the fixed monthly fee and s is the slope. From the first two points in the table, calculate the slope s = rise/run = 10/10 = 1.0. To calculate f, we can use the information in row 1 of the table to write the billing equation as $20 = f + 1.0(10)$ and solve for $f = 10$. So the monthly billing equation must be $B = 10 + 1.0T$. For this billing equation, the fixed fee is $10/month, the calling charge is $1/minute, and the total bill for a month with 1 hour of long-distance calls is $B = 10 + 1.0(60) = \$70$.

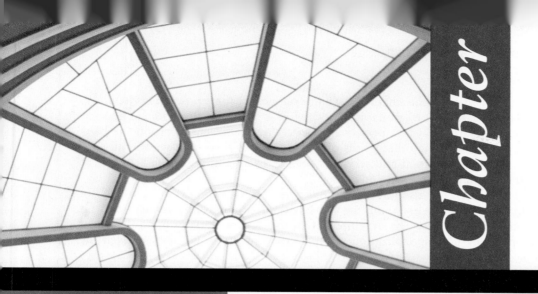

COMPARATIVE ADVANTAGE: THE BASIS FOR EXCHANGE

During a stint as a volunteer teacher in rural Nepal, a young economic naturalist employed a cook named Birkhaman, who came from a remote Himalayan village in neighbouring Bhutan. Although Birkhaman had virtually no formal education, he was spectacularly resourceful. His primary duties, to prepare food and maintain the kitchen, he performed with competence and dispatch. But he also had many other skills. He could thatch a roof, butcher a goat, and repair shoes. An able tinsmith and a good carpenter, he could sew, fix a broken alarm clock, and plaster walls. On top of all that, he was a local authority on home remedies.

Birkhaman's range of skills was broad even by Nepalese standards. But even the least skilled Nepalese villager can perform a wide range of services that most North Americans hire others to perform. The alternative to a system in which everyone is a jack-of-all-trades is one in which people *specialize* in particular goods and services, then satisfy their needs by trading among themselves. Economic systems based on specialization and the exchange of goods and services are generally far more productive than those with less specialization—and this is a large part of the reason why income per person in Nepal is less than one hundredth that in Canada. Our task in this chapter is to investigate why exchange and specialization can increase economic output. In doing so we will explore why people choose to exchange goods and services in the first place, rather than having each person produce his own food, cars, clothing, shelter, and the like.

Did this man perform most of his own services because he was poor, or was he poor because he performed most of his own services?

A major focus of this chapter is what economists call *comparative advantage.* Roughly, a person has a comparative advantage at producing a particular good or service, say haircuts, if that person is *relatively* more efficient at producing haircuts than at producing other goods or services. We will see that we can all consume more of *every* good and service if each of us specializes in the activities at which we have a comparative advantage.

This chapter will also introduce the *production possibilities curve,* which is a graphical method of describing the combinations of goods and services that an economy can produce. The development of this tool will allow us to see much more precisely how specialization enhances the productive capacity of even the simplest economy.

◼ 2.1 EXCHANGE AND OPPORTUNITY COST

The scarcity problem (see Chapter 1) reminds us that the opportunity cost of spending more time on any one activity is having less time available to spend on others. As the following example makes clear, this helps explain why everyone can do better by concentrating on those activities at which she performs best relative to others.

EXAMPLE 2.1

Will a top lawyer be better off if he prepares his own will?

Will Johnnie Cochran be better off if he writes his own will?

Attorney Johnnie Cochran gained international attention as the leader of the legal team that, against all odds, won O. J. Simpson's acquittal of the charge of murdering his former wife and her friend in 1994. By consensus, Cochran is one of the most able attorneys in the U.S. For example, when the *California Lawyer* magazine asked leading California attorneys whom they would hire if they were charged with a serious felony, Cochran's was the name most often mentioned. But although Cochran devotes virtually all of his working hours to high-profile litigation, he is also competent to perform a much broader range of legal services. Suppose, for example, that he could prepare his own will in two hours, only half as long as it would take any other attorney. Does that mean that Cochran will be better off if he prepares his own will?

On the strength of his talent as a litigator, Cochran earns several million dollars a year, which means that the opportunity cost of any time he spends preparing his will would be more than $1,000 per hour. Attorneys who specialize in property law typically earn far less than that amount. Cochran would have little difficulty engaging a competent property lawyer who could prepare his will for him for less than $800. So even though Cochran's considerable skills would enable him to perform this task more quickly than another attorney, it would not be in his interest to prepare his own will.

---

absolute advantage one person has an absolute advantage over another if he or she takes fewer hours to perform a task than the other person

comparative advantage one person has a comparative advantage over another if his or her opportunity cost of performing a task is lower than the other person's opportunity cost

In the preceding example, economists would say that Cochran has an **absolute advantage** at preparing his will but a **comparative advantage** at trial work. He has an absolute advantage at preparing his will because he can perform that task in less time than a property lawyer could. Even so, the property lawyer has a comparative advantage at preparing wills because his opportunity cost of performing that task is lower than Cochran's.

The point of Example 2.1 is not that people whose time is valuable should never perform their own services. That example made the implicit assumption that Cochran would have been equally happy to spend an hour preparing his will or preparing for a trial. If he was tired of trial preparation and felt it might be enjoyable to refresh his knowledge of property law, preparing his own will might then have made perfect sense! But unless he expected to gain special satisfaction from performing that task, he would almost certainly do better to hire a property lawyer. The property lawyer would also benefit, or else she would not have offered to prepare wills for the stated price.

THE PRINCIPLE OF COMPARATIVE ADVANTAGE

One of the most important insights of modern economics is that when two people (or two nations) have different opportunity costs of performing various tasks, they can increase the total value of available goods and services by trading with one another. The following simple example captures the logic behind this insight.

Will Rikke be better off if she updates her own Web page?	**EXAMPLE 2.2**

Consider the case of Rikke and Beth. Rikke is a professional bicycle mechanic who can repair a bicycle in 10 minutes. Rikke also knows hypertext markup language (HTML), and she can update a Web page in 20 minutes. It takes Beth 30 minutes to repair a bicycle and 30 minutes to update a Web page. Each regards the two tasks as roughly equal in pleasantness. These data are summarized in Table 2.1. The table shows that Rikke possesses an absolute advantage over Beth in both activities.

TABLE 2.1
Productivity Information for Rikke and Beth

	Time to update a Web page	Time to complete a bicycle repair
Rikke	20 minutes	10 minutes
Beth	30 minutes	30 minutes

But the fact that Rikke is a better programmer than Beth does *not* imply that Rikke will be better off if she updates her own Web page. If Rikke uses 20 minutes to update her Web page, the same 20 minutes cannot be used to repair bicycles. Because she can repair a bicycle in 10 minutes, Rikke incurs an opportunity cost of two bicycle repairs when she updates a Web page. If Beth spends 30 minutes to update a Web page, she cannot use the same 30 minutes to repair a bicycle. Table 2.1 shows that if Beth updates a Web page, the opportunity cost is one bicycle repair. Therefore, Beth's opportunity cost for updating a Web page is one-half of Rikke's. Like the property lawyer who has a comparative advantage over the trial lawyer in preparing wills, Beth has a comparative advantage over Rikke in programming. If we were to consider Rikke's and Beth's opportunity cost of repairing bicycles, we would also show the corollary: Because Rikke's opportunity cost of repairing a bicycle is half Beth's, Rikke has a comparative advantage at repairing bicycles.

Table 2.2 summarizes the data on opportunity costs. These data imply that if Rikke and Beth both spend part of their time at each task, the number of Web page updates and bicycle repairs will be smaller than if each specializes according to her comparative advantage.

TABLE 2.2
Opportunity Costs for Rikke and Beth

	Opportunity cost of updating a Web page	Opportunity cost of a bicycle repair
Rikke	2 bicycle repairs	0.5 Web page update
Beth	1 bicycle repair	1 Web page update

To see this, suppose that their community wants 16 Web page updates per day. If neither person specializes and if Rikke spends half her eight-hour workday updating Web pages, she can update 12 Web pages. By spending two hours programming, Beth can provide four more updates, for a total of 16 Web page updates per day. Out of Rikke's eight-hour workday, four hours will remain for repairing bicycles. At 10 minutes per repair, Rikke will repair 24 bicycles per day. Six hours remain out of Beth's eight-hour day. In six hours, she will repair 12 bicycles. Together, Rikke and Beth repair 36 bicycles per eight-hour day. These data are summarized in Part A of Table 2.3.

TABLE 2.3
The Gains When Rikke and Beth Specialize

Part A: Without Specialization				
	Time spent updating Web pages	Number of updated Web pages	Time spent repairing bicycles	Number of bicycles repaired
Rikke	4 hours	12	4 hours	24
Beth	2 hours	4	6 hours	12
Total output		16		36

Part B: With Specialization According to Comparative Advantage				
	Time spent updating Web pages	Number of updated Web pages	Time spent repairing bicycles	Number of bicycles repaired
Rikke	0 hours	0	8 hours	48
Beth	8 hours	16	0 hours	0
Total output		16		48
Net gain with specialization		0		12

Suppose each woman had specialized according to comparative advantage. In eight hours Beth would update 16 Web pages; in eight hours Rikke would repair 48 bicycles. Part B of Table 2.3 summarizes these data. With specialization, 12 more bicycles are repaired, and there is no reduction in the number of Web page updates. Specialization reduces the opportunity cost of the 16 Web page updates the community wants. Therefore, specialization creates 12 additional bicycle repairs!

"We're a natural, Rachel. I handle intellectual property, and you're a content-provider."

When computing the opportunity cost of one good in terms of another, we must pay close attention to the form in which the information is presented. In Example 2.2, we were told how many minutes each person needed to perform each task. Alternatively, we might be given data on each person's **productivity** in each task. A person's labour productivity is her output per hour of labour time. Her labour is an input to a production process. Thus in Exercise 2.1 below, Barb's productivity when she repairs bicycles is three repairs per hour. Work through the exercise to see how to proceed when information is presented in this alternative format.

productivity units of output per hour divided by units of input per hour

EXERCISE 2.1

Will Barb be better off if she updates her own Web page?
    The following table shows the productivity rates for Barb and Mina in HTML programming and repairing bicycles. Does the fact that Barb can program faster than Mina imply that Barb will be better off if she updates her own Web page?

	Productivity in programming	Productivity in bicycle repair
Mina	2 Web page updates per hour	1 repair per hour
Barb	3 Web page updates per hour	3 repairs per hour

The principle illustrated by Examples 2.1 and 2.2 is so important that we state it formally as one of the core ideas of the course:

The Principle of Comparative Advantage: Total output is largest when each person (or each country) concentrates on the activities for which his or her opportunity cost is lowest.

COMPARATIVE
ADVANTAGE

Indeed, the gains made possible from specialization based on comparative advantage constitute the rationale for market exchange. They explain why each person does not devote 10 percent of his time to producing cars, 5 percent to growing food, 25 percent to building housing, 0.0001 percent to performing brain surgery, and so on. By concentrating on those tasks at which we are relatively most productive, together we can produce vastly more than if we all tried to be self-sufficient.

This insight brings us back to Birkhaman the cook. Though Birkhaman's versatility was marvelous, he was not nearly as good a doctor as someone who has been trained in medical school nor as good a repairman as someone who spends each day fixing things. If several people with Birkhaman's talents had joined together, each of them specializing in one or two tasks, together they would have enjoyed more and better goods and services than each could possibly have produced on his own. Although there is much to admire in the resourcefulness of people who have learned through necessity to rely on their own skills, that path is no route to economic prosperity.

SOURCES OF COMPARATIVE ADVANTAGE

At the individual level, comparative advantage often appears to be the result of inborn talent. For instance, some people seem to be naturally gifted at programming computers, while others seem to have a special knack for fixing bicycles. But nobody is born knowing how to fix bicycles. Actual ability, at a particular point in time, is always the result of innate ability plus education, training, and experience.

To understand why some people, such as Johnnie Cochran, are so good at law while others are better at carpentry, we have to examine how those skills were developed. Similarly, at the national level, comparative advantage may derive

www.internationalecon.com/ v1.0/ch40/ch40.html Economics Study Centre

from differences in natural resources or from differences in society, culture, or institutions. Canada, which has one of the world's highest per capita endowments of farm and forest land, has a comparative advantage in the production of agricultural and forestry products. However, topography and climate explain why Canada produces so much wheat while New Zealand has so many sheep.

Seemingly noneconomic factors can also give rise to comparative advantage. For instance, the emergence of English as the de facto world language gives English-speaking countries a comparative advantage over non-English-speaking nations in the production of books, movies, and popular music. Technological change and governmental policies can also play a role.

2.1 ECONOMIC NATURALIST

How Does Comparative Advantage Arise and Why Might Countries Not take Advantage of It?

In 1890, Canadian pulp and paper was a small, insignificant industry with only very limited access to the American market. Forty years later, Canada was the world's largest papermaker and exported much of its product to the United States. Today, pulp and paper remains one of Canada's most important industries. How did Canada "create" a pulp and paper industry? How is this case relevant to today's trade disputes?

In the mid-nineteenth century, paper was produced in costly, small-scale operations. Rags, grasses, and straw provided the raw material. Beginning in 1851, a series of technological advances allowed cellulose to be isolated from wood and used as the raw material for paper. The new processes operated on a much larger scale and required large amounts of electricity. The new technology gave Canada, with its vast forests and large potential to produce hydroelectricity, a comparative advantage in the manufacture of paper. However, it was not clear that Canada would be able to benefit from its comparative advantage.

By 1900, the United States could not satisfy its growing demand for newsprint. The United States protected its pulp and paper industry from Canadian competition with high tariffs on imported pulp and paper and by imposing no duties on raw, imported pulpwood. This enabled the American pulp and paper industry to obtain inexpensive pulpwood from Canada and then to manufacture it into pulp and paper that it sold in the United States.

Under Canadian federalism, the provinces have the right to manage their natural resources. In 1902, Ontario placed an embargo on the export of pulpwood harvested from Crown lands. The embargo prevented pulpwood from being exported to the United States. No restrictions were imposed on the export of pulp and paper. The purpose was

to encourage pulp and paper manufactured in Ontario to be exported to the United States. By 1915, all other provinces had taken similar measures.

The United States responded to pressure from its own pulp and paper industry by increasing its tariffs on Canadian pulp and paper. This made the Canadian product more expensive to Americans and might have defeated efforts to develop a Canadian industry by causing the Americans to buy pulp and paper elsewhere. But there was nowhere else to buy. The higher tariffs simply caused American newspapers to pay more for Canadian newsprint. In 1913, the interests of the American newspaper industry prevailed over the interests of the American pulp and paper industry, and Congress removed the tariffs against Canadian pulp and newsprint. By 1929, Canada was producing more than twice as much newsprint as the United States and was the world's largest papermaker.

Comparative advantage obviously facilitated the creation of a Canadian pulp and paper industry, but other factors played a role, too. American demand for Canadian newsprint was growing rapidly, and the American newspaper industry's desire for access to inexpensive Canadian newsprint aligned with the interests of Canadian pulp and paper. Provincial governments undertook trade policies that capitalized on these factors. The United States removed its trade barriers to Canadian pulp and paper, and the Canadian industry flourished.[1]

Canada's current trade dispute with the United States over another forest product, softwood lumber, spans more than a century. Canada provides the United States with about 35 percent of its softwood lumber. Restrictions on the importation of Canadian lumber serve the interests of the American lumber industry, but they cost the American

[1]Adapted from B.D. Lesser, "Canada 'Creates' a Pulp and Paper Industry," in B.D. Lesser (ed.), *Four Case Studies on Aspects of the Canadian Economy*, Halifax: Nova Scotia Department of Education, 1977, pp. 1–2. See also Kenneth Norrie and Douglas Owram, *A History of the Canadian Economy*, 2nd ed., Toronto: Harcourt Brace & Company Canada, Ltd., 1996, pp. 256–257, 323–324.

construction industry about $1 billion annually because they increase U.S. lumber prices.[2] The interests of Canadian lumber and American construction converge in ways that could some day prove useful to Canadian negotiators but until now the political influence of U.S. lumber producers has been stronger. The softwood lumber case is an example of a failure to take advantage of comparative advantage due to protectionism. Some people (in this case, U.S. lumber producers) lose from greater trade, even if the potential gains from greater trade (in this case, for the U.S. construction industry) are larger than the total losses. If the losers from greater trade are not compensated for their losses, they have a self-interested reason to propose restraints on trade, and sometimes can do so successfully.

RECAP	EXCHANGE AND OPPORTUNITY COST

Gains from exchange are possible if trading partners have comparative advantages in producing different goods and services. An individual has a comparative advantage when his or her opportunity cost—measured in terms of other production opportunities foregone—is smaller than the corresponding opportunity costs of his or her trading partners. Maximum production is achieved if each person specializes in producing the good or service in which she has the lowest opportunity cost (the principle of comparative advantage). Comparative advantage makes specialization worthwhile even if one trading partner has an absolute advantage in every activity.

2.2 COMPARATIVE ADVANTAGE AND PRODUCTION POSSIBILITIES

Comparative advantage and specialization allow an economy to produce more than if each person tries to produce a little of everything. In this section we gain further insight into the advantages of specialization by first examining an imaginary economy with only one person and then noting how economic possibilities change as new people join the economy. Along the way, we will introduce a useful graph called the *production possibilities curve*, which can be used to describe the combinations of goods and services that a particular economy can produce.

PRODUCTION POSSIBILITIES IN A ONE-PERSON ECONOMY

We begin with a hypothetical economy consisting of a single worker who can produce two goods, sugar cane and Macadamia nuts. The worker lives on a small island, and "production" consists either of cutting sugar cane that grows on the island's central valley floor or picking Macadamia nuts that grow on trees on the hillsides overlooking the valley. The more time the worker spends cutting sugar cane, the less time she has available for picking nuts. If she wants more sugar cane, then she must make do with a smaller amount of nuts. Knowing how productive she is at each activity, we can easily summarize the various combinations of sugar cane and nuts she can harvest each day if she makes full use of her available working time. This menu of possibilities is known as the **production possibilities curve.**

As the following example illustrates, constructing the production possibilities curve for a one-person economy is a straightforward matter.

production possibilities curve a graph that describes the maximum amount of one good that can be produced for every possible level of production of the other good

---

[2]David Laband and Daowei Zhang, "America's Been Bushwhacked."

EXAMPLE 2.3

What is the production possibilities curve for an economy in which Susan is the only worker?

Consider a society consisting only of Susan, who allocates her production time between sugar cane and nuts. Each hour per day she devotes to cutting sugar cane yields 1.5 kg of cane, and each hour she devotes to harvesting nuts yields 3 kg of nuts. If Susan works a total of eight hours per day, describe her production possibilities curve—the graph that displays, for each level of sugar cane she cuts, the maximum amount of nuts that Susan can pick.

The vertical axis in Figure 2.1 shows Susan's daily production of sugar cane, and the horizontal axis shows her daily production of nuts. Let's begin by looking at two extreme allocations of her time. First, suppose she employs her entire workday (eight hours per day) cutting sugar cane. In that case, since she can cut 1.5 kg of sugar cane per hour, she would pick (8 hours/day)(1.5 kg/hour) = 12 kg per day of sugar cane and 0 kg of nuts. That combination of sugar cane and nuts is represented by point *A* in Figure 2.1, the vertical intercept of Susan's production possibilities curve.

FIGURE 2.1

Susan's Production Possibilities

For the production relationships given, the production possibilities curve is a straight line.

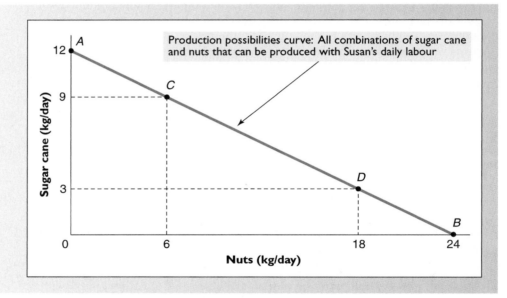

Now suppose, instead, that Susan devotes all her time to picking nuts. Since she can pick 3 kg of nuts per hour, her total daily production would be (8 hours/day)(3 kg/hour) = 24 kg of nuts. That combination is represented by point *B* in Figure 2.1, the horizontal intercept of Susan's production possibilities curve. Because Susan's production of each good is exactly proportional to the amount of time she devotes to that good, the remaining points along her production possibilities curve will lie on the straight line that joins *A* and *B*.

For example, suppose that Susan devotes six hours each day to cutting sugar cane and two hours to picking nuts. She will then produce (6 hours/day)(1.5 kg/hour) = 9 kg of sugar cane per day and (2 hours/day)(3 kg/hour) = 6 kg of nuts. This is the point labelled *C* in Figure 2.1. Alternatively, if she devotes two hours to sugar cane and six hours to nuts, she will get (2 hours/day)(1.5 kg/hour) = 3 kg of sugar cane per day and (6 hours/day)(3 kg/hour) = 18 kg of nuts. This alternative combination is represented by point *D* in Figure 2.1.

Since Susan's production possibilities curve (PPC) is a straight line, its slope is constant. The absolute value of the slope of Susan's PPC is the ratio of its vertical intercept to its horizontal intercept: (12 kg of sugar cane/day)/(24 kg of nuts/day) = 1/2 kg of sugar cane/1 kg of nuts. (Be sure to keep track of the units of measure on each axis when computing this ratio.) *This ratio means that Susan's opportunity cost of an additional kilogram of nuts is 1/2 kilogram of sugar cane.*

Note that Susan's opportunity cost of nuts can also be expressed as the following simple formula:

$$OC_{nuts} = \frac{\text{loss in sugar cane}}{\text{gain in nuts}},$$

where "loss in sugar cane" means the amount of sugar cane given up and "gain in nuts" means the corresponding increase in nuts. Likewise, Susan's opportunity cost of sugar cane is expressed by this formula:

$$OC_{sugar\ cane} = \frac{\text{loss in nuts}}{\text{gain in sugar cane}}.$$

To say that Susan's opportunity cost of an additional kilogram of nuts is 1/2 kg of sugar cane is equivalent to saying that her opportunity cost of 1 kg of sugar cane is 2 kg of nuts.

The production possibilities curve shown in Figure 2.1 illustrates the scarcity problem—the idea that because our resources are limited, having more of one good or service generally means having to settle for less of another (see Chapter 1). Although we generally specify the "price" of a commodity in dollar terms, economists think of the concept of "price" in more general terms—what a person has to give up in order to get something. Susan can have an additional kilogram of sugar cane if she wants, but only if she is willing to give up 2 kg of nuts. If Susan is the only person in the economy, her opportunity cost of producing a good becomes, in effect, its price. Thus, the price she has to pay for an additional kilogram of sugar cane is 2 kg of nuts; or equivalently, the price she has to pay for an additional kilogram of nuts is 1/2 kg of sugar cane.

Any point that lies either on the production possibilities curve or to the left of it is said to be an **attainable point,** meaning that it can be produced with currently available resources. In Figure 2.2, for example, points *A*, *B*, *C*, *D*, and *E* are attainable points. Points that lie to the right of the production possibilities curve

attainable point any combination of goods that can be produced using currently available resources

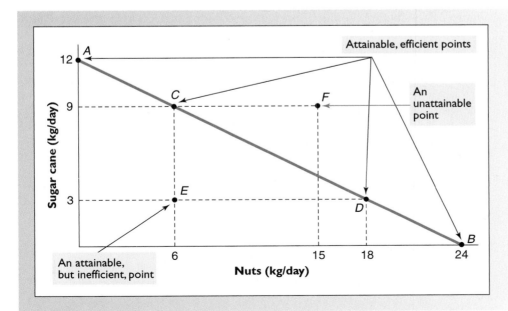

FIGURE 2.2

Attainable and Efficient Points on Susan's Production Possibilities Curve
Points that lie either on the production possibilities curve (for example, *A, C, D,* and *B*) or to its left (for example, *E*) are said to be attainable. Points that lie to the right the production possibilities curve (for example, *F*) are unattainable. Points that lie on the curve are said to be efficient, while those that lie within the curve are said to be inefficient.

unattainable point any combination of goods that cannot be produced using currently available resources

inefficient point any combination of goods for which currently available resources enable an increase in the production of one good without a reduction in the production of the other

efficient point any combination of goods for which currently available resources do not allow an increase in the production of one good without a reduction in the production of the other

are said to be **unattainable**, meaning that they cannot be produced using currently available resources. In Figure 2.2, *F* is an unattainable point because Susan cannot produce 9 kg of sugar cane per day *and* 15 kg of nuts. Points that lie within the curve are said to be **inefficient**, in the sense that existing resources would allow for production of more of at least one good without sacrificing the production of any other good. At *E*, for example, Susan is producing only 3 kg of sugar cane per day and 6 kg of nuts, which means that she could increase her harvest of sugar cane by 6 kg per day without giving up any nuts (by moving from *E* to *C*). Alternatively, Susan could pick as many as 12 additional kgs of nuts each day without giving up any sugar cane (by moving from *E* to *D*). An **efficient point** is one that lies on the production possibilities curve. At any such point, more of one good can be produced only by producing less of the other.

Why might Susan be at point E? Perhaps she has been using a glove, which slows her down—in economic terms, she is at point E because she is using an inefficient technique. By switching to an efficient technique, she gets more of both goods.

FACTORS THAT INFLUENCE THE PRODUCTION POSSIBILITIES CURVE

To see how the slope and position of the production possibilities curve depend on an individual's productivity, let's compare Susan's PPC to that of a person who is less productive in both activities.

EXAMPLE 2.4

How do changes in productivity affect the opportunity cost of nuts?

Suppose Tom can harvest 0.75 kg of nuts for each hour he devotes to picking nuts and 0.75 kg of sugar cane for each hour he spends cutting sugar cane. If Tom is the only person in the economy, describe the economy's production possibilities curve.

We can construct Tom's PPC the same way we did Susan's. Note first that if Tom devotes an entire workday (8 hours/day) to cutting sugar cane, he harvests (8 hours/day)(0.75 kg/hour) = 6 kg of sugar cane per day and 0 kg of nuts. Therefore, the vertical intercept of Tom's PPC is *A* in Figure 2.3. If instead he devotes all his time to picking nuts, he gets (8 hours/day)(0.75 kg/hour) = 6 kg of nuts per day and no sugar cane. That means the horizontal intercept of his PPC is *B* in Figure 2.3. As before, because Tom's production of each good is proportional to the amount of time he devotes to it, the remaining points on his PPC will lie along the straight line that joins these two extreme points.

FIGURE 2.3
Tom's Production Possibilities Curve
The less productive a person is, the closer to the origin is his PPC.

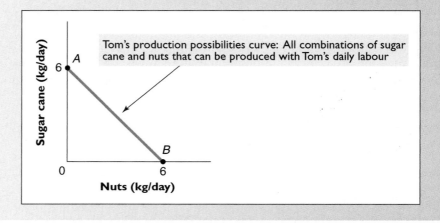

Tom's production possibilities curve: All combinations of sugar cane and nuts that can be produced with Tom's daily labour

How does Tom's PPC compare with Susan's? Note that because Tom is less productive than Susan at both activities, the horizontal and vertical intercepts of Tom's PPC lie closer to the origin than do Susan's (see Figure 2.4). For Tom, the opportunity cost of an additional kilogram of nuts is 1 kg of sugar cane, which is twice Susan's opportunity cost of nuts. This difference in opportunity costs shows up as a difference in the slopes of their PPCs: the absolute value of the slope of Tom's PPC is 1, whereas Susan's is 1/2.

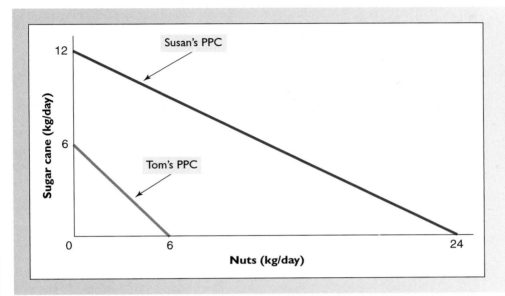

FIGURE 2.4

Individual Production Possibilities Curves Compared

Though Tom is less productive in both activities than Susan, Tom's opportunity cost of cutting sugar cane is only half Susan's.

But note too that while Tom is absolutely less efficient than Susan at harvesting sugar cane, his opportunity cost of sugar cane is only half Susan's. Whereas Susan must give up 2 kg of nuts to pick an additional kilogram of sugar cane, Tom must give up only 1 kg. This difference in opportunity costs is another example of the concept of comparative advantage. Although Tom is *absolutely* less efficient than Susan at harvesting sugar cane, he is *relatively* more efficient. That is, Susan has an absolute advantage in both sugar cane and nuts, but Tom has a comparative advantage in sugar cane. Susan's comparative advantage is in nuts.

Notice that the principle of comparative advantage is a relative concept— one that makes sense only when the productivities of two or more people (or countries) are being compared. To cement this idea, work through the following exercise.

EXERCISE 2.2

Suppose Susan can harvest 1.5 kg of sugar cane per hour or 3 kg of nuts per hour; Tom can pick 0.75 kg of sugar cane per hour and 2.25 kg of nuts per hour. What is Susan's opportunity cost of picking a kilogram of nuts? What is Tom's opportunity cost of picking a kilogram of nuts? Where does Susan's comparative advantage now lie?

PRODUCTION POSSIBILITIES IN A TWO-PERSON ECONOMY

Why have we spent so much time defining comparative advantage? As the next examples illustrate, a comparative advantage arising from disparities in individual opportunity costs can create gains for everyone.

EXAMPLE 2.5

How does the one-person economy's PPC change when a second person is added?

Suppose Susan can harvest 1.5 kg of sugar cane per hour or 3 kg of nuts and Tom can harvest 0.75 kg of sugar cane per hour or 0.75 kg of nuts. If Susan and Tom are the only two people in the economy and each works eight hours per day, describe the production possibilities curve for the economy as a whole.

To construct the PPC for a two-person economy, we use an approach similar to the one we used for a one-person economy. To find the vertical intercept of the PPC, we ask how much sugar cane they would have if both Susan and Tom worked full-time harvesting sugar cane. The answer is 18 kg per day (12 kg from Susan and 6 kg from Tom), so point *A* in Figure 2.5 is the vertical intercept of the PPC. Similarly, if Susan and Tom both worked full-time picking nuts, they would pick 30 kg of nuts per day (24 kg from Susan and 6 from Tom). Thus point *B* in Figure 2.5 is the horizontal intercept of the PPC.

FIGURE 2.5

The PPC for a Two-Person Economy

Initial nut production relies on Susan, whose opportunity cost of nuts is lower than Tom's. Once Susan is fully occupied picking nuts (point *D*), additional nut production must rely on Tom.

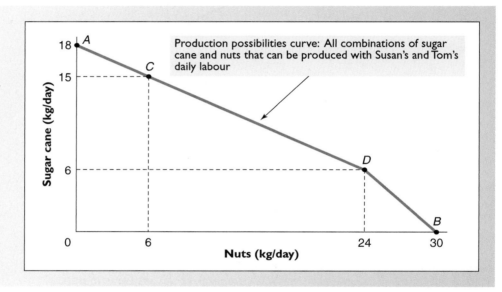

In contrast to the PPC for the one-person economy, however, the PPC for the two-person economy is not a straight line joining the two extreme points. To see why, suppose Susan and Tom were initially devoting all their time to harvesting sugar cane when they decided they wanted some nuts. How would they launch their nut production effort? They would want Susan to pick nuts, because her opportunity cost of picking nuts is only half Tom's. Thus, if Susan spent two hours picking nuts while Tom continued to devote all his time to sugar cane, they would lose 3 kg of sugar cane but gain 6 kg of nuts each day. Point *C* in Figure 2.5 represents this combination.

If Susan devotes all her time to picking nuts while Tom continues to devote all his time to sugar cane, they will end up at *D* in Figure 2.5, which represents 6 kg of sugar cane per day and 24 kg of nuts. If they want to expand nut production any further, Tom will have to take some of his time away from sugar cane. But in doing so, they gain only one additional kilogram of nuts for each kilogram of sugar cane they lose. Notice in Figure 2.5 how the slope of the PPC changes at point *D*. To the right of point *D*, the slope of the PPC reflects Tom's opportunity cost of sugar cane rather than Susan's.

> **To the left of point _D_ in Figure 2.5, what is the slope of the production possibilities curve, and what opportunity cost does this slope represent?**

The PPC for the two-person economy bends outward (is concave to the origin) because of individual differences in opportunity costs. As the following example shows, this distinctive shape represents expanded opportunities for both Susan and Tom.

What is the best way to achieve a given production goal?

Tom and Susan, a married couple, want 12 kg of sugar cane per day and 12 kg of nuts. If their productive abilities are as described in Example 2.5, what is the most effective way of dividing their labour?

Though Tom has a comparative advantage in harvesting sugar cane, even if he spends all his time harvesting sugar cane, he can cut only (8 hours/day)(0.75 kg/hour =) 6 kg per day. So Susan will have to harvest the additional 6 kg of sugar cane to achieve their production target of 12 kg. Since Susan is capable of harvesting (8 hours/day)(1.5 kg/hour) = 12 kg of sugar cane per day, she will need only four hours per day to harvest 6 kg. She can spend the remaining four hours picking nuts, which is exactly the amount of time she needs to pick their production target of 12 kg. In terms of their two-person production possibilities curve, this allocation of labour puts Susan and Tom at point _E_ in Figure 2.6.

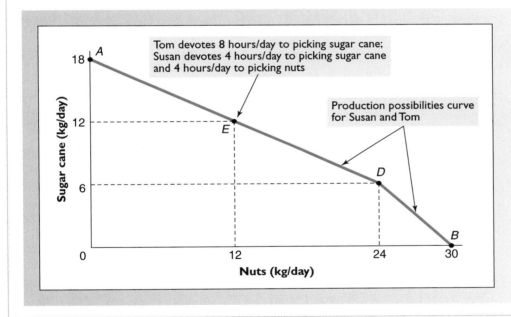

FIGURE 2.6
Optimal Assignment of Production Tasks in a Two-Person Economy
At the optimal division of labour (point _E_), Tom specializes completely in sugar cane, and Susan harvests only as much sugar cane as is needed to complete their production target.

Example 2.6 illustrates the general principle that when more than one opportunity is available, we are best off if we exploit the best opportunity first.

The Principle of Increasing Opportunity Cost: In expanding the production of any good, first employ those resources with the lowest opportunity cost. Only when all of the lowest cost resources are employed does it make economic sense to use resources that have higher opportunity costs.

INCREASING OPPORTUNITY COST

HOW MUCH DOES SPECIALIZATION MATTER?

In Example 2.6, Tom specialized completely in sugar cane, his area of comparative advantage (lowest opportunity cost). Susan did not specialize completely in picking nuts because if she had, the two would have harvested twice the nuts (24 kg) and half the sugar cane they wanted. Given what they wanted, Tom and Susan still did better through partial specialization than they could have if neither had specialized, as the following example demonstrates.

EXAMPLE 2.7

How much does specialization expand opportunity? (Part 1)

Suppose that in Example 2.6 Susan and Tom had divided their time so that each person's output consisted of half nuts and half sugar cane. How much worse off would they have been?

Tom can harvest equal quantities of both goods by spending four hours each day on the production of each, which yields (4 hours/day)(0.75 kg/hour) = 3 kg of sugar cane and (4 hours/day)(0.75 kg/hour) = 3 kg of nuts. Since Susan can harvest twice as many kilograms of nuts in an hour as she can sugar cane, to get equal quantities of both goods, she must devote twice as many hours to sugar cane as to nuts. Thus, she will need to spend two-thirds of a workday (16/3 hours/day) harvesting sugar cane and one-third of a workday (8/3 hours/day) picking nuts. Her output will be (16/3 hours/day)(1.5 kg/hour) = 8 kg of sugar cane per day and (8/3 hours/day)(3 kg/hour) = 8 kg of nuts. Their combined daily production will be only 11 kg of sugar cane and 11 kg of nuts—1 kg less of each good than when they specialized.

The relatively small gains from specialization that we saw in Example 2.7 might seem an insufficient explanation for the dramatic differences in the level of wealth across countries. While getting one extra kilogram of each of two goods by specializing is better than nothing, it is a small gain.

But a country that is more productive will have a higher national income, and it can invest more. For example, it can afford to provide more education for its population. It will also be able to put more resources into discovery and enhancement of technology, and into construction of machines and buildings. All these things increase productivity, which raises incomes, enabling even more investment. Small yearly investments can therefore cumulate over decades and cause a small initial advantage in productivity to widen, year after year. Thus, when we compare the living standards of the world's nations today, a large part of the differences we see is due to that cumulative advantage. However, as the next example illustrates, the gains from specialization are considerably larger when people are both absolutely *and* relatively more efficient at their respective specialties, and when the differences in opportunity costs are more pronounced.

EXAMPLE 2.8

How much does specialization of labour expand opportunity? (Part 2)

Susan can harvest 1 kg of sugar cane or 7 kg of nuts in an hour. Tom can harvest 7 kg of sugar cane or 1 kg of nuts in an hour. Draw their combined production possibilities curve. Assuming that the two want sugar cane and nuts in equal quantities, by how much will specialization increase their consumption?

Susan and Tom's combined PPC is shown in Figure 2.7. By working together, with Susan specializing in nuts and Tom specializing in sugar cane, the couple can have (8 hour/day)(7 kg/hour) = 56 kg of sugar cane and (8 hour/day)(7 kg/hour) = 56 kg of nuts each day. If the two had worked separately, each would have been able to pick only 7 kg of sugar cane and 7 kg of nuts each day, for a total of 14 kg of sugar cane and 14 kg of nuts a day—only one-fourth of what they picked when they specialized.

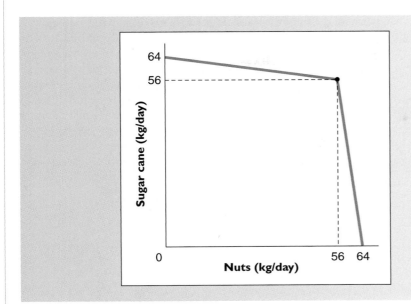

FIGURE 2.7
An Especially Useful Division of Labour
The gains from specialization are larger when differences in opportunity cost are larger and when individuals enjoy absolute advantage in their respective specialties.

In truth, the gains from specialization will often be far more spectacular than those shown in Example 2.8. One reason is that specialization not only capitalizes on preexisting differences in individual skills but also deepens those skills through practice and experience. It also eliminates many of the switching and start-up costs people incur when they move back and forth among numerous tasks. These gains apply not only to people but also to the tools and equipment they use. Breaking a task down into simple steps, each of which can be performed by a different machine, greatly multiplies the productivity of individual workers.

Even in simple settings, these factors can combine to increase productivity hundredsfold or even thousandsfold. Consider, for instance, Adam Smith's description of work in an eighteenth-century Scottish pin factory:

> One man draws out the wire, another straightens it, a third cuts it, a fourth points it, a fifth grinds it at the top for receiving the head; to make the head requires two or three distinct operations. ... I have seen a small manufactory of this kind where only ten men were employed ... [who] could, when they exerted themselves, make among them about twelve pounds of pins in a day. There are in a pound upwards of four thousand pins of middling size. Those ten persons, therefore, could make among them upwards of forty-eight thousand pins in a day. Each person, therefore, making a tenth part of forty-eight thousand pins, might be considered as making four thousand eight hundred pins in a day. But if they had all wrought separately and independently, and without any of them having been educated to this peculiar business, they certainly could not each of them have made twenty, perhaps not one pin in a day... .[3]

The gains in productivity that result from specialization are often prodigious. They constitute the single most important explanation for why societies that don't rely heavily on specialization and exchange are much less productive than those that do.

[3]Adam Smith, *The Wealth of Nations*, New York: Everyman's Library, E.P. Dutton, 1910 (1776), Book 1, p. 5; and *The Wealth of Nations*, with an introduction by Max Lerner and an introduction by Edwin Cannan. Edited by Edwin Cannan. New York, Random House, Inc., 1965 (1776), Book 1, Chapter 1, p. 5.

Of course, the mere fact that specialization boosts productivity does not mean that more specialization is always better than less, for specialization also entails costs. For example, most people appear to enjoy variety in the work they do, but variety tends to be one of the first casualties as workplace tasks become ever more narrowly specialized.

Indeed, Karl Marx argued forcefully that the fragmentation of workplace tasks often exacts a heavy psychological toll on workers. Thus, he wrote, "[A]ll means for the development of production ... mutilate the laborer into a fragment of a man, degrade him to the level of an appendage of a machine, destroy every remnant of charm in his work and turn it into hated toil... ."[4]

Charlie Chaplin's 1936 film, *Modern Times,* paints a vivid portrait of the psychological costs of repetitive factory work. As an assembly worker, Chaplin's only task, all day every day, is to tighten the nuts on two bolts as they pass before him on the assembly line. Finally he snaps and walks zombielike from the factory, wrenches in hand, tightening every nutlike protuberance he encounters.

Can specialization proceed too far?

Modern Times was filmed nearly seventy years ago, and since then industrial engineers have realized that good job design involves finding the right balance between the benefits and costs of specialization. The engineers and programmers who design and produce industrial robots that now do much of the work described by Chaplin's *Modern Times* are highly specialized. If you ever need brain surgery, you will be comforted if you know that before the surgeon opens your skull, he has already exposed and successfully treated a thousand other brains. Many people make interesting and challenging careers out of highly specialized work. Besides, failure to specialize imposes its own substantial costs.

We can expect to meet life's financial obligations in the shortest time—thereby freeing up more time to do whatever else we want—if we concentrate at least a significant proportion of our efforts on those tasks for which we have a comparative advantage.

A PRODUCTION POSSIBILITIES CURVE FOR A MANY-PERSON ECONOMY

Most actual economies, of course, consist of millions of workers. Even so, the process of constructing a production possibilities curve for an economy of that size is really no different from the process for a one- or two-person economy. But

---

[4]Karl Marx, *Das Kapital,* New York: Modern Library, 1936 (1856), pp. 708, 709.

since each worker's contribution to total output is extremely small in a large economy, production possibilities curves tend not to be kinked like the ones in preceding examples, but smoothly bowed, like the one shown in Figure 2.8.

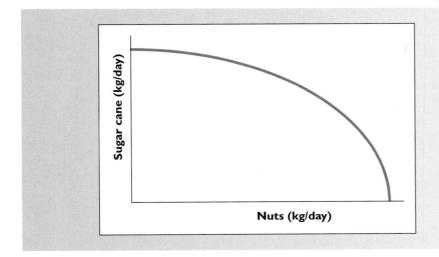

FIGURE 2.8
Production Possibilities Curve for a Large Economy
For an economy with millions of workers, the PPC is bowed outward from the origin (it is convex).

Like all production possibilities curves, the one in Figure 2.8 is downward-sloping, illustrating once again the problem of scarcity and the need to make trade-offs. If all available resources are currently engaged in the production of sugar cane and nuts, the only way to get more nuts is to sacrifice some sugar cane. Note also that the slope of the production possibilities curve in Figure 2.8 increases as the society moves toward greater production of nuts. Recall the principle of increasing opportunity cost: In expanding nut production, people turn first to those resources that are relatively efficient at picking nuts. Only when those resources have been deployed do they turn to less efficient resources. As more and more nuts are picked, the opportunity cost of picking additional nuts rises. Note that the principle of increasing opportunity cost applies to both goods shown in Figure 2.8. Thus, as more sugar cane is harvested, the opportunity cost of additional sugar cane rises.

INCREASING
OPPORTUNITY
COST

SPECIALIZATION, EXCHANGE, AND THE CIRCULAR FLOW OF INCOME AND EXPENDITURE

Specialization and exchange go together. If your professor spends most of her time teaching, she must depend on someone else to grow her food. The accountant will usually depend on someone else to make his clothes, and so on. We all are highly specialized in our work, and we all depend on the cooperation of many other individuals in obtaining the things we need and desire. Most of us do this by selling our labour in return for wages or salaries that we receive as money and which we can then spend to obtain the goods and services we want.

Figure 2.9 represents a very simple economy that has no government and does not engage in foreign trade. Labour is the only input used in this economy to produce goods and services. Simple though it is, Figure 2.9 is sufficient to represent the circular flow of expenditure and of exchange. Households, composed of individuals, sell labour services to firms. Firms use the labour they hire to produce goods and services, which they sell to households. The blue arrows in the upper half of Figure 2.9 indicate the flow of labour through the labour market to firms. The blue arrows in the lower half indicate the flow of goods and services from firms through markets for goods and services to households. Thus, the blue inner arrows indicate a flow of real (or physical) units.

FIGURE 2.9

The Circular Flow of Income and Expenditure
This diagram links income and expenditure in a highly simplified model of the economy. The outer set of arrows in red indicates money or dollar flows in the economy. The inner set of arrows in blue indicates the flows of real inputs and goods and services.

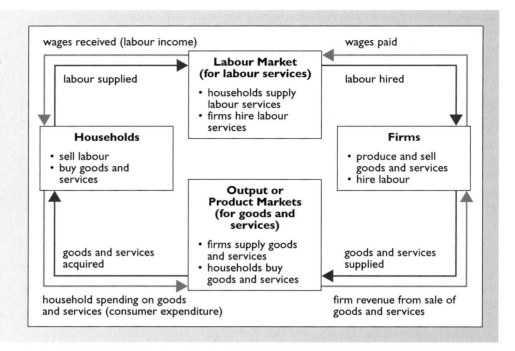

Firms pay wages and salaries to households for their labour. As indicated by the red arrows in the upper half of Figure 2.9, wages and salaries are expenditures that flow from firms through the labour market to households, where they are received as income. Red arrows in the lower half show payments flowing from households through markets for goods and services to firms. The expenditures of households are the income of firms. The red outer arrows represent monetary flows in the economy. In general, one party's expenditure is another's income.

Figure 2.9 becomes much more complicated in appearance if we make it more realistic and add boxes to represent capital markets, government, and foreign trade, and arrows to represent the flows of expenditure on, and goods received from, each. However, a simple principle remains—every transaction has both a buyer and a seller, so one person's sale is another's purchase.

| RECAP | COMPARATIVE ADVANTAGE AND PRODUCTION POSSIBILITIES |

For an economy that produces two goods, the production possibilities curve describes the maximum amount of one good that can be produced for every possible level of production of the other good. Attainable points are those that lie on or to the left of the curve, and efficient points are those that lie on the curve. The slope of the production possibilities curve tells us the opportunity cost of producing an additional unit of the good measured along the horizontal axis. The principle of increasing opportunity cost tells us that the slope of the production possibilities curve becomes steeper as we move downward to the right. The greater the differences among individual opportunity costs, the more bow-shaped the production possibilities curve will be, and the more bow-shaped is the production possibilities curve, the greater will be the potential gains from specialization. Specialization and exchange go together, and exchange can be characterized as a circular flow. In any transaction, one party's expenditure is another's income.

■ 2.3 COMPARATIVE ADVANTAGE AND INTERNATIONAL TRADE

The same logic that leads the individuals in an economy to specialize and exchange goods with one another also leads nations to specialize and trade among themselves. As with individuals, each trading partner can benefit from exchange, even though one may be more productive than the other in absolute terms.

Can a poor nation prosper by trading?

EXAMPLE 2.9

Susan and Tom are the only two workers in Islandia, a small island nation, and their production possibilities curve is as shown in Figure 2.10. Millions of workers live in the rest of the world. For simplicity, we will assume that each of them can produce 100 kg of nuts or 100 kg of sugar cane per hour. How does the opportunity to trade affect consumption opportunities in Islandia?

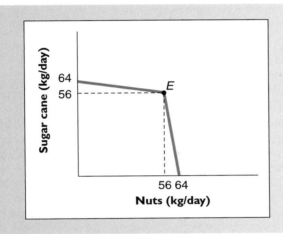

FIGURE 2.10
Production Possibilities Curve for Islandia

In the rest of the world, the opportunity cost of a kilogram of sugar cane is 1 kg of nuts. The market price of 1 kg of sugar cane will therefore be 1 kg of nuts. (If someone tried to charge, say, 1.5 kg of nuts for a kilogram of sugar cane, consumers could simply reduce their own nut harvest by a kilogram and harvest an extra kilogram of sugar cane instead.) Because Islandia is tiny relative to the rest of the world, 1 kg of sugar cane will exchange for exactly 1 kg of nuts in a market consisting of Islandia and the rest of the world. The opportunity to trade with Islandia therefore has no perceptible impact on the rest of the world.

But it has a profound impact on Susan and Tom. Suppose they were initially at point E on their PPC (Figure 2.10). Without the opportunity to trade, they would have to give up 7 kg of nuts to increase sugar cane by 1 kg. But with the opportunity to trade, they can purchase 1 kg of sugar cane in exchange for only 1 kg of nuts. If Islandians started at E and sold their entire 56 kg of nuts in the world market, they could buy an additional 56 kg of sugar cane, for a total of $56 + 56 = 112$ kg of sugar cane and $56 - 56 = 0$ kg of nuts. So point A in Figure 2.11 represents their maximum possible daily consumption of sugar cane once they can engage in trade.

Similarly, if they were initially at point E on their PPC and lacked the opportunity to trade, they would have to sacrifice 7 kg of sugar cane to obtain an additional kilogram of nuts. But if they could trade, they could get an extra kilogram of nuts at a cost of just 1 kg of sugar cane. If Islandians started at E and sold their entire 56 kg of sugar cane to the rest of the world, they could buy an additional 56 kilograms of nuts, for a total of $56 + 56 = 112$ kg of nuts and $56 - 56 = 0$ kg of sugar cane. So point A in Figure 2.11 represents the maximum possible sugar

FIGURE 2.11
**How Trade Expands
Islandia's Menu of
Possibilities**
The opportunity to trade
with the rest of the
world greatly expands the
consumption opportunities
of a smaller nation.

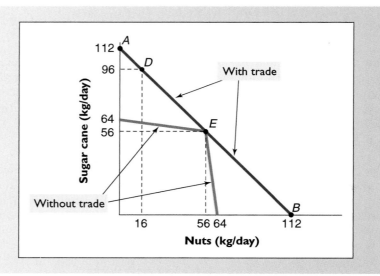

cane consumption, and point *B* represents their maximum possible nut consumption once they can engage in trade.

   A and *B* represent the two extreme points on Islandia's new menu of possibilities. By trading lesser quantities of sugar cane or nuts, it is also possible for Islandians to achieve any point along the straight line joining *A* and *B*. For example, if Islandians started at point *E* and sold 40 kg of nuts, they could buy an additional 40 kg of sugar cane, which would move them to point *D*, which has 56 + 40 = 96 kg of sugar cane and 56 − 40 = 16 kg of nuts. The opportunity to trade thus transforms Islandia's menu of possibilities from the PPC shown in Figure 2.10 to the one labelled *AB* in Figure 2.11. Trade gives Islandia the ability to consume *outside* its own production possibilities curve.

Refer to Example 2.9. What would Islandia's new menu of possibilities look like if each citizen in the rest of the world could harvest 100 kg of sugar cane per day, as before, but only 50 kg of nuts?

   How much does trade benefit the citizens of Islandia? The answer depends on which particular combination of sugar cane and nuts Islandians most prefer. Suppose, for example, that they most prefer the combination at point *E* in Figure 2.12 on the next page: 56 kg of sugar cane per day and 56 kg of nuts. The opportunity to trade would then be of no benefit to them, since that combination was available to them before trade became possible (see Figure 2.10).

   But suppose that in the absence of trade, Islandians would have chosen to harvest and consume only 28 kg of sugar cane and 60 kg of nuts per day (point *D* in Figure 2.12). The opportunity to trade would then be very valuable indeed, for it would enable the Islandians almost to double their consumption of sugar cane without reducing their nut consumption (by moving from *D* to *G* in Figure 2.12). Or they could increase their nut consumption from 60 to 84 kg per day without giving up any sugar cane (by moving from *D* to *F* in Figure 2.12). The gains from trade would also be valuable if the Islandians had initially chosen to produce at a point at which the opportunity cost of a kilogram of nuts was less than 1 kg of sugar cane—say, point *C* in Figure 2.12.

   The patterns displayed in this example are at least roughly indicative of actual patterns of international trade. The volume of trade has grown substantially over time, and with some important exceptions, no single nation produces more than a small fraction of the total supply of any good or service. Thus the price at which

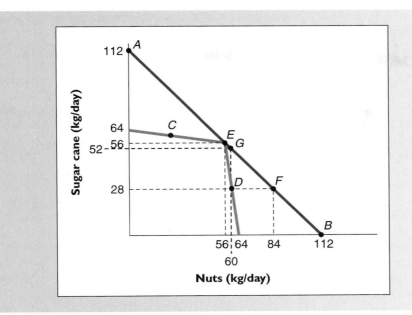

FIGURE 2.12

Gains from International Trade
If the small nation were originally at *D* on its PPC, the ability to trade with the rest of the world enables it to increase its consumption of nuts by 24 kg per day (by moving from *D* to *F*). Alternatively, it could increase its consumption of sugar cane by 24 kg per day (by moving from *D* to *G*).

one good exchanges for another on the world market is not much influenced by how much of a good a nation itself produces. The greater the difference between domestic opportunity costs and world opportunity costs, the more a nation benefits from the opportunity to trade with other nations.

CAN EXCLUSION FROM TRADE HURT A SMALL, POOR NATION?

Suppose the small nation of Figure 2.12 is trading with a superpower and is at point *F*, consuming 28 kg of sugar cane and 84 kg of nuts per day. The small nation is tiny compared to the superpower. Therefore, it cannot influence the price of nuts (or sugar cane). If the small nation loses access to trade and continues to consume 28 kg of sugar cane per day, it must reduce its consumption of nuts by almost 30 percent, from 84 kg to 60 kg per day, as described by point *D*. Whether the superpower trades with the smaller nation makes little difference to the superpower.

The importance of trade and comparative advantage to the smaller trading partner may influence the foreign policy of the larger nation. For example, in 1959, the revolution led by Fidel Castro overthrew the government of Cuban dictator Fulgencio Batista. In 1960, while moving into the Soviet orbit, Castro expropriated all American business interests in Cuba. The United States responded early in 1961 by breaking diplomatic relations and ceasing all its trade with Cuba. Since then, the United States has not traded with Cuba, thereby maintaining economic pressure on Castro's communist government. (Sugar is Cuba's most important export.)

EXERCISE 2.5

Refer to the answer to Exercise 2.4. Suppose that Figure 2.11 represents Islandia's circumstances of trade with a superpower. After Islandia and the superpower have been trading for many years, a dispute between them causes trade to cease. Will this cause hardship for Islandia? How?

DOES EVERYONE BENEFIT FROM TRADE?

The North American Free Trade Agreement (NAFTA) is a treaty that greatly reduces trade barriers among Canada, the United States, and Mexico. NAFTA is a contentious political issue, and discussions among world leaders about global trading arrangements are just as contentious. If international specialization and trade are so beneficial, why would anyone oppose them?

It is possible to accept the logic of comparative advantage and oppose freer trade on other grounds. Although international trade can increase the total value of goods and services produced, it does not guarantee that everyone will participate in those benefits. Some opponents of NAFTA feared that it would help Mexico exploit its comparative advantage in the production of goods made with unskilled labour. Some also feared that Mexico would not honour Canadian and U.S. labour standards and environmental policies. Consumers would benefit, but unskilled workers in Canada and the United States would confront the possibility of lower wages or unemployment, and global pollution might be aggravated. Also, the example of the small trading partner paired with a superpower suggests that the superpower can use trade as an instrument of foreign policy, thereby reducing the sovereignty of the smaller partner. The issue of sovereignty may be closely linked to the distribution of trade benefits. If foreigners own a large part of the small country's industry, much of the benefit of trade might flow to foreigners, not to the domestic population.

Opponents of trade agreements also fear that the agreements will lock existing patterns of comparative advantage into place, making it difficult to develop new, more desirable patterns. Recall the case of Canadian pulp and paper. The American pulp and paper industry would have preferred that Canada use its comparative advantage to supply pulpwood as raw material to the American industry. This would have been an obstacle to the development of a Canadian pulp and paper industry. Canadian provincial governments opted instead to use barriers to trade to support the development of a Canadian industry.

RECAP	**COMPARATIVE ADVANTAGE AND INTERNATIONAL TRADE**

Nations, like individuals, can benefit from exchange, even though one trading partner may be more productive than the other in absolute terms. The greater the difference between domestic opportunity costs and world opportunity costs, the more a nation can potentially benefit from exchange with other nations. But expansions of exchange do not guarantee that each individual citizen will do better. Unskilled workers in high-wage countries may be hurt in the short run by the reduction of barriers to trade with low-wage nations. International trade may also raise issues about the distribution of benefits between trading partners, national sovereignty, and the extent to which an existing pattern of comparative advantage might change over time.

■ SUMMARY

- **2.1** One person has an *absolute* advantage over another in the production of a good if she can produce more of that good than the other person. One person has a *comparative* advantage over another in the production of a good if she is relatively more efficient than the other person at producing that good, meaning that her opportunity cost of producing it is lower than her counterpart's. Specialization

based on comparative advantage is the basis for economic exchange. When each person specializes in the task at which she is relatively most efficient, the economic pie is maximized, making possible the largest slice for everyone.

- **2.1** At the individual level, comparative advantage may spring from differences in talent or ability or from differences in education, training, and experience. At the national level, sources of comparative advantage include these innate and learned differences, as well as differences in language, culture, institutions, climate, natural resources, and a host of other factors.

- **2.2** The production possibilities curve is a simple device for summarizing the possible combinations of output that a society can produce if it employs its resources efficiently. In a simple economy that produces only sugar cane and nuts, the PPC shows the maximum quantity of sugar cane production (vertical axis) possible at each level of nut production (horizontal axis). The slope of the PPC at any point represents the opportunity cost of nuts at that point, expressed in kilograms of sugar cane.

- **2.2** All production possibilities curves slope downward because of the scarcity problem, which implies that the only way to obtain more of one good is to accept less of another. In a nut/sugar cane economy whose workers

have different opportunity costs of picking nuts, the slope of the PPC becomes steeper with increasing production of nuts and movement down the curve. This change in slope illustrates the principle of increasing opportunity cost, which states that in expanding the production of any good, a society minimizes the opportunity cost by first employing those resources that are relatively efficient at producing that good. Only when all of the lowest cost resources are employed does it make economic sense to use resources that have higher opportunity costs.

- **2.2** The same logic that prompts individuals to specialize in their production and to exchange goods with one another also leads nations to specialize and trade with one another. On both levels, each trading partner can benefit from an exchange, even though one may have an absolute advantage for each good. For both individuals and nations, the benefits of exchange tend to be larger the larger are the differences between the trading partners' opportunity costs.

CORE

The Principle of Comparative Advantage
Total output is largest when each person (or each country) concentrates on the activities for which his or her opportunity cost is lowest.

The Principle of Increasing Opportunity Cost
In expanding the production of any good, first employ those resources with the lowest opportunity cost. Only when all of the lowest cost resources have been employed does it make economic sense to use resources that have higher opportunity costs.

KEY TERMS

absolute advantage (32)
attainable point (39)
comparative advantage (32)

efficient point (40)
inefficient point (40)
production possibilities curve (37)

productivity (35)
unattainable point (40)

REVIEW QUESTIONS

1. Explain what "having a comparative advantage" at producing a particular good or service means. What does "having an absolute advantage" at producing a good or service mean?

2. How will a reduction in the number of hours worked each day affect an economy's production possibilities curve?

3. How will technological innovations that boost labour productivity affect an economy's production possibilities curve?

4. Why does saying that people are poor because they do not specialize make more sense than saying that people perform their own services because they are poor?

5. What factors helped Canada to establish a pulp and paper industry?

6. What factors help Canada to be an exporter of grain?

7. What factors make it more difficult for Quebec to produce and sell movies, books, and popular music, compared to English-speaking Canada?

■ PROBLEMS

1. Consider a society whose only worker is Helen, who allocates her production time between cutting hair and baking bread. Each hour per day she devotes to cutting hair yields 4 haircuts, and each hour she devotes to baking bread yields 8 loaves of bread. If Helen works a total of 8 hours per day, graph her production possibilities curve.

2. Refer to Problem 1. Which of the points listed below is efficient? Which is attainable?
   a. 28 haircuts/day, 16 loaves/day
   b. 16 haircuts/day, 32 loaves/day
   c. 18 haircuts/day, 24 loaves/day

3. Determine whether the following statements are true or false, and briefly explain why.
   a. Toby can produce 5 L of apple cider or 70 g of feta cheese per hour. Kyle can produce 3 L of apple cider or 42 g of feta cheese per hour. Therefore, Toby and Kyle cannot benefit from specialization and trade.
   b. A doctor who can vacuum her office faster and more thoroughly than commercial cleaners is better off if she cleans her office herself.
   c. In an economy in which millions of workers each have different opportunity costs of producing two goods, the principle of comparative advantage implies that the slope of the production possibilities curve decreases in absolute value as more of the good on the horizontal axis is produced.

4. Nancy and Bill are auto mechanics. Nancy takes 4 hours to replace a clutch and 2 hours to replace a set of brakes. Bill takes 6 hours to replace a clutch and 2 hours to replace a set of brakes. If Bill and Nancy open a motor repair shop:
   a. If Nancy works only on clutches, and Bill works only on brakes both will be better off.
   b. Bill has a comparative advantage at replacing brakes.
   c. Nancy has an absolute advantage at replacing clutches.
   d. Nancy has a comparative advantage at replacing clutches.
   e. All but one of the above statements are correct.

5. Bob and Stella are a married couple. Bob takes 10 minutes to change a lightbulb and 2 minutes to fix a broken fuse. Stella takes 3 minutes to change a lightbulb and 30 seconds to fix a broken fuse. Which of the following statements is true?
   a. Stella has a comparative advantage at fixing fuses, because she can do it faster than Bob.
   b. Stella has a comparative advantage at changing lightbulbs and fixing fuses, because she can do both of them faster than Bob.
   c. Stella has an absolute advantage at changing lightbulbs and fixing fuses, because she can do both of them faster than Bob.
   d. Bob has a comparative advantage at fixing fuses, because Stella has a comparative advantage at changing lightbulbs.
   e. Stella has a comparative advantage at changing lightbulbs.

6. Kamal and Filipe are stranded together on a desert island. The raw materials on the island are suitable only for making beer and pizza, but their quantities are unlimited. What is scarce is labour. Filipe and Kamal each spend 10 hours a day making beer or pizza. The following table specifies *how much beer and pizza Filipe and Kamal can produce per hour.*

	Beer	Pizza
Filipe	I bottle per hour	0.2 pizza per hour
Kamal	I.5 bottles per hour	0.5 pizzas per hour

a. Draw the daily production possibilities curves (PPCs) for Filipe and Kamal.
b. Who has an absolute advantage in making pizza? in brewing beer?
c. Who has a comparative advantage in making pizza? in brewing beer?

Now suppose their preferences are as follows: Filipe wants 2 beers and as much pizza as he can eat each day; Kamal wants 2 pizzas and as much beer as he can drink each day.
d. If each man is self-reliant, how much beer and pizza will Filipe and Kamal eat and drink?
e. Suppose the two men decide to trade with each other. Draw their joint PPC, and give an example of a trade that will make each of them better off.

7. Rework Problem 6 with the following changes:
a. Each individual's productivity is shown in the table that follows, *which specifies the number of hours each man needs to produce a single unit of beer and pizza.*
b. Filipe wants 6 beers and as much pizza as he can eat each day, while Kamal wants 2 pizzas and as much beer as he can drink each day.

	Production time for 1 beer	Production time for 1 pizza
Filipe	5/4 hours	5/3 hours
Kamal	5 hours	5/2 hours

8. Suppose Filipe and Kamal's production possibilities curves from Problem 7 are combined. What would be the maximum number of pizzas available to Filipe and Kamal if they could buy or sell in a world market in which 1 beer could be exchanged for 1 pizza? What would be the maximum number of beers available to them?

9. Inlandia and Outlandia both can produce oranges and oil. Inlandia can produce up to 10 million metric tons of oranges per week or 5 million barrels of oil, or any combination of oil and oranges along a straight-line production possibilities curve linking those two points. Outlandia can produce up to 50 million metric tons of oranges per week or 1 million barrels of oil, or any combination along a straight-line production possibilities curve linking those points.
a. Does the principle of increasing opportunity cost apply in either of these two economies? Why or why not?
b. Suppose Inlandia and Outlandia sign a trade agreement in which each country will specialize in the production of either oil or oranges. According to the Principle of Comparative Advantage, which country will specialize in which commodity?
c. If Inlandia and Outlandia are the only two economies in the world that are open to international trade, what are the maximum and minimum prices that can prevail on the world market for a metric ton of oranges, in terms of barrels of oil?

10. Jay, Kay, and Dee are marooned alone on the Greek island of Skorpios. They must find a way to provide themselves with food and drinking water. The following table shows how many hours each person takes to produce one unit of food or one unit of water.

	Production time for 1 unit of food	Production time for 1 unit of drinking water
Jay	1 hour	2 hours
Kay	2 hours	1 hour
Dee	4 hours	6 hours

a. If each person can work for 12 hours a day and each person provides only for himself or herself, draw their individual PPCs.

b. Suppose Jay, Kay, and Dee decide to produce food and water cooperatively, so they can gain from trade. Draw their combined production possibilities curve.

c. If the trio wants, in aggregate, to consume 15 units of food and 12 units of water, who will specialize in food production? Who will specialize in water production? Will anyone divide his or her time between food and water production?

d. If the trio wants, in aggregate, to consume 6 units of water and as much food as possible, who will specialize in food and who will specialize in water? Will anyone divide his or her time between food and water production? How much food will be produced?

e. Suppose production is as in part (c). Dee suggests dividing the output equally among the three of them. Assuming that the amounts of food that Jay and Kay get under this arrangement are exactly what each would have chosen if he or she had lived and worked alone, is each of them strictly better off when they share? Explain.

■ ANSWERS TO IN-CHAPTER EXERCISES

2.1

	Productivity in programming	Productivity in bicycle repair
Mina	2 Web page updates per hour	1 repair per hours
Barb	3 Web page updates per hour	3 repairs per hour

The entries in the table tell us that Barb has an absolute advantage over Mina in both activities. While Barb can update 3 Web pages per hour, Mina can update only 2. Barb's absolute advantage over Mina is even greater in the task of fixing bicycles —3 repairs per hour versus Mina's 1.

But, as in Example 2.2, the fact that Barb is a better programmer than Mina does not imply that Barb will be better off if she updates her own Web page. Barb's opportunity cost of updating a Web page is 1 bicycle repair, whereas Mina must give up only half a bicycle repair to update a Web page. Mina has a comparative advantage over Barb at programming, and Barb has a comparative advantage over Mina at bicycle repair.

2.2 Susan's opportunity cost of picking a kilogram of nuts is 1/2 kg of sugar cane. But Tom's opportunity cost of picking a kilogram of nuts is now only 1/3 kg of sugar cane. So Tom has a comparative advantage at picking nuts, and Susan has a comparative advantage at cutting sugar cane.

2.3 The slope to the left of point D (in absolute value) is 1/2 kg of sugar cane per kilogram of nuts, which is Susan's opportunity cost of picking nuts.

2.4 In the rest of the world, the opportunity cost of a kilogram of nuts is now 2 kg of sugar cane, not 1 kg. This means that Islandians can now buy or sell a kilogram of nuts for 2 kg of sugar cane and can buy or sell a kilogram of sugar cane for 1/2 kg of nuts. So if Islandians start at point E and sell all 56 kg of nuts they produce, they can buy an additional 112 kg of sugar cane, for a total of 168 kg of sugar cane. This would put them at point A in the diagram on the next page. Alternatively, if they start at E and sell all 56 kg of sugar cane they produce, they can buy an additional 28 kg of nuts, for a total of 84 kg of nuts, which would put them at B. The straight line AB is their new menu of opportunities.

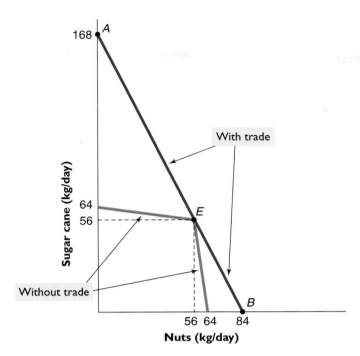

2.5 Loss of the opportunity to trade reduces Islandia's menu of possibilities from *AB* to its own production possibilities curve. If, when it was trading, Islandia selected a combination of nuts and sugar cane significantly different from the combination represented by point *E* in the graph above, loss of the opportunity to trade would cause Islandia significant hardship. (If, when it was trading, Islandia selected a point on *AB* quite close to *E*, loss of trade would cause Islandia only minor inconvenience.)

Chapter

3

Chapter Outline

3.1 **Markets and Prices**

3.2 **Markets and Social Welfare**

3.3 **Explaining Changes in Prices and Quantities**

SUPPLY AND DEMAND: AN INTRODUCTION

The stock of foodstuffs on hand at any moment in Toronto's grocery stores, restaurants, and private kitchens is sufficient to feed the city's 2.5 million residents for at most a week. Since most of these residents have nutritionally adequate and highly varied diets, and since almost no food is produced within the city, provisioning Toronto requires that millions of kilograms of food and drink be delivered to locations throughout the city each day.

No doubt many Torontonians, buying groceries at their favourite local markets or eating at their favourite Italian, Chinese, and Indian restaurants, give little or no thought to the nearly miraculous coordination of people and resources that is required to feed city residents daily. Even if the supplying of Toronto consisted only of transporting a fixed collection of foods to a given list of destinations each day, it would be quite an impressive operation, requiring at least a small army (and a well-managed one) to carry out.

The entire process is astonishingly more complex than that. For example, the system must somehow ensure that not only *enough* food is delivered to satisfy Torontonians' discriminating palates but also the *right kinds* of food. There mustn't be too much bacon and not enough eggs, or too much caviar and not enough canned tuna, and so on. Similar judgments must be made *within* each category of food and drink: There must be the right amount of Swiss cheese and the right amounts of provolone, Gorgonzola, and feta, and a different variety of herbs and seasonings for each type of cuisine.

But even this doesn't begin to describe the complexity of the decisions and actions required to provide our nation's largest city with its daily bread. Someone has to decide where each particular type of food gets produced, and how, and by whom. Someone must decide how much of each type of food gets delivered to *each* of the thousands of restaurants and grocery stores in the city. Someone must determine whether the deliveries should be made in big trucks or small ones, arrange that the trucks be in the right place at the right time, and ensure that fuel and qualified drivers are available.

Thousands of individuals must decide what role, if any, they will play in this collective effort. Some people—just the right number—must choose to drive food delivery trucks, rather than trucks that deliver lumber. Others must become the mechanics who fix these trucks, rather than carpenters who build houses. Others must become farmers, rather than architects or bricklayers. Still others must become chefs in upscale restaurants, or flip burgers at McDonald's, instead of becoming plumbers or electricians.

Yet despite the huge number and complexity of the tasks involved, somehow the supplying of Toronto manages to get done remarkably smoothly. A grocery store will occasionally run out of flank steak, or a diner will sometimes be told that someone else has just ordered the last serving of roast duck. But if episodes like these stick in memory, it is only because they are rare. For the most part, Toronto's food delivery system—like that of every other city in the country—functions so seamlessly that it attracts virtually no notice.

In this chapter we'll explore how markets allocate food, housing, and other goods and services, usually with remarkable efficiency despite the complexity of the tasks. To be sure, markets are by no means perfect, and our stress on their virtues is to some extent an attempt to counteract what most economists view as an underappreciation by the general public of their remarkable strengths. In the course of our discussion we will see why, under fairly general circumstances, markets function so smoothly. We will also discuss the circumstances under which markets, left to themselves, cannot be expected to function well.

To convey an understanding of how markets work is a major goal of this course, and in this chapter we provide only a brief introduction and overview. As the course proceeds we will discuss the economic role of markets in considerably more detail, paying attention to some of the problems of markets as well as their strengths.

No society—regardless of how it is organized—can escape the need to answer certain basic economic questions. For example, how much of our limited time and other resources should we devote to building housing, how much to the production of food, and how much to providing other goods and services? What techniques should we use to produce each good? Who should do each specific task? And how should the resulting goods and services be distributed among people? In Canada, as elsewhere, the market plays a crucial role. Therefore, we need to understand how (and why) markets can often successfully answer these questions—and also how (and why) they may sometimes fail.

3.1 MARKETS AND PRICES

Beginning with some basic concepts and definitions, we will explore how the interactions among buyers and sellers in markets determine the prices and quantities of the various goods and services traded in those markets. We begin by defining a market: The **market** for any good consists of all the potential buyers and sellers of that good. For any good, we should specify the time and the place at which it is bought and sold. So, for example, the market for hamburgers on a given day in a given place is just the set of people (or other economic actors, like firms) potentially able to buy or sell hamburgers at that time and location.

market the market for any good consists of all potential buyers and sellers of that good

In the market for hamburgers, sellers comprise the individuals and companies that either do sell—or might, under the right circumstances, sell—hamburgers. Similarly, buyers in this market include all individuals who buy—or might buy—hamburgers.

In most parts of Canada a cooked hamburger can still be had for less than $5. Where does the market price of hamburgers come from? Looking beyond hamburgers to the vast array of other goods that are bought and sold every day, we may ask, "Why are some goods cheap and others expensive?"

Adam Smith and other early economists (including Karl Marx) thought that the market price of a good was determined by its cost of production. But although costs surely do affect prices, they cannot explain why one of Pablo Picasso's paintings sells for so much more than one of A.J. Casson's.

Stanley Jevons and other nineteenth-century economists tried to explain price by focusing on the value people derived from consuming different goods and services. It certainly seems plausible that people will pay a lot for a good they value highly. Yet willingness to pay cannot be the whole story, either. A person deprived of water in the desert, for example, will be dead in a matter of hours, and yet water from a municipal system sells for a tiny fraction of a penny per litre. By contrast, human beings can get along perfectly well without gold, and yet gold sells for about $500 Canadian an ounce.

Cost of production? Value to the user? Which is it? The answer is that both matter. Writing in the late nineteenth century, the British economist Alfred Marshall was among the first to show clearly how costs and value interact to determine both the prevailing market price for a good and the amount of it that is bought and sold. Our task in the pages ahead will be to explore Marshall's insights and gain some practice in applying them. As a first step, we introduce the two main components of Marshall's pathbreaking analysis: the supply curve and the demand curve. [His famous analogy was that demand and supply are like the two blades of a scissors, since each by itself can explain little, but together they can cut through to the essence of many issues.[1]]

THE SUPPLY CURVE

supply curve a curve or schedule showing the total quantity of a good that sellers want to sell at each price

In the market for hamburgers, the **supply curve** of hamburgers is a simple schedule, or graph, that tells us, for each possible price of hamburgers, how many hamburgers all hamburger sellers together would be willing to sell at that price.

What does the supply curve of hamburgers look like? The answer is based on the logical assumption that people will be willing to produce and sell hamburgers as long as the price they receive for them is sufficient to cover their opportunity costs of supplying them. Thus, if what people could earn by selling hamburgers is not sufficient to compensate them for what they could have earned if they had spent their time and invested their money in some other way, they will not sell hamburgers. Otherwise, they will.

Figure 3.1 provides a possible illustration. Note that it shows the relationship between the *price* and *quantity* supplied of the same type and quality of good. Economists know perfectly well that some hamburgers are bigger than others (and consequently sell for a higher price), but we want to focus on the role played by prices

FIGURE 3.1

The Daily Supply Curve of Hamburgers in Downtown Toronto
At higher prices, sellers generally offer more units for sale. The supply curve is upward sloping.

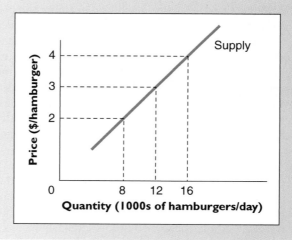

[1]"We might as reasonably dispute whether it is the upper or the under blade of a pair of scissors that cuts a piece of paper, as whether value is governed by utility or cost of production." Alfred Marshall, *Principles of Economics*, 8th ed., London: Macmillan & Co Ltd, 1964 (1920), p. 290.

in the market mechanism. So we will simplify by making the assumption that we can draw a supply curve for a particular type of hamburger; for example, one made with six ounces of well-done, grade A beef and garnished with relish. The most straightforward way to define "quantity supplied" in a given amount of time is "the number of units of a specific good, with given characteristics, produced and sold in a given market." We therefore think of other, similar goods (larger or smaller hamburgers, hotdogs, etc.) as being sold in other, different markets—recognizing that because these goods cater to similar wants, the markets for them are linked.

In general, people differ with respect to their opportunity costs of producing and selling hamburgers: For those with limited education and work experience, the opportunity cost of selling hamburgers is relatively low (because such individuals typically do not have a lot of high-paying alternatives). For others, the opportunity cost of selling burgers is of moderate value, and for still others—like rock stars and professional athletes—it is prohibitively high. Because of these differences among people in the opportunity cost of selling hamburgers, the daily supply curve of hamburgers will be *upward sloping* as shown in Figure 3.1, which exhibits a hypothetical supply curve for the hamburger market in downtown Toronto on a given day. (Although economists usually refer to demand and supply "curves," to keep things simple we often draw them as straight lines in examples.)

Why is the supply curve for hamburgers upward sloping? When the price of hamburgers is low—say, $2 per hamburger—only those people whose opportunity cost of selling hamburgers is less than or equal to that amount will offer hamburgers for sale. For the supply curve shown in Figure 3.1, the quantity supplied at a price of $2 will be 8000 hamburgers per day. In that example, 8000 hamburgers is the total quantity of hamburgers offered for sale by people whose opportunity cost of selling hamburgers is $2 per hamburger or less. If the price of a hamburger were to rise above $2, however, additional sellers would find it worthwhile to offer hamburgers for sale. For example, at a price of $3, Figure 3.1 shows that the quantity of hamburgers supplied is 12 000 per day, while at a price of $4, the quantity supplied is 16 000. The higher the price, the more people find it worthwhile to supply hamburgers.

The fact that the supply curve slopes upward may be seen as a consequence of the principle of increasing opportunity cost, discussed in Chapter 2. This principle tells us that as we expand the production of hamburgers, we turn first to those whose opportunity costs of producing hamburgers are lowest and only then to others with higher opportunity costs.

INCREASING OPPORTUNITY COST

Stated another way, the fact that the supply curve for a good is upward sloping reflects the idea that the cost of producing an additional unit of the good rises as we produce more of it. If sellers are currently supplying 12 000 hamburgers a day in Figure 3.1, for example, the opportunity cost of the last hamburger produced (including the cost of meat, bun, etc., as well as the value of the supplier's time) must be $3. (If sellers could produce a 12 001st hamburger for less than that, they would have an incentive to supply it, since they can sell it for $3, which is more than it cost them to produce it. And if the cost of producing the 12 000th hamburger were greater than $3, it would not have been offered for sale at that price.) By similar reasoning, when the total quantity of hamburgers is 16 000, the opportunity cost of producing another hamburger must be $4.

THE DEMAND CURVE

The supply curve, by itself, does not tell us how many hamburgers will be sold in downtown Toronto on a given day, or at what price those hamburgers will sell. To find the prevailing price and quantity, we also need the demand curve for hamburgers in this market. The **demand curve** is a graph that tells us the total quantity of hamburgers that buyers want to buy at various prices.

demand curve a curve or schedule showing the total quantity of a good that buyers want to buy at each price

Typically, the demand curve for a good is downward sloping with respect to the price of that good. For example, the demand curve for hamburgers tells us that the higher the price of hamburgers becomes, the fewer hamburgers buyers as a whole will want to buy. Thus the daily demand curve for hamburgers in downtown Toronto might look like the curve shown in Figure 3.2.

FIGURE 3.2

The Daily Demand Curve for Hamburgers in Downtown Toronto
The demand curve for any good is a generally downward-sloping function of its price. At lower prices, buyers generally want to purchase more units.

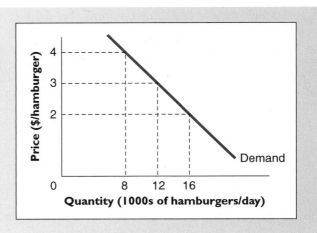

The demand curve in Figure 3.2 tells us that when the price of hamburgers is low—say, $2 per hamburger—buyers will want to buy 16 000 hamburgers per day, whereas they will want to buy only 12 000 at a price of $3 and only 8000 at a price of $4. The demand curve for hamburgers slopes downward for two reasons. First, as hamburgers become less expensive, some people switch to hamburgers from chicken sandwiches, pizza, and other foods that substitute for hamburgers. Second, people who already consumed hamburgers simply can buy more hamburgers when prices are lower.

MARKET EQUILIBRIUM

equilibrium a stable, balanced, or unchanging situation in which all forces at work within a system are cancelled by others

The concept of **equilibrium** is employed in both the physical and social sciences and is of central importance in economic analysis. We use the term "equilibrium" to denote a "state of rest" of the market under analysis. In general, a system is in equilibrium when there is no tendency for the system to change further. In physics, for example, a ball hanging from a spring is said to be in equilibrium when the spring has stretched sufficiently that the upward force it exerts on the ball is exactly counterbalanced by the downward force of gravity. In economics, a market is said to be in equilibrium when no participant in the market has any reason to alter his or her behaviour so that there is no tendency for production or prices in that market to change.

equilibrium price and equilibrium quantity the price and quantity of a good at the intersection of the supply and demand curves for the good

If we want to determine the final position of a ball hanging from a spring, (recognizing that it may bounce for a while, but will eventually settle down) we need to find the point at which the forces of gravity and spring tension are balanced and the system is in equilibrium. Similarly, if we want to find the price at which a good will sell (which we will call the **equilibrium price**) and the quantity of it that will be sold (the **equilibrium quantity**) (when the market has settled down), we need to find the equilibrium in the market for that good. The basic tools for finding the equilibrium in a market for some good are the supply and demand curves for that good. The price and quantity at which the supply and demand curves for the good intersect is such an equilibrium. For the hypothetical supply and demand curves for hamburgers in downtown Toronto, the equilibrium price will therefore be $3 per hamburger, and the equilibrium quantity of hamburgers sold will be 12 000 per day, as shown in Figure 3.3, which combines Figures 3.1 and 3.2.

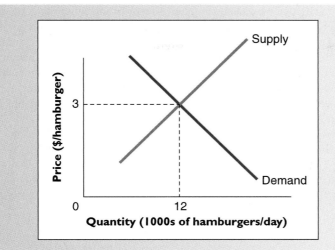

FIGURE 3.3
The Equilibrium Price and Quantity of Hamburgers in Downtown Toronto
The equilibrium quantity and price of a product are the values that correspond to the intersection of the supply and demand curves for that product.

In Figure 3.3, note that at the equilibrium price of $3 per hamburger, both sellers and buyers are "satisfied" in the following sense: Buyers are buying exactly the quantity of hamburgers they want to buy at that price (12 000 per day) and sellers are selling exactly the quantity of hamburgers they want to sell (also 12 000 per day). And since they are satisfied in this sense, neither buyers nor sellers face any incentives to change their behaviour.

Note the limited sense of the term *satisfied* in the definition of **market equilibrium.** It does not mean that sellers would not be pleased to receive a price higher than the equilibrium price. Rather, it means only that they are able to sell all they wish to sell at that price. Similarly, to say that buyers are satisfied at the equilibrium price does not mean that they would not like to have a higher income or that they would not be happy to pay less than the equilibrium price. Rather, it means only that, given their incomes, they are able to buy exactly as many units of the good as they want to at the equilibrium price.

Note also that if the price of hamburgers in our downtown Toronto market was anything other than $3, either buyers or sellers would not be satisfied. Suppose, for example, that the price of hamburgers was $4, as shown in Figure 3.4. At that price, buyers want to buy only 8000 hamburgers per day, but sellers want to sell 16 000. Since no one can force someone to buy a hamburger against his or her wishes, this means that buyers will buy only the 8000 hamburgers they want

market equilibrium occurs when all buyers and sellers are satisfied with their respective quantities at the market price

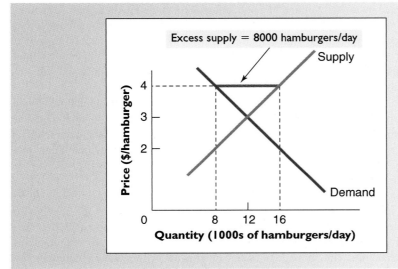

FIGURE 3.4
Excess Supply
When price exceeds the equilibrium price, there is excess supply, or surplus, that is equal to the difference between quantity supplied and quantity demanded.

excess supply, or surplus the difference between the quantity supplied and the quantity demanded when the price of a good exceeds the equilibrium price; sellers are dissatisfied when there is excess supply

to buy. So when the price exceeds the equilibrium price, sellers will be dissatisfied. At a price of $4 in this example, they are left with an **excess supply**, or **surplus**, of 8000 hamburgers per day. (Note that the term *surplus* has a different meaning when used to denote excess supply than when used to denote economic surplus.)

Conversely, suppose that the price of hamburgers in the downtown Toronto market was less than the equilibrium price, say, $2 per hamburger. As shown in Figure 3.5, buyers want to buy 16 000 hamburgers per day at that price, whereas sellers want to sell only 8000. Since sellers cannot be forced to sell hamburgers against their wishes, this time the buyers will be dissatisfied. At a price of $2 in this example, they experience an **excess demand**, or **shortage**, of 8000 hamburgers per day.

FIGURE 3.5

Excess Demand
When price lies below the equilibrium price, there is excess demand, the difference between quantity demanded and quantity supplied.

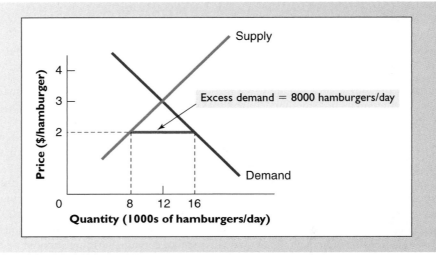

excess demand, or shortage the difference between the quantity supplied and the quantity demanded when the price of a good lies below the equilibrium price; buyers are dissatisfied when there is excess demand

Markets for goods and services often tend toward their respective equilibrium prices and quantities. The mechanisms by which this happens are implicit in our definitions of excess supply and excess demand. Suppose, for example, that the price of hamburgers in our hypothetical market was $4, leading to excess supply as shown in Figure 3.4. Because sellers are dissatisfied—because they sell more hamburgers than buyers want to buy, they have an incentive to take whatever steps they can to increase their sales. A simple strategy is for them to cut their price slightly. Thus, if one seller reduced his price from $4 to, say, $3.95 per hamburger, he could attract many of the buyers who had been paying $4 for hamburgers supplied by other sellers. Those sellers, to recover their lost business, would then have an incentive to match the price cut. But notice that if all sellers lowered their prices to $3.95, there would still be considerable excess supply in the hamburger market. So sellers would face continuing incentives to cut their prices. This pressure to cut prices will not go away until the price falls all the way to $3. At $3, excess supply is zero.

Conversely, suppose that price starts out less than the equilibrium price, say, $2 per hamburger. This time it is the buyers who are dissatisfied. A person who cannot get all the hamburgers she wants at a price of $2 has an incentive to offer a higher price, hoping to obtain hamburgers that would otherwise have been sold to other buyers. And sellers, for their part, will be only too happy to post higher prices as long as queues of dissatisfied buyers remain.

The upshot is that price has a tendency to move to its equilibrium level under conditions of either excess supply or excess demand. And when price reaches its equilibrium level, both buyers and sellers are satisfied simultaneously since they are able to buy or sell precisely the amounts they choose, given their incomes.

We emphasize that the mere fact that buyers and sellers are satisfied in this sense does not mean that markets automatically result in the best of all possible worlds. For example, a poor person may be satisfied with the one hamburger he chooses to buy each day at a price of $3, but still be hungry—in this case, he is satisfied only in the sense that he cannot buy a second hamburger without sacrificing other urgent purchases.

It is also important to emphasize that the equilibrating process depends on competition among many buyers and sellers, all of whom are small relative to the size of the market. If all sellers are small, no seller has the ability to increase the price of hamburgers above the equilibrium price by restricting the quantity supplied. For example, if all sellers are small, no seller can raise the price of hamburgers to $4 by restricting the quantity to 8000 hamburgers per day. Why? Because at $4, other sellers will be perfectly willing to compete for buyers by increasing the quantity of hamburgers, while offering a somewhat lower price.

Similarly, if all buyers are small, no buyer can reduce price below the equilibrium price, say to $2, by announcing that no more than $2 will be paid for a hamburger. Why? Because at $2 only 8000 hamburgers/day will be supplied, and other buyers will compete for hamburgers by offering a somewhat higher price.

SUPPLY AND DEMAND: AN ANALYSIS OF FOREIGN EXCHANGE MARKETS

Supply and Demand are (as Alfred Marshall put it) like the two blades of a scissors. Each, by itself, is incomplete—but together they can cut through to the essence of many economic issues. We can use the tools of Supply and Demand Analysis to explain both micro-markets where only a few thousand dollars change hands and also to understand the flow of the hundreds of billions of dollars that are traded every day in foreign exchange markets.

Every day in financial markets, people in the U.K., Norway, India, and many other countries around the world pay in pounds, kroner, and rupees to buy Canadian dollars. In the financial pages of your daily newspaper, you can read the exchange rate of one Canadian dollar that results from these trades. For example, you might read that today one Canadian dollar is worth $0.7541 U.S. or $1.0934 Australian or 0.7065 Euros; the financial pages provide the price of one Canadian dollar in terms of many other currencies. These prices are called **foreign exchange rates**. A *foreign exchange rate* is the price of one unit of a country's currency in terms of another country's currency and is determined in foreign exchange markets.

Analyzing the supply and demand for foreign exchange is a useful example of how competitive markets work because there are so many potential buyers and sellers, and foreign exchange markets adjust very quickly. As well, the foreign exchange rate is very important for the Canadian economy, so understanding how this market works is an important issue for any economics student. Nevertheless, there is a complication. When it comes to currencies, we can always express prices in two equivalent ways. We can either say, "Ten dimes equal a dollar" or, "One dime equals a tenth of a dollar." Saying it one way is just the flip side of the other —it is just a question of perspective—and the same is true of foreign currencies.

If you were to check the financial pages for the exchange rate of the Canadian dollar against the Euro, and find a quote of $1.4154 per Euro, the exchange rate being expressed is the price of one Euro in terms of Canadian dollars—one Euro will cost $1.4154. But one could equally well see this as the price of one Canadian dollar in terms of Euros (which we said in a previous paragraph was €0.7065.) If it takes $1.4154 to buy one Euro, then:

$$1€ = \$1.4154.$$

If we divide both sides of the expression by 1.4154, then:

$$\$1 = €0.7065,$$

foreign exchange rate the price of one unit of a country's currency in terms of another country's currency. Foreign exchange rates are determined in foreign exchange markets.

which simply says that it takes 0.7065 Euros to buy one Canadian dollar. Expressing the exchange rate one way answers the question: "What's the price of one Canadian dollar? i.e., How many Euros does it take to buy one Canadian dollar?" which is just the flip side of the question: "How many dollars does it take to buy one Euro?" Whenever the exchange rate of one currency is stated in terms of another, a reciprocal exchange rate can be obtained.[2] A discussion that shifts from an exchange rate to its reciprocal and back again can become quite confusing. For example, one news commentator might say, "Tonight, the exchange rate is $1.4154." A few minutes later, the next commentator might say, "Tonight, the exchange rate is 0.7065 Euros." It might not be clear to the viewer that both are quoting the same exchange rate. To avoid confusion on this point, in this textbook we will always be answering the question, "What is the price of one Canadian dollar?" Both commentators would agree that the price of one Canadian dollar is 0.7065 Euros. So it is important to stick to only one perspective. In this text we will look at the Canadian perspective: i.e., what is the price of one Canadian dollar?

Measured by the value of currency that is traded, the market in which U.S. and Canadian dollars are traded is the largest, whereas other markets (such as the market in which Japanese yen are exchanged for Canadian dollars) are much smaller. But the fundamental logic driving foreign exchange rates is the same around the world, so we can focus on a single market like the one in which Euros and Canadian dollars are traded.

When using supply and demand to analyze foreign exchange markets, it is important to be clear about what is being measured along each axis of our graphs. In Figure 3.6, the quantity of Canadian dollars is measured along the horizontal axis. The exchange rate, or the price of one Canadian dollar in terms of Euros, is measured along the vertical axis.

THE SUPPLY OF CANADIAN DOLLARS IN FOREIGN EXCHANGE MARKETS

First, consider the supply of Canadian dollars to the market in which Canadian dollars and Euros are traded. Who are the suppliers of Canadian dollars? Why do they want to supply Canadian dollars?

At any given time, the holders of Canadian dollars can use their dollars to buy Canadian goods and services, or Canadian financial assets. However, if they want to buy goods and services or financial assets in Europe, they must acquire Euros before they can make these purchases. Whether Canadian tourists buy their Euros before they leave or while they are cruising around France, Germany, Italy, and Spain, local people will only accept Euros. Similarly, a Canadian financial investor who wants to buy a German company's shares or bonds will need to acquire Euros to buy these assets. To obtain Euros, they will *supply* Canadian dollars. Figure 3.6 displays a hypothetical supply curve for Canadian dollars. Notice that on the vertical axis, the price of a Canadian dollar is quoted in Euros. The supply curve is upward sloping, showing that as price rises, a larger quantity of dollars is supplied.

Why does the supply curve slope upward? As any tourist knows, a low exchange rate means it is more expensive to have a good time while you are trav-

---

[2]If you have ever purchased foreign currency, you know that a bank or currency broker charges a higher price when selling foreign currency than it offers when buying. Bankers and currency brokers want to earn a net return for the services they provide, which they get from the spread between the buying and selling price. Since the spread is typically small, we will ignore it for now.

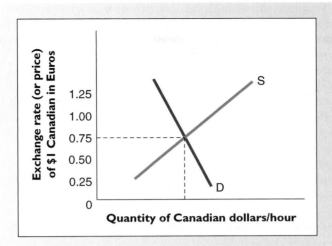

FIGURE 3.6
Supply and Demand for Canadian Dollars
The equilibrium exchange rate and quantity of dollars traded are given by the intersection of supply and demand.

elling—the lower the value of a Canadian dollar, the more Canadian dollars that are required to make any given purchase. If each Canadian dollar sold for only 0.25 Euros, a European vacation would be very expensive indeed. A 100 Euro hotel room in Paris is at the low end of the local market, but in Canadian dollars, it would cost $400—and many Canadians would look for a cheaper hotel (if they could find it). More important, many Canadians would decide that whatever the delights of Paris, it is just too expensive, and they would not go to Europe at all. When fewer Canadians travel, the quantity of Canadian dollars supplied to foreign exchange markets falls.

However, if each Canadian dollar were worth two Euros, the same 100 Euro hotel room would cost our traveller only $50 Canadian, and souvenirs and meals would be comparable bargains. Because the foreign exchange value (i.e., the price) of the Canadian dollar is higher, the fine wine and superb food of the best restaurants would look cheap to our lucky traveller. More Canadians would travel to Europe and they would stay longer and buy more goods and services. To buy more, they would require more Euros. To obtain more Euros, they would increase the quantity of Canadian dollars supplied to the foreign exchange market. In general, the higher the price (expressed in Euros) of one Canadian dollar, the greater the flow of Canadian tourists to Europe, the more each tourist buys, and the greater the quantity of Canadian dollars supplied to the foreign exchange markets. That is why the supply curve of Figure 3.6 has a positive slope.

Tourism is one important reason for Canadians to supply Canadian dollars to foreign exchange markets but there are many others. Canadians also want European goods and financial and real assets. To purchase them, Canadians must obtain Euros by supplying Canadian dollars in a foreign exchange market. When the foreign exchange value (or price) of the dollar rises, goods like Mercedes Benz cars and villas in the south of France cost fewer Canadian dollars. Therefore, Canadians are more likely to purchase them, which means that the quantity of Canadian dollars supplied increases. Just as before, the supply curve in Figure 3.6 slopes upward.

THE DEMAND FOR CANADIAN DOLLARS IN FOREIGN EXCHANGE MARKETS

Now consider the demand for Canadian dollars. Who are the demanders of Canadian dollars? Why would they want to buy Canadian dollars, and pay for them with Euros?

Many Canadians travel abroad, but tourism is also a major industry in Canada. Whether it is skiing at Whistler, whale watching off Cape Breton or visiting Niagara Falls, many Europeans are drawn to Canada for an experience that they cannot get at home. Of course, Canadians want to be paid in Canadian dollars for car rentals, hotel rooms, and restaurant meals. German and French tourists thus have to pay with their Euros for the Canadian dollars they buy in order to purchase the goods and services they want. The quantity of Canadian dollars they demand will depend on price per dollar—and when the exchange value, or price, of the Canadian dollar is low, vacations in Canada will seem like a great bargain to them.

The demand curve for Canadian dollars thus slopes down, because a lower exchange value (or price) for the dollar means that more European tourists will travel to Canada, stay longer, and buy more goods and services. To make more purchases they will have to buy more dollars, which they will pay for with Euros. A $150 hotel room in Toronto would only cost them 37.5 Euros if the price of the Canadian dollar were 0.25 Euros—so a Canadian vacation would be a "best buy," and more Europeans would take advantage of the bargain. On the other hand, if the exchange rate price were to rise to two Euros to the dollar, the same hotel room would cost them the equivalent of 300 Euros, and a Canadian vacation would be much less affordable.

Of course, tourism makes up only one part of the total demand for Canadian dollars. When Europeans buy Canadian goods (like wheat or aircraft) or Canadian assets (like Ontario bonds or Nova Scotia sea front properties) they need Canadian dollars to make their purchases. Therefore, the total demand for Canadian dollars is the sum of the dollars demanded by foreigners for all purchases of Canadian goods, services, financial assets, and real assets. But the basic logic is the same—a lower exchange rate (or the price of one Canadian dollar) will, other things being equal, increase the quantity of Canadian dollars demanded in foreign exchange markets.

When Canadians travel in Europe, they supply Canadian dollars to the foreign exchange market and when Europeans travel in Canada, they demand Canadian dollars. The price matters to both—but Canadian tourists supply more dollars when the exchange rate is high, whereas European tourists demand more dollars when the exchange rate is low. It is the function of the foreign exchange market to bring supply and demand into equilibrium. Figure 3.6 shows the market for Canadian dollars in equilibrium at a price, or exchange rate, of 0.75 Euro/Canadian dollar.

As Marshall said, like the two blades of a scissors, supply and demand *together* determine equilibrium. If tourism were the only reason for foreign exchange transactions, then equilibrium would occur when the supply of Canadian dollars (by Canadians travelling in Europe) is equal to the demand for Canadian dollars (by Europeans travelling in Canada). In the real world, there are many other reasons why Canadians want to supply Canadian dollars and why Europeans demand Canadian dollars—but in total, for all different types of transactions, the supply of, and demand for, Canadian dollars must balance in equilibrium.

RECAP   **MARKETS AND PRICES**

The *market* for a good consists of the actual and potential buyers and sellers of that good. For any given price, the *supply curve* shows the total quantity that suppliers of the good would be willing to sell, and the *demand curve* shows the total quantity that demanders would be willing to buy. Suppliers are willing to sell more at higher prices (supply curves slope upward) and demanders are willing to buy less at higher prices (demand curves slope downward).

Market equilibrium, the situation in which all buyers and sellers are satisfied with their respective quantities at the market price, occurs at the intersection of the supply and demand curves. The corresponding price and quantity are called the *equilibrium price* and the *equilibrium quantity.*

Prices and quantities tend to be driven toward their equilibrium values by the competitive actions of buyers and sellers. If the price is initially too high, resulting in excess supply, dissatisfied sellers will compete for buyers by cutting their prices to sell more. If the price is initially too low, resulting in excess demand, competition among buyers drives the price upward. This process continues until equilibrium is reached. The equilibrating process depends on competition among large numbers of small buyers and sellers.

■ 3.2 MARKETS AND SOCIAL WELFARE

When a market for a good is in equilibrium, the equilibrium price conveys important information to potential suppliers about the value that potential demanders place on that good. At the same time, the equilibrium price informs potential demanders about the opportunity cost of supplying the good. This rapid, two-way transmission of information is the reason that markets can coordinate an activity as complex as supplying Toronto with food and drink, even though no one person or organization oversees the process.

But are the prices and quantities determined in market equilibrium socially optimal in the sense of maximizing total economic surplus? That is, does equilibrium in unregulated markets always maximize the difference between the total benefits and total costs experienced by market participants? As we see in this section, the answer is "it depends": A market that is out of equilibrium always creates opportunities for individuals to arrange transactions that will increase their individual economic surplus. However, a market for a good that is in equilibrium maximizes total, society-wide economic surplus only when the supply and demand curves in the market fully reflect the costs and benefits associated with the production and consumption of that good.

When a market is out of equilibrium, it is always possible to identify mutually beneficial exchanges. When people have failed to take advantage of all mutually beneficial exchanges, we often say that there is "cash on the table"—the economist's metaphor for unexploited opportunities. When the price in a market is below the equilibrium price, there is cash on the table, because it will always be possible for a supplier to produce an additional unit at a cost that is lower than the price buyers are willing to pay.

efficient quantity the efficient quantity of a good is the quantity that results in the maximum possible economic surplus from producing and consuming the good

SMART FOR ONE, DUMB FOR ALL

The **efficient quantity** of any good is the quantity that maximizes the total economic surplus that results from producing and consuming the good. The *cost–benefit principle* tells us to keep expanding production of the good as long as the benefit of producing one more unit exceeds the cost of that additional unit. This means that the efficient quantity is that level of production for which the cost and benefit of one more unit of the good are the same.

When the quantity of a good is less than the efficient quantity, increasing its production will increase total economic surplus. By the same token, when the quantity of a good exceeds the efficient quantity, reducing its production will increase total economic surplus. **Economic efficiency** occurs when all goods and services in the economy are produced and consumed at levels that produce the maximum economic surplus for society.

Efficiency is an important social goal. Failure to achieve efficiency means that total economic surplus is smaller than it could have been. Movements toward

COST–
BENEFIT

economic efficiency condition that occurs when all goods and services are produced and consumed at their respective socially optimal levels

efficiency make the total economic pie larger, making it possible for everyone to have a larger slice. The importance of efficiency will be a recurring theme as we move forward, and we state it here as one of the core principles:

EFFICIENCY

The Efficiency Principle: Economic efficiency occurs when total economic surplus is maximized. Efficiency is an important social goal because, when the economic pie grows larger, everyone can potentially have a larger slice.

Is the market equilibrium quantity of a good efficient? That is, does it maximize the total economic surplus received by participants in the market for that good? When the market for a given good is in equilibrium, we can say that the cost *to the seller* of producing *an additional* unit of the good is the same as the benefit *to the buyer* of having *an additional* unit. If all costs of producing the good are borne directly by sellers, and if all benefits from the good accrue directly to buyers, it follows that the market equilibrium quantity of the good will equate the marginal cost and marginal benefit of the good. And this implies that the equilibrium quantity also maximizes total economic surplus.

But sometimes the production of a good entails costs that fall on people other than those who sell the good. These are referred to as *external costs*. This will be true, for instance, for goods whose production generates significant levels of environmental pollution. As extra units of these goods are produced, the extra pollution harms other people besides sellers. In the market equilibrium for such goods, the benefit *to buyers* of the last good produced is, as before, equal to the cost incurred by sellers to produce that good. But since producing that good also imposes pollution costs on others, we know that the *full* marginal cost of the last unit produced—the seller's private marginal cost plus the marginal pollution cost borne by others—must be higher than the benefit of the last unit produced. So in this case the market equilibrium quantity of the good will be higher than the socially optimal quantity. Total economic surplus would be higher if output of the good were lower. Yet neither sellers nor buyers have any incentive to alter their behaviour.

In Economic Naturalist 1.2 we discussed the environmental problems created by littering. If a brewery can sell beer in cans, without a deposit, the cash cost to consumers will be lower and the brewery will be able to sell more beer—but since some of those cans will be thrown away as litter, that littering is a social cost arising from the production and sale of beer cans, which is not being recognized in the price. Breweries often protest that their prices will be higher, and their production will be lower, if a deposit system is introduced—but without the deposit system, the social costs of litter are being ignored, and the market price will not fully reflect all the social costs of production.

Another possibility is that people other than those who buy the good may receive significant benefits from it. These are referred to as *external benefits*. For instance, when a beekeeper adds an additional hive to his apiary, his neighbour's apple orchard yields a larger crop because of the higher levels of pollination caused by the bees from the extra hive. From the perspective of society as a whole, the best thing to do would be to keep adding hives until their marginal cost is equal to their marginal benefit. The marginal benefit of a hive is the value of the extra honey *plus* the value of the extra apples. However, unless they are paid for pollination, beekeepers will add hives only up to the point that the cost of an extra hive is equal to the revenue from the extra honey. In this case, then, the market equilibrium quantity of beehives will be smaller than the quantity that maximizes total economic surplus. Yet individual beekeepers and individual consumers of honey have no incentive to alter their behaviour.

Situations like the ones just discussed provide examples of behaviours that we can call "smart for one but dumb for all." In each case, the individual actors are behaving rationally. They are pursuing their goals as best they can, and yet there remain unexploited opportunities for gain from the point of view of the whole society. The difficulty is that these opportunities cannot be exploited by individuals acting alone. In subsequent chapters we will see how people can often organize collectively to exploit such opportunities. In some cases buyers and sellers will realize that rational pursuit of individual goals is causing opportunities for social gain to remain unexploited, and they will devise ways to act on those opportunities. As we will see later, at least in some circumstances orchard owners will pay beekeepers for pollination provided by bees. If this occurs, an extra hive produces extra revenue from both additional honey and additional pollination. Individual actions then result in whatever number of hives maximizes total economic surplus. For now, we simply summarize this discussion in the form of the following core principle:

The Equilibrium Principle: A market in equilibrium leaves no unexploited opportunities for individuals but may not exploit all gains achievable through collective action.

EQUILIBRIUM

For the remainder of this chapter, we will confine our attention to markets in which the supply and demand curves capture all relevant costs and benefits. Our focus will be on using supply and demand analysis to predict and explain changes in equilibrium prices and quantities.

RECAP	MARKETS AND SOCIAL WELFARE

When the supply and demand curves for a good reflect all significant costs and benefits associated with the production and consumption of that good, the market equilibrium will result in the largest possible economic surplus. But if people other than buyers benefit from the good, or if people other than sellers bear costs because of it, rational behaviour on the part of individuals need not maximize economic surplus.

3.3 EXPLAINING CHANGES IN PRICES AND QUANTITIES

If we know how the factors that govern supply and demand curves are changing, we can make informed predictions about how prices and the corresponding quantities will change. But when describing changing circumstances in the marketplace, we must take care to recognize some important terminological distinctions. For example, we must distinguish between the meanings of the seemingly similar expressions **change in the quantity demanded** and **change in demand**. When we speak of a "change in the quantity demanded," we mean the change in quantity that people want to buy that occurs in response to a change in price. For instance, Figure 3.7(a) depicts an increase in the quantity demanded that occurs in response to a reduction in the price of tuna. When the price falls from $5 to $4 per can, the quantity demanded rises from 2000 to 4000 cans per day. By contrast, when we speak of a "change in demand," we mean a *shift in the entire demand curve*. For example, Figure 3.7(b) depicts an increase in demand, meaning that at every price the quantity demanded is higher than before. In summary, a change in the quantity demanded refers to a movement *along* the demand curve, and a change in demand means a *shift* of the entire curve.

change in the quantity demanded a movement along the demand curve that occurs in response to a change in price

change in demand a shift of the entire demand curve

FIGURE 3.7

An Increase in the Quantity Demanded versus an Increase in Demand

FIGURE 3.7

An Increase in the Quantity Demanded versus an Increase in Demand
Panel (a): An increase in quantity demanded is represented by a downward movement along the demand curve as price falls. Panel (b): An increase in demand is represented by an outward shift of the demand curve.

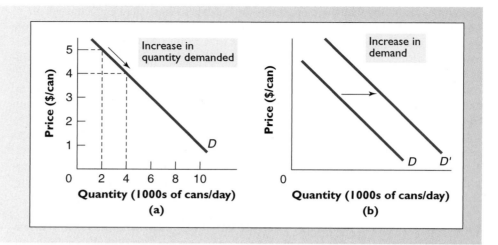

change in supply a shift of the entire supply curve

change in the quantity supplied a movement along the supply curve that occurs in response to a change in price

A similar terminological distinction applies on the supply side of the market. A **change in supply** means a shift in the entire supply curve, whereas **a change in the quantity supplied** refers to a movement along the supply curve.

Alfred Marshall's supply and demand model is one of the most useful tools of the economic naturalist. Once we understand the forces that govern the placements of supply and demand curves, we are suddenly in a position to make sense of a host of interesting observations in the world around us.

SHIFTS IN THE SUPPLY CURVE

To get a better feel for how the supply and demand model enables us to predict and explain price and quantity movements, it is helpful to begin with a few simple examples. Because the supply curve is based on costs of production, anything that changes production costs will shift the supply curve and hence will result in a new equilibrium quantity and price.

EXAMPLE 3.1

What will happen to the equilibrium price and quantity of new houses if the wage rate of carpenters falls?

Suppose the initial supply and demand curves for new houses are as shown by the curves *S* and *D* in Figure 3.8, resulting in an equilibrium price of $160 000 per house and an equilibrium quantity of 40 houses per month. A decline in the wage

FIGURE 3.8

The Effect on the Market for New Houses of a Decline in Carpenters' Wage Rates
When input prices fall, supply shifts right, causing equilibrium price to fall and equilibrium quantity to rise.

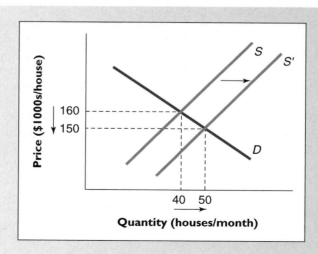

rate of carpenters reduces the cost of making new houses, and this means that, for any given price of houses, more builders can profitably serve the market than before. Diagrammatically, this means a rightward shift in the supply curve of houses, from S to S′. (A "rightward shift" in the supply curve can also be described as a "downward shift.")

Because carpenters make up only a tiny fraction of all potential home buyers, we may assume that lower wages have no significant effect on demand for houses. Thus, a reduction in carpenters' wages produces a significant rightward shift in the supply curve of houses, but no perceptible shift in the demand curve. We see from Figure 3.8 that the new equilibrium price, $150 000 per house, is lower than the original price, and the new equilibrium quantity, 50 houses per month, is higher than the original quantity.

Example 3.1 involved changes in the cost of an input in the production of a good—carpenters' labour in the production of houses. As the following case illustrates, supply curves also shift when technology changes.

3.1   ECONOMIC NATURALIST

Why has the consumption of French fries increased substantially during the last 25 years?

Commercial techniques for peeling, cutting, cooking, and storing French fries are much more sophisticated now than they were 25 years ago. Today, raw potatoes are processed into French fries in a few large plants, frozen, and shipped to restaurants and consumers. Once in restaurants and homes, French fries are easily cooked. In the United States, consumption of potatoes has increased by about 30 percent since 1977, most of it because Americans are eating more French fries and potato chips.[3]

In Figure 3.9, the curves labelled S and D depict the supply and demand curves for French fries during the late 1970s. The curve S′ represents the supply curve today. The increase in supply is the result of technological improvements in the production of French fries. As the graph shows, the equilibrium quantity of French fries has increased, and the price has decreased.

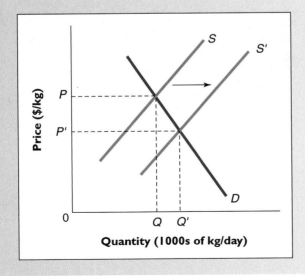

FIGURE 3.9

The Effect of Technical Change on the Market for French Fries
When new technology reduces the cost of production, supply shifts right, causing the equilibrium price to fall and the equilibrium quantity to rise.

[3]David M. Cutler, Edward L. Glaeser, and Jesse M. Shapiro, "Why have Americans Become More Obese?" *Journal of Economic Perspectives*, 17 (Summer 2003), p. 94.

Changes in input prices and technology are two of the most important factors that give rise to shifts in supply curves. In the case of agricultural commodities, weather may be another important factor, since good weather means larger crops—shifting the supply curves to the right. (Weather may also affect the supply curves of nonagricultural products through its effects on the national transportation system.) Expectations of future changes may also shift current supply curves, as when the expectation of poor crops from a current drought causes suppliers to withhold supplies from existing stocks in the hope of selling at higher prices in the future. An increase in a subsidy can also shift a supply curve to the right, as can an increase in the number of firms serving a market. A reduction in a subsidy or the number of firms in a market would shift a supply curve to the left. The next example shows how a change in the demand for European assets will affect the supply of Canadian dollars in the market for foreign exchange.

EXAMPLE 3.2

Suppose that as the European community becomes more closely integrated, the European economy shows ever stronger performance. Canadian investors perceive that rates of return earned on shares in European financial companies are improving significantly. What will happen to the exchange rate of the Canadian dollar and to the quantity of Canadian dollars traded?

If Canadians want to purchase more European assets, they will have to acquire more Euros to pay for them. Canadians can obtain more Euros by supplying more dollars to the market for Canadian dollars and accepting payment for their dollars in Euros. Therefore, in Figure 3.10, the supply curve for Canadian dollars shifts from S to S'. The exchange rate of one Canadian dollar in Euros decreases from P to P', and the quantity of dollars traded increases from Q to Q'.

FIGURE 3.10

An Increase in the Supply of Canadian Dollars
When the supply of Canadian dollars in the foreign exchange market increases, the equilibrium exchange rate decreases, and the equilibrium quantity of dollars traded increases.

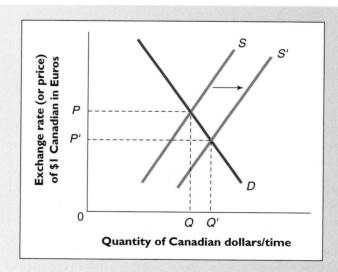

SHIFTS IN DEMAND

The preceding examples involved changes that gave rise to shifts in supply curves. Next, we'll look at what happens when demand curves shift. In the following example, the shift in demand results from events outside the particular market itself.

EXAMPLE 3.3

What will happen to the equilibrium price and quantity of tennis balls if court rental fees decline?

Let the initial supply and demand curves for tennis balls be as shown by the curves S and D in Figure 3.11, where the resulting equilibrium price and quantity are $1 per ball and 40 million balls per month, respectively. Tennis courts and tennis balls are what economists call **complements,** goods that are more valuable when used in combination than when used alone. Tennis balls, for example, would be of less value if there were no tennis courts on which to play. (Tennis balls would still have *some* value even without courts—for example, to the parents who pitch them to their children for batting practice.) As tennis courts become cheaper to use, people will respond by playing more tennis, and this will increase their demand for tennis balls. A decline in court rental fees will thus shift the demand curve for tennis balls rightward to D'. (A "rightward shift" of a demand curve can also be described as an "upward shift.")

complements two goods are complements in consumption if an increase in the price of one causes a leftward shift in the demand curve for the other

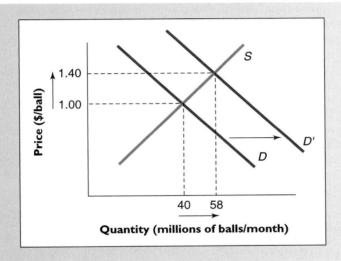

FIGURE 3.11
The Effect on the Market for Tennis Balls of a Decline in Court Rental Fees
When the price of a good's complement falls, demand for the good shifts right, causing equilibrium price and quantity to rise.

Note in Figure 3.11 that for the illustrative demand shift shown, the new equilibrium price of tennis balls, $1.40, is higher than the original price, and the new equilibrium quantity, 58 million balls per month, is higher than the original quantity.

EXAMPLE 3.4

What will happen to the equilibrium price and quantity of overnight letter delivery service as more people gain access to the Internet?

Suppose that the initial supply and demand curves for overnight letter deliveries are as shown by the curves S and D in Figure 3.12 and that the resulting equilibrium price and quantity are denoted P and Q. E-mail messages and overnight letters are examples of what economists call **substitutes,** meaning that, in many applications at least, the two serve similar functions for people. (Many noneconomists would call them substitutes, too. Economists don't *always* choose obscure terms for important concepts!) When two goods or services are substitutes, a decrease in the effective price of one will cause a leftward shift in the demand curve for the other. (A "leftward shift" in a demand curve can also be described as a "downward shift.") An increase in Internet access is, in effect, a decline in the price of a substitute for overnight delivery for affected users. Diagrammatically, this means a leftward shift in the demand curve for overnight delivery service to D' in Figure 3.12.

substitutes two goods are substitutes in consumption if an increase in the price of one causes a rightward shift in the demand curve for the other

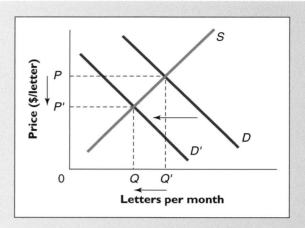

FIGURE 3.12

The Effect on the Market for Overnight Letter Delivery of a Decline in the Price of Internet Access
When the price of a substitute for a good falls, demand for the good shifts left, causing equilibrium price and quantity to fall.

As the figure shows, both the new equilibrium price P' and the new equilibrium quantity Q' are lower than the initial values P and Q. More widespread Internet access probably won't put Purolator and UPS out of business, but it will definitely cost them many customers.

To summarize, economists define goods as substitutes if an increase in the price of one causes a rightward shift in the demand curve for the other. By contrast, goods are complements if an increase in the price of one causes a leftward shift in the demand curve for the other.

The concepts of substitutes and complements enable you to answer questions like the one posed in the following exercise.

EXERCISE 3.1

How will a decline in airfares affect intercity (or long distance) bus fares and the price of hotel rooms in resort communities?

Demand curves are shifted not just by changes in the prices of substitutes and complements but also by other factors that change the amounts that people are willing to pay for a given good or service. One of the most important such factors is income.

3.2 ECONOMIC NATURALIST

When the price of oil rises, why do prices for houses in Calgary rise?

Calgary's economy is heavily dependent on the oil industry. If the price of oil rises, oil companies respond by exploring for more oil and by developing existing oil fields more intensively. As oil companies increase their activity, more people will be drawn to Calgary, some to work in the oil industry, others to supply more goods and services to the oil industry as it expands, and still others to supply goods and services to Calgary's rising population. (For example, if more families move to Calgary, more teachers will be required.) In addition, wages and salaries will tend to be bid up to attract more workers, there will be more opportunities to work overtime, and so on. Thus, individuals will tend to have higher incomes because of the oil boom. Because of a larger population and because at least some individuals will have higher incomes (and now may be able to afford to move out of apartments into houses), the demand curve for houses will shift to the right, as shown by the demand curve labelled D' in Figure 3.13. As a result, the equilibrium price and quantity of houses, P' and Q', will be higher than before.

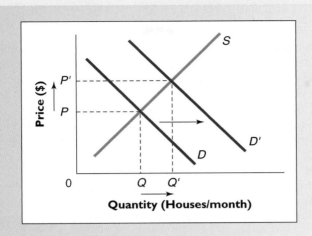

FIGURE 3.13

The Effect of an Increase in the Price of Oil on the Price of Houses in Calgary
An increase in income shifts demand for a normal good to the right, causing equilibrium price and quantity to rise.

Two factors caused the demand curve for houses in Calgary to shift to the right when the price of oil rose: the population of the city increased, and the income of individuals increased. Either effect by itself would have caused the demand curve to shift to the right; together, they reinforce each other. When incomes increase, the demand curves for most goods will shift to the right. In recognition of that fact, economists have chosen to call such goods **normal goods.**

Not all goods are normal goods, however. In fact, the demand curves for some goods actually shift leftward when income goes up, and such goods are called **inferior goods.**

When would having more money tend to make you want to buy less of something? In general, this will happen in the case of goods for which there are attractive substitutes that sell for only slightly higher prices. Apartments in an unsafe, inconveniently located neighbourhood are an example. Most residents would choose to move out of such neighbourhoods as soon as they could afford to, which means that an increase in income would cause the demand for such apartments to shift leftward.

Ground beef with high fat content is another example of an inferior good. For health reasons, most people prefer grades of meat with low fat content, and when they do buy high-fat meats it is usually a sign of budgetary pressure. When people in this situation receive higher incomes, they usually switch quickly to leaner grades of meat.

normal good a good whose demand curve shifts rightward when the incomes of buyers increase

inferior good a good whose demand curve shifts leftward when the incomes of buyers increase

EXERCISE 3.2

Normal and inferior goods were defined in terms of how their demand curves are affected by an increase in income. How will a *decrease* in income affect the demand for a normal good? an inferior good?

Preferences, or tastes, are another important factor that determines whether a given good will meet the cost–benefit test. Steven Spielberg's films *Jurassic Park* and *The Lost World* appeared to kindle a powerful, if previously latent, preference among children for toy dinosaurs. In the wake of these films, the demand for such toys shifted sharply to the right. And the same children who couldn't find enough dinosaur toys suddenly seemed to lose interest in toy designs involving horses and other present-day animals, whose respective demand curves shifted sharply to the left.

Expectations can also influence demand. For example, if many parents suddenly expect a special toy to be scarce during the holiday season, demand for the toy will increase before the holiday season.

EXAMPLE 3.5

What would happen to the exchange rate of the Canadian dollar if Europeans reduce their travel to Canada because they are afraid of SARS?

Severe Acute Respiratory Syndrome (SARS) first appeared in China late in 2002. The disease has no known cure, and it often kills its victims quickly. In early 2003, it spread to Canada, with outbreaks in Toronto and Vancouver, and the World Health Organization issued advisories against travelling to these cities. Out of fear of SARS, Europeans reduced their travel to Canada, both for business and for vacations. Demand by Europeans for Canadian dollars therefore decreased. Figure 3.14 shows demand for Canadian dollars decreasing from D to D'. As a result, the equilibrium exchange rate of one Canadian dollar in Euros decreased from P to P', and the equilibrium quantity decreased from Q to Q'. (Fortunately, the SARS epidemic was quickly brought under control. The effects of SARS on tourism lingered for a while, but fear of SARS gradually receded—which implies that the demand curve for Canadian dollars eventually shifted back to D.)

FIGURE 3.14

A Decrease in the Demand for Canadian Dollars

When the demand for Canadian dollars in the foreign exchange market decreases, the equilibrium exchange rate decreases and the equilibrium quantity of dollars traded decreases.

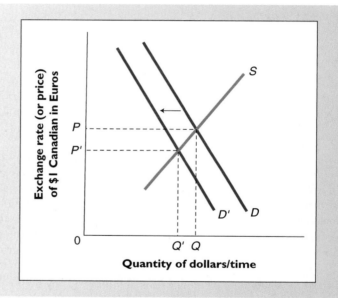

FOUR SIMPLE RULES

For supply and demand curves that have the conventional slopes (upward sloping for supply curves, downward sloping for demand curves), the preceding examples illustrate the four basic rules that govern how shifts in supply and demand affect equilibrium prices and quantities. These rules are summarized in Figure 3.15.

The qualitative rules summarized in Figure 3.15 hold for supply or demand shifts of any magnitude, provided the curves have their conventional slopes. But although it is easy enough for textbook authors to invent examples where only one thing is happening in a market, in the real world we often observe simultaneous changes in demand and supply. As the next example demonstrates, when both supply and demand curves shift at the same time, the direction in which equilibrium price or quantity changes will depend on the relative magnitudes of the shifts.

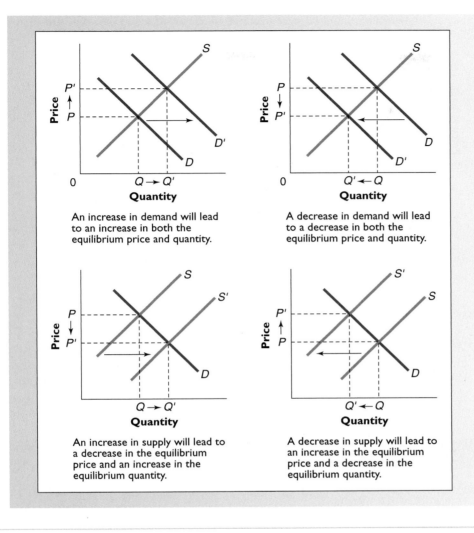

FIGURE 3.15

Four Rules Governing the Effects of Supply and Demand Shifts

An increase in demand will lead to an increase in both the equilibrium price and quantity.

A decrease in demand will lead to a decrease in both the equilibrium price and quantity.

An increase in supply will lead to a decrease in the equilibrium price and an increase in the equilibrium quantity.

A decrease in supply will lead to an increase in the equilibrium price and a decrease in the equilibrium quantity.

EXAMPLE 3.6

How do shifts in *both* demand and supply affect equilibrium quantities and prices?

What will happen to the equilibrium price and quantity in the corn tortilla chip market if both the following events occur: (1) researchers discover that the oils in which tortilla chips are fried are harmful to human health, and (2) the price of corn-harvesting equipment falls?

The discovery regarding the health effects of the oils will shift the demand for tortilla chips to the left, because many people who once bought chips in the belief that they were healthful will now switch to other foods. The decline in the price of harvesting equipment will shift the supply of chips to the right, because additional farmers will now find it profitable to enter the corn market. In Figure 3.16(a) and (b), the original supply and demand curves are denoted by *S* and *D*, while the new curves are denoted by *S'* and *D'*. Note that in both parts, the shifts lead to a decline in the equilibrium price of chips.

But note also that the effect of the shifts on equilibrium quantity cannot be determined without knowing their relative magnitudes. Taken separately, the demand shift causes a decline in equilibrium quantity, whereas the supply shift causes an increase in equilibrium quantity. The net effect of the two shifts thus depends on which of the individual effects is larger. In Figure 3.16(a), the demand shift dominates, so equilibrium quantity declines. In Figure 3.16(b), the supply shift dominates, so equilibrium quantity goes up.

FIGURE 3.16

The Effects of Simultaneous Shifts in Supply and Demand

When demand shifts left and supply shifts right, equilibrium price falls, but equilibrium quantity may either rise [panel (b)] or fall [panel (a)].

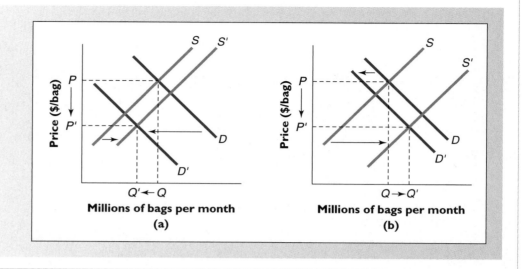

The following exercise asks you to consider a simple variation on the problem posed in Example 3.6.

EXERCISE 3.3

What will happen to the equilibrium price and quantity in the corn tortilla chip market if both the following events occur: (1) researchers discover that a vitamin found in corn helps protect against cancer and heart disease; and (2) a swarm of locusts destroys part of the corn crop?

3.3 ECONOMIC NATURALIST

Why do the prices of some goods, like airline tickets to Europe, go up during the months of heaviest consumption, while others, like sweet corn, go down?

Seasonal price movements for airline tickets are primarily the result of seasonal variations in demand. Thus, ticket prices to Europe are highest during the summer months because the demand for tickets is highest during those months, as shown in Figure 3.17(a) (where the w and s subscripts denote winter and summer values, respectively).

By contrast, seasonal price movements for sweet corn are primarily the result of seasonal variations in supply. The price of sweet corn is lowest in the summer months because its supply is highest during those months [Figure 3.17(b)].

FIGURE 3.17

Seasonal Variation in the Air Travel and Corn Markets

Panel (a): Prices are highest during the period of heaviest consumption when heavy consumption is the result of high demand. Panel (b): Prices are lowest during the period of heaviest consumption when heavy consumption is the result of high supply.

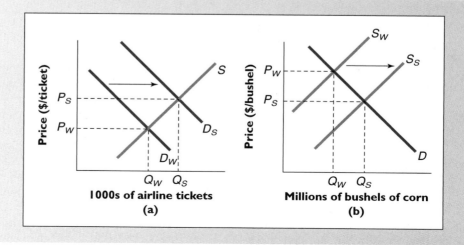

FACTORS CAUSING AN INCREASE IN SUPPLY (SUPPLY CURVE SHIFTS RIGHT)

1. A decrease in the cost of materials, labour, or other inputs used in the production of the good or service
2. An improvement in technology that reduces the cost of producing the good or service
3. An increase in a subsidy provided by government
4. An increase in the number of firms

When these factors move in the opposite direction, supply will shift left.

FACTORS CAUSING AN INCREASE IN DEMAND (DEMAND CURVE SHIFTS RIGHT)

1. A decrease in the price of complements to the good or service
2. An increase in the price of substitutes for the good or service
3. An increase in income (for a normal good)
4. An increased preference by demanders for the good or service
5. An increase in the population of potential buyers

When these factors move in the opposite direction, demand will shift left. When both supply and demand shift, it is often necessary to know the relative magnitudes of the shifts to determine if equilibrium price and equilibrium quantity increase or decrease.

SUMMARY

- **3.1** Eighteenth-century economists tried to explain differences in the prices of goods by focusing on differences in their cost of production. But this approach cannot explain why a conveniently located house sells for more than one that is less conveniently located. Early nineteenth-century economists tried to explain price differences by focusing on differences in what buyers were willing to pay. But this approach cannot explain why the price of a lifesaving appendectomy is less than that of a surgical facelift.

- **3.1** Alfred Marshall's model of supply and demand explains why neither cost of production nor value to the purchaser (as measured by willingness to pay) by itself is sufficient to explain why some goods are cheap and others are expensive. To explain variations in price, we must examine the interaction of cost and willingness to pay. As we saw in this chapter, goods differ in price because of differences in their respective supply and demand curves.

- **3.1** The supply curve is an upward-sloping line indicating the quantity sellers will offer at any given price. The demand curve is a downward-sloping line that tells what quantity buyers will demand at any given price. Market equilibrium occurs when the quantity buyers demand at the market price is exactly the same as the quantity that sellers offer. The equilibrium price–quantity pair is the one at which the demand and supply curves intersect. In equilibrium, market price measures both the value of the last unit sold to buyers and the cost of the resources required to produce it.

- **3.1** When the price of a good lies above its equilibrium value, there is an excess supply, or surplus, of that good. Excess supply motivates sellers to cut their prices, and price continues to fall until the equilibrium price is reached. When price lies below its equilibrium value, there is excess demand, or shortage. With excess demand, dissatisfied buyers are motivated to offer higher prices, and the upward pressure on prices persists until equilibrium is reached. The equilibrating process depends on competition among many small buyers and sellers. A remarkable feature of the market system is that, relying only on the tendency of people to respond in self-interested ways to market price signals, it somehow manages to coordinate the actions of literally billions of buyers and sellers worldwide.

- **3.2** When the supply and demand curves for a good reflect all significant costs and benefits associated with the production and consumption of that good, the market equilibrium price will guide people to produce and consume the quantity of the good that results in the largest possible economic surplus. This conclusion does not apply if others, beside buyers, benefit from the good (as when orchard owners benefit from beehives), or if others besides sellers bear costs because of the good (as when its production generates pollution). It also does not apply if competition among many small buyers and sellers is absent. In such cases, rational behaviour on the part of individuals does not result in the greatest gain for all.

- **3.2** The efficiency of markets in allocating resources does not eliminate social concerns about how goods and services are distributed among different people. For example, we often lament the fact that many buyers enter the market with too little income to buy even the most basic goods and services. If the difficulty is that the poor have too little money, one solution is to discover ways of boosting their incomes directly.

- **3.3** The basic supply and demand model is a primary tool of the economic naturalist. Changes in the equilibrium price of a good, and in the amount of it traded in the marketplace, can be predicted on the basis of shifts in its supply or demand curves. The following four rules hold for any good with a downward-sloping demand curve and an upward-sloping supply curve:

  1. An increase in demand will lead to an increase in equilibrium price and quantity.
  2. A reduction in demand will lead to a reduction in equilibrium price and quantity.
  3. An increase in supply will lead to a reduction in equilibrium price and an increase in equilibrium quantity.
  4. A decrease in supply will lead to an increase in equilibrium price and a reduction in equilibrium quantity.

- **3.3** Incomes, tastes, population, and the prices of substitutes and complements are among the factors that shift demand schedules. Supply schedules, in turn, are primarily governed by such factors as technology, input prices, and, for agricultural products, the weather. Changes in expectations can also shift supply and demand schedules.

◼ CORE

The Efficiency Principle
Economic efficiency occurs when total economic surplus is maximized. Efficiency is an important social goal because, when the economic pie grows larger, everyone can have a larger slice.

The Equilibrium Principle
A market in equilibrium leaves no unexploited opportunities for individuals but may not exploit all gains achievable through collective action.

◼ KEY TERMS

change in demand (71)
change in quantity demanded (71)
change in quantity supplied (72)
change in supply (72)
complements (75)
demand curve (61)
economic efficiency (69)
efficient quantity (69)

equilibrium (62)
equilibrium price (62)
equilibrium quantity (62)
excess demand (64)
excess supply (64)
foreign exchange rate (65)
inferior good (77)

market (59)
market equilibrium (63)
normal good (77)
shortage (64)
substitutes (75)
supply curve (60)
surplus (64)

◼ REVIEW QUESTIONS

1. Why isn't knowing how much it costs to produce a good sufficient to predict its market price?

2. Distinguish between the meaning of the expressions "change in demand" and "change in the quantity demanded."

3. Last year a government official proposed that gasoline price controls be imposed to protect the poor from rising gasoline prices. What evidence could you consult to discover whether this proposal was enacted?

4. Explain why, in unregulated markets, the equilibrium principle suggests that excess demand and excess supply tend to be fleeting.

5. Give an example of behaviour you have observed that could be described as "smart for one but dumb for all."

■ PROBLEMS

1. State whether the following pairs of goods are complements or substitutes. (If you think a pair is ambiguous in this respect, explain why.)
   a. Tennis courts and squash courts
   b. Squash racquets and squash balls
   c. Ice cream and chocolate
   d. Cloth diapers and disposable diapers

2. How would each of the following affect the Canadian market supply curve for wheat?
   a. A new and improved crop rotation technique is discovered.
   b. The price of fertilizer falls.
   c. The government offers new tax breaks to farmers.
   d. The Prairies suffer a drought.

3. Indicate how you think each of the following would affect demand in the indicated market:
   a. An increase in family income on the demand for winter vacations in the Caribbean
   b. A study linking beef consumption to heart disease on the demand for hamburgers
   c. A relaxation of immigration laws on the demand for elementary-school places
   d. An increase in the price of audiocassettes on the demand for CDs
   e. An increase in the price of CDs on the demand for CDs

4. A student at the University of Regina claims to have spotted a UFO outside Regina. How will his claim affect the supply of binoculars in Regina stores?

5. What will happen to the equilibrium price and quantity of oranges if the wages paid to farm workers rise?

6. How will an increase in the birthrate affect the equilibrium price of land?

7. What will happen to the equilibrium price and quantity of fish if it is discovered that fish oils help prevent heart disease?

8. What will happen to the equilibrium price and quantity of beef if the price of chicken feed increases?

9. Use supply and demand analysis to explain why hotel room rental rates near your campus during parents' weekend and graduation weekend might differ from the rates charged during the rest of the year.

10. How will a new law mandating an increase in required levels of automobile insurance affect the equilibrium price and quantity in the market for new automobiles?

11. Suppose the current issue of *The Globe and Mail* reports an outbreak of mad cow disease in Manitoba, as well as the discovery of a new breed of chicken that gains more weight than existing breeds from the same amount of food. How will these developments affect the equilibrium price and quantity of chicken sold in Canada?

12. What will happen to the equilibrium quantity and price of potatoes if population increases and a new, higher yielding variety of potato plant is developed?

13. What will happen to the equilibrium price and quantity of apples if apples are discovered to help prevent colds and a fungus kills 10 percent of existing apple trees?

14. What will happen to the equilibrium quantity and price of corn if the price of butter increases and the price of fertilizer decreases?

15. Tofu was available 25 years ago only from small businesses operating in Chinese quarters of large cities. Today tofu has become popular as a high-protein health food and is widely available in supermarkets throughout Canada. At the same time, production has evolved to become factory-based, using modern food-processing technologies. Draw a diagram with demand and supply curves depicting the market for tofu 25 years ago and the market for tofu today. Given the information above, what does the demand–supply model predict about changes in the quantity of tofu sold in Canada between then and now? What does it predict about changes in the price of tofu?

■ ANSWERS TO IN-CHAPTER EXERCISES

3.1 Travel by air and travel by bus are substitutes, so a decline in airfares will shift the demand for bus travel to the left, resulting in lower bus fares and fewer bus trips taken. Travel by air and the use of resort hotels are complements, so a decline in airfares will shift the demand for resort hotel rooms to the right, resulting in higher hotel rates and an increase in the number of rooms rented.

3.2 A decrease in income will shift the demand curve for a normal good to the left and will shift the demand curve for an inferior good to the right.

3.3 The vitamin discovery shifts the demand for chips to the right, and the crop losses shift the supply of chips to the left. Both shifts result in an increase in the equilibrium price of chips. But depending on the relative magnitude of the shifts, the equilibrium quantity of chips may either rise [panel (a) of the figure] or fall [panel (b) of the figure].

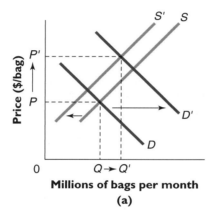

(a)

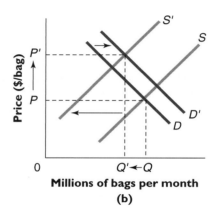

(b)

Competition and the Invisible Hand

■

Having grasped the basic core principles of economics, you are now in a position to sharpen your understanding of how consumers and firms behave. In Part 2 our focus will be on how things work in an idealized perfectly competitive economy in which consumers are perfectly informed and no firm has market power.

In our review of supply and demand in Part 1, we asked you simply to accept the law of demand, which says that demand curves are downward sloping. In Chapter 4 we will see that this law is a simple consequence of the fact that people spend their limited incomes in rational ways. We will also explore the concept of price elasticity, which describes the sensitivity of purchase decisions to variations in price. In Chapter 5 our focus will shift to the seller's side of the market, where our task will be to see why upward-sloping supply curves are a consequence of production decisions taken by firms whose goal is to maximize profit.

Our agenda in Chapter 6 is to develop more carefully and fully the concept of economic surplus introduced in Part 1 and to investigate the conditions under which unregulated markets generate the largest possible economic surplus. We will also explore why attempts to interfere with market outcomes often lead to unintended and undesired consequences.

Finally, in Chapter 7 we will investigate how economic forces cause the invisible hand of the marketplace to guide profit-seeking firms and satisfaction-seeking consumers in ways that, to a surprising degree, serve society's ends. These forces encourage aggressive cost cutting by firms, even though the resulting gains to society will eventually take the form of lower prices, not higher profits. We will also see why misunderstanding competitive forces often results in costly errors, both in everyday decision making and in government policy.

DEMAND: THE BENEFIT SIDE OF THE MARKET

Many illicit drug users commit crimes to finance their addiction. The connection between drugs and crime has led to calls for more vigorous efforts to stop the smuggling of illicit drugs. But can such efforts reduce the likelihood that your laptop computer will be stolen in the next month?

If attempts to reduce the supply of illicit drugs are successful, our basic supply and demand analysis predicts an increase in price (caused by a leftward shift in the supply curve for drugs). The law of demand tells us that drug users will respond by consuming a smaller quantity of drugs. But the amount of crime drug users commit depends not on the *price* or *quantity* of drugs they consume but rather on their *total expenditure* on drugs. Depending on the specific characteristics of the demand curve for illicit drugs, a price increase might reduce total expenditure on drugs, but it could also raise total expenditure.

Suppose, for example, that extra RCMP anti-smuggling efforts shift the supply curve in the market for illicit drugs to the left, as shown in Figure 4.1 where *P* is price and *Q* is quantity. As a result, the equilibrium quantity of drugs would fall from 5000 kg to 4000 kg per day, and the price of drugs would rise from $500 to $800 per kilogram. The total amount spent on drugs, which had been $2 500 000 per day (5000 kg/day times $500/kg), rises to $3 200 000 per day (4000 kg/day times $800/kg). In this case, then, efforts to stem the supply of drugs actually increases the likelihood of your laptop being stolen.

Other benefits from stemming the flow of illicit drugs might still outweigh the resulting increase in crime. But knowing that the policy might increase drug-related crime would clearly be useful to law enforcement authorities.

This chapter will explore the demand side of the market in greater depth than was possible in Chapter 3. Whether or not total expenditure on illicit drugs actually increases when the price of drugs increases depends crucially on the *size* of the change in prices *relative* to the *size* of the change in the quantity consumed of illicit drugs. In Chapter 3, we merely asked you to accept as an intuitively plausible claim that the quantity demanded of a good or service declines as its price rises. This relationship is known as the law of demand, and we will see how it emerges as a simple consequence of the assumption that people spend their limited incomes in rational ways.

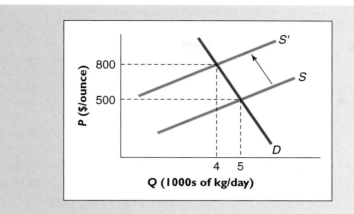

FIGURE 4.1

The Effect of Extra RCMP Patrols on the Market for Illicit Drugs
More policing shifts supply leftward and reduces the quantity demanded but may actually increase the total amount spent on drugs.

We will also explore the relationship between the price for which a good sells and the total amount that consumers spend on it. In the illicit drug example just considered, the increase in price led to an increase in total spending. In many other cases, an increase in price will lead to a reduction in total spending. Why this difference? The underlying phenomenon that explains this pattern, we will see, is elasticity of demand, a measure of the extent to which quantity demanded responds to variations in price.

4.1 NEEDS, WANTS, AND THE LAW OF DEMAND

When a good or service is scarce, it must somehow be rationed among competing users. In most markets, monetary prices perform that task. But although the demand curve is usually described as a relationship between the quantity demanded of a good and its monetary price, the relationship is really much more general. The demand curve is a relationship between the quantity demanded and *all* costs—monetary and nonmonetary—associated with acquiring a good. We can thus restate the **law of demand** as follows:

The Law of Demand: Other things remaining equal, people will purchase a smaller quantity of the goods or services they want as the cost of purchasing one more unit of them increases.

By stating the law of demand this way, we can see it as a direct consequence of the cost–benefit principle, which says that an activity will be pursued if (and only if) its benefits are at least as great as its costs. Recall that we measure the benefit of an activity by the highest price we would be willing to pay to pursue it. When the cost of an activity rises, it is more likely to exceed the highest price we are willing to pay for it, and we are therefore less likely to pursue that activity.

The law of demand stresses that a "cost" is the sum of *all* the sacrifices—monetary and nonmonetary, implicit and explicit—we must make to engage in an activity.

How much are you willing to pay for the latest Alanis Morisette CD? The answer will clearly depend on how you feel about her music. To Morisette's die-hard fans, buying the new release might seem absolutely essential; they would pay a steep price indeed. But those who do not like Morisette's music may not be willing to buy it at any price.

In everyday language, we distinguish between goods and services people need and those they merely want. For example, we might say that someone wants a ski vacation in the Rockies, but what he really needs is a few days off from his daily routine; or that someone wants a house with a view, but what she really needs is

Could reducing the supply of illegal drugs cause an increase in drug-related burglaries?

COST–
BENEFIT

shelter from the elements. Sometimes, of course, we hear other people protesting that they "need" something (like a third cup of coffee) that they could easily do without. However, in analyzing how markets work, the crucial issue is how much individuals are willing and able to pay for a good. Why individuals purchase a good (whether it is, for them, a "need" or a "want") is not usually of much interest to the good's sellers. What ultimately matters in the market place is whether or not individuals have the money to buy a good, and are willing to spend it on the good—at the price that they have to pay to get it.

■ 4.2 CHOICES AND THE LAW OF DEMAND

www.tfc-charts.w2d.com/ learning/law_of_demand.html Law of Demand Website

The scarcity problem reminds us that although our resources are finite, our appetites for good things are boundless. Even if we had unlimited bank accounts, we would quickly run out of the time and energy needed to do all the things we wanted to do. Our challenge is to use our limited resources to fulfill our desires to the greatest possible degree. And that leaves us with this practical question: How should we allocate our incomes among the various goods and services that are available? To answer that question, it helps to begin by recognizing that the goods and services we buy are not ends in themselves but rather means for satisfying our desires.

MEASURING WANTS: THE CONCEPT OF UTILITY

utility the sense of well-being, satisfaction, or pleasure a person derives from consuming a good or service.

Economists use the concept of **utility** to represent the satisfaction people derive from their consumption activities. The assumption is that people try to allocate their incomes so as to maximize their satisfaction, a goal referred to as *utility maximization.*

We begin by imagining that the utility associated with different activities can be measured. The nineteenth-century British economist Jeremy Bentham argued that it would be possible to measure utility if someone could invent an "utilometer." If such a device did exist, we could use it to assign a numerical utility value to every activity—watching a movie, eating a cheeseburger, and so on. The utilometer would measure utility in utils, much as a thermometer measures temperature in degrees Fahrenheit or Celsius.

If the consumer's goal is to maximize the total number of utils obtained from the goods consumed, how can one find that maximum—the combination of goods that provides the most "bang for the buck?"

Let's begin with an unusually simple problem, the one facing a consumer who reaches the front of the line at a free ice cream stand. How many cones of ice cream should this person, whom we will call Lamar, ask for? Table 4.1 shows the relationship between the total number of ice cream cones Lamar eats per hour and the total utility, measured in utils per hour, he derives from them.

TABLE 4.1
Lamar's Total Utility from Ice Cream Consumption

Cone quantity (cones/hour)	Total utility (utils/hour)
0	0
1	100
2	150
3	175
4	187
5	184

Note that the measurements in the table are stated in terms of cones per hour and utils per hour. Why "per hour"? Because without an explicit time dimension, we would have no idea whether a given quantity was a lot or a little. Five ice cream cones in a lifetime is not many, but five in an hour would be more than most of us would care to eat.

As the entries in Table 4.1 show, Lamar's total utility increases with each cone he eats, up to the fourth cone. Eating four cones per hour makes him happier than eating three, which makes him happier than eating two, and so on. But beyond four cones per hour, consuming more ice cream actually makes Lamar less happy. The fifth cone reduces his total utility from 187 utils per hour to 184 utils per hour.

We can display the utility information in Table 4.1 graphically, as in Figure 4.2. Note in the graph that the more cones per hour Lamar eats, the more utils he gets—but again only up to the fourth cone. Once he moves beyond four cones, his total utility begins to decline. Lamar's happiness reaches a maximum of 187 utils when he eats four cones per hour. At that point he has no incentive to eat the fifth cone, even though it is absolutely free. Eating the fifth cone actually makes him worse off. He probably feels sick.

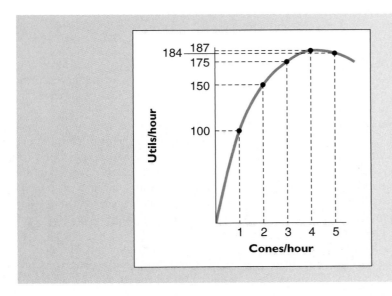

FIGURE 4.2

Lamar's Total Utility from Ice Cream Consumption
For most goods, utility rises at a diminishing rate with additional consumption.

Table 4.1 and Figure 4.2 illustrate another important aspect of the relationship between utility and consumption—namely, that the additional utility from additional units of consumption declines as total consumption increases. Thus, although one cone per hour is a *lot* better—by 100 utils—than zero, four cones per hour is just a *little* better than three (just 12 utils worth).

The term **marginal utility** denotes the amount by which total utility changes when consumption changes by one unit. In Table 4.2, the third column shows the marginal utility values that correspond to changes in Lamar's level of ice cream consumption. For example, the second entry in column 3 represents the increase in total utility (measured in utils per cone) when Lamar's consumption rises from one cone per hour to two. Note that the marginal utility entries in column 3 are placed midway between the rows of the preceding columns, to indicate that marginal utility corresponds to the movement from one consumption quantity to the next. Thus, we would say that the marginal utility of moving from one to two cones per hour is 50 utils per cone.

marginal utility the additional utility gained from consuming an additional unit of a good

Law of Diminishing Marginal Utility: As consumption of a good increases beyond some point, the additional utility gained from an additional unit of the good tends to decline.

TABLE 4.2
Lamar's Total and Marginal Utility from Ice Cream Consumption

Cone quantity (cones/hour)	Total utility (utils/hour)	Marginal utility (utils/cone)
0	0	
		100
1	100	
		50
2	150	
		25
3	175	
		12
4	187	
		−3
5	184	

$$\text{Marginal utility} = \frac{\text{change in utility}}{\text{change in consumption}}$$
$$= \frac{150 \text{ utils} - 100 \text{ utils}}{2 \text{ cones} - 1 \text{ cone}}$$
$$= 50 \text{ utils/cone}$$

This pattern of diminishing marginal utility holds true not just for Lamar but also for most consumers of most goods. If we have one brownie or one Ferrari, we are happier than we are with none; if we have two, we will be even happier—but not twice as happy, and so on.

Suppose Lamar has waited several hours in the lineup for ice cream. What will he do when he gets to the front of the line? At that point, the opportunity cost of the time he spent waiting is a sunk cost and hence is irrelevant to his decision about how many cones to order. And since there is no monetary charge for the cones, the cost of ordering an additional one is zero. According to the cost–benefit criterion, Lamar will therefore continue to order cones as long as the marginal benefit (here, the marginal utility he gets from an additional cone) is greater than or equal to zero. Thus, he will order four cones.

In this highly simplified example, Lamar's utility-maximization problem is just like the one he would confront if he were deciding how much water to drink from a public fountain. (Solution: Keep drinking until the marginal utility of water declines to zero.)

COST–
BENEFIT

ALLOCATING A FIXED INCOME BETWEEN TWO GOODS

Most of us confront considerably more complex purchase decisions than the one Lamar faced. For one thing, we generally must make decisions not just about a single good but about many—and the cost of consuming additional units will rarely be zero.

To see how to proceed in more complex cases, suppose Lamar must decide how to spend his fixed income on two different goods, each with a positive price. Should he spend all his income on one of the goods or part of it on each? The law of diminishing marginal utility suggests that spending all our income on a single good is not usually a good strategy. Rather than devoting more and more money to the purchase of a good we already consume in large quantities (and whose marginal utility is therefore relatively low), we generally do better to spend that money on other goods we consume in small quantities, and whose marginal utility therefore will likely be higher.

The simplest way to illustrate how economists think about the spending decisions of a utility-maximizing consumer is to work through an example like the following.

EXAMPLE 4.1

How many vanilla ice cream cones and chocolate sundaes will Lamar consume?

Suppose the free ice cream bonanza is over, and Lamar now has a fixed income of $10 per week to spend at the ice cream parlour. His two favourite choices are vanilla cones and chocolate sundaes. Sundaes sell for $2 and vanilla cones for $1. The number of utils Lamar derives from consuming different amounts of each are as shown in Table 4.3. If Lamar's goal is to maximize the utility he derives from his $10 weekly spending on ice cream, how much of each will he eat, if he maximizes utility?

TABLE 4.3
Utility from Two Types of Ice Cream Consumption

Vanilla cones per week	Utils/week from cones	Chocolate sundaes per week	Utils/week from sundaes
0	0	0	0
1	36	1	50
2	50	2	80
3	60	3	105
4	68	4	120
5	75	5	130
6	80	6	138
7	84	7	144
8	82	8	148
9	81	9	150
10	80	10	151

Lamar wants to maximize the total number of utils he gets from eating two types of ice cream—cones and sundaes—on a $10 weekly budget. His spending limit, or *budget constraint,* is $10. One way Lamar can solve his problem is to list all the combinations of cones and sundaes that cost $10 per week and then choose the one that delivers the highest total utility. Suppose he spends the entire $10 on cones. At $1 apiece, that gives him 10 cones per week, yielding a total utility of 80 utils per week.

Now compare that with what happens if Lamar splits up his budget. Suppose, for example, that he buys only six cones, which leaves $4 to spend on sundaes

TABLE 4.4
Affordable Combinations of Cones and Sundaes

Cone/sundae combinations	Total utility (utils/week)
10 cones, 0 sundaes	80 + 0 = 80
8 cones, 1 sundae	82 + 50 = 132
6 cones, 2 sundaes	80 + 80 = 160
4 cones, 3 sundaes	68 + 105 = 173
2 cones, 4 sundaes	50 + 120 = 170
0 cones, 5 sundaes	0 + 130 = 130

(enough to buy two per week). That gives him 80 utils/week from cones + 80 utils/week from sundaes = 160 utils/week, or twice as many utils per week as he got by spending all his income on cones.

Table 4.4 shows the various cone and sundae combinations Lamar can buy without exceeding his $10 weekly budget constraint.

A glance at the table shows that Lamar's *optimal combination* of goods is four cones per week and three sundaes. His total utility from that combination is 173 utils per week—more than he'd get from any of the other affordable combinations. In other words, the **optimal combination** is the *affordable* combination that delivers *maximum total utility*.

optimal combination of goods the affordable combination that yields the highest total utility

---

EXERCISE 4.1

In Example 4.1, the combination of 8 cones per week and 4 sundaes per week gives a total utility of 202 utils per week. Why is that combination not Lamar's best choice?

THE RATIONAL SPENDING RULE

If Lamar is to achieve the highest possible utility from the $10 per week he spends on ice cream, he must divide his purchases between the two types so that the marginal utility of the last dollar spent on each good is as large as possible. (If it were not, he could achieve higher total utility by spending his last dollar differently.) Let us refer to Table 4.3 to see if that condition is satisfied when Lamar buys four cones per week and three sundaes.

Note that the marginal utility of Lamar's third sundae is 25 utils (the difference between the 105 utils he gets from three sundaes and the 80 utils he gets from two). And since the third sundae costs him $2, his marginal utility per dollar is 25 utils/$2, or 12.5 utils per dollar. Could he have gotten more utils per dollar had he spent $2 on cones instead? Spending $1 more on cones would move him from four cones per week to five, which would increase his total utility from cones by seven utils per week (the difference between the 75 utils he gets from five cones and the 68 utils he gets from four). Buying a sixth cone would increase his total utility by only five utils, for a total increase of 12 utils, significantly less than the 25 utils he sacrifices by not purchasing the third sundae. Shifting more money to cones would thus prevent Lamar from achieving the largest total utility possible, given his weekly budget for ice cream.

Note that when Lamar allocates his budget optimally (that is, when he buys four cones per week and three sundaes), he receives 12.5 utils per dollar from his last purchase of sundaes but only eight utils per dollar from his last purchase of vanilla cones. If this discrepancy strikes you as a problem, your economic intuition has served you well. Since Lamar is getting more bang for his buck (more utils per dollar) from the last sundae he purchases than from the last cone, it would seem that he ought to spend more on sundaes and less on cones.

The way the example is structured, however, Lamar can purchase cones and sundaes *only in whole-number amounts*. Spending more on sundaes would thus require a move from three sundaes a week to four. And because buying a fourth sundae would yield only 7.5 utils per dollar—less than he would get by spending the same amount on cones—Lamar is better off if he consumes only three sundaes.

In actual experience, the inability to divide goods and services into fractional amounts is seldom an insurmountable problem. After all, if Lamar could do better by consuming, say, 3.2 sundaes per week instead of 3, he could accomplish that by consuming 32 sundaes every 10 weeks (which works out to an average of 3.2 per week).

Whenever goods can be consumed in fractional quantities, we can use the following important rule—the **Rational Spending Rule**—to solve the consumer's allocation problem.

The Rational Spending Rule: To maximize utility, spending must be allocated across goods so that the marginal utility per dollar is the same for each good.

The Rational Spending Rule tells us that if Lamar can purchase ice cream in fractional amounts, he should continue shifting from cones to sundaes until the marginal utility per dollar he obtains from the two goods becomes equal.

The Rational Spending Rule can be expressed as a simple formula. If we use MU_C to denote Lamar's marginal utility from cone consumption (measured in utils per cone) and P_C to denote the price of cones in dollars (measured in dollars per cone), then the ratio MU_C/P_C will represent Lamar's marginal utility per dollar spent on cones. Similarly, if we use MU_S to denote Lamar's marginal utility from sundae consumption, and P_S to denote the price of sundaes, then MU_S/P_S will represent his marginal utility per dollar spent on sundaes. The marginal utility per dollar will be exactly the same for the two types—and hence total utility will be maximized—when the following simple equation is satisfied:

The Rational Spending Rule for Two Goods:

$$\frac{MU_C}{P_C} = \frac{MU_S}{P_S}.$$

(4.1)

The Rational Spending Rule follows directly from the Cost–Benefit Principle and is easily generalized to apply to spending decisions regarding large numbers of goods. In its most general form, it says that in order to maximize utility, the ratio of marginal utility to price must be the same for each good the consumer buys. If the ratio were higher for one good than for another, the consumer could always increase her total utility by buying more of the first good and less of the second.

COST–
BENEFIT

HOW INCOME AND THE PRICES OF SUBSTITUTES AFFECT DEMAND

In Chapter 3 we made the plausible assumption that the demand for any good or service depends on income and the prices of substitutes. As you apply the Rational Spending Rule to work through the following exercises, you will see *why* more clearly.

EXERCISE 4.2

Refer to Example 4.1. How will Lamar allocate his spending between cones and sundaes if he has $14 per week rather than $10 per week to spend on ice cream?

From among the combinations of goods that are affordable, the utility-maximizing consumer chooses the combination that provides the highest total utility. Extra income stimulates demand by enlarging the set of affordable combinations—by making it possible to buy more of each good than before.

Since people typically have somewhat different tastes, Lamar's responses to having more income will not necessarily be the same as those of someone else. In general, the market demand for a commodity is determined both by the *ability* of potential consumers to pay and by their *willingness* to pay—so the distribution of income always matters, in determining the demand for commodities.

EXERCISE 4.3

Suppose that Lamar again has a budget of $10 per week to allocate between vanilla ice cream cones and chocolate sundaes. The utilities he derives from different quantities of each are again as given in Example 4.1, and chocolate sundaes again sell for $2 apiece. How many units of each type will Lamar buy if the price of vanilla cones is $2 rather than $1?

If you worked through Exercise 4.3 successfully, you saw that a rise in the price of cones caused Lamar to increase his consumption of sundaes. Now consider a more streamlined way of explaining why a change in the price of one good affects demands for other goods. When consumption goods can be purchased in fractional quantities, the Rational Spending Rule requires that the ratio of marginal utility to price be the same for all goods. This means that if the price of one good goes up, the ratio of its current marginal utility to its new price will be lower than for other goods. Consumers can then increase their total utility by devoting smaller proportion of their incomes to that good and a larger proportion to others. When the price of a vanilla ice cream cone increased, Lamar decreased his consumption of cones *and* increased his consumption of sundaes.

The impact of higher cone prices on Lamar's consumption of cones can be broken down into two effects. These two effects are known as the *income effect* and the *substitution effect.*

To define the income effect, recall that before the price of a cone increased, Lamar maximized his total utility by spending $10 to purchase 4 cones and 3 sundaes per week. However, after the price of a cone rose to $2, Lamar needed $14 per week to purchase this same combination of cones and sundaes. Lamar is clearly worse off because of the price increase. His weekly budget of $10 for ice cream cannot buy as much as it did when cones cost only $1 each—Lamar's real income has decreased. In general, if Lamar considers vanilla ice cream cones to be a normal good, he will purchase a smaller quantity of them whenever his real income is reduced. The *income* effect is the change in quantity demanded of a good that occurs because a change in the price of the good changes the real income of the person who purchases it.

When the price of a vanilla ice cream cone increased from $1 to $2, its price relative to the price of a chocolate ice cream sundae rose. (One could equally say that the price of sundaes relative to cones fell.) Suppose that after the price of cones increased, Lamar's income was increased by $4 per week so that if he wanted to, he could purchase 4 cones and 3 sundaes per week, just as he had before the price increase. Even if Lamar was compensated in this fashion for his loss of purchasing power, the rational spending rule tells us that he will reduce his weekly consumption of cones and increase his weekly consumption of sundaes—he will *substitute* the good that now has a relatively lower price for the good whose relative price has simultaneously increased until the rational spending rule is fulfilled. When real income is held constant, the change in the quantity demanded of a good whose relative price has changed is known as the *substitution effect.*

> **income effect** The change in quantity demanded of a good that occurs because a change in the price of the good changes the real income of the person who purchases it.

> **substitution effect** The change in quantity demanded of a good whose relative price has changed that occurs when a consumer's real income is held constant.

EXERCISE 4.4

Suppose that when the price of vanilla ice cream cones increases from $1 to $2, Lamar is the lucky winner of a prize from a local dairy that gives him an extra $4 per week to spend on vanilla ice cream cones and chocolate sundaes. According to the rational spending rule, how many cones and how many sundaes will Lamar purchase each week?

RECAP	CHOICES AND THE LAW OF DEMAND

The scarcity problem challenges us to allocate our incomes among the various goods that are available so as to fulfill our desires to the greatest possible degree. The optimal combination of goods is that affordable combination that yields the highest total utility. For goods that are perfectly divisible, the Rational Spending Rule tells us that the optimal combination is one for which the marginal utility per dollar is the same for each good. If this condition is not satisfied, the consumer can increase her utility by spending less on goods for which the marginal utility per dollar is lower and more on goods for which the marginal utility per dollar is higher.

▰ 4.3 APPLYING THE RATIONAL SPENDING RULE

The real payoff from learning the law of demand and the Rational Spending Rule lies not in working through hypothetical examples but in using these abstract concepts to make sense of the world around you. To encourage you in your efforts to become an economic naturalist, we turn now to a sequence of examples.

SUBSTITUTION AT WORK

In the first of these examples, we focus on the role of substitution. When the price of a good or service goes up, rational consumers generally turn to less expensive substitutes. Unable to meet the payments on a new car? Then buy a used one, or rent an apartment on a bus or subway line. French restaurants too pricey? Then go out for Chinese food, or eat at home more often. National Hockey League tickets too high? Watch the game on television, or read a book. Can't afford a book? Check one out of the library, or download some reading matter from the Internet. Once you start to think about it, there are many opportunities to substitute one good for another.

4.1   E C O N O M I C   N A T U R A L I S T

Why do contractors sometimes dismantle old houses in Halifax almost board-by-board, then rebuild them, being careful always to leave the supporting skeleton intact? Would it not be cheaper to demolish old houses and start over?

This practice is observed much more frequently on projects located near the core of the city, where land is much more expensive. The old houses were built when zoning regulations permitted them to be much closer together and cover more of the lot. New houses would have to be farther apart to meet newer zoning rules. Each new house would require more land and would be more expensive, and there would be fewer of them in the same space. Few people would be able to afford new houses on large lots near the core of the city. However, given the opportunity, they can choose to live near the core in more tightly spaced houses and spend what they save in other ways—perhaps on cottages in the country or on travel. Contractors respond to this choice by *rebuilding* old houses, which are not required to observe the newer spacing requirements. The heritage character of the city is retained, an unintended benefit.

An especially vivid illustration of substitution occurred during the late 1970s, when fuel shortages brought on by interruptions in the supply of oil from the Middle East led to sharp increases in the price of gasoline and other fuels. In a variety of ways—some straightforward, others remarkably ingenious—consumers changed their behaviour to economize on the use of energy. They formed carpools; switched to public transportation; bought lower-powered cars; moved closer to work; took fewer trips; turned down their thermostats; installed insulation, storm windows, and solar heaters; and bought more efficient appliances.

As the next example points out, consumers not only abandon a good in favour of substitutes when it gets more expensive but also return to that good when real prices return to their original levels.

4.2   E C O N O M I C   N A T U R A L I S T

Why did people turn to four-cylinder cars in the 1970s, only to shift back to six- and eight-cylinder cars in the 1990s?

At the beginning of 1973, the price of light crude oil on world markets was about $2.10 per barrel. (Oil prices on world markets are quoted in U.S. dollars.) Major disruptions of oil supplies occurred in 1974 and 1979. By early 1981, light crude oil was selling for more than $37.00, and prices of other grades had increased by similar magnitudes. Prices of refined products, including gasoline, also increased dramatically. Cars with four-cylinder engines use much less gasoline than those with six- or eight-cylinder engines, which most people were driving at the time. Hence, the demand for cars with four-cylinder engines rose, while V8 engines sold poorly. After 1980, fuel supplies stabilized, though the price of gasoline continued to rise slowly. Nevertheless, by the end of the 1980s, the proportion of cars sold with six- and eight-cylinder engines was rising. Why this reversal?

To explain the reversal, we must focus on the changes in the **real price** of gasoline. When someone decides how big an engine to choose, what matters is not the **nominal price** of gasoline but the price of gasoline *relative* to all other goods. On average, the nominal prices of all goods and services sold in Canada have been rising continually since the 1930s. (Some nominal prices have been rising more rapidly, some less rapidly, and some have even fallen; but on average, they have been rising.) From 1974 until early 1981, the nominal price of gasoline rose much more rapidly than the average rate of increase for all nominal prices in the economy. After 1981, the pattern began to reverse. Though the nominal price of gasoline was rising, it rose more slowly than the average rate of increase for all nominal prices. Thus from 1974 to 1981, the price of gasoline *relative to other goods and services* was rising. After 1981, *its relative price fell sharply* and remained low until the late 1990s. In 1999, the nominal price of a litre of gasoline actually represented a lower cost in terms of other goods and services than did the 1973 price. Its real price, that is, its opportunity cost, was actually quite low. The decline in the real price of gasoline (along with rising average incomes) accounts for the reversal of the trend toward smaller engines.

Will people continue to choose cars with large engines? Much of the answer depends on what happens to the real price of gasoline.

real price dollar price of a good relative to the average dollar price of all other goods and services

nominal price absolute price of a good in dollar terms

"We motored over to say hi!"

© The New Yorker Collection 1993 Edward Koren from cartoonbank.com
All Rights Reserved.

A sharp decline in the real price of gasoline also helps account for the explosive growth in sport utility vehicles since 1990. Almost 4 million SUVs were sold in the United States in 2001, up from only 750 000 in 1990. Gasoline has always been more expensive in Canada; nevertheless, during the 1990s it was cheaper in Canada than it had been during the 1970s. Sales of SUVs rose in Canada, too. Some SUVs—like the Ford Excursion—weigh almost 3500 kg and burn more than 23.5 litres per 100 km when driven on city streets. Vehicles like these would have been dismal failures during the 1970s but have been hot sellers in the cheap energy environment of recent years. Whether sport utility vehicles will continue to sell in large numbers will be determined in large part by what happens to the price of gasoline.

THE IMPORTANCE OF INCOME DIFFERENCES

The most obvious difference between the rich and the poor is that the rich have higher incomes. To explain why the wealthy generally buy larger houses than the poor, we need not assume that the wealthy feel more strongly about housing than the poor. A much simpler explanation is that the total utility from housing, as with most other goods, increases with the amount consumed.

HOW THE DISTRIBUTION OF INCOME AFFECTS DEMAND

People whose incomes differ substantially spend their incomes in different ways. For example, the proportion of income a person spends on food tends to fall as income rises, whereas the proportion of income spent on foreign travel tends to rise as income rises. This observation suggests that the demand for specific goods may differ from one city to another, not just because of differences in *average* incomes but also because of differences in the way income is distributed among people.

 4.3   ECONOMIC NATURALIST

Why does a house with a view cost more in Vancouver than in Prince Rupert?

In cities such as Vancouver or Prince Rupert, B.C., some proportion of homesites are located on hillsides with commanding views. Most homeowners think that having a view is desirable. If lots with views sold for the same price as lots without views, virtually every homeowner would buy a lot with a view. Since homesites with views are in limited supply, however, they command a significant price premium. But why is this premium more in Vancouver than in Prince Rupert?

Vancouver attracts executives and entrepreneurs from the entire west coast, people who earn significantly more than the top earners in Prince Rupert. The result is that the effective demand for homesites with views is much stronger in Vancouver than in Prince Rupert. In both cities the houses with views tend to go to the highest earners,

but the premium for a view is much higher in Vancouver because its top earners make so much more money.

To illustrate, suppose the supply of homesites with views is essentially fixed in each city, as indicated by the vertical supply curves shown in Figure 4.3, and that people in both cities have identical tastes regarding views. But because the incomes of the top earners in Vancouver are much higher than the incomes of the top earners in Prince Rupert, the demand curve for homesites with views in Vancouver lies significantly to the right of the corresponding demand curve for Prince Rupert. And that explains the significantly higher premium for views in Vancouver. In general, prices in the market place depend on the distribution of income, because changes in the distribution of income shift the demand curves of commodities.

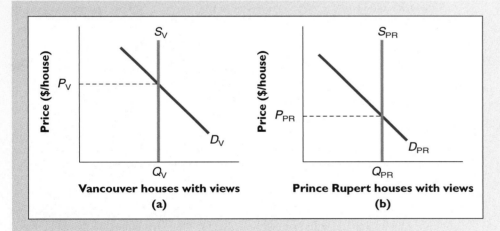

FIGURE 4.3

The Price for a House with a View

If the average income level is the same in two cities, then the city in which income is more unequally distributed, as in panel (a), will have higher demand for luxury goods such as homesites with views.

RECAP   **APPLYING THE RATIONAL SPENDING RULE**

Application of the rational spending rule highlights the important roles of income and substitution in explaining differences in consumption patterns —among individuals, among communities, and across time. The rule also highlights the fact that real, as opposed to nominal, prices and income are what matter. The demand for a good falls when the real price of a substitute falls or the real price of a complement rises. Patterns of demand may differ between communities of the same average real-income level if the distributions of income within those communities differ significantly.

▬ 4.4 INDIVIDUAL AND MARKET DEMAND CURVES

If we know what each individual's demand curve for a good looks like, how can we use that information to construct the market demand curve for the good? We must add together the individual demand curves, a process that is straightforward but requires care.

HORIZONTAL ADDITION

Suppose that there are only two buyers—Smith and Wong—in the market for canned tuna and that their demand curves are as shown in Figure 4.4(a) and (b). To construct the market demand curve for canned tuna, we simply announce a sequence of prices and then add the quantity demanded by each buyer at each price. For example, at a price of $4 per can, Smith demands six cans per week [Figure 4.4(a)] and Wong demands two cans per week [Figure 4.4(b)], for a market demand of eight cans per week [Figure 4.4(c)].

FIGURE 4.4

Individual and Market Demand Curves for Canned Tuna

The quantity demanded at any price on the market demand curve in panel (c) is the sum of the individual quantities in panels (a) and (b) demanded at that price.

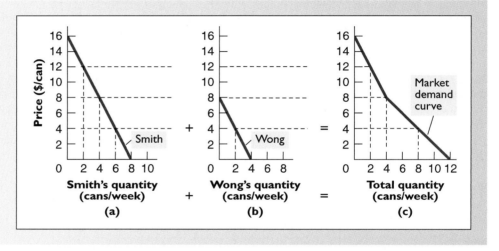

The process of adding individual demand curves to get the market demand curve is known as *horizontal addition,* a term used to emphasize that we are adding quantities, which are measured on the horizontal axes of individual demand curves.

Figure 4.5(a) illustrates the special case in which each of 1000 consumers in the market has the same demand curve. To get the market demand curve in this case, we simply multiply each quantity on the representative individual demand curve by 1000 [Figure 4.5(b)].

FIGURE 4.5

The Individual and Market Demand Curves When All Buyers Have Identical Demand Curves

When individual demand curves are identical, we get the market demand curve by multiplying each quantity on the individual demand curve by the number of consumers in the market.

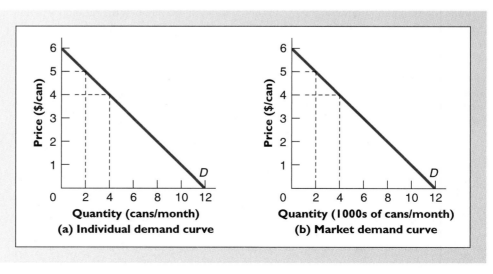

THE STRAIGHT-LINE DEMAND CURVE

So far, we have only predicted that the demand curve for a good or service slopes downward—with no predictions about the specific shape of the curve. It is often convenient, however, to draw demand curves as downward-sloping straight lines, as we did in Chapter 3.

Market demand curves may be shown not only in graphical form but in two other forms as well. The market demand relationship can be shown as a table. For example, the linear market demand curve shown in Figure 4.5(b) may be also represented as Table 4.5.

TABLE 4.5
The Market Demand for Canned Tuna in Tabular Form

Price ($/can)	Quantity (1000s of cans/month)
0	12
1	10
2	8
3	6
4	4
5	2
6	0

Market demand can also be expressed algebraically. Because economists have adopted the convention of plotting price on the vertical axis and quantity on the horizontal axis, we write the general formula of a straight-line demand curve as follows:

$$P = b - mQ, \qquad (4.2)$$

where P denotes the price of the good, usually measured in dollars per unit; Q denotes the quantity demanded, in physical units per unit of time; b denotes the vertical intercept of the demand curve, and $-m$ represents its slope.

To illustrate, suppose we want to write the equation for the market demand curve shown in Figure 4.6, which is the same as the one in Figure 4.5(b).

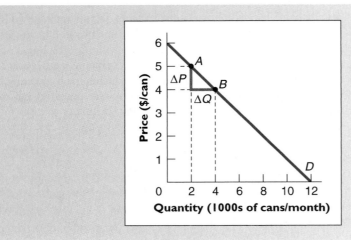

FIGURE 4.6
The Market Demand Curve for Canned Tuna

To begin, we can see from the graph that *b*, the vertical intercept of the demand curve, is 6. The slope is the ratio of the vertical distance between any two points on the line (the "rise") to the corresponding horizontal distance (the "run"). For example, if we look at the segment of the demand curve between the points labelled A and B, the rise is $\Delta P = -1$ (since the line falls a vertical distance of 1 unit between A and B), and the corresponding run is $\Delta Q = 2000$. Thus the slope of the demand curve shown is $-m = \Delta P/\Delta Q = -1/2000$. Knowing both the slope and vertical intercept of the demand curve, we also know that its equation must be

$$P = 6 - \left(\frac{1}{2000}\right) Q.$$

To check that this equation is indeed correct, consider whether it works for points A and B. Does the equation hold, for example, if we let $P = 5$ and $Q = 2000$? Calculations confirm that $5 = 6 - (1/2000)(2000)$. Similarly, we can verify that $4 = 6 - (1/2000)(4000)$.

In short, the demand relationship can be expressed as a curve, a table, or an equation—all say the same thing but in different ways.

EXERCISE 4.5   **Find the equation of the linear demand curve for movie tickets shown in the following diagram.**

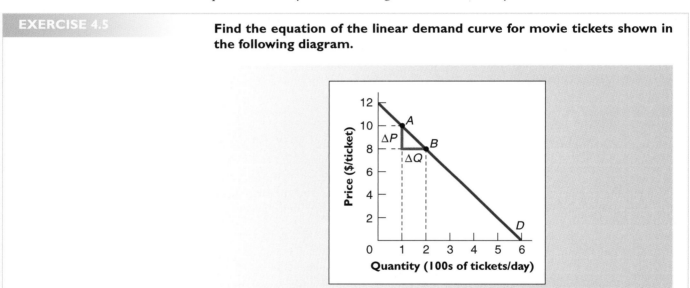

TOTAL EXPENDITURE

Given the market demand curve for a good, the total amount consumers spend on the good will depend on the price for which it is sold. And by definition, the total expenditure on a good per day is simply the number of units bought each day times the price for which it sells.

To illustrate, calculate how much moviegoers will spend on tickets each day if the demand curve is as shown in Figure 4.7 and the price is $2 per ticket. The demand curve tells us that at a price of $2 per ticket, 500 tickets per day will be sold, so total expenditure at that price will be $1000 per day. If tickets sell not for $2 but for $4 apiece, 400 tickets will be sold each day, so total expenditure at the higher price will be $1600 per day.

The same point can be made in another way. In Figure 4.7, the area of the green rectangle, representing a quantity of 500 tickets/day and price of $2, is $1000/day. The area of the rectangle containing the black lines is $1600/day. Thus, we see that the total revenue represented by the area of the rectangle containing the black lines is greater by $600/day.

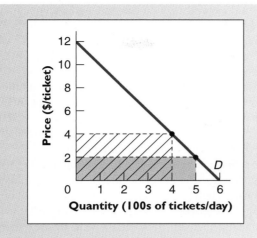

FIGURE 4.7

The Demand Curve for Movie Tickets
An increase in price from $2 to $4 per ticket increases total expenditure on tickets.

Note that the total amount consumers spend on a product each day must equal the total amount sellers of the product receive. That is, the terms **total expenditure** and **total revenue** are simply two sides of the same coin.

It might seem that an increase in the market price of a product should always result in an increase in the total revenue received by sellers. But although that happened in the case we just saw, it need not always be so. When the price of a good rises, people will buy less of it, but the two factors that govern total revenue—price and quantity—move in opposite directions. When price goes up and quantity goes down, the product of the two may go either up or down.

Note, for example, that for the demand curve shown in panel (a) of Figure 4.8 (which is the same as the one we just saw in Figure 4.7), a rise in price from $8 to $10

total expenditure = total revenue the dollar amount consumers spend on a product is equal to the dollar amount sellers receive

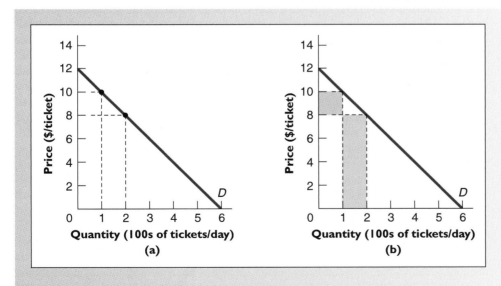

FIGURE 4.8

The Demand Curve for Movie Tickets
An increase in price from $8 to $10 per ticket results in a fall in total expenditure on tickets. Panel (a) shows the total expenditure when price is $8 per ticket and the total expenditure when price is $10 per ticket. At $8, $P \times Q$ = $8 × 200 tickets = $1600. At $10, $P \times Q$ = $10 × 100 tickets = $1000. Panel (b) shows the reduction in total expenditure caused because 100 fewer tickets are sold when the price rises from $8 to $10 (green rectangle). It also shows the increase in total expenditure caused because each of the 100 tickets are sold at $2 more per ticket (blue square) when the price rises from $8 to $10.

per ticket will cause total expenditure on tickets to go down. Thus people will spend $1600 per day on tickets at a price of $8, but only $1000 per day at a price of $10.

Panel (b) of Figure 4.8 makes the same point in a different way. The increase in price from $8 to $10 causes the quantity of tickets to fall from 200 to 100 per day. By itself, this causes total daily revenue to fall by $800: $8 × (−100 tickets) = −$800. The area of the green rectangle in panel (b) represents this drop in total revenue. At $10 per ticket, only 100 tickets are sold, but each of them sells for $2 more. Therefore, total daily revenue must rise by $2 × 100 tickets = $200. The area of the blue square in panel (b) of Figure 4.8 represents the increase in total revenue. The net change is the sum of the two offsetting changes: −$800 + $200 = −$600/day. This is consistent with the reduction from $1600 to $1000/day shown just previously.

These examples illustrate a general rule: a price increase will produce an increase in total revenue whenever it is greater, in percentage terms, than the corresponding percentage reduction in quantity demanded. Although the two price increases (from $2 to $4 and from $8 to $10) were of the same absolute value—$2 in each case—they are much different when expressed as a percentage of the original price. An increase from $2 to $4 represents a 100 percent increase in price, whereas an increase from $8 to $10 represents only a 25 percent increase in price. And although the quantity reductions caused by the two price increases were equal in absolute terms, they too are very different when expressed as percentages of the quantities originally sold. Thus, although the decline in quantity demanded was 100 tickets per day in each case, it was just a 20 percent reduction in the first case (from 500 units to 400) but a 50 percent reduction in the second (from 200 units to 100). In the second case, the negative effect on total expenditure of the 50 percent quantity reduction outweighs the positive effect of the 25 percent price increase. The reverse happens in the first case: The 100 percent increase in price (from $2 to $4) outweighs the 20 percent reduction in quantity (from five units to four units).

Example 4.2 provides further insight into the relationship between total revenue and price.

EXAMPLE 4.2

For the demand curve shown in Figure 4.9, draw a separate graph showing how total expenditure varies with the price of movie tickets.

FIGURE 4.9

The Demand Curve for Movie Tickets

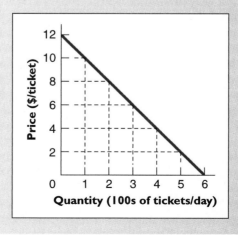

The first step in constructing this graph is to calculate total expenditure for a sample of prices on the demand curve and record the results, as in Table 4.6.

The next step is to plot total expenditure at each of the prices on a graph, as in Figure 4.10. Finally, sketch the curve by joining these points. (If greater accuracy is required, you can use a larger sample of prices than the one shown in Table 4.6.)

TABLE 4.6
Total Expenditure as a Function of Price

Price ($/ticket)	Total expenditure ($/day)
12	0
10	1000
8	1600
6	1800
4	1600
2	1000
0	0

Note in Figure 4.10 that as the price per ticket increases from 0 to $6, total expenditure increases. But as the price rises from $6 to $12, total expenditure decreases. Total expenditure reaches a maximum of $1800 per day at a price of $6.

The pattern observed in Example 4.2 holds true in general. For a straight-line demand curve, the maximum value of price times quantity occurs at the price that lies on the midpoint of the demand curve.

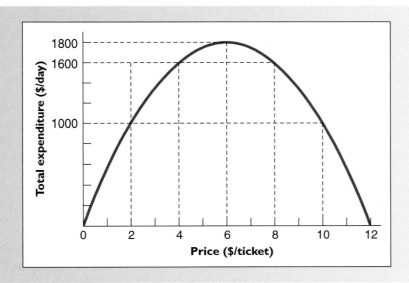

FIGURE 4.10
Total Expenditure as a Function of Price
For a good whose demand curve is a straight line, total expenditure reaches a maximum at the price corresponding to the midpoint of the demand curve.

RECAP   **INDIVIDUAL AND MARKET DEMAND CURVES**

To generate the market demand curve for a good, we add the individual demand curves of market participants horizontally. Although demand curves for actual goods will seldom be straight lines, they often can be well approximated as straight lines, especially when our concern is with the effects of small variations in quantity or price.

Total expenditure on a good is the product of its price and the quantity bought. Total revenue received by the seller of a good is the product of its price and the quantity sold. Because the quantity bought equals the quantity sold, total revenue must equal total expenditure. For a straight-line demand curve, price times quantity reaches a maximum at the price on the midpoint of the demand curve.

▌4.5 PRICE ELASTICITY OF DEMAND

When the price of a good or service rises, the quantity demanded falls. But as we have seen, to predict the effect of the price increase on total expenditure, we must also know by how much quantity will fall. The quantity demanded of some goods, such as salt, is not very sensitive to changes in price. Indeed, even if the price of salt were to double, or to fall by half, most people wouldn't alter their consumption of it. For other goods, however, the quantity demanded is extremely responsive to changes in price. As Table 4.8 (page 107) shows, for example, a significant increase in the price of green peas will cause consumption to fall sharply.

price elasticity of demand the percentage change in the quantity demanded of a good that results from a 1 percent change in its price

The **price elasticity of demand** for a good is a measure of the responsiveness of the quantity demanded of that good to changes in its price. Formally, the price elasticity of demand for a good is defined as the percentage change in the quantity demanded that results from a 1 percent change in its price. For example, if the price of beef falls by 1 percent and the quantity demanded rises by 2 percent, then the price elasticity of demand for beef has a value of −2.

elastic the demand for a good is elastic with respect to price if its price elasticity of demand is greater than one

Strictly speaking, the price elasticity of demand is negative (or zero) because price changes move in the opposite direction from changes in quantity demanded. However, for convenience, we can drop the negative sign and speak of price elasticities in terms of absolute value. The demand for a good is said to be **elastic** with respect to price if the absolute value of its price elasticity is greater than one. It is said to be **inelastic** if the absolute value of its price elasticity is less than one. Finally, demand is said to be **unit elastic** if the absolute value of its price elasticity is equal to one.

inelastic the demand for a good is inelastic with respect to price if its price elasticity of demand is less than one

unit elastic the demand for a good is unit elastic with respect to price if its price elasticity of demand is equal to one

ELASTICITY AND TOTAL EXPENDITURE

Sellers of goods and services often have a strong interest in being able to answer such questions as "Will consumers spend more on my product if I sell more units at a lower price or fewer units at a higher price?" As it turns out, the answer to this question depends critically on the price elasticity of demand. Suppose, for example, that the business manager of a rock band knows that 5000 tickets to the band's weekly summer concerts can be sold if the price is set at $20 per ticket. If the price elasticity of demand for tickets is equal to 3.0, will total ticket revenue go up or down in response to a 10 percent increase in the price of tickets?

Total revenue from ticket sales is currently ($20/ticket)(5000 tickets/week) = $100 000/week. The fact that the price elasticity of demand for tickets is 3 implies that a 10 percent increase in price will produce a 30 percent reduction in the number of tickets sold, which means that ticket sales will fall to 3500/week. Total expenditure on tickets will therefore fall to (3500 tickets/week)($22/ticket) = $77 000/week, which is significantly less than the current total expenditure. (Remember that because they are equal, total revenue and total expenditure are interchangeable.)

This example illustrates the following important rule regarding the relationship between price elasticity of demand and the effect of a price increase on total revenue:

For a product whose price elasticity of demand is greater than one, an increase in price will reduce total revenue, and a reduction in price will increase total revenue.

Let's look at the intuition behind this rule. Total expenditure is the product of price and quantity. If demand for a product is elastic, the percentage change in quantity will be larger than the corresponding percentage change in price. Thus, the change in units sold will more than offset the change in revenue per unit sold.

Now let us see how total spending responds to a price increase when demand is *inelastic* with respect to price. Suppose that in the case just considered, the elasticity of demand for tickets is not 3.0 but 0.5. How will total revenue respond to a 10 percent increase in ticket prices? This time the number of tickets sold will fall by only 5 percent to 4750 tickets/week, which means that total expenditure on tickets will rise to (4750 tickets/week)($22/ticket) = $104 500/week, or $4500/week more than the current total expenditure level.

As this example illustrates, the effect of a price change on total expenditure when demand is inelastic runs in the opposite direction from the effect when demand is elastic:

For a product whose price elasticity of demand is less than one, an increase in price will increase total expenditure, and a reduction in price will reduce total expenditure.

Again, the intuition behind this rule is straightforward. For a product whose demand is inelastic with respect to price, the percentage change in quantity demanded will be smaller than the corresponding percentage change in price. Thus, the change in revenue per unit sold will more than offset the change in the number of units sold.

Finally, if demand is unit elastic, a change in price does not change total expenditure:

For a product whose demand is unit elastic, neither an increase nor a decrease in price changes total expenditure.

If demand is unit elastic and the price increases, quantity will decrease by an exactly offsetting percentage; if the price decreases, quantity will increase by an exactly offsetting percentage. In both cases, price times quantity will be unchanged. Therefore, total expenditure will be unchanged.

Recall from the discussion of Figures 4.9 and 4.10 that for a straight-line demand curve, as price rises from a very low value, total expenditure rises from zero to a maximum at the price read from the midpoint of the demand curve. As price continues to increase, total expenditure decreases until it reaches zero at the price read from the vertical intercept of the demand curve. It follows that as price is increased continuously from zero along a linear demand curve, elasticity rises from a value very close to zero until the demand curve becomes unit elastic at its midpoint. As price continues to rise, demand becomes elastic. Elasticity approaches infinity as the vertical intercept of demand is approached.

The same statement can be produced by the converse argument in which price is decreased continuously from its value at the vertical intercept to zero. Labels in Figure 4.9 indicate values for price elasticity of demand as price increases from zero (or, conversely, decreases from the price read at the vertical intercept of demand).

The relationship between elasticity and the effect of a price change on total expenditure is summarized in Table 4.7, where the Greek letter epsilon (ϵ) is used to denote elasticity.

TABLE 4.7
Elasticity and the Effect of a Price Change on Total Expenditure

$\epsilon > 1$	Price increase causes reduction in total expenditure	Price reduction causes increase in total expenditure
$\epsilon = 1$	Price increase causes no change in total expenditure	Price reduction causes no change in total expenditure
$\epsilon < 1$	Price increase causes increase in total expenditure	Price reduction causes reduction in total expenditure

DETERMINANTS OF PRICE ELASTICITY OF DEMAND

COST–
BENEFIT

What factors determine the price elasticity of demand for a good or service? To answer this question, recall that before a rational consumer buys any product, the product must first pass the cost–benefit test. For instance, consider a good (such as a dorm refrigerator) that, if you buy it at all, you buy only one unit. Suppose that, at the current price, you have decided to buy it. Now imagine that the price goes up by 10 percent. Will a price increase of this magnitude be likely to cause the good to fail the cost–benefit test and make you change your mind? The answer will depend on factors such as the following.

Substitution Possibilities When the price of a product you want to buy goes up significantly, you are likely to ask yourself, "Is there some other good that can do roughly the same job but for less money?" If the answer is yes, then you can escape the effect of the price increase by simply switching to the substitute product. But if the answer is no, you are more likely to stick with your current purchase.

These observations suggest that the price elasticity of demand will tend to be higher for products for which close substitutes are readily available. Salt, for example, has no close substitutes, which is one reason that the demand for it is highly inelastic. Note, however, that while the quantity of salt people demand is highly insensitive to price, the same cannot be said of the demand for any specific brand of salt. After all, despite what salt manufacturers say about the special advantages of their own labels, consumers tend to regard one brand of salt as a virtually perfect substitute for another. Thus, if Windsor were to raise the price of its salt significantly, people would simply switch to some other brand.

The vaccine against rabies is another product for which there are essentially no attractive substitutes. A person who is bitten by a rabid animal and does not take the vaccine faces a certain and painful death. So most people in that position would pay any price they could afford rather than do without the vaccine.

If the price of salt were to double, would you use less of it?

Budget Share Suppose the price of key rings suddenly were to double. How would that affect the number of key rings you buy? If you're like most people, it would have no effect at all. Think about it—a doubling of the price of a 25 cent item that you buy only every year or two is simply nothing to worry about. By contrast, if the price of the new car you were about to buy suddenly doubled, you would definitely want to check out possible substitutes, such as a used car or a smaller new model or using public transit. If you already own a car, you might consider keeping it longer. The larger the share of your budget an item represents the greater is your incentive to look for substitutes when the price of the item rises. Big-ticket items therefore tend to have higher price elasticities of demand.

Time Home appliances come in a variety of models, some more energy-efficient than others. As a general rule, the more efficient an appliance is, the higher its price. If you were about to buy a new air conditioner and the electricity rates suddenly rose sharply, it would be in your interest to buy a more efficient machine than you had originally planned. But suppose you had already bought the machine before you learned of the rate increase. In all likelihood, it would not pay you to discard the machine right away and replace it with a more efficient model. Rather, you would wait until the machine wore out, or until you moved, before making the switch. As this example illustrates, substitution of one product or service for another may take time. Some substitutions occur in the immediate aftermath of a price increase, but many others take place years or even decades later. For this reason, the price elasticity of demand for any good or service will be higher in the long run than in the short run.

SOME REPRESENTATIVE ELASTICITY ESTIMATES

As the entries in Table 4.8 show, the price elasticities of demand for different products often differ substantially—in this sample, ranging from a high of 2.80 for green peas to a low of 0.18 for theatre and opera tickets. This variability is explained in part by the determinants of elasticity just discussed. Patrons of theatre and opera, for example, tend to have high incomes, implying that the shares of their budgets devoted to these items are likely to be small. What is more, theatre and opera patrons are often highly knowledgeable and enthusiastic about these art forms; for many of them, there are simply no acceptable substitute forms of entertainment.

TABLE 4.8
Price Elasticity Estimates for Selected Products

Good or service	Price elasticity
Green peas	2.80
Restaurant meals	1.63
Automobiles	1.35
Electricity	1.20
Beer	1.19
Movies	0.87
Air travel (foreign)	0.77
Shoes	0.70
Coffee	0.25
Theatre, opera	0.18

SOURCE: These short-run elasticity estimates are taken from the following sources: Ronald Fisher, *State and Local Public Finance*, Chicago: Irwin, 1996; H. S. Houthakker and Lester Taylor, *Consumer Demand in the United States: Analyses and Projections*, 2nd ed., Cambridge, MA: Harvard University Press, 1970; L. Taylor, "The Demand for Electricity: A Survey," *Bell Journal of Economics*, Spring 1975; K. Elzinga, "The Beer Industry," in *The Structure of American Industry*, Walter Adams, ed., New York: Macmillan, 1977.

Why is the price elasticity of demand more than 14 times larger for green peas than for theatre and opera performances? The answer cannot be that income effects loom any larger for green peas than for theatre tickets. Even though the average consumer of green peas earns much less than the average theatre or opera patron, the share of a typical family's budget devoted to green peas is surely very small. What differentiates green peas from theatre and opera performances is that there are so many more close substitutes for peas than for opera and theatre. The lowly green pea, which is mostly found in the canned goods or frozen foods sections of supermarkets, just does not seem to have inspired a loyal consumer following.

USING PRICE ELASTICITY OF DEMAND

An understanding of the factors that govern price elasticity of demand is necessary not only to make sense of consumer behaviour, but also to design effective public policy. Consider, for example, the debate about how taxes affect smoking among teenagers.

4.4   E C O N O M I C   N A T U R A L I S T

Will a higher tax on cigarettes curb teenage smoking?

In a debate that has also occurred in Canada, consultants hired by the tobacco industry testified in the U.S. Congress against higher cigarette taxes aimed at curbing teenage smoking. The main reason teenagers smoke is that their friends smoke, these consultants testified, and they concluded that higher taxes would have little effect. Does the consultants' testimony make economic sense?

The consultants are almost certainly right that peer influence is the most important determinant of teen smoking. But that does not imply that a higher tax on cigarettes would have little impact on adolescent smoking rates. Because most teenagers have small disposable incomes (that is, most have little money to spend at their own discretion), cigarettes constitute a significant share of a teenage smoker's budget. The price elasticity of demand is thus likely to be far from negligible. For at least some teenage smokers, a higher tax would make smoking unaffordable.

And among those who could afford the higher prices, at least some others would choose to spend their money on other things rather than pay the higher prices.

Given that the tax would affect at least *some* teenage smokers, the consultants' argument begins to unravel. If the tax deters even a small number of smokers directly through its effect on the price of cigarettes, it will also deter others indirectly by reducing the number of peer role models who smoke. And those who refrain because of these indirect effects will in turn no longer influence others to smoke, and so on. So even if the direct effect of higher cigarette taxes on teen smoking is small, the cumulative effects may be extremely large. The mere fact that peer pressure may be the primary determinant of teen smoking does not imply that higher cigarette taxes will have no significant impact on the number of teens who smoke.

CALCULATING PRICE ELASTICITY

Price elasticity of demand is the percentage change in quantity demanded that occurs in response to a 1 percent change in price. For example, if a 5 percent increase in price causes quantity demanded to fall by 10 percent, the price elasticity of demand is 10 percent/5 percent = 2.0. By defining elasticity in this way, we can construct a simple formula that enables us to calculate the price elasticity of demand for a product using only minimal information about its demand curve.

Suppose we let P represent the current price of a good and Q the quantity demanded at that price. Similarly, let ΔP represent a small change in the current price and ΔQ the resulting change in quantity demanded. (See Figure 4.11.) The expression $\Delta P/P$ will then stand for the proportion by which price changes when P changes by ΔP, and $\Delta Q/Q$ will stand for the corresponding proportion by which quantity changes. The formula for price elasticity may then be written as

$$\text{Price elasticity} = \epsilon = \frac{\text{Percentage change in quantity}}{\text{Percentage change in price}} = \left(\frac{\Delta Q}{Q}\right)\bigg/\left(\frac{\Delta P}{P}\right). \qquad (4.3)$$

An attractive feature of this formula for elasticity is its straightforward graphical interpretation. Thus, if we want to calculate the price elasticity of demand at point A on the linear demand curve shown in Figure 4.11, we can begin by rewriting the right-hand side of equation 4.3 as $(P/Q)(\Delta Q/\Delta P)$. And since the slope of the demand curve is equal to $\Delta P/\Delta Q$, $\Delta Q/\Delta P$ is the reciprocal of that slope: $\Delta Q/\Delta P = 1/\text{slope}$. So the price elasticity of demand at point A, denoted ϵ_A, has the following simple formula:

$$\epsilon_A = \left(\frac{P}{Q}\right)\left(\frac{1}{\text{slope}}\right). \qquad (4.4)$$

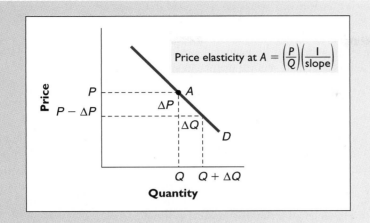

FIGURE 4.11
A Graphical Interpretation of Price Elasticity of Demand
Price elasticity of demand at any point along a straight-line demand curve is the ratio of price to quantity at that point times the reciprocal of the slope of the demand curve.

To illustrate how convenient this graphical interpretation of elasticity can be, suppose we want to find the price elasticity of demand at point A on the demand curve in Figure 4.12. The slope of this demand curve is the ratio of its vertical intercept to its horizontal intercept: $20/5 = 4$, so $1/\text{slope} = 1/4$. (Actually, the slope is -4, but we ignore the minus sign for convenience, since price elasticity always has the same sign.) The ratio P/Q at point A is $8/3$, so the price elasticity at point A is equal to $(P/Q)(1/\text{slope}) = (8/3)(1/4) = 2/3$.

Because Equation 4.4 can be used to calculate elasticity at any point on a demand curve, it is often called the **point elasticity** formula for price elasticity of demand. As another example, consider point B in Figure 4.12. Equation 4.4 gives price elasticity at point B:

point elasticity of demand elasticity calculated at a specific point on a demand curve

$$\epsilon_B = (12/2)(1/4) = 3/2.$$

So far, we have considered only small changes in the price. For small changes, the price we start at is very nearly the same as the price we end up at, but for larger changes this is not true. Suppose that we begin at point A with a price of $8 and increase it to $12, which is the price at point B. Should we calculate elasticity at point A, where price is $8, or at point B where price is $12? If we use point A, elasticity is $2/3$; if we use point B, elasticity is $3/2$. Because A and B are two different points, the same change in price over the same section of the demand curve produces two quite different values for elasticity. The choice between the two different values is arbitrary.

Because elasticity changes from point to point on the demand curve, the **arc elasticity** formula is sometimes used to calculate "average" elasticity for a segment of a demand curve:

arc elasticity of demand elasticity calculated between the endpoints of a segment of a demand curve

$$\text{arc } \epsilon = \dfrac{\dfrac{\Delta Q}{(Q_1 + Q_2)/2}}{\dfrac{\Delta P}{(P_1 + P_2)/2}} = \dfrac{\dfrac{\Delta Q}{Q_1 + Q_2}}{\dfrac{\Delta P}{P_1 + P_2}} = \left(\dfrac{P_1 + P_2}{Q_1 + Q_2}\right)\left(\dfrac{1}{\text{slope}}\right) \qquad (4.5)$$

where P_1 and Q_1 are price and quantity, respectively, at one point on a demand curve, and where P_2 and Q_2 are price and quantity, respectively at a second point. Therefore:

$$\Delta Q = Q_1 - Q_2,$$
$$\Delta P = P_1 - P_2.$$

Notice that equation 4.5 uses the average of P_1 and P_2 and the average of Q_1 and Q_2.

We can use equation 4.5 to calculate "average" elasticity over the segment of the demand curve defined by points A and B in Figure 4.12. We simply let points A and B be our first and second points, respectively.

$$\text{arc } \epsilon = \left(\frac{8 + 12}{3 + 2}\right)\left(\frac{1}{4}\right) = 1$$

The value of elasticity obtained by the arc formula falls between the elasticity values obtained by using the point formula to find elasticity at point A and at point B. However, the arc formula is not entirely satisfactory. Why? The value it gives actually is incorrect at both points A and B. In this example, price increased by 50 percent. Therefore, the value produced by the arc formula is considerably different from elasticity at either point A or point B.

However, a small price change will define a small segment of the demand curve. Points A and B in Figure 4.12 would have been much closer together if the price increase had been 5 percent, not 50 percent. Therefore, elasticity would not have been nearly so much greater at B than at A. Because the difference is smaller, it is less relevant. But the smaller difference in elasticity at the two points also makes the arc formula less relevant. From now on, unless we explicitly state otherwise, we will be referring to the point form when discussing price elasticity.

EXERCISE 4.6

What is the price elasticity of demand when *P* = 4 on the demand curve in Figure 4.12?

FIGURE 4.12

Calculating Price Elasticity of Demand
The price elasticity of demand at *A* is given by (*P/Q*)(1/slope) = (8/3)(1/4) = 2/3.

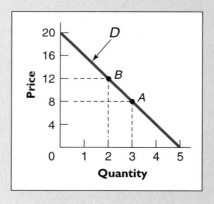

PRICE ELASTICITY CHANGES ALONG A STRAIGHT-LINE DEMAND CURVE

Our point elasticity formula makes it clear that price elasticity has a different value at every point along a straight-line demand curve. The slope of a straight-line demand curve is constant, which means that 1/slope is also constant. But the price–quantity ratio, *P/Q*, declines as we move down the demand curve. Thus, the elasticity of demand declines steadily as we move downward along a straight-line demand curve.

If we recall that elasticity is the percentage change in quantity demanded divided by the corresponding percentage change in price, this pattern makes sense. After all, a price movement of a given absolute size is small in percentage terms when it occurs near the top of the demand curve, where price is high, but large in percentage terms when it occurs near the bottom of the demand curve, where price is low. Likewise, a quantity movement of a given absolute size is large in percentage terms when it occurs near the top of the demand curve, where quantity is low, and small in percentage terms when it occurs near the bottom of the curve, where quantity is high. Figure 4.13 illustrates how price elasticity of demand changes as price decreases along a linear demand curve. Begin with the highest price shown on the demand curve in Figure 4.13, which appears as point a. Point a is the demand curve's vertical intercept. As price decreases from point a, elasticity decreases continuously from a very high value to a value of one at the demand curve's midpoint, to a very low value as price approaches zero. To put it a little differently, as price decreases from point a, the demand curve, which initially is highly elastic, becomes less elastic. It reaches unit elasticity at its midpoint and becomes highly inelastic as price approaches zero.

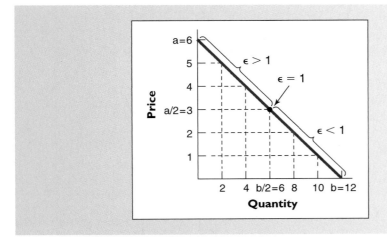

FIGURE 4.13
Price Elasticity Regions along a Straight-Line Demand Curve
Demand is elastic on the top half, unit elastic at the midpoint, and inelastic on the bottom half of a straight-line demand curve.

To see more clearly why elasticity follows this pattern again refer to Figure 4.13 and note that when price is $5, quantity demanded is 2. Suppose that if price is reduced by $1, quantity demanded increases by 2, from 2 to 4. As you can see, a 20 percent reduction of price causes a 100 percent increase in quantity. Therefore, price elasticity of demand is 5 (i.e., 100%/20% = 5). Now suppose that we start with a price of $2. Figure 4.13 shows that quantity demanded will be 8. Let us again reduce price by one dollar, from $2 to $1. Suppose that a reduction in price of one dollar again causes quantity demanded to increase by 2. This time, a reduction of $1 represents a reduction of 50 percent from the original price. And when quantity increases by 2 (from 8 to 10), the increase in quantity is 25 percent. Thus a 50 percent reduction in price causes a 25 percent increase in quantity. Therefore, price elasticity of demand is ½ (i.e., 25%/50% = ½). *As price decreases from high to low values along a linear demand curve, price elasticity of demand decreases from high to low values.*

THREE SPECIAL CASES

Three special cases constitute important exceptions to the general rule that elasticity declines along straight-line demand curves. Note that the horizontal demand curve in Figure 4.14(a) has a slope of zero, which means that the reciprocal of its slope is infinite. Price elasticity of demand is thus infinite at every point along a horizontal demand curve. Such demand curves are said to be **perfectly elastic**. The economic meaning of a perfectly horizontal demand curve is that even a small decline in price would mean that consumers would demand an infinitely large amount of the good in question—which does not seem very sensible. In practice, the price elasticity of demand may be very large, but it is not literally infinite, and the demand curve is not exactly horizontal.

In contrast, the demand curve in Figure 4.14(b) is vertical, which means that consumers want to consume exactly the same amount, regardless of price. While such goods may be rare, one can think of examples (e.g., rabies vaccine, for people who have been bitten by a rabid dog). Price elasticity of demand is exactly

perfectly elastic the demand for a good is perfectly elastic with respect to price if its price elasticity of demand is infinite

FIGURE 4.14

Perfectly Elastic, Perfectly Inelastic, and Unit Elastic Demand Curves

The horizontal demand curve in panel (a) is perfectly elastic, or infinitely elastic, at every point. Even the slightest increase in price leads consumers to desert the product in favour of substitutes. The vertical demand curve in panel (b) is perfectly inelastic at every point. Consumers do not, or cannot, switch to substitutes even in the face of large increases in price. The demand curve in panel (c) represents a case of unit elastic demand. Regardless of the price selected, total expenditure is unchanged. In this example, total expenditure is $28 no matter what price is selected.

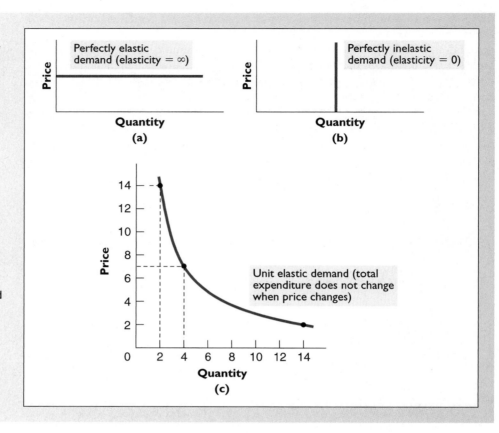

perfectly inelastic the demand for a good is perfectly inelastic with respect to price if its price elasticity of demand is zero

zero at every point along the curve. For this reason, vertical demand curves are said to be **perfectly inelastic.**

Panel (c) of Figure 4.14 provides an example of a third special case, that of a demand curve that is unit elastic at every point. No matter what price is selected on a unit-elastic demand curve, total revenue always is the same—for the demand curve in panel (c), price times quantity always is $28. The area of any rectangle defined by a price–quantity combination on the demand curve of panel (c) is equal to the area of any other rectangle defined by a different price–quantity combination on the demand curve. Therefore, the demand curve of panel (c) is a rectangular hyperbola. All demand curves that are unit elastic at every possible price are rectangular hyperbolas.

RECAP   **PRICE ELASTICITY OF DEMAND**

The price elasticity of demand for a good is the percentage change in the quantity demanded that results from a 1 percent change in its price. Mathematically, the elasticity of demand at a point along a demand curve is equal to $(P/Q)(1/\text{slope})$, where P and Q represent price and quantity and $(1/\text{slope})$ is the reciprocal of the slope of the demand curve at that point.

For a product whose price elasticity is greater than one, an increase in price will reduce total expenditure, and a reduction in price will increase total expenditure. For a product whose price elasticity of demand is less than one, an increase in price will increase total expenditure, and a reduction in price will reduce total expenditure.

The price elasticity of demand for a good or service tends to be larger when substitutes for the good are more readily available, when the good's share in the consumer's budget is larger, and when consumers have more time to adjust to a change in price.

■ 4.6 INCOME ELASTICITY AND CROSS-PRICE ELASTICITY OF DEMAND

Elasticity is an important concept in economics. There are many instances in which a change in one variable causes a change in some other variable—for example, the demand for a particular good may change if incomes change, or if the price of another good changes. So far in this chapter, we have looked at a change in a good's own price, and how much the quantity of it demanded will change as a result. However, the concept of elasticity can be used in many other contexts. Economists use the concept of elasticity—the size of two percentage changes relative to each other—to quantify the responses of demand to changes in income or prices of other goods.

The elasticity concept is used to show whether a change in one variable (such as income or price) causes a large or small change in another variable (such as demand or quantity demanded). To know whether the magnitude of a change is large or small, it must be measured relative to something else. It makes little sense to say something like, "A $1 increase in the price of oil causes a decline of 100 000 barrels in consumption," if we do not know whether $1 is a large or small percentage of price or whether 100 000 barrels is 0.001 percent, 1 percent, 10 percent, or some other percentage of total consumption. However, if we know the percentage change of a variable, we know the relative size of the change. Thus, an elasticity coefficient can tell us with a single number if a given percentage change in one variable causes a relatively large or small percentage change in another variable. Income elasticity and cross-price elasticity are two very commonly used elasticity coefficients.

Income elasticity of demand is the percentage change in the quantity demanded of a good in response to a 1 percent change in income. Equation 4.6 gives the formula for income elasticity of demand:

income elasticity of demand the percentage change in the quantity demanded of a good in response to a 1 percent change in income

$$\text{Income elasticity} = \frac{\text{percentage change in quantity demanded}}{\text{percentage change in income}} = \left(\frac{\Delta Q}{Q}\right) \Big/ \left(\frac{\Delta I}{I}\right) \qquad (4.6)$$

where I is income and the other terms are as defined previously. Income elasticity is often used to classify goods as normal or inferior. If a good's income elasticity of demand is positive, the good is a normal good. If income elasticity is negative, the good is an inferior good. As an example, suppose that as the income of a society rises, there is a decrease in the quantity purchased of single-speed bicycles with balloon tires. A single-speed bicycle would be an inferior good. If the quantity purchased of bicycles with many gears and specialized tires increases as a society's income increases, multi-geared bicycles are a normal good.

In Chapter 3, shifts of demand curves were used to define inferior and normal goods. Notice that definitions of inferior and normal goods made in terms of income elasticity are consistent with the definitions made in Chapter 3.

EXERCISE 4.7

If a 10 percent increase in income causes the number of students who choose to attend private universities to rise by 5 percent, what is the income elasticity of demand for private universities?

Cross-price elasticity of demand for two goods is the percentage change in the quantity demanded of one good in response to a 1 percent change in the price of a second good.

cross-price elasticity of demand for two goods the percentage change in the quantity demanded of one good in response to a 1 percent change in the price of a second good

For example, the cross-price elasticity of peanuts with respect to the price of cashews is the percentage change in the quantity demanded of peanuts arising from a 1 percent change in the price of cashews. Equation 4.7 gives the formula for cross-price elasticity of demand:

$$\text{Cross-price elasticity} = \frac{\text{percentage change in quantity of good } X}{\text{percentage change in price of good } Y} \qquad (4.7)$$

$$= \left(\frac{\Delta Q_X}{Q_X}\right)\bigg/\left(\frac{\Delta P_Y}{P_Y}\right)$$

where Q_X is the quantity demanded of one good (e.g., peanuts), P_Y is the price of another, different good (e.g., cashews), ΔP_Y is a small change in the price of Y, and ΔQ_X is the resulting change in the quantity demanded of good X.

If the price of cashews increases, the quantity of peanuts purchased will increase because people will substitute peanuts for cashews—cross-price elasticity will be positive. If cross-price elasticity is positive, the two goods are substitutes.

On the other hand, consider the relationship between the price of gasoline and the quantity of tires purchased. If the price of gasoline increases, causing people to drive less, they will wear out fewer tires. The quantity of tires purchased will decrease, and cross-price elasticity will be negative. If cross-price elasticity is negative, the two goods are complements.

In Chapter 3, shifts of demand curves were used to define complements and substitutes. Notice that definitions of substitutes and complements made in terms of cross-price elasticity are consistent with the definitions made in Chapter 3.

✦ 4.5   ECONOMIC NATURALIST

Why does Maxwell's Plum in Halifax sell beer at $5.00 per mug, but give free peanuts to its patrons?

In most cases, people who eat more peanuts become thirstier and drink more beer. In terms of cross-price elasticity of demand, a reduction in the price of peanuts (in this case to zero) will increase the quantity of beer consumed. Because beer and peanuts are complements, the sign of the cross-price elasticity coefficient is positive. The managers figure that the profits on the extra beer they sell will more than compensate for the value of peanuts they give away. If you also apply the definition of complements from Chapter 3, you know the demand for beer will increase when the price of peanuts is reduced to zero. The increase in demand not only enables the managers to sell more beer, it increases the price they can charge, and sales are strong, even at $5 per mug. Thus they sell beer for $5 per mug. You may be able to offer similar explanations for other pricing patterns of food and beverages (and other goods and services: for example computer printers and ink cartridges).

RECAP	INCOME ELASTICITY AND CROSS-PRICE ELASTICITY OF DEMAND

Income elasticity of demand is the percentage change in the quantity demanded that results from a 1 percent change in income. It can be calculated by using equation 4.6. If income elasticity is positive, the good is a normal good. If income elasticity is negative, the good is an inferior good.

Cross-price elasticity of demand is the percentage change in the quantity demanded of one good divided by a 1 percent change in the price of another good. It can be calculated by using equation 4.7. If cross-price elasticity is positive, the goods are substitutes; if cross-price elasticity is negative, the goods are complements.

SUMMARY

- **4.1** The rational consumer allocates income among different goods so that the marginal utility gained from the last dollar spent on each good is the same. This rational spending rule gives rise to the law of demand, which states that other things being equal, people will purchase a smaller quantity of the goods and services they want as the cost of purchasing one more unit of them increases. Here, *cost* refers to the sum of all monetary and nonmonetary sacrifices—explicit and implicit—that must be made to engage in the activity.

- **4.2** The ability to substitute one good for another is an important factor behind the law of demand. Because virtually every good or service has at least some substitutes, economists prefer to speak in terms of wants rather than of needs. We face choices, and describing our demands as needs is misleading because it suggests we have no options.

- **4.3** The demand curve is a schedule that shows the quantity of a good people want to buy at various prices. Demand curves can be used to summarize the price–quantity relationship for a single individual, but more commonly we employ them to summarize that relationship for an entire market. At any quantity along a demand curve, the corresponding price represents the amount by which the consumer (or consumers) would benefit from having an additional unit of the product. For this reason, the demand curve is sometimes described as a summary of the benefit side of the market.

- **4.5** The price elasticity of demand is a measure of how strongly buyers respond to changes in price. It is the percentage change in quantity demanded that occurs in response to a 1 percent change in price. The demand for a good is elastic with respect to price if its price elasticity is more than one, inelastic if its price elasticity is less than one, and unit elastic if its price elasticity is equal to one.

- **4.5** A decrease in price will increase total expenditure on a good if demand is elastic, but reduce it if demand is inelastic. An increase in price will increase total expenditure on a good if demand is inelastic but reduce it if demand is elastic. Total expenditure on a good reaches a maximum when price elasticity of demand is equal to one.

- **4.5** Goods such as salt, which occupy only a small share of the typical consumer's budget and have few or no good substitutes, tend to have low price elasticity of demand. Goods such as new cars of a particular make and model, which occupy large budget shares and have many attractive substitutes, tend to have high price elasticity of demand. Price elasticity of demand is higher in the long run than in the short run because people often need time to adjust to price changes.

- **4.5** The price elasticity of demand at a point along a demand curve can also be expressed as the formula $\epsilon = (\Delta Q/Q)/(\Delta P/P)$. Here, P and Q represent price and quantity at that point, and ΔQ and ΔP represent small changes in price and quantity. For straight-line demand curves, this formula can also be expressed as $\epsilon = (P/Q)(1/\text{slope})$. Because we express price elasticity of demand as an absolute value, these formulations tell us that price elasticity declines as we move down a straight-line demand curve.

- **4.6** Income elasticity of demand is the percentage change in the quantity demanded of good that arises from a 1 percent change in income. If the income elasticity of demand for a good is positive, the good is a normal good. If income elasticity of demand is negative, the good is an inferior good.

- **4.6** Cross-price elasticity of demand is the percentage change in the quantity demanded of a good that arises from a 1 percent change in the price of a different good. If cross-price elasticity is positive, the two goods are substitutes; if it is negative, the two goods are complements.

KEY TERMS

arc elasticity of demand (109)
cross-price elasticity of demand (113)
elastic (104)
income effect (94)
income elasticity of demand (113)
inelastic (104)
law of demand (87)

law of diminishing marginal utility (89)
marginal utility (89)
nominal price (96)
optimal combination of goods (92)
perfectly elastic (111)
perfectly inelastic (112)
point elasticity of demand (109)

price elasticity of demand (104)
rational spending rule (93)
real price (96)
substitution effect (94)
total expenditure (101)
total revenue (101)
unit elastic (104)
utility (88)

■ REVIEW QUESTIONS

1. Why does the law of diminishing marginal utility encourage people to spread their spending across many different types of goods?

2. Under what conditions will an increase in the price of a product lead to a reduction in total spending for that product?

3. Why do economists pay little attention to the algebraic sign of the elasticity of demand for a good with respect to its own price, yet they pay careful attention to the algebraic sign of the elasticity of demand for a good with respect to another good's price?

4. Why does the elasticity of demand for a good with respect to its own price decline as we move down along a straight-line demand curve?

5. Suppose the cross-price elasticity of demand for firewood with respect to the price of fuel oil is positive. If the price of fuel oil rises, what will happen to the quantity demanded of firewood? Why? What will happen to the demand curve for firewood? Why?

6. Large numbers of motor scooters are used for transportation in many cities of the Third World. Do you think that in the third world motor scooters are an inferior or a normal good? What about automobiles? Explain.

■ PROBLEMS

1. In which type of restaurant do you expect the service to be more prompt and courteous: an expensive gourmet restaurant or an inexpensive diner? Explain your answer.

2. Carlos has a weekly allowance of $24, all of which he spends on pizza and movie rentals, whose prices are $6 and $3, respectively. His total utility is the sum of the utility he derives from all the pizza he eats and all the movies he sees. If total utility derived from each varies with the amounts consumed as shown in the following table, and pizzas and movie rentals are consumable only in integer amounts, how many pizzas and how many movie rentals will Carlos consume each week?

Pizzas/week	Utils/week from pizza	Movie rentals/ week	Utils/week from rentals
0	0	0	0
1	20	1	40
2	38	2	46
3	54	3	50
4	68	4	54
5	80	5	56
6	90	6	57
7	98	7	57
8	104	8	57

3. Mila's current marginal utility from consuming orange juice is 75 utils per 30 mL, and her marginal utility from consuming coffee is 50 utils per 30 mL. If orange juice costs 25 cents per 30 mL and coffee costs 20 cents per 30 mL, is Mila maximizing her total utility from the two beverages? If so, explain how you know. If not, how should she rearrange her spending?

4. The following schedule shows the number of packs of bagels bought in Quebec City each day at a variety of prices.

Price of bagels ($/pack)	Number of packs purchased per day
6	0
5	3 000
4	6 000
3	9 000
2	12 000
1	15 000
0	18 000

a. Graph the daily demand curve for packs of bagels in Quebec City.
b. Derive an algebraic expression for the demand schedule you graphed.
c. Calculate the price elasticity of demand at the point on the demand curve where the price of bagels is $3.
d. If all bagel shops increased the price of bagels from $3 to $4, what would happen to total revenue?
e. Calculate the price elasticity of demand at a point on the demand curve where the price of bagels is $2.
f. If bagel shops increased the price of bagels from $2 to $3, what would happen to total revenue?
g. Show on your graph for part (a) the inelastic and elastic regions of the demand curve.

5. Refer to the data presented for Problem 4 above.
a. Calculate the price elasticity of demand for bagels at the point on the demand curve where price is $4.
b. Is your answer for part (a) the same as the answer you obtained for part (c) of Problem 4, when price was $3? If there is a difference, explain why it occurs.
c. Suppose that the price of bagels is reduced from $4 to $3. If you use the value you calculated for elasticity in part (a) of this problem, by what percentage would expect quantity to increase?
d. Suppose the price of bagels is increased from $3 to $4. If you use the value you calculated for elasticity in part (c) of Problem 4, by what percentage would you expect quantity to decrease? Do your answers for (c) and (d) of this problem exactly offset each other? Explain.
e. Use the arc elasticity formula to estimate price elasticity of demand for the segment of the demand curve defined by prices of the $3 and $4. Is your answer different from the other values of elasticity you calculated for this problem? Why or why not?

6. Refer to the table for Problem 4.
a. Calculate arc elasticity of demand when price increases from $1 to $2 per bagel.
b. Compare the answer you obtained for (a) with the answer you obtained for part (e) of Problem 5.
c. Explain any difference you discover when you make the comparison requested at (b).

7. Suppose chartered banks decide to greatly reduce the availability of student loans that are guaranteed against default by the Canadian government.
a. What would you expect to happen to the demand for credit cards by students?
b. What would you expect to happen to the quantity of credit cards issued to students? to the willingness of students to incur debt at the much higher rates of interest charged on credit cards?
c. Are credit cards a substitute, albeit an imperfect one, for student loans? What sign (positive or negative) would you expect for the cross-price elasticity of demand for credit cards with respect to interest rates charged to students for other forms of credit?

8. Perhaps you have noticed that the baby boomers are aging. In general, their incomes have increased as they have aged. It has been reported that the quantity of wine consumed has been rising over time, but the quantity of beer has changed very little, if at all.
   a. Based on this information, would you expect income elasticity of demand for wine to be positive or negative? What about beer? Explain.
   b. Would this evidence indicate that wine is an inferior or a normal good? What about beer? Explain.
   c. It is reported that as people age, their incomes decline and their consumption of prescription drugs increases. If you consider only this information, would you conclude that prescription drugs are a normal or an inferior good? Explain.
   d. As people age, what do you think happens to their marginal utility of prescription drugs? to their demand for prescription drugs? On taking these considerations into account, would you modify the answer you provided at (c)? Explain.

9. Suppose, while rummaging through your uncle's closet, you found the original painting of *Dogs Playing Poker,* a valuable piece of art. You decided to set up a display in your uncle's garage. The demand curve to see this valuable piece of art is $P = 12 - 2Q$, where P is dollars per visit and Q is the number of visitors per day.
   a. Draw the demand curve for the painting.
   b. How many people would view the painting if you charged them nothing?
   c. What is the price elasticity of demand when the price is $4?

10. Is the demand for a particular brand of car, like a Chevrolet, likely to be more or less price elastic than the demand for all cars? Why?

11. Among the following groups—senior executives, junior executives, and students—which is likely to have the most and which is likely to have the least price-elastic demand for membership in the Association of Business Professionals? Why?

12. At point A on the following demand curve, how will a 1 percent increase in the price of the product affect total expenditure on the product? Why?

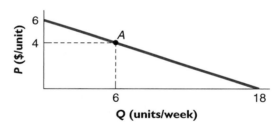

13. Andy is selling Economics Department T-shirts. The vertical axis of his demand curve measures the price of T-shirts in dollars, and the horizontal axis measures the quantity demanded in T-shirts per week. The absolute value of the slope of his demand curve is 2, and if Andy's goal is to maximize revenue from selling the T-shirts, the price he should charge, in dollars, will be: (Notice that problem 13 *does not* refer to the demand curve in the figure above, which pertains to problem 12 only.)
   a. Half as large as the number of shirts he will sell at that price.
   b. Twice as large as the number of shirts he will sell at that price.
   c. Equal to the number of shirts he will sell at that price.
   d. Low enough to sell as many T-shirts as possible.
   e. There is not enough information here to answer this question.

■ ANSWERS TO IN-CHAPTER EXERCISES

4.1 To buy 8 cones per week and 4 sundaes would cost $16, which is $6 more than Lamar has to spend.

4.2 See table next page. Suppose Lamar starts with his previous optimal combination—4 cones per week and 3 sundaes—then allocates his additional $4 one step at a time—either by spending $2 on an additional sundae or by spending that same $2 on 2 more cones. If he buys a fourth sundae for $2, he'll get 15 extra utils, or 7.5 utils per dollar. For the same money, he could buy 2 additional cones, which would give him 12 extra utils, or 6 utils per dollar. Since the first option is better, Lamar should spend the first $2 of his additional $4 weekly ice cream budget on sundaes. That gives him 4 cones and 4 sundaes, with an additional $2 to spend. He can spend it either on a fifth sundae or on 2 more cones. If he buys the fifth sundae, he will get 10 extra utils, or 5 utils per dollar. If he buys 2 more cones, he will get 12 extra utils, or 6 utils per dollar. So cones are the better choice this time. Proceeding in this manner, Lamar ends up buying 6 cones per week and 4 sundaes, a combination that yields 200 utils per week. The increase in his income has increased his demands for both cones and sundaes.

Vanilla cones per week	Utils/week from cones	Chocolate sundaes per week	Utils/week from sundaes
0	0	0	0
1	36	1	50
2	50	2	80
3	60	3	105
4	68	4	120
5	75	5	130
6	80	6	138
7	84	7	144
8	82	8	148
9	81	9	150
10	80	10	151

4.3   As we saw earlier, when the price of cones was $1 apiece, Lamar's best option was to buy 4 cones per week and 3 sundaes. But with the price of cones now $2 instead of $1, he cannot afford to buy 4 cones and 3 sundaes (they would cost him $14, or $4 more than his $10 weekly budget). So he needs to cut back, and the best place to start is with the good that delivers less marginal utility per dollar. The marginal utility per dollar delivered by the fourth cone is now only 8 utils/$2 = 4 utils per dollar, much less than the marginal utility per dollar delivered by the third sundae (which is still 12.5 utils per dollar). At 3 cones and 3 sundaes a week, he is still spending $2 too much, and the solution is to reduce consumption of cones still further (since giving up the third cone sacrifices only 5 utils per dollar, or less than he'd lose by giving up a sundae). Having cut back to 2 cones and 3 sundaes, he is spending exactly $10 per week. Now suppose he cuts his cone consumption from 2 to 1. By so doing he will lose another 14 utils, or 7 utils per dollar saved. And if he then spends that $2 on an additional sundae, he'll gain 15 utils, or 7.5 utils per dollar. So Lamar's best option this time is to consume 1 cone and 4 sundaes per week, which gives him a total of 156 utils per week.

4.4   Having answered Problem 4.3, you know that when Lamar's budget for ice cream remains at $10 per week, he consumes 1 cone and 4 sundaes per week after the price of cones increases to $2. When his budget for ice cream increases by $4, Lamar has the $14 per week that is necessary to purchase his original combination of cones and sundaes. According to Table 4.3, Lamar will obtain 7 additional utils per dollar if he increases his consumption of cones from 1 to 2 per week. This is better than the 5 additional utils per dollar he will obtain if he increases his consumption of sundaes from 4 to 5 per week. Therefore, Lamar spends $2 to buy an additional cone. He still has $2 per week to spend. Table 4.3 tells us that Lamar will obtain an additional 5 utils per dollar whether he increases his consumption of cones from 2 to 3 per week or his consumption of sundaes from 4 to 5 per week. Since Lamar doesn't care whether he eats an additional cone or an additional sundae, let us arbitrarily assume that he consumes an additional cone. He will then be spending $14 to consume 3 cones and 4 sundaes per week. This is one less cone and one more sundae than Lamar consumed before the price of cones increased. With his real income constant, Lamar purchases one less cone. The reduction of one cone is the *substitution effect* of the increase in the price of cones from $1 to $2.

If Lamar had not received the $4 that kept his real income constant, his budget for ice cream would be unchanged at $10 per week. The solution to Problem 4.3 shows that Lamar then would reduce his purchase of cones not to 3 but to 1. The further reduction by 2 cones is the *income effect* of the increase in the price of cones from $1 to $2. The *total effect* of the price change is the sum of the substitution effect plus the income effect (−1 cone − 2 cones = −3 cones).

4.5   The vertical intercept of this demand curve is 12, and its slope is $\Delta P/\Delta Q = -2/100 = -1/50$. So the equation for this demand curve is $P = 12 - (1/50)Q$.

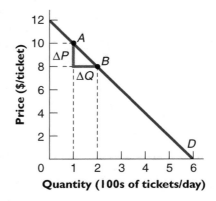

4.6   At point A in the following diagram, $P/Q = 4/4 = 1$. The slope of this demand curve is $20/5 = 4$, so $\epsilon = 1(1/\text{slope}) = 1/4$.

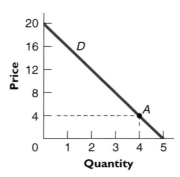

4.7   Income elasticity = percentage change in quantity demanded/percentage change in income = 5 percent/10 percent = 0.5.

Chapter 5

PERFECTLY COMPETITIVE SUPPLY: THE COST SIDE OF THE MARKET

Cars took more than 50 hours to be assembled in the 1970s but now are built in fewer than 8 hours. Similar productivity growth has occurred in many other manufacturing industries. Yet in many service industries, productivity has grown only slowly, if at all. For example, the same number of musicians is required to play Mozart's *String Quartet* today as in 1800. And it still takes a barber much the same amount of time to cut someone's hair as it always has.

Given the spectacular growth in manufacturing workers' productivity, it is no surprise that their real wages have risen more than fivefold during the past 100 years. But how can we explain why real wages for service workers have risen just as much? If barbers and musicians are no more productive than they were one hundred years ago, why are they now paid five times as much?

Remember that the opportunity cost of pursuing any given occupation is the most one could have earned in some other occupation. Most people who become barbers or musicians instead could have chosen jobs in manufacturing. If workers in service industries were not paid roughly as much as they could have earned in other occupations, many of them would not have been willing to work in service industries in the first place.

The trajectories of wages in manufacturing and service industries illustrate the intimate link between the prices at which goods and services are offered for sale in the market and the opportunity cost of the resources required to produce them. Whereas our focus in Chapter 4 was on the buyer's side of the market, our focus here is on the seller's side. Earlier, we saw that the demand curve is a graph that tells how many units buyers want to purchase at different prices. Our task here is to gain insight into the factors that shape the supply curve, which tells how many units suppliers want to sell at different prices.

Although the demand side and the supply side of the market differ in several ways, many of these differences are superficial. Indeed, the behaviour of both buyers and sellers is, in an important sense, fundamentally the same. After all, the two groups confront similar questions—in the buyer's case, "Will I be better off if I buy another unit?" and in the seller's case, "Will I be better off if

COST–
BENEFIT

I sell another unit?" What is more, buyers and sellers use the same criterion for answering these questions: A rational consumer will buy another unit if its benefit exceeds its cost, and a rational seller will sell another unit if its production cost is less than the extra revenue that results from selling it (the familiar cost–benefit principle again).

■ 5.1 PROFIT-MAXIMIZING FIRMS AND PERFECTLY COMPETITIVE MARKETS

To explore the nature of the supply curve of a product more fully, we must say more about the goals of the organizations that supply the product and the kind of economic environment in which they operate. In virtually every economy, goods and services are produced by a variety of organizations that have a host of different motives. Food banks supply food because their organizers and donors want to help people in need, the local government fixes potholes because the mayor was elected on a promise to do so, karaoke singers perform because they like public attention, and car wash employees are driven primarily by the hope of making enough money to pay their rent.

PROFIT MAXIMIZATION

Why are barbers paid five times as much now as in 1900, even though they require about as much time to cut hair now as they did then?

profit the total revenue a firm receives from the sale of its product minus all costs— explicit and implicit—incurred in producing it

profit-maximizing firm a firm whose primary goal is to maximize the difference between its total revenues and total costs

factor of production an input used in the production of a good or service

perfectly competitive market a market in which no individual supplier has significant influence on the market price of the product

price taker (perfectly competitive firm) a firm that has no influence over the price at which it sells its product

Notwithstanding this rich variety of motives, *most* goods and services offered for sale in a market economy are sold by private firms whose main reason for existing is to earn **profit** for their owners. A firm's profit is the difference between the total revenue it receives from the sale of its product and all costs it incurs, both explicit and implicit, in producing that product.

A **profit-maximizing firm** is one whose primary goal is to maximize the amount of profit it earns. It combines factors of production to produce a good or service. A **factor of production** is an input such as labour or machinery used in the production of a good or service. In this text, we start with the assumption that goods are sold by profit-maximizing firms in **perfectly competitive markets,** which are markets in which each individual firm has no influence over the market price of the products they sell. Any single firm, being just one of many sellers of the product, cannot hope to charge more than its rivals and has no motive to charge less. Because of their inability to influence market price, **perfectly competitive firms** are often described as **price takers.**

Four conditions are required to produce a perfectly competitive market:

1. **All firms sell the same standardized product.** Although this condition is almost never literally satisfied, it holds as a rough approximation for many markets. Thus the markets for concrete building blocks of a given size, or for apples of a given variety, may be described in this way. This condition implies that buyers are willing to switch from one seller to another if by so doing they can obtain a lower price.
2. **The market has many buyers and sellers, each of which buys or sells only a small fraction of the total quantity exchanged.** This condition implies that individual buyers and sellers will be price takers, regarding the market price of the product as a fixed number beyond their control. For example, a single farmer's decision to plant fewer acres of wheat would have no appreciable impact on the market price of wheat, just as an individual consumer's decision to become a vegetarian would have no perceptible effect on the price of beef.
3. **Productive resources are mobile.** This condition implies that if a potential seller identifies a profitable business opportunity in a market, he or she will be able to obtain the labor, capital, and other productive resources neces-

sary to enter that market. By the same token, sellers who are dissatisfied with the opportunities they confront in a given market are free to leave that market and employ their resources elsewhere.

4. **Buyers and sellers are well informed.** This condition means that buyers and sellers know the market price and quality of the standardized product that is sold in the market. They are aware of the relevant opportunities available to them. If that were not so, buyers would be unable to seek out sellers who charge the lowest prices, and sellers would have no means of deploying their resources in the markets in which they would earn the most.

Economists know perfectly well that many real world markets do not fit this model. For example, because Microsoft's share of the market for operating systems for desktop computers exceeds 90 percent, the market is far from being perfectly competitive. Microsoft has significant control over the prices it charges. It is not a price taker. If Microsoft were to raise the price of its latest edition of its Windows operating system by, say, 20 percent, some consumers might switch to Macintosh or Linux, and others might postpone their next upgrade; but many—perhaps even most—would continue with their plans to buy.

In this text, we will analyze markets that are not perfectly competitive in detail in Part 3. Nevertheless, it is useful to start with an analysis of perfect competition, both as a benchmark of comparison and because some industries are closer to perfect competition than to any other type of market. Agriculture is one example. The market faced by a wheat farmer in Manitoba comes very close to meeting the first three conditions of perfect competition. First, wheat is grown on vast expanses of land in Canada, the United States, Australia, Argentina, and other parts of the world. The farmer's land is a tiny part of what the world uses to grow wheat. The farmer is one of thousands of wheat farmers, each of whom grows a tiny part of the world's total crop. Although the Canadian Wheat Board acts as sole sales agent for Western Canadian wheat exports in foreign markets, the world market price is beyond its control. Second, although there are different grades of wheat, the quality of a given batch of wheat is graded according to known practices and is highly standardized. Third, commodity markets publish the price of each grade of wheat, making information on the quality and price of wheat readily available. Contrary to the third condition, most farmers cannot easily move into or out of agriculture—but some could switch to other crops. Nevertheless, the farmer in Manitoba, like other wheat farmers, cannot obtain a price for wheat that is higher than the going price and has no reason to accept a lower price. All farmers must take the price of wheat as given; therefore, our Manitoban farmer, like other farmers, is a price taker.

www.cwb.ca
Canadian Wheat Board

THE DEMAND CURVE FACING A PERFECTLY COMPETITIVE FIRM

From the perspective of an individual firm in a perfectly competitive market, what does the demand curve for its product look like? Since the firm produces only a very small part of industry output and can sell as much or as little as it wants at the prevailing market price, the demand curve facing the firm is perfectly elastic at the market price. Figure 5.1(a) shows the market demand and supply curves intersecting to determine a market price of P_0. Figure 5.1(b) shows that the product demand curve D_i as faced by any individual firm in this market is a horizontal line at the market price level P_0.

Since a perfectly competitive firm has no control over the market price of its product, it must accept the price established in the industry by the intersection of the industry supply and demand curves. The perfectly competitive firm has only one choice to make—the output level that enables it to make as much profit as it can. As we investigate how the competitive firm responds to this challenge, we will see that some costs are more important than others.

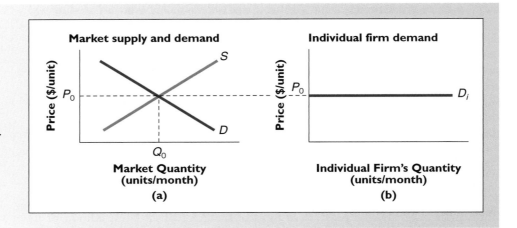

PRODUCTION IN THE SHORT RUN

One crucial aspect of a firm's decision-making is the fact that it can take much longer to implement some decisions than others (e.g., designing and building a new factory may take 12 to 18 months, but new workers can usually be hired in a week). Thus, economists often distinguish between the long run, when all of a firm's factors of production can be changed, and the short run, when some factors of production cannot be changed. In analyzing the supply decision of the firm, it is useful to begin with the short run. To gain a deeper understanding of how market supply is linked to a firm's costs, we must first consider how a firm's costs shape the firm's supply curve. After we have developed the relationship between a firm's costs and its supply curve, we can investigate how the supply curves of many firms form a market supply curve.

In our "Economic Naturalist 1.1" example in Chapter 1, we considered the social problem of littering, but we did not explicitly look at the production of beverage containers. Suppose they are produced by a perfectly competitive firm which has to decide how many containers to produce. The firm in question is a small company that makes glass bottles. To keep things simple, suppose that the silica sand required for making bottles is available free from a nearby desert, and that the only costs the firm incurs are the wages it pays its employees and the lease payment on its bottle-making machine. The employees and the machine are the firm's two factors of production. In more complex examples, factors of production might also include land, buildings, entrepreneurship, energy, and other items, but for now we consider only labour and capital.

short run a period of time
sufficiently short that at least
one of the firm's factors of
production cannot be varied

The **short run** is the period of time during which at least one of the firm's factors of production cannot be varied. (In our example, we assume that workers can be hired by the day (so the firm can vary employment from one day to the next), but that new machinery takes time to design, manufacture and install—so for our bottle maker, the short run is that period during which the firm cannot alter the size of its bottle-making machine.) By contrast, the **long run** is a period of sufficient length that all the firm's factors of production are variable.

long run a period of time of
sufficient length that all the
firm's factors of production
are variable

The bottle-making firm has to decide how many workers to hire each day. From experience it knows that Table 5.1 represents the relationship between the number of workers and total daily output. A technological relationship between inputs and output is known as a **production function**. Thus, columns 1 and 2 of Table 5.1 represent a short-run production function (short run because we are assuming the size of the firm's bottle-making machine is fixed—in fact, everything is fixed except labour). Graphs or mathematical relationships also can represent production functions.

production function a
technological relationship
between inputs and output

TABLE 5.1
Employment and Output for a Glass-Bottle Maker

(1) Total number of employees/day	(2) Total number of bottles/day	(3) Marginal product	(4) Average product (2) ÷ (1)
0	0		
		90	
1	90		90
		110	
2	**200**		100
		60	
3	260		87
		40	
4	**300**		75
		38	
5	338		68
		33	
6	371		62
		29	
7	**400**		57
11	**500**		45
16	**600**		38
22	**700**		32

Columns 1 and 2 in Table 5.1 determine the entries in column 3, which displays **marginal product**. Marginal product is the increase in total output caused by an increase of *one* unit in the variable factor of production, holding all other factors of production and technology fixed. A **variable factor of production** changes as output changes. In this case, labour is the only variable factor of production, so marginal product is about a *change* in the amount of labour employed. The bottle-making machine is the **fixed factor of production**. A fixed factor of production cannot be changed in the short run; therefore, it does not change as output changes. Column 3 answers the question "How much does daily output increase when one *more* worker is hired?" It shows that, if employment increases from two to three workers/day, total daily output rises from 90 to 200 bottles, for an increase of 110 bottles/day. Hence, marginal product is 110. Each entry in column 3 is determined in this way. Also, because marginal product is about a change from one amount of labour to another, each entry in column 3 appears between two corresponding entries in column 2.

Notice that once output of bottles increases to more than 200/day, the marginal product of labour begins to decline. In other words, given that at least one factor of production and technology is fixed, beyond some point the marginal product of labour decreases as successively more units of labour are employed in the bottle factory. Economists call this the **law of diminishing marginal returns**.

When marginal product is decreasing, increasingly more labour is required to produce an additional 100 bottles. The pattern is highlighted by the boldface

marginal product the increase in total output caused by an increase of one unit in the variable factor of production, holding technology and all other inputs constant

variable factor of production an input whose quantity can be altered in the short run

fixed factor of production an input whose quantity cannot be altered in the short run

law of diminishing marginal returns a property of the relationship between the amount of a good or service produced and the amount of a variable factor required to produce it; the law says that when technology and at least one factor of production is fixed, beyond some point marginal product of the variable input diminishes

entries of Table 5.1. For example, if the daily output of bottles is to rise from 200 to 300, labour must be increased by two—from two to four employees. But to increase daily output from 300 to 400 bottles, labour must increase by three—from four to seven employees. Beyond the marginal product at seven employees, no entries appear in column 3. This is because the table adds employees one by one only until seven are reached. Adding employees one at a time makes it easy to show marginal product. However, in order to reduce the size of Table 5.1, the next entry after seven employees is eleven employees; therefore, the increment is four employees. The additional four employees cause output to increase from 400 to 500 bottles/day, for an increase of 100. Beyond seven employees, it simplifies the table to show production of bottles increasing by increments of 100/day and to omit entries for marginal product.

average product total output divided by total units of the variable factor of production

Column 4 of Table 5.1 shows **average product** of labour. Average product is total output divided by units of the variable factor of production, or simply output per unit of variable input. For example, the fourth entry in column 4 is calculated as 300/4 = 75. Output per unit of labour is also referred to as the average productivity of labour.

The law of diminishing marginal returns always refers to situations in which technology and at least one factor of production is fixed. In the current example, technology, or knowledge of methods of producing bottles, is fixed, as is the size of the bottle-making machine. Diminishing marginal returns often arise because as workers are added, increasingly more workers must share the same workspace and tools. Space around the bottle-making machine will become increasingly crowded as employees are added. Workers might get in each other's way (or on each other's nerves), causing breakage to increase and requiring more visits to the first aid station and more time for removing broken glass from the work area. It is easy to believe that workers are less productive when they work under cramped, stressful conditions.

◼ 5.2 GRAPHING THE RELATIONSHIPS AMONG TOTAL, AVERAGE, AND MARGINAL VALUES

INCREASING
OPPORTUNITY
COST

Figure 5.2 highlights relationships among total, average, and marginal values by graphing information from Table 5.1. Knowledge of these relationships will be helpful when we study how the law of diminishing marginal returns interacts with the principle of increasing opportunity cost. Panel (a) graphs total output of bottles/day against employees/day and thus plots the tabular production function shown in Table 5.1. Panel (a) shows total output increasing over the entire range that is plotted. Panel (b) graphs the average and marginal product of labour. Both rise to a maximum, then decrease.

Consider marginal product, which reaches a maximum between one and two employees/day, then declines. Initially, each successive employee adds a larger amount to total output—the second employee's marginal product is greater than the first employee's. However, the third employee's addition to total output, his marginal product, is less than the second employee's. Diminishing marginal returns appear with the third employee. Thereafter, each successive employee adds a smaller amount to total output. When panels (a) and (b) are taken together, Figure 5.2 provides a picture of the relationship between total output and marginal product. Provided marginal product is positive, total output always rises as labour increases. However, the graph of marginal product shows that total output rises first by increasing amounts, then by decreasing amounts. Thus marginal product increases to a maximum and then begins to decline as diminishing marginal returns to labour take effect.

Note that the broken line that is perpendicular to the horizontal axis of Panel (b) of Figure 5.2 intersects maximum marginal product and extends into Panel (a). In Panel (a), it passes through the point where the slope of the production function is

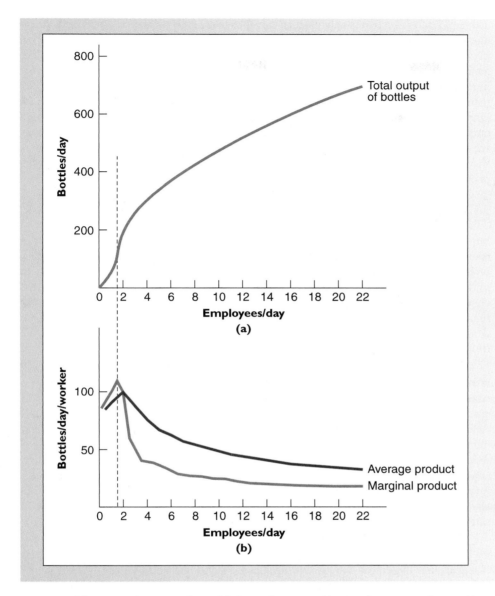

FIGURE 5.2

A Short-Run Production Function for a Glass Bottle Maker

Panel (a) shows a production function, which summarizes the technological relationship between daily use of a variable input (labour) and total daily output. Panel (b) shows marginal product, which is the increase in total daily output caused when one more unit of labour is used each day. Panel (b) also shows the average product of labour, which is total output divided by units of labour. The quantity of labour where marginal product reaches its maximum is also the quantity of labour where the slope of the production function is at a maximum. Diminishing marginal product of labour causes the production function to flatten as successive additional units of labour add smaller and smaller increments to total output.

greatest. Thus, as the quantity of labour increases beyond two employees/day, marginal product decreases, as shown in Panel (b). Moreover, as the quantity of labour is increased beyond two employees/day, the law of diminishing marginal returns causes the slope of the production function in Panel (a) to decrease. The slope of the production function can be defined as the change in output of bottles divided by the change in units of labour. Each increase of labour by one unit is associated with an increase in output of bottles; therefore, the slope of the production function is equal to marginal product. Whether one refers to Panel (a) or Panel (b), beyond the point where two workers are employed, diminishing marginal returns cause successive units of labour to add smaller and smaller increments to total output. Panel (a) and Panel (b) therefore provide two different pictures of the same effect. Panel (b) also shows four elements of the relationship between average and marginal product:

1. Maximum marginal product occurs to the left of maximum average product.
2. Marginal product intersects average product at its maximum.
3. If marginal product exceeds average product, then average product is rising.
4. If marginal product is less than average product, then average product is falling.

Table 5.1 also illustrates this pattern. Suppose one worker/day is employed. Average product is 90. Now let the number of employees/day rise to two. Marginal product is 110. Because the amount added by the additional employee exceeds the average product of 90, the output of the additional employee increases the average. As Table 5.1 shows, the average product with two employees/day is 100, 10 more than the average product with one employee. Now let the number of employees/day increase from two to three. The marginal product of a third employee is 60, which is less than the average product of two employees. Thus, we expect average product to fall when a third employee is added, and Table 5.1 shows this. At 87, the average product of three employees is less than the average product of two employees.

CHOOSING OUTPUT TO MAXIMIZE PROFIT

Suppose the lease payment for the firm's bottle-making machine is $40/day, and it must be paid whether or not the firm makes any bottles. This payment is both a fixed cost (since it does not depend on the number of bottles per day the firm makes) and, for the duration of the lease, a sunk cost. For short, we'll refer to this cost as the company's *capital cost*. In Examples 5.1 to 5.3, we'll explore how the firm's decisions about how many workers to hire and how many bottles to make depend on the price of bottles, the wage rate, and the cost of capital. Labour is the only variable input.

EXAMPLE 5.1

If bottles sell for $35/hundred and if the employee's wage is $10/day, how many bottles should the firm described above produce each day?

The firm's goal is to maximize its profit, which is the difference between the revenue it collects from the sale of bottles and the cost of its labour and capital. Table 5.2 shows how the daily number of bottles produced (denoted Q) is related to the

TABLE 5.2
Employment, Output, Revenue, Costs, and Profit

(1) Total number of employees/day	(2) Q (Total bottles/ day)	(3) Total revenue ($/day)	(4) Marginal revenue ($)	(5) Total labour cost ($/day)	(6) Total fixed cost ($/day)	(7) Total cost ($/day)	(8) Marginal cost ($)	(9) Profit ($/day)
		$0.35 × (2)		$10 × (1)		(5) + (6)		(3) − (7)
0	0	0		0	40	40		−40
2	200	70		20	40	60		10
			35				20	
4	300	105		40	40	80		25
			35				30	
7	400	140		70	40	110		30
			35				40	
11	500	175		110	40	150		25
			35				50	
16	600	210		160	40	200		10
			35				60	
22	700	245		220	40	260		−15

Notes: Employee's wage = $10/day
       Price of bottles = $35/hundred = $0.35/bottle

firm's revenue, employment, costs, and profit. Columns 1 and 2 of Table 5.2 reproduce the bold-faced entries in columns 1 and 2 of Table 5.1. Columns 4 and 8 of Table 5.2 compare the additional revenue obtained from selling 100 more bottles/day with the cost of making them. We will show that these two columns identify the daily output of bottles that maximizes profit.

To see how the entries in Table 5.2 are constructed, examine the revenue, cost, and profit values that correspond to 200 units of output (row 2). Total revenue is $70, the company's receipts from selling 200 bottles at $35/hundred. To make 200 bottles, the firm had to employ two workers (see column 1). At a wage of $10/hour, that translates into $20 of total labour cost. When the firm's fixed capital cost of $40/day is added to its total labour cost, we get the total cost entry of $60/day in column 7. The firm's daily profit is total revenue − total cost = $70 − $60 = $10, the entry in column 9.

Having decided to produce 200 bottles/day, which requires two workers/day, can the firm increase its profits by hiring more workers and producing more bottles? If it produces and sells more bottles, clearly the firm's revenues will rise. However, because it must hire more labour to produce more bottles, its costs will also rise.

How can the firm decide if it will make greater profit by increasing production? To answer this crucial question, the firm must compare its marginal revenue with its marginal cost. **Marginal revenue** is the increase in total revenue obtained by producing and selling one more unit of output. For a perfectly competitive firm, marginal revenue equals the price of its product. **Marginal cost** is the increase in total cost incurred by producing one more unit of output (in Table 5.2, a unit of output is 100 bottles). When the firm compares marginal revenue with marginal cost, it is applying the cost–benefit principle.

If the firm increases its daily output by 100 bottles (from 200 to 300 bottles/day), its total revenue will rise by $35/day. That is, its marginal revenue will be $35, which is the first entry in column 4. Because it must hire two more workers/day (which increases its employees from two to four) to produce another 100 bottles/day, the firm must incur a marginal cost of $20. The first entry in column 8 is $20. We see that if the firm produces and sells 100 more bottles, then it will increase its total revenue by $15 more than it increases its total cost. Therefore, its profit increases by $15/day.

In fact, whenever marginal revenue is greater than marginal cost, the firm can increase its profit by producing and selling more output. If marginal revenue is less than marginal cost, the firm will reduce its profit by producing more output. Indeed, if marginal revenue is less than marginal cost, the firm can improve profit by reducing output. If we apply this logic, comparisons of the entries in columns 4 and 8 tell us that the bottle-making firm will maximize profit if it increases its output to 400 bottles/day, thereby employing seven workers/day. Inspection of column 9 confirms that by producing 400 bottles/day, the firm's resulting daily profit of $30 will be the largest possible.

marginal revenue the increase in total revenue obtained by producing and selling one more unit of output

marginal cost the increase in total cost incurred by producing one more unit of output

COST–
BENEFIT

COST–
BENEFIT

We have discovered the firm's profit-maximizing output by asking whether an increase in output will increase profits. A comparison of marginal revenue with marginal cost gives the answer. Suppose we had asked a different question: how many workers will the firm employ to maximize profit? To answer, we again use the cost–benefit principle and compare the marginal revenue with the marginal cost of hiring another worker. As was the case for Example 5.1, let price/bottle be 35 cents (or $35/100 bottles) and the daily wage rate be $10. Suppose the firm has hired two workers. Table 5.1 shows that marginal product of a third worker is 60 bottles per day. Because each bottle sells for 35 cents, the value of a third worker's marginal product is $0.35 × 60 = $21/day. The worker's wage rate is $10/day, so marginal cost of the worker is $10/day. Thus, by adding a third worker, the firm

COST–
BENEFIT

increases its profit by $11/day. By working from Table 5.1 and continuing to compare the value of a worker's marginal product with the marginal cost of the worker, we find that the firm will maximize profits by employing seven workers. Table 5.1 shows that seven workers will produce 400 bottles/day. Whether we look for the firm's profit-maximizing output or the firm's profit-maximizing number of employees, we get the same answer: hire seven workers and produce 400 bottles/day.

EXAMPLE 5.2

Same as Example 5.1, except now bottles sell for $45/hundred.

If the price of bottles rises, but costs do not change, it is reasonable to expect that the firm will produce more bottles. As seen in columns 3, 4, and 7 of Table 5.3, an increase in selling price increases total revenue, marginal revenue, and profit. However, costs are unaffected. Therefore, in Table 5.3 we reproduce only total and marginal cost from Table 5.2. Total and marginal cost in Table 5.3 (columns 5 and 6) are identical to total and marginal cost in Table 5.2 (columns 7 and 8). Comparison of marginal revenue with marginal cost in Table 5.3 shows the firm will maximize profits by increasing daily output to 500 bottles. This means the firm will employ 11 workers. Column 7 confirms that when 500 bottles/day are produced and sold, profits are maximized at $75/day.

TABLE 5.3
Employment, Output, Revenue, Costs, and Profit

(1) Total number of employees/day	(2) Q(Total bottles/ day)	(3) Total revenue ($/day)	(4) Marginal revenue ($)	(5) Total cost ($/day)	(6) Marginal cost ($)	(7) Profit ($/day)
		$0.45 × (2)				(3) − (5)
0	0	0		40		−40
2	200	90		60		30
			45		20	
4	300	135		80		55
			45		30	
7	400	180		110		70
			45		40	
11	500	225		150		75
			45		50	
16	600	270		200		70
			45		60	
22	700	315		260		55

Notes: Employee's wage = $10/day
Price of bottles = $45/hundred = $0.45/bottle

EXAMPLE 5.3

Same as Example 5.1, except now the wage rate is $14/hour.

If costs rise and the price/bottle remains at $0.35, we would expect the firm to produce fewer bottles. With a higher wage rate, labour costs are higher at every level of output, as shown in column 5, Table 5.4.

TABLE 5.4
Employment, Output, Revenue, Costs, and Profit

(1) Total number of employees/day	(2) Q (Total bottles/ day)	(3) Total revenue ($/day)	(4) Marginal revenue ($)	(5) Total labour cost ($/day)	(6) Total fixed cost ($/day)	(7) Total cost ($/day)	(8) Marginal cost ($)	(9) Profit ($/day)
		$0.35 × (2)		$14 × (1)		(5) + (6)		(3) − (7)
0	0	0		0	40	40		−40
2	200	70		28	40	68		2
			35				28	
4	300	105		56	40	96		9
			35				42	
7	400	140		98	40	138		2
			35				56	
11	500	175		154	40	194		−19
			35				70	
16	600	210		224	40	264		−54
			35				84	
22	700	245		308	40	348		−103

Notes: Employee's wage = $14/day
Price of bottles = $35/hundred = $0.35/bottle

Marginal cost is increased at every level of output (column 8). When marginal revenue (column 4) is compared with marginal cost, we find that 300 bottles/day is the greatest output for which marginal revenue exceeds marginal cost. Thus, the firm will maximize profit by producing 300 bottles/day. Column 9 shows that this produces a daily profit of $9, the largest possible. The firm will produce 100 bottles fewer than when the wage rate was $10 per day, and it will employ three fewer workers/day.

PRICE EQUALS MARGINAL COST: THE SELLER'S SUPPLY RULE

The fact that the firm's profit-maximizing quantity of output does not generally depend on its fixed costs is an immediate consequence of the cost–benefit principle, which says that a firm will increase its output if, and only if, the *extra* benefit exceeds the *extra* cost. If the firm increases production by 100 bottles/day, its benefit is the extra revenue it gets, which in this case is simply the price of 100 bottles. The cost of increasing production by 100 bottles is by definition the marginal cost of producing 100 bottles—the amount by which total variable cost and, hence, total cost increase when bottle production rises by 100/day. The cost–benefit principle thus tells us that the perfectly competitive firm will increase production as long as the price of the product is greater than marginal cost.

When the law of diminishing marginal returns applies (that is, when at least one factor of production is fixed), marginal cost goes up as the firm increases production. Under these circumstances, the perfectly competitive firm's best option is to supply that level of output for which price and marginal cost are exactly equal.

Note from Table 5.2 that if the firm's capital cost had been any more than $70/day, it would have made a loss at *every* possible level of output. As long as it

COST–
BENEFIT

**www.strategis.ic.gc.ca/
sc_ecnmy/engdoc/
homepage.html
Strategis/Government
of Canada**

still had to pay its fixed cost, however, its best option would have been to continue producing 400 bottles/day. It is better, after all, to experience a smaller loss than a larger one. If a firm in that situation expected conditions to remain the same, though, it would want to get out of the bottle business as soon as its equipment lease expired.

A NOTE ON THE FIRM'S SHUTDOWN CONDITION

It might seem that a firm that can sell as much output as it wants at a constant market price would *always* do best in the short run by producing and selling the output level for which price equals marginal cost. But there is an important exception to this rule. Suppose, for example, that the market price of the firm's product falls so low that its revenue from sales is smaller than its total variable cost when price equals marginal cost. The firm will then minimize losses by ceasing production for the time being. By shutting down, it will suffer a loss equal to its fixed costs. But by remaining open, it would suffer an even larger loss. A firm's losses need never exceed its total fixed costs.

| EXERCISE 5.1 | In Example 5.1, suppose bottles sold, not for $35/hundred, but for only $5/hundred. Calculate the profit corresponding to each level of output, as in Example 5.1, and verify that the firm's best option is to cease operations in the short run. |

GRAPHING MARGINAL COST

To plot the marginal cost curve for a specific firm, we would need to know how total cost changes for every possible change in output. In Examples 5.1 to 5.3, however, we know the firm's cost for only a small sample of production values. Even with this limited information, though, we can construct a reasonable approximation of the firm's marginal cost curve. For instance, note in Example 5.1 and Table 5.2 that when the firm expands production from 200 to 300 bottles/day, its marginal cost is $20. When we graph the marginal cost curve, what output level does this $20 marginal cost correspond to? Strictly speaking, it corresponds neither to 200 nor to 300 but to the movement between the two. On the graph we thus show the $20 marginal cost value corresponding to an output level midway between 200 and 300 bottles/day, namely, 250 bottles/day, as in Figure 5.3. Similarly, when the firm in Example 5.1 expands from 300 to 400 bottles/day, its marginal cost is $30, so we plot a marginal cost of $30 with the output level 350 in Figure 5.3. Proceeding in this fashion, we generate the marginal cost curve shown in the diagram.

FIGURE 5.3

The Firm's Marginal Cost of Production

The firm's cost goes up by $20 when it expands production from 200 to 300 bottles/day. The marginal cost of the increased output is thus $20. By convention we plot that value at a point midway between 200 and 300 bottles/day.

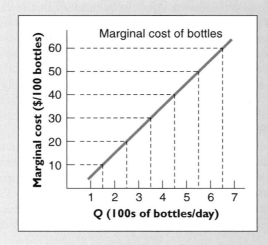

Suppose the market price facing the seller whose marginal cost curve is shown in Figure 5.3 is $35/hundred. If the firm's goal is to make as much profit as possible, how many bottles will it sell? It will sell the quantity for which marginal cost is equal to $35/hundred, and as we see in Figure 5.4, that quantity is 400 bottles/week, just as we concluded in Example 5.1.

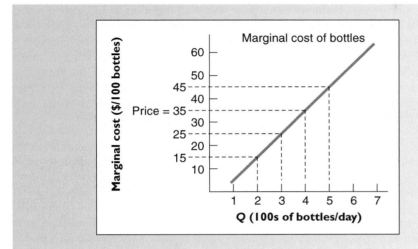

FIGURE 5.4
Price = Marginal Cost: The Perfectly Competitive Firm's Profit-Maximizing Supply Rule
If price exceeds marginal cost, the firm can increase its profit by increasing production and sales. If price is less than marginal cost, the firm can increase its profit by producing and selling less output.

To gain further confidence that 400 must be the profit-maximizing quantity when the price is $35/hundred, first suppose that the firm had sold some amount less than that, say, only 300 bottles/day. Its benefit from producing and selling one bottle would then be the bottle's market price, here 35 cents (since bottles sell for $35/hundred, each individual bottle sells for 35 cents). The cost of producing one more bottle is equal (by definition) to the firm's marginal cost, which at 300 bottles/day is only $25/100 = 25 cents (see Figure 5.4). So by selling the 201st bottle for 35 cents and producing it for an extra cost of only 25 cents, the firm will increase its profit by 35 − 25 = 10 cents/day. Similarly, we can show that for *any* quantity less than the level at which price equals marginal cost, the seller can boost profit by increasing production.

Conversely, suppose the firm is currently selling more than 400 bottles/day—say, 500—at a price of $35/hundred. From Figure 5.4 we see that marginal cost at an output of 500 is $45/100 = 45 cents per bottle. If the firm then reduces its output by one bottle/day, it would cut its costs by 45 cents while losing only 35 cents in revenue. As before, its profit would grow by 10 cents/day. The same argument can be made regarding any quantity larger than 400, so if the firm is currently selling an output at which price is less than marginal cost, it can always increase profits by producing and selling fewer bottles.

We have thus established that if the firm were selling fewer than 400 bottles/day, it could earn more profit by increasing production, and that if it were selling more than 400, it could earn more by reducing output. It follows that at a market price of $35/hundred, the seller maximizes profit by selling 400 units per week, the quantity for which price and marginal cost are exactly the same.

For a bottle price of $25/hundred, calculate the profit corresponding to each level of output, as in Example 5.1, and verify that the profit-maximizing output is 300 bottles/day.   **EXERCISE 5.2**

As further confirmation of the claim that the perfectly competitive firm maximizes profit by setting price equal to marginal cost, note in Figure 5.4 that when marginal cost is equal to a price of $45/hundred, the corresponding quantity is

500 bottles/day. This is the same as the profit-maximizing quantity we identified for that price in Table 5.3.

Notice that as price changes, we move from one point to another on the firm's marginal cost curve. At a price of 25 cents, the firm produces and sells 300 bottles each day; at 35 cents, the quantity is 400 bottles/day, and so on. As price rises, the firm is increasing its output along a fixed marginal cost curve.

Table 5.4 presents a different case: Price was held constant at $35 per hundred bottles, while the cost of labour increased. This caused marginal cost to increase at each level of output. In such a case, the entire marginal cost curve shifts. Figure 5.5 illustrates this. The marginal cost curve *MC* in Figure 5.5 is identical to the marginal cost curve in Figure 5.4. Marginal cost data from Table 5.4 are also plotted in Figure 5.5 and labelled *MC'*. It is clear that when the cost of labour rises and causes marginal cost to increase, the entire marginal cost curve shifts to the left. This causes the firm to reduce its daily output of bottles from 400 to 300.

FIGURE 5.5

A Shift of the Marginal Cost Curve
Price of bottles = $35/100. Labour cost increases from $10 to $14/day and causes *MC* to shift to *MC'*.

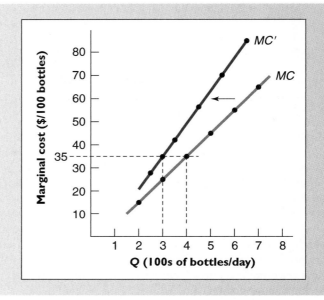

THE "LAW" OF SHORT-RUN SUPPLY

The law of demand tells us that consumers buy less of a product when its price rises. The analogous law of supply says that producers offer more of a product for sale when its price rises. Because perfectly competitive supply curves are essentially marginal cost curves, and because the law of diminishing marginal returns implies that marginal cost curves are upward sloping in the short run, the supply curve is upward sloping in the short run.

Although the short-run supply curve slopes up, the long-run supply curve may not. In the long run, the law of diminishing marginal returns does not necessarily apply. (Recall that it applies only if at least one factor of production is fixed.) Because in the long run firms can vary the amounts of *all* factors of production they use, they can often double their production by simply doubling the amount of each input they use. In such cases costs would be exactly proportional to output, and the firm's marginal cost curve in the long run would be horizontal, not upward sloping. So for now we'll say only that the "law" of supply holds as stated in the short run but not necessarily in the long run. The theory of costs in the long run is discussed in Chapter 7. For both the long run and the short run, however, *the perfectly competitive firm's supply curve is its marginal cost curve.*[1]

---

[1]Again, this rule holds subject to the provision that total revenue exceeds variable production cost at the output level for which price equals marginal cost.

A perfectly competitive market has many firms and each is a price taker. When the market price increases, each firm increases its output along its short-run supply curve. Therefore, we can get the total supply response of all firms by adding the supply responses of all the individual firms. This will provide a market supply curve.

A short-run market supply curve is shown in Figure 5.6, where it is assumed that 1000 identical bottle makers are serving the market. The quantity supplied at each price is the quantity supplied by one seller multiplied by 1000. For example, at a price of $35, Figure 5.6 shows that one bottle maker will produce and sell 400 bottles/day. One thousand such bottle makers will supply 400 000 bottles/day (400 × 1000). A similar calculation will show that 600 000 bottles/day will be supplied if price is $55, and so on. Because the supply curve resulting from these calculations is derived from the individual short-run supply curves of 1000 bottle makers, it is a short-run market supply curve.

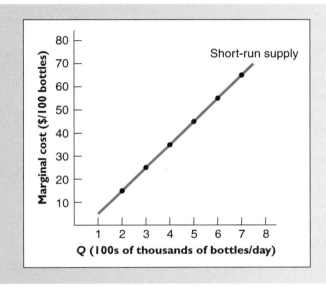

FIGURE 5.6
Short-Run Market Supply: One Thousand Identical Bottle Makers

Every quantity of output along the market supply curve represents the summation of all the quantities individual sellers offer at the corresponding price. So the correspondence between price and marginal cost exists for the market supply curve as well as for the individual supply curves that lie behind the market supply curve. That is, *for every price–quantity pair along the market supply curve, price will be equal to each seller's marginal cost of production.*

This is why the supply curve represents the cost side of the market, whereas the demand curve represents the benefit side of the market. At every point on a market demand curve, price represents what buyers would be willing to pay for an additional unit of the product—and this, in turn, is how we measure the amount by which they would benefit by having an additional unit of the product. Likewise, at every point on a market supply curve, price measures what it would cost producers to increase production by one unit.

RECAP   THE COMPETITIVE FIRM'S SUPPLY CURVE

The perfectly competitive firm faces a horizontal demand curve for its product, meaning that it can sell any quantity it wants at the market price. As a result, market price is also marginal revenue for a perfect competitor. In the short run, the firm chooses the level of output that maximizes its profits.

> It will maximize profit by choosing the output level for which marginal cost is equal to the market price of its product (provided market price exceeds minimum average variable cost—as will be shown). When it chooses its output level, the firm simultaneously chooses the number of workers it will employ. The perfectly competitive firm's supply curve is its marginal cost curve, which is upward sloping in the short run because of the law of diminishing returns. Adding the supply responses of all firms in a market provides the market supply curve.

5.3 COST, PROFIT MAXIMIZATION, AND SUPPLY IN THE SHORT RUN: ADDITIONAL GRAPHS

Why add more graphs of costs, especially when it will take some work to understand them? As we have seen, if diminishing marginal returns are in effect, marginal cost increases as the firm increases output. We will see that the law of diminishing marginal returns also influences average cost (i.e., cost per bottle in the case of our bottle maker). But some costs are fixed (like factory rent) while others (like wages paid) are variable. Because marginal cost is derived from changes in the amount of variable input, marginal cost is a variable cost. But total costs include fixed and variable costs, so average total cost per bottle is influenced by fixed costs, too. A graph provides a picture that greatly aids verbal description. Additional cost graphs will help us to discover more about how the law of diminishing marginal returns shapes the firm's short-run costs. Because it influences short-run costs, the law of diminishing marginal returns also influences the perfectly competitive firm's profit-maximizing rate of output.

DIMINISHING MARGINAL RETURNS AND SHORT-RUN COSTS

Table 5.1 is adapted from panel (a) of Table 5.5. Column 3 shows that the marginal product of a second worker is 110 bottles/day. Because we assumed the wage rate to be $10, the cost of increasing output by 110 bottles/day is $10. Marginal cost ($MC$) is as the change in total cost (ΔTC) divided by the change in output (ΔQ):

$$MC = \Delta TC/\Delta Q. \tag{5.1}$$

Therefore, when output is increased from 90 to 200 bottles the marginal cost of one bottle is about 9 cents ($10/110 = $0.09). (Notice that $0.09/ bottle is the same as $9/100 bottles.) When a third worker is added, the marginal product of that worker is 60. Therefore, the marginal cost of a bottle rises to 17 cents ($10/60 = $0.17). Column 5 of Table 5.5 shows the value of marginal cost that corresponds to each value of marginal product in column 3. In each case, marginal cost is $10 (the wage rate) divided by marginal product. If additional workers add increasingly more to output (as in the first two entries of column 3), marginal product is rising. It follows (as we see in the first two entries of column 5) that marginal cost is falling.

Subsequent entries reverse this pattern, because after the second worker, additional workers add less and less to total output. When marginal product declines, marginal cost rises. In general, marginal product and marginal cost move in opposite directions—if marginal product rises, marginal cost falls; if marginal product falls, marginal cost rises.

A similar relationship exits between average product and average variable cost. Column 5 of Table 5.2 shows total labour cost at various levels of output. Since the firm's payments for labour represent the only costs that vary as the bot-

variable cost any cost that changes as the firm changes its output

TABLE 5.5

The Law of Diminishing Marginal Returns and Short-Run Costs for a Glass-Bottle Maker (at a daily wage of $10)

	Panel (a)			Panel (b)		Panel (c)	
(1) Total number of employees/day	(2) Q (bottles/ day)	(3) Marginal product[a] in bottles/ day	(4) Average product in bottles/ day	(5) Marginal cost ($)	(6) Average variable cost ($/bottle)	(7) Average fixed cost ($/bottle)	(8) Average total cost ($/bottle)
			(2) ÷ (1)	$10 ÷ (3)	$10 ÷ (4)	$40 ÷ (2)	(6) + (7)
0	0						
		90		0.11			
1	90		90		0.11	0.44	0.55
		110		0.09			
2	200		100		0.10	0.20	0.30
		60		0.17			
3	260		87		0.12	0.15	0.27
		40		0.25			
4	300		75		0.13	0.13	0.26
		38		0.26			
5	338		68		0.15	0.12	0.27
		31		0.32			
7	400		57		0.18	0.10	0.275
		25		0.40			
11	500		45		0.22	0.08	0.30

Notes: [a]Marginal product is the increase in total output caused by hiring one more worker; however, the second-last entry in column (1) shows two more workers being hired (an increase from five to seven). Two more workers cause total output to increase by 62 bottles (from 338 to 400). Therefore, marginal product is 62/2 = 31, the second-last entry of column (3). By the same reasoning, the last entry in column 3 is 100/4 = 25. Strictly speaking, these calculations provide approximations. They are not exact.

tle maker of Table 5.2 changes its output, total labour cost is also total variable cost (*TVC*). (Of course, if the firm had additional costs, such as energy usage that varied with output, those costs also would be variable costs.) Average variable cost (*AVC*) is total variable cost divided by total output (*Q*):

$$AVC = TVC/Q. \tag{5.2}$$

Equation 5.1 can be used to calculate average variable cost directly from columns 2 and 5 of Table 5.2. However, a slightly different method will emphasize that average product and average variable cost move in opposite directions.

Column 4 of Table 5.1 provides column 4 of Table 5.5; both columns provide values of average product. Average product is output per unit of variable input. To keep the example simple, we are assuming that labour is our only variable input, so average product in this example is output per worker. If the wage rate is $10 per day, $10 is the average cost per worker. Thus, we can obtain average variable cost by dividing average cost per worker by average product:

$$AVC = \$10/\text{average product}.$$

Columns 4 and 6 of Table 5.5 shows how, when average product rises, average variable cost falls (and vice versa). This pattern, too, is general. The law of diminishing marginal returns influences average variable cost through its effect on average product. Panel (b) of Table 5.5 displays the data on marginal cost and average variable cost that arise from the data on production provided in panel (a).

The relationship between product and cost curves is shown in Figure 5.7. Panel (a) is similar to panel (b) of Figure 5.2, except that the marginal and average product curves have been smoothed in Figure 5.7. Notice that panel (a) of Figure 5.7 preserves the relationship between marginal and average product that appears in panel (b) of Figure 5.2. The two panels of Figure 5.7 show that when marginal product reaches its maximum, marginal cost is at its minimum. And when average product reaches its maximum, average variable cost is at its minimum. In addition, just as marginal product intersects average product at maximum average product, marginal cost intersects average variable cost at minimum average variable cost. The case for the relationship between marginal and average cost is analogous to the case already made for marginal and average product. The two sets of curves are mirror images of each other.

FIGURE 5.7
The Relationship between Product Curves and Cost Curves

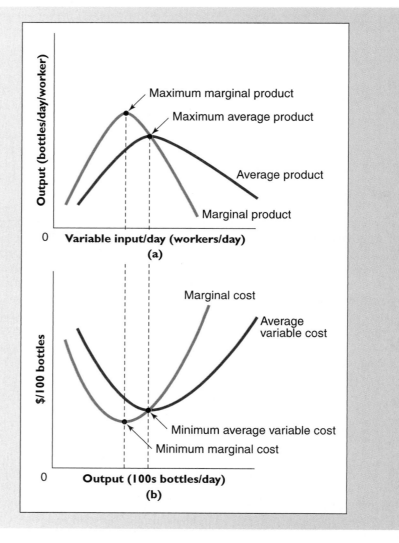

Marginal cost and average variable cost from Table 5.5 are graphed as smooth curves in Figure 5.8. To separate the effect of diminishing marginal returns from the effect of fixed cost on cost per bottle, we must add two more short-run costs to our picture. These are average fixed cost (*AFC*) and average total cost (*ATC*), which appear in panel (c) of Table 5.5. Once we have included

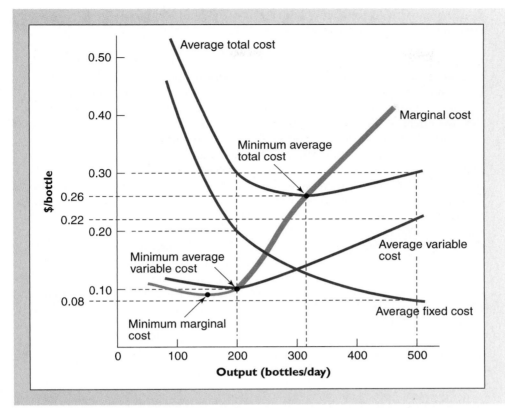

FIGURE 5.8

Short-Run Average and Marginal Cost Curves for a Glass-Bottle Maker
Wage rate = $10/day and total fixed cost = $40/day. The firm's short-run supply curve is given by the short-run marginal cost above minimum average variable cost.

these two costs, we will discover that in the short run, cost per unit of output is influenced by two opposing trends.

Fixed costs represent the cost of fixed factors of production, which do not vary with the firm's output. Average fixed cost (*AFC*) is total fixed cost (*TFC*) divided by total output (*Q*).

$$AFC = TFC/Q. \qquad (5.3)$$

Average fixed cost appears in column 7 of Table 5.5. It is calculated assuming that the bottle maker's total fixed cost is $40/day. As the daily output of bottles rises, $40 is divided over an ever larger number of bottles, and the graph of average fixed cost in Figure 5.8 approaches the horizontal axis as an asymptote. It becomes ever smaller but never touches the horizontal axis. Decreasing average fixed cost is often said to arise from "spreading the overhead."

Average total cost is the sum of average variable cost and average fixed cost:

$$ATC = AFC + AVC. \qquad (5.4)$$

Entries in columns 6 and 7 of Table 5.5 are summed to provide average total cost in column 8, and then average total cost is graphed as a smooth curve in Figure 5.8. Since average fixed cost always decreases when output increases, by itself, average fixed cost will cause average total cost to decrease when output increases.

Marginal cost intersects average variable cost at its minimum, which occurs at an output of 200 bottles per day. At higher rates of output, marginal cost is above average variable cost, and average variable cost is rising. Thus, beyond 200 bottles/day, the law of diminishing marginal returns means that marginal productivity is falling, which pulls down average productivity, which causes average variable cost to rise. By itself, rising average variable cost will cause average total cost to rise. In this example, at rates of output greater than 200 bottles/day, decreasing average fixed cost and the law of diminishing marginal returns are exerting opposing effects on average total cost.

Marginal cost intersects average total cost at its minimum point, which occurs at a higher rate of output (about 320 bottles per day) than does minimum average variable cost. In Figure 5.8, as output increases from 200 to 320 bottles/day, the effect of decreasing average fixed cost on average total cost dominates the effect of diminishing marginal returns, and average total cost decreases. Beyond 320 bottles, the effect of diminishing marginal returns dominates, and average total cost increases. Because output of about 320 bottles/day minimizes cost per bottle (i.e., average total cost), the **short-run cost-minimizing quantity of output** for the firm's factory is 320 bottles/day. When a factory exceeds its cost-minimizing quantity of output, the decrease in average total cost that is accomplished by spreading fixed cost over more and more output is more than offset by the increase in average variable cost caused by diminishing marginal returns. This causes average total cost to rise. Whether it is profitable for a firm to exceed its cost-minimizing quantity of output depends entirely on the price of the product it sells.

Because fixed costs are spread more thinly as output increases, average total cost and average variable costs converge as output increases. (Remember that $ATC = AFC + AVC$, and that AFC decreases as output increases.) Note in Figure 5.8 that average total cost is 30 cents at both 200 and 500 bottles/day. However, at 200 bottles/day, average fixed cost is 20 cents and average variable cost is 10 cents. At 500 bottles/day, average fixed cost is 8 cents, and average variable cost is 22 cents. At the higher rate of output, average fixed cost is a smaller component and average variable cost is a larger component of average total cost.

short-run cost-minimizing quantity of output the quantity of output at which a factory reaches minimum average total cost

WHEN TO SHUT DOWN THE FIRM

COST–
BENEFIT

If a firm's revenue from sales is smaller than its total variable costs, the cost–benefit principle tells the firm to shut down to minimize its losses. This rule can be restated in terms of the price the firm receives for what it sells. If a firm shuts down, its losses will be equal to its total fixed costs. In Figure 5.8, lowest possible average variable cost is obtained at 200 bottles/day, where average variable cost is 10 cents. Average variable cost was defined in equation 5.2:

$$AVC = TVC/Q. \qquad (5.2)$$

This can be rewritten to define total variable cost:

$$TVC = AVC \times Q. \qquad (5.5)$$

Therefore, when 200 bottles are produced, total variable cost is calculated as

$$TVC = AVC \times Q = \$0.10 \times 200 = \$20.$$

If the firm's revenue from sales drops below $20, the firm will shut down if it wants to minimize losses. If its revenue rises above this, the firm will operate if it wants to minimize short-run losses.

As a corollary, if the price/bottle drops below 10 cents, the firm will minimize short-run losses by shutting down. If it increases above 10 cents, it will be better off if it continues to produce bottles. Why? Consider a price of 11 cents per bottle. If the firm minimizes average variable cost by producing 200 bottles/day, each bottle sold will bring revenue sufficient to pay average variable cost plus one more penny that can be used to defray fixed costs. The firm's daily losses will be total fixed cost *less* $2. Conversely, suppose price per bottle drops to 9 cents, one cent below minimum average variable cost. Each bottle sold will bring a price that is one penny less than minimum average variable cost. At this price, the firm will not be able to defray any of its fixed cost. Further, if the firm minimizes average variable cost by producing 200 bottles/day, each of the 200 bottles will contribute on average one cent more to costs than to revenues. Therefore, the firm's daily losses will be total fixed costs *plus* $2. But if the firm shuts down, its daily losses will equal its total fixed costs. In other words, if price drops below minimum average variable cost, the firm should supply nothing, and minimum average variable cost is the firm's **short-run shutdown point.** We determined previously that a firm's short-run supply curve is its short-run marginal cost curve, but we left out an important qualification—that a firm's short-run supply curve is its short-run marginal cost curve *above minimum average variable cost.* Therefore, the heavy marginal cost curve above minimum average variable cost in Figure 5.8 gives the firm's short-run supply curve. The positively sloped short-run supply curve is consistent with the principle of increasing opportunity cost.

The firm's cost curves can also be used to show explicitly an economic loss or profit. Figure 5.9 shows that if market price is 35 cents, the bottle maker will produce 400 bottles per day. Cost per bottle will be 27.5 cents for a profit of 7.5 cents per bottle. Thus, total profit will be $30/day (0.075 × 400). This is represented by the shaded rectangle in Figure 5.9. Further, just as losses cause firms to leave an industry in the long run, profits in a perfectly competitive industry will be eroded in the long run as new firms, attracted by profits, enter the industry.

short-run shutdown point a firm's minimum average variable cost; if price drops below minimum average variable cost, the firm will minimize its losses by shutting down

INCREASING
OPPORTUNITY
COST

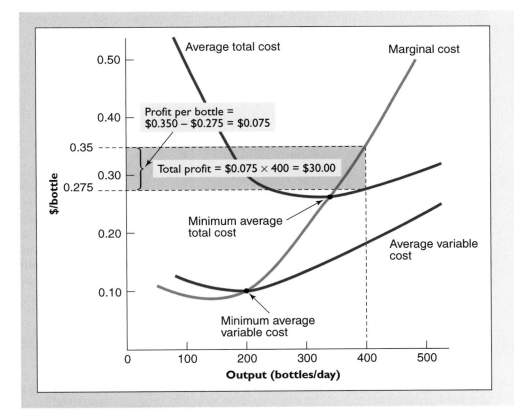

FIGURE 5.9
Costs and Profit for a Glass-Bottle Maker
Price per bottle = $0.35; wage rate = $10/day; total fixed costs = $40/day.

RECAP	**COSTS, PROFIT MAXIMIZATION, AND SUPPLY IN THE SHORT RUN**

The graphs in this section produce several results concerning diminishing marginal returns and short-run costs:

• The law of diminishing marginal returns means that marginal cost increases as output increases, which causes the firm's short-run supply curve to have a positive slope.

- The perfectly competitive firm's short-run supply curve is its short-run marginal cost curve above minimum average variable cost.
- If price is less than minimum average variable cost, the firm can minimize losses by shutting down.
- Minimum average total cost occurs at a higher rate of output than does minimum average variable cost. The opposing effects of diminishing marginal returns and the spreading of fixed cost over higher rates of output cause this result.
- Whether it is profitable for a firm to exceed its short-run cost-minimizing quantity of output depends solely on the price the firm receives for its product.

In the long run, as shown in Chapter 7, firms have more flexibility to adjust to changes in costs and markets.

■ 5.4 DETERMINANTS OF SUPPLY REVISITED

What factors give rise to changes in supply? (Again, remember that a *change in supply* refers to a shift in the entire supply curve, as opposed to a movement along the curve, which we call a *change in the quantity supplied*.) A seller will offer more units if the benefit of selling extra output goes up relative to the cost of producing it. And since the benefit of selling output in a perfectly competitive market is a fixed market price beyond the seller's control, our search for factors that influence supply naturally focuses on the cost side of the calculation. Examples 5.1 to 5.3 suggest why the following five factors, among others, will affect whether a product is profitable to produce. They will affect whether a product satisfies the cost–benefit test for a given supplier.

TECHNOLOGY

This chapter has so far focused on the short run, but in the long run, the most important determinant of production cost is technology. Improvements in technology make it possible to produce additional units of output at lower cost. This shifts each individual supply curve outward and hence shifts the market supply curve outward as well. Over time, the introduction of more sophisticated machinery has resulted in dramatic increases in the number of goods produced per hour of effort expended. Every such development gives rise to an outward shift in the market supply curve.

INPUT PRICES

Whereas technological change generally (although not always) leads to gradual shifts in supply, changes in the prices of important inputs can give rise to large supply shifts literally overnight. For example, the price of crude oil, which is the most important input in the production of gasoline, rose suddenly in 1979, and the resulting leftward shift in supply caused gasoline prices to rise almost immediately. The same phenomenon occurred in 2000. However, prices decreased following the destruction of the World Trade Center in New York City on September 11, 2001, apparently because of reduced demand for fuel.

Similarly, when wage rates rise, the marginal cost of any business that employs labour also rises, shifting supply curves to the left. When interest rates fall, the opportunity cost of capital equipment also falls, causing supply to shift to the right.

THE NUMBER OF SUPPLIERS

Just as demand curves shift to the right when population grows, supply curves also shift to the right as the number of individual suppliers grows.

EXPECTATIONS

Expectations about future price movements can affect how much sellers choose to offer in the current market. Suppose, for example, that recyclers expect the future price of aluminum to be much higher than the current price because of the growing use of aluminum components in cars. The rational recycler would then have an incentive to withhold aluminum from the market at today's lower price, thereby having more available to sell at the higher future price. Conversely, if recyclers expected next year's price of aluminum to be lower than this year's, their incentive would be to offer more aluminum for sale in today's market.

CHANGES IN PRICES OF OTHER PRODUCTS

Apart from technological change, perhaps the most important determinant of supply is variation in the prices of other goods and services that sellers might produce. Prospectors, for example, search for those precious metals for which the surplus of benefits over costs is greatest. When the price of silver rises, many people stop looking for gold and start looking for silver. Conversely, when the price of platinum falls, many platinum prospectors shift their attention to gold.

■ 5.5 APPLYING THE THEORY OF SUPPLY

Whether the activity is producing new soft drink containers or recycling used ones, or indeed any other production activity at all, the same logic governs all supply decisions: Can I make more money if I sell one more unit? In perfectly competitive markets (and in any other setting in which sellers can sell as much as they want to at a constant price) the gain from selling one more unit is just its sale price. The increase in costs is the marginal cost of production. Hence, to maximize profit, keep increasing output until marginal cost is equal to the price of the product. This logic helps us understand many market outcomes, for example, why recycling efforts are more intensive for some products than others.

★ 5.1   ECONOMIC NATURALIST

When recycling is left to private market forces, why are many more aluminum beverage containers recycled than glass ones?

In both cases, recyclers gather containers until their marginal costs are equal to the containers' respective redemption prices. When recycling is left to market forces, the redemption price for a container is based on what companies can sell it (or the materials in it) for. Aluminum containers can be easily processed into scrap aluminum, which commands a high price, and this leads profit-seeking companies to offer a relatively high redemption price for aluminum cans. By contrast, the glass from which glass containers are made has only limited resale value, and this leads profit-seeking companies to offer much lower redemption prices for glass containers.

If the redemption price for aluminum cans is high many people will be induced to track down these cans, whereas the low redemption prices for glass containers will lead most people to ignore the glass containers. If recycling is left completely to market forces, then we would expect to see aluminum soft drink containers more quickly recycled than glass containers. This is in fact the pattern we do see in jurisdictions without recycling laws. As Figure 5.10 shows, as the redemption price of aluminum containers increases, suppliers of recycling services will recycle more aluminum containers. A similar graph could be drawn for glass containers. More aluminum and fewer glass containers are recycled in jurisdictions without recycling laws, a simple consequence of the fact that the supply curves of container recycling services are upward sloping. Of course, whether it is worthwhile to collect and recycle aluminum cans at all depends on the price of aluminum scrap.

FIGURE 5.10

The Supply Curve of Aluminum Container Recycling Services

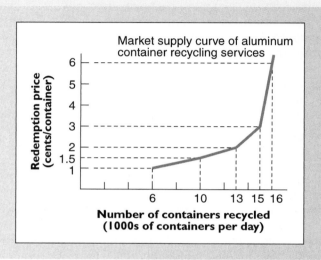

The acquisition of valuable raw materials is only one of two important benefits from recycling. The second benefit is that, by removing litter, recycling makes the environment more pleasant for everyone. Economic Naturalist 5.1 does not explicitly discuss the benefits of reduced litter. However, such benefits may well be large enough to justify incurring extra costs in order to obtain them. Such situations are analyzed in Chapter 10.

■ 5.6 THE PRICE ELASTICITY OF SUPPLY

DEFINING AND CALCULATING ELASTICITY OF SUPPLY

price elasticity of supply the change in quantity supplied arising from a 1 percent change in price

On the buyer's side of the market, we use price elasticity of demand to measure the responsiveness of quantity demanded to changes in price. On the seller's side of the market, the analogous measure is **price elasticity of supply,** which is defined as the percentage change in quantity supplied that occurs in response to a 1 percent change in price. For example, if a 1 percent increase in the redemption price of glass containers leads to a 2 percent increase in the quantity supplied, the price elasticity of supply of recycled glass containers would be 2.0.

The mathematical formula for price elasticity of supply at any point is the same as the corresponding expression for price elasticity of demand:

$$\text{Price elasticity of supply} = \frac{\text{\% change in Quantity}}{\text{\% change in Price}} = \frac{\Delta Q/Q}{\Delta P/P}, \qquad (5.6)$$

elastic supply supply is elastic if price elasticity of supply is greater than one

inelastic supply supply is inelastic if price elasticity of supply is less than one

where P and Q are the price and quantity at that point, ΔP is a small change in the initial price, and ΔQ is the resulting change in quantity. If price elasticity of supply is less than one, **supply** is **inelastic;** if it is greater than one, **supply** is **elastic.**

As with the corresponding expression for price elasticity of demand, equation 5.6 can be rewritten as follows:

$$\text{price elasticity of supply} = \left(\frac{P}{Q}\right)\left(\frac{\Delta Q}{\Delta P}\right) \tag{5.7}$$

Since $\Delta Q/\Delta P$ is the reciprocal of the slope of the supply curve, equation 5.7 can be rewritten as:

$$\text{price elasticity of supply} = \left(\frac{P}{Q}\right)\left(\frac{1}{\text{slope}}\right) \tag{5.8}$$

Equation 5.8 is the same expression we saw for price elasticity of demand in Chapter 4 (equation 4.4).

Price and quantity are always positive, as is the slope of the typical short-run supply curve, which implies that price elasticity of supply will be a positive number at every point.

Generally, price elasticity of supply will change from point to point along a supply curve. (An exception occurs when a straight-line supply curve passes through the origin.)

Elasticity is not constant along straight-line supply curves like the one in Figure 5.11, those that do not pass through the origin. Although the slope of this supply curve is equal to 1 at every point, the ratio P/Q declines as we move to the right along the curve. Elasticity at A is equal to $(4/2)(1) = 2$ and declines to $(5/3)(1) = 5/3$ at B.[2]

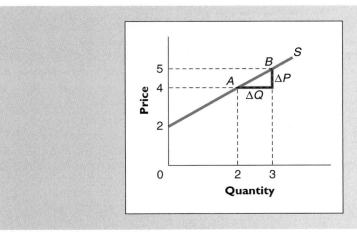

FIGURE 5.11

A Supply Curve for Which Price Elasticity Declines As Quantity Rises

For the supply curve shown, 1/slope is the same at every point, but the ratio P/Q declines as Q increases. So elasticity = $(P/Q)(1/\text{slope})$ declines as quantity increases, though it never falls to 1. It is always elastic.

On the buyer's side of the market, two important polar cases are demand curves with infinite price elasticity and zero price elasticity. As Examples 5.4 and 5.5 illustrate, analogous polar cases exist on the seller's side of the market.

EXAMPLE 5.4

What is the elasticity of supply of land on Montreal Island?

Land on Montreal Island sells in the market for a price, just as aluminum or corn or automobiles or any other product. The demand for land on the island is a downward-sloping function of its price. For all practical purposes, however, its supply of land on the island is completely fixed. No matter whether its price is high or low, the same amount of it is available in the market. The supply curve of such a good is vertical, and its price elasticity is zero at every price. Supply curves like the one in Figure 5.12 are said to be **perfectly inelastic**.

perfectly inelastic supply curve a supply curve whose elasticity with respect to price is zero

---

[2]The price elasticity of a linear supply curve that intersects the vertical axis is always greater than one. If a linear supply curve passes through the origin, it is unit elastic. If a linear supply curve intersects the horizontal axis, its price elasticity is less than one.

FIGURE 5.12

A Perfectly Inelastic Supply Curve
Price elasticity of supply is zero at every point along a vertical supply curve.

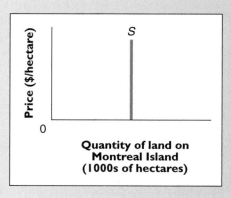

EXAMPLE 5.5

What is the elasticity of supply of lemonade?

Suppose that the ingredients required to bring a cup of lemonade to market and their respective costs are listed as follows:

Paper cup	2.0 cents
Lemon	3.8 cents
Sugar	2.0 cents
Water	0.2 cents
Ice	1.0 cents
Labour (30 seconds @ $6/hour)	5.0 cents

If these proportions remain the same no matter how many cups of lemonade are made and the inputs can be purchased in any quantities at the stated prices, draw the supply curve of lemonade and compute its price elasticity.

Since each cup of lemonade costs exactly 14 cents to make, no matter how many cups are made, the supply curve of lemonade is a horizontal line at 14 cents/cup (Figure 5.13). The price elasticity of supply of lemonade is infinite.

FIGURE 5.13

A Perfectly Elastic Supply Curve
The elasticity of supply is infinite at every point along a horizontal supply curve.

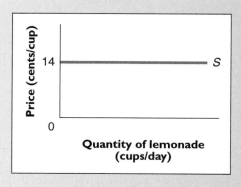

perfectly elastic supply curve
a supply curve whose elasticity with respect to price is infinite

Whenever additional units of a good can be produced by using the same combination of inputs, purchased at constant prices, more of the supply curve of that good will be horizontal. Such supply curves are said to be **perfectly elastic**. Because all factors of production were assumed to be variable, the example describes what happens when the law of diminishing marginal returns does not apply. For the specific production process described, the marginal cost curve is horizontal—at 14 cents/cup—not upward sloping.

DETERMINANTS OF SUPPLY ELASTICITY

Examples 5.5 and 5.6 suggest some of the factors that govern the elasticity of supply of a good or service. The lemonade case in Example 5.5 was one whose production process was essentially like a cooking recipe. For such cases, we can exactly double our output by doubling each ingredient. If the price of each ingredient remains fixed, the marginal cost of production for such goods will be constant, and hence they have horizontal supply curves. Again, when all factors of production can be increased, the law of diminishing returns does not apply, and so the supply curve need not be upward sloping.

Example 5.4 of land on Montreal Island is a contrast in the extreme. For all practical purposes, the supply of land on the island is fixed.

The terms on which additional amounts of the inputs to the production process can be obtained are key to determining elasticity of supply. In general, the more easily additional units of these inputs can be acquired, the higher the price elasticity of supply will be. The following four factors (among others) govern the ease with which additional inputs can be acquired by a producer.

Flexibility of Inputs To the extent that production of a good requires inputs that are also useful for the production of other goods, it is relatively easy to lure additional inputs away from their current uses, making supply of that good relatively elastic with respect to price. Thus, the fact that lemonade production requires labour with only minimal skills means that a large pool of workers could shift from other activities to lemonade production if a profit opportunity arose. Brain surgery, by contrast, requires elaborately trained and specialized labour, which means that even a large price increase would not increase the quantity of brain surgeons, except after a long time lag.

Mobility of Inputs If inputs can be easily transported from one site to another, an increase in the price of a product in one market will enable a producer in that market to summon inputs from other markets. For example, the supply of agricultural products is made more elastic with respect to price by the willingness of thousands of farmworkers to migrate northward from Mexico during the growing season. The supply of entertainment is similarly made more elastic by the willingness of entertainers to hit the road. Circus performers, lounge singers, comedians, and even exotic dancers often spend a substantial fraction of their time away from home. For instance, according to a 1996 *New York Times* article, the top exotic dancers "basically follow the action, so the same entertainers who worked the Indianapolis 500 now head to Atlanta for the Olympics."

For most goods, the price elasticity of supply increases each time a new canal is dug, or when a new highway is built, or when the telecommunications network improves, or indeed when any other development makes it easier to find and transport inputs from one place to another.

Ability to Produce Substitutes The inputs required to produce finished diamond gemstones include raw diamond crystal, skilled labour, and elaborate cutting and polishing machinery. In time, the number of people with the requisite skills can be increased, as can the amount of specialized machinery. The number of raw diamond crystals buried in the earth is probably fixed in the same way that real estate on Montreal Island real estate is fixed, but unlike the island's real estate, rising prices will encourage miners to spend the effort required to find a larger proportion of those crystals. Still, the supply of natural gemstone diamonds tends to be relatively inelastic because of the difficulty of augmenting the number of diamond crystals.

The day is close at hand, however, when gemstone makers will be able to produce synthetic diamond crystals that are indistinguishable from real ones. Indeed, there are already synthetic crystals that fool even highly experienced jewellers. The introduction of a perfect synthetic substitute for natural diamond crystals would increase the price elasticity of the supply of diamonds (or, at any rate, the price elasticity of supply of gemstones that look and feel just like diamonds).

Time Because it takes time for producers to switch from one activity to another and because it takes time to build new capital goods and train additional skilled workers, the price elasticity of supply will be higher for most goods in the long run than in the short run. In the short run, a manufacturer's inability to augment existing stocks of capital equipment and skilled labour may make it impossible to expand output beyond a certain limit. But if a shortage of managers is the bottleneck, new MBAs can be graduated in only two years if they have a bachelor's degree. Or if a shortage of legal staff is the problem, new lawyers can be trained in three years. In the long run, firms can always buy new equipment, build new factories, and hire additional skilled workers.

The conditions that gave rise to the perfectly elastic supply curve for lemonade in Example 5.5 are also satisfied for many other products in the long run. If a product can be copied (in the sense that any company can acquire the design and other technological information required to produce it) and if the inputs needed for its production are used in roughly fixed proportions and are available at fixed market prices, then the long-run supply curve for that product will be horizontal. But as we will presently see, many products do not satisfy these conditions, and their supply curves remain steeply upward sloping, even in the long run.

UNIQUE AND ESSENTIAL INPUTS: THE ULTIMATE SUPPLY BOTTLENECK

Fertile agricultural land is, for example, a historically scarce resource. As the English economist David Ricardo noted over 175 years ago, one can increase agricultural output by adding more inputs, such as labour or fertilizer, to a given amount of land, or one can expand the area under cultivation. But since it makes sense to use the most fertile land first, as the amount of land under cultivation expands, eventually less fertile land will have to be used. When all the best land has been used, farmers can start using even more inputs to squeeze a higher yield from their acreage, or turn to land with inherently lower productivity—either way, the costs of production will rise. Thus, when an essential input into production is inherently limited in availability, the supply curve will be upward sloping, even in the long term.[3]

RECAP	**PRICE ELASTICITY OF SUPPLY**

The price elasticity of supply of a good is the percentage change in the quantity supplied that results from a 1 percent change in its price. Mathematically, the elasticity of supply at a point on a supply curve is equal to $(P/Q)(1/\text{slope})$, where P and Q represent price and quantity and $1/\text{slope}$ is the reciprocal of the slope of the supply curve at that point.

Elasticity of supply for a good tends to be larger when the inputs required for its production are also widely used to produce other goods, when inputs are more mobile, when production is possible using substitutes for existing inputs, and when suppliers have more time to augment their productive capacities. If the inputs needed for a good's production are used in roughly fixed proportions and are available at fixed market prices, then the long-run supply curve will be horizontal. In the long run, the only goods that tend to have upward-sloping supply curves are those whose production requires essential inputs that cannot be duplicated.

---

[3]David Ricardo, *The Principles of Political Economy and Taxation,* with an introduction by Donald Winch, London: Everyman's Library, Dent, 1973 (1817), pp. 33–47.

■ SUMMARY

- **5.1** The supply curve for a good or service is a curve that for any price tells us the quantity sellers want to supply at that price. The prices at which goods and services are offered for sale in the market depend, in turn, on the opportunity cost of the resources required to produce them.

- **5.2** Supply curves are upward sloping, at least in the short run, because of the law of diminishing marginal returns. The law of diminishing marginal returns says that when technology and at least one factor of production is held fixed, beyond some point marginal product of the variable factor of production diminishes.

- **5.3** For perfectly competitive markets—or, more generally, for markets in which individual sellers can sell whatever quantity they want at a constant price—the seller maximizes profit by selling that quantity of output for which price equals marginal cost. This rule pertains provided price exceeds minimum average variable cost. The supply curve for the seller thus coincides with the marginal cost curve above minimum average variable cost. The marginal cost curve measures the cost of producing additional units of output. This is why we sometimes say the supply curve represents the cost side of the market (in contrast to the demand curve, which represents the benefit side of the market).

- **5.3** The law of diminishing marginal returns directly affects short-run marginal cost. If marginal product is increasing, short-run marginal cost is decreasing; if marginal product is decreasing, short-run marginal cost is increasing. Also, marginal product intersects average product at maximum average product, and marginal cost intersects average variable cost at minimum average variable cost. Both intersections occur at the same quantity of output. Thus, short-run marginal cost is a mirror image of marginal product, and average variable cost is a mirror image of average product.

- **5.3** If a firm shuts down, it will make no sales. Therefore, it will receive no revenue, and its losses will be equal to its total fixed costs. Thus, a firm's losses need never exceed its total fixed costs. Further, if the price of its product falls below minimum average variable cost, the perfectly competitive firm will minimize losses by shutting down. The perfectly competitive firm's short-run supply curve therefore is positively sloped and coincides with a short-run marginal cost curve above minimum average variable cost.

- **5.3** The law of diminishing marginal returns causes the perfectly competitive firm's short run supply curve to slope upward. As output increases above the quantity that minimizes average variable cost, the law of diminishing marginal returns also causes average variable cost to increase. Increasing average variable cost causes cost per unit (i.e., average total cost) to increase.

- **5.3** Average fixed cost always decreases as the quantity of output increases, and thus tends to reduce average total cost. However, diminishing marginal returns cause average total cost to rise. As output increases beyond the quantity that minimizes average total cost, the effect of diminishing marginal returns dominates, and average total cost increases.

- **5.4** An important terminological distinction from the demand side of the market also applies on the supply side of the market. *A change in supply* means a shift in the entire supply curve, whereas *a change in the quantity supplied* means a movement along the supply curve. The factors that cause supply curves to shift include technology, input prices, the number of sellers, expectations of future price changes, and the prices of other products that firms might produce.

- **5.6** Price elasticity of supply is defined as the percentage change in quantity supplied that occurs in response to a 1 percent change in price. The mathematical formula for the price elasticity of supply at any point is $(\Delta Q/Q)/(\Delta P/P)$, where P and Q are the price and quantity at that point, ΔP is a small change in the initial price, and ΔQ is the resulting change in quantity. This formula can also be expressed as $(P/Q)(1/\text{slope})$, where $1/\text{slope}$ is the reciprocal of the slope of the supply curve.

- **5.6** The price elasticity of supply of a good depends on how difficult or costly it is to acquire additional units of the inputs involved in producing that good. In general, the more easily additional units of these inputs can be acquired, the higher the price elasticity of supply will be. It is easier to expand production of a product if the inputs used to produce that product are similar to inputs used to produce other products, if inputs are relatively mobile, or if an acceptable substitute for existing inputs can be developed. And like the price elasticity of demand, the price elasticity of supply is greater in the long run than in the short run. Except for the existence of unique and essential inputs, all goods and services would have highly elastic supply curves in the long run. There are no fixed costs in the long run; thus, the long run affords more flexibility in adjusting costs than does the short run.

■ KEY TERMS

average product (126)
elastic supply (144)
factor of production (122)
fixed factor of production (125)
inelastic supply (144)
law of diminishing marginal returns (125)
long run (124)
marginal cost (129)

marginal product (125)
marginal revenue (129)
perfectly competitive firm (122)
perfectly competitive market (122)
perfectly elastic supply curve (146)
perfectly inelastic supply curve (145)
price elasticity of supply (144)
price taker (122)
production function (124)

profit (122)
profit-maximizing firm (122)
short run (124)
short-run cost-minimizing quantity of output (140)
short-run shutdown point (141)
variable cost (136)
variable factor of production (125)

■ REVIEW QUESTIONS

1. Explain why you would expect supply curves to slope upward based on the principle of increasing opportunity cost.

2. Which do you think is more likely to be a fixed factor of production for an ice cream producer during the next two months, its factory building or its workers who operate the machines? Explain.

3. Economists often stress that diminishing marginal returns result from increasingly more workers using the same workspace and tools. With this in mind, explain why it would be impossible to feed all the people on earth with food grown in a single flowerpot, even if unlimited water, labour, seed, fertilizer, sunlight, and other inputs were available.

4. True or false: The perfectly competitive firm should *always* produce the output level for which price equals marginal cost.

5. What is the effect of diminishing marginal product on short-run marginal cost? Why is short-run mar-

ginal cost a mirror image of marginal product? Why is average variable cost a mirror image of average product?

6. If average fixed cost always decreases as the quantity of output rises, why does it not follow that cost per unit of output always decreases as output rises?

7. Why does minimum average variable cost occur at a smaller quantity of output than minimum average total cost?

8. A firm's losses need never exceed its total fixed costs. Why? Why does this imply that a perfectly competitive firm's short-run supply curve is given by its short-run marginal cost curve above minimum average variable cost?

9. Does a firm maximize profits by minimizing cost per unit of output? Why or why not?

10. Why is supply elasticity higher in the long run than in the short run?

■ PROBLEMS

1. Zoe is trying to decide how to divide her time between her job as a wedding photographer, which pays $27/hour for as many hours as she chooses to work, and as a fossil collector, in which her pay depends both on the price of fossils and the number of fossils she finds. Earnings aside, Zoe is indifferent between the two tasks, and the number of fossils she can find depends on the number of hours a day she searches, as shown in the following table.

Hours/day	Total fossils/day
1	5
2	9
3	12
4	14
5	15

a. Derive a table with price in dollar increments from $0 to $30 in the first column and the quantity of fossils Zoe is willing to supply per day at that price in the second column.

b. Plot these points in a graph with price on the vertical axis and quantity per day on the horizontal axis. What is this curve called?

2. A price-taking firm makes air conditioners. The market price of one of their new air conditioners is $120. Its total cost information is given in the following table.

Air conditioners/day	Total cost ($/day)	Marginal cost ($)
1	100	
2	150	
3	220	
4	310	
5	405	
6	510	
7	650	
8	800	

a. Complete the column labelled "Marginal cost."

b. How many air conditioners will the firm produce per day if its goal is to maximize its profit?

c. Does your answer to (b) imply that the firm is setting marginal revenue equal to marginal cost? Why or why not?

3. The Paducah Slugger Company makes baseball bats out of lumber supplied to it by Acme Sporting Goods, which pays Paducah $10 for each finished bat. Paducah's only factors of production are lathe operators and a small building with a lathe. The number of bats per day it produces depends on the number of employee-hours per day, as shown in the following table.

Number of bats/day	Number of employee-hours/day
0	0
5	1
10	2
15	4
20	7
25	11
30	16
35	22

a. If the wage is $15/hour and Paducah's daily capital cost for the lathe and building is fixed at $60, what is the profit-maximizing quantity of bats?

b. What would be the profit-maximizing number of bats if the capital cost were not $60/day but only $30?

4. In problem 3, how would Paducah's profit-maximizing level of output be affected if the government imposed a tax of $10/day on the company? What would Paducah's profit-maximizing level of output be if the government imposed a tax of $2 per bat?

5. Explain how the following would affect supply in the indicated market:
a. An increase in the world price of honey in the market for beeswax candles.

    b. An increase in the world price of cauliflower in the market for cabbage. (Assume the demand for cabbage does not shift.)

    c. An increase in the world price of ice cream in the market for ice cream.

6. How would each of the following affect the Canadian market supply curve for corn?

    a. A new high-yielding strain of corn is discovered.

    b. The price of fertilizer falls.

    c. The government offers corn farmers a subsidy of $1/bushel.

7. Which of the following are true? Why? The price elasticity of supply for Basmati rice (an aromatic strain of rice) is likely to be:

    a. Higher in the long run than the short run, because farmers cannot easily change their decisions about how much Basmati rice to plant once the current crop has been planted.

    b. High, because consumers have a lot of other kinds of rice and other staple foods to choose from.

    c. Low in both the long run and short run, because rice farming requires only unskilled labour.

    d. High in both the long run and the short run because the inputs required to produce Basmati rice can easily be duplicated.

8. What are the respective price elasticities of supply at A and B on the supply curve shown in the following figure?

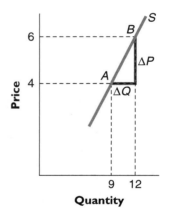

9. The supply curves for the only two firms in a competitive industry are given by $P = 2Q_1$ and $P = 2 + Q_2$, where Q_1 is the output of firm 1 and Q_2 is the output of firm 2. What is the market supply curve for this industry? (*Hint:* Graph the two curves side by side, then add their respective quantities at a sample of different prices.)

10. Consider two companies, Slap-Shot and Slapstick. Both companies make hockey sticks. Slap-Shot's contract with its employees says that if it lays off any of its workers, it must pay each of them severance pay. Slapstick's contract does not include a similar clause.

    a. In which case does it make sense to say that labour represents a fixed cost? Why?

    b. Suppose the price of hockey sticks decreases so that both companies are making losses. If price continues to decrease, which company will shut down first? That is, which company will have the lower shutdown price? Why?

    c. If the price of hockey sticks drops low enough to cause both companies to shut down, which company will suffer the greater loss? Why?

11. A union is negotiating a new contract with its employer. The employer says that it cannot pay higher wages because it already is making losses. In fact, says the employer, it can make good case for reducing wages.

    a. Why would an employer operate at a loss?

    b. Suppose that the employer's annual losses are $1 million and its total fixed costs are $2 million per year. Does the union have any room to bargain for increased wages? Consider two different cases: (i) The union is convinced that over the next three years the employer will run the factory until it falls apart, then move its operations to Southeast Asia. The union believes this will happen regardless of any agreement between the employer and the union. (ii) The union believes the employer is considering moving its operations to Southeast Asia, but it will not move if it can modernize its factory and reach an agreement that will be consistent with a modest increase in wages.

ANSWERS TO IN-CHAPTER EXERCISES

5.1 The profit figures corresponding to a price of $5/hundred are as shown in the last column of the following table, where we see that the profit-maximizing output (which here means the loss-minimizing output) is 0 bottles/day. Note that the company actually loses $40/day at that output level. But it would lose even more if it produced any other amount. If the company expects conditions to remain unchanged, it will want to go out of the bottle business as soon as its equipment lease expires.

Q (bottles/day)	Total revenue ($/day)	Total labour cost ($/day)	Total cost ($/day)	Profit ($/day)
0	0	0	40	−40
100	5	10	50	−45
200	10	20	60	−50
300	15	40	80	−65
400	20	70	110	−90
500	25	110	150	−125
600	30	160	200	−170
700	35	220	260	−225

5.2 The profit figures corresponding to a price of $25/hundred are as shown in the last column of the following table, where we see that the profit-maximizing output (which here means the loss-minimizing output) is 300 bottles/day. Note that the company actually loses $5/day at that output level. But as long as it remains committed to its daily lease payment of $40, it would lose even more if it produced any other amount. If the company expects conditions to remain unchanged, it will want to go out of the bottle business as soon as its equipment lease expires.

Q (bottles/day)	Total revenue ($/day)	Total labour cost ($/day)	Total cost ($/day)	Profit ($/day)
0	0	0	40	−40
100	25	10	50	−25
200	50	20	60	−10
300	75	40	80	−5
400	100	70	110	−10
500	125	110	150	−25
600	150	160	200	−50
700	175	220	260	−85

EFFICIENCY AND EXCHANGE

I n Canada today, most of our economic lives depend on markets. As we decide daily on what to buy and what to sell, we pay close attention to the prices of goods and services. As Chapter 3 has discussed, it is the interaction of supply and demand in markets that determines those prices, so market processes are fundamentally important to our consumption, savings, and labour market decisions.

But is this the way economic life *should* be organized? What can we expect markets to do well? What can we expect markets to do badly? What sorts of social issues *should* be addressed by government regulation? Which issues should be left to the market?

For generations, people have debated the role that markets can, or should, play in determining social and economic outcomes. And although it is easy to see why a billionaire might be happy with the outcomes that markets produce, it is less obvious why low-income families struggling to pay their bills should think that a market allocation of resources is desirable. But if poor people could expect to be even worse off under an alternative system, should both the rich and the poor agree that market solutions are the most efficient answers to society's problems?

If a market transaction is voluntary, then one can at least say that both the buyer and the seller think it will make them better off. After all, nobody would voluntarily buy a good or service if she did not think it would improve her well-being—and nobody would voluntarily sell that good or service if he thought the transaction would make him worse off. Thus, a voluntary exchange must necessarily improve the expected welfare of both buyer and seller. Both the billionaire who buys a new company and the minimum wage worker who buys a loaf of bread do so because each thinks that purchase improves their own well-being.

Under what conditions, however, will these individually self-oriented decisions add up to a social optimum, in the long run? Under what conditions could everyone in society be made better off by *preventing* some voluntary market transactions? Is there a cost to society of interfering in the market mechanism, and if so, what is it? Students of the market system would argue that in certain wide domains, markets are remarkable instruments, but they would acknowledge that markets do not solve several important problems. Markets will not automatically provide a distribution of income or of the benefits of international trade that most people would consider fair. They will not guarantee that workplaces will be free of hazards. They will not necessarily provide the means for people to learn new skills when old ones become obsolescent, and so on. Economists also would caution that the phrases, "free enterprise" and "free markets," do not convey the same technical meaning that "perfect competition" does. When "free markets" and "free enterprise" are not clearly defined, we cannot know what an advocate of them really is seeking.

Be this as it may, markets can help a society to meet its goals. This does not mean that markets can solve all problems. Nevertheless, it is a bad idea to prevent markets from performing those functions for which they are ideally suited. In this chapter we will explore why many tasks are best left to the market. We will develop more carefully the concept of economic surplus introduced in Chapter 1, and we will explore the conditions under which unregulated markets generate the largest possible economic surplus. We will also discuss why attempts to interfere with market outcomes can lead to unintended and undesired consequences.

■ 6.1 MARKET EQUILIBRIUM AND EFFICIENCY

As noted in Chapter 3, the mere fact that markets coordinate the production of a large and complex list of goods and services is reason enough to marvel at them. But under some conditions markets not only produce these goods but also produce them as efficiently as possible.

The term **efficient**, as economists use it, has a particular technical meaning. When we say that market equilibrium is efficient, we mean simply this: *If markets are perfectly competitive and if price and quantity take anything other than their equilibrium values, a transaction that will make at least some people better off without harming others can always be found.* This concept of efficiency is also known as **Pareto efficiency,** after Vilfredo Pareto, the nineteenth-century Italian economist who introduced it.

efficient (or Pareto-efficient) a situation is efficient if no change is possible that will help some people without harming others

Recall that in a perfectly competitive market, every buyer and seller is a price taker: no buyer or seller has any power to influence product price. Significant departures from perfect competition confer on some buyers or sellers the ability to influence the price of the product they sell. In doing so, self-interested sellers will influence price in their favour. Perfect competition prevents the abuse of economic power by diffusing power so widely that no one has any power to abuse. As we will see in Chapter 8, departures from perfect competition can prevent potential Pareto-efficient transactions from being realized.

By now you may be asking, "Why study perfect competition? Why not study markets in which buyers and sellers can influence the price of their product?" Although most markets may not be perfectly competitive, there are three good reasons for studying perfect competition:

1. Some markets (e.g., foreign exchange, many agricultural products) are closer to perfect competition than to other market types.
2. It is easier to analyze perfect competition and then proceed to other market types than it is to do the reverse.
3. Perfect competition provides a benchmark against which the efficiency of other market types can be compared.

With the third point in mind, we proceed to the following examples. They employ the cost–benefit principle to show that welfare-enhancing (i.e., Pareto-efficient) transactions become possible whenever a perfectly competitive market is out of equilibrium.

COST–
BENEFIT

EXAMPLE 6.1

Why is holding the price of milk below its equilibrium level inefficient?

Suppose the supply and demand curves for milk are as shown in Figure 6.1 and the current price of milk is $1/litre. Describe a transaction that will benefit both buyer and seller.

FIGURE 6.1

A Market in Which Price Is below the Equilibrium Level
In this market, milk is currently selling for $1/litre, $0.50 below the equilibrium price of $1.50/litre.

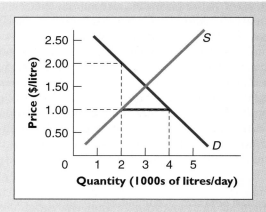

At a price of $1, sellers offer only 2000 litres of milk a day. At that quantity, buyers value an extra litre of milk at $2 (the price on the demand curve that corresponds to 2000 litres a day and that represents what buyers are willing to pay for an additional litre). We also know that the cost of producing an extra litre of milk is only $1 (the price that corresponds to 2000 litres a day on the supply curve, which equals marginal cost).

Furthermore, a price of $1/litre leads to excess demand of 2000 litres/day, which means that many dissatisfied buyers cannot buy as much milk as they want at the going price. Now suppose a supplier sells an extra litre of milk to the most eager of these buyers for $1.25, as in Figure 6.2. Since the extra litre cost only $1 to produce, the seller is $0.25 better off than before. And since the most eager buyer values the extra litre at $2, that buyer is $0.75 better off than before. In sum, the transaction creates an extra $1 of economic surplus out of thin air!

FIGURE 6.2

How Excess Demand Creates an Opportunity for a Surplus-Enhancing Transaction
At a market price of $1/litre, the most intensely dissatisfied buyer is willing to pay $2 for an additional litre, which a seller can produce at a cost of only $1. If this buyer pays the seller $1.25 for the extra litre, the buyer gains an economic surplus of $0.75 and the seller gains an economic surplus of $0.25.

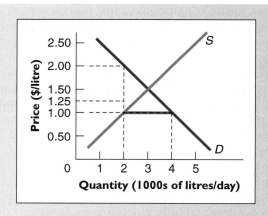

If the price of milk rises to $1.25/litre for all purchasers, those who previously purchased 2000 litres of milk for $1/litre will be worse off. However, the sellers of those 2000 litres will be better off by the same monetary amount by which the purchasers are worse off. Therefore, it is possible for the sellers to exactly compensate the purchasers for their loss, while at the same time total economic surplus has been increased by $1. In other words, providing that compensating payments can be made to those who lose when the price of milk rises, it is possible for additional buyers and additional sellers to be better off while no one is worse off. Thus, milk selling for only $1/litre cannot be efficient. Indeed, if milk sells for *any* price below $1.50/litre (the market equilibrium price), we can design a transaction in which each participant's benefit exceeds his or her cost, which means that selling milk for any price less than $1.50/litre cannot be efficient.

EXERCISE 6.1

In Example 6.1, suppose that milk initially sells for 50 cents/litre. Describe a transaction that will create additional economic surplus for both buyer and seller without causing harm to anyone else.

EXAMPLE 6.2

Why is holding the price of milk above its equilibrium level inefficient?

Suppose the current price of milk is $2/litre with the same demand and supply curves as in Example 6.1. Describe a transaction that would benefit both buyer and seller.

With the price at $2/litre, the quantity supplied is 4000 litres/day, but the quantity demanded is only 2000 litres/day. There is an excess supply of 2000 litres/day (see Figure 6.3). If all 4000 litres are to be sold, the demand curve shows that price must be reduced to $1/litre. At 4000 litres/day, buyers value an additional litre of milk at only $1. However, the supply curve indicates that at 4000 litres/day, the marginal cost of a litre of milk is $2. Therefore, if 4000 litres/day

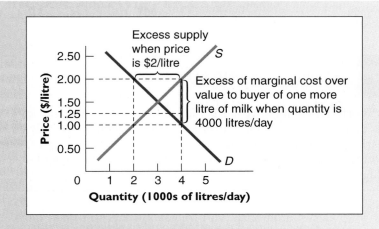

FIGURE 6.3

How Excess Supply Creates an Opportunity for a Surplus-Enhancing Transaction

If a price of $2/litre is imposed, suppliers will bring a quantity of 4000 litres/day to the market. Marginal cost of a litre is $2 when the daily quantity is 4000 litres. However, at a daily quantity of 4000 litres, the value to purchasers of an extra litre is only $1. Therefore, if a marginal producer pays a marginal buyer $1.25 to reduce daily consumption by 1 litre, the marginal buyer will be better off by $0.25. At the same time, if the marginal producer reduces daily production by 1 litre, costs are reduced by $2. By paying $1.25 to avoid $2 of costs, the marginal producer is better off by $0.75. The transaction causes total economic surplus to increase by $1.

are being produced and sold, a producer of milk could pay a buyer $1.25 to reduce consumption by one litre, and the buyer would be better off by $0.25. At the same time, by reducing the daily production of milk by one litre, the producer would reduce her total cost of production by $2. If the producer avoids $2 of cost by making a payment of $1.25, the producer is better off by $0.75. As in Example 6.1, the new transaction creates $1 of additional economic surplus. If market price is any price above equilibrium price, we can design a similar surplus-enhancing transaction. Hence, it cannot be efficient to sell milk for more than $1.50/litre. If a price above equilibrium price is imposed in a perfectly competitive market, reducing price to the equilibrium price will enhance total economic surplus.

Indeed, the market equilibrium price is the *only* price at which buyers and sellers cannot design a surplus-enhancing transaction. In this specific, limited sense, free markets are said to allocate goods and services efficiently.

Actually, to claim that market equilibrium is always efficient even in this limited sense is an overstatement. The claim holds only if markets are perfectly competitive and if the demand and supply curves satisfy certain other restrictions. For example, market equilibrium will not be efficient if the individual marginal cost curves that add up to the market supply curve fail to include all relevant costs of producing the product. As we saw in Chapter 3, for example, if production generates pollution that harms others, then the true cost of expanding output will be higher than indicated by the market supply curve. The equilibrium output will be inefficiently large and the equilibrium price inefficiently low.

Likewise, market equilibrium will not be efficient if the individual demand curves that make up the market demand curve do not capture all the relevant benefits of buying additional units of the product.

We will take up such market imperfections in greater detail in later chapters. For now, we will confine our attention to perfectly competitive markets whose demand curves capture all relevant benefits and whose supply curves capture all relevant costs. For such goods, market equilibrium will always be efficient in the particular sense described earlier.

RECAP   **EQUILIBRIUM AND EFFICIENCY**

When a perfectly competitive market is not in equilibrium a transaction can always be made in which both buyer and seller benefit. A perfectly competitive market in equilibrium is said to be efficient, or Pareto-efficient, meaning that no reallocation is possible that will benefit some people without harming others.

6.2 ECONOMIC SURPLUS

total economic surplus the total economic surplus in a market is the sum of all the individual economic surpluses gained by buyers and sellers who participate in the market

In Chapter 1, we first encountered the concept of economic surplus, which in a buyer's case is the difference between the most she would have been willing to pay for a product and the amount she actually pays for it. The same concept applies to sellers of goods and services, for whom economic surplus is the difference between what they are paid for the goods they sell and the smallest amount they would have been willing to accept. In any given market, **total economic surplus** is the sum of all economic surplus attributable to participation in that market by buyers and sellers. Stated another way, it is a measure of the total amount by which buyers and sellers benefit from their participation in the market. A perfectly competitive market maximizes its economic surplus when it reaches equilibrium price and quantity. This is the reason for removing obstacles that prevent a perfectly competitive market from reaching equilibrium.

CALCULATING ECONOMIC SURPLUS

Consider a hypothetical market for a service with 11 potential buyers and 11 potential sellers. Suppose that the buyers and sellers live in a neighbourhood of 11 houses, each with a similar driveway. As morning dawns, the neighbourhood wakens to a common Canadian scene. During the night, a heavy blanket of snow has covered the ground. All the driveways are covered to the same depth. A teenager lives in each household, and for the right price, has the time to shovel one driveway—it does not matter which one. After considering her opportunity costs, Anna is willing to shovel a driveway for no less than $1; Beth, however, requires at least $2, Celine wants at least $3, and so on for all 11 teenagers. Each teenager wants $1 more than the previous one to shovel a driveway. When the 11 teenagers are arranged from lowest to highest according to the minimum price each will accept for shovelling a driveway, supply forms the staircase-shaped supply curve shown in Figure 6.4. Each teenager's minimum price is a **supplier's reservation price**.

supplier's (or seller's) reservation price the lowest price a supplier will accept in return for providing a good or service

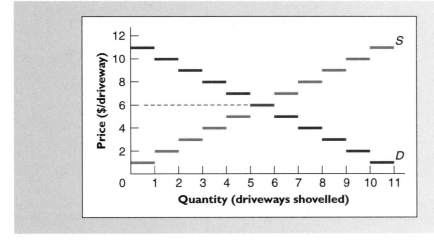

FIGURE 6.4
A Market with Discrete Supply and Demand Curves
When a product can be sold only in whole-number amounts, its demand and supply curves have the staircase shapes shown.

All heads of household will pay to have their driveways shovelled, provided an acceptable price is charged for shovelling. Angela's reservation price (the maximum price she is willing to pay) for having her driveway cleared is $11, Bernard's reservation price is $10, Claude's is $9, and so on for all heads of household. Each head is willing to pay $1 less than the previous one. Each head's maximum price is a **demander's reservation price**. When the potential purchasers are arranged from highest to lowest reservation price, demand forms the staircase-shaped demand curve in Figure 6.4. The supply and demand curves of Figure 6.4 can be thought of as discrete counterparts of the traditional continuous supply and demand curves.

Let us assume that everyone has full information about the price paid for shovelling a driveway, and that in the end, every homeowner pays the same price for having a driveway cleared. The equilibrium price in Figure 6.4 is $6/driveway, and the equilibrium quantity is six driveways. (This means that five driveways are not shovelled and five teenagers do not shovel.) Shovelling the sixth driveway produces no surplus for either the buyer or the seller because both have the same reservation price. But the first five driveways yielded surpluses for both buyers and sellers. Angela, the owner of the first driveway, for example, would have been willing to pay as much as $11 to have it shovelled, but since the market price was

demander's (or buyer's) reservation price the highest price a demander will offer in order to obtain a good or service

consumer surplus the economic gain of the buyers of a product, as measured by the cumulative difference between their respective reservation prices and the price they actually paid

producer surplus the economic gain of the sellers of a product as measured by the cumulative difference between the price received and their respective reservation prices

only $6, she realized a surplus of $5. Likewise, Anna, the teenager who shovelled the first driveway, would have been willing to clear it for as little as $1, so she also received a surplus of $5. Bernard, owner of the second driveway, would have been willing to pay as much as $10 to have it shovelled, and Beth, who cleared the driveway, was willing to shovel for $2. Thus, both Bernard and Beth received a surplus of $4. Similarly, the owners of the third, fourth, and fifth driveways receive surpluses of $3, $2, and $1, respectively, and so do the three teenagers who clear those driveways.

If we add all the buyers' surpluses, we get a total of $15 of buyers' surplus for each storm. This total is often referred to as **consumer surplus**. Similarly, the sum of the corresponding surpluses for sellers is also $15/storm. This total is often referred to as **producer surplus**. As we'll see in later examples, the surplus received by buyers and sellers need not always be the same. The total economic surplus for this market is the sum of consumer surplus and producer surplus, or $30/storm, which corresponds to the combined blue and green areas in Figure 6.5.

FIGURE 6.5

Consumer and Producer Surplus
Consumer surplus (blue region) is the cumulative difference between the most that buyers are willing to pay for each unit and the price they actually pay. Producer surplus (green region) is the cumulative difference between the price at which producers sell each unit and the smallest amounts they would be willing to accept.

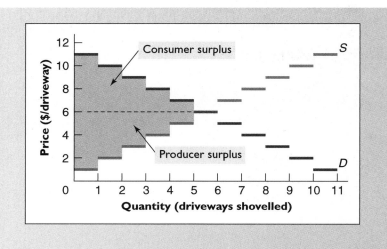

Perhaps you are thinking that the reservation prices stated for at least some of the six teenagers who shovelled driveways in this example are too low. Who would shovel even a very short driveway for $1?

Suppose we accept this argument and raise the reservation price for every teenager by $2. Supply then becomes the discrete supply curve shown in Figure 6.6. Demand in Figure 6.6 is the same as in Figures 6.4 and 6.5. The equilibrium price rises to $7/driveway, and five driveways are shovelled (not six, as previously). Also, if you calculate the producers' and consumers' surplus, you will find that both have decreased to $10, for a total surplus of $20.

But why would the available surplus fall just because the teenagers raised their reservation prices? Remember that the teenagers determined their reservation prices by considering their opportunity costs. If Anna states her reservation price to be $1, she is saying that by using her time to shovel a driveway, she is foregoing some alternate use of her time worth $1. If the best alternate use of her time (her opportunity cost) is worth only $1, she gains $5 (the excess of the market price over her opportunity cost) by shovelling a driveway. Why would her reservation price increase? Suppose a new recreation centre opens in the neighbourhood. It offers several interesting activities, and members of the neighbourhood have free access to the centre. Anna now has something better to do with her time, so her opportunity cost is higher. Thus, she raises her reservation price to $3. The market price for shovelling a driveway is $7, so Anna's surplus is $4. It is still worth $11 to Angela to have her driveway cleared. Since she pays Anna $7, Angela's surplus is $4. The total surplus from this transaction is $8, not $10 as in

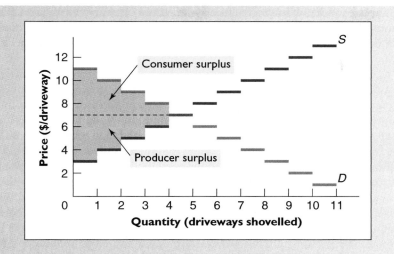

FIGURE 6.6
Consumer and Producer Surplus
Consumer and producer surplus are defined the same as in Figure 6.5. However, when the teenagers raise their reservation prices for shovelling snow because they have better alternative uses for their time, the sizes of both the consumer and the producer surplus are reduced. The producers (teenagers) have a smaller surplus because they have a better alternative use of their time. The consumers (homeowners) have a smaller surplus because the market price has risen. Therefore, because opportunity cost has risen and the supply has shifted up, the total of consumer and producer surplus is reduced in Figure 6.6 compared with Figure 6.5.

the previous example. The total surplus that can be created by providing a service worth $11 depends on the opportunity cost of the resources used to provide that service. Other things being equal, if the opportunity cost rises, the surplus is smaller; if it falls, the surplus is larger.

EXERCISE 6.2

Calculate producer surplus and consumer surplus for a market like the one just described, except that the buyers' reservation prices for each driveway are $2 higher than before. (That is, how big would the surpluses be if the demand and supply curves were as shown in the following diagram?)

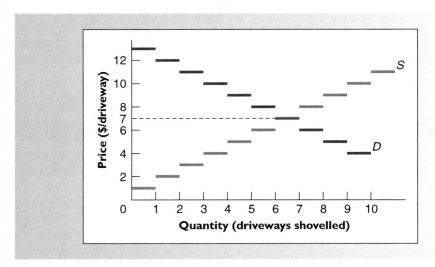

Now suppose we want to measure total economic surplus in a market with conventional straight-line supply and demand curves. As Example 6.3 illustrates, this task is a simple extension of the method used for discrete supply and demand curves.

EXAMPLE 6.3

How much do buyers and sellers benefit from their participation in the market for milk?

Consider the market for milk whose demand and supply curves are shown in Figure 6.7, which has an equilibrium price of $2/litre and an equilibrium quantity of 4000 litres/day. How much total economic surplus do the participants in this market reap?

FIGURE 6.7

Supply and Demand in the Market for Milk

For the supply and demand curves shown, the equilibrium price of milk is $2/litre and the equilibrium quantity is 4000 litres/day.

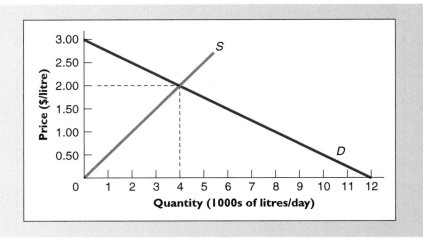

In Figure 6.7, note first that, as in Figures 6.5 and 6.6, the last unit exchanged generates no surplus at all, either for buyers or sellers. Note also that for all milk sold up to 4000 litres/day, buyers receive consumer surplus and sellers receive producer surplus, just as in Figures 6.5 and 6.6. For sellers, the surplus is the cumulative difference between market price and marginal cost. For buyers, the surplus is the cumulative difference between the most they would be willing to pay for milk (as measured on the demand curve) and the price they actually pay.

Total consumer surplus received by buyers in the milk market is thus the blue triangle between the demand curve and the market price in Figure 6.8. Note that this area is a right triangle whose vertical arm is $h = \$1/$litre and whose horizon-

FIGURE 6.8

Total Economic Surplus in the Market for Milk

Consumer surplus is the area of the blue triangle ($2000/day). Producer surplus is the area of the green triangle ($4000/day). Total economic surplus is the sum of the two, or $6000/day.

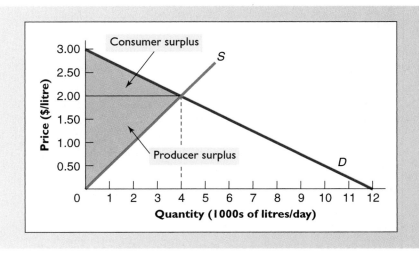

tal arm is b = 4000 litres/day. And since the area of any triangle is equal to $(\frac{1}{2})bh$, consumer surplus in this market is equal to

$$(\tfrac{1}{2})(4000 \text{ litres/day})(\$1/\text{litre}) = \$2000/\text{day}.$$

Likewise, total producer surplus is the green triangle between the supply curve and the market price. The height of this triangle is h = $2/litre and the base is b = 4000 litres/day, so producer surplus is equal to

$$(\tfrac{1}{2})(4000 \text{ litres/day})(\$2/\text{litre}) = \$4000/\text{day}.$$

The total economic surplus from this milk market is the sum of consumer and producer surplus, or $6000/day.

A useful way of thinking about this surplus is to ask, "What is the highest price consumers and producers would pay, in the aggregate, for the right to continue participating in the milk market?" For buyers, the answer is $2000/day, since that is the amount by which their combined benefits exceed their combined costs. Sellers would pay up to $4000/day, since that is the amount by which their combined benefits exceed their combined reservation prices. Together, then, buyers and sellers would be willing to pay up to $6000/day for the right to continue participating in this market.

That economic surplus is the amount by which buyers and sellers benefit from participating in a market sheds further light on the claim that market equilibrium is efficient. At any price other than the equilibrium price, the total economic surplus produced by a market will be less than it would be at the equilibrium price. Stated another way, the equilibrium price and quantity serve to maximize the total economic surplus created by a market.

EFFICIENCY IS NOT THE ONLY GOAL

The fact that market equilibrium maximizes economic surplus is an attractive feature, to be sure. Bear in mind, however, that "efficient" does not mean the same thing as "good." For example, the market for milk may be in equilibrium at a price of $2/litre, yet many poor families may be unable to afford milk for their children at that price.

Our conclusion about efficiency is based on the assumption that the attributes of buyers and sellers are predetermined. That is, we assume that the tastes of buyers and the distribution of income among individuals have already been established. Supply and demand then generate a particular set of prices and quantities as outcomes in markets. The market outcomes are based on buyers' tastes and the underlying distribution of income. If either tastes or the distribution of income were to change, market outcomes typically would also change. Thus, the prices and quantities that we observe as equilibrium outcomes in markets are *conditional* on tastes and the distribution of income.

Furthermore, as Chapter 11 will discuss in more detail, an important part of our assumption of "perfect competition" is the assumption of "perfect information." Under the assumptions sufficient to produce perfect competition, the combined effects of individual cost–benefit decisions give rise to the supply and demand curves for each good produced in an economy and to a Pareto-efficient outcome for each of these goods. If we are concerned about inequality in the distribution of attributes like income, we should not be surprised to discover that markets do not always yield outcomes we like.

Most of us could agree, for example, that the world would be a better one if poor families had enough income to feed their families adequately. The claim that equilibrium in the market for milk is efficient means simply that *taking people's incomes as given,* the resulting allocation of milk cannot be altered so as to help some people without at the same time harming others.

To this a critic of the market system might respond: So what? As such critics rightly point out, imposing costs on others may be justified if doing so will help those with sufficiently important unmet demands. For example, most people would prefer to fund homeless shelters with their tax dollars rather than let the homeless freeze to death. Arguing in these terms, policymakers in some jurisdictions responded to rapid increases in the price of oil in the late 1970s by imposing price controls on home heating oil. And many of us might agree that if the alternative had been to take no action at all, price controls might have been justified in the name of social justice.

But the concept of market efficiency makes clear that there *must* be a better alternative policy. Price controls generally prevent the market from reaching equilibrium, which means foregoing transactions that would benefit some people without harming others.

WHY EFFICIENCY IS IMPORTANT

Efficiency is important because it enhances our ability to achieve other goals. Whenever a perfectly competitive market is out of equilibrium, it is always possible to generate additional economic surplus. A larger economic surplus means that potentially it is possible to make at least some people better off without making anyone worse off.

RECAP | **ECONOMIC SURPLUS**

The economic surplus generated by a market is the total dollar amount by which buyers and sellers benefit from their participation in that market. It is the sum of consumer surplus and producer surplus. Consumer surplus is the cumulative difference between what buyers would have been willing to pay for the product and the price they actually do pay. Graphically it is the area between the demand curve and the market price. Producer surplus is the cumulative difference between the market price and the reservation prices at which producers would have been willing to make their sales. Graphically it is the area between market price and the supply curve.

Total economic surplus in a perfectly competitive market is maximized when exchange occurs at the equilibrium price. But the fact that equilibrium is "efficient" in this sense does not mean the same as "good." All markets can be in equilibrium, yet many people may lack sufficient income to buy even basic goods and services. However, when economic surplus is maximized, it is possible to pursue other goals more fully.

■ 6.3 THE COST OF PREVENTING PRICE ADJUSTMENTS

PRICE CEILINGS

During the winter of 2000–01 the price of crude petroleum was more than twice what it had been two years before. In the aftermath of the destruction of New York's World Trade Center on September 11, 2001, the price of oil fell, but in the months preceding the war in Iraq in 2003, it fluctuated considerably as oil traders re-evaluated their estimates of the likelihood of general interruption of oil supplies from the Middle East. However, recent fluctuations in the international price of oil have actually been relatively small, compared with some of the energy crises in Canada's history.

Early in 1973, before the Yom Kippur War between Israel and the states of Egypt and Syria, the world price of oil was about U.S.$2/barrel (bbl). With the war, which occurred late in 1973, the world price more than quadrupled in the first of two oil "shocks." Concerned about the impact of much more expensive oil, the Canadian government restricted exports of crude oil and refined products and froze the domestic price of crude oil. It also announced that the interprovincial oil pipeline, which until then had piped oil from Western Canada only as far east as the Ottawa Valley, would be extended to Montreal. Further, to maintain a uniform price of oil across the country, exports of oil from Western Canada would be taxed and the resulting revenue used to subsidize the price of oil "east of Montreal." Revenue derived from export taxes was approximately sufficient to maintain the subsidized price of oil in Eastern Canada, and the policy covered its financial costs until the late 1970s. Nevertheless, after 1973, producers in Western Canada, primarily Alberta, would have much preferred to sell their oil at high world prices. Not long after freezing the domestic price of oil, the federal government began to allow the Canadian price of oil to rise at a controlled rate. In mid-1978, the world price was about U.S.$13/bbl. The Canadian price was about $10/bbl.

The second oil shock came in 1980 in the aftermath of the Iranian Revolution. The world price rose rapidly until it exceeded U.S.$30/bbl. Because the domestic Canadian price was rising at a slow, controlled rate, it was only about half the world price. Western provinces, primarily Alberta, were greatly aggrieved that they were required to sell oil at half the price available in the export market. (More than 20 years later, memories of this still contribute to a sense of Western alienation. The period of 1961–73, when oil producers in Western Canada benefited from selling oil at higher prices in a protected North American market, has been largely forgotten.) Because exports to the United States were reduced and because the differential between the controlled Canadian price and the world price had widened, taxes on exported oil were not sufficient to maintain the subsidized price on oil imported into Eastern Canada. By 1980, keeping the price of oil in Eastern Canada at about half the world price was costing the federal treasury billions of dollars per year in excess of what it could raise by taxing exports of oil from Western Canada. The consumption of oil in Eastern Canada was being heavily subsidized at the expense of oil profits in Western Canada (primarily Alberta) and the federal treasury. This set the stage for the National Energy Program of 1980.

Before discussing the National Energy Program, let us use Example 6.4 to illustrate why a price control on oil will cause loss of economic surplus.

www.statcan.ca
Statistics Canada

How much is an economic surplus reduced by price controls? **EXAMPLE 6.4**

Suppose the demand and supply curves for oil are as shown in Figure 6.9, in which the equilibrium price is $14/bbl. And suppose that legislators pass a law setting the maximum price at $10/bbl. How much lost economic surplus does this policy cost society?

First, let's calculate the surplus without price controls. If this market is not regulated, 3000 bbl/day will be sold at a price of $14/bbl. In Figure 6.10, the economic surplus received by buyers is the area of the blue triangle. Since the height of this triangle is $6/bbl and its base is 3000 bbl/day, its area is equal to (½)(3000 bbls/day)($6/bbl) = $9000/day. The economic surplus received by producers is the area of the green triangle. Since this triangle also has an area of $9000/day, total economic surplus in this market will be $18 000/day.

If the price of oil is prevented from rising above $10/bbl, only 1000 bbl/day will be sold, and the total economic surplus will be reduced by the area of the

FIGURE 6.9

Economic Surplus in an Unregulated Market for Oil

For the supply and demand curves shown, the equilibrium price of oil is $14/bbl, and the equilibrium quantity is 3000 bbl/day. Consumer surplus is the area of the blue triangle ($9000/day). Producer surplus is the area of the green triangle (also $9000/day).

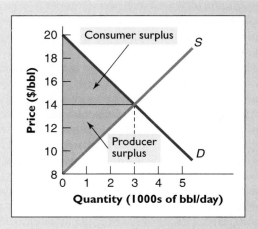

lined triangle in Figure 6.10. Since the height of this triangle is $8/bbl, and its base is 2000 bbl/day, its area is (½)(2000 bbl/day)($8/bbl) = $8000/day. Producer surplus falls from $9000/day in the unregulated market to the area of the green triangle, or (½)(1000 bbl/day)($2/bbl) = $1000/day, which is a loss of $8000/day. Thus, given the way we have drawn the supply and demand curves in this example, the loss in total economic surplus is equal to the loss in producer surplus, which means that the new consumer surplus must be the same as the original consumer surplus. To verify that, note that consumer surplus under controls is the area of the blue figure, which is again $9000/day. (*Hint:* To compute this area, first split the figure into a rectangle and a triangle.) By preventing the oil market from reaching equilibrium, price controls waste $8000 of producer surplus per day without creating any additional surplus for consumers!

FIGURE 6.10

The Economic Waste Caused by Price Controls

By limiting output in the oil market to 1000 bbl/day, price controls cause a loss in economic surplus of $8000/day (area of the lined triangle).

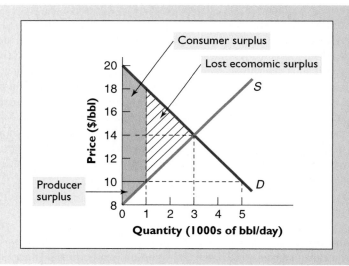

Defenders of price controls might respond that those who managed to buy some oil at the lower price received welcome budget relief. While this is true, the same objective could be accomplished in a much less costly way. Income could be transferred to those who pay more for oil in order to compensate them for their loss. But will income actually be transferred? On reflection, the answer to this question may be yes, *if the alternative is to impose price controls that would be even more costly than the income transfers.* After all, the **price ceiling** as implemented ends up costing oil sellers $8000/day in lost economic surplus. So they

price ceiling a maximum allowable price, specified by law

ought to be willing to pay some amount up to $8000/day in additional taxes to escape the burden of controls.

If the price ceiling is removed, all those who previously purchased oil at $10/bbl will be worse off. Nevertheless, producer surplus will rise by more than enough to offset any reduction in consumer surplus. By transferring some of the greater producer surplus to consumers, it is still possible to make some (or all) people better off without making anyone worse off—Pareto efficiency is possible.

This point is so important that we will state it another way. Think of economic surplus as a pie to be divided among the market participants. If the price of oil is limited to no more than $10/bbl, total economic surplus is $10 000/day. If the price of oil is allowed to rise to its equilibrium price, total economic surplus rises to $18 000/day. *In effect, removal of the price ceiling creates a larger pie. With a larger pie, it is possible for every participant to have a larger piece of pie.* Price controls in a perfectly competitive market prevent buyers and sellers from making mutually advantageous transactions by preventing transactions that pass the cost–benefit test.

But this raises another interesting question. Why would price ceilings ever persist? Surely any political leader worth the name would seize an opportunity to abolish price controls in order to make some people better off without making anyone worse off. What better way could there be to get votes? Yet, the National Energy Program of 1980 provided, not for dropping price controls, but for continuing to use them for the next 10 years.

In 1980 the Government of Canada argued that to control the disruption caused by the high and volatile price of oil, the Canadian price should not be tied to the world price but should rise at a much slower, controlled rate. A higher price would give Canadians an incentive to economize on their use of oil and encourage new oil discoveries. A slow, controlled rate of increase would permit users of oil to make a more orderly adjustment to higher prices. The Canadian price was based on the cost of producing oil from a variety of Canadian sources. Further, the price of oil would be the same for all users of oil in the country.

www.canada.gc.ca
Government of Canada

Why in 1980 did the Canadian government find price controls on oil to be politically viable? Removal of a price ceiling increases producer surplus and has the potential to be Pareto-efficient. However, more than 75 percent of Canada's oil industry was owned by foreign companies, most of them American. Some Canadians believed that an increased producer surplus just would have flowed out of the country into the hands of foreign owners. If this happened, the producer surplus generated by higher prices would have been unavailable to compensate Canadians who would have been paying higher energy prices. The transfers that might have compensated them would have been impossible to make.

However, suppose that it would have been possible to retain a significant part of an increased producer surplus in Canada. People in those parts of the country that did not produce oil might not have believed that they would receive any of the surplus as compensation for paying higher energy prices—they might have believed that compensation was possible, but not that it would actually happen.

Payment of compensation to oil consumers outside Alberta would have required taxes to be levied on oil producers in Alberta and the revenue paid to people outside Alberta. Only the federal government could make such payments. However, the Government of Alberta had the constitutional right to levy royalties on oil. Whatever part of the surplus the Government of Alberta kept in its hands by levying royalties on oil would have been unavailable to the federal government for compensating consumers, or for any other purpose. Price controls might have been seen as a more effective way than taxation for the federal government to transfer some economic surplus to its constituency, the majority of whom lived in parts of the country that did not produce oil.

Faced with selling oil at half the world price, the government of Alberta threatened to reduce the amount of oil delivered to the interprovincial pipeline. In

1981, Ottawa and Edmonton agreed that the domestic price of oil would increase rapidly. However, the world price of oil soon began to decline, and by 1985 the contest over oil revenues was moot. Nevertheless, another dramatic increase in the world price of oil could trigger a similar contest.

WHY DISTRIBUTION IS IMPORTANT

Even if removal of price controls would increase total economic surplus, would everyone be in favour? If some people have reason to believe that none of an increased economic surplus will be transferred to them, they have no reason to support removal of price controls. If they believe that they will have an absolutely smaller piece of a larger pie, they will generally oppose the removal of price controls. *The success of any policy designed to make a society's economic pie as large as possible is linked to how the pie is distributed among members of the society.* If a policy makes the pie larger but provides smaller pieces to some members of society, it will attract opposition from those who receive the smaller pieces. In analyzing whether a policy is Pareto-efficient, remember that a world of difference exists between *actual* and *potential* compensation. For a policy to be Pareto-efficient, it must include an appropriate system for distributing the economic surplus. It may be costly to design and administer a system that provides individuals with incentives to enhance an economic surplus. If members of a society believe such a system will not be available, they have no reason to support the policy; indeed, they may have reason to oppose it. To the extent that incentives to help create a surplus are reduced, it becomes more difficult for a society to create a surplus.

ELASTICITY AND THE SIZE OF TOTAL ECONOMIC SURPLUS

Thus far, we have not considered the impact price elasticity of supply or demand can have on the size of total economic surplus that is at stake when a price ceiling is implemented. The impact can be large, as we will see by comparing two rental markets, one of which has greater elasticity of supply than does the other.

Consider a city (like Winnipeg), where new apartments can be constructed either by making buildings taller or by extending new construction further out on the plain. Compare this to another city (like Vancouver), hemmed in on all sides by either mountains or the sea. With very few vacant lots, new apartments can be constructed, but only by making buildings taller. Given these different situations, the long-run supply of apartments will be more elastic in Winnipeg than in Vancouver. We will assume that both cities have the same demand curve for apartments.

Suppose the supply and demand curves for rental housing in Winnipeg are as shown in panel (a) of Figure 6.11. (To keep things simple, assume we are dealing with a market for similar, one-bedroom apartments.) The equilibrium rent in this market is $200/month, and the equilibrium quantity is 4000 apartments/month. The area of the blue triangle in panel (a) represents renters' consumer surplus:

$$\text{consumer surplus} = (\tfrac{1}{2})bh = (\tfrac{1}{2})(4000 \text{ apartments/month})(\$800)$$
$$= \$1\,600\,000/\text{month}.$$

Landlords' producer surplus is represented by the green triangle in panel (a), Figure 6.11:

$$\text{producer surplus} = (\tfrac{1}{2})bh = (\tfrac{1}{2})(4000 \text{ apartments/month})(\$200)$$
$$= \$400\,000/\text{month}.$$

Total economic surplus in the Winnipeg market is the sum of consumer and producer surplus, which is $2\,000\,000/month.

FIGURE 6.11

Economic Surplus in Two Unregulated Housing Markets

For the supply and demand curves shown in panel (a) (Winnipeg), consumer surplus is $1 600 000/month (area of the blue triangle) and producer surplus is $400 000/month (area of the green triangle). Total economic surplus in Winnipeg's rental market is $2 000 000/month. For panel (b) (Vancouver), consumer surplus also is $1 600 000/month, but producer surplus (area of the green figure) is $700 000/month. Total economic surplus in Vancouver's rental market is $2 300 000/month. Because the two markets are identical except for elasticity of supply, the difference arises solely because supply is less elastic in Vancouver than in Winnipeg.

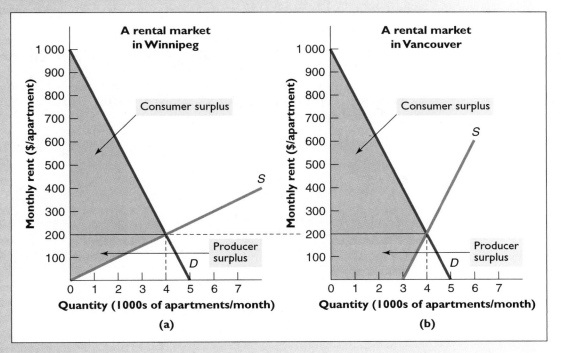

Now consider panel (b) of Figure 6.11, which portrays a rental market in Vancouver (again, for similar, one-bedroom apartments). The demand curve, equilibrium price, and equilibrium quantity of apartments are identical in panels (a) and (b). Therefore, consumer surplus in Vancouver is the same as in Winnipeg—$1 600 000/month. However, the supply curve for apartments in Vancouver is less elastic than in Winnipeg. Producer surplus in Vancouver [the green area of panel (b)] is calculated as the area of the rectangle with base zero to three *plus* the area of the triangle with the base three to four. This is $700 000/month. Therefore, in Vancouver:

$$\text{total economic surplus} = \text{consumer surplus} + \text{producer surplus}$$
$$= \$2\ 300\ 000/\text{month}.$$

Thus, calculations confirm the visual impression given by Figure 6.11, and total economic surplus is $300 000/month larger in Vancouver than in Winnipeg. The difference arises solely because supply is less elastic in Vancouver than in Winnipeg, which causes producer surplus to be larger in Vancouver.

ELASTICITY OF SUPPLY AND LOSS OF TOTAL ECONOMIC SURPLUS WITH RENT CONTROL

Historically, rent control has been introduced when a rapid increase in demand causes rents to rise dramatically. Resource booms and wartime mustering of troops at central points are typical causes. Landlords realize that they can charge more, and renters discover that apartments they have occupied for years quickly become more expensive.

Suppose that for historical reasons, rents in Vancouver and Winnipeg have been capped at $100/month—an identical price ceiling has been imposed on both markets. With rents capped at $100/month, Figure 6.12 shows that 2000 apartments/month are supplied in the Winnipeg market and 3500 are supplied in the Vancouver market. Because the reduction in apartments is smaller in Vancouver, we might expect the reduction in total economic surplus from the price ceiling to be smaller in Vancouver than in Winnipeg. The reduction in total economic surplus in Winnipeg is equal to the area of the triangle that contains the black lines in panel (a) of Figure 6.12:

$$(\tfrac{1}{2})bh = (\tfrac{1}{2})(2000 \text{ apartments/month})(\$500) = \$500\,000/\text{month}.$$

In comparison, the area of the triangle in panel (b) of Figure 6.12 containing the black lines gives the reduction in total economic surplus stemming from an identical price ceiling in Vancouver:

$$(\tfrac{1}{2})bh = (\tfrac{1}{2})(500 \text{ apartments/month})(\$200) = \$50\,000/\text{month}.$$

FIGURE 6.12

Lost Surplus and Redistribution of Surplus Arising from a Price Ceiling

When rent is prevented from rising above $100/month in Winnipeg [panel (a)], the triangle containing the black lines represents the decrease in total economic surplus ($500 000/month). The rectangle outlined in black represents the amount transferred from landlords to renters by the rent control ($200 000/month). When the same ceiling is imposed on rental housing in Vancouver [panel (b)], the reduction in total economic surplus is represented by the triangle containing the black lines ($50 000/month). The area of the rectangle outlined in black represents the amount transferred from landlords to renters by the price ceiling on rental housing in Vancouver ($350 000/month). In Vancouver, the loss of economic surplus is much smaller and the redistributive effect much larger compared with Winnipeg. Because the two markets are identical except for supply, the difference arises entirely because supply is less elastic in Vancouver.

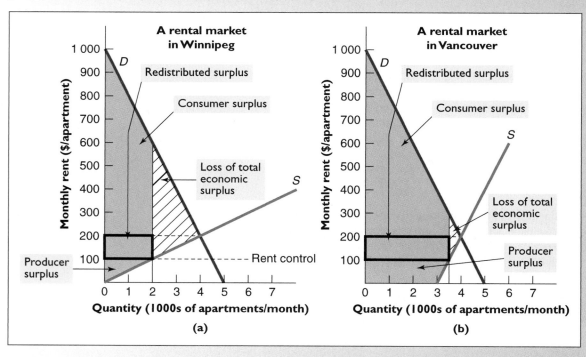

Thus, calculations confirm the visual impression given by Figure 6.12. The loss of total economic surplus in Vancouver is one-tenth the size of the loss in the Winnipeg rental market. The difference arises entirely because suppliers in Vancouver make a much smaller response to a reduction in price than do suppliers in Winnipeg—supply is less elastic in Vancouver. The likely differences in effect are outlined below.

ELASTICITY OF SUPPLY AND THE DISTRIBUTIVE EFFECTS OF RENT CONTROL

Suppose that for whatever reasons, rent control has existed for some time in Winnipeg and Vancouver. If rent control in Winnipeg is removed, the number of apartments supplied will rise from 2000 to 4000/month. Because of this, total economic surplus will rise by $500 000/month. Further, renters who choose to rent the 2000 new apartments and the landlords who choose to make them available will be better off. However, unless they are compensated, the renters who previously paid $100/month for each of 2000 apartments will be worse off after rent control is removed. They will be worse off by ($100/month)(2000 apartments) = $200 000/month. The same $200 000/month is transferred to landlords, making them be better off. Landlords will favour removal of rent control. The rectangle that is outlined in black in panel (a) of Figure 6.12 represents the monthly amount transferred from renters to landlords when rent control in Winnipeg is removed. Because total economic surplus is larger by $500 000/month, it is possible to compensate those renters who pay more when rent control is removed. It is possible for renters of old apartments, renters of new apartments, and landlords all to be better off. However, without actual compensation, the renters of the 2000 apartments will have good reason to oppose removal of rent control.

An identical price ceiling in the Vancouver rental market does not produce the same quantitative effects on consumer and producer surplus as in Winnipeg. Because the supply curve is less elastic in Vancouver, rent control produces a smaller reduction in the quantity of apartments supplied in Vancouver than in Winnipeg. Further, the consumer surplus under rent control in Vancouver is the area of the blue figure in panel (b), Figure 6.12. The blue figure also can be divided into a rectangle and a triangle and its area calculated as

$$(3500 \text{ apartments/month})(\$200) + (\tfrac{1}{2})(3500 \text{ apartments/month})(\$700)$$
$$= \$1\ 925\ 000/\text{month}.$$

In Vancouver, rent control actually increases consumer surplus from $1 600 000/month in the uncontrolled market to $1 925 000/month in the controlled market. At the same time, *total* economic surplus is $50 000/month more in the uncontrolled market because with removal of rent control, 500 more apartments become available.

By itself, though, removing rent control will not be Pareto-efficient—simple removal of rent control will not make some individuals better off while making no one worse off. Why? Landlords who collect $200/month for each of 3500 apartments where previously they collected $100 obviously will be better off by an amount equal to the area of the rectangle in panel (b), Figure 6.12, that is outlined in black. Its area is

$$(\$100/\text{month})(3500 \text{ apartments}) = \$350\ 000/\text{month}.$$

However, unless they receive compensation, the renters of those apartments will be worse off by the same amount, and will have reason to oppose removal of rent control. The rectangle outlined in black represents a transfer from renters to landlords when rent control is removed.

Notice that in Vancouver, the transfer ($350 000/month) arising from removal of rent control is much larger than in Winnipeg ($200 000/month). In Vancouver, the transfer affects renters of more apartments (3500/month) than in Winnipeg (2000/month). Further, when rent control is removed, fewer new apartments become available in Vancouver (500/month) than in Winnipeg (2000/month). Therefore, the increase in total economic surplus is much smaller in Vancouver ($50 000/month) than it is in Winnipeg ($500 000/month). Also, in Vancouver the renters of 500 new apartments and the landlords who supply them will be better off. However, this will be a smaller group than in Winnipeg, where 2000 new apartments become available. All of this arises from one basic point: *Other things remaining equal, the less elastic supply is, the smaller the loss of total economic surplus arising from a price control and the larger its redistributive impact.* A similar analysis could be made for price elasticity of demand.

What form do rent controls actually take? Richard Arnott reports that where they are used in North America, rent controls have evolved into forms that govern relationships between landlords and tenants. The controls try to take into account market imperfections, incentives that operate on landlords and tenants, distributive effects, and the effect of controls on the availability of rental housing. New York City provides an important exception. There, rent control takes the form of a ceiling price, consequently raising the issue of housing shortages and lost economic surplus.[1]

Rent controls are an example of a price ceiling. When implemented as a ceiling price, rent controls prevent landlords from charging more than a specified amount for rental housing. Tenants lucky enough to find a rent-controlled apartment often end up paying less than they would have in the absence of rent controls. But rent controls also prevent the housing market from reaching equilibrium and are thus inefficient. Alternatives to rent controls that will do even more for tenants can always be found, though implementing Pareto-efficient compensation will not necessarily be easy.

The reduction in economic surplus caused by a price ceiling constitutes waste, though again the size of the lost surplus depends on elasticity of both supply and demand. Further, elasticity of supply will affect the size of the distributional impact of a price ceiling.

EXERCISE 6.3

How much total economic surplus would have been lost in Winnipeg and Vancouver if the rent ceiling had been set at $150 instead of $100?

Compared with a price ceiling, a better policy would be to give low-income tenants some additional income and then let them bid for housing in a perfectly competitive market. Those who complain that no one would be willing to give low-income tenants extra money must be asked to explain why people would be willing to tolerate rent controls, which are *more* costly than income transfers. Logically, if people are willing to support rent controls on a competitive market, they should be even more eager to support income transfers to low-income tenants.

That is not to say that low-income tenants reap no benefit at all from rent controls on competitive markets. Again, those who are lucky enough to find an apartment that meets their needs often end up paying substantially less than they would in an unregulated market. The point is that more can be done for those with low incomes. Their problem is that they have too little income, so the sim-

---

[1]Richard Arnott, "Time for Revisionism on Rent Control?" *Journal of Economic Perspectives*, 9 (Winter 1995), 99–120. Arnott also reports that New York's experience is similar to that of a number of European cities where rent control has had a major effect on housing markets.

plest solution may be not to regulate the prices of the goods they and others buy but to give them more money.

PRICE FLOORS

Whereas a price ceiling prevents sellers from charging more than a specified amount, a **price floor** guarantees that suppliers will receive at least a specified amount for their product. But unlike a price ceiling, which attempts to hold price below its equilibrium level, a price floor attempts to peg price above its equilibrium level. And unlike the imposition of a price ceiling, in which the government's only responsibility is to impose penalties on sellers who charge too much, the imposition of a price floor requires the government to become an active participant on the buyer's side of the market. When price is pegged above the equilibrium level, an excess supply develops, which consumers cannot be forced to buy against their wishes.

price floor a minimum allowable price, specified by law

Agricultural price supports are an example of a price floor. They represent another attempt by the government to prevent markets from reaching equilibrium to provide benefits for some citizens. But as Example 6.5 demonstrates, price ceilings and price floors do have one fundamental characteristic in common: Both stand in the way of actions that satisfy the cost–benefit test, and both therefore reduce total economic surplus.

COST–
BENEFIT

By how much do price supports for wheat reduce total economic surplus?

EXAMPLE 6.5

Suppose the supply and demand for wheat are as shown in Figure 6.13. The government offers to buy as much wheat as necessary to clear the market at a price of $40/metric ton. Assuming that the government then gives the wheat it buys to the consumers who value it most, by how much will price supports reduce the total economic surplus generated in the wheat market?

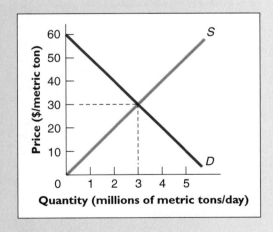

FIGURE 6.13
Equilibrium in an Unregulated Wheat Market
In the absence of a government price support, 3 million metric tons of wheat/day are sold at a price of $30/metric ton.

Without the price support, the equilibrium price in this market would be $30/metric ton. With the price support set at $40/metric ton, the public purchases 2 million metric tons/month and the government purchases the remaining 2 million metric tons offered by farmers at that price. If the government then gives the wheat to the consumers who value it most, the total quantity consumed is 4 million metric tons/month. The first million metric tons that are given away effectively restore the economic surplus that would have been produced had the market been left unregulated (see Figure 6.14), since the cost of producing this wheat is the same as before and the same consumers end up getting it. But the second million metric tons the government gives away cost farmers more to produce (as measured by the supply curve) than what buyers were willing to pay for it (as measured by the demand curve). The resulting reduction in economic surplus is represented by the area of the blue triangle in Figure 6.14, which is $10 million/month.

FIGURE 6.14

Lost Surplus from Price Supports for Wheat
A price support of $40/metric ton results in 4 metric tons of wheat/month being produced, of which the government buys half and the public buys half. Lost economic surplus from the program is equal to $10 million/month.

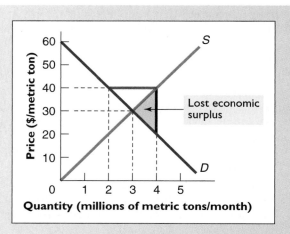

EXERCISE 6.4

In Example 6.5, by how much would total economic surplus be reduced by the price support if none of the wheat purchased by the government were given to consumers?

FIRST-COME–FIRST-SERVED POLICIES

Governments are not the only institutions that attempt to promote social goals by preventing markets from reaching equilibrium. Some universities, for example, attempt to protect access for low-income students to concerts and sporting events by selling a limited number of tickets below the market-clearing price on a first-come–first-served basis.

The commercial airline industry was an early proponent of the use of the first-come–first-served allocation method, which it used to ration seats on overbooked flights. Throughout the industry's history, most airlines have routinely accepted more reservations for their flights than there are seats on those flights. Most of the time, this practice causes no difficulty, because many reservation holders do not show up to claim their seats. Indeed, if airlines did not overbook their flights, most flights would take off with many empty seats, forcing airlines to charge higher ticket prices to cover their costs.

The only real difficulty is that every so often, more people actually do show up for a flight than there are seats on the plane. Until the late 1970s, airlines dealt with this problem by boarding passengers on a first-come–first-served basis. For example, if 120 people showed up for a flight with 110 seats, the last 10 people to arrive were "bumped," or forced to wait for the next available flight.

The bumped passengers often complained bitterly, and no wonder, since many of them ended up missing important business meetings or family events. As the following example illustrates, there was, fortunately, a simple solution to this problem, one that in the United States was almost blocked by a public interest group that failed to appreciate how rich and poor alike can benefit when an efficient policy replaces an inefficient one.

✦ 6.1   ECONOMIC NATURALIST

Why are there now fewer complaints about being bumped from an overbooked flight?

In 1978, airlines abandoned their first-come–first-served policy in favour of a new procedure. Since then, their practice has been to solicit volunteers to give up their seats on oversold flights in return for a cash payment or free ticket.

Now, the only people who give up their seats are those who volunteer to do so in return for compensation. Hence, the almost complete disappearance of complaints about being bumped from overbooked flights.

Example 6.6 illustrates how we might attempt to quantify the loss in surplus that results from first-come–first-served policies.

Which of the two policies—first-come–first-served or compensation for volunteers—is more efficient?

EXAMPLE 6.6

The difficulty with the first-come–first-served policy is that it gives little weight to the interests of passengers with pressing reasons for arriving at their destination on time. Such passengers can sometimes avoid losing their seats by showing up early, but passengers coming in on connecting flights often cannot control when they arrive. And the cost of showing up early is likely to be highest for precisely those people who place the highest value on not missing a flight (such as business executives, whose opportunity cost of waiting in airports is high). How big is the efficiency loss that results from first-come–first served?

For the sake of illustration, suppose that 37 people show up for a flight with only 33 seats. One way or another, four people will have to wait for another flight. Suppose we ask each of them, "What is the most you would be willing to pay to fly now rather than wait?" Typically, different passengers will have different reservation prices for avoiding the wait. Suppose the person who is most willing to pay would pay up to $60 rather than miss the flight, that the person willing to pay the second highest amount would pay up to $59, that the person willing to pay the third highest amount would pay up to $58, and so on. In that case, the person with the smallest reservation price for avoiding the wait would have a reservation price of $24. For the entire group of 37 passengers, the average reservation price for avoiding the wait would be ($60 + $59 + $58 + ... + $24)/37 = $42.

Given the difficulty of controlling airport arrival times, the passengers who get bumped under the first-come–first-served policy are not likely to differ systematically from others with respect to their reservation price for not missing the flight. On average, then, the total cost imposed on the four bumped passengers would be four times the average reservation price of $42, or $168. As far as those four passengers are concerned, that total is a pure loss of consumer surplus.

How does this cost compare with the cost imposed on bumped passengers when the airline compensates volunteers? Suppose the airline solicits volunteers by conducting an informal auction, increasing its cash compensation offer by $1 increments until it has the desired number of volunteers. As the incentive to stay behind rises, more people will volunteer; those whose reservation prices are the lowest will volunteer first. In this example, offers below $24 would generate no volunteers. An offer of $24 would generate one volunteer; an offer of $25 would generate two volunteers; and so on. A compensation payment of $27 to each volunteer would generate the necessary four volunteers.

What is the net cost of the compensation policy? While the airline pays out (4)($27) = $108 in compensation payments, not all that amount represents lost economic surplus. Thus, the passenger whose reservation price for missing the flight is $24 receives a net gain in economic surplus of $3—the difference between the $27 compensation payment and her $24 reservation price. Similarly, those whose reservation prices were $25 and $26 receive a net gain of $2 and $1, respectively. The cost of the cash compensation policy net of these gains is thus $108 − $6 = $102, or $66 less than under the first-come–first-served policy.

The compensation policy is more efficient than the first-come–first-served policy because it establishes a market for a scarce resource that would otherwise be allocated by nonmarket means. Figure 6.15 shows the supply and demand curves for seats under the compensation policy. In this market, the equilibrium price of not having to wait is $27. People who choose not to volunteer at that price incur an opportunity cost of $27 to not miss the flight. The four people who do volunteer accept $27 as ample compensation—indeed, more than ample for three of them.

FIGURE 6.15

Equilibrium in the Market for Seats on Oversold Flights

The demand curve for remaining on the flight is generated by plotting the reservation prices in descending order. The equilibrium compensation payment for volunteers who give up their seats is $27— the price at which four passengers volunteer to wait and the remaining 33 choose not to wait.

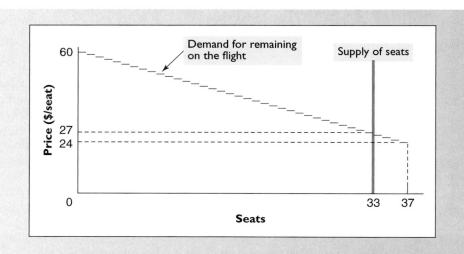

In practice, transactions like the one called for in Example 6.6 would be cumbersome to administer. Typically, the seller is in a position to solve such problems more easily by offering cash payments to elicit volunteers, and then financing those cash payments by charging slightly higher prices. Buyers, for their part, are willing to pay the higher prices because they value the seller's promise not to cancel their reservations without compensation.

RECAP   THE COST OF BLOCKING PRICE ADJUSTMENTS IN PERFECTLY COMPETITIVE MARKETS

When price adjustments are blocked in perfectly competitive markets, total economic surplus is reduced. Loss of economic surplus is wasteful and to be avoided. If price controls have been implemented for historical reasons, removal of the controls will increase total economic surplus, making it possible for at least some individuals to better off without anyone becoming worse off. However, if no one is to be worse off, compensation must be paid to those who pay more when price controls are removed. Removal of a price ceiling will make anyone who previously could make purchases at the ceiling price worse off unless they receive compensating payments. Removal of a price floor will make those who previously could sell at the floor price worse off unless they receive compensating payments.

■ 6.4 TAXES AND EFFICIENCY

WHO PAYS A TAX IMPOSED ON SELLERS OF A GOOD?

If we are going to have public services such as roads, fire fighters, or national defence, somebody has to pay—and that means taxes. Some may argue that corporations can better afford to pay taxes than consumers, but suppose they pass the tax on? Who, in the end, actually bears the burden of taxation?

EXAMPLE 6.7

How will the imposition of a tax of $1/kilogram collected from potato farmers affect the equilibrium price and quantity of potatoes?

Suppose the demand and supply curves for potatoes are shown by *D* and *S* in Figure 6.16, resulting in an initial equilibrium price and quantity of $3/kilogram and 3 million kilograms/month, respectively. From the farmers' perspective, the imposition of a tax of $1/kilogram is essentially the same as a $1 increase in the marginal cost of producing each kilogram of potatoes. Thus the tax can be seen as an upward shift in the supply curve by $1/kilogram.

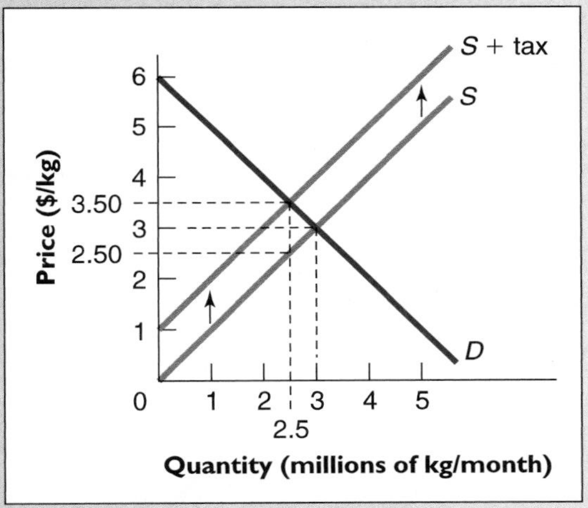

FIGURE 6.16

The Effect of a Tax on the Equilibrium Quantity and Price of Potatoes
With no tax, 3 million kilograms of potatoes are sold each month at a price of $3/kilogram. With a tax of $1/kilogram collected from sellers, consumers end up paying $3.50/kilogram (including tax), while sellers receive only $2.50/kilogram (net of tax). Equilibrium quantity falls from 3 million kilograms/month to 2.5 million.

As shown in Figure 6.16, the new equilibrium price (including the tax) will be $3.50, and the new equilibrium quantity will be 2.5 million kilograms/month. The net price per kilogram received by producers is $1 less than the price paid by the consumer, or $2.50. Even though the tax was collected entirely from potato sellers, the burden of the tax fell on both buyers and sellers—on buyers, because they pay $0.50/kilogram more than before the tax, and on sellers, because they receive $0.50/kilogram less than before the tax.

The burden of the tax need not fall equally on buyers and sellers. Indeed, as the following example illustrates, a tax levied on sellers may end up being paid almost entirely by buyers.

ECONOMIC NATURALIST

How will a tax on cars affect automobile prices in the long run?

Denmark is a country that does not have any automobile industry. All the cars sold in Denmark are imported. Honda, Volkswagen, Peugeot, and all the world's other car companies are quite willing to supply the Danish market, but they want to make as much profit per car from sales in Denmark as they make from sales anywhere else. If the inputs required to produce each car cost $10 000, how will the long-run equilibrium price of automobiles be affected if a tax of $100/car is levied on manufacturers?

The fact that the long-run marginal cost of making cars is constant means that the long-run supply curve of cars is horizontal at $10 000/car. A tax of $100/car effec-

tively raises marginal cost by $100/car and thus shifts the supply curve upward by exactly $100. If the demand curve for cars is as shown by curve *D* in Figure 6.17, the effect is to raise the equilibrium price of cars by exactly $100, to $10 100. The equilibrium quantity falls from 2 million cars/month to 1.9 million. (In fact, Denmark has much higher taxes on automobiles than this example would suggest—indeed, Danish prices for cars are nearly the highest in the world. But although the manufacturer initially pays excise taxes, they are passed on to buyers in higher prices, and Danish consumers ultimately bear the *entire* burden of these taxes.)

Although the long-run supply curve shown in Figure 6.17 is in one sense an extreme case (since its price elasticity is infinite), it is by no means an unrepresentative one. As we discussed in Chapter 5, the long-run supply curve will tend to be horizontal when it is possible to acquire more of all the necessary inputs at constant prices. As a first approximation, this can be accomplished for many goods and services in a typical economy.

FIGURE 6.17

The Effect of a Tax on Sellers of a Good with Infinite Price Elasticity of Supply

When the supply curve for a good is perfectly elastic, the burden of a tax collected from sellers falls entirely on buyers.

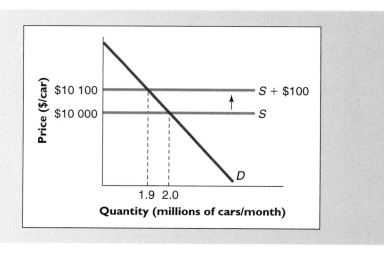

For goods with perfectly elastic supply curves, the entire burden of any tax is borne by the buyer.[2] That is, the increase in the equilibrium price is exactly equal to the tax. For this empirically relevant case, then, there is special irony in the common political practice of justifying taxes on business by saying that businesses have greater ability to pay than consumers.

HOW A TAX COLLECTED FROM A SELLER AFFECTS ECONOMIC SURPLUS

We saw earlier that perfectly competitive markets distribute goods and services efficiently if demand curves reflect all relevant benefits and supply curves reflect

---

[2]In the example given, the tax was collected from sellers. If you go on to take intermediate microeconomics, you will see that the same conclusions apply when a tax is collected from buyers.

all relevant costs. In Example 6.8, we will consider how the imposition of a tax on a product might affect a market's efficiency.

EXAMPLE 6.8

How does a tax on potatoes affect economic efficiency?

Suppose the supply and demand for potatoes are as shown by the curves S and D in Figure 6.18. How would the imposition of a tax of $1/kilogram, collected from potato sellers, affect total economic surplus in the potato market?

In the absence of a tax, 3 million kilograms of potatoes/month would be sold at a price of $3/kilogram, and the resulting total economic surplus would be $9 million/month (the area of the pale blue triangle in Figure 6.18).

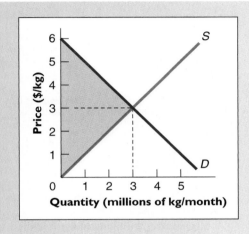

FIGURE 6.18

The Market for Potatoes without Taxes
Without taxes, total surplus in the potato market equals the area of the pale blue triangle, $9 million/month.

With a tax of $1/kilogram collected from potato sellers, the new equilibrium price of potatoes would be $3.50/kilogram (of which sellers receive $2.50, net of tax), and only 2.5 million kilograms of potatoes would be sold each month (see Figure 6.19). The total economic surplus reaped by buyers and sellers in the potato market would be the area of the pale blue triangle shown in Figure 6.19, which is $6.25 million/month, or $2.75 million less than before.

This drop in surplus may sound like an enormous loss. But it is a misleading figure, because it fails to take account of the value of the additional tax revenue collected, which is equal to $2.5 million/month ($1/kilogram on 2.5 million kilograms of potatoes). That revenue is available for transfer payments to households,

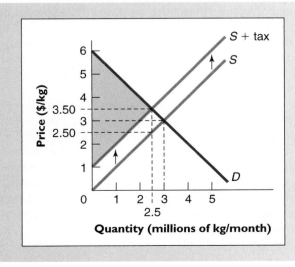

FIGURE 6.19

The Effect of a $1/Kilogram Tax on Potatoes
A $1/kilogram tax on potatoes would cause an upward shift in the supply curve by $1. Total surplus would shrink to the area of the pale blue triangle, $6.25 million/month.

to reduce other taxes, or to fund public services—all of which provide benefits to households. For example, potato tax revenue could fund total transfer payments to households of $2.5 million/month. So although buyers and sellers lose $2.75 million/month in economic surplus from their participation in the potato market, they also enjoy a $2.5 million in services or transfer payments. On balance, then, their net reduction in economic surplus is $0.25 million.

Graphically, the loss in economic surplus caused by the imposition of the tax can be shown as the area of the small pale blue triangle in Figure 6.20. This loss in surplus is often described as the **deadweight loss** from the tax.

FIGURE 6.20

The Deadweight Loss Caused by a Tax

For the market shown, the loss in economic surplus caused by a tax of $1/kilogram of potatoes equals the area of the small pale blue triangle, or $250 000/month.

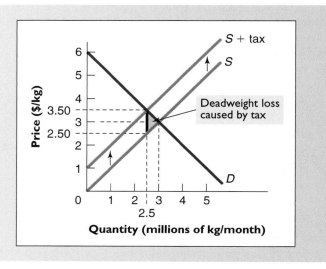

COST–BENEFIT

deadweight loss the deadweight loss caused by a policy is the reduction in economic surplus that results from adoption of that policy

A tax typically reduces economic surplus because a tax drives a wedge between the price that consumers actually pay and the price that producers actually receive. That "tax wedge" distorts the basic cost–benefit criterion that would ordinarily guide efficient decisions about production and consumption. In Example 6.8, the cost–benefit test tells us that we should expand potato production up to the point at which the benefit of the last kilogram of potatoes consumed (as measured by what buyers are willing to pay for it) equals the cost of producing it (as measured by the producer's marginal cost). That condition was satisfied in the potato market before the tax, but it is not satisfied once the tax is imposed. In Figure 6.20, for example, note that when potato consumption is 2.5 million kilograms/month, the value of an additional kilogram of potatoes to consumers is $3.50, whereas the cost to producers is only $2.50, not including the tax. (The cost to producers, including the tax, is $3.50/kilogram, but again we note that this tax is not a cost to society as a whole because it offsets other taxes that would otherwise have to be collected.)

Is a tax on potatoes necessarily "bad"? Does it lower total economic surplus? To answer this question, we must first identify the best alternative to taxing potatoes. You may be tempted to say, "Don't tax anything at all!" On a moment's reflection, however, you will realize that this is surely not the best option. After all, a country that taxed nothing could not pay for even the most minimal public services, such as road maintenance, fire protection, and national defence. And a country without at least minimal defence capability could not hope to maintain its independence for long. (In Chapter 14 we will consider why we often empower government to provide public goods.) On balance, if taxing potatoes were the best way to avoid doing without highly valued public services, then a small dead-weight loss in the potato market would be worth it.

So the real question is whether one can find a more efficient tax. Are there other things we could tax that would be better than taxing potatoes? The problem with a tax on any activity is that if market incentives encourage people to pursue the "right" amount of the activity (that is, the surplus-maximizing amount), then a tax will encourage them to pursue too little of it. As economists have long recognized, this observation suggests that taxes will cause smaller deadweight losses if they are imposed on goods for which the equilibrium quantity is not highly sensitive to changes in prices.

TAXES, ELASTICITY, AND EFFICIENCY

Suppose the government put a tax of 50 cents/kilogram on table salt. How would this affect the amount of salt you and others use? In Chapter 4 we saw that the demand for salt is highly inelastic with respect to price, because salt has few substitutes and occupies only a minuscule share in most family budgets. Because the imposition of a tax on table salt would not result in a significant reduction in the amount of it consumed, the deadweight loss from this tax on would be relatively small. More generally, the deadweight loss from a per-unit tax imposed on the seller of a good will be smaller the smaller the price elasticity of demand for the good is.

Figure 6.21 illustrates how the deadweight loss from a tax declines as the demand for a good becomes less elastic with respect to price. In both parts, the original supply and demand curves yield an equilibrium price of $2/unit and an equilibrium quantity of 24 units/day. The deadweight loss from a tax of $1/unit imposed on the good shown in panel (a) is the area of the pale blue triangle in panel (a), which is $2.50/day. The demand curve D_2 in panel (b) is less elastic at the equilibrium price of $2 than the demand curve D_1 in panel (a), which follows from the fact that P/Q is the same in both cases, while 1/slope is smaller in panel (b). The deadweight loss from the same $1/unit tax imposed on the good in panel (b) is the area of the pale blue triangle in panel (b), which is only $1.50/day.

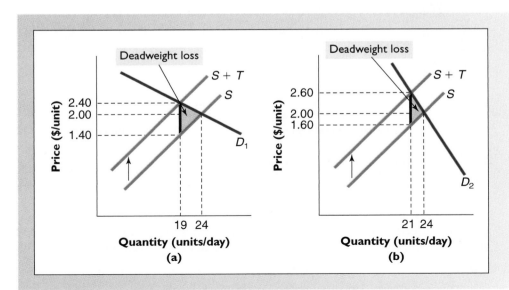

FIGURE 6.21

Elasticity of Demand and the Deadweight Loss from a Tax
At the equilibrium price and quantity, price elasticity of demand is smaller for the good shown in panel (b) than for the good shown in panel (a). The area of the deadweight loss triangle in panel (b) ($1.50/day) is smaller than the area of the deadweight loss triangle in panel(a) ($2.50/day).

ECONOMIC NATURALIST

6.3

Why did 60,000 people risk imprisonment rather than pay a tax on salt?

Because salt has no real substitutes, it could be called a "necessity," and in very poor countries, even a small tax on salt might be significant to some households. So when the British rulers of colonial India decided to institute a tax on salt, there were widespread protests. Those who felt the burden of the tax most keenly were the poorest of India's poor. In March 1930, Mahatma Gandhi led a massive march of protest to gather salt from the sea, rather than pay the tax. More than 60,000 people were imprisoned, but in the spring of 1931, the British permitted the making of salt for personal use. Although British colonial administrators may have known their economics, there is more to tax policy than efficiency. The march to the sea was one of Gandhi's most effective protests: though its immediate purpose was to protest against the tax, it also focused attention on the momentous ethical question of whether India, or any country, should be a colony at all. India became an independent nation in 1947, thus beginning the dissolution of the British Empire.[3]

The reduction in equilibrium quantity that results from a tax on a good will also be smaller the smaller the elasticity of supply of the good is. In Figure 6.22, for example, the original supply and demand curves for the markets portrayed in panels (a) and (b) yield an equilibrium price of $2/unit and an equilibrium quantity of 72 units/day. The deadweight loss from a tax of $1/unit imposed on the good shown in panel (a) is the area of the pale blue triangle in panel (a), which is $7.50/day. The supply curve S_2 in panel (b) is less elastic at the equilibrium price than the supply curve S_1 in panel (a), again because P/Q is the same in both cases, while 1/slope is smaller in panel (b). The deadweight loss from the same $1/unit tax imposed on the good in panel (b) is the area of the pale blue triangle in panel (b), which is only $4.50/day.

FIGURE 6.22

Elasticity of Supply and the Deadweight Loss from a Tax

At the equilibrium price and quantity, price elasticity of supply is smaller for the good shown in panel (b) than for the good shown in panel (a). The area of the deadweight loss triangle in panel (b) ($4.50/day) is smaller than the area of the deadweight loss triangle in panel (a) ($7.50/day).

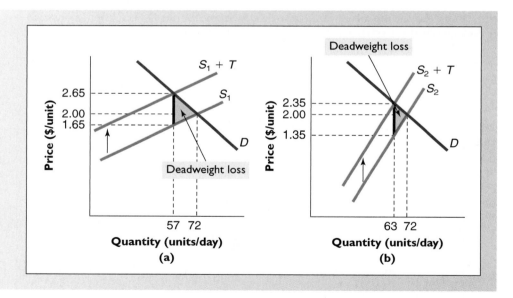

Similarly, the deadweight loss from a tax imposed on a good whose supply curve is perfectly inelastic will be zero. This explains why many economists continue to favour the tax Henry George advocated in the nineteenth century. George

[3]Encylopædia Britannica, 15th ed. (1986), vol. 5, p. 109; vol. 19, p. 652.

proposed that all taxes on labour and goods be abolished and replaced by a single tax on land. Such a tax, he argued, would cause no significant loss in economic surplus because the supply of land is almost perfectly inelastic. If either demand or supply is highly inelastic, then the equilibrium quantity changes little when a tax is imposed.

If demand for a good is highly inelastic, then much the same amount of the good is consumed, regardless of how much tax is added to consumer prices. If the supply of the good is highly inelastic, then producers will supply about the same amount of the good, whatever the producer price is. And if the equilibrium quantity produced and sold in the market changes little, the deadweight loss of taxation will be correspondingly small.

TAXES, EXTERNAL COSTS, AND EFFICIENCY

Even more attractive than taxing goods with inelastic supply or demand, from an efficiency standpoint, is taxing activities that people tend to pursue to excess. We mentioned activities that generate environmental pollution as one example; in later chapters we will discuss others. Whereas a tax on land does not reduce economic surplus, a tax on pollution can actually increase total economic surplus. Taxes on activities that cause harm to others have a "double dividend:" they generate revenue to pay for useful public services and at the same time discourage people from pursuing the harmful activities. The notion that taxes always and everywhere constitute an obstacle to efficiency simply does not withstand careful scrutiny. For example, Bob's willingness to pay to be inoculated against measles depends on how much that vaccination reduces his personal chances of contracting the disease. However, because vaccination also reduces the chances that Bob will transmit measles to Sue, vaccination provides benefits to Sue (and to others) that are not captured in his own private "willingness to pay." If all individuals act like Bob, and just pay attention to their own private benefits from vaccination, the equilibrium quantity of vaccination will be inefficiently low. However, a tax could be used to fund governmental provision of an efficient quantity of vaccinations.

RECAP   TAXES AND EFFICIENCY

A tax levied on each unit of a seller's product has the same effect on equilibrium quantity and price as a rise in marginal cost equal to the amount of the tax. The burden of a tax imposed on sellers will generally be shared among both buyers and sellers. In the extreme case of a good whose elasticity of supply is infinite, the entire burden of the tax is borne by buyers.

A tax imposed on a product whose supply and demand curves embody all relevant costs and benefits associated with its production and use will result in a deadweight loss—a reduction in total economic surplus in the market for the taxed good. Such taxes may nonetheless be justified if the value of the public services financed by the tax outweighs this deadweight loss. In general, the deadweight loss from a tax on a good will be smaller the smaller are the good's price elasticities of supply and demand. Taxes on activities that generate harm to others may produce a net gain in economic surplus, even apart from the value of the public services they finance.

▣ SUMMARY

- **6.1** In a perfectly competitive market when the supply and demand curves for a product capture all the relevant costs and benefits of producing and consuming that product, then market equilibrium for that product will be efficient. In such a market, if price and quantity do not equal their equilibrium values, a transaction can be found that will make at least some people better off without harming others. This assumes that a system for actually making such transactions is in place.

- **6.2** Total economic surplus is a measure of the amount by which participants in a market benefit by participating in it. It is the sum of total consumer surplus and total producer surplus in the market. For an individual buyer, the economic surplus from a transaction is the difference between the most the buyer would have been willing to pay and the amount actually paid. For an individual seller, the economic surplus from a transaction is the difference between the revenue received and the lowest amount at which the seller would have been willing to make the sale. Total economic surplus in a market is the sum of all producer and consumer surplus in that market. One of the attractive properties of market equilibrium is that it maximizes the value of total economic surplus.

- **6.2** Efficiency should not be equated with a social optimum. If we believe that the distribution of income among people is unjust, we will not like the results produced by the intersection of the supply and demand curves based on that income distribution, even if those results are efficient.

- **6.2** Even so, efficiency is important because it enhances our ability to achieve other goals. Whenever a perfectly competitive market is out of equilibrium, the economic pie can be made larger. And with a larger pie, everyone can have a larger slice, provided a system is in place for distributing the larger pie so that at least some individuals are actually made better off and no one is actually made worse off.

- **6.3** Regulations or policies that prevent competitive markets from reaching equilibrium—such as rent controls, price supports for agricultural products, and first-come–first-served allocation schemes—are often defended on the equity grounds. But such schemes reduce economic surplus, meaning that alternatives under which everyone is better off are conceivable.

- **6.4** Critics often complain that taxes make the economy less efficient. A tax will indeed reduce economic surplus if the supply and demand curves in the market for the taxed good reflect all the relevant costs and benefits of its production and consumption. But this decline in surplus has to be compared with the increase in economic surplus made possible by public goods financed with the proceeds of the tax. The best taxes are ones imposed on activities that would otherwise be pursued to excess, such as activities that generate environmental pollution. Such taxes are "best" because they do not reduce economic surplus; they actually increase it.

▣ KEY TERMS

consumer surplus (160)
deadweight loss (180)
demander's (or buyer's) reservation
price (159)

efficient (or Pareto-efficient) (155)
price ceiling (166)
price floor (173)
producer surplus (160)

supplier's (or seller's) reservation
price (159)
total economic surplus (158)

▣ REVIEW QUESTIONS

1. Why do economists emphasize efficiency as an important goal of public policy?

2. You are an MP considering how to vote on a policy that would reduce the economic surplus of workers by $1 million/year but increase the economic surplus of retirees by $10 million/year. What additional measure might you combine with the policy to ensure that the overall result is a better outcome for everyone?

3. How do elasticity of supply and elasticity of demand affect the size of the economic surplus a perfectly competitive market can offer?

4. How does elasticity of supply affect the loss of economic surplus caused by a price ceiling?

5. How does elasticity of supply affect the distributive impact of a price ceiling?

6. Why does the loss in total economic surplus directly experienced by participants in the market for a good that is taxed overstate the overall loss in economic surplus that results from the tax?

7. Why is compensating volunteers to relinquish their seats on overbooked flights more efficient than a policy of first-come–first-served?

8. Why do price supports reduce economic surplus?

PROBLEMS

1. Calculate the producer and consumer surplus for the market whose demand and supply curves are shown as follows.

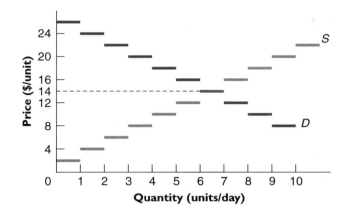

2. Suppose the weekly demand curve for wristwatches in Winnipeg is given by the equation $P = 12 - 0.25Q$, and the weekly supply of wristwatches is given by the equation $P = 6 + 0.75Q$, where P is the dollar price of a wristwatch and Q is the quantity of wristwatches measured in 100s. Sketch the weekly demand and supply curves in Winnipeg, and calculate:
   a. The weekly consumer surplus
   b. The weekly producer surplus
   c. The maximum weekly amount that producers and consumers in Winnipeg would be willing to pay to be able to buy and sell wristwatches in any given week

3. Refer to problem 2. Suppose a coalition of high-school students succeeds in persuading the local government to impose a price ceiling of $7.50 on wristwatches, on the grounds that local suppliers are taking advantage of teenagers by charging exorbitant prices.
   a. Calculate the weekly shortage of wristwatches that will result from this policy.
   b. Calculate the total economic surplus lost every week as a result of the price ceiling.
   c. In the face of the price ceiling, describe a transaction that would benefit both a buyer and a seller of wristwatches.

4. The Kubak crystal caves are renowned for their stalactites and stalagmites. The warden of the caves offers a tour each afternoon at 2 P.M. sharp. Only four people per day can see the caves without disturbing their fragile ecology. Occasionally, however, more than four people want to see the caves on the same day. The following table shows the list of people who wanted to see the caves on September 24, 2004, together with their respective times of arrival and reservation prices for taking the tour that day.

	Arrival time	Reservation price ($)
Herman	1:48	20
Jon	1:50	14
Kate	1:53	30
Jack	1:56	15
Penny	1:57	40
Fran	1:59	12
Faith	2:00	17

    a. If the tour is free and the warden operates it on a first-come–first-served basis, what will the total consumer surplus be for the four people who get to go on the tour on that day?

    b. Suppose the warden solicits volunteers to postpone their tour by offering increasing amounts of cash compensation until only four people still want to see the caves that day. If he gives each volunteer the same compensation payment, how much money will he have to offer to generate the required number of volunteers? What is the total economic surplus under this policy?

    c. Why is the compensation policy more efficient than the first-come–first-served policy?

    d. Describe a way of financing the warden's compensation payments that will make everyone, including the warden, either better off or no worse off than under the first-come–first-served approach.

5. Suppose the weekly demand for a certain good, in thousands of units, is given by the equation $P = 8 - Q$, and the weekly supply of the good by the equation $P = 2 + Q$, where P is the price in dollars.

    a. Calculate the total weekly economic surplus generated at the market equilibrium.

    b. Suppose a per-unit tax of $2, to be collected from sellers, is imposed in this market. Calculate the direct loss in economic surplus experienced by participants in this market as a result of the tax.

    c. How much government revenue will this tax generate each week? If the revenue is used to offset other taxes paid by participants in this market, what will be their net reduction in total economic surplus?

6. a. Graph the supply and demand equations given in problem 5.

    b. Now suppose that weekly demand for a good is the same as in problem 5, but weekly supply is $P = (5/3)Q$. Graph supply and demand on a pair of axes separate from the axes you used for 6(a).

    c. Determine equilibrium price and quantity implied by the equations given in 6(b). and compare with equilibrium price and quantity implied by the equations given in problem 5.

    d. Calculate the total surplus implied by the equations given in 6(b). Compare this with your answer for problem 5(a). Explain any difference you find, using no more than four sentences.

7. Refer to in-chapter Exercise 6.1. Suppose that a price ceiling of $0.50/litre is in effect for milk. Suppose the price ceiling is removed, and that equilibrium price and quantity are established, but nothing else happens. Who are the winners and losers when the price ceiling is removed? By how much do they win or lose?

8. A price support for milk will lead to a loss of economic efficiency because: (Choose one.):

    a. It will raise the marginal cost of milk above the marginal benefit of milk to consumers.

    b. It will cause a reduction in economic surplus.

    c. It will lead consumers to buy less milk than they would otherwise have bought.

    d. All of the above.

9. The government of Islandia, a small island nation, imports heating oil at a price of $2/litre and makes it available to citizens at a price of $1/litre. If Islandians' demand curve for heating oil is given by $P = 6 - Q$, where P is the price per litre in dollars and Q is the quantity in millions of litres per year, how much economic surplus is lost as a result of the government's policy?

10. Refer to problem 9. Suppose each of the one million Islandian households has the same demand curve for heating oil.

    a. Write an equation that gives an individual household's demand for oil.

    b. How much consumer surplus would each household lose if it had to pay $2/litre instead of $1/litre for heating oil, assuming there were no other changes in the household budget?

c. With the money saved by not subsidizing oil, by how much could the Islandian government afford to cut each family's annual taxes?

d. If the government abandoned its oil subsidy and implemented the tax cut, by how much would each family be better off?

e. How does the resulting total gain for the one million families compare with your calculation of the lost surplus in problem 9?

11. Is a company's producer surplus the same as its profit? (*Hint:* A company's total cost is equal to the sum of all marginal costs incurred in producing its output, plus any fixed costs.)

ANSWERS TO IN-CHAPTER EXERCISES

6.1 At a price of 50 cents/litre, there is excess demand of 4000 litres/day. Suppose a seller produces an extra litre of milk (marginal cost = 50 cents) and sells it to the buyer who would value it most (reservation price = $2.50) for $1.50. Both buyer and seller will gain an additional economic surplus of $1, and no other buyers or sellers will be hurt by the transaction.

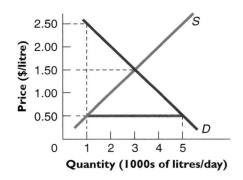

6.2 The new equilibrium price becomes $7/unit. Consumer surplus is now $(13 - 7) + (12 - 7) + (11 - 7) + (10 - 7) + (9 - 7) + (8 - 7) = \$21$. Producer surplus is $(7 - 1) + (7 - 2) + (7 - 3) + (7 - 4) + (7 - 5) + (7 - 6) = \$21$. Total economic surplus is $42.

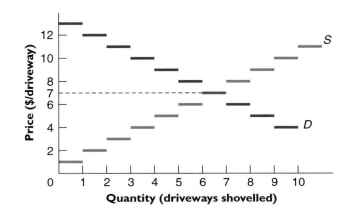

6.3 The new lost surplus is the area of the lined triangle in the following figure: $(\frac{1}{2})(\$250/\text{month})(1000 \text{ apartments/month}) = \$125\,000/\text{month}$.

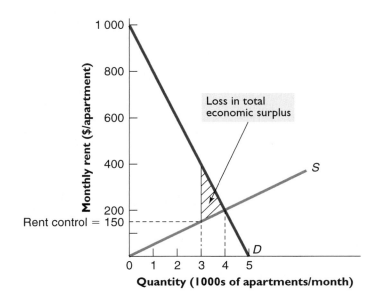

6.4 With the price support set at $40/metric ton, the public again purchases 2 million metric tons/month, and the government purchases the remaining 2 million metric tons farmers offer at that price. If none of the wheat purchased by the government goes to consumers, it will generate no benefit. So compared to the case without price supports, the lost benefit is equal to the area under the demand curve between 2 million and 3 million metric tons/month. The cost of producing the extra 1 million metric tons/month, which is the area under the supply curve between 3 million and 4 million metric tons/month, is also lost. The total loss in economic surplus caused by the price support is thus the area of the pale blue region shown in the following diagram, which is $70 million/month.

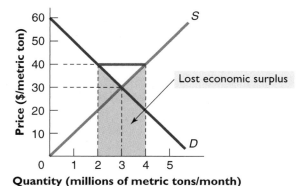

Notice that though the loss in total economic surplus is $70, the government actually pays $40 × 2 million metric tons = $80 million/month for the 2 million metric tons it purchases. You can unravel this paradox as follows: Producers receive a producer surplus of $20 million on the wheat the government buys [½($20 × 2 million metric tons) = $20 million]. In addition, when price is supported at $40/metric ton, consumers reduce their consumption from 3 to 2 million metric tons. Consumers thus lose a consumer surplus of 1/2($20 × 1 million metric tons) = $10 million. When the two effects are taken together, the net effect is an increase of $10 million in economic surplus: $20 million − $10 million = $10 million. Therefore, the monthly loss in total economic surplus is actually $10 million less than what the government pays for the wheat it buys: $80 million − $10 million = $70 million.

THE QUEST FOR PROFIT AND THE INVISIBLE HAND

C onsider the choice of ethnic cuisine in any small North American city. Twenty-five years ago, the city might have offered one or two Greek, a few Italian, and a few Chinese restaurants. Today, the same city with roughly the same population might have added Spanish, Indian, Thai, Japanese, Mexican, Vietnamese, and other restaurants. In some other industries, the choice is likely to have narrowed; the numbers of shoe repair and watch repair shops have probably declined.

Rare indeed is the marketplace in which buyers and sellers remain static for extended periods. Our small city is likely to have more body-piercing studios and fewer gas stations. Even in the same profession, the type of services provided probably has changed. For example, relatively more veterinarians might specialize in treatment of household pets and fewer in agricultural livestock.

Driving these changes is the businessowner's quest for profit. Businesses migrate to industries and locations in which profit opportunities abound and desert those whose prospects appear bleak. In perhaps the most widely quoted passage from his landmark treatise, *The Wealth of Nations,* Adam Smith wrote:

> It is not from the benevolence of the butcher, the brewer, or the baker that we expect our dinner, but from their regard of their own interest. We address ourselves not to their humanity, but to their self-love, and never talk to them of our necessities, but of their advantage.[1]

Smith went on to argue that although the entrepreneur "intends only his own gain," he is "led by an invisible hand to promote an end which was no part of his intention." As Smith saw it, even though self-interest is the prime mover of economic activity, the end result is an allocation of goods and services that serves society's collective interests remarkably well. If producers are offering "too much" of one product and "not enough" of another, profit opportunities immediately alert entrepreneurs to that fact and provide incentives for them to take remedial action. All the while, the system exerts relentless pressure on pro-

[1]Adam Smith, *The Wealth of Nations,* New York: Everyman's Library, E.P. Dutton, 1910 (1776), Book I, and *The Wealth of Nations* with an introduction by Max Lerner and an introduction by Edwin Cannan. Edited by Edwin Cannan. New York, Random House, Inc., 1965 (1776), Book I, Chapter II, p.14.

Why do most North American cities now have more tattoo parlours and fewer watch repair shops than in 1972?

ducers to hold the price of each good close to its cost of production, and indeed to reduce that cost in any ways possible.

Our task in this chapter is to gain deeper insight into the nature of the forces that guide the invisible hand. What exactly does "profit" mean? How is it measured, and how does the quest for it serve society's ends? And if competition holds price close to the cost of production, why do some entrepreneurs become fabulously wealthy? We will also discuss cases in which misunderstanding of Smith's theory results in costly errors, both in everyday decision making and in the realm of government policy.

■ 7.1 THE CENTRAL ROLE OF ECONOMIC PROFIT

The economic theory of business behaviour is built on the assumption that the firm's goal is to maximize its profit. So we must be clear at the outset about what, exactly, profit means.

THREE TYPES OF PROFIT

The economist's understanding of profit is different from the accountant's, and the distinction between the two is important in understanding how the invisible hand works. Accountants define the annual profit of a business as the difference between the revenue it takes in over the year and its **explicit costs** for the period, which are the actual payments the firm makes to its factors of production and other suppliers. Profit thus defined is called **accounting profit:**[2]

$$\text{accounting profit} = \text{total revenue} - \text{explicit costs}.$$

explicit costs the actual payments a firm makes to its factors of production and other suppliers

accounting profit the difference between a firm's total revenue and its explicit costs

Accounting profit is the most familiar profit concept in everyday discourse. It is the one that companies use, for example, when they provide statements about their profits in press releases or annual reports.

Particularly in the small business sector, however, the owners of a company may supply labour or other resources (e.g., land) to the firm without making an explicit charge for salary or rent. Economists, therefore, define profit as the difference between the firm's total revenue and not just its explicit costs but also its **implicit costs,** which are the opportunity costs of all the resources supplied by the firm's owners. Profit thus defined is called **economic profit:**

$$\text{economic profit} = \text{total revenue} - \text{explicit costs} - \text{implicit costs}.$$

implicit costs all the firm's opportunity costs of the resources supplied by the firm's owners and for which the owners do not make an explicit charge

economic or excess profit the difference between a firm's total revenue and the sum of its explicit and implicit costs

To illustrate the difference between accounting profit and economic profit, consider a firm with $400 000 in total annual revenue. The firm incurs explicit costs of $250 000/year to lease its building and pay its employees. The owners of this firm also have invested $1 million in the shares of the company to finance the firm's operations. This firm's accounting profit, then, is the difference between its total revenue of $400 000/year and its explicit costs of $250 000/year, or $150 000/year.

However, explicit costs often are only part of the opportunity costs a firm incurs. Some opportunity costs are implicit. To calculate a firm's economic profit, we must include both explicit and implicit opportunity costs. Suppose the current annual interest rate on savings accounts is 10 percent. Suppose, too, that this is the best alternate use of the funds the owners have invested. Had the owners not put their funds into the firm, they could have earned an additional $100 000/year

[2]For most firms, there will not be an exact match between the timing of payments and the actual use of resources. For example, when a firm ships goods to a customer toward the end of one financial year, the cheque that pays for the goods may actually be received some time in the next financial year. As well, a machine that is bought this year will normally produce output for several years in the future before wearing out. Therefore, the cost of the machine this year is the out-of-pocket costs of use plus the change in its value (i.e., depreciation). Accountants therefore have to devise rules in order to allocate receipts and explicit costs to the correct financial year—but the basic point remains.

interest by depositing their $1 million in a savings account. So the firm's economic profit is $400 000/year − $250 000/year − $100 000/year = $50 000/year.

Note that this economic profit is smaller than the accounting profit by exactly the amount of the firm's implicit costs—the $100 000/year opportunity cost of the resources supplied by the firm's owners. This difference between a business's accounting profit and its economic profit is called its **normal profit. Normal profit is simply the opportunity cost of the resources supplied to a business by its owners.** A normal profit is just sufficient to hold a firm in an industry, but it provides no incentive for new firms to enter the industry.

Figure 7.1 illustrates the difference between accounting and economic profit. Panel (a) represents a firm's total revenues, while panels (b) and (c) show how these revenues are apportioned among the various cost and profit categories.

Examples 7.1 to 7.5 illustrate why the distinction between accounting and economic profit is so important.

normal profit the opportunity cost of the resources supplied by the firm's owners; normal profit = accounting profit − economic profit

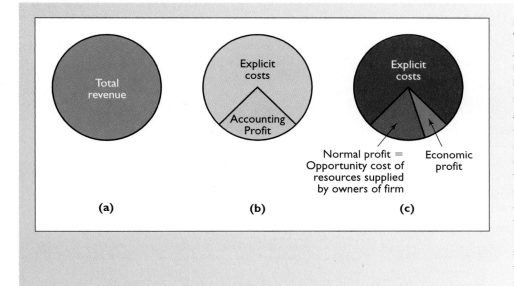

(a) (b) (c)

FIGURE 7.1

The Difference between Accounting Profit and Economic Profit
Panel (a): A firm's total revenues. Panel (b): Accounting profit is the difference between total revenue and explicit costs. Panel (c): Normal profit is the opportunity cost of all resources supplied by firm's owners. Economic profit is the difference between total revenue and all costs, explicit and implicit (also equal to the difference between accounting profit and normal profit).

"All I know, Harrison, is that I've been on the board forty years and have yet to see an excess profit."

EXAMPLE 7.1

Should Bernard Buffet stay in the farming business?

Bernard Buffet is a farmer who lives near Regina. His annual expenses are $6000 to lease the land he farms plus $4000 for equipment rental and supplies. The only input he supplies is his own labour, and he considers farming just as attractive as his only other employment opportunity, which is managing a retail store at a salary of $11 000/year. Apart from the matter of pay, Bernard is indifferent between farming and being a manager. Wheat sells for a constant price per bushel in an international market too large to be affected by changes in one farmer's wheat production. Bernard's revenue from wheat sales is $22 000/year. What is his accounting profit? his economic profit? his normal profit? Will he remain a wheat farmer?

As shown in Table 7.1, Bernard's accounting profit is $12 000/year, the difference between his $22 000 annual revenue and his $10 000 yearly payment for land, equipment, and supplies. His economic profit is that amount less the opportunity cost of his labour, which is the $11 000/year he could have earned as a store manager. Thus, he is making an economic profit of $1000/year. Finally, his normal profit is the $11 000 opportunity cost of the only resource he supplies, namely, his labour. Since Bernard likes the two jobs equally well, he will be better off by $1000/year if he remains in farming.

TABLE 7.1
Revenue, Cost, and Profit Summary for Example 7.1

Total revenue ($/year)	Explicit costs ($/year)	Implicit costs ($/year)	Accounting profit (= total revenue − explicit costs) ($/year)	Economic profit (= total revenue − explicit costs − implicit costs) ($/year)	Normal profit (= implicit costs) ($/year)
22 000	10 000	11 000	12 000	1 000	11 000

EXAMPLE 7.2

If Bernard's annual revenue falls by $2000, will he stay in farming?

Refer to Example 7.1. How will Bernard's economic profit change if his annual revenue from wheat production is not $22 000 but $20 000? Will he continue to farm?

As shown in Table 7.2, Bernard's accounting profit is now $10 000, the difference between his $20 000 annual revenue and his $10 000/year payment for land, equipment, and supplies. His economic profit is that amount minus the

TABLE 7.2
Revenue, Cost, and Profit Summary for Example 7.2

Total revenue ($/year)	Explicit costs ($/year)	Implicit costs ($/year)	Accounting profit (= total revenue − explicit costs) ($/year)	Economic profit (= total revenue − explicit costs − implicit costs) ($/year)	Normal profit (= implicit costs) ($/year)
20 000	10 000	11 000	10 000	−1 000	11 000

opportunity cost of his labour—again, the $11 000/year he could have earned as a store manager. So Bernard is now earning a negative economic profit, −$1000/year. As before, his normal profit is $11 000/year, the opportunity cost of his labour. Although an accountant would say Bernard is making an annual profit of $10 000, that amount is less than a normal profit for his activity. An economist would therefore say that Bernard is making an **economic loss** of $1000/year. Since Bernard likes the two jobs equally well, he will be better off by $1000/year if he leaves farming to become a manager.

economic loss an economic profit that is less than zero

If Bernard makes an economic profit in farming, he will prefer farming to his best alternative occupation. If he makes a negative economic profit as a farmer, he will prefer his best alternative occupation to farming. When he makes a normal profit (i.e., when his economic profit is zero), Bernard will be indifferent between farming and his best alternative occupation; he will have no reason to leave farming.

Recall that in Example 7.2, Bernard was making an economic loss of $1000 annually. His expenditures included $6000/year to lease land. You might think that if Bernard could save enough money to buy his land, his best option would be to remain a farmer. After all, he no longer would be spending $6000 to lease land. But as Example 7.3 makes clear, that impression is based on a failure to perceive the difference between accounting profit and economic profit.

Does owning the land make a difference?

EXAMPLE 7.3

Suppose Bernard's Uncle Warren, who owns the farmland Bernard has been renting, dies and leaves Bernard that parcel of land. If the land could be rented to some other farmer for $6000/year, will Bernard remain in farming?

As shown in Table 7.3, if Bernard continues to farm his own land, his accounting profit will be $16 000/year, or $6000 more than before. But his economic profit will be the same as before (−$1000/year) because Bernard must deduct the $6000/year opportunity cost of farming his own land. The reduction of $6000 in explicit costs is exactly offset by an increase of $6000 in implicit costs. If other farmers have tastes like Bernard's and face similar outside employment opportunities, the normal profit from owning and operating a farm like his will be $17 000/year, the opportunity cost of the land and labour provided by the farmer. But since Bernard earns an accounting profit of only $16 000, he will again do better to abandon farming for the managerial job.

TABLE 7.3
Revenue, Cost, and Profit Summary for Example 7.3

Total revenue ($/year)	Explicit costs ($/year)	Implicit costs ($/year)	Accounting profit (= total revenue − explicit costs) ($/year)	Economic profit (= total revenue − explicit costs − implicit costs) ($/year)	Normal profit (= implicit costs) ($/year)
20 000	4 000	17 000	16 000	−1 000	17 000

Needless to say, Bernard would be wealthier as an owner than he was as a renter. But the question of whether to remain a farmer is answered the same way whether Bernard rents his farmland or owns it.

EXAMPLE 7.4

What would happen to land values if *all* farmers around Regina earned less than normal profit?

Suppose the conditions confronting Bernard Buffet in Example 7.2 are essentially the same as those confronting all other farmers around Regina; that is, all earn less than a normal profit. What economic changes will result?

We have been assuming that if a farmer leaves farming, he can do something else. As an alternative to farming, Bernard can manage a store. Some farmland may not have alternative uses—either it is farmed or it is not used for anything. If all farmers around Regina are making economic losses, some farmers will switch to other activities. This will reduce the demand for farmland, and, especially if there are no competing uses for farmland, the market price of farmland will fall. As its market price falls, the opportunity cost of farmland to any individual farmer will fall. If Bernard owns his own land, the payment any other farmer is willing to make for use of that land will fall as the demand for farmland declines. The price of farmland will continue to fall until farmers around Regina can once again earn a normal profit. Specifically, the price of land will fall until the yearly rental for a farm like Bernard's is only $5000, for at that rent the accounting profit of those who farmed their own land would be $16 000/year, exactly the same as normal profit. Their economic profit would be zero.

EXAMPLE 7.5

What will happen to land values if all farmers earn *more* than a normal profit?

Suppose wheat growers farm 800 hectares of their own land, which sells for $100/hectare. Each farm's revenue from wheat sales is $20 000/year. Equipment and other supplies cost $4000/year, and the current annual interest rate on savings accounts is 5 percent. Farmers can earn $11 000/year in alternative jobs that they like equally as well as farming. What is normal economic profit for these farmers? How much accounting profit will they earn? How much economic profit? Is their economic situation stable? If not, how is it likely to change?

As shown in Table 7.4, accounting profit—the difference between the $20 000 annual revenue and the $4000 annual expense for equipment and supplies—is $16 000/year, as in Example 7.3. Normal profit is the opportunity cost of the farmer's time and land—$11 000 for his time and $4000 for his land (since had he sold the land for $80 000 and put the money in the bank at 5 percent interest, he would have earned $4000/year in interest)—for a total of $15 000. Accounting profit thus exceeds normal profit by $1000/year, which means that farmers are earning an economic profit of $1000/year.

TABLE 7.4
Revenue, Cost, and Profit Summary for Example 7.5

Total revenue ($/year)	Explicit costs ($/year)	Implicit costs ($/year)	Accounting profit (= total revenue − explicit costs) ($/year)	Economic profit (= total revenue − explicit costs − implicit costs) ($/year)	Normal profit (= implicit costs) ($/year)
20 000	4 000	15 000	16 000	1 000	15 000

To see whether this situation is stable, we must ask whether people have an incentive to change their behaviour. Consider the situation from the perspective of a manager who is earning $11 000/year. To switch to farming, he would need to borrow $80 000 to buy land, which would mean interest payments of $4000/year. With $20 000/year in revenue from wheat sales and $4000/year in expenses for supplies and equipment, in addition to $4000/year in interest payments, the manager would earn an accounting profit of $12 000/year. And since that amount is $1000/year more than the opportunity cost of the manager's time, he will want to switch to farming. Indeed, *all* managers will want to switch to farming because at current land prices, a farmer can make an economic profit.

As we know from the equilibrium principle, however, such situations are not stable. There is only so much farmland to go around, so as demand for farmland increases, its price will begin to rise. The price will keep rising until there is no longer any incentive for managers to switch to farming.

EQUILIBRIUM

How much must the price of land rise to eliminate the incentive to switch? If 800 hectares of land sold for $100 000 (that is, if land sold for $125/hectare), the interest on the money borrowed to buy a farm would be $5000/year, an amount that would reduce economic profit to zero and make workers indifferent between farming or being a manager. But if land sells for anything less than $125/hectare, there will be excess demand for farmland.

A farm is a type of firm. A **firm** is an organization that combines factors of production to produce a good or service or some combination of goods and services. A perfectly competitive firm produces one good of uniform quality.

A wheat farm is a firm that combines factors of production to produce wheat. We will continue to use a wheat farm as an example in what follows. Keep in mind, however, that what we are describing as pertaining to a wheat farm operating in a perfectly competitive market would pertain to any perfectly competitive firm.[3]

firm an organization that combines factors of production to produce a good or service or some combination of goods and services; a perfectly competitive firm produces one good of uniform quality

WHAT HAPPENS IF ALL FARMERS MAKE AN ECONOMIC PROFIT?

Consider panel (a) of Figure 7.2. Assume that technology and the stock of capital used on the farm are fixed. Durable inputs to the production process, such as tools, machinery, and buildings, constitute the stock of **capital**. The curve labelled ATC_s is a graph of average total cost for different quantities of wheat produced by an 800-hectare farm. Because the size of the farm, capital, and technology cannot be changed quickly, in the short run they are fixed, so ATC_s is a short-run cost curve. Given a farm of 800 hectares, ATC_s represents the lowest cost per unit of wheat that can be achieved for any given quantity of wheat. For example, ATC_s shows that if 12 000 bushels (bu) are produced, the cost per bushel will be $2.12. If 12 000 bushels are produced on an 800-hectare farm, it is not possible to reduce the cost per bushel below $2.12. Notice, too, that if the farm produces 10 000 bushels of wheat per year, the cost per bushel will be $2.10. Given that the size of Bernard's farm and its capital stock are fixed, this is the lowest cost per bushel that can be achieved.

capital any durable inputs to the production process, such as tools, machinery, and buildings

The curve labelled MC_s in panel (a) is the marginal cost curve for wheat. For example, if Bernard chooses to produce 12 000 bu/year, marginal cost is $2.20— when 12 000 bu/year are being produced, one more bushel can be produced for $2.20. Because the size of Bernard's farm and the amount of capital being used are fixed, MC_s is a short-run marginal cost curve.

Panel (b) of Figure 7.2 represents the market for wheat. To be consistent with panel (a), which gives a short-run picture for one farm, panel (b) gives a short-run

[3]The Canadian Wheat Board influences the marketing of Canadian wheat; however, to keep things simple, we do not analyze the effects of the Canadian Wheat Board in what follows.

FIGURE 7.2

The Firm, the Market, and a Shift in the Short-Run Supply: Responses of a Wheat Farm and the Wheat Market
Panel (a) pertains to the firm's short-run supply cost and shows its marginal cost curve for wheat. Panel (b) pertains to the market for wheat and shows the shift of the short-run supply curve in response to an increase in demand.

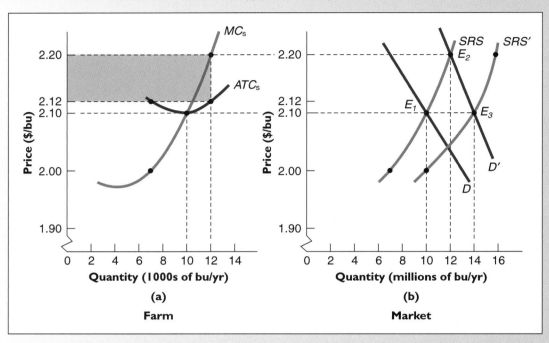

picture of the market. In the short run, the number of farms serving the market, the size of each farm, and the amount of capital each farm uses are fixed. If we say that the wheat industry is the group of farms that supplies the market for wheat, the number of firms in the wheat industry is fixed in the short run.

To keep things simple, we assume that initially 1000 identical farms supply wheat to the wheat market. When 1000 farms serve the market, the short-run supply curve SRS of panel (b) pertains. Suppose equilibrium price is $2.10/bu, as determined by SRS and the demand curve D. Like all the other wheat farmers, Bernard is a price taker, and his marginal revenue equals market price. To maximize profit, Bernard produces the quantity of wheat that causes price to equal marginal cost. Thus, panel (a) shows that Bernard will produce 10 000 bu/year of wheat. Panel (b) shows that when 1000 identical farmers make the same decision, 10 million bu/yr of wheat are supplied to the wheat market:

$$1000 \text{ farms} \times 10\ 000 \text{ bu/farm/yr} = 10\ 000\ 000 \text{ bu/yr.}$$

Further, because price per bushel equals cost per bushel, each farmer makes a normal profit by producing 10 000 bu/yr. Short-run equilibrium in the market is at E_1—the intersection of demand curve D and short-run supply curve SRS.

Now suppose that because a virulent strain of potato bug appears, the world's supply of potatoes is greatly reduced, and the price of potatoes rises dramatically. As a result, consumers reduce consumption of potatoes and increase consumption of bread and pasta. The demand for wheat increases to D' [panel (b)], causing the price of wheat to rise to $2.20/bu. Following the rule for maximizing profits, Bernard increases the amount of wheat he produces to 12 000 bu/yr [panel (a)], as do every one of the 1000 wheat farmers. Thus, panel (b) shows the new equilibrium E_2, where demand curve D' intersects supply curve SRS. At a price of $2.20, 12 million bu/yr are supplied to the wheat market.

Panel (a) shows that if price is $2.20/bu and 12 000 bushels/yr are supplied, average total cost will be $2.12/bu. Therefore, a farmer makes an economic profit of $0.08/bu:

$$\$2.20/bu - \$2.12/bu = \$0.08/bu.$$

The area of the green rectangle in panel (a) represents Bernard's total economic profit per year:

$$\$0.08/bu \times 12\ 000\ bu/yr = \$960.00/yr.$$

This is an amount in excess of Bernard's normal profit. Each of the 1000 identical wheat farmers is earning the same annual economic profit. As long as price is $2.20/bu, and no new farmers can enter the market to supply wheat, the farmers will continue to make this economic profit.

But what happens if new farmers can enter the wheat market? (One way this could happen is if farmers switch crops—e.g., farmers who are now producing canola or soybeans decide to grow wheat instead.) This would allow the number of wheat farms to increase, which would increase the size of the wheat industry. Any change in the number of farms that supply wheat is a long-run adjustment. Can economic profit persist in the long run? Remember that economic profit is a return in excess of opportunity cost. If other individuals perceive that by supplying wheat, they can make an economic profit, new farmers will enter the market and supply wheat. As they do so, short-run supply will increase, and competition in the wheat market will cause price to fall. According to the equilibrium principle, farmers will enter the wheat market until the price of wheat falls low enough to reduce economic profit to zero. Panel (b) of Figure 7.2 shows the long-run equilibrium E_3 where price returns to $2.10/bu when short-run supply has increased to SRS', and the quantity of wheat supplied has risen to 14 million bu/yr. At a price of $2.10/bu, Bernard again produces 10 000 bushels/yr, where cost per bushel is minimized. At the same time, 400 new wheat farmers have entered the market, increasing the total number of identical wheat farms to 14 000. Each farm produces 10 000 bu/yr, each farmer makes a normal profit, cost per bushel is minimized, and the total quantity of wheat supplied is 140 million bu/yr:

EQUILIBRIUM

$$14\ 000\ farms \times 10\ 000\ bu/farm/year = 140\ 000\ 000\ bu/yr.$$

By assuming that participants in a perfectly competitive market are free to enter (or leave) the market, we see that in the long run, economic profit will be competed away by new suppliers.

RECAP	THE CENTRAL ROLE OF ECONOMIC PROFIT

A firm's accounting profit is the difference between its revenue and the sum of all explicit costs it incurs. Economic profit is the difference between the firm's revenue and *all* costs it incurs—both explicit and implicit. Normal profit is the opportunity cost of the resources supplied by the owners of the firm.

■ 7.2 HOW COMPETITION AFFECTS THE SIZE OF FIRMS

Suppose that the curve labelled *ATC*1 in panel (a), Figure 7.3, is the average total cost curve for a 400-hectare wheat farm. Curve *ATC*2 is the average total cost curve for an 800-hectare wheat farm. The smaller farm will show an economic loss if price is $2.10/bu. However, if demand rises from D to D' [see panel (b)], price rises to $2.20/bu, and at this price, the smaller farm will show an economic profit. However, in the long run farms can buy new machinery or change their size—and new farms can enter the industry. We have shown that at $2.20/bu, entry of new suppliers will cause supply to increase until economic profit is zero. Under perfect competition, if 800-hectare farms earn an economic profit, the number of 800-hectare farms will increase until, in accord with the equilibrium principle, price falls in the long run to $2.10/bu, and 800-hectare farms are making only a normal profit. At $2.10/bu, 400-hectare farms make an economic loss. In the long run, farms at that size will tend to disappear, either withdrawing from farming or combining with larger farms.

EQUILIBRIUM

FIGURE 7.3
Scale and Market Equilibrium: Two Sizes of Wheat Farm and the Market
Panel (a) shows the cost curves for farms of two different sizes or scales of operation. Panel (b) shows that even if demand increases from D to D', a price of $2.20/bu cannot persist. Entry of new farms will shift supply from SRS to SRS' and price will return to $2.10/bu.

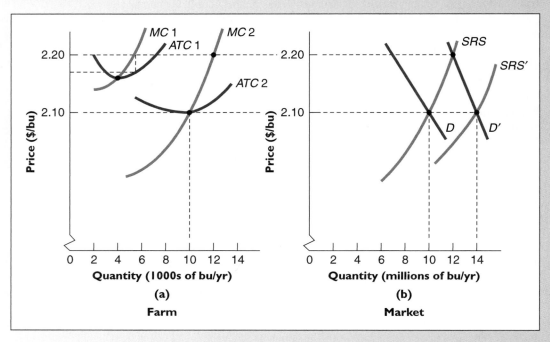

(a) Farm   (b) Market

Of course, farms could be of many sizes other than 400 and 800 hectares. Figure 7.4 pertains when farms of five different sizes are possible. It shows five short-run average total cost curves. Each short-run average cost curve pertains to a farm of given size. Suppose the smallest farm considered in Figure 7.4 is 250 hectares, and that $ATC1$ pertains to that firm. If this farm produces 2000 bushels per year, $ATC1$ shows cost will be $2.17/bu. If the farm produces a different quantity of wheat, its cost per bushel will be different. Curve $ATC2$ pertains to the next largest farm, and so on, with $ATC5$ pertaining to the largest farm. Thus, each average total cost curve shows cost per unit of wheat for different quantities produced by a farm of given size. Curve $ATC3$ of Figure 7.4 pertains to an 800-hectare farm; therefore, $ATC3$ is identical to ATC in Figure 7.2.

The heavy blue curve, labelled $LRAC$, is the long-run average cost curve. It shows the lowest cost per bushel that can be obtained for any quantity of wheat, given that farms of different sizes are possible. Consider 8000 bu/yr. Reading

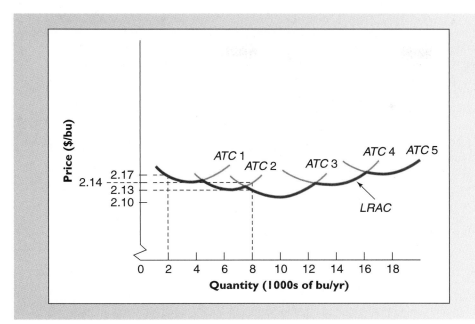

FIGURE 7.4
Long-Run Average Cost

from *ATC*3, we see that if 8000 bushels per year are produced, cost per bushel will be $2.13. However, a smaller farm, whose costs are represented by *ATC*2, can also produce 8000 bushels. Figure 7.4 shows that if it does, the smaller farm's cost will be $2.14/bu. Nevertheless, $2.14 does not appear on *LRAC* because in the long run, it is possible to achieve a cost lower than $2.14/bu when producing 8000 bushels by choosing a farm of the next larger size. In general, any part of any short-run average total cost curve that lies above *LRAC* cannot be part of the long-run average cost curve. Why? Because by definition, **long-run average cost** is the minimum cost per unit that can be achieved for a given level of output, assuming that technology is constant. In the long run, all factors of production, and therefore all costs, are variable. Thus, the size of a farm can change. Long-run average cost for any quantity of wheat is always determined by referring to the size of farm that achieves minimum cost per unit for that quantity of output.

Because all factors of production, all costs, and the size of a firm are variable in the long run, managers of a firm can plan the best way to combine factors of production. They can also choose the best size for the firm. Therefore, the long run is also referred to as a firm's planning horizon. When Bernard considers the long run, he presumably will try to plan the most profitable combination of factors of production for his farm, including the most profitable size of his farm. Notice that in the long run, he can choose the size of his farm; indeed, he can choose whether to continue farming.

The size of a farm can be varied almost continually. When this is taken into account, the long-run average cost curve takes the smooth shape shown in panel (a) of Figure 7.5. In the long run, competition will cause farms to gravitate toward the size that minimizes long-run average cost. As shown in panel (b), in long-run perfectly competitive equilibrium, minimum long-run average cost equals market price. Farms that are either too small or too large to produce at minimum long-run average cost will disappear in the long run.

long-run average cost the lowest cost per unit that can be achieved for a given level of output when all factors of production, all costs, and the size of the firm are variable, but technology is constant

LONG-RUN MARKET SUPPLY

Long-run market supply can be developed from short-run market supply curves, such as those shown in Figure 7.2. The cost curves in panel (a) and the demand and short-run market supply curves in panel (b) of Figure 7.6 are the same as

FIGURE 7.5

Long-Run Equilibrium in a Perfectly Competitive Market

The long-run average cost curve is shown in panel (a), while panel (b) shows that market price equals minimum long-run average cost.

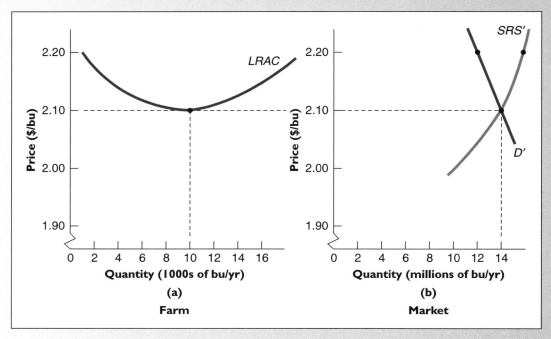

(a)

Farm

(b)

Market

the cost, demand, and short-run supply curves shown in Figure 7.2. However, in Figure 7.6, the equilibrium point of D and SRS is joined with the equilibrium point of D' and SRS' to form the long-run market supply curve, which is labelled LRS. Recall that in the long run, the number of farms that produce wheat can rise or fall. Panel (b) of Figure 7.6 shows that if demand rises from D to D', in the long run, the quantity of wheat exchanged in the wheat market rises from $Q1$ to $Q3$. However, when long run adjustments are complete, the quantity of wheat produced by the farm represented in panel (a) is the same as it was before demand increased from D to D'. In the long run, the entire increase from $Q1$ to $Q3$ is accomplished by the entry of new farms, each producing at its minimum long-run average cost. The number of farms has increased, but the quantity of wheat produced by each farm is unchanged. Further, because long-run market supply in Figure 7.6 is horizontal, market price returns to what it was before demand increased from D to D'.

Long-run market supply is horizontal because we assumed that as the number of farms serving the wheat market rises, the prices that farmers pay for the factors of production they employ remain constant. However, it may well be that as the number of farms increases, prices paid for factors of production used by farmers are bid up. This would cause the cost curves of individual farms to shift up, and long-run market supply will have a positive slope. Suppose, for example, that as the number of farms increases, the prices of land and other inputs are bid up. Figure 7.7 shows this case. As the number of farms increases in response to an increase in the demand for wheat, from the point of view of individual farmers, long-run average cost increases from $LRAC1$ to $LRAC2$, as shown in panel (a). As a result, even after long-run adjustments are complete, market price is higher. Thus, panel (b) shows long-run market supply with a positive slope. Of course, those who owned land before its price was bid up benefit because their land has become more valuable. In the same way, if the demand for

FIGURE 7.6

Long-Run Supply (LRS) in a Perfectly Competitive Market—Case I: Constant Opportunity Cost of Inputs

Panel (a) shows the firm's long-run average cost curve, while panel (b) shows the demand, and short-run and long-run market supply curves. Long-run market supply is horizontal and pertains to a constant cost industry.

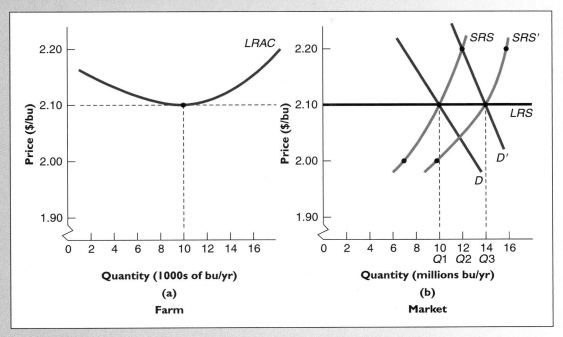

FIGURE 7.7

Long-Run Supply in a Perfectly Competitive Market—Case II: Cost of Inputs Rises as Short-Run Supply Increases

Panel (a): As the number of farms increases in response to an increase in the demand for wheat, long-run average cost increases from *LRAC*1 to *LRAC*2. Panel (b): After long-run adjustments are complete, market price is higher, so long-run market supply has a positive slope and pertains to an increasing cost industry.

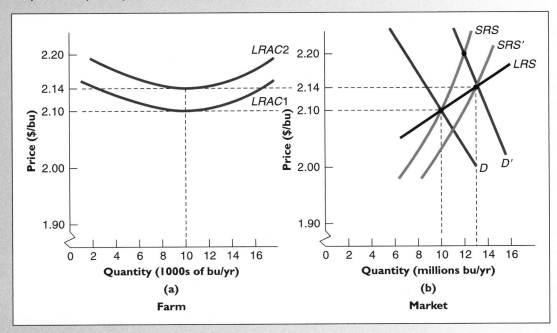

**www.uvic.ca/econ
University of Victoria**

wheat falls and causes the value of land to decline, landowners will see the value of land decrease.[4]

THE EFFECT OF MARKET FORCES ON ECONOMIC PROFIT

A firm's normal profit is just a cost of doing business. Thus the owner of a firm that earns no more than a normal profit has managed only to recover the opportunity cost of the resources invested in the firm. By contrast, the owner of a firm that makes a positive economic profit earns more than the opportunity cost of the invested resources; the owner earns a normal profit and then some. Naturally, everyone would be delighted to earn more than a normal profit, and no one wants to earn less. The result is that those markets in which firms are earning an economic profit tend to attract additional resources, whereas markets in which firms are experiencing economic losses tend to lose resources.

EQUILIBRIUM

The net result of these resource movements is that in the long run, when new firms can easily enter the industry, all firms will tend to earn zero economic profit. They would all, of course, like to make more, but the dynamics of entry into and exit from the market will mean that in long-run equilibrium, nobody does.

7.1   # ECONOMIC NATURALIST

Why do supermarket checkout lines all tend to be roughly the same length?

Pay careful attention the next few times you go grocery shopping, and you'll notice that the lines at all the checkout stations tend to be roughly the same length. Suppose you saw one line that was significantly shorter than the others as you wheeled your cart toward the checkout area. Which line would you choose? The shorter one, of course. Everyone else will do the same, and the short line will quickly lengthen. You and the other shoppers will probably check the load in each other's carts and the speed of the cashiers, too. Lines will quickly adjust so that expected waiting time is equalized.

EXERCISE 7.1   **Use the equilibrium principle to explain why the cars in a subway train all tend to be equally crowded during rush hour.**

RECAP	**HOW COMPETITION AFFECTS THE SIZE OF FIRMS**

When a firm's accounting profit is exactly equal to the opportunity cost of the inputs supplied by the firm's owners, the firm's economic profit is zero. Industries in which firms earn a positive economic profit attract new firms. Firms leave industries in which they sustain economic loss. In each case the adjustments continue until economic profit equals zero.

If a market initially is in a long-run, perfectly competitive equilibrium, an increase in demand causes market price to rise. In the short run, the number of firms serving a market does not change. Firms already in the market respond to the higher price by increasing their output, causing the quantity exchanged on the market to increase. The higher market price lets existing firms earn an economic profit. That economic profit attracts new firms, which enter the market until competition reduces economic profit to zero.

---

[4]It is conceptually possible for long-run average cost to shift down as the number of firms serving a market increases. In this case, long-run market supply would have a negative slope. The empirical relevance of this case is doubtful.

> When long-run adjustments are complete, more firms are supplying the market, and each firm is operating at minimum long-run average cost and earning a normal profit. If the prices of factors of production used by the firms are not bid up as new firms enter, market price will return to what it was before the increase in demand, and the long-run market supply curve will be horizontal. If prices of factors of production rise as new firms enter, long-run market supply will have a positive slope. If a decrease in demand causes economic losses in a perfectly competitive market, a similar set of adjustments occurs, though working in the opposite direction.

▊ 7.3 FIRM SIZE AND THE SHAPE OF THE LONG-RUN AVERAGE COST CURVE

Figure 7.5 shows minimum long-run average cost occurring at a single quantity of output. This implies that a farm of only one size can achieve minimum long-run average cost. If this is true, in the long run, wheat farms will all be the same size. However, it is possible, perhaps even likely, that minimum long-run average cost can be achieved over a range of output, and by farms of a number of different sizes. This possibility is represented in Figure 7.8.

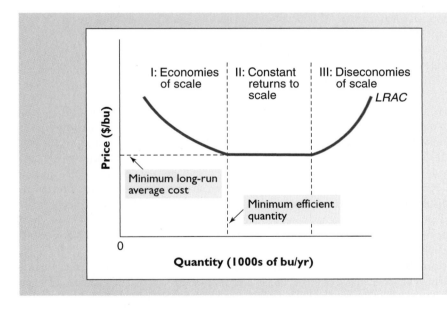

FIGURE 7.8
Long-Run Average Cost and Returns to Scale
The curve *LRAC* portrays economies of scale, constant returns to scale, and diseconomies of scale.

The long-run average cost curve, *LRAC*, of Figure 7.8 is divided into sections I, II, and III, which represent economies of scale, constant returns to scale, and diseconomies of scale, respectively. **Scale** refers to the size of a firm relative to other possible sizes of firms serving a particular market. Over section I, **economies of scale** are achieved as the size, or scale, of an operation increases and causes long-run average cost to decrease as output increases.

Economies of scale can arise because specialization and division of labour can be greater in a larger firm than a smaller one. Adam Smith noted in 1776 that this can be a very important factor in manufacturing even so simple an item as a pin.[5]

scale the size of a firm relative to other possible sizes of firms serving a particular market

economies of scale a situation in which long-run average cost decreases as a firm's output increases

---

[5]Adam Smith, *The Wealth of Nations*, with introductions by Max Lerner and Edwin Cannan. Edited by Edwin Cannan. New York, Random House, Inc., 1965 (1776), Book I, Chapter I, p. 4.

He noted that in the seventeenth century the manufacturing of pins was divided into as many as 18 different tasks—one worker straightened the wire, another cut it, another fastened the head, and so on. Workers are much more productive if they specialize because they learn a limited set of tasks well, and they spend less time moving from one task to another. The same type of economies could be important on a wheat farm. For example, a large farm might be better able than a small one to use a custom combining crew at harvest time.

Economies of scale may also occur because some factors of production, and therefore some costs of setup, are indivisible. Some minimal amount of an **indivisible factor of production** is necessary if a productive activity, even of minimal size, is to occur at all. Presumably any farm, regardless of how small it is, requires a tractor sufficiently large to be capable of basic tasks such as pulling machinery that will till the soil. (It probably is technically possible to manufacture very small tractors, but beyond some point, a small tractor is not useful. A very small one would just get lost in the weeds.) The cost of an indivisible factor of production is an **indivisible cost**.

A third source of economies of scale depends on geometry. If, for example, you wanted to build a round silo, you would find that the cost of materials and labour depends on the amount of materials needed, which depends on the circumference of the silo (which geometry tells us is equal to $2\pi rh$, where r is the radius of the silo and h is its height). However, the storage capacity of the silo depends on the volume of the silo (which is equal to $\pi r^2 h$). Capacity thus increases more than proportionately as the radius of the silo increases. Similarly, constructing additional capacity for pipelines and oil refineries inherently increases output more than proportionately to the cost of adding additional capacity.

Over section II of *LRAC* in Figure 7.8, **constant returns to scale** are in effect. If constant returns to scale are in effect, and everything that the firm needs for production is just "scaled up" (e.g., the firm uses 2/3 more capital, 2/3 more labour, 2/3 more raw material, etc.) then output goes up by exactly the same proportion (i.e., by 2/3). With constant returns to scale, long-run average cost is constant as output changes. That is, a change in the scale of an operation leaves long-run average cost unchanged. Notice that the boundary between section I and section II indicates a **minimum efficient quantity** of output. The minimum efficient quantity is the smallest quantity of output that will achieve minimum long-run average cost. The presence of constant returns to scale means that firms of a number of different sizes can simultaneously earn normal profits. Thus, firms of different sizes can simultaneously serve a market, all of them making a normal profit. For example, with constant returns to scale, farms of different sizes could produce wheat while earning a normal profit.

Section III of *LRAC* portrays **diseconomies of scale**. With diseconomies of scale, long-run average cost increases as output increases. If output always increased in the same proportion as the scale of a firm increased, diseconomies would not exist. Do we want twice as much wheat? With constant returns to scale in wheat production, twice as much wheat could be obtained by doubling the size of a farm without causing any increase in cost per unit of wheat. Do we again want twice as much wheat? Just double the size of the farm again, and so on. However, if diseconomies of scale appear, output will increase less than in proportion to an increase in scale, causing long-run average cost to increase as output increases.

Two reasons are commonly given for diseconomies of scale. First, as a firm becomes larger, it becomes increasingly difficult (i.e., costly) to organize and coordinate. Second, the larger a firm becomes, the more difficult (i.e., costly) it may be to develop and maintain smooth labour relations. If labour relations become acrimonious (or even less than collegial) as the size of a firm increases, teamwork suffers and long-run average cost increases as output increases.

indivisible factor of production a factor of production that must be available in some minimum amount if a productive activity, even of minimal size, is to occur at all

indivisible cost the cost of an indivisible factor of production

constant returns to scale a situation in which long-run average cost does not change as scale changes

minimum efficient quantity the smallest quantity of output that will achieve minimum long-run average cost

diseconomies of scale a situation in which long-run average cost increases as a firm's output increases

> | **RECAP** | **FIRM SIZE AND THE SHAPE OF THE LONG-RUN AVERAGE COST CURVE** |
>
> If long-run average cost decreases as the relative size, or scale, of a firm increases, economies of scale are present; if long-run average cost remains constant as the scale of a firm increases, constant returns to scale are present. Diseconomies of scale are present when long-run average cost rises as the scale of a firm increases. If constant returns to scale are present, it is possible for firms of different sizes to be present in a market that has reached long-run, perfectly competitive equilibrium.

◼ 7.4 THE INVISIBLE HAND THEORY

TWO FUNCTIONS OF PRICE

Prices in competitive markets serve two important and distinct functions. The first, the **rationing function of price**, is to distribute scarce goods among potential claimants, assuring that those who get them are the ones who are able and willing to pay the most. Thus, if three people want the only antique clock for sale at an auction, the clock goes home with the person who bids the most for it. The second function, the **allocative function of price**, is to direct productive resources to different sectors of the economy. Resources leave markets in which price cannot cover the cost of production and enter those in which price exceeds the cost of production.

Both the allocative and rationing functions of price underlie Adam Smith's celebrated **theory of the invisible hand** of the market. Recall that Smith thought the market system channels the interests of individual buyers and sellers so as to promote the greatest good for society. He argued that under the correct circumstances, legitimate competition among buyers and sellers would cause self-interest to promote the common good. Under carefully specified circumstances, the carrot of economic profit and the stick of economic loss would cause existing supplies in any market to be allocated efficiently. The same carrot and stick would also cause resources to be allocated across markets to produce the most efficient possible mix of goods and services.

Of course, two related questions arise. What are the correct circumstances? What is legitimate competition? Modern scholars who study Smith's work are struck by the incisiveness and subtlety he brings to these questions, and a few lines (or pages) cannot do justice to his answers. However, it is clear that for Smith, the "right" circumstances include competition among a large number of small participants in markets, none of whom have any power to influence market price. But it is equally clear that for Smith, a large number of small competitors is far from sufficient to harmonize unbridled pursuit of self-interest with the common good. Social institutions play a central role in aligning self-interest with the common good, and a commercial society cannot function well without institutions of justice that protect lives, the security of person and property, and the rights that arise from contracts freely made with others. Justice, says Smith, "...is the main pillar that upholds the whole edifice [of society]." Remove justice and "...the immense fabric of human society...must in a moment crumble into atoms."[6]

To take an extreme case, violence can be an effective way to eliminate competition for those able to wield it with greatest force. Competition will not arise from

rationing function of price distributes scarce goods to those consumers who value them most highly

allocative function of price directs resources away from overcrowded markets and toward markets that are underserved

invisible hand theory a theory stating that under carefully specified circumstances, the actions of independent, self-interested buyers and sellers will often result in the most efficient allocation of resources

[6]Adam Smith, *The Theory of Moral Sentiments.* Vol. I of *The Glasgow Edition of the Works and Correspondence of Adam Smith*, edited by D.D. Raphael and A.L. MacFie, 6 vols. Oxford, Clarendon Press, 1976 (1759), pp. 84, 86.

someone who is dead, cowed by threats of violence, or deprived of property without due process. But, says Smith, a society that permits this kind of competitive strategy among its members cannot become a commercial state. To take a less extreme case, suppose contracts could be broken without consequence. Pareto exchange would not occur because no one could be confident that once made, a bargain would be kept. If it is well known that delivery of goods might be met with arbitrary withholding of payment, or worse yet, violence, if one presses for payment, there is no incentive in the first place to produce goods to be offered in exchange. Under such circumstances, it would be very difficult, if not impossible, for a society to produce an economic surplus. Thus, societies need laws (and courts to enforce them) to ensure competition takes legitimate forms—i.e., no one interferes with the liberty of others to compete on equal footing nor impedes the ability of others to pursue their own self-interest in whatever way they want. A society that cannot provide a regular administration of justice cannot become a successful commercial state.[7]

We must emphasize that Smith's invisible hand theory does not mean that market allocation of resources is optimal in every way. It simply means that markets are efficient in the limited technical sense discussed in Chapter 6. Thus, if the current allocation differs from the market equilibrium allocation, the invisible hand theory implies that we can reallocate resources in a way that makes some people better off without harming others. We can gain additional insight into Smith's theory by working through a series of simple examples.

EXAMPLE 7.6

What happens in a city with "too many" hairstylists and "not enough" aerobics instructors?

According to the invisible hand theory, the efficient number of haircuts and aerobics classes for a community are determined by the intersections of the respective supply and demand curves. For a specific community, suppose that means 50 haircuts/day and 20 aerobics classes/day, as shown in Figure 7.9. Why would 55 haircuts/day and 15 aerobics classes be worse? What resource movements would occur in response to those production levels?

FIGURE 7.9

An Imbalance in the Markets for Haircuts and Aerobics Classes

In a town with too many haircuts and not enough aerobics classes, hairstylists will suffer economic losses and aerobics instructors will enjoy economic profits. Eventually, stylists will leave haircutting for other occupations, and others will become aerobics instructors. The shift in resources will continue until all economic profits and losses are eliminated.

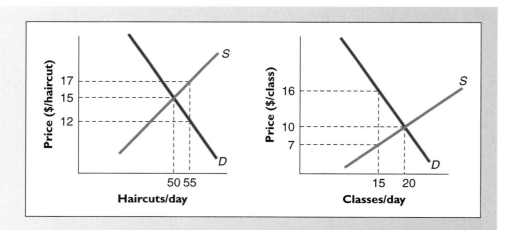

[7]Adam Smith, *The Wealth of Nations,* with introductions by Max Lerner and Edwin Cannan. Edited by Edwin Cannan. New York, Random House, Inc., 1965 (1776), Book IV, Chapter IX and Book V, Chapter III, pp. 651, 862.

Note that when the market for haircuts is in equilibrium, the $15 value that buyers receive from the last haircut purchased is exactly equal to the $15 cost of producing it, which includes a salary sufficient to cover the stylist's opportunity cost. If instead stylists offer 55 haircuts/day, the last haircut will fail the cost-benefit test: Its value ($12) will be less than the stylist's marginal cost of producing it ($17). By contrast, if aerobics instructors offer five fewer aerobics classes than the market equilibrium number, the value of the last lesson ($16) will be far higher than the instructor's marginal cost of producing it ($7).

**COST–
BENEFIT**

By definition, a situation in which there are "too many" hairstylists and "too few" aerobics instructors is one in which stylists earn less than the opportunity cost of their time, while aerobics instructors earn more than the opportunity cost of theirs. Stated another way, stylists earn an economic loss and aerobics instructors earn an economic profit. Over time, economic losses will induce some stylists to leave the haircutting market, and economic profits will lure new instructors to the aerobics teaching market. These resource movements will continue until there are only enough stylists to provide 50 haircuts/day and enough aerobics instructors to provide 20 classes/day—the equilibrium output levels in the two markets.

Those people who leave the haircutting market will not necessarily enter the aerobics teaching market. Indeed, given the sheer number of occupations a former hairstylist might choose to pursue, the likelihood of such a switch is low. Nor does the invisible hand theory imply an immediate adjustment of resources. In some markets, especially labour markets, the required movements might take months or even years. But if the supply and demand curves remain stable, the markets will eventually reach equilibrium prices and quantities.

THE IMPORTANCE OF FREE ENTRY AND EXIT

The allocative function of price cannot operate unless firms can enter new markets and leave existing ones easily. If new firms could not enter a market in which existing firms were making a large economic profit, economic profit would not tend to fall to zero over time, and price would not tend to gravitate toward the cost of production.

Forces that inhibit firms from entering new markets are sometimes called **barriers to entry**. In the book publishing market, for example, the publisher of a book enjoys copyright protection granted by the government. Copyright law forbids other publishers from producing and selling their own editions of protected works. This barrier allows the price of a popular book to remain significantly above its cost of production for an extended period, all the while generating an economic profit for its publisher. (A copyright provides no *guarantee* of a profit, and indeed most new books actually generate an economic loss for their publishers.)

barrier to entry any force that prevents firms from entering a new market

Barriers to entry may result from practical constraints as well as legal ones. Some economists, for example, have argued that the compelling advantages of product compatibility have created barriers to entry in the computer software market. Since more than 90 percent of new desktop computers come with Microsoft's Windows software already installed, rival companies have difficulty selling other operating systems, whose use would prevent most users from exchanging files with friends and colleagues. This fact, more than any other, explains Microsoft's spectacular profit history.

No less important than the freedom to enter a market is the freedom to leave. If firms know that a market, once entered, is difficult or impossible to leave, they become reluctant to enter the market in the first place. Barriers to exit thus become barriers to entry. Without reasonably free entry and exit, then, the implications of Adam Smith's invisible hand theory cannot be expected to hold.

All things considered, however, producers enjoy a high degree of freedom of entry in most North American markets. Because free entry is one of the defining characteristics of a perfectly competitive market, unless otherwise stated, we will assume its existence.

ECONOMIC RENT VERSUS ECONOMIC PROFIT

Microsoft chairman Bill Gates is one of the two or three wealthiest people on the planet, largely because the problem of compatibility prevents rival suppliers from competing effectively in the many software markets dominated by his company. Yet numerous people have become fabulously rich even in markets with no conspicuous barriers to entry. If market forces push economic profit toward zero, how can that happen?

The answer to this question hinges on the distinction between economic profit and **economic rent.** Most people think of rent as the payment they make to a landlord or the supplier of a dorm refrigerator, but the term *economic rent* has a different meaning. Economic rent is that portion of the payment for an input that is above the lowest price the supplier would accept for that input. Suppose, for example, that the lowest price a landowner would accept for a hectare of land is $100/year. That is, suppose he is willing to lease it to a farmer as long as he receives an annual payment of at least $100, but for less than that amount he would rather leave it fallow. If a farmer gives him an annual payment not of $100 but of $1000, the landowner's economic rent from that payment will be $900/year.

Economic profit is like economic rent in that it, too, may be seen as the difference between what someone is paid (the businessowner's total revenue) and the lowest amount she would accept for remaining in business (the sum of all her costs, explicit and implicit). But whereas competition pushes economic profit toward zero, it has no such effect on the economic rent for inputs that cannot be replicated easily. For example, although the lease payments for land may remain substantially above the landowner's lowest acceptable price, year in and year out, new land cannot come onto the market to reduce or eliminate the economic rent through competition. There is, after all, only so much land to be had.

As Example 7.7 illustrates, economic rent can accrue to people as well as land.

economic rent that part of the payment for a factor of production that exceeds the owner's reservation price, the price below which the owner would not supply the factor

---

EXAMPLE 7.7

How much economic rent will a talented chef get?

A community has 100 restaurants, 99 of which employ chefs of normal ability at a salary of $30 000/year, the same as the amount they could earn in other occupations that are equally attractive to them. But the 100th restaurant has an unusually talented chef. Because of her reputation, diners are willing to pay 50 percent more for the meals she cooks than for those prepared by ordinary chefs. Assume owners of the 99 restaurants with ordinary chefs each collect $300 000/year in revenue, which is just enough to pay all costs, ensuring that each earns exactly a normal profit. If the talented chef's opportunities outside the restaurant industry are the same as those of ordinary chefs, how much will she be paid by her employer at equilibrium? How much of her pay will be economic rent? How much economic profit will her employer earn?

Because diners are willing to pay 50 percent more for meals cooked by the talented chef, the owner who hires her will take in total receipts not of $300 000/year but of $450 000. In the long run, competition should assure that the talented chef's total pay each year will be $180 000/year, the sum of the $30 000 that ordinary chefs get and the $150 000 in extra revenues for which she is solely responsible. Since the talented chef's lowest acceptable price is the amount she could earn outside the restaurant industry—by assumption, $30 000/year, the same as for ordinary chefs—her economic rent is $150 000/year. The economic profit of the owner who hires her will be zero.

Since the talented chef's opportunities outside the restaurant industry are no better than an ordinary chef's, why is it necessary to pay the talented chef so much? Suppose her employer were to pay her only $60 000, which they both would consider a generous salary, since it is twice what ordinary chefs earn. The employer would then earn an economic profit of $120 000/year, since his annual revenue would be $150 000 more than that of ordinary restaurants, but his costs would be only $30 000 more.

But this economic profit would create an opportunity for the owner of some other restaurant to bid the talented chef away. For example, if the owner of a competing restaurant were to hire the talented chef at a salary of $70 000, the chef would be $10 000/year better off, and the rival owner would earn an economic profit of $110 000/year rather than his current economic profit of zero. Furthermore, if the talented chef is the sole reason that a restaurant earns a positive economic profit, the bidding for that chef should continue as long as any economic profit remains. Some other owner will pay her $80 000, still another $90 000, and so on. Equilibrium will be reached only when the talented chef's salary has been bid up to the point that no further economic profit remains—in Example 7.7, at an annual paycheque of $180 000.

This bidding process assumes, of course, that the reason for the chef's superior performance is that she possesses some personal talent that cannot be copied. If instead it were the result of, say, training at a culinary institute in France, then her privileged position would erode over time as other chefs sought similar training.

Whether the talented chef can be hired away also depends on a particular structure of information. If the chef is to get the economic rent, it must be the chef who is famous, not the restaurant. If the fame lies with the restaurant, the restaurant will capture the economic rent. This matter is discussed in Chapter 12.

THE EFFECT OF COST-SAVING INNOVATIONS

When economists speak of perfectly competitive firms, they have in mind firms whose contribution to total market output is too small to have a perceptible impact on market price. As explained in Chapter 5, such firms are often called price takers: They take the market price of their product as given and then produce that quantity of output for which marginal cost equals that price.

This characterization of the competitive firm gives the impression that the firm is essentially a passive actor in the marketplace. Yet for most firms, that is anything but the case. As Example 7.8 illustrates, even those firms that cannot hope to influence the market prices of their products have very powerful incentives to develop and introduce cost-saving innovations.

EXAMPLE 7.8

How do cost-saving innovations affect economic profit?

Forty merchant marine companies operate supertankers that carry oil from the Middle East to the east coast of Canada. The cost per trip, including a normal profit, is $500 000. Suppose an engineer at one of these companies develops a more efficient propeller design that results in fuel savings of $20 000/trip. How will this innovation affect the company's accounting and economic profits? Will these changes persist in the long run?

At first, the reduction in a single firm's costs will have no impact on the market price of transoceanic shipping services. The firm with the more efficient propeller will thus earn an economic profit of $20 000/trip (since its total revenue will be the same as before, while its total costs are now $20 000/trip lower). As other firms learn about the new design, however, they will (assuming that it cannot be patented) begin to adopt it, causing their individual supply curves to shift downward (since the marginal cost per trip at these firms will drop by $20 000). The shift in these individual supply curves will cause the market supply curve to shift, which in turn will result in a lower market price for shipping and a decline in economic profit at the firm where the innovation originated. When all firms have adopted the new efficient design, the long-run supply curve for the industry will have shifted downward by $20 000/trip, and each company will again be earning only a normal profit. At that point, any firm that did *not* adopt the new propeller design would suffer an economic loss of $20 000/trip.

The incentive to come up with cost-saving innovations to reap economic profit is one of the most powerful forces on the economic landscape. Its beauty, in terms of the invisible hand theory, is that competition among firms assures that the resulting cost savings will be passed along to consumers in the long run.

RECAP | **THE INVISIBLE HAND THEORY**

In economies with competitive markets, the allocative and rationing functions of prices guide resources to their most highly paid uses. Prices influence how much of each type of good gets produced (the allocative function). Firms enter those industries in which prices are sufficiently high to sustain an economic profit and leave those in which low prices result in an economic loss. Prices also direct existing supplies of goods to the buyers who are able and willing to pay for them (the rationing function).

Economic rent is the amount by which the payment to a factor of production exceeds the supplier's lowest acceptable price. Unlike economic profit, which is driven toward zero by competition, economic rent may persist for extended periods, especially in the case of factors with special talents that cannot easily be duplicated.

Early adopters of cost-saving innovations enjoy temporary economic profits. But as additional firms adopt the innovations, the resulting downward supply shift causes price to fall. In the long run, economic profit returns to zero, and all cost savings are passed on to consumers.

■ 7.5 THE INVISIBLE HAND IN ACTION

To help develop your intuition about how the invisible hand works, we will examine how it helps us gain insight into patterns we observe in a variety of different contexts.

THE INVISIBLE HAND IN REGULATED MARKETS

The carrot of economic profit and the stick of economic loss guide resource movements in regulated markets no less than in unregulated ones. Consider the taxi industry, which many cities regulate by licensing cabs. These licences are often called medallions, because they are sometimes issued in the form of a metal shield that must be affixed to the hood of the cab, where enforcement officials can easily see it. Cities that regulate cabs in this fashion typically issue fewer medallions than the equilibrium number of taxicabs that would appear in an unregulated market. If medallions can be bought and sold in the marketplace, the issuance of taxi medallions alters the equilibrium quantity of taxicabs but does not change the fundamental rule that resources flow in response to profit and loss signals.

Why do some taxicab medallions sell for more than $250 000?

Because most cities issue far fewer taxi medallions than would-be taxi owners could operate profitably, the equilibrium passenger fare is higher than the direct cost of operating a taxicab. Suppose the cost of operating a cab full-time—including car, fuel, maintenance, depreciation, and the opportunity cost of the driver's time, but excluding the purchase price of a medallion—is $40 000/year, and a cab in full-time operation will collect $60 000/year in fares. If the annual interest rate on savings accounts is 8 percent, how much will a medallion cost at equilibrium? Will the owner of a medallion earn an economic profit?

If the medallion were free and could not be sold to others, its owner would earn an economic profit of $20 000/year, the difference between $60 000 in fares and $40 000 in operating cost. But the equilibrium principle tells us that the lure of this economic profit would induce outsiders to enter the taxi industry, which could be done by purchasing an owner's medallion.

EQUILIBRIUM

How much would the entrant be willing to pay for a medallion? If one were available for, say, $100 000, would it be a good buy? Since $100 000 in the bank would earn only $8000/year in interest, but would bring $20 000 in earnings if used to purchase a taxi medallion, the answer must be yes. In fact, when the annual interest rate is 8 percent, a rational buyer's lowest acceptable price for a stream of economic profits of $20 000/year is the amount of money the buyer would have to put in the bank to earn that much interest each year—namely, $250 000. At any amount less than that, medallions would be underpriced.

Clearly, the owner of a $250 000 medallion has a valuable asset. The opportunity cost of using it to operate a taxi is forgone interest of $20 000/year. So the medallion owner who takes in $60 000 in fares actually covers only the cost of the resources invested in the operation. The owner's economic profit is zero. From the perspective of the medallion owner, the $20 000 difference between the owner's fares and explicit costs is an economic rent.

EXERCISE 7.2

How much would the medallion in the preceding example sell for if the annual interest rate were not 8 percent but 4 percent?

THE INVISIBLE HAND: DO POLICIES CREATE OUTCOMES OR INCENTIVES?

As Example 7.9 suggests, failure to understand the invisible hand may lead to policies that produce outcomes contrary to what is intended. The invisible hand suggests that without careful attention to policy design, it is possible to inadvertently build incentives into a policy that subvert its goals.

EXAMPLE 7.9

How will an irrigation project affect the incomes of poor farmers?

Suppose unskilled workers must choose between working in a textile mill at $8000/year and growing rice on a rented parcel of farmland. One worker can farm an 80-hectare rice parcel, which rents for $5000/year. Such farms yield $16 000/year in revenue, and the total nonlabour costs of bringing the crop to market are $3000/year. The net incomes of rice farmers are thus $8000/year, the same as those of textile workers. A legislator has introduced a bill to fund an irrigation project that would double the output of rice on farms operated by tenant farmers. If the contribution of the legislator's district to the total supply of rice is too small to affect the price, how will the project affect the incomes of tenant farmers over the long run?

The direct effect of the project will be to double rice yields, which means that each farmer will sell $32 000 worth of rice per year rather than $16 000. If nothing else changed, farmers' incomes would rise from $8000/year to $24 000/year. But the equilibrium principle tells us that farmers cannot sustain this income level. From the perspective of textile workers, there is an opportunity to triple their

EQUILIBRIUM

incomes, and many will want to switch to farming. But since the supply of land is fixed, farm rents will rise as textile workers begin bidding for them. They will continue to rise as long as farmers can earn more than textile workers. The long-run effect of the project, then, will be to raise the rent on rice farms, from $5000/year to $21 000/year (since at the higher rent the incomes of rice farmers and textile workers will again be the same). Thus the irrigation project will increase the wealth of landowners but will have no long-run effect on the incomes of tenant farmers. Thus, landlords are the real beneficiaries of the state-funded irrigation project. It would not have surprised Adam Smith to learn that, appearances not withstanding, landlords were the real champions of state-funded irrigation. If fact, given his keen understanding of incentives, he might have been surprised if this were not the case.

RECAP	**THE INVISIBLE HAND IN ACTION**

The quest for advantage guides resources not only in perfectly competitive markets but also in heavily regulated ones. Firms can almost always find ways to expand sales in markets in which the regulated price permits an economic profit or to withdraw service from markets in which the regulated price results in an economic loss.

The invisible hand helps us to understand that without attention to the incentives they create, policies may produce outcomes contrary to what is expected. An irrigation program that makes land more productive, for example, will raise the incomes of tenant farmers only temporarily. In the long run, the gains from such projects tend to be captured as rents to landowners.

■ 7.6 THE DISTINCTION BETWEEN AN EQUILIBRIUM AND A SOCIAL OPTIMUM

MARKET EQUILIBRIUM AND INCENTIVES

EQUILIBRIUM

The examples discussed in the preceding section illustrate the equilibrium principle, which tells us that when a market reaches equilibrium, no further opportunities for gain are available to individuals—there is no incentive to change behaviour. This principle implies that the market prices of resources that people own will eventually reflect their economic value. (As we will see in later chapters, the same cannot be said of resources that are not owned by anyone, such as fish in international waters.)

The equilibrium principle is sometimes misunderstood to mean that there are *never* any valuable opportunities to exploit. For example, the story is told of two economists on their way to lunch when they spot what appears to be a $100 bill lying on the sidewalk. When the younger economist stoops to pick up the bill, his older colleague restrains him, saying, "That can't be a $100 dollar bill." "Why not?" asks the younger colleague. "If it were, someone would have picked it up by now," the older economist replies.

The equilibrium principle means not that there are *never* any unexploited opportunities but that there are none when the market is *in equilibrium*. Occasionally a $100 bill does lie on the sidewalk, and the person who first spots it and picks it up gains a windfall. Likewise, when a company's earnings prospects improve significantly, *somebody* must be the first to recognize the opportunity, and that person can make a lot of money by purchasing the stock quickly.

Nevertheless, when a market is in equilibrium, no additional opportunities are available *to individuals*. But equilibrium does not imply that the resulting allocation is necessarily best from the point of view of society as a whole.

THE FALLACY OF COMPOSITION—SMART FOR ONE, DUMB FOR ALL

Adam Smith's profound insight was that the individual pursuit of self-interest often promotes the broader interests of society. But unlike some of his modern disciples, Smith was under no illusion that is *always* the case. Note, for example, Smith's elaboration on his description of the entrepreneur led by the invisible hand "to promote an end which was no part of his intention":

> Nor is it *always* the worse for society that it was no part of it. By pursuing his own interest he *frequently* promotes that of society more effectively than when he really intends to promote it. [emphasis added][8]

As Smith was well aware, the individual pursuit of self-interest often does not coincide with society's interest. In Chapter 3 we cited activities that generate environmental pollution as an example of conflicting economic interests, noting that behaviour in those circumstances may be described as smart for one but dumb for all. As the following example suggests, extremely high levels of investment in earnings forecasts can also be smart for one, dumb for all.

 7.3   ECONOMIC NATURALIST

Are there "too many" smart people working as corporate earnings forecasters?

Stock analysts use complex mathematical models to forecast corporate earnings. The more analysts invest in the development of these models, the more accurate the models become. Thus, the analyst whose model produces a reliable forecast sooner than others can reap a windfall buying stocks whose prices are about to rise. Given the speed with which stock prices respond to new information, however, the results of even the second-fastest forecasting model may come too late to be of much use. Individual stock analysts thus face a powerful incentive to make ever greater investments in their models in the hope of generating the fastest forecast. Does this incentive result in the socially optimal level of investment in forecast models?

Beyond some point, increased speed of forecasting is of little benefit to society as a whole, whose interests suffer little when the price of a stock moves to its proper level a few hours more slowly. If *all* stock analysts invested less in their forecasting models, *someone's* model would still produce the winning forecast, and the resources that might otherwise be devoted to fine-tuning the models could be put to more valued uses. Yet if any one individual invests less, she can be sure the winning forecast will not be hers.

The invisible hand went awry in the situation just described because the individual benefit from an investment was larger than the benefit of that investment to society as a whole. In later chapters we will discuss a broad class of investments with this property. In general, the efficacy of the invisible hand depends on the extent to which the individual costs and benefits of actions taken in the marketplace coincide with the respective costs and benefits of those actions to society. These exceptions notwithstanding, some of the most powerful forces at work in competitive markets clearly promote society's interests.

[8]Adam Smith, *The Wealth of Nations,* New York: Everyman's Library, E.P. Dutton, 1910 (1776), Book I; and *The Wealth of Nations*, with an introduction by Max Lerner and an introduction by Edwin Cannan. Edited by Edwin Cannan. New York, Random House, Inc., 1965 (1776), Book IV, Chapter II, p.423.

RECAP	EQUILIBRIUM VERSUS SOCIAL OPTIMUM

A market in equilibrium is one in which no additional opportunities for gain remain available to individual buyers or sellers. The equilibrium principle describes powerful forces that help push markets toward equilibrium. But even if all markets are in equilibrium, the resulting allocation of resources need not be socially optimal. Equilibrium will not be socially optimal when the costs or benefits to individual participants in the market differ from those experienced by society as a whole.

■ SUMMARY

- **7.1** Accounting profit is the difference between a firm's revenue and its explicit expenses. It differs from economic profit, which is the difference between revenue and the sum of the firm's explicit and implicit costs. Normal profit is the difference between accounting profit and economic profit. It is the opportunity cost of the resources supplied to a business by its owners.

- **7.1** The quest for economic profit is the invisible hand that drives resource allocation in market economies. Markets in which businesses earn an economic profit tend to attract additional resources, whereas markets in which businesses experience an economic loss tend to lose resources. If economic profits entice new firms to enter a market, that market's short-run supply curve shifts to the right, causing a reduction in the price of the product. Prices will fall until economic profits are eliminated. By contrast, if economic losses cause firms to leave a market, the short-run supply curve will shift left, increasing the price of the product. Prices will rise until economic losses are eliminated. In the long run, market forces drive economic profits and losses toward zero.

- **7.2** In the short run, the size (or scale) of a firm's capital stock can not change. Also, the number of firms serving a market does not change. Thus, in the short run, any changes to the quantity supplied to a perfectly competitive market are accomplished when a fixed number of firms, each of fixed size, change their rates of output. If market price changes in the short run, each firm changes its rate of output to maximize profit, but it does not change its scale. Further, short-run market supply curves do not shift in the short run.

- **7.2** In the long run, individual firms can change their scale of operation, and the number of firms serving a market can change. Therefore, in the long run, short-run mar-

ket supply curves can shift. When long-run equilibrium is established in a perfectly competitive market, each firm has selected a scale of operation and rate of output that minimizes long-run average cost. Thus, in long-run perfectly competitive equilibrium, market price equals minimum long-run average cost. In the long run, an increase in the quantity supplied to a market implies that the number of firms serving the market will increase and that every firm in the market will operate at minimum long-run average cost. The converse applies for a decrease in market supply.

- **7.3** Economies of scale occur when long-run average cost decreases as the scale of a firm increases. Constant returns to scale occur when long-average cost remains unchanged as the scale of a firm increases. Diseconomies of scale occur when long-run average cost increases as the scale of a firm increases.

- **7.4** When market supply and demand curves reflect the underlying costs and benefits to society of the production of a good or service, the quest for economic profit ensures not only that existing supplies are allocated efficiently among individual buyers, but also that resources are allocated across markets in the most efficient way possible. In any allocation other than the one generated by perfect competition, resources could be rearranged so as to benefit some people without harming others.

- **7.4** Economic rent is the portion of the payment for an input that exceeds the lowest price a supplier will accept for that input. If a chef with unique talent is willing to work for as little as $30 000/year, but is paid $180 000, he earns an economic rent of $150 000/year. Although the invisible hand drives economic profit toward zero over the long run, economic rent can persist indefinitely, because replicating the services of very talented individuals is impossible. Talented individuals who are responsible for the superior performance of a business will tend to capture the resulting financial gains as economic rents.

• **7.5** Failure to understand the logic of Adam Smith's invisible hand often compromises the design of regulatory programs. For instance, when regulation prevents firms from lowering prices to capture business from rivals, firms generally find other ways in which to compete. Many programs have been compromised by failure to consider how incentives change people's behaviour.

• **7.5** The equilibrium principle implies that if someone owns a valuable resource, the market price of that resource will fully reflect its economic value. This princi-

ple does not imply that lucrative opportunities never exist, but rather that such opportunities cannot exist when markets are in equilibrium.

• **7.6** Exceptions to the invisible hand theory arise when the benefit of an investment to an individual differs from its benefit to society as a whole. Such conflicting incentives give rise to behaviour that is smart for one but dumb for all. Despite such exceptions, the invisible hand works remarkably well much of the time. One of the market system's most important contributions to social well-being is the pressure it creates to adopt cost-saving innovations. Competition among firms ensures that the resulting cost savings are passed along to consumers in the long run.

KEY TERMS

accounting profit (190)	economic or excess profit (190)	indivisible factor of production (204)
allocative function of price (205)	economic rent (208)	invisible hand theory (205)
barrier to entry (207)	economies of scale (203)	long-run average cost (199)
capital (195)	explicit costs (190)	minimum efficient quantity (204)
constant returns to scale (204)	firm (195)	normal profit (191)
diseconomies of scale (204)	implicit costs (190)	rationing function of price (205)
economic loss (193)	indivisible cost (204)	scale (203)

REVIEW QUESTIONS

1. Why do most cities in North America now have more radios but fewer radio repair shops than they did in 1960?

2. How can a businessowner who earns $10 million/year from his or her business credibly claim to earn zero economic profit?

3. Why do market forces drive economic profit but not economic rent toward zero?

4. Is it possible for the short-run market supply to show that quantity supplied increases only if price increases, and for the long-run market supply to indicate that market price does not increase as quantity supplied increases? Why or why not?

5. Is it possible for individual firms to experience diseconomies of scale while long-run market supply simultaneously is horizontal? Why or why not?

PROBLEMS

1. True or false: Explain why the following statements are true or false:
   a. The economic maxim that when in equilibrium, a market provides no economic profits means that there are never any unexploited opportunities to make economic profits.
   b. Firms in competitive environments make no accounting profit when the market is in long-run equilibrium.
   c. Firms that can introduce cost-saving innovations can make an economic profit in the short run.

2. Explain why new software firms that give away their software products at a short-run economic loss are nonetheless able to sell their stock at positive prices.

3. John Jones owns and manages a café in Collegetown. His monthly revenue is $5000. Monthly expenses are shown in the following list:

Labour	$2000
Food and drink	500
Electricity	100
Vehicle lease	150
Rent	500
Interest on loan for equipment	1000

    a. Calculate John's monthly accounting profit.

    b. John could earn $1000/month as a recycler of aluminum cans. However, he prefers to run the café. In fact, he would be willing to pay up to $275/month to run the café rather than to recycle. Is the café making an economic profit? Will John stay in the café business? Explain.

    c. Suppose the café's revenues and expenses remain the same, but recyclers' earnings rise to $1100/month. Is the café still making an economic profit? Explain.

    d. Suppose that instead of borrowing $100 000 at a monthly interest rate of 10 percent to buy equipment, John had invested $100 000 of his own money in equipment. How would your answers to parts (a) and (b) change?

    e. If John can earn $1000/month as a recycler and he likes recycling just as well as running the café, how much additional revenue would the café have to collect each month to earn a normal profit?

4. Suppose the city of Vancouver has 200 advertising companies, 199 of which employ designers of normal ability at a salary of $100 000/year. Paying this salary, each of the 199 firms makes a normal profit on $500 000 in revenue. However, the 200th company employs Janus Jacobs, an unusually talented designer. This company collects $1 000 000 in revenues because of Jacobs's talent.

    a. How much will Jacobs earn? What proportion of his annual salary will be economic rent?

    b. Why won't the advertising company for which Jacobs works be able to earn an economic profit?

5. Explain carefully why, in the absence of a patent, a technical innovation invented and pioneered in one tofu factory will cause the supply curve for the entire tofu industry to shift to the right. What will finally halt the rightward shift?

6. The government of the Republic of Self-Reliance has decided to limit imports of machine tools to encourage development of locally made machine tools. To do so, the government offers to sell a small number of machine tool import licences. Operating a machine tool import business costs $30 000, excluding the cost of the import licence. An importer of machine tools can expect to collect total receipts of $50 000/year. If the annual interest rate is 10 percent, for how much will the government be able to auction the import licences? Will the owner of a licence earn an economic profit?

7. Unskilled workers in a poor cotton-growing region must choose between working in a factory for $6000/year or being tenant cotton farmers. One farmer can work a 120-hectare farm, which rents for $10 000/year. Such farms yield $20 000 worth of cotton each year. The total nonlabour cost of producing and marketing the cotton is $4000/year. A local politician whose motto is "working people come first" has promised that if he is elected, his administration will fund a fertilizer, irrigation, and marketing scheme that will triple cotton yields on tenant farms at no charge to tenant farmers.

    a. If the market price of cotton was unaffected by this policy and no new jobs were created in the cotton-growing industry, how would the project affect the incomes of tenant farmers in the short run? in the long run?

    b. Who would reap the benefit of the scheme in the long run? How much would they gain each year?

8. You have a friend who is a potter. He holds a permanent patent on an indestructible teacup whose sale generates $30 000/year more revenue than production costs. If the annual interest rate is 20 percent, what is the market value of his patent?

9. You have an opportunity to buy an apple orchard that produces $125 000/year in accounting profit. To run the orchard, you would have to give up your current job, which pays $50 000/year. If you found both jobs equally satisfying, and the annual interest rate is 10 percent, what is the highest price you would be willing to pay for the orchard?

10. Louisa, a renowned chef, owns one of the 1000 spaghetti restaurants in Sicily. Each restaurant serves 100 plates of spaghetti a night at $5/plate. Louisa knows she can develop a new sauce at the same cost as the current sauce, which would be so tasty that all 100 000 spaghetti eaters would buy her spaghetti at $10/plate. There are two problems: Developing the new sauce would require some experimental cost, and the other spaghetti producers could figure out the recipe after one day.
    a. What is the highest experimental cost Louisa would be willing to incur?
    b. How would your answer change if Louisa could enforce a year-long patent on her new sauce? (Assume that the interest rate is zero.)

■ ANSWERS TO IN-CHAPTER EXERCISES

7.1 Most people who travel by subway prefer a seat that gives them a bit of room to stretch out or read or otherwise relax. However, many people travel at rush hour and though they prefer to have a bit of extra space, most of them also prefer not to wait for later trains that will be less crowded. Passengers thus act on opportunities to find a bit of extra space until an equilibrium is established and all the cars are equally crowded.

7.2 If the taxi medallion were available free, it would still command an economic profit of $20 000/year. So its value is still the answer to the question "How much would you need to put in the bank to generate interest earnings of $20 000/year?" When the interest rate is 4 percent/year, the answer is $500 000, or twice what the medallion was worth at an interest rate of 8 percent.

Part 3

Market Imperfections

■

We now leave the frictionless world of perfect competition to investigate what happens in the real world, when people and firms interact in markets with a variety of imperfections. Not surprisingly, the invisible hand that served society so well in the perfectly competitive world may go astray in this new environment.

Our focus in Chapter 8 will be on how markets served by only one or a small number of firms differ from those served by perfectly competitive firms. We will see that although monopolies often escape the pressures that constrain the profits of their perfectly competitive counterparts, the two types of firms also have many important similarities.

In Chapters 1 to 8 economic decision makers confront an environment that is essentially fixed. In Chapter 9, however, we will discuss cases in which people can expect their actions to alter the behaviour of others, as when a firm's decision to advertise or launch a new product induces a rival to follow suit. Interdependent actions of this sort are the rule rather than the exception, and we will explore how to take them into account, using simple theories of games.

In Chapter 10 we will investigate how the allocation of resources is affected when activities generate costs or benefits that accrue to people not directly involved in those activities. We will see that if parties cannot easily negotiate with one another, the self-interested actions of individuals may not lead to efficient outcomes.

Although the invisible hand assumes that buyers and sellers are perfectly informed about all relevant options, this assumption is almost never satisfied in practice. In Chapter 11 we will explore how basic economic principles can help imperfectly informed individuals and firms make the best use of the limited information they possess.

MONOPOLY AND OTHER FORMS OF IMPERFECT COMPETITION

I n the late 1990s, there was a craze throughout North America for Pokémon cards. Unlike ordinary playing cards, which could be bought in most stores for only a dollar or two, a deck of Pokémon cards sold for as much as $15. And since Pokémon cards cost no more to manufacture than ordinary playing cards, their producer earned an enormous economic profit.

In a normal competitive market, entrepreneurs would see this economic profit as cash on the table. It would entice them to offer Pokémon cards at slightly lower prices so that eventually the cards would sell for roughly their cost of production, just as ordinary playing cards do. But Pokémon cards were on the market for several years, and that did not happen because the cards were copyrighted, i.e., the firm owning the copyright had an exclusive licence to sell them.

A holder of a copyright is an example of an **imperfectly competitive firm,** or **price setter,** that is, a firm with at least some latitude to set its own price. The competitive firm, by contrast, is a price taker, a firm with no influence over the price of its product.

This chapter focuses on the ways in which markets served by imperfectly competitive firms differ from those served by perfectly competitive firms. One salient difference is the imperfectly competitive firm's ability, under certain circumstances, to charge more than its cost of production. But if the producer of Pokémon cards could charge any price it wanted, why does it charge only $15? Why not charge $100, or even $1000? We will see that even though such a company may be the only seller of its product, its pricing freedom is far from absolute. We will also see how some imperfectly competitive firms manage to earn an economic profit, even in the long run, and even without government protections like copyright. We will also explore why the ability of Adam Smith's invisible hand to produce economically efficient outcomes is compromised in a world served by imperfectly competitive firms.

■ 8.1 IMPERFECT COMPETITION

The perfectly competitive market is an ideal type; the actual markets we encounter in everyday life differ from the ideal in varying degrees. In a somewhat arbitrary classification scheme, economics texts usually distinguish among three types of imperfectly competitive market structures.

DIFFERENT FORMS OF IMPERFECT COMPETITION

Furthest from the perfectly competitive ideal is the **pure monopoly,** a market in which a single firm is the lone seller of a unique product. The producer of Pokémon cards is a pure monopolist, as are many providers of electric power. If the residents of Montreal don't buy their electricity from Hydro Quebec, they simply do without.

Somewhat closer to the perfectly competitive ideal is **oligopoly,** the market structure in which only a few rival firms sell a given product. Examples include the market for long-distance telephone service, in which firms like Primus, Sprint, and MCI are the principal providers. Closer still to perfect competition is the market structure known as **monopolistic competition,** which typically consists of a relatively large number of firms selling slightly differentiated products that are reasonably close substitutes for one another. Examples include local gasoline markets in which stations differ not so much in the gas they sell as in their physical locations.

As we will see in the next section, one essential characteristic differentiates all three types of imperfectly competitive firms from perfectly competitive firms. Because pure monopoly, oligopoly, and monopolistic competition represent three different types of *imperfectly competitive* markets, the firms that participate in any of these three market types can be called *imperfectly competitive* firms.

THE ESSENTIAL DIFFERENCE BETWEEN PERFECTLY AND IMPERFECTLY COMPETITIVE FIRMS

In a perfectly competitive market, each individual firm produces a standardized commodity and provides such a small share of the total quantity supplied to the market that no individual firm is capable of influencing market price. A perfectly competitive firm can no more change the market price than a child with a bucket can change the level of the sea. Since market price is fixed by supply and demand for the industry as a whole, each individual firm in a perfectly competitive industry decides how much to produce *given* the market price—thus, a perfectly competitive firm is a *price taker*. This is not the case in an imperfectly competitive market where the share of the total quantity supplied to a market by an imperfectly competitive firm is large enough to influence market price. Thus, an imperfectly competitive firm must make its decisions about how much to produce *knowing that the quantity it produces will affect the market price*. An imperfectly competitive firm, therefore, is a *price setter*.

A single, common feature differentiates all imperfectly competitive firms from their perfectly competitive counterparts: *whereas the perfectly competitive firm faces a perfectly elastic demand curve for its product, the imperfectly competitive firm faces a downward-sloping demand curve.*

In the perfectly competitive industry, supply and demand curves intersect to determine an equilibrium market price. At that price, the perfectly competitive firm can sell as many units as it wants. It cannot charge more than the market price. If it tries to do so, it will sell nothing because a multitude of competitors stands ready to sell at the market price. Nor does it have any incentive to charge less than the market price, because it can sell as many units as it wants to at the

price setter or imperfectly competitive firm a firm with at least some latitude to set its own price

pure monopoly a market in which there is only one supplier of a unique product with no close substitutes

oligopoly a market in which there are only a few rival sellers (each of which is called an oligopolist)

monopolistic competition a market structure in which a large number of firms sell slightly differentiated products that are reasonably close substitutes for one another

www.hydroquebec.com
Hydro-Quebec

market price. The perfectly competitive firm's demand curve is thus a horizontal line at the market price, as we saw in Chapter 5.

By contrast, if a local gasoline retailer—an imperfect competitor—charges a few pennies more than its rivals for a gallon of gas, some of its customers may desert it. But others will remain, perhaps because they are willing to pay a little extra to continue stopping at their most convenient location. An imperfectly competitive firm thus faces a negatively sloped demand curve. Figure 8.1 summarizes this contrast between the demand curves facing perfectly competitive and imperfectly competitive firms.

FIGURE 8.1

The Demand Curves Facing Perfectly and Imperfectly Competitive Firms
Panel (a): The demand curve confronting a perfectly competitive firm is perfectly elastic at the market price. Panel (b): The demand curve confronting an imperfectly competitive firm is downward sloping.

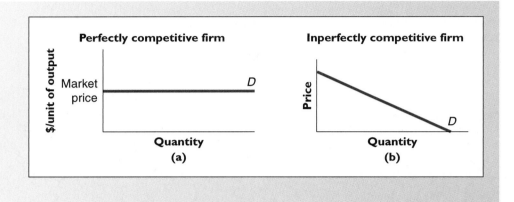

If the Petro Canada station on Quinpool Road raised its gasoline prices by 1 cent/litre, would all its customers shop elsewhere?

> **RECAP** | **IMPERFECT COMPETITION**
>
> Perfect competition is an ideal case, at best only approximated in actual industries. Economists study three other types of market structure that differ in varying degrees from perfect competition: monopoly, a market with only one seller of a unique product; oligopoly, a market served by only a few rival sellers; and monopolistic competition, a market in which many firms sell products that are close, but imperfect, substitutes for one another. The demand curve confronting a perfectly competitive firm is perfectly elastic at the market price, while the demand curve confronting an imperfectly competitive firm is downward sloping.

■ 8.2 FIVE SOURCES OF MARKET POWER

market power a firm's ability to raise the price of a good without losing all its sales

Firms that confront downward-sloping demand curves are sometimes said to enjoy **market power,** a term that refers to their ability to raise the prices of their products without losing all their sales. A perfectly competitive firm has no market power. If it attempts to charge a price higher than market price, it will lose all of its sales to other perfect competitors. When a firm has market power, it can increase the price of its product and lose only part of its sales (at least for small increases in price). The greater the market power of firms in an industry, the less competitive that industry. However, even a firm with market power cannot sell any quantity at any price it wants. All it can do is pick a price–quantity combination along its demand curve. If the firm chooses to raise its price, it is choosing a different point on its demand curve. A higher price means a smaller quantity demanded by consumers, which means the quantity sold by the firm is smaller. If price is increased too much (to the price represented by the vertical intercept of the demand curve, or higher), quantity demanded falls to zero and the firm sells nothing.

Why do some firms have market power while others do not? Since market power often carries with it the ability to charge a price above the cost of production, such power tends to arise from factors that limit competition. In practice, the following factors often confer such power: exclusive control over inputs, economies of scale, patents, licences or franchises, and network economies.

EXCLUSIVE CONTROL OVER IMPORTANT INPUTS

If a single firm controls an input essential to the production of a given product, that firm will have market power. For example, to the extent that some tenants are willing to pay a premium for office space that provides a spectacular view, the owner of a building with such views has market power.

ECONOMIES OF SCALE (NATURAL MONOPOLIES)

Figure 7.8 in Chapter 7 shows that economies of scale occur if long-run average cost decreases when a firm increases its scale of operation. For example, if by increasing the size of its generators and other factors of production by 10 percent, an electric utility increases output of electricity by more than 10 percent, its long-run average cost (or cost per unit) of electricity will decrease. The electric utility will be experiencing economies of scale usually present in the production of electricity. When significant economies of scale are present, a market tends to be served by only a few sellers. If economies of scale are still present when the quantity supplied by a single seller is large enough to serve an entire market, a single seller will monopolize the market, because the largest firm has the lowest costs and can drive competitors out of business. Having a large number of sellers would result in significantly higher costs per unit. A monopoly that results from economies of scale is called a **natural monopoly**.

natural monopoly a monopoly that results from economies of scale

PATENTS

Patents give the inventors or developers of new products the exclusive right to sell those products for a specified time. By insulating sellers from competition for an interval, patents enable innovators to charge higher prices to recoup their product's development costs. Pharmaceutical companies, for example, spend millions of dollars on research in the hope of discovering new drug therapies for serious illnesses. In Canada, a patent insulates a new drug from competition for 20 years from the date an application for a patent is filed. For the life of the patent, only the patent holder may legally sell the drug. This protection enables the patent holder to set a price above the marginal cost of production to recoup the cost of the research on the drug. In the same way, copyrights protect the authors of published works (such as this textbook).

LICENCES OR FRANCHISES

If you check intercity bus services in your part of the country, you will probably find that where service is provided between any two points, only one company operates the buses. In many cities, only one company provides cable television services. The Government of Canada has given Canada Post the exclusive right to provide a national postal service. In such cases, government has granted monopoly rights to one firm. Usually the stated objective is to obtain regulatory outcomes that might not be available if the market were left to itself. In an open market for intercity bus transportation, competitors might reduce standards of safety and comfort. Open competition in cable television services could result in costly duplication of services. Canada Post will deliver letters for the same price to many locations,

www.canadapost.ca
Canada Post

regardless of how remote they are. Private couriers might offer delivery to remote locations only with reduced frequency and a much higher price, if at all.

In many industries, franchising and licencing are also common. A company with a unique product or service (e.g., McDonald's hamburgers, Molly Maid cleaners) will sell the right to use their technology, and often their brand name, to another firm in a specific local market. The franchise usually includes a guarantee that the franchisor will not sell any other franchises in the same market area. Thus the purchaser of a franchise obtains a local monopoly of the production of that specific good or service.

NETWORK ECONOMIES

Although most of us do not care what brand of dental floss others use, many products become much more valuable to us as more people use them. In the case of home recorders, for instance, the VHS format's defeat of the competing Beta format was explained not by its superior picture quality—indeed, on most important technical dimensions, Beta was regarded by experts as superior to VHS. Rather, VHS won simply because it managed to gain a slight sales edge on the initial version of Beta, which could not record programs longer than one hour. Although Beta later corrected this deficiency, the VHS lead proved insuperable. Once the fraction of consumers owning VHS passed a critical threshold, the reasons for choosing it became compelling—variety and availability of tape rental, access to repair facilities, the capability to exchange tapes with friends, and so on.

A similar network economy helped to account for the dominant position of Microsoft's Windows operating system, which, as noted earlier, is currently installed in more than 90 percent of all personal computers. Because Microsoft's initial sales advantage gave software developers a strong incentive to write for the Windows format, the inventory of available software in the Windows format is now vastly larger than that for any competing operating system. And although general-purpose software like word processors and spreadsheets continues to be available for multiple operating systems, specialized professional software and games usually appear first—and often only—in the Windows format. This software gap and the desire to achieve compatibility for file sharing gave people a good reason for choosing Windows, even if, as in the case of many Apple Macintosh users, they believed a competing system was otherwise superior.

Firmly entrenched network economies are essentially economies of scale. When network economies are of value to the consumer, a product's quality increases as the number of users increases, so we can say that any given quality level can be produced at lower cost as sales volume increases. Thus network economies may be viewed as just another form of economies of scale in production, and that is how we will treat them here.

The most enduring of the sources of market power is economies of scale. Although it may be costly to do so, by constructing a taller building, a real estate developer can provide more offices with a view. Patents and copyrights do insulate their owners from competition, but firms often can evade patents and copyrights by making slight changes in design. Intercity buses face competition from automobiles and airlines. If cable television companies charge too much for their services, consumers can rent videotapes or buy satellite dishes. Similarly, Canada Post faces the competition of couriers, e-mail, and fax machines.

RECAP	**FIVE SOURCES OF MARKET POWER**

A firm's power to raise its prices without losing its entire market stems from exclusive control of important inputs, patents and copyrights, licenses, economies of scale, or network economies. By far the most important and enduring of these are economies of scale and network economies.

■ 8.3 ECONOMIES OF SCALE AND THE IMPORTANCE OF FIXED COSTS

As we saw in Chapter 1, variable costs are those that vary with the level of output produced, while fixed costs are independent of output. Strictly speaking, there are no fixed costs in the long run, because all inputs can be varied. Nevertheless, as indicated in Chapter 7, economies of scale can arise from indivisible costs, which are costs of indivisible factors of production. For some products, a minimum amount of an indivisible factor of production is necessary before even the smallest quantity of the product can be produced. However, once a sufficient amount of the indivisible factor has been acquired, marginal cost may be quite low.

Consider the production of computer software. Once a decision has been made to develop a package of software, one-time start-up costs must be incurred to write and test it. The start-up costs are fixed. They are the costs of indivisible factors of production that must be put in place before even one copy of the software can be produced. Once the start-up costs are incurred and the software is developed, additional copies of the software can be produced at very low marginal cost. A good such as software, whose production entails large fixed costs and low variable costs, will be subject to significant economies of scale. Because by definition fixed costs do not increase as output increases, the average cost of production for such goods will decline sharply as output increases.

To illustrate, consider a production process for which total cost is given by equation 8.1

$$TC = TFC + MQ \qquad (8.1)$$

where TFC is total fixed cost, M is marginal cost (assumed constant, which is critical in this illustration), and Q is the total quantity of output produced. Because marginal cost is constant, it also is equal to average variable cost (AVC). For a production process with this simple total cost function, total variable cost is simply MQ, the product of marginal cost and quantity. Panel (a) of Figure 8.2 graphs total cost (TC) for a firm whose total cost is given by equation 8.1. Notice that the vertical intercept (TFC) in panel (a) of Figure 8.2 gives the firm's total fixed cost. (In this discussion, definitions of different categories of cost are the same as those used in Chapter 5.)

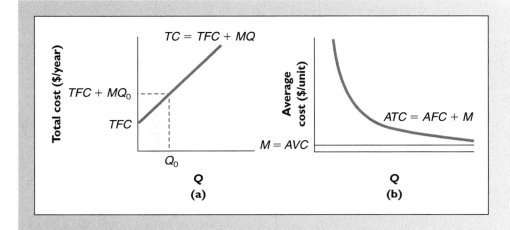

FIGURE 8.2

Total and Average Costs for a Production Process with Economies of Scale

For a firm whose total cost curve of producing Q units of output per year is TC = TFC + MQ, total cost in panel (a) rises at a constant rate as output grows, while average total cost in panel (b) declines. Average total cost is always higher than marginal cost for this firm, but the difference becomes less and less significant as output increases to higher and higher levels.

To find average total cost (*ATC*), divide equation 8.1 by *Q*:

$$TC/Q = TFC/Q + M \qquad (8.2)$$

Notice that as *Q* increases, *TFC/Q* must decrease. Because *M* is constant, this implies that as *Q* increases, *TC/Q* also must decrease. Therefore, as the quantity of output rises, cost per unit decreases because total fixed cost is spread over more and more units of output.

Equation 8.2 can be rewritten as:

$$ATC = AFC + AVC = AFC + M \qquad (8.3)$$

where *ATC* is average total cost, *AVC* is average variable cost, $ATC = TC/Q$, and $AVC = TVC/Q = M$. Panel (b) of Figure 8.2 shows an average total cost curve (*ATC*) that corresponds to equations 8.2 and 8.3. Panel (b) also shows the constant marginal cost, *M*, which is equal to constant average variable cost (*AVC*). The average total cost curve in panel (b) shows that cost per unit (i.e., average total cost) always decreases as output increases. And, though average total cost is always higher than marginal cost for this firm, the difference between the two diminishes as output grows. At extremely high levels of output, average cost is very close to marginal cost *(M)*. When the firm is spreading its fixed cost over an extremely large volume of output, average fixed cost becomes almost insignificant.

If you compare the average total cost curve in Figure 5.8 of Chapter 5 with average total cost in Figure 8.2, you will notice a striking difference. Although in Figure 8.2 average total cost always decreases as output increases, Figure 5.8 provides a quite different picture. In Figure 5.8 average total cost reaches a minimum and thereafter increases as quantity of output increases. A critical difference exists in the assumptions used in these two figures. In Figure 5.8, beyond a certain point, the law of diminishing marginal returns causes short-run marginal cost and average variable cost to increase. In Figure 8.2 short-run marginal cost and average variable cost remain constant at *M*. Therefore, in Figure 8.2, the law of diminishing marginal returns never causes marginal cost and average variable cost to increase with increases in output. As a result, the spreading of total fixed cost over an increasingly large quantity of output must always cause average total cost to decrease.

As Examples 8.1 and 8.2 illustrate, the importance of economies of scale depends on how large fixed cost is in relation to marginal cost.

EXAMPLE 8.1

Two manufacturers of video game consoles, Sony and Microsoft, each have fixed costs of $200 000 and marginal costs of $0.80/game. Sony makes PlayStation and Microsoft makes Xbox. Suppose each holds a large share of the market they serve. If Microsoft produces 1 million units/year and Sony produces 1.2 million units/year, how much lower will Sony's average production cost be?

TABLE 8.1
Costs for Two Video Game Producers (1)

	Microsoft	Sony
Annual production	1 000 000	1 200 000
Fixed cost	$200 000	$200 000
Variable cost	$800 000	$960 000
Total cost	$1 000 000	$1 160 000
Average cost per game	$1.00	$0.97

Table 8.1 summarizes the relevant cost categories for the two firms. Note in the bottom row that Sony enjoys only a 3 cent average cost advantage over Microsoft. Even though Microsoft produces 20 percent fewer copies of its video game than Sony, it does not suffer a significant cost disadvantage because fixed cost is a relatively small part of total production cost.

The next example shows how the picture changes when fixed cost looms large relative to marginal cost.

EXAMPLE 8.2

Now suppose Microsoft and Sony each have fixed costs of $10 000 000 and marginal costs of $0.20/video game. Again, Microsoft and Sony each hold a large share of the market they serve. If Microsoft produces 1 million units/per year and Sony produces 1.2 million units/year, how much lower will Sony's average production cost be?

TABLE 8.2
Costs for Two Video Game Producers (2)

	Microsoft	Sony
Annual production	1 000 000	1 200 000
Fixed cost	$10 000 000	$10 000 000
Variable cost	$200 000	$240 000
Total cost	$10 200 000	$10 240 000
Average cost per game	$10.20	$8.53

The relevant cost categories for the two firms are now summarized in Table 8.2. The bottom row shows that Sony enjoys a $1.67 average cost advantage over Microsoft, substantially larger than in Example 8.1.

If the video games the two firms produce are essentially similar, the fact that Sony can charge significantly lower prices and still cover its costs should enable it to attract customers away from Microsoft. As more and more of the market goes to Sony, its cost advantage will become self-reinforcing. Table 8.3 shows how a shift of 500 000 units from Microsoft to Sony would cause Microsoft's average cost to rise to $20.20/unit, while Sony's average cost would fall to $6.08/unit.

TABLE 8.3
Costs for Two Video Game Producers (3)

	Microsoft	Sony
Annual production	500 000	1 700 000
Fixed cost	$10 000 000	$10 000 000
Variable cost	$100 000	$340 000
Total cost	$10 100 000	$10 340 000
Average cost per game	$20.20	$6.08

Table 8.3 shows that by spreading a much larger output over the same total fixed cost, Sony accomplishes a large cost advantage over Microsoft.

The fact that a firm cannot long survive at a severe cost disadvantage helps to explain why the videogame market is served by only a small number of firms. Consider the case of Sony, Microsoft, Nintendo, and Sega. Sony launched

PlayStation 2 in 2000. In 2001 Microsoft launched Xbox, and Nintendo launched Game Cube. Press reports indicated that by mid-2004, Sony had sold nearly 71 million game consoles. Microsoft had sold fewer than 15 million, and Nintendo fewer than 14 million. The reports hardly mentioned Sega, a company that once led the industry with its Sega-Genesis.

In mid-2004, video game fans were eagerly anticipating the next generation of game consoles. Any manufacturer that could come up with the right combination of an early launch and attractive features stood to establish a self-reinforcing cost advantage.[1] Sony, Nintendo, and Microsoft had begun to jockey for position. Would a new generation of PlayStation again dominate the market? Or, would another leader emerge? Maybe the answer will be obvious by the time you read this.

EXERCISE 8.1	**Use the costs given in Example 8.2. How big will Sony's unit cost advantage be if it sells 2 000 000 units/year, while Microsoft sells only 200 000?**

During recent decades an increasing share of the value embodied in the goods and services we buy stems from fixed investment in research and development. For example, in 1984 some 80 percent of the cost of a computer was in its hardware (which has relatively high marginal cost); the remaining 20 percent was in its software. But by 1990 those proportions were reversed. Fixed cost now accounts for about 85 percent of total costs in the computer software industry, whose products are included in a growing share of ordinary manufactured goods.

8.1   ECONOMIC NATURALIST

Why does Intel sell the overwhelming majority of all microprocessors used in personal computers?

The fixed investment required to produce a new leading-edge microprocessor such as Intel's Pentium IV chip is more than $2 billion. But once the chip has been designed and the manufacturing facility built, the marginal cost of producing each chip is only pennies. This cost pattern explains why Intel currently sells more than 80 percent of all microprocessors. Of course, new generations of chips will continue to be developed, and the fixed costs of developing them will be high.

Economies of scale can be conferred by large fixed costs. If economies of scale occur over quantities of output that are a large share of the market being served, the perfectly competitive pattern of many small firms, each producing only a small share of its industry's total output, disappears. For this reason, we must develop a clear sense of how the behaviour of firms with market power differs from that of the perfectly competitive firm.

RECAP	**ECONOMIES OF SCALE AND THE IMPORTANCE OF FIXED COSTS**

Research, design, engineering, and other fixed costs account for an increasingly large share of all costs required to bring products successfully to market. For products with large fixed costs, marginal cost is often substantially lower than average total cost, and average total cost declines, often sharply, as output grows. This cost pattern explains why many industries are dominated by either a single firm or a small number of firms.

---

[1]Notice that in the case of video games, network economies can play an important role is establishing a cost advantage. If it appeared that one system would dominate the market, software developers would have a strong incentive to tailor their software to that system. Selling to the dominant firm would cause the fixed costs of developing and writing software to be spread over a larger quantity of output.

8.4 PROFIT MAXIMIZATION FOR THE MONOPOLIST

Regardless of whether a firm is a price taker or a price setter, economists assume that it wants to maximize its profit. Both types of firm choose the quantity of output that results in the greatest possible difference between total revenue and total cost. But there are some important differences in how the two types of firm choose the quantity of output that maximizes profit. To help focus attention on these differences, we begin with a brief review of how the perfectly competitive firm chooses its level of output.

THE PERFECTLY COMPETITIVE FIRM'S DECISION RULE: A REVIEW

Recall from Chapter 5 that a perfectly competitive firm is one firm among many, all of whom are producing the same product. As the following example reminds us, the competitive firm maximizes profit by selling that quantity of output at which marginal cost equals the market price.

How many watermelons will a farmer produce?   **EXAMPLE 8.3**

Consider a perfectly competitive watermelon farmer whose marginal cost is shown in Figure 8.3. If this grower can sell as many metric tons of melons as he chooses at a price of $200/metric ton, how many metric tons will he sell to maximize his profit?

A competitive firm, or a monopolist for that matter, will expand its production if and only if the benefit of doing so exceeds the cost. If the farmer in this example were producing only 12 metric tons/year, his marginal cost would be $160/metric ton, while his benefit from expanding production would be the market price for which he can sell the melons, $200/metric ton. So this farmer will expand his production of melons until he reaches 18 metric tons/year, the quantity at which marginal cost exactly equals the market price.

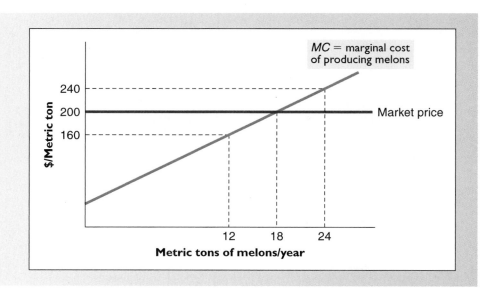

For both the perfectly competitive firm and the monopolist, the marginal benefit of increasing output by one unit is the additional revenue the firm will receive if it sells one additional unit of output. In both cases, this marginal benefit is called the firm's **marginal revenue**. For the perfectly competitive firm, marginal revenue is exactly equal to the market price of the product.

marginal revenue the increase in total revenue obtained by producing and selling one more unit of output

MARGINAL REVENUE FOR THE MONOPOLIST

COST–
BENEFIT

The logic of profit maximization is precisely the same for the monopolist as for the perfectly competitive firm. In both cases, the firm increases output as long as the benefit of doing so exceeds the cost. The calculation of marginal cost is also precisely the same for the monopolist as for the perfectly competitive firm. *The only significant difference between the two cases concerns the calculation of marginal revenue.*

As we saw in Chapter 5, marginal revenue for a competitive firm is simply the market price. If that price is $6, then the marginal benefit of selling an extra unit is exactly $6. *To a monopolist, in contrast, the marginal benefit of selling an additional unit is strictly less than the market price.* Examples 8.4 to 8.6 make it clear that although the perfectly competitive firm can sell as many units it wants at the market price, the monopolist can sell an additional unit only if it reduces the price. And when the monopolist reduces the price, it affects the revenue received from each unit it is currently offering for sale.

EXAMPLE 8.4

How much extra revenue would a monopolist get by increasing its output?

A monopolist with the demand curve shown in Figure 8.4 is currently selling two units of output at a price of $6/unit. What would be its marginal benefit from selling an additional unit?

This monopolist's total revenue from the sale of two units/week is ($6/unit)(2 units/week) = $12/week. Its total revenue from the sale of three units/week would be $15/week. The difference—$3/week—is the marginal revenue from the sale of the third unit each week. Note that this amount is not only smaller than the original price ($6) but smaller than the new price ($5) as well. Marginal revenue is $2 less than the new price because the two units that previously sold for $6 each now sell for $5 each, a decrease of $1 per unit or $2 in total.

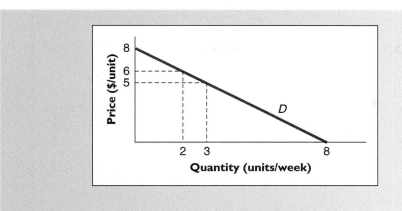

FIGURE 8.4
The Monopolist's Benefit from Selling an Additional Unit
The monopolist shown receives $12/week in total revenue by selling 2 units/week at a price of $6 each. This monopolist could earn $15/week by selling 3 units/week at a price of $5 each. Thus the benefit from selling the third unit would be $15 − $12 = $3, which is less than its selling price of $5.

EXERCISE 8.2

Calculate marginal revenue for the monopolist in Example 8.4 as it increases output from 3 to 4 units/week, and then from 4 to 5 units/week.

Consider again the monopolist whose demand curve is shown in Figure 8.4. In Example 8.4 and Exercise 8.1, we saw that a sequence of increases in output—from two to three, from three to four, and from four to five—could yield marginal revenue of $3, $1, and −$1, respectively. The first two columns of Table 8.4 just report in tabular form the same information that is in Figure 8.4. They display the demand relationship—the relationship between the price the firm charges and the quantity the firm will be able to sell. Column three reports total revenue, which is equal to price times quantity (i.e., the product of the first two columns). When the firm considers increasing production by one unit, it will want to ask, "How much does total revenue increase when production is increased by one unit?" Economists call the answer to this question *marginal revenue*. Marginal revenue is reported in column four.

TABLE 8.4
Marginal Revenue for a Monopolist

Price	Quantity Sold	Total Revenue	Marginal Revenue
6	2	12	
			+3
5	3	15	
			+1
4	4	16	
			−1
3	5	15	

Note that in Table 8.4, the marginal revenue values are displayed between the two quantity figures to which they correspond. For example, when the firm increased its output from two units/week to three, its marginal revenue was $3/unit. Strictly speaking, this marginal revenue corresponds to neither quantity but to the movement between the two quantities, hence its placement in the table. Likewise, in moving from three to four units/week, the firm earned marginal revenue of $1/unit. Therefore, the figure is placed midway between the quantities of three and four, and so on.

To graph marginal revenue as a function of quantity, we plot marginal revenue for the movement from two to three units of output per week ($3) at a quantity of 2.5, because 2.5 lies midway between two and three. Similarly, we plot the marginal revenue for the movement from three to four units/week ($1) at a quantity of 3.5 units/week, and the marginal revenue for the movement from four to five units/week ($-$1) at a quantity of 4.5. The resulting marginal revenue curve *MR,* is shown in Figure 8.5.

FIGURE 8.5

Marginal Revenue in Graphical Form

Because a monopolist must reduce price to sell an extra unit, not only for the extra unit sold but also for all units that it sells, marginal revenue from the sale of the extra unit is less than its selling price.

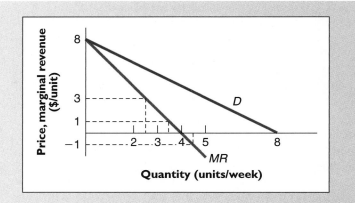

More generally, consider a monopolist with a straight-line demand curve whose vertical intercept is *a* and whose horizontal intercept is Q_0, as shown in Figure 8.6. This monopolist's marginal revenue curve will also have a vertical intercept of *a,* and it will be twice as steep as the demand curve. Thus, its horizontal intercept will be not Q_0, but $Q_0/2$, as shown in Figure 8.6.

FIGURE 8.6

The Marginal Revenue Curve for a Monopolist with a Straight-Line Demand Curve

For a monopolist with the demand curve shown, the corresponding marginal revenue curve has the same vertical intercept as the demand curve, and a horizontal intercept only half as large as that of the demand curve.

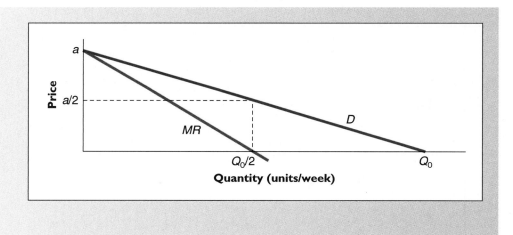

Marginal revenue curves can also be expressed algebraically. If the formula for the monopolist's demand curve is $P = a - bQ$, then the formula for its marginal revenue curve will be $MR = a - 2bQ$. If you have had calculus, this relationship is easy to derive,[2] but even without calculus you can verify it by working

---

[2]For those who have had an introductory course in calculus, marginal revenue can be expressed as the derivative of total revenue with respect to output. If $P = a - bQ$, then total revenue will be given by $TR = PQ = aQ - bQ^2$, which means that $MR = dTR/dQ = a - 2bQ$.

through a few numerical examples. First, translate the formula for the demand curve into a diagram, and then construct the corresponding marginal revenue curve graphically. Reading from the graph, write the formula for that marginal revenue curve.

What is the marginal revenue curve that corresponds to a specific demand curve?

EXAMPLE 8.5

Find the equation for the marginal revenue curve for the monopolist whose demand curve is given by $P = 10 - (\frac{1}{2})Q$.

    We use the fact that the marginal revenue curve has the same vertical intercept as the demand curve and a horizontal intercept half as large as the demand curve's horizontal intercept. Since the demand curve has a slope of $-1/2$ and since the marginal revenue curve is twice as steep as the demand curve, the slope of the marginal revenue curve must be -1. And since the marginal revenue curve has the same vertical intercept as the demand curve, its formula must be $MR = 10 - Q$. To confirm the pattern shown in Figures 8.5 and 8.6, graph the equations for demand and marginal revenue.

THE MONOPOLIST'S PROFIT-MAXIMIZING DECISION RULE

Having derived the monopolist's marginal revenue curve, we are now in a position to describe how the monopolist chooses the quantity of output that maximizes profit. As in the case of the perfectly competitive firm, the cost–benefit principle says that the monopolist will continue to increase output as long as the gain from doing so exceeds the cost. At the current level of output, the benefit from increasing output is the marginal revenue value that corresponds to that quantity of output. The cost of an increase in output is the marginal cost at that additional quantity of output. Whenever marginal revenue exceeds marginal cost, the firm will increase its output. Conversely, whenever marginal revenue is less than marginal cost, the firm will reduce its output. *Profit is maximized at the level of output for which marginal revenue precisely equals marginal cost.*

COST–
BENEFIT

    When the monopolist's profit-maximizing rule is stated in this way, we can see that the perfectly competitive firm's rule is actually a special case of the monopolist's rule. When the perfectly competitive firm expands output by one unit, its marginal revenue exactly equals the product's market price (because the perfectly competitive firm can increase sales by a unit without having to decrease the price of existing units). So when the perfectly competitive firm equates price with marginal cost, it is also equating marginal revenue with marginal cost.

What is the monopolist's profit-maximizing quantity of output?

EXAMPLE 8.6

Consider a monopolist with the demand and marginal cost curves shown in panel (a) of Figure 8.7. If this firm is currently producing 12 units/week, will it increase or decrease production? What is the profit-maximizing quantity of output?

    In panel (b) of Figure 8.7, we begin by constructing the marginal revenue curve that corresponds to the monopolist's demand curve. It has the same vertical intercept as the demand curve, and its horizontal intercept is half as large. Note that the monopolist's marginal revenue at 12 units/week is zero, which is clearly less than its marginal cost of $3/unit. Therefore this monopolist will earn a higher profit by reducing production until marginal revenue equals marginal cost, which occurs at an output of 8 units/week. At the profit-maximizing quantity of output, the firm will charge $4/unit, the price that corresponds to eight units/week on the demand curve.

FIGURE 8.7

The Demand, Marginal Revenue, and Marginal Cost Curves for a Monopolist

Panel (a) shows that price equals marginal cost when price is $3 and output is 12 units/week. However, a monopolist's price is always greater than its marginal revenue. Therefore, the monopolist's marginal revenue is less than its marginal cost, and it will reduce its output. Panel (b) shows that the monopolist will maximize its profit when price is $4/unit and output is 8 units/week.

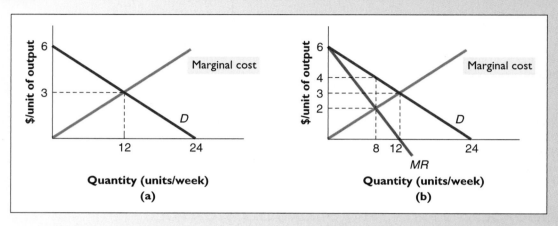

EXERCISE 8.3

Find the profit-maximizing price and quantity of output for a monopolist with the demand curve P = 12 − Q and the marginal cost curve MC = 2Q, where P is the price of the product in dollars per unit and Q is output in units per week.

MONOPOLY: A GRAPHICAL SUMMARY

If we consider a monopoly that is due to the firm having a licence, patent, or franchise for a unique product, it is quite possible that the firm has a U-shaped cost curve similar to those we developed in Chapters 5 and 7. Panel (a) of Figure 8.8 portrays such a monopolist, operating in the short run. The monopolist's demand curve is labelled D, MR is marginal revenue, ATC is average total cost, and MC is marginal cost. The monopolist maximizes profit when it produces the quantity Q_M, where marginal revenue equals marginal cost. By selecting the price P_M, the monopolist determines that quantity sold will be Q_M. By choosing a price, the monopolist also implicitly chooses the quantity it can sell at that price—the monopolist chooses a point on its demand curve. Point B in panel (a) of Figure 8.8 is the point on the monopolist's demand curve that it chooses when it chooses the quantity of output that maximizes profit.

When the quantity of output is Q_M, average total cost is AC_M, which is read from curve ATC. Profit per unit of output is the difference between price and average total cost:

$$\text{Profit/unit} = P_M - AC_M.$$

Total profit is obtained by multiplying profit/unit by the quantity of units produced:

$$\text{Total profit} = (P_M - AC_M)Q_M.$$

The monopolist's profit is represented by the green rectangular area in panel (a) of Figure 8.8. It is the area obtained by multiplying profit/unit times the quantity of units.

FIGURE 8.8

Monopoly: A Graphical Summary

The monopolist portrayed in panel (a) maximizes profit by choosing price P_M and quantity Q_M as defined by point B on the demand curve. At quantity Q_M, average total cost is AC_M; therefore, total profit is represented by the green rectangle. The same monopolist is portrayed in panel (b), and the same demand curve is shown in both panels. When marginal cost decreases from MC to MC', the monopolist moves from point B to point C on its demand curve; it reduces price to P_M' and increases quantity to Q_M'. The monopolist's profits are higher with the cost reduction and the new price–quality combination.

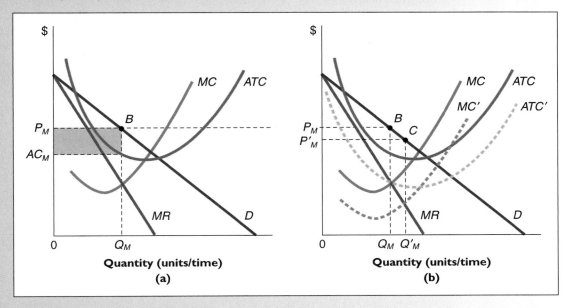

Suppose a technological improvement in production efficiency reduces the monopolist's costs. This is shown in panel (b) of Figure 8.8 by the downward shift of ATC to ATC' and MC to MC'. Nothing has happened to consumers, so the monopolist's demand curve is unchanged from panel (a). However, with the new marginal cost curve, it will be profitable for the monopolist to increase quantity to Q_M' and reduce price to P_M'. Notice that in choosing the new profit maximizing price and quantity, the monopolist has moved from point B on its demand curve to point C—it has chosen a new point on its demand curve. The monopolist did not move from one point to another on a supply curve. Given its cost structure, a monopolist chooses the point on its demand curve that maximizes profit. Indeed, one could say that a monopolist does not really have a "supply curve," since a monopolist always chooses the point on the *industry demand curve* that maximizes profit.

RECAP	PROFIT MAXIMIZATION FOR THE MONOPOLIST

Both the perfectly competitive firm and the monopolist maximize profit by choosing the quantity of output at which marginal revenue equals marginal cost. But whereas marginal revenue equals market price for the perfectly competitive firm, marginal revenue is always less than market price for the monopolist. A monopolist chooses the point on its demand curve that maximizes profit.

▣ 8.5 WHY THE INVISIBLE HAND BREAKS DOWN UNDER MONOPOLY

In our discussion of equilibrium in perfectly competitive markets in Chapter 6, we considered conditions under which the self-serving pursuits of consumers and firms were consistent with the broader interests of society as a whole. Let us explore whether the same conclusion holds true for the case of imperfectly competitive firms.

Consider the monopolist in Example 8.6. Is this firm's profit-maximizing output level efficient from society's point of view? For any given level of output, the corresponding price on the demand curve indicates the amount buyers would be willing to pay for an additional unit of output. When the monopolist is producing 8 units/week, the marginal benefit to society of an additional unit of output is thus $4 [see panel (b) of Figure 8.7]. And since the marginal cost of an additional unit at that output level is only $2 (again, see Figure 8.7), society would gain a net benefit of $2/unit if the monopolist were to expand production by one unit above the profit-maximizing level. As long as marginal cost is less than marginal benefit to society, total economic surplus will increase if output increases by another unit. Both panels of Figure 8.7 show that as long as output is less than 12 units, total economic surplus will increase if output is increased by one more unit. Because monopoly causes total economic surplus to be smaller than the maximum possible, the profit-maximizing monopolist is socially inefficient.

Recall that the existence of inefficiency means that the economic pie is smaller than it might be. If that is so, why does the monopolist not simply increase production? The answer is that the monopolist would gladly do so, if only there were some way to maintain the price of existing units and reduce the price of only the extra units. As a practical matter, however, that is not always possible.

Consider again the monopolist in Example 8.6, whose demand, marginal revenue, and marginal cost curves are taken from panel (b) of Figure 8.7 and reproduced in Figure 8.9. For the market served by this monopolist, what is the socially efficient level of output?

At any output level, the cost to society of an additional unit of output is the same as the cost to the monopolist, namely, the amount shown on the monopolist's marginal cost curve. The marginal benefit *to society* (not to the monopolist) of an extra unit of output is simply the amount people are willing to pay for it, which is the amount shown on the monopolist's demand curve. To achieve social efficiency, the monopolist should increase production until the marginal benefit to society equals the marginal cost, which in this case occurs at a level of 12 units/week. Social efficiency is thus achieved at the output level at which the market demand curve intersects the monopolist's marginal cost curve.

The fact that marginal revenue is less than price for the monopolist results in a deadweight loss. For the monopolist just discussed, the size of this deadweight loss is equal to the area of the pale blue triangle in Figure 8.9, which is $(\frac{1}{2})(\$2/\text{unit})(4 \text{ units/week}) = \$4/\text{week}$. That is the amount by which total economic surplus is reduced because the monopolist produces too little.

For a monopolist, profit maximization occurs when marginal cost equals marginal revenue. Since the monopolist's marginal revenue is always less than price, the monopolist's profit-maximizing output level is always below the socially efficient level. Under perfect competition, by contrast, profit maximization occurs when marginal cost equals the market price—the same criterion that must be satisfied for social efficiency. This difference indicates that although the invisible hand may cause self-interest to serve the common good under perfectly competitive conditions, it will not do so under monopoly.

If perfect competition is socially efficient and monopoly is not, why is monopoly legal? The nation's legislators have tried to limit the extent of monopoly through antitrust laws. But even the most enthusiastic proponents of those laws

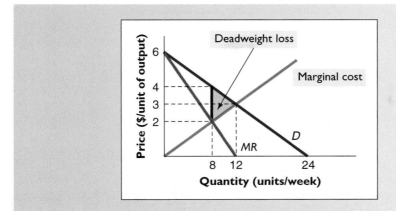

FIGURE 8.9

The Deadweight Loss from Monopoly

A loss in economic surplus results because the profit-maximizing level of output (8 units/week) is less than the socially optimal level of output (12 units/week). This deadweight loss is the area of the pale blue triangle, $4/week.

recognize the limited utility of the legislative approach, since the alternatives to monopoly often entail problems of their own.

Suppose, for example, that a monopoly results from a patent that prevents all but one firm from manufacturing some highly valued product. Would society be better off without patents? The problem is that eliminating patent protection would discourage innovation. If patents were eliminated, anyone would be free to copy a new product as soon as it appeared. The innovator would have no way to recover developmental costs. Virtually all successful industrial nations grant some form of patent protection, which gives firms a chance to recover research and development costs. Nevertheless, the appropriate length of a patent is open to debate: too long, and the inefficiency of monopoly will outweigh the benefits of innovation; too short, and costs arising from loss of innovation will outweigh the benefits of the greater efficiency that occurs when monopoly is reduced.

At the same time, research need not be conducted only by firms in the private sector; universities, government laboratories, and foundations all conduct research. Although, for example, the pharmaceutical industry develops and patents many drugs; some important drugs, such as penicillin and the polio vaccine, were discovered and developed by research conducted in the public sector.[3] If citizens were willing to pay the higher taxes necessary to fund more drug research in universities or other public research institutes, and if those institutions made their research results freely available, successful drugs could be rapidly copied and produced by many firms. A competitive market for drugs would be the result, in which drug producers would only have to cover their direct costs of production (which are typically rather small). Prices would be much lower, since monopoly profits would be competed away and since drug companies would not have to recover their development and testing costs (which are often huge—particularly since drug companies also have to cover the costs of their unsuccessful research). If the public sector paid for drug research, citizens would pay more in taxes, but less in drug prices.

Which is the better solution? The answer depends, in part, on one's perspective. Humanity as a whole receives the benefits of more public knowledge about effective drug treatments—if it is not subject to patent protection, the drug research that is published by Canadian scientists will benefit people around the world.[4] If this research is done by the public sector, Canadians will have to finance *all* the costs but would receive only *part* of the benefits. The alternative is to do drug research in the private sector and to enforce the patent laws that prevent

[3]For a discussion of private and public sector research and development of therapeutic drugs see Dean Baker, "Patent Medicine," *American Prospect, 12*(2), 29 January 2001.

[4]In Chapter 14, we will discuss the concept of "public goods" in more detail. A pure "public good" is both "non-rival" and "non-excludable." A "private good" is both "rival" and "excludable." These terms are all defined in Chapter 14.

competition in drug production—in which case, taxes will be lower, and drug prices will be higher. One argument for doing pharmaceutical research in the private sector is the fact that multi-national drug firms can use their worldwide sales revenue to finance research. If taxpayers in each country consider only the potential benefits of improved drugs to themselves, they may not be as willing to pay for "enough" research. However, one implication of higher drug prices is that people who cannot afford to pay for their drugs will have to do without—at the cost of preventable suffering and, sometimes, an early death. Since Canadians are, on average, relatively prosperous and can (usually) afford to purchase drugs, relatively few Canadians will be in this position. However, in the poor countries of this world there are many millions of people who cannot afford to pay. In recent years, the high prices charged by multinational drug companies for the retroviral drugs needed to combat HIV-AIDS has been a particularly important issue in sub-Saharan Africa, where the AIDS epidemic has affected large sectors of the population—but the issue is actually much broader in scope. Economic analysis is a crucial tool for understanding the costs and benefits of these policy choices—choices that can literally be a matter of life or death.

Or suppose that the market in question is a natural monopoly—one that, because of economies of scale, is most cheaply served by a single firm. Would society do better to require this market to be served by many small firms, each with higher average costs of production? An increase in the number of competitors might reduce the deadweight monopoly loss, but offsetting, higher costs would be incurred because each of the competing firms would be operating on a smaller, less efficient scale.

In short, we live in an imperfect world. Monopoly is socially inefficient, but the alternatives to monopoly are not perfect, either. To determine whether one arrangement would be better for society than another requires that the costs and benefits of each be compared. Accurate measurement of costs and benefits may be very difficult to achieve. By itself, however, this is not a sufficient reason to avoid attempts to measure costs and benefits.

THE DISTRIBUTIVE EFFECT OF MONOPOLY

As we have already shown, monopoly reduces total economic surplus by the amount of the deadweight loss. In the case of Figure 8.9, the deadweight loss was calculated as $4/week. However, a monopoly also redistributes the remaining economic surplus in favour of the monopolist. When compared to the socially

FIGURE 8.10

The Distributive Effect of Monopoly

Not only does monopoly reduce total economic surplus by the amount of the deadweight loss, it redistributes the remaining surplus in favour of the monopolist. With the monopoly price, the area containing the black lines represents the producer's surplus. The producer's (monopolist's) surplus is made larger by making the consumers' surplus smaller.

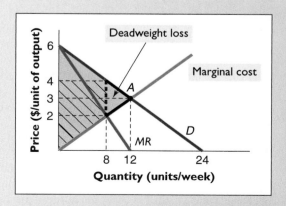

efficient outcome, the monopolist's surplus is larger because the consumers' surplus is smaller.

Consider Figure 8.10, where demand, marginal revenue, and marginal cost are the same as in Figure 8.9. At the socially efficient price ($3) and quantity (12 units/week), the area of the blue triangle represents the consumer surplus. (The blue triangle partially overlaps the figure containing the black lines.) Therefore,

$$\text{Consumer surplus} = (\tfrac{1}{2})(\$3)(12 \text{ units/week}) = \$18/\text{week}.$$

The area of the green triangle represents the producer surplus. (The green triangle also partially overlaps the figure containing the black lines.) As a result,

$$\text{Producer surplus} = (\tfrac{1}{2})(\$3)(12 \text{ units/week}) = \$18/\text{week}.$$

(In this example, the producer surplus equals the consumer surplus, but this is an artifact coincidental to the way the supply and demand curves are drawn.)

Total economic surplus with the socially efficient price and quantity is the sum of consumer and producer surplus.

$$\begin{aligned}\text{Total economic surplus} &= \text{consumer surplus} + \text{producer surplus} \\ &= \$18/\text{week} + \$18/\text{week} = \$36/\text{week}\end{aligned}$$

As shown in the previous section, the monopoly price and quantity are $4 and 8 units/week, respectively. Further, the monopoly causes a deadweight loss of $4/week. Thus, total economic surplus decreases by $4/week. Therefore,

$$\begin{aligned}\text{Total economic surplus under monopoly} &= \$36/\text{week} - \$4/\text{week} \\ &= \$32/\text{week}.\end{aligned}$$

However, this is only part of the story, because the monopoly also redistributes the smaller economic surplus. At the monopoly price, the area of the blue triangle above the figure containing the black lines represents consumer surplus:

$$\text{Consumer surplus under monopoly} = (\tfrac{1}{2})(\$2)(8 \text{ units/week}) = \$8/\text{week}.$$

In addition, the figure containing the black lines represents the monopolist's producer surplus. The figure can be divided into a rectangle and a triangle, which permits the following calculation:

$$\begin{aligned}\text{Producer surplus under monopoly} &= (\tfrac{1}{2})(\$2)(8 \text{ units/week}) + (\$2)(8 \text{ units/week}) \\ &= \$8/\text{week} + \$16/\text{week} = \$24/\text{week}.\end{aligned}$$

Notice that at $24/week the monopolist's producer surplus is $6 more than it would be at the socially efficient price and quantity. The consumer surplus at $8/week is $10 less. Taken together, the two effects cause total economic surplus to decrease by $4/week, which is consistent with what was calculated earlier. Even though total economic surplus is smaller, the monopolist's producer surplus is larger because part of the smaller total economic surplus has been redistributed from consumers to the monopolist. The monopolist's producer surplus can also be interpreted as profit.

Notice, too, that for a given marginal cost curve, the steepness of the demand curve affects the magnitude of the deadweight loss and the redistribution caused by monopoly. Suppose that a demand curve steeper than demand curve D in Figure 8.10 intersected marginal cost at point A. Total economic surplus at the socially efficient price and quantity would be larger, and so would the deadweight loss and redistribution caused by monopoly.

RECAP	WHY THE MONOPOLIST PRODUCES "TOO LITTLE" OUTPUT

The monopolist maximizes profit at the output level for which marginal revenue equals marginal cost. Because its profit-maximizing price exceeds marginal revenue, and hence also marginal cost, the benefit to society of the last unit produced (the market price) must be greater than the cost of the last unit produced (the marginal cost). So the output level for an industry served by a profit-maximizing monopolist is smaller than the socially optimal level of output. Monopoly also causes total economic surplus to be smaller than it would be with a socially efficient solution. Moreover, it distributes the smaller surplus in favour of the monopolist, causing the absolute size of the monopolist's surplus to be larger and the absolute size of the consumer surplus to be smaller.

8.6 USING DISCOUNTS TO EXPAND THE MARKET

Monopoly is inefficient because the monopolist's benefit from expanding output is less than society's. Return to Figure 8.9, which shows that if the monopolist charges $4, it will sell 8 units per week. Suppose the monopolist reduces price to $3. What benefit will the monopolist receive? The monopolist's additional benefit is the additional revenue it receives when it reduces its price. Thus the answer can be divided into two parts. First, at $3 the monopolist will sell 4 more units for a total of 12 units per week. Because it sells 4 more units, the monopolist's weekly revenue will increase by $12:

$$\$3 \times 4 \text{ units/week} = \$12/\text{week}.$$

Second, all 8 units/week the monopolist sold when price was $4 now sell for $3 each—each of these 8 units sells for $1 less than it did previously. Because it has reduced price by $1/unit on each of 8 units, the monopolist's weekly revenue decreases by $8:

$$-\$1 \times 8 \text{ units/week} = -\$8/\text{week}.$$

Taken together, these two effects show that if the monopolist reduces price from $4 to $3, its weekly revenue will increase by $4:

$$\$12/\text{week} - \$8/\text{week} = \$4/\text{week}.$$

Figure 8.9 shows that the monopolist will not reduce price to $3/unit because if it does, its increase in costs will exceed its increase in revenue.

At the same time, the demand curve of Figure 8.9 shows that at a price of $3/unit, buyers are willing to purchase 12 units/week. That is, if price were reduced from $4 to $3, buyers would increase their purchases from 8 to 12 units per week. Buyers are willing to pay $3 for each of those 4 additional units. Therefore, we can infer that buyers attach a value of at least $12 to the 4 additional units. These buyers would be better off if they could buy at a $3 price.

Clearly, the monopolist would like to have the added revenue ($12) from selling more output, but it would like to avoid the loss in revenue ($−8) from charging a lower price and having to sell all its output at that same lower price. Would the monopolist not be better off if it could somehow charge a different price to each of its different consumers? Would society also be better off?

To say that monopoly is inefficient means that it is possible to make some people better off without harming others. Why, for example, does the monopolist of Figure 8.9 not charge two prices? Why not sell the first 8 units/week at a price of $4, and then reduce the price for more price-sensitive buyers? Would this not increase the size of the economic pie in a fashion consistent with the efficiency principle?

EFFICIENCY

PRICE DISCRIMINATION DEFINED

Sometimes the monopolist does precisely that. Charging different buyers different prices for essentially the same good or service is a practice known as **price discrimination.** Examples of price discrimination include senior citizens' and children's discounts on movie tickets, supersaver discounts on air travel, and rebate coupons on retail merchandise.

price discrimination the practice of charging different buyers different prices for essentially the same good or service

Attempts at price discrimination seem to work effectively in some markets, but not in others. Buyers are not stupid, after all; if the monopolist periodically offered a 50 percent discount on the $8 list price, those who were paying $8 might anticipate the next price cut and postpone their purchases to take advantage of it. In some markets, however, buyers may not know how the price they pay compares to the prices paid by other buyers (or simply may not take the trouble to find out). Alternatively, the monopolist may be in a position to prevent some groups from buying at the discount prices made available to others. In such cases, a monopolist must be able to do two things: (1) separate its market into submarkets, each with a different demand curve, and charge a different price in each submarket; (2) prevent buyers from buying at a low price in one submarket and reselling at a higher price in another submarket. If the monopolist cannot do both, it will not be able to practise price discrimination. If it can do both, it can practise price discrimination.

8.2   E C O N O M I C   N A T U R A L I S T

Why do many movie theatres offer discount tickets to students?

Whenever a firm offers a discount, the goal is to target that discount to buyers who would not purchase the product without it. People with low incomes generally have lower reservation prices for movie tickets than people with high incomes. Because students generally have lower disposable incomes than working adults, theatre owners can increase ticket sales by charging lower prices to students than to adults. Student discounts are one practical way of doing so. Offering student discounts also entails no risk of some people buying the product at a low price and then reselling it to others at a higher price.

HOW PRICE DISCRIMINATION AFFECTS OUTPUT

Examples 8.7 to 8.9 show how the ability to price-discriminate affects the monopolist's profit-maximizing level of output. First we will consider a baseline case in which the monopolist must charge the same price to every buyer.

How many manuscripts will Carla type?

EXAMPLE 8.7

Carla supplements her income as a teaching assistant by typing term papers for undergraduates. There are 8 students/week for whom she might type. Each student must submit one paper. Each student's reservation price for having Carla type his or her paper appears in the following table.

Student	Reservation price
A	$40
B	38
C	36
D	34
E	32
F	30
G	28
H	26

Carla is a profit maximizer. If each paper takes her two hours to type, and she could work elsewhere for $14.50 per hour, the opportunity cost of her time to type each paper is $29. If she must charge the same price to each student, how many papers will she type? How much profit will she make?

Table 8.5 summarizes Carla's total and marginal revenue at various output levels. To generate the amounts in the total revenue column, we simply multiplied the corresponding reservation price by the number of students whose reservation prices were at least that high. For example, to type 4 papers/week (for students *A, B, C,* and *D*), Carla must charge a price no higher than *D*'s reservation price ($34). So her total revenue when she types 4 papers/week is (4)($34) = $136/week. Carla will increase the number of students she serves as long as her marginal revenue exceeds the opportunity cost of her time. Marginal revenue, or the difference in total revenue that results from adding another student, is shown in the last column of Table 8.5.

TABLE 8.5
Total and Marginal Revenue from Typing

Student	Reservation price ($/paper)	Total revenue ($/week)	Marginal revenue ($/paper)
			40
A	40	40	
			36
B	38	76	
			32
C	36	108	
			28
D	34	136	
			24
E	32	160	
			20
F	30	180	
			16
G	28	196	
			12
H	26	208	

Note that if Carla were typing 2 papers/week, her marginal revenue from typing a third paper would be $32. Since that amount exceeds her $29 opportunity cost, she will type the third paper. But since the marginal revenue of typing a fourth paper would be only $28, Carla will not type a fourth paper. She will type 3 papers/week. The total opportunity cost of the time required to type the 3 papers is $(3)(\$29) = \$87$, so Carla's profit is $\$108 - \$87 = \$21$/week.

EXAMPLE 8.8

What is the socially efficient number of papers Carla can type?

Again, suppose that Carla's opportunity cost of typing is $29/paper and that she could type as many as 8 papers/week for students whose reservation prices remain as given in Table 8.5. What is the socially efficient number of papers Carla can type?If she must charge the same price to each student, what will her profit be if she types the socially efficient number of papers?

Refer to Table 8.5. Students *A* to *F* are willing to pay more than Carla's opportunity cost, so serving these students is socially efficient. But students *G* and *H* are unwilling to pay at least $29 for Carla's services. The socially efficient outcome, therefore, is for Carla to type 6 papers/week. To attract that number, she must charge a price no higher than $30/paper. Her total revenue will be $(6)(\$30) = \$180$/week, slightly more than her total opportunity cost of $(6)(\$29) = \$174$/week. Her profit will thus be only $6/week.

EXAMPLE 8.9

If Carla can price discriminate, how many papers will she type?

Suppose Carla is a shrewd judge of human nature. After a moment's conversation with a student, she can discern that student's reservation price. The reservation prices of her potential customers remain as given in Table 8.5. If Carla can charge students their respective reservation prices, how many papers will she type, and how much profit will she make?

Refer again to Table 8.5. Carla will type papers for students *A* to *F* and charge each exactly his or her reservation price. Because students *G* and *H* have reservation prices below $29, Carla will not type their papers. Carla's total revenue will be $\$40 + \$38 + \$36 + \$34 + \$32 + \$30 = \$210$/week. Her total opportunity cost of typing 6 papers is $(6)(\$29) = \$174$/week, so her profit will be $\$210 - \$174 = \$36$/week, $30/week more than when she was constrained to charge each customer the same price.

A monopolist who can charge each buyer exactly his or her reservation price is called a **perfectly discriminating monopolist**. Notice that when Carla was discriminating among customers in this way, her profit-maximizing level of output was exactly the same as the socially efficient level of output: 6 papers/week. With a perfectly discriminating monopoly, there is no loss of efficiency. All buyers who are willing to pay a price high enough to cover marginal cost will be served.

perfectly discriminating monopolist a firm that charges each buyer exactly his or her reservation price

Notice, too, that although total economic surplus is maximized by a perfectly discriminating monopolist, consumers would have little reason to celebrate if they found themselves dealing with such a firm. A monopolist that practises perfect price discrimination captures the entire economic surplus. Total economic surplus and producer surplus are the same. Therefore, when price discrimination is perfect, consumer surplus is zero.

PRICE DISCRIMINATION: A GRAPHICAL SUMMARY

The situation for Carla and her clients can also be portrayed graphically. The data from Table 8.5 are graphed in Figure 8.11. Because Carla cannot sell partially typed papers, continuous lines cannot represent her demand and marginal revenue schedules. Therefore, demand is graphed in panels (a) and (b) as a series of points. However, in both panels the points are connected by a straight line to show how Carla's demand curve would appear if she had the option of typing term papers in whatever fractions she wanted. The line is labelled D. Likewise, marginal revenue is graphed in panel (a) as a series of points that are connected by a straight line that is labeled MR. The opportunity cost of the time Carla spends to type each paper is $29. Therefore, her marginal cost is constant at $29. It is graphed as a series of points in both panels (a) and (b). The points are connected by a horizontal line with a vertical intercept at $29 to show how Carla's marginal cost curve would appear if she had any reason to type fractions of term papers. Because marginal cost is constant, it is equal to average cost; therefore, the graph of the marginal cost data is labelled MC = AC.

FIGURE 8.11

Two Monopoly Pricing Strategies

In both panels, the demand for Carla's typing services is graphed as a series of discrete points. In panel (a) she is portrayed as a monopolist who charges the same price to all her clients; therefore, she sets her price at $36 and types 3 papers. In panel (b) she practises perfect price discrimination, charging each client his or her reservation price. She types 6 papers, the socially efficient quantity, but captures the entire economic surplus.

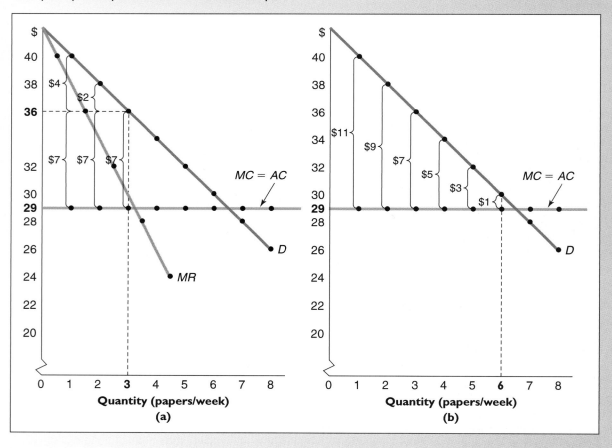

Panel (a) illustrates what Carla will do if she must charge one price to all her clients. She will choose a price of $36 and type 3 papers because the third paper is the last paper for which marginal revenue exceeds marginal cost. Carla's total opportunity cost is $87. Carla's profit/paper is $36 − $29 = $7. Therefore, her total profit is ($7/paper) × 3 papers = $21. The total profit can also be regarded as Carla's producer's surplus. Carla's total revenue for typing the 3 papers is ($36)3 = $108, which equals the sum of total cost and total profit. Notice, too, that each of Carla's 3 clients receives a consumer's surplus equal to the difference between the student's reservation price and the price Carla charges. Thus student A's consumer's surplus is $40 − $36 = $4. In the same way, students B and C each have a consumer's surplus of $2 and $0, respectively; therefore, total consumers' surplus is $6.

When Carla practises perfect price discrimination, a different picture emerges. As panel (b) shows, she charges each student his reservation price and types 6 papers. Her opportunity cost is $29 for each paper she types. Her profit on each paper is the difference between the client's reservation price and $29. Thus her profit on the first paper is $40 − $29 = $11; on the second, it is $38 − $29 = $9, and so on through the sixth paper, which gives her a total profit of $36. Again, her profit can also be interpreted as her producer's surplus. Notice two results that emerge from Panel (b). First, with perfect price discrimination, Carla maximizes total economic surplus—she produces the socially efficient quantity. Second, Carla captures the entire total economic surplus—there is no consumers' surplus.

In practice, of course, perfect price discrimination can never occur, because no seller knows each and every buyer's precise reservation price. But even if some sellers did know, practical difficulties would stand in the way of their charging a separate price to each buyer. For example, in many markets the seller would be unable to prevent buyers who bought at low prices from reselling to other buyers at higher prices, capturing some of the seller's business in the process. Despite these difficulties, price discrimination is widespread. But it is generally *imperfect price discrimination,* that is, price discrimination in which at least some buyers are charged less than their reservation prices.

PERFECT PRICE DISCRIMINATION: THE ESSENTIAL ISSUE

However, firms with some market power, not only monopolists, always have an incentive to price discriminate. When such firms develop new, improved mechanisms for price discrimination, two things happen: (1) their total output increases and gets closer to the socially efficient level of production, and (2) their share of the total economic surplus increases. If a monopolistic firm could *perfectly* price-discriminate, it would produce exactly the socially optimal amount, but would also capture the entire consumer surplus, as well as the entire producer surplus. In this case, the key issue is not the *amount* of economic surplus but the *distribution* of economic surplus. Would it be a good idea if the monopolist captured the entire economic surplus in an industry? Would your answer depend on whether the owner of the monopoly in question is: (a) a multinational corporation whose shareholders are all rich foreigners; (b) a charitable foundation that spends all its revenue on combating poverty; or (c) owned equally by all citizens? Typically, students have different answers to the question of the desirability of a perfectly discriminatory monopolist, depending on how they think the profits of that monopoly will be distributed.

THE HURDLE METHOD OF PRICE DISCRIMINATION

The profit-maximizing seller's goal is to charge each buyer the highest price that buyer is willing to pay. Two primary obstacles prevent sellers from achieving this goal. First, sellers do not know exactly how much each buyer is willing to pay. And second, they need some means of excluding those who are willing to pay a high price from buying at a low price. These are formidable problems, which no seller can hope to solve completely.

One common method by which sellers achieve a crude solution to both problems is to require buyers to overcome some obstacle to be eligible for a discount price. This method is called the **hurdle method of price discrimination.** For exam-

hurdle method of price discrimination the practice by which a seller offers a discount to all buyers who overcome some obstacle

ple, the seller might sell a product at a standard list price and offer a rebate to any buyer who takes the trouble to mail in a rebate coupon.

COST–BENEFIT

The hurdle method solves both the seller's problems, provided that buyers with low reservation prices are more willing than others to jump the hurdle. Because the decision to jump the hurdle is subject to the cost–benefit test, such a link seems to exist. As noted earlier, buyers with low incomes are more likely than others to have low reservation prices (at least in the case of normal goods). Because of the low opportunity cost of their time, they are more likely than others to take the trouble to send in rebate coupons. Rebate coupons thus target a discount toward those buyers whose reservation prices are low and who might not buy the product otherwise.

perfect hurdle one that completely segregates buyers whose reservation prices lie above some threshold from others whose reservation prices lie below it, imposing no cost on those who jump the hurdle

A **perfect hurdle** is one that separates buyers precisely according to their reservation prices, and in the process imposes no cost on those who jump the hurdle. With a perfect hurdle, the highest reservation price among buyers who jump the hurdle will be lower than the lowest reservation price among buyers who choose not to jump the hurdle. In practice, perfect hurdles do not exist. Some buyers will always jump the hurdle, even though their reservation prices are high. And hurdles will always exclude at least some buyers with low reservation prices. Even so, many commonly used hurdles do a remarkably good job of targeting discounts to buyers with low reservation prices.

Once you grasp the principle behind the hurdle method of price discrimination, you will begin to see many examples of it. Monopolistic competitors, oligopolists, and monopolists all have incentives to practise price discrimination. Next time you visit a grocery, hardware, or appliance store, for instance, notice how many different product promotions include cash rebates. Temporary sales are another illustration of the hurdle method. Stores usually sell their merchandise at the "regular" price, but periodically they offer special sales at a significant discount. The hurdle requires taking the trouble to find out when and where the sales occur and then going to the store during that period. This technique works because buyers with low reservation prices are more likely to monitor advertisements carefully and buy only during sale periods.

To give another example, book publishers typically launch a new book in hardcover form at a price from $20 to $30. A year later they bring out a paperback edition priced between $5 and $15. In this instance, the hurdle requires the buyer to wait an extra year and to accept a slight reduction in the quality of the finished product. People who are strongly concerned about price wait for the paperback edition, while those with high reservation prices usually pay for the hardcover.

Or take the example of automobile producers, who typically offer several different models with different trim and accessories. Although GM's actual cost of producing a Cadillac may be only $2000 more than its cost of producing a Chevrolet, the Cadillac's selling price may be $10 000 to $15 000 higher than the Chevrolet's. Buyers with low reservation prices purchase the Chevrolet, while those with high reservation prices are more likely to choose the Cadillac.

Commercial air carriers have perfected the hurdle method to an extent matched by almost no other seller.[5] Their supersaver fares are often less than half their regular coach fares. To be eligible for these discounts, travellers must purchase their tickets 7 to 21 days in advance, and their journey must include a Saturday night stayover. Vacation travellers can more easily satisfy these restrictions than business travellers, whose schedules often change at the last moment and whose trips seldom involve Saturday stayovers. And—no surprise—the business traveller's

---

[5] Jules Dupuit, a distinguished civil engineer, analyzed price discrimination more than 150 years ago. He had observed that railroads and providers of other public services charged different prices to different categories of customers and that the differences were unrelated to differences in cost. In 1933, Joan Robinson used a technical argument to show that discriminatory pricing between submarkets could either increase or decrease output compared to single price monopoly. Robinson suggested that cases where price discrimination increased total output would be more common than cases that reduced it.

reservation price tends to be much higher than the vacation traveller's.[6] Moreover, it is easy for airlines to practise price discrimination because it is easy for them to prevent people from buying discounted tickets and then selling them to travellers who have high reservation prices. Requiring all passengers to show photo identification may enhance the security of air transportation. It also tells airline personnel that the passenger is the original purchaser of the ticket. He did not buy a discounted ticket from someone else because he learned only yesterday of his urgent need to travel and is avoiding the purchase of an expensive ticket. Though managers of airlines may complain about the costs of enhanced security, they will never complain about the costs of requiring passengers to show photo identification.

Many sellers employ not just one hurdle but several by offering deeper discounts to buyers who jump successively more difficult hurdles. For example, movie producers release their major films to first-run theatres at premium prices, then several months later to neighbourhood theatres at a few dollars less. Still later they make the films available on pay-per-view cable channels, then release them on video, and finally permit them to be shown on network television. Each successive hurdle involves waiting a little longer, and in the case of the televised versions, accepting lower quality. These hurdles are remarkably effective in segregating moviegoers according to their reservation prices.

Recall that the efficiency loss from single-price monopoly occurs because to the monopolist the benefit of expanding output is smaller than the benefit to society as a whole. The hurdle method of price discrimination reduces this loss by giving the monopolist a practical means of cutting prices for price-sensitive buyers only. In general, the more finely the monopolist can partition a market using the hurdle method, the smaller the efficiency loss and the greater the share of total economic surplus captured by the monopolist. Hurdles are not perfect, however, and some degree of efficiency will inevitably be lost.

8.3 ECONOMIC NATURALIST

Why are U.S. drug companies now concerned about U.S. citizens shopping for prescriptions in Canada when they never were in the past?

High though the prices of prescription drugs may seem to Canadians, for many years they have been significantly lower in Canada (and Mexico) than in the U.S. Busloads of American senior citizens in border states have, therefore, long come across the border to fill their prescriptions in Canada. Seniors tend to have lower income and greater need for drugs than nonseniors. Although these people were purchasing the same drugs, made by the same companies, at lower prices in Canada than they would have had to pay in the U.S., U.S. drug companies did not attempt to interfere. The time necessary to make the trip to Canada meant that only low income people, who had lots of time available, would make the effort necessary to purchase drugs in Canada—and they might not have had the income necessary to purchase as many drugs at the higher prices charged in the U.S. Cross-border shopping for prescription drugs can therefore be seen as an example of the hurdle method of price discrimination—a way that U.S.

drug companies could charge higher prices to the large majority of their customers who do not have the time to travel to Canada, while also profiting from the additional sales made at lower Canadian prices to cross-border shoppers.

However, the "hurdle" method of price discrimination relies on the cost of the hurdle to potential consumers. In a social sense, it is inefficient to make people travel to another country to buy something that they could get from their corner drugstore. As Internet use has spread in the population, Internet-based pharmacies in Canada, which deliver by courier or parcel post, have started to target a broader U.S. market. It is no longer necessary to travel to Canada to obtain prescriptions at the lower Canadian price because the Internet has removed the hurdle. U.S. drug companies have become seriously concerned and can be expected to press the Canadian government for policies that keep prices of Canadian prescription drugs as high as they are in the U.S.

[6]Jules Dupuit, "On the Measurement of the Utility of Public Works," translated by R.H. Barback, *International Economic Papers*, no. 2, London: MacMillan 1952, (1844), pp. 83–110. Jules Dupuit, "On Tolls and Transport Charges," translated by R.H. Barback, *International Economic Papers*, no. 11, London: MacMillan 1962, (1849), pp. 7–31. Joan Robinson, *Economics of Imperfect Competition*, London: Macmillan and Co., Limited, 1933, pp. 170–208. Also Robert B. Ekelund, Jr. and Robert F. Hebert, *A History of Economic Theory and Method*, 4th ed., New York: McGraw-Hill, 1997, pp. 267–280, 455.

> **RECAP** | **USING DISCOUNTS TO EXPAND THE MARKET**
>
> A price-discriminating seller is one who charges different prices to different buyers for essentially the same good or service. A common method of price discrimination is the hurdle method, which involves granting a discount to buyers who jump over a hurdle, such as mailing in a rebate coupon. An effective hurdle is one that is more easily cleared by buyers with low reservation prices than by buyers with high reservation prices. In many cases, such a hurdle enables the seller to expand output and thereby reduce the deadweight loss from monopoly pricing. The amount of increase in output and the magnitude of the distributional implications of price discrimination will depend on characteristics such as the elasticity of the demand curves in submarkets.

■ 8.7 MONOPOLISTIC COMPETITION: A BLEND OF COMPETITION AND LIMITED MARKET POWER

How should we think of a firm like GAP, which has a *monopoly* in sales of a particular line of clothing but faces *competition* from Old Navy and a large number of other clothing companies? Monopolistic competition is a market structure characterized by three features: First, many firms serve the market. Second, the firms sell *differentiated* products that nevertheless are reasonably close substitutes for each other. Third, there are no barriers to entry. Thus, product differentiation is the *sole* feature that distinguishes monopolistic competition from perfect competition.

PRODUCT DIFFERENTIATION AND MARKET POWER

A monopolistically competitive firm differentiates its product from competing products by advertising or by some functional feature. When we look at markets for many consumer goods—for example, toothpaste, breakfast cereal, laundry detergent, or bottled water, we see many varieties of essentially the same product competing for our dollars. In some cases, the differentiation is largely artificial (bottled water is a prime example), and the point of advertising is to create product differentiation in the consumer's mind. In other cases (e.g., automobiles or stereos) there are real differences in the characteristics of different goods even though they perform the same function. However, whether real or artificial, product differentiation provides the monopolistic competitor with a limited degree of market power. Thus the monopolistic competitor faces a downward sloping demand curve. However, if barriers to entry are absent (nearly anybody can, for example, hire an advertising agency and start bottling water), a monopolistic competitor in long run equilibrium earns a normal rate of return.[7]

Consider Figure 8.12, which represents a monopolistically competitive firm in short run equilibrium. The firm has used advertising to differentiate its product; therefore, its demand curve, represented by D, is downward sloping. Also, because the firm incurs expenses by advertising, its long-run average cost curve, represented by $LRAC$, is higher than it would be for a comparable perfectly competitive firm. (Recall that the perfect competitor does no advertising.) The monopolistic competitor represented in Figure 8.12 maximizes profit by selecting price P

[7]Edward Chamberlin developed the theory of monopolistic competition in order to analyze markets that combined a high degree of competition with product differentiation. Edward Chamberlin, *The Theory of Monopolistic Competition* (Cambridge: Harvard University Press), 1938.

and output Q because this is where marginal revenue equals marginal cost (represented by MR and MC). Average cost is C; therefore, the monopolistic competitor realizes an economic profit, represented by the green rectangle.

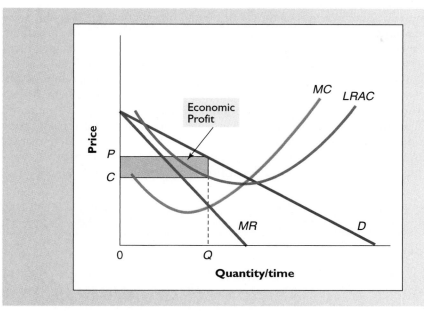

FIGURE 8.12

A Monopolistically Competitive Firm in Short-Run Equilibrium
In the short run, a monopolistically competitive firm earns an economic profit by differentiating its product.

However, if there are no barriers to entry in monopolistic competition, this economic profit cannot persist. New firms will be attracted by the promise of economic profit to enter the market. Each new firm will supply a somewhat different but competing product. New firms will continue to enter the market as long as the "typical" firm is making economic profits (i.e., more than is necessary to pay the opportunity cost of capital, labour, and entrepreneurship). Eventually, when enough new firms have entered the market, long-run equilibrium will occur with the typical firm making zero economic profit. This situation is represented in Figure 8.13. The cost curves in Figure 8.13 are identical to those in Figure 8.12. And, just as before, the firm chooses the price and quantity that cause marginal revenue to equal marginal cost. However, compared with Figure 8.12, the firm's demand curve has shifted to the left. As Figure 8.13 shows, the monopolistic

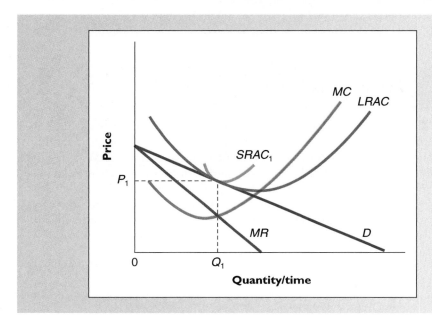

FIGURE 8.13

A Monopolistically Competitive Firm in Long-Run Equilibrium
In the long run, competition causes a monopolistically competitive firm to earn a normal profit.

competitor in long-run equilibrium earns only a normal profit. Because the firm's demand curve slopes downward, demand is tangent to the firm's long-run average cost curve at quantity Q_1 and price P_1. Both Q_1 and P_1 are smaller than P and Q, respectively, of Figure 8.12.

In long-run equilibrium, even though the firm is earning a normal profit, *price exceeds marginal cost*. Furthermore, quantity Q_1 is too small to achieve minimum long-run average cost. As Figure 8.13 shows, the firm chooses the scale of operation that is represented by the short-run average cost curve that is labeled $SRAC_1$. This scale is too small to fully realize economies of scale. Even having chosen $SRAC_1$, the firm produces quantity Q_1, which is too small to reach the lowest short-run average cost that can be accomplished, given $SRAC_1$. As well, the monopolistically competitive firm has advertising costs, which perfectly competitive firms do not. All these features cause a monopolistically competitive market to produce a smaller total economic surplus than its perfectly competitive counterpart, thus making monopolistic competition inefficient.

ECONOMIC NATURALIST

Why is there such a wide range of prices for Scotch whisky?

A typical liquor store will feature several varieties of generic blended Scotch whisky and a selection of single-malt Scotches, the most expensive of which may retail for four or five times the price of the most inexpensive blended Scotch whisky. This range of prices pertains for bottles containing the same amount of Scotch, all with approximately the same alcohol content, and all produced in the same part of the world using much the same technique. Why does single-malt Scotch sell for so much more?

Each producer of single malt Scotch has a monopoly—the production of a particular distillery. If consumers can be convinced that there is something unique, and extra desirable, about "the peaty aroma" or "the purity of rainfall" of that particular distillery, then "monopoly" or market power can be created. Success in differentiating a product means that consumers will pay a higher price for the product because they like the qualities it offers. (Indeed, producers of

blended Scotch whiskys also differentiate their products, and the price of the most expensive blended Scotch is much higher than the least expensive.) At the same time, the theory of monopolistic competition hypothesizes that economic profits cannot persist in the long run. If Figure 8.12 represented the situation of a "typical" distillery of specialty Scotch, the existence of economic profit would provide an incentive for new producers to invest in building distilleries. When economic profits are present, the producers of "no name" whiskys also have an incentive to invest in an advertising campaign extolling the virtues of their products and helping them to sell more. Both types of market entry would steal some customers from the firm represented in Figure 8.12, which would experience a decrease of demand. But, even though large differences in prices persist, a monopolistic competitor in long-run equilibrium earns only a normal profit, as shown in Figure 8.13.

RECAP   MONOPOLISTIC COMPETITION

Monopolistic competition is a market structure in which a large number of firms sell differentiated products that compete with each other. Product differentiation is the sole feature that distinguishes monopolist competition from perfect competition. Monopolistic competition is inefficient because advertising makes costs higher than they need to be, monopolistic competitors chose inefficiently small scales of operation, and they operate their plants with excess capacity. The theory of monopolistic competition can be used to analyze markets that combine a high degree of competition with product differentiation.

▩ SUMMARY

- **8.1** Our concern in this chapter was the conduct and performance of the imperfectly competitive firm, a firm that has at least some latitude to set its own price. Economists often distinguish among three different types of imperfectly competitive firms: the pure monopolist, the lone seller of a product in a given market; the oligopolist, one of only a few rival sellers of a given product; and the monopolistic competitor, one of a relatively large number of firms that sell similar though slightly differentiated products.

- **8.1** Although advanced courses in economics devote much attention to differences in the behaviour among these three types of firms, our focus was on the common feature that differentiates them from perfectly competitive firms. Whereas the perfectly competitive firm faces an infinitely elastic demand curve for its product, the imperfectly competitive firm faces a downward-sloping demand curve.

- **8.2** Firms with market power have limited ability to increase the price of their product without losing all their sales. Market power stems from exclusive control over important inputs, from economies of scale, from patents, from licences or franchises, and from network economies. The most important and enduring of these five sources of market power is economies of scale.

- **8.3** Large fixed cost may cause marginal cost to be less than average total cost. Such a situation can be an important factor in economies of scale.

- **8.4** Unlike the perfectly competitive firm, for which marginal revenue exactly equals market price, the imperfectly competitive firm's marginal revenue is always less than its price. This shortfall reflects the fact that to sell more output, the firm must reduce the price not only to additional buyers but to existing buyers as well. For the imperfectly competitive firm with a straight-line demand curve, the marginal revenue curve has the same vertical intercept and a horizontal intercept that is half as large as the intercept for the demand curve.

- **8.5** Whereas the perfectly competitive firm maximizes profit by producing at the level at which marginal cost equals the market price, the imperfectly competitive firm maximizes profit by equating marginal cost with marginal revenue, which is significantly lower than the market price. The result is an output level that is best for the imperfectly competitive firm but smaller than the level that would be best for society as a whole. Total economic surplus is smaller, and it is distributed less in favour of consumers and more in favour of the firm than is the case for the socially efficient price and quantity. At the profit-maximizing level of output, the benefit of an extra unit of output (the market price) is greater than its cost (the marginal cost). At the socially efficient level of output, where the marginal cost curve intersects the market demand curve, the benefit and cost of an extra unit are the same.

- **8.6** In many cases, both the firm and its potential customers can do better if the firm can grant discounts to price-sensitive buyers. The extreme example is the perfectly discriminating monopolist, who charges each buyer exactly his or her reservation price. Such producers are socially efficient, because they sell to every buyer whose reservation price is at least as high as the marginal cost. However, a monopolist that practises perfect price discrimination will capture the entire economic surplus. Under perfect price discrimination, consumer surplus will be zero.

- **8.6** One common method of targeting discounts toward price-sensitive buyers is the hurdle method of price discrimination, in which the buyer becomes eligible for a discount only after overcoming some obstacle, such as mailing in a rebate coupon. This technique works well because those buyers who care most about price are more likely than others to jump the hurdle. Although the hurdle method reduces the efficiency loss associated with single-price monopoly, it does not completely eliminate it.

- **8.7** Monopolistic competition is a market structure in which many firms sell differentiated products that compete with each other. It is inefficient because advertising increases costs unnecessarily, firms chose inefficiently small scales of operation and operate their plants with excess capacity, and price is greater than marginal cost. The theory of monopolistic competition can be used to analyze markets characterized by differentiated products and substantial competition.

▩ KEY TERMS

hurdle method of price discrimination (245)
imperfectly competitive firm (221)
marginal revenue (230)
market power (222)

monopolistic competition (221)
natural monopoly (223)
oligopoly (221)
perfect hurdle (246)

perfectly discriminating monopolist (243)
price discrimination (241)
price setter (221)
pure monopoly (221)

■ REVIEW QUESTIONS

1. What important characteristic do all three types of imperfectly competitive firm share?

2. True or false: A firm with market power can sell whatever quantity it wants at whatever price it chooses.

3. Why do most successful industrial societies offer patents and copyright protection, even though these protections enable sellers to charge higher prices?

4. Why is marginal revenue always less than the price for a monopolist but equal to the price for a perfectly competitive firm?

5. Explain how a monopoly that charges a single price transfers part of a smaller total economic surplus from consumers to itself.

6. Explain how a monopolist can use price discrimination to transfer part or all of total economic surplus to itself.

7. Explain how a monopolist that practises price discrimination can be more efficient than a monopolist that charges one price to all buyers.

8. True or false: Because a natural monopolist charges a price greater than marginal cost, it necessarily earns a positive economic profit.

9. Explain why monopolistic competition is an inefficient market structure.

■ PROBLEMS

1. Two car manufacturers, Saab and Volvo, have fixed costs of $1 billion and marginal costs of $10 000/car. If Saab produces 50 000 cars/year and Volvo produces 200 000, calculate the average production cost for each company. Based on these costs, which company's market share do you think will grow in relative terms?

2. State whether the following statements are true or false, and explain why.
   a. In a perfectly competitive industry, the industry demand curve is horizontal, whereas for a monopoly it is downward sloping.
   b. Perfectly competitive firms have no control over the price they charge for their product.
   c. For a natural monopoly, average cost declines as the number of units produced increases over the relevant output range.

3. State whether the following statements are true, false, or uncertain, and explain why. A single-price profit-maximizing monopolist:
   a. Causes excess demand, or shortages, by selling too few units of a good or service.
   b. Chooses the output level at which marginal revenue begins to increase.
   c. Always charges a price above the marginal cost of production.
   d. Also maximizes marginal revenue.
   e. None of the above statements is true.

4. State whether the following statements are true, false, or uncertain, and explain why. If a monopolist could perfectly price-discriminate:
   a. The marginal revenue curve and the demand curve would coincide.
   b. The marginal revenue curve and the marginal cost curve would coincide.
   c. Every consumer would pay a different price.
   d. Marginal revenue would become negative at some output level.
   e. The resulting pattern of exchange would still be socially inefficient.

5. What is the socially desirable price for a natural monopoly to charge? Why will a natural monopoly that attempts to charge the socially desirable price invariably suffer an economic loss?

6. TotsPoses, Inc., a profit-maximizing business, is the only photography business in town that specializes in portraits of small children. Sven, who owns and runs TotsPoses, expects to encounter an average of eight customers per day, each with a reservation price shown in the following table.

Customer	Reservation price ($/photo)
A	50
B	46
C	42
D	38
E	34
F	30
G	26
H	22

a. If the marginal cost of each photoportrait is $12, how much should Sven charge if he must charge a single price to all customers? At this price, how many portraits will Sven produce each day? What will be his economic profit?

b. How much consumer surplus is generated each day at this price?

c. What is the socially efficient number of portraits?

d. Sven is very experienced in the business and knows the reservation price of each of his customers. If he is allowed to charge any price he likes to any consumer, how many portraits will he produce each day, and what will his economic profit be?

e. In this case, how much consumer surplus is generated each day?

f. Suppose Sven is permitted to charge two prices. He knows that customers with a reservation price above $30 never bother with coupons, whereas those with a reservation price of $30 or less always use them. At what level will Sven set the list price of a portrait? At what level should he set the discount price? How many photoportraits will he sell at each price?

g. In this case, what is Sven's economic profit, and how much consumer surplus is generated each day?

7. Suppose that the Charlottetown Cinema is a local monopoly whose demand curve for adult tickets on Saturday night is $P = 12 - 2Q$, where P is the price of a ticket in dollars and Q is the number of tickets sold in hundreds. The demand for children's tickets on Sunday afternoon is $P = 8 - 3Q$, and for adult tickets on Sunday afternoon, $P = 10 - 4Q$. On both Saturday night and Sunday afternoon, the marginal cost of an additional patron, child or adult, is $2.

a. What is the marginal revenue curve in each of the three submarkets?

b. What price will the cinema charge in each of the three markets if its goal is to maximize profit?

8. Suppose you are a monopolist in the market for a specific video game. Your demand curve is given by $P = 80 - Q/2$, and your marginal cost curve is $MC = 10$. Your fixed costs equal $400.

a. Graph the demand and marginal cost curve.

b. Derive and graph the marginal revenue curve.

c. Calculate and indicate on the graph the monopoly price and quantity.

d. What is your profit?

e. What is the level of consumer surplus?

9. Indira is a second-grader who sells lemonade on a street corner in your neighbourhood. She is the only seller in her neighbourhood. Each cup of lemonade costs Indira 20 cents to produce; she has no fixed costs. The reservation prices for the 10 people who walk by Indira's lemonade stand each day are listed in the following table.

Person	A	B	C	D	E	F	G	H	I	J
Reservation Price	$1.00	$0.90	$0.80	$0.70	$0.60	$0.50	$0.40	$0.30	$0.20	$0.10

Indira knows the distribution of reservation prices (that is, she knows that one person is willing to pay $1, another $0.90, and so on), but she does not know any specific individual's reservation price.
   a. Calculate the marginal revenue of selling an additional cup of lemonade. (Start by figuring out the price Indira would charge if she produced only one cup of lemonade and calculate the total revenue; then find the price Indira would charge if she sold two cups of lemonade; and so on.)
   b. What is Indira's profit-maximizing price?
   c. At that price, what are Indira's economic profit and total consumer surplus?
   d. What price will Indira charge if she wants to maximize total economic surplus?
   e. Now suppose Indira can tell the reservation price of each person. What price would she charge each person if she wanted to maximize profit? Compare her profit to the total surplus calculated in part (d).

10. Refer to problem (10) and its table. This time, suppose that a number of other children are selling lemonade in Indira's neighbourhood. However, Indira's family owns a greenhouse in which a few lemon and lime trees are growing (along with many other plants). They are the only lemon and lime trees anywhere near Indira's town. On the advice of an older sister, Indira blends juice from freshly picked lemons and limes into her lemonade. She posts paper signs at her corner advertising that her lemonade uses juice from the freshest lemons and limes that can be found anywhere. Her signs also state that her lemonade has a wonderful, unique flavour because she uses a special blend of lemon and lime juices. Suppose that Indira's variable cost remains at $0.20 per cup. However, her signs cost $1.00 to make. Indira knows the distribution of reservation prices (that is, she knows one person is willing to pay $1.00 and so on), but she does not know any specific individual's reservation price.
   a. Given the assumptions for this problem, is Indira selling in a perfectly competitive market or a monopolistically competitive market? Why?
   b. What price will Indira charge? How many cups of lemonade will she sell? Explain.
   c. Suppose Indira operates her stand five days per week. Because of wear and tear, she must replace her signs once per week. Also, her sister has advised her that she can keep the attention of her customers if she changes the colour and design of the signs each week. What are Indira's total *weekly* costs? Would her costs be higher or lower if she were selling in a perfectly competitive market? How much higher or lower? Explain.
   d. Calculate Indira's *weekly* economic profit. When making your calculations, include the data given in (c). Also, assume that the variable cost of lemonade includes the opportunity cost of Indira's time.
   e. If Indira is a monopolistic competitor, will her profits persist in the long run? Why or why not?

11. Consider the market for taxicab drivers in a city. Assume that each driver owns and drives her own cab—she is the owner-operator of a small business. Each driver also pays for the services of a dispatcher.
   a. Assume the market for taxi services is perfectly competitive. Use a graph to show the price a driver will charge and the number of kilometers she will drive in long-run equilibrium. Explain.
   b. Now assume that the market for taxi services is monopolistically competitive and answer (a). Explain your answer.
   c. Suppose a driver's shift is 10 hours long. Will a driver do more driving per shift if the market is perfectly competitive or monopolistically competitive? Why? In which case will a passenger pay a higher price for a trip? Why?
   d. Suppose the opportunity cost of a driver's time is $10/hour. How much will a driver earn when the market for taxi services is in long-run equilibrium and the market is perfectly competitive? What if the market is monopolistically competitive? If your answers are the same, explain why. If they are not the same, explain why not.
   e. Your answer to (c) should reveal that a driver will drive fewer kilometers during a 10-hour shift if the market is monopolistically competitive. Your answer to (d) should reveal that in long-run equilibrium, a driver will earn $10/hour for each

hour of a 10-hour shift, regardless of whether the market is perfectly or monopolistically competitive. How is it possible for a driver to drive less in a monopolistically competitive market yet earn the opportunity cost of her time?

■ ANSWERS TO IN-CHAPTER EXERCISES

8.1 The relevant cost figures are as shown in the following table, which shows that Sony's unit-cost advantage is now $50.20 − $5.20 = $45.00.

	Microsoft	**Sony**
Annual production	200 000	2 000 000
Fixed cost	$10 000 000	$10 000 000
Variable cost	$40 000	$400 000
Total cost	$10 040 000	$10 400 000
Average cost per game	$50.20	$5.20

8.2 When the monopolist expands from three to four units/week, total revenue rises from $15 to $16/week, which means that the marginal revenue from the sale of the fourth unit is only $1/week. When the monopolist expands from four to five units/week, total revenue drops from $16 to 15/week, which means that the marginal revenue from the sale of the fifth unit is actually negative, or −$1/week.

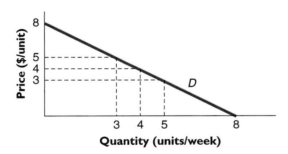

8.3 For the demand curve $P = 12 − Q$, the corresponding marginal revenue curve is $MR = 12 − 2Q$. Equating MR and MC, we solve the equation $12 − 2Q = 2Q$ for $Q = 3$. Substituting $Q = 3$ into the demand equation, we solve for the profit-maximizing price, $P = 12 − 3 = 9$.

THINKING STRATEGICALLY

At a dinner party in 1997, actor Robert DeNiro pulled singer Tony Bennett aside for a moment. "Hey, Tony—there's a film I want you in," DeNiro said. He was referring to the project that became the 1999 Warner Brothers hit comedy *Analyze This,* in which the troubled head of a crime family, played by DeNiro, seeks the counsel of a psychotherapist, played by Billy Crystal. In the script, both the mob boss and his therapist are big fans of Bennett's music.

Bennett heard nothing further about the project for almost a year. Then his son and financial manager, Danny Bennett, got a phone call from Warner Brothers, in which the studio offered Tony $15 000 to sing "Got the World on a String" in the movie's final scene. As Danny described the conversation, "... they made a fatal mistake. They told me they had already shot the film. So I'm like: 'Hey, they shot the whole film around Tony being the end gag and they're offering me $15 000?'"[1]

Warner Brothers paid $200 000 for Bennett's performance.

In business negotiations, as in life, timing can be everything. If executives at Warner Brothers had thought the problem through carefully, they would have negotiated with Bennett *before* shooting the movie. At that point Bennett would have realized that the script could be rewritten if he asked too high a fee. By waiting, studio executives left themselves with no other option than to pay Bennett's price.

The payoff to many actions depends not only on the actions themselves but also on when they are taken and how they relate to actions taken by others. In previous chapters, economic decision makers confronted an environment that was essentially fixed. This chapter will focus on cases in which people must consider the effect of their behaviour on others. For example, an imperfectly competitive firm will want to weigh the likely responses of rivals when deciding whether to cut prices or to increase the advertising budget. Interdependencies of this sort are the rule rather than the exception in economic and social life. To make sense of the world we live in, then, we must take these interdependencies into account.

[1] As quoted by Geraldine Fabrikant, "Talking Money with Tony Bennett," *The New York Times,* May 2, 1999, Money & Business, p. 1.

9.1 THE THEORY OF GAMES

In chess, tennis, or any other game, the payoff to a given move depends on what your opponent does in response. In choosing your move, therefore, you must anticipate your opponent's responses, how you might respond, and what further moves your own response might elicit. In such situations, payoffs to different actors depend on the actions their opponents take. The theory of games, developed by mathematicians, economists, and other behavioural scientists, uses logical deduction to explore the consequences arising when small numbers of interdependent competitors use different strategies. It can be used to study warfare, crime, and other topics that some might not regard as subjects of conventional economics. Its name notwithstanding, game theory is often used to study strategies that have momentous outcomes.

If all economic markets were perfectly competitive, there would be no need for economists to study game theory. In a perfectly competitive market, each firm is such a small part of the total industry that its decisions have only an infinitesimal impact on the profitability of any and all other individual firms in the market (and vice versa). If, for example, one perfectly competitive firm changes its quantity of output, there is no impact on market price because the firm's production is such a small fraction of total industry output. Therefore, no firm needs to consider what the response of other firms to its own decisions might be. However, in imperfectly competitive markets, each firm's decisions *will* affect the profitability of other firms' decisions. When the other firms react by changing their own decisions, they affect the initial firm. In such circumstances, firms need to find *strategies* about how best to respond to the decisions of their competitors.

THE THREE ELEMENTS OF A GAME

Any game has three **basic elements**: the players, the list of possible actions (or strategies) each player can choose from, and the payoffs the players receive for each combination of strategies. How these elements combine to form the basis of a theory of behaviour will become clear in the context of the following illustrative examples.

basic elements of a game the players, the strategies available to each player, and the payoffs each player receives for each possible combination of strategies

---

Will Pepsi spend more money on advertising?

EXAMPLE 9.1

Imagine that Pepsi and Coca Cola are the only makers of cola drinks. Both are earning economic profits of $6000/day. However, both want to increase their profits. Assume the following: If Pepsi increases its advertising expenditures in this market by $1000/day and Coca Cola spends no more on advertising than it does now, Pepsi's profit will increase to $8000/day and Coca Cola's will decrease to $2000. If both spend $1000 on advertising, each will earn an economic profit of $5500/day. These payoffs are symmetric, so if Pepsi stands pat while Coca Cola increases its spending by $1000, Pepsi's economic profit will fall to $2000/day, and Coca Cola's will increase to $8000. If each must decide independently whether to increase spending on advertising, what should Pepsi do?

Think of this situation as a game. What are its three elements? The players are the two soft drink companies, each of which must choose one of two strategies: to raise spending by $1000 or to leave it the same. The payoffs are the economic profits that correspond to the four possible scenarios resulting from their choices. One way to summarize the relevant information about this game is to display the players, strategies, and payoffs in the form of a simple table called a **payoff matrix** (see Table 9.1).

payoff matrix a table that describes the payoffs in a game for each possible combination of strategies

TABLE 9.1
The Payoff Matrix for an Advertising Game

		Coca Cola	
		Raise spending on advertisements	Leave spending on advertisements the same
Pepsi	Raise spending on advertisements	$5500 for Pepsi $5500 for Coca Cola	$8000 for Pepsi $2000 for Coca Cola
	Leave spending on advertisements the same	$2000 for Pepsi $8000 for Coca Cola	$6000 for Pepsi $6000 for Coca Cola

Confronted with the payoff matrix in Table 9.1, what should Pepsi do? The essence of strategic thinking is to begin by looking at the situation from the other party's point of view. Suppose Coca Cola assumes that Pepsi will raise its spending on advertising (the top row in Table 9.1). In that case, Coca Cola's best option would be to follow suit (the left column in Table 9.1). Why is the left column Coca Cola's best response when Pepsi chooses the top row? Coca Cola's economic profits, given in the upper left cell of Table 9.1, will be $5500 as compared with only $2000 if it keeps spending constant (see the upper right cell).

Alternatively, suppose Coca Cola assumes that Pepsi will not change its expenditures on advertising (that is, Pepsi will choose the bottom row in Table 9.1). In that case, Coca Cola would still do better to increase spending, because it would earn $8000 (the lower left cell) as compared with only $6000 if it keeps spending constant (lower right cell). In this particular game, no matter which strategy Pepsi chooses, Coca Cola will earn a higher economic profit by increasing its spending on advertising. And since this game is perfectly symmetric, a similar conclusion holds for Pepsi: No matter which strategy Coca Cola chooses, Pepsi will do better by increasing its spending on advertisements.

dominant strategy one that yields a higher payoff no matter what the other players in a game choose

When one player has a strategy that yields a higher payoff no matter which choice the other player makes, that player is said to have a **dominant strategy.** Not all games involve dominant strategies, but both players in this game have one, and that is to increase spending on advertisements. For both players, to leave ad spending the same is a **dominated strategy**—one that leads to a lower payoff than an alternative choice, regardless of the other player's choice.

dominated strategy any other strategy available to a player who has a dominant strategy

Notice, however, that when each player chooses the dominant strategy, the resulting payoffs are smaller than if each had left spending unchanged. When Pepsi and Coca Cola increase their spending on advertisements, each earns only $5500 in economic profits as compared to the $6000 each would have earned without the increase. (We will say more below about this apparent paradox. Notice that we now have an alternative to monopolistic competition (Chapter 8) as an explanation of excessive advertising.)

NASH EQUILIBRIUM

A game is said to be in equilibrium if each player's strategy is the best he or she can choose, given the other players' strategies. This definition of equilibrium is sometimes called a **Nash equilibrium,** after the Nobel laureate John Nash, who developed the concept in the early 1950s. When a game is in equilibrium, no player has any incentive to deviate from his or her current strategy.

Nash equilibrium any combination of strategies in which each player's strategy is his or her best choice, given the other players' strategies

If each player in a game has a dominant strategy, as in Example 9.1, equilibrium occurs when each player follows that strategy. But even in games in which not every player has a dominant strategy, we can often identify an equilibrium outcome. Consider, for instance, the following variation on the advertising game in Example 9.1.

EXAMPLE 9.2

Will Coca Cola spend more money on advertising?

Suppose Pepsi and Coca Cola are the only makers of cola drinks. Their payoff matrix for advertising decisions is shown in Table 9.2. Does Pepsi have a dominant strategy? Does Coca Cola? If each firm does the best it can, given the incentives facing the other, what will be the outcome of this game?

TABLE 9.2
Equilibrium When One Player Lacks a Dominant Strategy

		Coca Cola	
		Raise spending on advertisements	Leave spending on advertisements the same
Pepsi	Raise spending on advertisements	$3000 for Pepsi $8000 for Coca Cola	$8000 for Pepsi $4000 for Coca Cola
	Leave spending on advertisements the same	$4000 for Pepsi $4000 for Coca Cola	$5000 for Pepsi $2000 for Coca Cola

In this game, no matter what Pepsi does, Coca Cola will do better to increase its advertising, so raising the advertising budget is a dominant strategy for Coca Cola. Pepsi, however, does not have a dominant strategy. If Coca Cola raises its spending, Pepsi will do better to stand pat; if Coca Cola stands pat, however, Pepsi will do better to spend more. But even though Pepsi does not have a dominant strategy, we can still predict what is likely to happen in this game. After all, Pepsi's managers know what the payoff matrix is, so they can predict that Coca Cola will spend more on advertisements (since that is Coca Cola's dominant strategy). Thus, the best strategy for Pepsi, given the prediction that Coca Cola will spend more on ads, is to keep its own spending constant. If both players do the best they can, taking account of the incentives each faces, this game will end in the lower left cell of the payoff matrix: Coca Cola will raise its spending on advertisements and Pepsi will not. (Note that when both players are positioned in the lower left cell, neither has any incentive to change its strategy.)

EXERCISE 9.1

What will Pepsi and Coca Cola do if their payoff matrix is modified as follows?

		Coca Cola	
		Raise spending on advertisements	Leave spending on advertisements the same
Pepsi	Raise spending on advertisements	$3000 for Pepsi $8000 for Coca Cola	$4000 for Pepsi $5000 for Coca Cola
	Leave spending on advertisements the same	$8000 for Pepsi $4000 for Coca Cola	$5000 for Pepsi $2000 for Coca Cola

> **RECAP** **THE THEORY OF GAMES**
>
> The three elements of any game are the players, the list of strategies from which they can choose, and the payoffs to each combination of strategies. Players in some games have a dominant strategy, one that yields a higher payoff regardless of the strategies chosen by other players.
>
> Equilibrium in a game occurs when each player chooses the strategy that yields the highest payoff available, given the strategies chosen by other players. Such a combination of strategies is called a Nash equilibrium.

▦ 9.2 THE PRISONER'S DILEMMA

prisoner's dilemma a game in which each player has a dominant strategy, and when each plays it, the resulting payoffs are smaller than if each had played a dominated strategy

The game in Example 9.1 belongs to an important class of games called the **prisoner's dilemma.** In the prisoner's dilemma, when each player chooses his dominant strategy, the result is unattractive to the group of players as a whole.

THE ORIGINAL PRISONER'S DILEMMA

Example 9.3 recounts the original scenario from which the prisoner's dilemma drew its name.

EXAMPLE 9.3

Should the prisoners confess?

Two prisoners, Horace and Jasper, are being held in separate cells for a serious crime that they did in fact commit. The prosecutor, however, has only enough hard evidence to convict them of a minor offence, for which the penalty is a year in jail. Each prisoner is told that if one confesses while the other remains silent, the confessor will go free and the other will spend 20 years in prison. (A confession by one prisoner implicates the other.) If both confess, they will get an intermediate sentence of five years. (These payoffs are summarized in Table 9.3.) The two prisoners are not allowed to communicate with one another. Do they have a dominant strategy? If so, what is it?

TABLE 9.3
The Payoff Matrix for a Prisoner's Dilemma

		Jasper	
		Confess	Remain silent
Horace	Confess	5 years for each	0 years for Horace 20 years for Jasper
	Remain silent	20 years for Horace 0 years for Jasper	1 year for each

In this game, the dominant strategy for each prisoner is to confess. No matter what Jasper does, Horace will get a lighter sentence by confessing. If Jasper confesses, Horace will get five years (upper left cell) instead of 20 (lower left cell). If Jasper remains silent, Horace will go free (upper right cell) instead of spending a year in jail (lower right cell). Because the payoffs are perfectly symmetric, Jasper will also do better to confess, no matter what Horace does. The difficulty is that when each follows his dominant strategy and confesses, both will do worse than if each had shown restraint. When both confess, they each get five years (upper left cell) instead of the one year they would have gotten by remaining silent (lower right cell). Hence the name of this game, the prisoner's dilemma.

GM and Ford must both decide whether to invest in a new process. Games 1 and 2 below show how their profits depend on the decisions they make. Which of these games is a prisoner's dilemma?

EXERCISE 9.2

Game 1
Ford

		Not invest	Invest
GM	Not invest	10 for each	4 for GM 12 for Ford
	Invest	12 for GM 4 for Ford	5 for each

Game 2
Ford

		Not invest	Invest
GM	Not invest	4 for GM 12 for Ford	5 for each
	Invest	10 for each	12 for GM 4 for Ford

The prisoner's dilemma is one of the most powerful metaphors in all of human behavioural science. Countless social and economic interactions have payoff structures analogous to the one confronted by the two prisoners. Some of those interactions occur between only two players, as in the examples just discussed; many others involve larger groups. But regardless of the number of players involved, the common thread is one of conflict between the narrow self-interest of individuals and the broader interests of larger communities. The issue is whether individuals can co-ordinate their actions, and end up better off, by *not* acting in their narrow self-interest.

PRISONER'S DILEMMAS CONFRONTING IMPERFECTLY COMPETITIVE FIRMS

A **cartel** is any coalition of firms that conspire to restrict production for the purpose of earning an economic profit. As we will see in the next example, the problem confronting oligopolists who are trying to form a cartel is a classic illustration of the prisoner's dilemma.

cartel a coalition of firms that agree to restrict output for the purpose of earning an economic profit

---

🍁 9.1   **E C O N O M I C   N A T U R A L I S T**

Why are cartel agreements notoriously unstable?

Consider a market for bottled water served by only two firms, Aquapure and Mountain Spring. Each firm can draw water free from a mineral spring located on its own land. Customers supply their own bottles. Rather than compete with one another, the two firms decide to collude by selling water at the price a profit-maximizing pure monopolist would charge. Under their agreement (which constitutes a cartel), each firm would produce and sell half the quantity of water demanded by the market at the monopoly price (see Figure 9.1). The agreement is not legally enforceable, however, which means that each firm has the option of charging less than the agreed price. If one firm sells water for less than the other firm, it will capture the entire quantity demanded by the market at the lower price.

FIGURE 9.1

The Market Demand for Mineral Water

Faced with the demand curve shown, a monopolist with zero marginal cost would produce 1000 bottles/day (the quantity at which marginal revenue equals zero) and sell them at a price of $1.00/bottle.

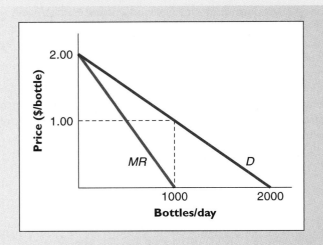

Why is this agreement likely to collapse?

Since the marginal cost of mineral water is zero, the profit-maximizing quantity for a monopolist with the demand curve shown in Figure 9.1 is 1000 bottles/day, the quantity for which marginal revenue equals marginal cost. At that quantity, the monopoly price is $1/bottle. If the firms abide by their agreement, each will sell half the market total, or 500 bottles/day at a price of $1/bottle, for an economic profit of $500/day.

But suppose Aquapure reduced its price to $0.90/bottle. By underselling Mountain Spring, Aquapure would capture the entire quantity demanded by the market, which, as shown in Figure 9.2, is 1100 bottles/day. Aquapure's economic profit would rise from $500/day to ($0.90/bottle) (1100 bottles/day) = $990/day, almost twice as much as before. In the process, Mountain Spring's economic profit would fall from $500/day to zero. Rather than see its economic profit disappear, Mountain Spring would match Aquapure's price cut, recapturing its original 50 percent

share of the market. But when each firm charges $0.90/bottle and sells 550 bottles/day, each earns an economic profit of ($0.90/bottle)(550 bottles/day) = $495/day, or $5/day less than before.

Suppose we view the cartel agreement as an economic game in which the two available strategies are to sell for $1/bottle or to sell for $0.90/bottle. The payoffs are the economic profits that result from these strategies. Table 9.4 shows the payoff matrix for this game. Each firm's dominant strategy is to sell at the lower price, yet in following that strategy, each earns a lower profit than if each had sold at the higher price.

The game does not end with both firms charging $0.90/bottle. Each firm knows that if it cuts the price a little further, it can recapture the entire market, and in the process earn a substantially higher economic profit. At every step the rival firm will match any price cut, until the price falls to the marginal cost—in this example, zero.

FIGURE 9.2

The Temptation to Violate a Cartel Agreement

By cutting its price from $1/bottle to $0.90/bottle, Aquapure can sell the entire market quantity demanded at that price, 1100 bottles/day, rather than half the monopoly quantity of 1000 bottles/day.

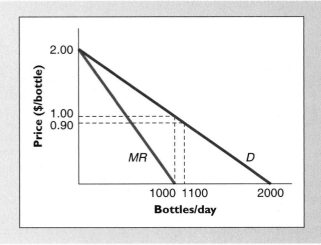

TABLE 9.4
The Payoff Matrix for a Cartel Agreement

		Mountain Spring	
		Charge $1/bottle	Charge $0.90/bottle
Aquapure	Charge $1/bottle	$500/day for each	0 for Aquapure $990/day for Mt. Spring
	Charge $0.90/bottle	$990/day for Aquapure 0 for Mt. Spring	$495/day for each

Cartel agreements confront participants with the economic incentives inherent in the prisoner's dilemma, which explains why such agreements have historically been so unstable. Usually a cartel involves not just two firms, but several, a situation that can make retaliation against price cutters extremely difficult. In many cases, discovering which parties have broken the agreement is difficult. For example, the Organization of Petroleum Exporting Countries (OPEC), is a cartel of oil producers that was formed in 1960. The cartel came to prominence in the 1970s when it restricted oil production. However, it has no practical way to prevent member countries from increasing their sales by secretly offering to sell oil below the cartel price.

9.2   ECONOMIC NATURALIST

How did the American Congress unwittingly solve the television advertising dilemma confronting cigarette producers in the United States?

In 1970, the American Congress enacted a law making cigarette advertising on television illegal after January 1, 1971. As evidenced by the steadily declining proportion of Americans who smoke, this law seems to have achieved its stated purpose of protecting citizens against a proven health hazard. But the law also had an unintended effect, which was to increase the economic profit of cigarette makers, at least in the short run. In the year before the law's passage, manufacturers spent more than $300 million on advertising, about $60 million more than they spent during the year after the law was enacted. Much of the saving in advertising expenditures in 1971 was reflected in higher cigarette profits at year-end. But if eliminating television advertising made companies more profitable, why did the manufacturers not eliminate the ads on their own?

When an imperfectly competitive firm advertises its product, its demand curve shifts rightward, for two reasons. First, people who have never used that type of product learn about it, and some buy it. Second, people who consume a different brand of the product may switch brands. The first effect boosts sales industrywide; the second merely redistributes existing sales.

Although advertising produces both effects in the cigarette industry, its primary effect is brand switching. Thus, the decision of whether to advertise confronts the individual firm with a prisoner's dilemma. Table 9.5 shows the payoffs facing a pair of cigarette producers trying to decide whether to advertise. If both firms advertise on TV (upper left cell), each earns a profit of only $10 million/year as compared to a profit of $20 million/year for each if neither advertises (lower right cell). Clearly, both will benefit if neither advertises.

But note the powerful incentive that confronts each firm. RJR sees that if Philip Morris does not advertise, RJR can earn higher profits by advertising ($35 million/year) than by not advertising ($20 million/year). RJR also sees that if Philip Morris does advertise, RJR will again earn more by advertising ($10 million/year) than by not advertising ($5 million/year). Thus, RJR's dominant strategy is to advertise. And because the payoffs are symmetric, Philip Morris's dominant strategy also is to advertise. So when each firm behaves rationally from its own point of view, the two together do worse than if they had both shown restraint. The American Congressional ban on advertising forced cigarette manufacturers to do what they could not have accomplished on their own.

TABLE 9.5
Cigarette Advertising as a Prisoner's Dilemma

		Philip Morris	
		Advertise on TV	Do not advertise on TV
RJR	Advertise on TV	$10 million/year for each	$35 million/year for RJR $5 million/year for Philip Morris
	Do not advertise on TV	$5 million/year for RJR $35 million/year for Philip Morris	$20 million/year for each

THE PRISONER'S DILEMMA IN EVERYDAY LIFE

As the following example makes clear, the prisoner's dilemma helps the economic naturalist to make sense of human behaviour not only in the world of business, but in other domains of life as well.

9.3   ECONOMIC NATURALIST

Why do people often stand at concerts, even though they can see just as well when everyone sits?

A few years ago, an economic naturalist went with friends to hear Diana Ross sing. They bought good seats, some 20 rows from the stage. But before Ross had finished her first song, several people in front of them rose to their feet, presumably to get a better view. In doing so, they blocked the line of sight for others behind them, forcing those people to stand to see better. Before long, the entire crowd was standing. Then a few people in the front rows climbed atop their seats, blocking the views of those behind them and forcing them to stand on their seats too. The seats had fold-up bottoms, so from time to time someone who stood too close to the pivot point would tumble as the seat popped into its vertical position. All things considered, the outcome was far less satisfactory than if everyone had remained seated. Why this pattern of self-defeating behaviour?

To understand what happened at the concert, note that standing is self-defeating only when viewed from the group's perspective. From the individual's perspective, however, standing passes the cost–benefit test. No matter what others do, an individual sees better by standing than by sitting. Suppose for the sake of discussion that you and other members of the audience would be willing to pay $2 to avoid standing and $3 to get a better view (or avoid having a worse one). In this multiperson prisoner's dilemma, you are one player and the rest of the audience is the other. The two strategies are to stand or to sit. Suppose everyone is seated to begin with. The payoffs you and others face will depend on the combination of strategies that you and others choose, as shown Table 9.6.

COST–
BENEFIT

Since standing is tiring and the view is no better when everyone stands than when everyone sits, why do people often stand at concerts?

TABLE 9.6
Standing Versus Sitting at a Concert as a Prisoner's Dilemma

		Others	
		Stand	Sit
You	Stand	−$2 for each	$1 for you −$3 for others
	Sit	−$3 for you $1 for others	0 for each

The payoff of 0 in the lower right cell of the payoff matrix reflects the fact that when everyone remains seated, everyone is just as well off as before. Your payoff of −$3 in the lower left cell reflects the fact that if you sit while others stand, you will have a worse view. Your payoff of −$2 in the upper left cell reflects the fact that when you and others stand, you must endure the $2 cost of standing, even though you don't get a better view. Finally, your $1 payoff in the upper right cell represents the difference between your $3 benefit and your $2 cost of standing when you stand while others sit.

These payoffs mean that your dominant strategy is to stand. If others stand, you will get −$2 by standing, which is better than the −$3 you will get by sitting. If others sit, you will get $1 by standing, which is better than the $0 you will get by sitting. Since this game is symmetric, the dominant strategy for others is also to stand. Yet when everyone stands, everyone gets a payoff of −$2, which is $2 worse than if everyone had remained seated. As in all prisoner's dilemmas, the choice that is more attractive from the perspective of the individual turns out to be less attractive from the perspective of the group.

RECAP	THE PRISONER'S DILEMMA

The prisoner's dilemma is a game in which each player has a dominant strategy and in which the payoff to each player when each chooses that strategy is smaller than if each had chosen a dominated strategy. Incentives analogous to those found in the prisoner's dilemmas help to explain a broad range of behaviour in business and everyday life—among them, excessive spending on advertising, cartel instability, standing at concerts, and shouting at parties.

▀ 9.3 GAMES IN WHICH TIMING MATTERS

In the games discussed so far, players were assumed to choose their strategies simultaneously, and which player moved first didn't particularly matter. For example, in the prisoner's dilemma, players would follow their dominant strategies even if they knew in advance what strategies their opponents had chosen. But in other situations, such as the negotiations between Warner Brothers and Tony Bennett described at the beginning of this chapter, timing is of the essence.

www.gametheory.net
Game Theory

THE ULTIMATUM BARGAINING GAME

Another such game is illustrated in Example 9.4.

EXAMPLE 9.4

Should Torben accept Kamal's offer?

Kamal and Torben are subjects in an experiment. The experimenter begins by giving $100 to Kamal, who must then propose how to divide the money between himself and Torben. Kamal can propose any division he chooses, provided the proposed amounts are whole dollars and he offers Torben at least $1. Suppose Kamal proposes $X for himself and $(100 − X) for Torben, where X is a whole number no larger than 99. Torben must then say whether he accepts the proposal. If he does, each will get the proposed amount. But if Torben rejects the proposal, each player will get zero, and the $100 will revert to the experimenter. If Kamal and Torben know they will play this game only once, and each wants to make as much money for himself as possible, what should Kamal propose?

A payoff matrix is not a useful way to summarize the information in this game, because it says nothing about the timing of each player's move. For games in which timing matters, a **decision tree**, or **game tree**, is more useful. This type of diagram describes the possible moves in the sequence in which they may occur and lists the final payoffs for each possible combination of moves.

decision tree (or game tree)
a diagram that describes the possible moves in a game in sequence and lists the payoffs that correspond to each possible combination of moves

The decision tree for the game in Example 9.4 is shown in Figure 9.3. At *A*, Kamal begins the game by making his proposal. At *B*, Torben responds to Kamal's proposal. If he accepts (the top branch of the tree), Kamal will get $X and Torben will get $(100 − X). If he refuses (the bottom branch of the tree), both will get nothing.

FIGURE 9.3

Decision Tree for Example 9.4

This decision tree shows the possible moves and payoffs for the game in Example 9.4 in the sequence in which they may occur.

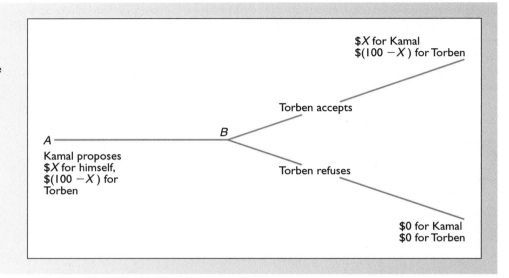

In thinking strategically about this game, the key for Kamal is to put himself in Torben's shoes and imagine how he might react to various proposals. If Torben's goal is to make as much money as possible, Kamal predicts that Torben will accept his offer, no matter how small, because the alternative is to reject it and get nothing. For instance, suppose Kamal proposes $99 for himself and only $1 for Torben (see Figure 9.4). At *B*, Torben's best option is to accept the offer. This is a Nash equilibrium, because neither player has any incentive to deviate from the strategy he chose.

This type of game has been called the **ultimatum bargaining game,** because of the power of the first player to confront the second player with a take-it-or-leave-it offer. Torben could refuse a one-sided offer from Kamal, but doing so would make him worse off than if he accepted it.

ultimatum bargaining game one in which the first player has the power to confront the second player with a take-it-or-leave-it offer

FIGURE 9.4

Kamal's Best Strategy in an Ultimatum Bargaining Game

Because Kamal can predict that Torben will accept any positive offer, Kamal's income-maximizing strategy at *A* is to offer Torben the smallest positive amount possible, $1.

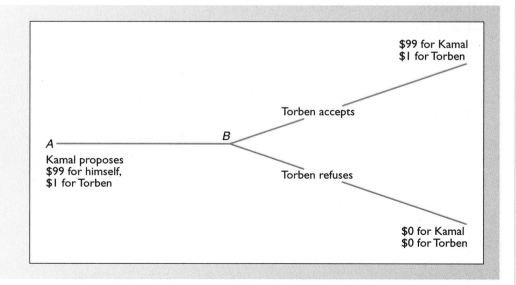

Example 9.5 illustrates the importance of the timing of moves in determining the outcome of the ultimatum bargaining game.

What will Torben's acceptance threshold be?   EXAMPLE 9.5

Suppose we change the rules of the ultimatum bargaining game slightly so that Torben has the right to specify *in advance* the smallest offer he will accept. Once Torben announces this number, he is bound by it. If Kamal's task is again to propose a division of the $100, what amount will maximize Torben's gains?

This seemingly minor change in the rules completely alters the game, because Torben now has the first move. Once Torben announces that $Y is the smallest offer he will accept, his active role in the game is over. If Y is $60 and Kamal proposes anything less for Torben, his offer will be rejected automatically. The decision tree for this game is shown in Figure 9.5.

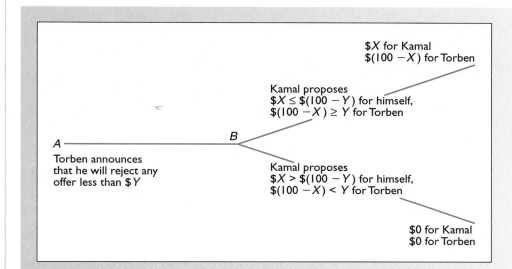

FIGURE 9.5
The Ultimatum Bargaining Game with an Acceptance Threshold
If Torben can commit himself to a minimum acceptable offer threshold at *A*, he will fare dramatically better than in the standard ultimatum bargaining game.

When Torben announces that $Y is the smallest offer he will accept, the best Kamal can do is to propose $(100 − Y) for himself and $Y for Torben. If he proposes any amount less than $Y for Torben, both will get nothing at all. Since this reasoning holds for any value of Y less than $100, Torben's best bet is to announce an acceptance threshold of $99—the largest whole number that is less than $100. The equilibrium outcome of the game will then be $99 for Torben and only $1 for Kamal, exactly the opposite of the outcome when Kamal had the first move.

CREDIBLE THREATS AND PROMISES

Why couldn't Torben have threatened to refuse a one-sided offer in the original version of the game? Although nothing prevented him from doing so, such a threat would not have been credible. In the language of game theory, a **credible threat** is one that is in the threatener's interest to carry out when the time comes to act. The problem in the original version of the game is that Torben would have no reason to carry out his threat to reject a one-sided offer in the event he actually received one. Once Kamal announced such an offer, refusing it would not pass the cost–benefit test.

The concept of a credible threat figured prominently in the negotiations between Warner Brothers managers and Tony Bennett over the matter of Mr. Bennett's fee for performing in *Analyze This*. Once most of the film had been shot,

credible threat a threat to take an action that is in the threatener's interest to carry out

COST–
BENEFIT

managers knew they couldn't credibly threaten to refuse Mr. Bennett's salary demand, because at that point the cost to adapt the film to another singer would have been prohibitive. In contrast, a similar threat made before production of the movie had begun would have been credible.

"Listen to me, John. Tell them this is our final offer. Let 'em know we'll take an option at twenty-five million over five years—not a penny more, not a minute longer! If they balk, stall them for time and get back to me."

Here is another example in which one person suffers as a result of the inability to make a credible threat.

EXAMPLE 9.6

Is it safe to steal Veronica's briefcase?

When Veronica travels out of town on business, she usually brings along an expensive briefcase. A stranger sees her waiting for a plane in the airport, takes a liking to her briefcase and assumes that because Veronica is an economist, she must be a self-interested, rational person. The stranger considers whether to walk off with Veronica's briefcase, knowing that she is watching, and can call the police immediately. If the cost to Veronica of pressing charges in the event her briefcase is stolen exceeds the value of the briefcase, can the stranger safely steal it?

Provided the thief's assumptions about Veronica are correct, he can get away with his crime. To press charges once her briefcase has been stolen, Veronica must call the police and will probably miss her flight home. Months later, she will have to return to testify at the thief's trial, and she may have to endure hostile cross-examination by the thief's attorney. Since these costs clearly exceed the value of the briefcase, a rational, self-interested person would simply write off the briefcase. But if Veronica could somehow have made a credible threat to press charges in the event her briefcase was stolen, she could have deterred the thief. The problem is that the thief knows the cost of retaliation will exceed the benefit, so the threat is not credible.

---

credible promise a promise to take an action that is in the promiser's interest to keep

Just as in some games credible threats are impossible to make, in others **credible promises** are impossible. A credible promise is one that is in the interests of the promiser to keep when the time comes to act. In Example 9.7, both players suffer because of their inability to make a credible promise.

EXAMPLE 9.7

Will the businessowner open a remote office?

The owner of a thriving business wants to start up an office in a distant city. If she hires someone to manage the new office, she can afford to pay a weekly salary of $1000—a premium of $500 over what the manager would otherwise be able to earn—and still earn a weekly economic profit of $1000 for herself. The owner's concern is that she will not be able to monitor the manager's behaviour. The owner knows that by managing the remote office dishonestly, the manager can boost his take-home pay to $1500 while causing the owner an economic loss of $500/week. If the owner believes that all managers are selfish income maximizers, will she open the new office?

The decision tree for the remote office game is shown in Figure 9.6. At *A*, the managerial candidate promises to manage honestly, which brings the owner to *B*, where she must decide whether to open the new office. If she opens it, they reach *C*, where the manager must decide whether to manage honestly. If the manager's only goal is to make as much money as he can, he will manage dishonestly (bottom branch at *C*), since that way he will earn $500 more than by managing honestly (top branch at *C*).

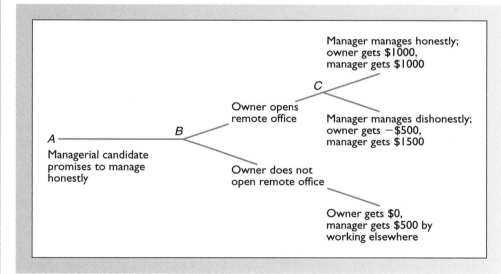

FIGURE 9.6

Decision Tree for the Remote Office Game
The best outcome is for the manager to open the office at *B* and for the manager to manage the office honestly at *C*. But if the manager is purely self-interested and the owner knows it, this path will not be an equilibrium outcome.

So if the owner opens the new office, she will end up with an economic loss of $500. If she had not opened the office (bottom branch at *B*), she would have realized an economic profit of zero. Since zero is better than −$500, the owner will choose not to open the remote office. In the end, the opportunity cost of the manager's inability to make a credible promise is $1500: the manager's forgone $500 salary premium and the owner's forgone $1000 return.

Smith and Jones are playing a game in which Smith has the first move at *A* in the following decision tree. Once Smith has chosen either the top or bottom branch at *A*, Jones, who can see what Smith has chosen, must choose the top or bottom branch at *B* or *C*. If the payoffs at the end of each branch are as shown, what is the equilibrium outcome of this game? If before Smith chose, Jones could make a credible commitment to

choose either the top or bottom branch when his turn came, what would he do?

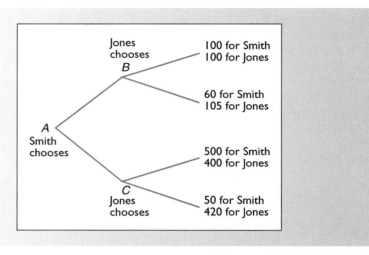

COMMITMENT PROBLEMS

Games like the one in Exercise 9.3, as well as the prisoner's dilemma, the cartel game, the ultimatum bargaining game, and the remote office game, confront players with a **commitment problem,** a situation in which they have difficulty achieving the desired outcome because they cannot make credible threats or promises. If both players in the prisoner's dilemma (Example 9.3) could make a binding promise to remain silent, both would be assured of a shorter sentence. Hence the logic of the underworld code of *omerta,* under which the family of anyone who provides evidence against a fellow mob member is killed. A similar logic explains the adoption of military arms control agreements, in which opponents sign an enforceable pledge to curtail weapons spending.

A **commitment device** is a way of solving the commitment problem by ensuring that a particular strategy will not be chosen, either because the individual cannot now make that choice, or will no longer find it in his or her interest to do so. For example, one way of reducing robberies from gas stations and convenience stores is to have all the cash placed in a safe that the clerk cannot open. The "locked cashbox strategy" makes it impossible for the clerk to choose the "Yes, I will give you the money" option when confronted with a hold-up. It is thus pointless to threaten the clerk and try to hold up such a store.

The commitment devices just discussed—the underworld code of *omerta* and the military arms control agreements—all work because they change the material incentives facing the decision makers. But as Example 9.8 illustrates, changing incentives in precisely the desired way is not always practical.

commitment problem a situation in which people cannot achieve their goals because of an inability to make credible threats or promises

commitment device a way of changing incentives so as to make otherwise empty threats or promises credible

EXAMPLE 9.8

Will Angelo leave a tip when dining on the road?

Angelo has just finished a $100 steak dinner at a restaurant on the Trans-Canada Highway, some 500 km from home. The waiter provided good service. If Angelo cares only about himself, will he leave a tip?

Once the waiter has provided good service, there is no way for him to take it back if the diner fails to leave a tip. In restaurants patronized by local diners, failure to tip is not a problem, because the waiter can simply provide poor service the next time a nontipper comes in. Repeated interaction makes it easier to develop credible commitments and threats. But the waiter lacks that leverage with out-of-town diners. Having already received good service, Angelo must choose between paying $100 or $115 for his meal. If he is an essentially selfish person, the former choice may be an appealing one.

RECAP	GAMES IN WHICH TIMING MATTERS

The outcomes in many games depend on the timing of each player's move. For such games, the payoffs are best summarized by a decision tree rather than a payoff matrix.

The inability to make credible threats and promises often prevents people from achieving desired outcomes in many games. Games with this property are said to confront players with commitment problems. Such problems can sometimes be solved by employing commitment devices—ways of changing incentives to facilitate making credible threats or promises.

▪ 9.4 THE STRATEGIC ROLE OF PREFERENCES

In all the games we have discussed so far, players were assumed to care only about obtaining the best possible outcome for themselves. Thus each player's goal was to get the highest monetary payoff, the shortest jail sentence, the best chance of survival, and so on. The irony, in most of these games, is that players do not attain the best outcomes. Better outcomes can sometimes be achieved by altering the material incentives selfish players face, but not always.

Adam Smith is best known for his book, *The Wealth of Nations*, which emphasized the "invisible hand" of self-interested economic behaviour, but he was also the author of *The Theory of Moral Sentiments*, in which he said, "The regard to those general rules of conduct, is what is properly called a sense of duty, a principle of the greatest consequence in human life... ." Further, "... upon the tolerable observance of these duties depends the very existence of human society, which would crumble into nothing if mankind were not generally impressed with a reverence for these important rules of conduct."[2]

As Example 9.9 illustrates, in a society in which people are strongly conditioned to develop moral sentiments—feelings of guilt when they harm others, feelings of sympathy for their trading partners, feelings of outrage when they are treated unjustly—commitment problems arise less often than in more narrowly self-interested societies.

In a moral society, will the businessowner open a remote office?　　　　　　　　　　　**EXAMPLE 9.9**

Consider again the owner of the thriving business who is trying to decide whether to open an office in a distant city (Example 9.7). Suppose the society in which she lives is one in which all citizens have been strongly conditioned to behave honestly. Will she open the remote office?

Suppose, for instance, that the managerial candidate would suffer guilt pangs if he embezzled money from the owner. Most people would be reluctant to assign a monetary value to guilty feelings. But for the sake of discussion, let's suppose

---

[2]Adam Smith, *The Theory of Moral Sentiments*, Part III, Ch. V, 6th ed., abridged and reprinted in Robert L. Heilbroner, ed., with the assistance of Laurence J. Malone, *The Essential Adam Smith*, New York: W.W. Norton & Company, 1986, pp. 110, 112.

that those feelings are so unpleasant that the manager would be willing to pay at least $10 000 to avoid them. On this assumption, the manager's payoff if he manages dishonestly will not be $1500 but ($1500 − $10 000) = −$8500. The new decision tree is shown in Figure 9.7.

FIGURE 9.7

The Remote Office Game with an Honest Manager

If the owner can identify a managerial candidate who would choose to manage honestly at C, she will hire that candidate at B and open the remote office.

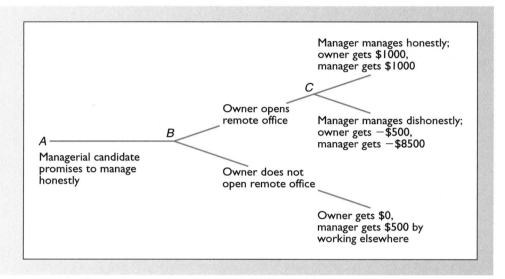

In this case, the best choice for the owner at *B* will be to open the remote office, because she knows that at *C* the manager's best choice will be to manage honestly. The irony, of course, is that the honest manager in this example ends up richer than the selfish manager in Example 9.8, who earned only a normal salary.

ARE PEOPLE FUNDAMENTALLY SELFISH?

As Example 9.9 suggests, the assumption that people are self-interested in the narrow sense of the term does not always capture the full range of motives that govern choice in strategic settings. Think, for example, about the last time you had a meal at an out-of-town restaurant. Did you leave a tip? If so, your behaviour was quite normal. Researchers have found that tipping rates in restaurants patronized mostly by out-of-town diners are essentially the same as in restaurants patronized mostly by local diners.

Reflect also on how you would behave in some of the other games we have discussed. In the ultimatum game, what would you do if the other player proposed $99 for himself and only $1 for you? Would you reject the offer? If so, you are not alone. The ultimatum game provides a very clean test of the hypothesis of selfish behaviour. Economists have therefore studied it extensively and have discovered similar results in a variety of contexts. In actual fact, the most common proposal by the first player in this game is not a 99-1 split, but a 50-50 split. And, on the few occasions when the first player does propose a highly one-sided split, the second player almost always rejects it. Subjects who reject the offer often mention the satisfaction they experienced at having penalized the first player for an "unfair" offer.

Indeed, there are many exceptions to the outcomes predicted on the basis of the assumption that people are self-interested in the most narrow sense of the term. People who have been treated unjustly often seek revenge even at ruinous cost to themselves. Every day people walk away from profitable transactions whose terms they believe to be "unfair." The British spent vast sums to defend the desolate Falkland Islands, even though they had little empire left against which to deter future aggression. (The Argentine writer Jorge Luis Borges likened the

Falklands war to two bald men fighting over a comb.) In these and countless other ways, people do not seem to be pursuing self-interest as narrowly defined. And if motives beyond narrow self-interest are significant, we must take them into account when we attempt to predict and explain human behaviour.

PREFERENCES AS SOLUTIONS TO COMMITMENT PROBLEMS

Economists tend to view preferences as ends in themselves. Taking them as given, they calculate what actions will best serve those preferences. This approach to the study of behaviour is widely used by other social scientists and by game theorists, military strategists, philosophers, and others. In its standard form, it assumes purely self-interested preferences for present and future consumption of goods of various sorts, leisure pursuits, and so on. Concerns about fairness, guilt, honour, sympathy, and the like typically play no role.

Preferences clearly affect the choices people make in strategic interactions. Sympathy for one's trading partner can make a businessperson trustworthy even when material incentives favour cheating. A sense of justice can prompt a person to incur the costs of retaliation, even when incurring those costs will not undo the original injury. It can also induce people to reject one-sided offers, even when their wealth would be increased by accepting them.

Note, however, that although preferences can clearly shape behaviour in these ways, that alone does not solve commitment problems. The solution to such problems requires not only that a person *have* certain preferences, but also that others have some way of *discerning* them. Unless the businessowner can identify the trustworthy employee, that employee cannot land a job whose pay is predicated on trust. If the predator can identify a person whose character will motivate retaliation, that person is not likely to become a victim. And unless a person's potential trading partners can identify him as someone predisposed to reject one-sided offers, he will not be able to deter such offers.

From among those whom we might engage in ventures requiring trust, can we identify reliable partners? If people could make *perfectly* accurate character judgments, they could always steer clear of dishonest persons. That people continue to be victimized at least occasionally by dishonest persons suggests that perfectly reliable character judgments are either impossible to make or prohibitively expensive.

Vigilance in the choice of trading partners is an essential element in solving (or avoiding) commitment problems, for if there is an advantage in being honest and being perceived as such, there is an even greater advantage in only *appearing* to be honest. After all, a liar who appears trustworthy will have better opportunities than one who glances about furtively, sweats profusely, and has difficulty making eye contact. Indeed, the liar will have the same opportunities as an honest person but will get higher payoffs because the liar will exploit them to the fullest.

In the end, the question of whether people can make reasonably accurate character judgments is an empirical one. Experimental studies have shown that even based on brief encounters involving strangers, subjects are adept at predicting who will cooperate and who will defect in prisoner's dilemma games. For example, in one experiment in which only 26 percent of subjects defected, the accuracy rate of predicted defections was more than 56 percent. One might expect that predictions regarding those we know well would be even more accurate.

Do you know someone who would return an envelope containing $1000 in cash to you if you lost it at a crowded concert? If so, then you accept the claim that personal character helps people to solve commitment problems. As long as honest individuals can identify at least some others who are honest, and can interact selectively with them, honest individuals can prosper in a competitive environment.

| RECAP | THE STRATEGIC ROLE OF PREFERENCES |

Most applications of the theory of games assume that players are self-interested in the narrow sense of the term. In practice, however, many choices, such as leaving tips in out-of-town restaurants, appear inconsistent with this assumption.

The fact that people seem driven by a more complex range of motives makes behaviour more difficult to predict but also creates new ways of solving commitment problems. Psychological incentives can often serve as commitment devices when changing players' material incentives is impractical. For example, people who are able to identify honest trading partners and interact selectively with them are able to solve commitment problems that arise from lack of trust.

■ SUMMARY

• **9.1** Economists use the mathematical theory of games to analyze situations in which the payoffs of one's actions depend on the actions taken by others. Games have three basic elements: the players; the list of possible actions, or strategies, from which each player can choose; and the payoffs the players receive for those strategies. The payoff matrix is the most useful way to summarize this information in games in which the timing of the players' moves is not decisive. In games in which the timing of moves does matter, a decision tree provides a much more useful summary of the information.

• **9.1** A dominant strategy is one that yields a higher payoff regardless of the strategy chosen by the other player. In some games, such as the prisoner's dilemma, each player has a dominant strategy. The equilibrium occurs in such games when each player chooses his or her dominant strategy. In other games, not all players have a dominant strategy.

• **9.2** Although the equilibrium outcome of any game is any combination of choices in which each player does the best

he can, given the choices made by others, the result is often unattractive from the perspective of players as group. The prisoner's dilemma has this feature. The incentive structure of this game helps explain such disparate social dilemmas as excessive advertising, the underworld code of *omerta*, and failure to reap the potential benefits of interactions requiring trust.

• **9.3** Individuals can often resolve these dilemmas if they can make binding commitments to behave in certain ways. Some commitments, such as those involved in military arms control agreements, are achieved by altering the material incentives confronting the players.

• **9.4** Commitments can also be achieved by relying on psychological incentives to counteract material payoffs. Moral sentiments like guilt, sympathy, and a sense of justice often foster better outcomes than can be achieved by narrowly self-interested players. For this type of commitment to work, the relevant moral sentiments must be discernible to one's potential trading partners.

■ KEY TERMS

basic elements of a game (257)
cartel (261)
commitment device (270)
commitment problem (270)
credible promise (268)

credible threat (267)
decision tree (265)
dominant strategy (258)
dominated strategy (258)
game tree (265)

Nash equilibrium (258)
payoff matrix (257)
prisoner's dilemma (260)
ultimatum bargaining game (266)

■ REVIEW QUESTIONS

1. Explain why a military arms race is an example of a prisoner's dilemma.

2. Why did Warner Brothers make a mistake by waiting until the filming of *Analyze This* was almost finished before negotiating with Tony Bennett to perform in the final scene?

3. Suppose General Motors is trying to hire a small firm to manufacture the door handles for Ford sedans. The task requires an investment in expensive capital equipment that cannot be used for any other purpose. Why might the president of the small firm refuse to undertake this venture without a long-term contract for supply that includes fixing the price of the door handles?

4. Would you be irrational to refuse a one-sided offer in an ultimatum bargaining game if you knew that you would be playing that game many times with the same partner?

5. Describe the commitment problem that narrowly self-interested diners and waiters would confront at restaurants located on the Trans-Canada Highway. Given that in such restaurants tipping does seem to assure reasonably good service, do you think people are always selfish in the narrowest sense?

■ PROBLEMS

1. In studying for his economics final, Sam is concerned about only two things: his grade and the amount of time he spends studying. A good grade will give him a benefit of 20; an average grade, a benefit of 5; and a poor grade, a benefit of 0. By studying a lot, Sam will incur a cost of 10; by studying a little, a cost of 6. Moreover, if Sam studies a lot and all other students study a little, he will get a good grade and they will get poor ones. But if they study a lot and he studies a little, they will get good grades and he will get a poor one. Finally, if he and all other students study the same amount of time, everyone will get average grades. Other students share Sam's preferences regarding grades and study time.
   a. Model this situation as a two-person prisoner's dilemma in which the strategies are to study a little and to study a lot, and the players are Sam and all other students. Include the payoffs in the matrix.
   b. What is the equilibrium outcome in this game? From the students' perspective, is it the best outcome?

2. Consider the following "dating game," which has two players, A and B, and two strategies, to buy a movie ticket or a baseball ticket. The payoffs, given in points, are as shown in the following matrix. Note that the highest payoffs occur when both A and B attend the same event.

		B	
		Buy movie ticket	Buy baseball ticket
A	Buy movie ticket	2 for A 3 for B	0 for A 0 for B
	Buy baseball ticket	I for A I for B	3 for A 2 for B

Assume that players A and B buy their tickets separately and simultaneously. Each must decide what to do knowing the available choices and payoffs but not what the other has actually chosen. Each player believes the other to be rational and self-interested.
   a. Does either player have a dominant strategy?
   b. How many potential equilibriums are there? (*Hint:* To see whether a given combination of strategies is an equilibrium, ask whether either player could get a higher payoff by changing his or her strategy.)

    c. Is this game a prisoner's dilemma? Explain.

    d. Suppose player *A* gets to buy his or her ticket first. Player *B* does not observe *A*'s choice but knows that *A* chose first. Player *A* knows that player *B* knows he or she chose first. What is the equilibrium outcome?

    e. Suppose the situation is similar to part (d), except that player B chooses first. What is the equilibrium outcome?

3. Blackadder and Baldrick are rational, self-interested criminals imprisoned in separate cells in a dark medieval dungeon. They face the prisoner's dilemma displayed in the following matrix.

		Blackadder	
		Confess	Deny
Baldrick	Confess	5 years for each	0 years for Baldrick 20 years for Blackadder
	Deny	0 years for Blackadder 20 years for Baldrick	1 year for each

Assume that Blackadder is willing to pay $1000 for each year by which he can reduce his sentence below 20 years. A corrupt jailer tells Blackadder that before he decides whether to confess or deny the crime, she can tell him Baldrick's decision. How much is this information worth to Blackadder?

4. The owner of a thriving business wants to open a new office in a distant city. If he can hire someone who will manage the new office honestly, he can afford to pay that person a weekly salary of $2000 ($1000 more than the manager would be able to earn elsewhere) and still earn an economic profit of $800. The owner's concern is that he will not be able to monitor the manager's behaviour and that the manager would therefore be in a position to embezzle money from the business. The owner knows that if the remote office is managed dishonestly, the manager can earn $3100 while causing the owner an economic loss of $600/week.

    a. If the owner believes that all managers are narrowly self-interested income maximizers, will he open the new office?

    b. Suppose the owner knows that a managerial candidate is a devoutly religious person who condemns dishonest behaviour and who would be willing to pay up to $15 000 to avoid the guilt she would feel if she were dishonest. Will the owner open the remote office?

5. Imagine yourself sitting in your car in a campus parking lot that is currently full, waiting for someone to pull out so that you can park your car. Somebody pulls out, but at the same moment a driver who has just arrived overtakes you in an obvious attempt to park in the vacated spot before you can. Suppose this driver was willing to pay up to $10 to park in that spot and up to $30 to avoid getting into an argument with you. (That is, the benefit of parking is $10, and the cost of an argument is $30.) At the same time the other driver guesses, accurately, that you too would be willing to pay up to $30 to avoid a confrontation and up to $10 to park in the vacant spot.

    a. Model this situation as a two-stage decision tree in which the other driver's bid to take the space is the opening move and your strategies are (1) to protest and (2) not to protest. If you protest (initiate an argument), the rules of the game specify that the other driver has to let you take the space. Show the payoffs at the end of each branch of the tree.

    b. What is the equilibrium outcome?

    c. What would be the advantage of being able to be able to communicate credibly to the other driver that your failure to protest would be a significant psychological cost to you?

6. Newfoundland's fishing industry has recently declined sharply due to overfishing, even though fishing companies were supposedly bound by a quota agreement. If all fishing companies had abided by the agreement, yields could have been maintained at high levels.
   a. Model this situation as a prisoner's dilemma in which the players are Company *A* and Company *B* and the strategies are to keep the quota and break the quota. Include appropriate payoffs in the matrix. Explain why overfishing is inevitable in the absence of effective enforcement of the quota agreement.
   b. Provide another environmental example of a prisoner's dilemma.
   c. In many potential prisoner's dilemmas, a way out of the dilemma for a would-be cooperator is to make reliable character judgments about the trustworthiness of potential partners. Explain why this solution is not available in many situations involving degradation of the environment.

7. Consider the following game, called matching pennies, which you are playing with a friend. Each of you has a penny hidden in your hand, facing either heads up or tails up (you know which way the one in your hand is facing). On the count of "three" you simultaneously show your pennies to each other. If the face-up side of your coin matches the face-up side of your friend's coin, you get to keep the two pennies. If the faces do not match, your friend gets to keep the pennies.
   a. Who are the players in this game? What are each player's strategies? Construct a payoff matrix for the game.
   b. Is there a dominant strategy? If so, what?
   c. Is there an equilibrium? If so, what?

8. Consider the following game. Harry has four quarters. He can offer Sally from one to four of them. If she accepts his offer, she keeps the quarters Harry offered her and Harry keeps the others. If Sally declines Harry's offer, they both get nothing ($0). They play the game only once, and each cares only about the amount of money he or she ends up with.
   a. Who are the players? What are each player's strategies? Construct a decision tree for this ultimatum bargaining game.
   b. Given their goal, what is the optimal choice for each player?

9. Two airplane manufacturers are considering the production of a new product, a 150-passenger jet. Both are deciding whether to enter the market and produce the new plane. The payoff matrix is as shown (payoff values are in millions of dollars).

		Airbus	
		Produce	Do not produce
Boeing	Produce	−5 for each	100 for Boeing 0 for Airbus
	Do not produce	0 for Boeing 100 for Airbus	0 for each

   The implication of these payoffs is that the market demand is large enough to support only one manufacturer. If both firms enter, both will sustain a loss.
   a. Identify two possible equilibrium outcomes in this game.
   b. Consider the effect of a subsidy. Suppose the European Union decides to subsidize the European producer, Airbus, with a cheque for $25 million if it enters the market. Revise the payoff matrix to account for this subsidy. What is the new equilibrium outcome?
   c. Compare the two outcomes (pre- and post-subsidy). What qualitative effect does the subsidy have?

10. Jill and Jack both have two pails that can be used to carry water down a hill. Each makes only one trip down the hill, and each pail of water can be sold for $5. Carrying the pails of water down requires considerable effort. Both Jill and Jack would be willing to pay $2 each to avoid carrying one bucket down the hill and an additional $3 to avoid carrying a second bucket down the hill.

a. Given market prices, how many pails of water will each fetch from the top of the hill?

b. Jill and Jack's parents are worried that the two children don't cooperate enough with one another. Suppose they make Jill and Jack share their revenues from selling the water equally. Given that both are self-interested, construct the payoff matrix for the decisions Jill and Jack face regarding the number of pails of water each should carry. What is the equilibrium outcome?

◼ ANSWERS TO IN-CHAPTER EXERCISES

9.1 No matter what Coca Cola does, Pepsi will do better to leave ad spending the same. No matter what Pepsi does, Coca Cola will do better to raise ad spending. So each player will play its dominant strategy: Coca Cola will raise its ad spending, and Pepsi will leave its ad spending the same.

		Coca Cola	
		Raise spending on advertisements	Leave spending on advertisements the same
Pepsi	Raise spending on advertisements	$3000 for Pepsi $8000 for Coca Cola	$4000 for Pepsi $5000 for Coca Cola
	Leave spending on advertisements the same	$8000 for Pepsi $4000 for Coca Cola	$5000 for Pepsi $2000 for Coca Cola

9.2 In game 1, no matter what Ford does, GM will do better to invest, and no matter what GM does, Ford will do better to invest. Each has a dominant strategy, but in following it, each does worse than if it had not invested. So game 1 is a prisoner's dilemma. In game 2, no matter what Ford does, GM again will do better to invest; but no matter what GM does, Ford will do better *not* to invest. Each has a dominant strategy, and in following it, each gets a payoff of 10—which is 5 more than if each had played its dominated strategy. So game 2 is not a prisoner's dilemma.

Game 1
Ford

		Do not invest	Invest
GM	Do not invest	10 for each	4 for GM 12 for Ford
	Invest	12 for GM 4 for Ford	5 for each

Game 2
Ford

		Do not invest	Invest
GM	Do not invest	4 for GM 12 for Ford	5 for each
	Invest	10 for each	12 for GM 4 for Ford

9.3 Smith assumes that Jones will choose the branch that maximizes his payoff, which is the bottom branch at either *B* or *C*. So Jones will choose the bottom branch when his turn comes, no matter what Smith chooses. Since Smith will do better (60) on the bottom branch at *B* than on the bottom branch at *C* (50), Smith will choose the top branch at *A*. So the equilibrium in this game is for Smith to choose the top branch at *A* and Jones to choose the bottom branch at *B*. Smith gets 60, and Jones gets 105. If Jones could make a credible commitment to choose the top branch no matter what, both would do better. Smith would choose the bottom branch at *A* and Jones would choose the top branch at *C*, giving Smith 500 and Jones 400.

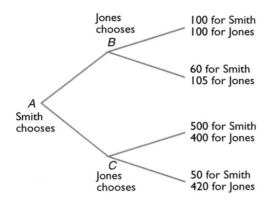

Chapter **10**

EXTERNALITIES AND PROPERTY RIGHTS

A droll television ad for a British brand of pipe tobacco opens with a distinguished looking gentleman sitting quietly on a park bench, smoking his pipe and reading a book of poetry. Before him lies a pond, unrippled except for a mother duck swimming peacefully with her ducklings. Suddenly a raucous group of teenage boys bursts onto the scene with a remote-controlled toy warship. Yelling and chortling, they launch their boat and manoeuvre it in aggressive pursuit of the terrified ducks.

Interrupted from his reverie, the gentleman looks up from his book and draws calmly on his pipe as he surveys the scene before him. He then reaches into his bag, pulls out a remote control of his own, and begins manipulating the joystick. The scene shifts underwater, where a miniature submarine rises from the depths of the pond. Once the boys' boat is in the sub's sights, the gentleman pushes a button on his remote control. Seconds later, the boat is blown to smithereens by a torpedo. The scene fades to a close-up of the tobacco company's label.

Many market transactions generate costs or benefits that accrue to people not directly involved in those transactions. These effects are often unintended. They are called **external costs** and **benefits—externalities,** for short. From the pipe smoker's point of view, the noise generated by the marauding boys was an external cost. And had others been disturbed by the boys' rowdiness, they may well have regarded the pipe smoker's retaliatory gesture as an external benefit. The boys will have a different view of the situation. If the smoker has his tranquillity, they cannot have the fun they derive from their toy warship. The boys can argue that the smoker's tranquillity imposes a cost on them for which they are not compensated. Thus the problem is reciprocal, and it is the problem of scarcity. If the smoker has his tranquillity, the boys are deprived of their recreation. If the boys have their recreation, the smoker is deprived of his tranquillity. (Surely, there is no real threat to the ducks. They can easily fly away.) The pond cannot simultaneously provide recreation for the boys and tranquillity for the smoker and others.

How is the pond to be allocated between its competing uses? There is no market through which an answer can be provided. There is no mechanism that will enable the smoker to pay the boys to go away, or for the boys (or their parents) to pay the smoker to be tranquil somewhere else. For one thing, it appears that neither of the two parties has the right to demand and receive payment. Besides, other users of the pond are affected too, and it seems quite impractical to include them in negotiations about the pond. We must also question the smoker's method of determining how the pond will be used. Can a society function well if differences are resolved by blowing up property or by relying on other forms of violent conflict?

This chapter focuses on how externalities affect the allocation of resources and on methods of resolving the problems caused by externalities. Adam Smith's theory of the invisible hand applies to an ideal marketplace in which externalities do not exist. Smith's structure included a system of justice that secured everyone's right to pursue his or her self-interest on equal footing with everyone else. In such situations, Smith argued, the self-interested actions of individuals would lead to socially efficient outcomes. We will see that when the parties affected by externalities can easily negotiate with one another, the invisible hand will still produce an efficient outcome.

But in many cases, such as the scene depicted in the tobacco ad, negotiation is impractical. In those cases, the self-interested actions of individuals will simply not lead to efficient outcomes. Because externalities are widespread, the attempt to forge solutions to the problems they cause is one of the most important rationales, not only for the existence of government but also for a variety of other forms of collective action, including compliance with norms of behaviour.

external cost (or negative externality) A cost that arises from an activity undertaken by an individual, firm, or other economic agent and that is borne by others because the cost is not incorporated in market prices the agent pays

external benefit (or positive externality) A benefit received by others that arises from an activity undertaken by an individual, firm, or other economic agent for which the agent is not compensated in the market price paid for the good or service involved

externality an external cost or benefit of an activity

▬ 10.1 HOW EXTERNAL COSTS AND BENEFITS AFFECT RESOURCE ALLOCATION

The way in which externalities distort the allocation of resources can be seen clearly in the next several examples.

Does the honeybee keeper face the right incentives? (Part 1)　　　　　**EXAMPLE 10.1**

Phoebe earns her living as a keeper of honeybees. Her neighbours on all sides grow apples. Because bees pollinate apple trees as they forage for nectar, the more hives Phoebe keeps, the larger the harvests will be in the surrounding orchards. However, apple blossoms produce little nectar, so bees produce little honey when they forage on apple blossoms. If there is no way for orchard owners to compensate Phoebe for pollination and if she takes only her own costs and benefits into account in deciding how many hives to keep, will she keep the socially optimal number of hives?

For the orchard owners, Phoebe's hives constitute an external benefit. If she takes only her own personal costs and benefits into account, she will add hives only until the added revenue she gets from the last hive just equals the cost of adding it. But since the orchard owners also benefit from additional hives, the total benefit of adding another hive at that point will be greater than its cost. Phoebe, then, will keep too few hives.

Does the honeybee keeper face the right incentives? (Part 2)　　　　　**EXAMPLE 10.2**

As in Example 10.1, Phoebe earns her living as a keeper of honeybees. But now her neighbours are not apple growers but an elementary school and a nursing home. The more hives Phoebe keeps, the more students and nursing home residents will be stung by bees. If Phoebe takes only her own costs and benefits into account in deciding how many hives to keep, will she keep the socially optimal number of hives?

For the students and nursing home residents, Phoebe's hives constitute an external cost. If she considers only her own costs and benefits in deciding how many hives to keep, she will continue to add hives until the added revenue from the last hive is just enough to cover its cost. But since Phoebe's neighbours also incur costs when she adds a hive, the benefit of the last hive at that point will be smaller than its cost. Phoebe, in other words, will keep too many hives.

Every activity involves costs and benefits. When all the relevant costs and benefits of an activity accrue directly to the person who carries it out—that is, when the activity generates no externalities—the level of the activity that is best for the individual will be best for society as a whole. But when an activity generates externalities, individual self-interest does not produce the best allocation of resources. Individuals who consider only their own costs and benefits will tend to engage too much in activities that generate external costs and too little in activities that generate external benefits. When an activity generates both external benefits and external costs, private and social interests will coincide only in the unlikely event that the opposing effects offset one another exactly.

THE GRAPHICAL PORTRAYAL OF EXTERNALITIES

The effects of externalities on resource allocation can be portrayed graphically, as in Figure 10.1. In panel (a), Private MC (for marginal cost) is the supply curve of a product whose production is accompanied by an external cost of XC per unit. The market equilibrium level of output is Q_{pvt}, the output level at which the demand curve D intersects Private MC. Note that Q_{pvt} is larger than the socially optimal level of output, Q_{soc}, the output level at which the demand curve intersects Social MC. Social MC, the socially optimal supply curve of the product, is the result of adding the external cost XC to every value along Private MC.

FIGURE 10.1

How External Costs and Benefits Affect Resource Allocation
The market equilibrium level of output (Q_{pvt}) is larger than the socially optimal level (Q_{soc}) for products accompanied by external costs [panel (a)] but smaller than the socially optimal level for products accompanied by external benefits [panel (b)].

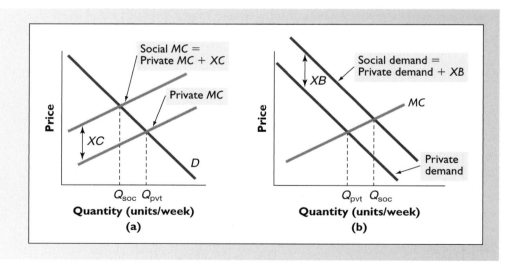

In Figure 10.1(b), private demand is the demand curve for a product whose production generates an external benefit of XB per unit. The market equilibrium quantity of this good, Q_{pvt}, is the output level at which private demand intersects the supply curve of the product *(MC)*. This time Q_{pvt} is smaller than the socially optimal level of output, Q_{soc}. The output level at which MC intersects the socially optimal demand curve (social demand), is Q_{soc}. The socially optimal demand curve is the result of adding the external benefit XB to every value along private demand.

Externalities thus distort the allocation of resources in an otherwise efficient market. When externalities are present, the individual pursuit of self-interest will not result in the largest possible economic surplus. And when it does not, the outcome is by definition inefficient.

THE COASE THEOREM

To say that a situation is inefficient means that it can be rearranged in a way that would make at least some people better off without harming others. Such situations, we have seen, are a source of creative tension. For example, we saw that because monopoly pricing results in an inefficiently low output level, the potential for gain gives monopolists an incentive to make discounts available to price-sensitive buyers. And, when orchard owners want more pollination than beekeepers will provide on their own accord, orchard owners have an incentive to pay beekeepers to locate hives near their orchards. If beekeepers want access to crops that do not require pollination by honeybees but that produce abundant nectar, they have an incentive to pay crop owners for access to the crops. **Side payments** from orchard owners to bee keepers can increase the number of hives near orchards, and remedy any under-supply of hives.[1] The next examples illustrate how the inefficiencies that result from externalities create incentives for remedial action.

www.hmco.com/hmco/
college/economics/taylor/
micro/student/exercise/
mitaylor/coase.htm
Coase Theorem

side payments a payment made by one party to another in compensation for an external cost or benefit

---

EXAMPLE 10.3

Will Chabar dump toxins in the river? (Part 1)

Chabar's factory produces a toxic waste by-product. If Chabar dumps it in the river, he causes damage to Fitch, a fisherman located downstream. The toxins are short-lived and cause no damage to anyone other than Fitch. At a cost, Chabar can filter out the toxins, in which case Fitch will suffer no damage at all. The relevant gains and losses for the two individuals are listed in Table 10.1.

TABLE 10.1
Costs and Benefits of Eliminating Toxic Waste (Part 1)

	With filter	Without filter
Gains to Chabar	$100/day	$130/day
Gains to Fitch	$100/day	$50/day

If the law does not penalize Chabar for dumping toxins in the river, and if Chabar and Fitch cannot communicate with one another, will Chabar operate with or without a filter? Is that choice socially efficient?

Since Chabar earns $30/day more without a filter than with one, his natural incentive is to operate without one. But if he does, the outcome is socially inefficient. Thus, when Chabar operates without a filter, the total daily gain to both parties is only $130 + $50 = $180, compared to $100 + $100 = $200 if Chabar had operated with a filter. The daily cost of the filter to Chabar is only $130 − $100 = $30, which is smaller than its daily benefit to Fitch of $100 − $50 = $50. The fact that Chabar does not install the filter implies a lost daily surplus of $20.

---

[1]Stephen N.S. Cheung reported that beekeepers and orchard owners frequently pay each other for provision of pollination and access to crops. If a market is established so that side payments are consistently possible, the externality is internalized. It is no longer an externality. (Stephen N.S. Cheung, "The Fable of the Bees: An Economic Investigation," *The Journal of Law & Economics*, v. 16 (April 1973), pp. 11–33.)

EXAMPLE 10.4

Will Chabar dump toxins in the river? (Part 2)

Suppose the costs and benefits of using the filter are as in Example 10.3 except that Chabar and Fitch can now communicate with one another at no cost. Even though the law does not require him to do so, will Chabar use a filter?

Recall from Chapter 6 the observation that when the economic pie grows larger, everyone can have a larger slice. Because use of a filter would result in the largest possible economic surplus, it would enable both Chabar and Fitch to have a larger net gain than before. Fitch thus has an incentive to *pay* Chabar to use a filter. For example, suppose Fitch offers Chabar $40/day to compensate him for operating with a filter. Both Chabar and Fitch will then be exactly $10/day better off than before, for a total daily net gain of $20.

EXERCISE 10.1

In Example 10.4, what is the largest whole-dollar amount by which Fitch could compensate Chabar for operating with a filter and still be better off than before?

Coase theorem if at no cost, people can negotiate the purchase and sale of the right to perform activities that cause externalities, they can always arrive at efficient solutions to the problems caused by externalities

Ronald Coase, a professor at the University of Chicago Law School, was the first to see clearly that if people can negotiate with one another at no cost over the right to perform activities that cause externalities, they have the incentive to arrive at an efficient solution. This insight, which is often called the **Coase theorem,** is a profoundly important idea, one for which Coase (rhymes with "dose") was awarded the 1991 Nobel Prize in Economics.[2]

Why, you might ask, should Fitch pay Chabar to filter out toxins that would not be there in the first place if not for Chabar's factory? The rhetorical force of this question is undeniable. Yet Coase points out that externalities are reciprocal in nature. The toxins do harm Fitch, to be sure, but preventing Chabar from emitting them would penalize Chabar, by exactly $30/day. Why should Fitch necessarily have the right to harm Chabar? Indeed, as Example 10.5 illustrates, even if Fitch had that right, his incentive is to exercise it only if filtering the toxins proved the most efficient outcome.

EXAMPLE 10.5

Will Chabar dump toxins in the river? (Part 3)

Suppose the law says that Chabar may *not* dump toxins in the river unless he has Fitch's permission. If the relevant costs and benefits of filtering the toxins are as shown in Table 10.2, and if Chabar and Fitch can negotiate with one another at no cost, what are Chabar's incentives to filter the toxins?

TABLE 10.2
Costs and Benefits of Eliminating Toxic Waste (Part 3)

	With filter	Without filter
Gains to Chabar	$100/day	$150/day
Gains to Fitch	$100/day	$70/day

[2]Ronald Coase, "The Problem of Social Cost," *Journal of Law & Economics*, v. 3 (October 1960), pp. 1–44.

Note that this time the most efficient outcome is for Chabar to operate without a filter, for the total daily surplus in that case will be $220 as compared to only $200 with a filter. Under the law, however, Fitch has the right to insist that Chabar use a filter. We might expect him to exercise that right, since his own gain would rise from $70 to $100/day if he did so. But because this outcome yields less surplus, we know that each party can do better.

Suppose, for example, that Chabar gives Fitch $40/day in return for Fitch's permission to operate without a filter. Each would then have a net daily gain of $110, which is $10 better for each of them than if Fitch had insisted that Chabar use a filter. Chabar's pollution harms Fitch, sure enough, but failure to allow the pollution would have caused even greater harm to Chabar.

These examples illustrate the point that when externalities are a source of inefficiency, the affected parties have the incentive to search for the outcome with the highest total economic surplus. Externalities are hardly rare and isolated occurrences. And because externalities can distort the allocation of resources, recognizing them and dealing intelligently with them is important. Consider the following example of an externality that arises among six farmers.

Will Bob Grow Genetically Modified Barley?   **EXAMPLE 10.6**

The regulation of genetically modified foodstuffs is an important area of disagreement between the European Union and the United States. In Europe, consumer resistance to genetically modified foods is very strong, and the European Union has often banned their importation. Because European consumers shun foods that contain genetically modified components, the EU requirement that labels identify foods with any genetically modified ingredients is tantamount to a ban on importation. In the U.S., foods containing genetically modified ingredients are not separately identified. Therefore, products such as genetically modified wheat or barley are sold in the U.S. as easily as unmodified products.

Consider then the case of Bob and his five neighbours, who are now all growing barley near Humboldt, Saskatchewan. Bob's barley is traditionally shipped to the U.S. market, while his neighbours have traditionally sold their crops (at the same price) to European buyers. Bob is considering the possibility of growing a new type of genetically modified barley with a higher yield and expects that his net profit from switching to genetically modified seed would be $100. However, his five neighbours are concerned. They cannot prevent some of Bob's seeds from blowing onto their land, but if that happens, and if their European consumers fear that their crops contain some genetically modified seed, they will lose access to European markets and have to sell their barley in the U.S. But, if all Saskatchewan barley producers have similar responses, Bob's neighbours can expect that increased supply to the U.S. will cause U.S. barley prices to drop. If barley prices drop, the neighbours will be better off switching to another crop, but will lose profits of $80 each.

Table 10.3 shows the benefit that Bob will realize if he decides to grow genetically modified barley and the external cost that his decision will impose on his neighbours. If Bob has the legal right to grow whatever crop he wants, and if he exercises that right, Table 10.3 shows that there will be a net loss to society (+$100 − $400 = −$300). However, this potential loss can also be seen as the incentive Bob's neighbours have to get him to *not* exercise his right. If each of his five neighbours were to contribute $21, they could pay him $105 not to switch to genetically modified barley, thus avoiding an $80 loss (and therefore being better off), while Bob would be better off by $5 if he accepted their side payment and did not grow genetically modified barley.

TABLE 10.3
The Effects of Growing Genetically Modified Barley

	Bob's Profits	Losses for Bob's Neighbours	Net Gain/Loss
Bob grows genetically modified barley	+$100	(−$80 each) × 5 = −400	−300

We obtain the same outcome (no genetically modified barley) if we reverse the legal onus. If Bob does *not* have the right to grow genetically modified barley, and if he has to obtain the permission of his neighbours to do so, his potential gain of $100 is not enough to compensate his neighbours for their losses, so he cannot afford to buy them off. Therefore, regardless of whether Bob has the legal right to grow what he wants, or whether his neighbours have the right to prevent him from growing genetically modified crops without their permission, he will not grow genetically modified barley. The direction of payment between Bob and his neighbours is of no consequence to his decision: it is the same whether he has to pay his neighbours for the external costs they bear if he grows genetically modified barley or whether they have to pay him not to grow genetically modified barley.

Notice that in this example, the legal system defines rights—it establishes who must pay whom, but regardless of how those rights are assigned, the response to the problem of scarcity is the same.

Suppose the legal system gives Bob the right to grow genetically modified barley. Bob is then entitled to be paid by his neighbours if he foregoes that right. Alternatively, the legal system could state that Bob does not have the right to grow genetically modified barley. This means that if Bob wants the right, he must obtain it by paying his neighbours a price that they consider acceptable. However, regardless of the direction of payment specified by the law between Bob and his neighbours, Bob continues to grow conventional barley and does not reallocate his land to genetically modified barley. Neither do his neighbours reallocate their land to other, alternative crops. They, too, continue to grow conventional barley. Thus, the legal specification of rights has no effect on how Bob and his neighbours choose to use their land: they have the same response to the problem of scarcity. Bob and his neighbours continue to grow conventional barley regardless of who must pay whom. Of course, the legal system does affect the distribution of net financial benefits. Bob is better off if he is entitled to receive payments from his neighbours, but his neighbours are better off if they are entitled to receive payments from him.

However, we need to consider the example more carefully before we conclude that the distribution of net benefits is always the only thing affected when the legal system determines who must pay whom. Bob's decision is the same regardless of who pays whom, *provided that negotiations between him and his neighbours are costless and perfectly informed.* As Table 10.3 shows, whether Bob has the right to grow genetically modified barley (and his neighbours have to pay him not to exercise that right) or whether Bob does not have that right (and has to pay his neighbours to get their permission), it is socially inefficient for Bob to grow genetically modified barley, so he does not grow it. But the assumption that negotiations are costless and perfectly informed is very important. Recall that we assumed that if Bob and others like him grew genetically modified barley, barley that previously went to Europe would be sold in the U.S. market, causing prices there to drop. But if the price of barley dropped for Bob's neighbours, it would drop for Bob, too. Why did Bob not include this own potential loss in his calculations?

If he is fully informed, Bob already knows the incentives that confront his neighbours. He knows that if he grows genetically modified barley, his neighbours and others like them would minimize their losses by switching to other crops. Thus Bob knows that the supply of barley to the U.S. will be unaffected and he also knows that the price of barley will not drop.

However, suppose Bob's information about his neighbours' incentives is incomplete, and we consider how some of them might change their behaviour. Suppose one of Bob's neighbours (let's call him Dan) observes that Bob is receiving $105 in side payments for *not* doing something. If Dan decides that he too would like to be paid for *not* growing genetically modified barley, he can *threaten* to grow genetically modified barley, and demand a side payment. In fact, Dan is not the only one who is *potentially* eligible for side payments—any of Bob's neighbours can also state that they are about to grow genetically modified barley. Who, then, will pay the side payments and who will receive them?

The assumption of "perfect information" underlying the Coase argument is really quite a strong presumption, since it rules out the possibility of posturing, bluffing, and other strategic behaviour. Such game playing is more likely if the legal system is one where Bob (or Dan or anybody else) has to be paid to *not* exercise a legal right that is his and that he could easily exercise. In general, imperfect information and transaction costs often mean that a system of side payments may not be able to function effectively. However, we still get the socially efficient outcome if the legal system requires Bob to compensate his neighbours for their losses because his gain from growing the new crop is not enough (+$100) to pay them the full value of their $400 loss (5 × −$80 = −$400).

LEGAL REMEDIES FOR EXTERNALITIES

We have seen that efficient solutions to externalities can be found whenever the affected parties can negotiate with one another at no cost, or at least at a cost that is less than the surplus that could be gained by negotiating. Thus, we find that beekeepers and orchard owners do negotiate over what otherwise would be external benefits. But, negotiation is not always practical. A motorist with a noisy muffler, for example, imposes costs on others, yet they cannot flag him down and offer him a compensation payment to fix his muffler. If they could, we would then have to worry that some people might drive around with noisy mufflers, just to attract payments from those who are bothered by the noise. In recognition of this difficulty, most governments simply require that cars have working mufflers. Indeed, the explicit or implicit purpose of a large share—perhaps the lion's share—of laws is to solve problems caused by externalities. The goal of such laws is to help people achieve the solutions they might have reached had they been able to negotiate with one another.

When negotiation is costly, the task of adjustment generally falls on the party who can accomplish it at the lowest cost. For example, many municipal noise ordinances also place the burden of adjustment on those who can accomplish it at lowest cost. Consider, for example, the restrictions on loud party music, which may take effect at a later hour on weekends than on weekdays. This pattern reflects both the fact that the gains from loud music tend to be larger on weekends and the fact that such music is more likely to disturb people on weekdays. By setting the noise curfew at different hours on different days of the week, the law places the burden on partygoers during the week and on sleepers during the weekend. Similar logic explains why noise ordinances allow motorists to honk their horns in most neighbourhoods but not in the immediate vicinity of a hospital. The following two examples provide cases in which government influences the level of externalities. In the first example, laws and regulations are used to control external costs. In the second, subsidies encourage the provision of external benefits.

ECONOMIC NATURALIST

Why do many governments enact laws that limit the discharge of environmental pollutants?

Limitations on the discharge of pollutants into the environment are perhaps the clearest examples of laws aimed at solving problems caused by externalities. The details of these laws reflect the cost–benefit principle. The discharge of toxic wastes into rivers, for example, tends to be most strictly regulated on those waterways whose commercial fishing or recreational uses are most highly valued. On other waterways, the burden of adjustment is likely to fall more heavily on fishermen, recreational boaters, and swimmers. Similarly, air quality regulations tend to be strictest in the most heavily populated regions of the country, where the marginal benefit of pollution reduction is the greatest, although control of pollution from motor vehicles is an exception. Regulations require all motor vehicles of the same age and vintage to carry the same pollution control equipment regardless of where they are driven.

In all these cases, although it is possible to imagine a legal system that determines who must pay whom in compensation for external costs and then makes provision for payments to take place, that system might be quite cumbersome. For example, the legal system could give Toronto the right to charge a pollution tax on every litre of gasoline sold in the metropolitan area. The tax could be varied according to differences in air quality at different times, across regions of the city, etc. It could even be increased for vehicles with particularly noxious exhaust fumes. Revenues generated by the tax could be used to prevent, correct, or compensate for harm caused by pollution. However, the costs of making such a system work would likely be quite high, and its practicality questionable. Instead, emissions from motor vehicles are controlled by regulations that require manufacturers to install pollution control equipment. When compared with alternative systems of control, the regulations apparently pass the cost–benefit test.

ECONOMIC NATURALIST

Why does government subsidize activities that generate external benefits?

The laws discussed in the preceding examples are meant to regulate activities that generate external costs. But government also uses the law to encourage activities that generate external benefits. The planting of trees on hillsides, for example, benefits not just the landowner but also his neighbours by limiting the danger of flooding. In recognition of

this fact, many jurisdictions subsidize the planting of trees. Similarly, governments spend millions of dollars each year in support of basic research, an implicit acknowledgment of the external benefits associated with the generation of new knowledge.

EXTERNAL BENEFITS AND THE USE OF SUBSIDIES

Laws and regulations are often used to control external costs. Governments can also use subsidies to encourage external benefits.

It is worth emphasizing that the effectiveness of laws and regulations designed to correct externalities is closely related to existing norms or conventions of behaviour. For example, traffic signals would be far less effective if most people simply ignored them. Most people observe most laws of their own accord, and although the police and courts suppress the exceptions, compliance generally is greater than can be explained by the sheer weight of enforcement. However, if infractions are difficult to detect, compliance may be reduced and enforcement less effective. If infractions are easy to detect, the reverse is true.

If public support for a law is so low that a large number of people refuse to comply with it, the law is likely to be repudiated. The repeal of prohibition in the United States provides a particularly striking example. In 1919 the United States passed a constitutional amendment that prohibited the manufacture, transportation, and consumption of alcoholic beverages. Problems with enforcement were so severe that the amendment was repealed in 1933.

THE OPTIMAL AMOUNT OF EXTERNAL COSTS IS NOT ZERO

Curbing pollution and other external costs entails both costs and benefits. According to the cost–benefit principle, the largest total economic surplus from abating pollution will occur when the marginal cost of abatement equals its marginal benefit. In general, the marginal cost of abatement rises with the amount of pollution eliminated. (Following the principle of increasing opportunity cost, polluters can use the cheapest cleanup methods first and then turn to more expensive ones.) And the law of diminishing marginal utility suggests that beyond some point, the marginal benefit of pollution reduction tends to fall as more pollution is removed. Since marginal cost increases and marginal benefit decreases as pollution is reduced, the marginal cost and marginal benefit curves almost always intersect at less than the maximum reduction of pollution. The intersection of the two curves instead marks the socially optimal level of pollution reduction. If pollution is curtailed by any less than that amount, society will gain more than it will lose by pushing the cleanup effort a little further. But if regulators push beyond the point at which the marginal cost and benefit curves intersect, society will incur costs that exceed the benefits. The existence of a socially optimal level of pollution reduction implies the existence of a socially optimal level of pollution. That level will almost always be greater than zero.

COST–
BENEFIT

INCREASING
OPPORTUNITY
COST

Because people think of pollution as bad, many cringe when they hear the phrase "socially optimal level of pollution." How can any positive level of pollution be socially optimal? But to speak of a socially optimal level of pollution is not the same as saying that pollution is good. It merely recognizes that though society has an interest in cleaning up the environment, the cleanup incurs costs. The underlying idea is no different from the idea of an optimal level of dirt in an apartment. After all, even if you spent the whole day, every day, vacuuming your apartment, there would be *some* dirt left in it. And because you have better things to do than vacuum all day, you probably tolerate substantially more than the minimum possible amount of dirt. A dirty apartment is not good, nor is pollution in the air you breathe. But in both cases, the cost–benefit principle states that the cleanup effort is to be increased only until the marginal benefit equals the marginal cost.

RECAP   **EXTERNAL COSTS AND BENEFITS**

Externalities occur when the costs or benefits of an activity accrue to people other than those directly involved in the activity. The Coase theorem says that when affected parties can negotiate with one another without cost, activities will be pursued at efficient levels, even in the presence of external costs or benefits. But when negotiation is prohibitively costly, inefficient behaviour generally results. Activities that generate external costs are pursued to excess, while those that generate external benefits are pursued too little. Laws and regulations are often adopted in an effort to alter inefficient behaviour that results from externalities. The effectiveness of laws and regulations will be related to social norms of behaviour.

■ 10.2 PROPERTY RIGHTS AND THE TRAGEDY OF THE COMMONS

People who grow up in the industrialized nations tend to take the institution of private property for granted. Our intuitive sense is that people have the right to own any property they acquire by lawful means and to do with that property much as they see fit.

Our intuitive idea of property is probably that of a physical object (as in "That's *my* shirt"), but property rights are much more complex than simple possession (consider, for example, a record company's property right to receive royalty payments when music is digitally reproduced). Our attitudes to "property" sometimes depend on what type of property is under consideration. In recent years, many people who would never even consider walking off with somebody else's shirt have downloaded songs for free from the Internet.

The extent of property rights has, moreover, changed substantially over time in advanced industrial countries. In the nineteenth century in Britain, for example, it was taken for granted that in buying a country estate, a new owner also purchased the right to renovate the local castle however he pleased, no matter how ugly the changes or how old the castle. Today, because the U.K. electorate wants to preserve its inheritance of historic architecture (which is highly important for the tourism industry), heritage preservation laws restrict what owners can do to "listed" buildings. Because these conservation laws have wide public support, they are generally observed. Economic analysis can help to design laws that will produce socially efficient outcomes, but one must also realize that the observance of those laws crucially depends on whether people think they are "fair" or "reasonable." For instance, the Internet has made it easy to copy music without paying for it, even though the law states that musical artists are entitled to royalties when their music is copied. If millions of people continue to copy music files, it will not be practical to enforce the law on file sharing and it will fall into disuse.

THE PROBLEM OF UNPRICED RESOURCES

To understand the laws that govern the use of property, we must begin by asking why societies created the institution of private property in the first place. The following examples, which show what happens to property that nobody owns, suggest why private property rights may sometimes help to produce socially efficient outcomes.

| EXAMPLE 10.7 | How many steers will villagers send onto the commons? |

A village has five residents, each of whom has accumulated savings of $100. Each villager can use the money to buy a government bond that pays 13 percent interest per year or to buy a year-old steer, send it onto the commons to graze, and sell it after one year. The price the villager will get for the two-year-old steer depends on the amount of weight it gains while grazing on the commons, which in turn depends on the number of one-year-old steers sent onto the commons, as shown in Table 10.4.

The price of a two-year-old steer declines with the total number of steers grazing on the commons, because the more steers, the less grass is available to each. The villagers make their investment decisions one at a time, and the results are public. If each villager decides how to invest individually, how many one-year-old steers will be sent onto the commons, and what will be the village's total income?

If a villager buys a $100 government bond, he will earn $13 of interest income at the end of one year. Thus, he will send a one-year-old steer onto the commons if and only if that steer will command a price of at least $113 when it is two years old. When each villager chooses in this self-interested way, we can expect four

TABLE 10.4
The Relationship between Hard Size and Steer Price

Number of steers on the commons	Price per two-year-old steer ($)	Income per steer ($/year)
1	126	26
2	119	19
3	116	16
4	113	13
5	111	11

villagers to send a steer onto the commons. (Actually, the fourth villager would be indifferent between investing in a one-year-old steer or buying a bond, since he would earn $13 either way. For the sake of discussion, we will assume that in the case of a tie, people choose to be cattle ranchers.) The fifth villager, seeing that he would earn only $11 by sending a fifth steer onto the commons, will choose instead to buy a government bond. As a result of these decisions, the total village income will be $65/year—$13 for the one bondholder and 4($13) = $52 for the four cattle ranchers.

Has Adam Smith's invisible hand produced the most efficient allocation of these villagers' resources? We can tell at a glance that it has not, since their total village income is only $65—precisely the same as it would have been had the possibility of cattle raising not existed. The source of the difficulty will become evident in Example 10.8.

What is the socially optimal number of steers to send onto the commons?

EXAMPLE 10.8

Suppose the five villagers in Example 10.7 confront the same investment opportunities as before, except that this time they are free to make their decisions as a group rather than individually. How many one-year-old steers will they send onto the commons, and what will be their total village income?

This time the villagers' goal is to maximize the income received by the group as a whole. When decisions are made from this perspective, a one-year-old steer will be sent onto the commons only if its marginal contribution to village income is at least $13, the amount that could be earned from a government bond. As the entries in the last column of Table 10.5 indicate, the first steer clearly meets this criterion, since it contributes $26 to total village income. But the second steer

TABLE 10.5
Marginal Income and the Socially Optimal Herd Size

Number of steers on the commons	Price per two-year-old steer ($)	Income per steer ($/year)	Total income from steers ($/year)	Total village income ($/year)	Marginal village income ($/year)
1	126	26	26	78	13
2	119	19	38	77	−1
3	116	16	48	74	−3
4	113	13	52	65	−9
5	111	11	55	55	−10

does not. Sending that steer onto the commons increases the village's income from raising cattle from $26 to $38, a gain of just $12. The $100 required to buy the second one-year-old steer would thus have been better invested in a government bond. Worse, the collective return from sending a third steer is only $10; from a fourth, only $4; and from a fifth, only $3.

In sum, when investment decisions are made with the goal of maximizing total village income, the best choice is to buy four government bonds and send only a single one-year-old steer onto the commons. The resulting village income will be $78: $26 from sending the single steer and $52 from the four government bonds. That amount is $13 more than the total income that resulted when villagers made their investment decisions individually. Once again, moving from an inefficient allocation to an efficient one causes the economic pie to grow larger. And when the pie grows larger, everyone can have a larger slice. For instance, if the villagers agree to pool their income and share it equally, each will get $15.60, or $2.60 more than before.

EXERCISE 10.2

How would your answers to Examples 10.7 and 10.8 differ if the interest rate were not 13 percent but 11 percent/year?

Why do the villagers in Examples 10.7 and 10.8 do better when they make their investment decisions collectively? The answer is that when individuals decide alone, they ignore the fact that sending another steer onto the commons will cause existing steers to gain less weight. Their failure to consider this externality makes the return from sending another steer seem misleadingly high to each of them as an individual.

tragedy of the commons the tendency for a resource that has no price to be used until its marginal benefit falls to zero

The grazing land on the commons is a valuable economic resource. When no one owns it, no one has any incentive to take the opportunity cost of using it into account. And when that happens, people will tend to use it until its marginal benefit is zero. This problem, and others similar to it, are known as the **tragedy of the commons**. The tragedy of the commons occurs because one person's use of commonly held property imposes an external cost on others by making the property less valuable. The tragedy of the commons also provides a vivid illustration of the equilibrium principle (see Chapter 3). Each individual villager behaves rationally by sending an additional steer onto the commons, yet the overall outcome falls far short of the attainable ideal.

EQUILIBRIUM

THE EFFECT OF PRIVATE OWNERSHIP

As Example 10.9 illustrates, private ownership of the village's grazing land offers one possible solution to the tragedy of the commons.

EXAMPLE 10.9

How much will a buyer pay for the right to control the village commons?

Suppose the five villagers face the same investment opportunities as before, except that this time they decide to auction off the right to use the commons to the highest bidder. Assuming that villagers can borrow as well as lend at an annual interest rate of 13 percent, what price will the right to use the commons fetch? How will the owner of that property right use it, and what will be the resulting village income?

To answer these questions, simply ask yourself what you would do if you had complete control over how the grazing land were used. As we saw in Example 10.8, the most profitable way to use this land is to send only a single steer to graze on it. If you do so, you will earn $26/year. Since the opportunity cost of the $100 you spent on the single yearling steer is the $13 in interest you could have earned from a bond, your economic profit from sending a single steer onto the commons will be $13 per year, provided you can use the land for free. But you cannot; to finance your purchase of the property right, you must borrow money (since you used your $100 savings to buy a one-year-old steer).

What is the most you will pay for the right to use the commons? Since its use generates an income of $26/year, or $13 more than the opportunity cost of your investment in the steer, the most you will pay is $100 (because that amount used to purchase a bond that pays 13 percent interest would also generate income of $13/year). If the land were sold at auction, $100 is precisely the amount you would have to pay. Your annual earnings from the land would be exactly enough to pay the $13 interest on your loan and cover the opportunity cost of not having put your savings into a bond.

Note that when the right to use the land is auctioned to the highest bidder, the village achieves a more efficient allocation of its resources, because the owner has a strong incentive to take the opportunity cost of more intensive grazing fully into account. Total village income in this case will again be $78. If the annual interest on the $100 acquired from selling the land rights is shared equally among the five villagers, each will again have an annual investment income of $15.60.

The logic of maximizing economic surplus helps to explain why the most commercial nations have well-developed private property laws. It also reminds us of the importance of compliance with laws and regulations. Some traditional societies have developed implicit rules of use for their commonly owned resources that have the effect of considering opportunity costs. However, such arrangements are difficult for larger, more complex commercial societies to use. In such societies property that belongs to everyone belongs, in effect, to no one. Not only is its potential economic value never fully realized, it usually ends up being of no value at all. Likewise, property rights that are not enforced by a legal system or that people completely ignore are tantamount to no property rights at all.

Bear in mind, however, that in most countries the owners of private property are not free to do *precisely* as they want with it. For example, local zoning laws may give the owner of a lot in a residential area the right to build a three-storey house but not a six-storey house. Here, too, the logic of maximizing economic surplus applies, for a fully informed and rational legislature would define property rights so as to create the largest possible total economic surplus. In practice, of course, such ideal legislatures never really exist. Yet the essence of politics is the cutting of deals that make people better off. If a legislator could propose a change in the property laws that would enlarge the total economic surplus, she could also propose a scheme that would give each of her constituents a larger slice, thus enhancing her chances for reelection.

As an economic naturalist, challenge yourself to use this framework when thinking about the various restrictions imposed on private property laws: zoning laws that constrain what you can build and what types of activities you can conduct on your land; traffic laws that constrain what you can do with your car; employment and environmental laws that constrain how you can operate your business. Your understanding of these and countless other laws will be enhanced by the insight that everyone can gain when the private property laws are defined so as to create the largest total economic surplus.

WHEN PRIVATE OWNERSHIP IS IMPRACTICAL

Do not be misled into thinking that the law provides an *ideal* resolution of all problems associated with externalities and the tragedy of the commons. Defining and enforcing efficient property rights entails costs, after all, and sometimes, as in the following examples, the costs outweigh the gains.

ECONOMIC NATURALIST

Why are blackberries in public parks picked too soon?

Wild blackberries grow profusely at the edge of a wooded area in a crowded city park. The blackberries taste best if left to ripen fully, but they taste reasonably good if picked and eaten a few days early. Will the blackberries be left to ripen fully?

Obviously, the costs of defining and enforcing the property rights to blackberries growing in a public park are larger than the potential gains, so the blackberries will remain common property. That means that whoever picks them first gets them. Even though everyone would benefit if people waited until the berries were fully ripe, everyone knows that those who wait are likely to end up with no berries at all. And that means that the berries will be eaten too soon.

ECONOMIC NATURALIST

Why does London, England, impose a tax of £5 on every vehicle that enters the central business district during business hours?

By 2001, traffic congestion in London was spiralling out of control. Motorists in central London spent 50 percent of their time in traffic jams. An estimated £2 to £4 million worth of time was being wasted every week. Everyone knew it was a problem, but drivers kept crowding onto the roads. Each person thought of roads as "common property" and considered only their own costs of travel time, ignoring the greater congestion and the increase in travel time that their presence on the roads caused. London mayor Ken Livingstone (a well-known left-wing politician) ran for election pledging to tackle traffic congestion. He did it by using the market mechanism, and charging a price for using the central city roads during the day!

Since February 2002, motorists entering designated central zones between 7:00 A.M. and 6:30 P.M. pay £5 a day. Around 230 cameras match car licence plates against a database of vehicles whose drivers have paid the charge, with a fine of £80 levied on any motorist who fails to pay before midnight. The revenues have been used to subsidize more frequent bus service. When the charge came into operation, traffic levels instantly fell by 20 percent.

Here are some further examples of the type of tragedy of the commons that are not easily solved by defining private ownership rights.

Harvesting Whales in International Waters Each individual whaler knows that harvesting an extra whale reduces the breeding population and hence the size of the future whale population. But the whaler also knows that any whale that is not harvested today will be taken by some other whaler. One solution would be to define and enforce property rights to whales. But the oceans are vast, and the behaviour of whalers is hard to monitor. And even if their behaviour could be monitored, the concept of national sovereignty would make international enforcement of property rights problematic.

Controlling Multinational Environmental Pollution Each individual polluter may know that if he and all others pollute, the damage to the environment will be greater than the cost of not polluting. But if the environment is common property into which all are free to dump, each has a powerful incentive to pollute. If all polluters live under the jurisdiction of a single government, enforcing laws and regulations that limit the discharge of pollution may be practical. But if polluters come from many different countries, solutions are much more difficult to implement. Thus, the Mediterranean Sea has long suffered serious pollution, because none of the many nations that border it has an economic incentive to consider the effects of its discharges on other countries.

As the world's population continues to grow, the absence of an effective system of international property rights will become an economic problem of increasing significance.

> **RECAP** **PROPERTY RIGHTS AND THE TRAGEDY OF THE COMMONS**
>
> When a valuable resource has a price of zero, people will continue to exploit it as long as its marginal benefit remains positive. The tragedy of the commons describes situations in which valuable resources are squandered because users do not bear the opportunity cost of using them. In many cases, an efficient remedy for such waste is to define and enforce rights to use the valuable property. But this solution is difficult to implement for resources such as the oceans and the atmosphere, because no single government has the authority to enforce property rights for these resources.

10.3 POSITIONAL EXTERNALITIES

In professional sports and a host of other competitive situations, the rewards people receive typically depend not only on how they perform in absolute terms but also on how they perform relative to their closest rivals. In these situations, competitors have an incentive to take actions that will increase their odds of winning. Someone who consistently wins major tennis tournaments will claim big prizes and be presented with lucrative opportunities to endorse products. Second- or third-place finishers will claim smaller prizes and will receive fewer and less valuable opportunities to make endorsements. Nevertheless, runners-up will earn at least the opportunity cost of their efforts; otherwise, they will stop being professional tennis players and enter some other occupation.

PAYOFFS THAT DEPEND ON RELATIVE PERFORMANCE

Suppose an individual tennis player can increase her chances of winning by hiring a personal fitness trainer and a sports psychologist, provided no other player does so. If she does not hire a trainer and a psychologist and her competitors do, her chances of winning will be greatly reduced. If every player knows this situation to be the case, they all will hire personal fitness trainers and sports psychologists, because anyone who fails to do so will have greatly diminished chances of winning tournaments.

   Now suppose that spectators and those who pay athletes to endorse products will pay exactly the same amount regardless of whether the players hire personal trainers and sports psychologists—to the fans and sponsors, tournaments are of the same value either way. If additional resources are employed to obtain what spectators and sponsors regard as the same output, there can be no gain for spectators, sponsors, and athletes as a group. Indeed, when more resources are employed to obtain the same thing, total economic surplus must be smaller. To the extent that each contestant's payoff depends on his or her relative performance, then, the incentive to undertake such investments will be excessive from a collective point of view.

   Consider the following example.

 10.5   E C O N O M I C   N A T U R A L I S T

Why do some football players take anabolic steroids?

The offensive linemen of many National Football League teams currently average more than 330 pounds. In the 1970s, by contrast, offensive linemen in the league averaged barely 280 pounds, and the all-decade linemen of the 1940s averaged only 229 pounds. Size and strength are the two cardinal virtues of an offensive lineman, and other things being equal, the job will go to the larger and stronger of two rivals.

Size and strength, in turn, can be enhanced by the consumption of anabolic steroids. But if all players consume these substances, the rank ordering of players by size and strength—and hence the question of who lands the jobs—will be largely unaffected. And since the consumption of anabolic steroids entails potentially serious long-term health consequences, as a group football players are clearly worse off if they consume these drugs. So why do some football players take steroids?

The problem here is that contestants for starting berths on the offensive line confront a prisoner's dilemma like the one analyzed in Chapter 9. Consider two closely matched rivals—Smith and Jones—who are competing for a single position. If neither takes steroids, each has a 50 percent chance of winning the job and a starting salary of $1 million/year. If both take steroids, each again has a 50 percent chance of winning the job. But if one takes steroids and the other does not, the first is sure to win the

job. Notice we are assuming that even if steroids did not exist and linemen averaged 229 pounds, the starting salary would be $1 million/year. And, if steroids are used and the average lineman weighs 330 pounds, the starting salary is still $1 million/year. In either case, the loser ends up selling insurance for $30 000/year. Neither likes the fact that the drugs may have adverse health consequences, but each would be willing to take that risk in return for a shot at the big salary. Given that steroids do exist, the two competitors face the payoff matrix shown in Table 10.6.

Clearly, the dominant strategy for both Smith and Jones is to take steroids. Yet when they do so, each gets only the third-best outcome, whereas they could have gotten the second-best outcome by not taking the drugs. Hence the attraction of rules that forbid the consumption of anabolic steroids. Of course, the issue of compliance and enforcement is again present.

TABLE 10.6
Payoff Matrix for Steroid Consumption

		Jones	
		Do not take steroids	Take steroids
Smith	Do not take steroids	Second best for each	Best for Jones Worst for Smith
	Take steroids	Best for Smith Worst for Jones	Third best for each

POSITIONAL ARMS RACES

positional externality occurs when an increase in one person's performance reduces the expected reward of another's in situations in which reward depends on relative performance

When used to maintain relative position, the use of steroids is an example of a **positional externality.** Whenever the payoffs to one contestant depend at least in part on how he or she performs relative to a rival, any step that improves one contestant's relative position must necessarily worsen the other's. The example of standing at concerts discussed in Chapter 9 (Economic Naturalist 9.3) is another instance of a positional externality. Just as the invisible hand of the market is weakened by the presence of conventional externalities, it is also weakened by positional externalities. Why? Because positional externalities often lead contestants to engage in an escalating series of mutually offsetting investments in performance enhancement. We call such spending patterns **positional arms races.**

positional arms race a series of mutually offsetting investments in performance enhancement that is stimulated by a positional externality

POSITIONAL ARMS CONTROL AGREEMENTS

positional arms control agreement an agreement in which contestants attempt to limit mutually offsetting investments in performance enhancement

Because positional arms races produce inefficient outcomes, people have an incentive to curtail them. Steps taken to reduce positional arms races, such as nuclear non-proliferation agreements, similar in effect to rules against anabolic steroids, may therefore be thought of as **positional arms control agreements.**

"I don't know why McGillicuddy is so pleased with himself. We're all wee, darlin' men here."

Once you become aware of positional arms races, you will begin to see examples of them almost everywhere. You can hone your skills as an economic naturalist by asking these questions about every competitive situation you observe: What form do the investments in performance enhancement take? What steps have contestants taken to limit these investments? Sometimes positional arms control agreements are achieved by the imposition of formal rules or by the signing of legal contracts. Some examples of this type of agreement follow.

Roster Limits Major League Baseball permits teams to have only 25 players on the roster during the regular season. The Canadian Football League sets its roster limit at 39, the National Basketball Association at 12. Why these limits? In their absence, any team could increase its chance of winning by simply adding players. Inevitably, other teams would follow suit. However, it is on the plausible assumption that, beyond some point, larger rosters do not add much to the entertainment value for fans. Roster limits are thus a sensible way to deliver sports entertainment at a more reasonable cost.

Arbitration Agreements In the business world, contracting parties often sign a binding agreement that commits them to arbitration in the event of a dispute. By doing so, they sacrifice the option of pursuing their interests as fully as they might want to later, but they also insulate themselves from costly legal battles. Binding arbitration can also be used to limit the costs that might arise from strikes and lockouts.

Mandatory Starting Dates for Kindergarten A child who is a year or so older than most of her kindergarten classmates is likely to perform better, in relative terms, than if she had entered school with children her own age. And since most parents are aware that admission to prestigious universities and eligibility for top jobs on graduation depend largely on *relative* academic performance, many are tempted to keep their children out of kindergarten a year longer than necessary. Yet there is no social advantage in holding *all* children back an extra

www.cfl.ca
Canadian Football League

year, since their relative performance would essentially be unaffected. In many jurisdictions, therefore, the law requires children who reach their fifth birthday before December 1 of a given year to start kindergarten the same year.

SOCIAL NORMS AS POSITIONAL ARMS CONTROL AGREEMENTS

In some cases, social norms may take the place of formal agreements to curtail positional arms races. Some familiar examples follow.

Work Effort Norms In many workplaces, there is competition for promotions, and employers can use the probability of promotion as an incentive to increase the work effort of their labour force. Firms can let it be known (formally or informally) that working late without overtime, coming in on weekends, and taking work home are all activities that increase a worker's chances of getting promoted. Obviously, the owners of the firm will benefit because if many of their workers provide extra labour for no extra pay, profits will increase. However, only one worker will actually be promoted. When each worker decides individually to increase her effort, she only takes into account the (positive) impact the extra hours of work have on her own chances of promotion. But she does not consider the fact that an increase in the probability of her own promotion necessarily decreases the probability of promotion for each of her co-workers and that as a result, she decreases their well-being. In the end, when each worker decides individually, each supplies offsetting amounts of overtime, so everyone's chance of promotion is unchanged.

In such a labour market, it is the *relatively* hardest working person who gets the prize (this has often been called the "tournament" or "rat-race" model). Each worker's decision to increase labour supply creates an externality for other workers by reducing their probability of promotion. As workers compete against each other for relative position, the firm is better off, but workers as a group get less leisure. Thus, for any given final equilibrium of hours worked, all workers would be better off if they could sign an enforceable agreement that everyone reduce work hours by x hours.

In practice, workers often realize that, as a group, they will be better off if there is an informal agreement among them to *not* compete in some ways—and although traditions at each workplace do differ, strong workplace norms about *nobody* doing extra work at particular times (e.g., on Christmas day) are often the result.

Fashion Norms Social norms regarding dress and fashion often change quickly because of positional competitions. Consider, for instance, the person who wants to be on the cutting edge of fashion. In some North American social circles during the 1950s, that goal could be accomplished by having pierced ears. But as more and more people adopted the practice, it ceased to communicate avant-garde status. At the same time, those who wanted to make a conservative fashion statement gradually became freer to have their ears pierced.

During the 1960s and 1970s, a person could be on fashion's cutting edge by wearing two earrings in one earlobe. But by the 1990s multiple ear piercings had lost much of their social significance, the threshold of cutting-edge status having been raised to upward of a dozen piercings of each ear, or a smaller number of piercings of the nose, eyebrows, or other body parts. A similar escalation has taken place in the number, size, and placement of tattoos.

The increase in the required number of tattoos or body piercings has not changed the value of avant-garde fashion status to those who desire it. Being on the outer limits of fashion has much the same meaning now as it once did. So to the extent that there are costs associated with body piercings, tattoos, and other steps required to achieve avant-garde status, the current fashions are wasteful compared to earlier ones. In this sense, the erosion of social norms against tattoos

Is being on fashion's cutting edge more valuable now than in the 1950s?

© Associated Press

and body piercings has produced a social loss. Of course, the costs associated with this loss are small in most cases. Yet since each body piercing entails a small risk of infection, the costs will continue to rise with the number of piercings. And once those costs reach a certain threshold, support may mobilize on behalf of social norms that discourage body mutilation.

Norms of Taste   Similar cycles occur with respect to behaviours considered to be in bad taste. In the 1950s, for example, prevailing norms prevented major national magazines from accepting ads that featured photographs of nude figures. Naturally, advertisers had a powerful incentive to chip away at such norms in an effort to capture the reader's limited attention. And indeed, taboos against nudes in photographs have eroded in the same way as taboos against body mutilation.

Consider, for instance, the evolution of perfume ads. First came the nude silhouette; then, increasingly well-lighted and detailed nude figures; and more recently, photographs of what appear to be group sex acts. Each innovation achieved just the desired effect: capturing the reader's instant and rapt attention. Inevitably, however, other advertisers followed suit, causing a shift in our sense of what is considered attention-grabbing. Photographs that once would have shocked readers now often draw little more than a bored glance.

"We're looking for the kind of bad taste that will grab—but not appall."

Opinions differ, of course, about whether this change is an improvement. Many believe that the earlier, stricter norms were ill-advised, the legacy of a more prudish and repressive era. Yet even people who take that view are likely to believe that *some* kinds of photographic material ought not to be used in magazine advertisements. Obviously, what is acceptable will differ from person to person, and each person's threshold of discomfort will depend in part on current standards. But as advertisers continue to break new ground in their struggle to capture attention, the point may come when people begin to mobilize in favour of stricter standards of "public decency." Such a campaign would provide yet another example of a positional arms control agreement.

■ SUMMARY

- **10.1** Externalities are the costs and benefits of activities that accrue to people who are not directly involved in those activities. When all parties affected by externalities can negotiate with one another at no cost, the invisible hand of the market will produce an efficient allocation of resources. According to the Coase theorem, the allocation of resources is efficient in such cases because the parties affected by externalities can compensate others for taking remedial action.

- **10.1** Negotiation over externalities is often impractical, however. In these cases, the self-serving actions of individuals typically will not lead to efficient outcomes. The attempt to forge solutions to the problems caused by externalities is one of the most important rationales for collective action. Sometimes collective action takes the form of laws and government regulations that alter the incentives facing those who generate, or are affected by, externalities. Such remedies work best when they place the burden of accommodation on the parties who can accomplish it at the lowest cost. Traffic laws, zoning laws, and environmental protection laws are examples. Social norms can help to make such rules more effective.

- **10.1** Curbing pollution and other external costs entails costs as well as benefits. The optimal amount of pollution reduction is the amount for which the marginal benefit of further reduction just equals the marginal cost. In general, this formula implies that the socially optimal level of pollution, or of any other external cost, is greater than zero.

- **10.2** When grazing land and other valuable resources are owned in common, no one has an incentive to take the opportunity cost of using those resources into account.

This problem is known as the tragedy of the commons. Defining and enforcing private rights that govern the use of valuable resources is often an effective solution to the tragedy of the commons. Not surprisingly, most economically successful nations have well-developed institutions of private property. Some traditional societies deal with the problem by developing implicit rules of use concerning commonly owned resources that have the effect of considering opportunity costs. This approach is difficult for large commercial societies to use. In such societies, property that belongs to everyone belongs, in effect, to no one. Not only is its potential economic value never fully realized; it usually ends up having no value at all.

- **10.2** The difficulty of enforcing property rights in certain situations explains a variety of inefficient outcomes, such as the excessive harvesting of whales in international waters. The excessive pollution of seas that are bordered by many countries also results from a lack of enforceable property rights.

- **10.3** Situations in which people's rewards depend on how well they perform in relation to their rivals can give rise to positional externalities. In these situations, any step that improves one side's relative position necessarily worsens the other's. Positional externalities tend to spawn positional arms races—escalating patterns of mutually offsetting investments in performance enhancement. Collective measures to curb positional arms races are known as positional arms control agreements. These collective actions may take the form of formal regulations or rules, such as rules against anabolic steroids in sports, workplace norms, and binding arbitration agreements. Informal social norms can also curtail positional arms races.

■ KEY TERMS

Coase theorem (284)	positional arms control agreement	positional externality (296)
external benefit (281)	(296)	side payment (283)
external cost (281)	positional arms race (296)	tragedy of the commons (292)
externality (281)		

■ REVIEW QUESTIONS

1. What incentive problem explains why the freeways in cities like Toronto suffer from excessive congestion?

2. How would you explain to a friend why the optimal amount of freeway congestion is not zero?

3. If Parliament could declare any activity that imposes external costs on others to be illegal, would such legislation be advisable?

4. Why does the Great Salt Lake, which is located wholly within the state of Utah, suffer lower levels of pollution than Lake Erie, which is bordered by several states on the American side and by Ontario on the Canadian side?

5. Explain why the wearing of high-heeled shoes might be viewed as the result of a positional externality. Further, how could high-heeled shoes create external costs?

PROBLEMS

1. Determine whether the following statements are true or false, and briefly explain why:
   a. A given reduction of total emissions by a polluting industry will be achieved at the lowest possible total cost when the cost of the last unit of pollution curbed is equal for each firm in the industry.
   b. In an attempt to lower their costs of production, firms sometimes succeed merely in shifting costs to outsiders.

2. Phoebe keeps a bee farm next door to an apple orchard. She chooses her optimal number of beehives by selecting the honey output level at which her private marginal benefit from beekeeping equals her private marginal cost.
   a. Assume that Phoebe's private marginal benefit and marginal cost curves from beekeeping are normally shaped. Draw a diagram of them.
   b. Phoebe's bees help to pollinate the blossoms in the apple orchard, increasing the fruit yield. Show the social marginal benefit from Phoebe's beekeeping in your diagram.
   c. Phoebe's bees are Africanized killer bees that aggressively sting anyone who steps into their flight path. Phoebe, fortunately, is naturally immune to the bees' venom. Show the social marginal cost curve from Phoebe's beekeeping in your diagram.
   d. Indicate the socially optimal quantity of beehives on your diagram. Is it higher or lower than the privately optimal quantity? Explain.
   e. Should Phoebe be banned from keeping Africanized killer bees?

3. Suppose the supply curve of boom box rentals in Stanley Park is given by $P = 5 + 0.1Q$, where P is the daily rent per unit in dollars and Q is the quantity of units rented in hundreds per day. The demand curve for boom boxes is $20 - 0.2Q$. If each boom box imposes $3/day in noise costs on others, by how much will the equilibrium number of boom boxes rented exceed the socially optimal number?

4. Refer to Problem 3. How would the imposition of a tax of $3/unit on each daily boom box rental affect efficiency in this market?

5. Suppose the law says that Jones may *not* emit smoke from his factory unless he gets permission from Smith, who lives downwind. If the relevant costs and benefits of filtering the smoke from Jones's production process are as shown in the following table, and if Jones and Smith can negotiate with one another at no cost, will Jones emit smoke?

	Jones emits smoke	Jones does not emit smoke
Surplus for Jones	$200	$160
Surplus for Smith	400	420

6. John and Karl can live together in a two-bedroom apartment for $500/month, or each can rent a single-bedroom apartment for $350/month. Aside from the rent, the two would be indifferent between living together and living separately, except for one problem: John leaves dirty dishes in the sink every night. Karl would be willing to pay up to $175/month to avoid John's dirty dishes. John, for his part, would be willing to pay up to $225 to be able to continue his sloppiness. Will John and Karl be better off if they live together? If they do, will there be dirty dishes in the sink? Explain.

7. How, if at all, would your answer to Problem 6 differ if John would be willing to pay up to $30/month to avoid giving up his privacy by sharing quarters with Karl?

8. Barton and Statler are neighbours in an apartment complex in downtown Saskatoon. Barton is a concert pianist, and Statler is a poet working on an epic poem. Barton rehearses his concert pieces on the baby grand piano in his front room, which is directly below Statler's study. The following matrix shows the monthly payoffs to

Barton and Statler when Barton's front room is and is not soundproofed. The sound-proofing will be effective only if it is installed in Barton's apartment.

	Soundproofed	Not soundproofed
Gains to Barton	$100/month	$150/month
Gains to Statler	$120/month	$ 80/month

a. If Barton has the legal right to make any amount of noise he wants and he and Statler can negotiate with one another at no cost, will Barton install and maintain soundproofing? Explain. Is his choice socially efficient?

b. If Statler has the legal right to peace and quiet and can negotiate with Barton at no cost, will Barton install and maintain soundproofing? Explain. Is his choice socially efficient?

c. Does the attainment of an efficient outcome depend on whether Barton has the legal right to make noise, or Statler the legal right to peace and quiet?

9. Refer to Problem 8. Barton decides to buy a full-sized grand piano. The new payoff matrix is as follows:

	Soundproofed	Not soundproofed
Gains to Barton	$100/month	$150/month
Gains to Statler	$120/month	$ 60/month

a. If Statler has the legal right to peace and quiet and Barton and Statler can negotiate at no cost, will Barton install and maintain soundproofing? Explain. Is this outcome socially efficient?

b. Suppose that Barton has the legal right to make as much noise as he likes and that negotiating an agreement with Barton costs $15/month. Will Barton install and maintain soundproofing? Explain. Is this outcome socially efficient?

c. Suppose Statler has the legal right to peace and quiet, and it costs $15/month for Statler and Barton to negotiate any agreement. (Compensation for noise damage can be paid without incurring negotiation cost.) Will Barton install and maintain soundproofing? Is this outcome socially efficient?

d. Why does the attainment of a socially efficient outcome now depend on whether Barton has the legal right to make noise?

10. A village has six residents, each of whom has accumulated savings of $100. Each villager can use this money either to buy a government bond that pays 15 percent interest per year or to buy a one-year-old llama, send it onto the commons to graze, and sell it after one year. The price the villager gets for the two-year-old llama depends on the quality of the fleece it grows while grazing on the commons. That in turn depends on the animal's access to grazing, which depends on the number of llamas sent to the commons, as shown in the following table:

Number of llamas on the commons	Price per two-year-old llama ($)
1	122
2	118
3	116
4	114
5	112
6	109

The villagers make their investment decisions one after another, and their decisions are public.

a. If each villager decides individually how to invest, how many llamas will be sent onto the commons, and what will be the resulting net village income?

b. What is the socially optimal number of llamas for this village? Why is that different from the actual number? What would net village income be if the socially optimal number of llamas were sent onto the commons?

c. The village committee votes to auction the right to graze llamas on the commons to the highest bidder. Assuming villagers can both borrow and lend at 15 percent annual interest, what price will the right fetch at auction? How will the new owner use the right, and what will be the resulting village income?

ANSWERS TO IN-CHAPTER EXERCISES

10.1 Since Fitch gains $50/day when Chabar operates with a filter, he could pay Chabar as much as $49/day and still come out ahead.

10.2 The income figures from the different levels of investment in cattle would remain as before, as shown in the table. What is different is the opportunity cost of investing in each steer, which is now $11/year instead of $13. The last column of the table shows that the socially optimal number of steers is now two instead of one. And if individuals still favour holding cattle, all other things being equal, they will now send five steers onto the commons instead of four, as shown in the middle column.

Number of steers on the commons	Price per two-year-old steer ($)	Income per steer ($/year)	Total income from steers ($/year)	Total village income ($/year)	Marginal village income ($/year)
1	126	26	26	70	15
2	119	19	38	71	1
3	116	16	48	70	−1
4	113	13	52	63	−7
5	111	11	55	55	−12

THE ECONOMICS OF INFORMATION

Years ago, a naive young economist bought a used car. It had a sunroof and a great stereo and no rust despite 150,000 kilometres on the odometer. It looked like a good deal at the time, and his younger brother (who said he knew a lot about cars) told him it was a bargain. So he drove the car around the block, paid the lawyer who had owned it $1500 and then drove it away.

The proud first-time owner had his first bad surprise when he paid $400 to have the car safety checked. His second bad surprise occurred 900 kilometres later when the transmission lost reverse, first, and fourth gears while he was trying to accelerate after going through a toll-booth. With the remaining gears, the car limped home and sat forlornly in its parking spot for several months, dripping oil from a leaking engine seal, before being towed off (because the brakes had seized) and sold to the local scrap yard for $50.

The modern version of Adam Smith's invisible hand theory presumes that buyers are fully informed about the myriad ways in which they might spend their money—what goods and services are available, what prices they sell for, how long they last, how frequently they break down, and so on. Up to now, we have assumed that all buyers and sellers in a market possess "perfect information." They all have the same complete, accurate information on the good being traded. Perfect information means that there is no uncertainty about the quality, or any other characteristic, of the good being traded, that all potential buyers and sellers know the prices that are being charged, and that they obtain all this information at no cost. But of course no one is ever really *fully* informed about anything. Still, life goes on, and most people muddle through somehow.

In the days after his car became immobile, the budding economist pondered the economics of information. Maybe, before buying, he should have invested a bit more in acquiring better information about this vehicle. Maybe he should have hired a mechanic to check the car out, rather than relying on the unpaid services of his brother. Maybe he should have taken more time to test-drive the vehicle and to read its service history.

Consumers employ a variety of strategies for gathering information, some of which are better than others. They read *Consumer Reports,* talk to family and friends, visit stores, and so on. All these activities have a cost, but they increase a potential buyer's knowledge of which seller offers the best price, and they reduce the uncertainty that consumers would otherwise have about the quality of a commodity.

However, although it was clear to the young economist (in retrospect—after 900 kilometres) that he had made a bad deal, based on bad information, he also noticed that there were two themes in the "economics of information" that could help explain *why* he had had bad information. He should certainly have invested more time, money, and effort in acquiring more data. The first theme of "information economics" emphasizes that the process of acquiring information is a process of *investment*. Like all processes of investment, acquiring information necessitates the use of scarce resources.

Our young economist's investment in information had clearly been suboptimal. Nevertheless, even if he had fully researched the vehicle, the previous owner would still have had an advantage—the seller knew a lot about the car that he was unlikely ever to reveal. He knew the history of the vehicle, the conditions under which it had been driven, and the problems that had already emerged. And he had a strong incentive not to disclose any information that would hinder his ability to sell the car. The second theme in the economics of information emphasizes that in such circumstances, there is an *asymmetry of information* between the buyer and seller. No amount of investment in information can fully offset this asymmetry.

This chapter will begin by considering how our conclusions about markets are affected by the problem of optimal investment in information. It will then consider the implications of asymmetric information. We should also stress that in practice many markets may not be very far from "perfect information." For example, when you purchase 2 × 4 lumber from your local building supply dealer, it is fairly easy to compare prices on such a standardized product, and you can easily check for obvious quality flaws. When there is little uncertainty about price or quality, and when both parties have the same information, the assumption of "perfect information" can be a reasonable one. However, the art of doing good economics is recognizing when we need to make a different assumption.

The economics of information is a relatively new subject. In 2001, George Akerlof, Michael Spence, and Joseph Stiglitz shared the Nobel Prize in Economics for their work in developing this field. Their work can be used to help identify those situations in which additional information is most likely to prove helpful, and those situations in which information is inherently imperfect.

www.uvic.ca/econ/
nobel.html
Nobel Prize for Economics

■ 11.1 HOW THE INTERMEDIARY ADDS VALUE

One of the most common problems consumers confront is the need to choose among different versions of a product whose many complex features they do not fully understand. As Example 11.1 illustrates, in such cases consumers can sometimes rely on the knowledge of others.

How should a consumer decide which pair of skis to buy?

EXAMPLE 11.1

You need a new pair of skis, but the technology has changed considerably since you bought your last pair, and you do not know which of the current brands and models would be best for you. Skis R Us has the largest selection, so you go there and ask for advice. The salesperson appears to be well informed; after asking about your experience level and how aggressively you ski, he recommends the Salomon X-Scream 9. You buy a pair for $600, then head back to your apartment and show them to your roommate, who says that you could have bought them on the Internet for only $400. How do you feel about your purchase? Are the different prices charged by the two suppliers related to the services they offer? Were the extra services you got by shopping at Skis R Us worth the extra $200?

Internet retailers can sell for less because their costs are so much lower than those of full-service retail stores. Those stores, after all, must hire knowledgeable salespeople, put their merchandise on display, rent space in expensive shopping malls, and so on. Internet retailers and mail-order houses, by contrast, typically employ unskilled telephone clerks, and they store their merchandise in cheap warehouses. But if you are a consumer who does not know which is the right product for you, the extra expense of shopping at a specialty retailer is likely to be a good investment. Spending $600 on the right skis is smarter than spending $400 on the wrong ones.

Many people believe that wholesalers, retailers, and other agents who assist manufacturers in the sale of their products play a fundamentally different economic role from the one played by those who actually make the products. In this view, the production worker is the ultimate source of economic value added. Sales agents are often disparaged as mere intermediaries, parasites on the efforts of others who do the real work.

"On the one hand, eliminating the middleman would result in lower costs, increased sales, and greater consumer satisfaction; on the other hand, we're the middleman."

On a superficial level, this view might seem to be supported by the fact that many people will go to great lengths to avoid paying for the services of sales agents. Many manufacturers cater to them by offering consumers a chance to "buy direct" and sidestep the intermediary's commission. But on closer examination, we can see that the economic role of sales agents is essentially the same as that of production workers. Consider Example 11.2.

EXAMPLE 11.2

How does better information affect economic surplus?

Ellis has just inherited a rare Babe Ruth baseball card issued during the great slugger's rookie year. He would like to keep the card but has reluctantly decided to sell it to pay some overdue bills. His reservation price for the card is $300, but he is hoping to get significantly more for it. He has two ways of selling it: He can place a classified ad in the local newspaper for $5, or he can list the card on eBay, the Internet auction service. If he sells the card on eBay, the fee will be 5 percent of the winning bid.

Because Ellis lives in a small town with few potential buyers of rare baseball cards, the local buyer with the highest reservation price is willing to pay $400 at most. If Ellis lists the card on eBay, however, a much larger number of potential buyers will see it. If the two eBay shoppers who are willing to pay the most for Ellis's card have reservation prices of $900 and $800, respectively, how much larger will the total economic surplus be if Ellis sells his card on eBay? (For the sake of simplicity, assume that the eBay commission and the classified ad fee equal the respective costs of providing those services.)

In an eBay auction, each bidder reports his or her reservation price for an item. When the auction closes, the bidder with the highest reservation price wins, and the price he or she pays is the reservation price of the second highest bidder. So in this example, the Babe Ruth baseball card will sell for $800 if Ellis lists it on eBay. Net of the $40 eBay commission, Ellis will receive a payment of $760, or $460 more than his reservation price for the card. Ellis's economic surplus will thus be $460. The winning bidder's surplus will be $900 − $800 = $100, so the total surplus from selling the card on eBay will be $560.

If Ellis instead advertises the card in the local newspaper and sells it to the local buyer whose reservation price is $400, then Ellis's surplus (net of the newspaper's $5 fee) will be only $95, and the buyer's surplus will be $0. Thus, total economic surplus will be $560 − $95 = $465 larger if Ellis sells the card on eBay than if he lists it in the local newspaper.

eBay provides a service by making information available to people who can make good use of it. A real increase in economic surplus results when an item ends up in the hands of someone who values it more highly than the person who otherwise would have bought it. That increase is just as valuable as the increase in surplus that results from manufacturing cars, growing corn, or any other productive activity.

RECAP   **HOW THE INTERMEDIARY ADDS VALUE**

In a world of incomplete information, sales agents and other intermediaries add genuine economic value by increasing the extent to which goods and services are allocated to the consumers who value them most. When a sales agent causes a good to be purchased by a person who values it by $20 000 more than the person who would have bought it in the absence of a sales agent, that agent augments total economic surplus by $20 000, an achievement on a par with the production of a $20 000 car.

■ 11.2 THE OPTIMAL AMOUNT OF INFORMATION

Without a doubt, having more information is better than having less. But information is generally costly to acquire. In most situations, the value of additional information will decline beyond some point. And because of the principle of increasing opportunity cost, people tend to gather information from the cheapest sources first before turning to more costly ones. Typically, then, the marginal benefit of information will decline, and its marginal cost will rise, as the amount of information gathered increases.

INCREASING
OPPORTUNITY
COST

THE COST–BENEFIT TEST

Information gathering is, in one important respect, an activity like any other. The cost–benefit principle tells us that a rational consumer will continue to gather

COST–
BENEFIT

information as long as its marginal benefit exceeds its marginal cost. If the relevant marginal cost and marginal benefit curves are as shown in Figure 11.1, a rational consumer will acquire I^* units of information, the amount for which the marginal benefit of information equals its marginal cost.

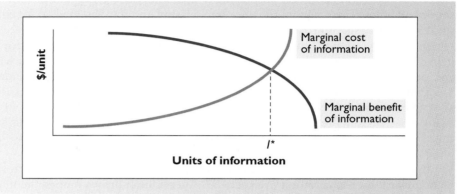

FIGURE 11.1

The Optimal Amount of Information

For the marginal cost and benefit curves shown, the optimal amount of information is I^*. Beyond that point, additional information costs more to acquire than it is worth.

Figure 11.1 can also be interpreted as showing the optimal level of ignorance. When the cost of acquiring information exceeds its benefits, acquiring additional information simply does not pay. If information could be acquired free, decision makers would, of course, be glad to have it. But when the cost of acquiring the information exceeds the gain in value from the decision it will facilitate, people are better off remaining ignorant.

free-rider problem an incentive problem in which too little of a good or service is produced because nonpayers cannot be excluded from using it

THE FREE-RIDER PROBLEM

Does the invisible hand ensure that the optimal amount of advice will be made available to consumers in the marketplace? The next example suggests one reason that it might not.

 ECONOMIC NATURALIST

Why is finding a knowledgeable salesclerk often difficult?

People can choose for themselves whether to bear the extra cost of retail shopping. Those who value advice and convenience can pay slightly higher prices, while those who know what they want can buy for less from a mail-order house.

The market would provide the optimal level of retail service except for one practical problem, namely, that consumers can make use of the services offered by retail stores without paying for them. After benefiting from the advice of informed salespersons and after inspecting the merchandise, the consumer can return home and buy the same item from an Internet retailer or mail-order house. Not all consumers do so, of course. But the fact that customers can benefit from the information provided by retail stores without paying for it is an example of the **free-rider problem**, an incentive problem that results in too little of a good or service being produced. Because retail stores have difficulty recovering the cost of providing information, private incentives may yield less than the socially optimal level of retail service.

EXERCISE 11.1   **Apart from its possible contribution to free-rider problems, how is increased access to the Internet likely to affect total economic surplus?**

"In reply to your inquiry regarding the Burke garden hoe, please visit our Worldwide Web home page at: http://www.burke1903.com."

TWO GUIDELINES FOR RATIONAL SEARCH

In practice, of course, the exact value of additional information is difficult to know, so the amount of time and effort we should invest in acquiring it is not always obvious. But as Examples 11.3 and 11.4 suggest, the cost–benefit principle provides a strong conceptual framework for thinking about this problem.

COST–
BENEFIT

EXAMPLE 11.3

Will a person living in Paris, Ontario, be better off if she spends more or less time searching for an apartment than someone living in Paris, France?

Suppose that rents for one-bedroom apartments in Paris, Ontario, vary between $300 and $500/month, with an average rent of $400/month. Rents for similar one-bedroom apartments in Paris, France, vary between $2000 and $3000/month, with an average rent of $2500. In which city will a rational person expect to spend a longer time searching for an apartment?

In both cities, visiting additional apartments entails a cost, largely, the opportunity cost of one's time. For simplicity, let us assume that the marginal costs of searching—i.e., the time and expense of visiting one more apartment—are the same in both places. In both cities, the more apartments someone visits, the more likely it is that he or she will find one near the lower end of the rent distribution. But because rents are higher and are spread over a broader range in Paris, France, the expected saving from further time spent searching will be greater there than in Paris, Ontario. And so a rational person will expect to spend more time searching for an apartment in Paris, France.

Example 11.3 illustrates the principle that spending additional search time is more likely to be worthwhile for expensive items than for cheap ones. For example, we should spend more time searching for a good price on a diamond engagement ring than for a good price on a stone made of cubic zirconium; more time searching for a low fare from a city within Canada to Sydney, Australia, than for a low fare to Sydney, Nova Scotia; and more time searching for a car than for a bicycle. By extension, hiring an agent—someone who can assist with a search—is more likely to be a good investment in searching for something expensive than for something cheap. For example, people typically engage real estate agents to help them find a house, but they seldom hire agents to help them buy a litre of milk.

EXAMPLE 11.4

Who can expect to search longer for a job?

Both Tom and Tim are looking for a job. They both have the same qualifications, and they both figure that in today's labour market, each will have to distribute one hundred résumés in order to get a job offer. If Tom has a car, and Tim does not, and if all the available jobs are in the suburbs and require each job applicant to deliver their résumés in person, who is likely to spend the least amount of time unemployed?

In both cases, the benefits of job search are the same—but the costs are different. If Tim has to walk or take public transit to apply for a job, his job search time is less effective than Tom's, and he is likely to remain jobless for longer.

Example 11.4 makes the point that when searching becomes more costly, we can afford to do less of it. As a result, the outcomes we can expect in the market will tend to be poorer.

THE GAMBLE INHERENT IN SEARCH

expected value of a gamble the sum of the possible outcomes of the gamble multiplied by their respective probabilities

fair gamble a gamble whose expected value is zero

better-than-fair gamble a gamble whose expected value is positive

risk-neutral person someone who would accept any gamble that is fair or better than fair

risk-averse person someone who would refuse any fair gamble

Suppose you are in the market for a one-bedroom apartment and have found one that rents for $400 per month. Should you rent it or search further in hopes of finding a cheaper apartment? Even in a large market with many vacant apartments, there is no guarantee that searching further will turn up a cheaper or better apartment. Searching further entails a cost, which might outweigh the gain. In general, someone who engages in further search must accept certain costs in return for unknown benefits. Thus, further search invariably carries an element of risk.

In thinking about whether to take any gamble, a helpful first step is to compute its **expected value**—the average amount you would win (or lose) if you played that gamble many times. To calculate the expected value of a gamble with more than one outcome, we first multiply each outcome by its corresponding probability of occurring, and then sum the resulting values. For example, suppose you win $1 if a coin flip comes up heads and lose $1 if it comes up tails. Since ½ is the probability of heads (and also the probability of tails), the expected value of this gamble is $(½)($1) + (½)(-$1) = 0$. A gamble with an expected value of zero is called a **fair gamble**. If you played this gamble a large number of times, you would not expect to make money, but you also would not expect to lose money.

A **better-than-fair gamble** is one with a positive expected value. (For example, a coin flip in which you win $2 for heads and lose $1 for tails is a better-than-fair gamble.) A **risk-neutral person** is someone who would accept any gamble that is fair or better than fair. A **risk-averse person** is someone who would refuse to take any fair gamble.

EXERCISE 11.2

Consider a gamble in which you win $4 if you flip a coin and it comes up heads and lose $2 if it comes up tails. What is the expected value of this gamble? Would a risk-neutral person accept it?

In Example 11.5 we apply these concepts to the decision of whether to search further for an apartment.

EXAMPLE 11.5

Are you better off if you search further for an apartment?

You have arrived in Montreal for a one-month summer visit and are searching for a one-bedroom sublet for the month. Vacant one-bedroom apartments in the neighbourhood in which you want to live are identical in every respect. Nevertheless, 80 percent of them rent for $400 and 20 percent for $360. To discover the rent for a vacant apartment, you must visit it in person. The first apartment you visit rents for $400. If you are risk-neutral and your opportunity cost of visiting an additional apartment is $6, will you visit another apartment or rent the one you have found?

If you visit one more apartment, you have a 20 percent chance of finding one that rents for $360 and an 80 percent chance of finding one that rents for $400. If it is the former, you will save $40 in rent, but if it's the latter, you will face the same rent as before. Since the cost of a visit is $6, visiting another apartment is a gamble with a 20 percent chance to win $40 − $6 = $34 and an 80 percent chance of losing $6 (which means "winning" −$6). The expected value of this gamble is thus (0.20)($34) + (0.80)(−$6) = $2. Visiting another apartment is a better-than-fair gamble, and since you are risk-neutral, you will take it.

Refer to Example 11.5. Suppose you visit another apartment and discover it rents for $400. If you are risk-neutral, will you visit a third apartment?

THE COMMITMENT PROBLEM WHEN SEARCH IS COSTLY

When most people search for an apartment, they want a place to live not for just a month but for a year or more. Most landlords, for their part, are also looking for long-term tenants. Similarly, few people accept a full-time job in their chosen field unless they expect to hold the job for several years. Firms, too, generally prefer employees who will stay for extended periods. Finally, when most people search for mates, they are looking for someone with whom to settle down.

Because in all these cases search is costly, examining every possible option will never make sense. Apartment hunters do not visit every vacant apartment, nor do landlords interview every possible tenant. Job seekers do not visit every employer, nor do employers interview every job seeker. And not even the most determined searcher can manage to date every eligible potential mate. In these and other cases, people are rational to end their searches, even though they know a more attractive option surely exists out there somewhere.

But herein lies a difficulty. What happens when, by chance, a more attractive option comes along after the search has ceased? Few people would rent an apartment if they thought the landlord would kick them out the moment another tenant came along who was willing to pay higher rent. Few landlords would be willing to rent to a tenant if they expected her to move out the moment she discovers a cheaper apartment. Employers, job seekers, and people who are looking for mates would have similar reservations about entering relationships that could be terminated once a better option happened to come along.

This potential difficulty in maintaining stable matches between partners in ongoing relationships would not arise in a world of perfect information. In such a world, everyone would find the best possible relationship, so no one would be tempted to renege. But when information is costly and the search must be limited, there will always be the potential for existing relationships to dissolve because a better partner fortuitously appears.

In most contexts, people solve this problem not by conducting an exhaustive search (which is usually impossible, in any event) but by committing themselves to remain in a relationship once a mutual agreement has been reached to terminate the search. Thus, landlords and tenants sign a lease that binds them to one another for a specified period, usually one year. Employees and firms enter into employment contracts, either formal or informal, under which each promises to honour his or her obligations to the other, except under extreme circumstances. And in most countries a marriage contract penalizes those who abandon their spouses. Entering into such commitments limits the freedom to pursue one's own interests at a later date. Yet most people freely accept such restrictions, because they know the alternative is failure to solve the search problem.

RECAP	**THE OPTIMAL AMOUNT OF INFORMATION**

Additional information creates value, but it is also costly to acquire. A rational consumer will continue to acquire information until its marginal benefit equals its marginal cost. Beyond that point, it is rational to remain uninformed.

Markets for information do not always function perfectly. Free-rider problems often hinder retailers' efforts to provide information to consumers.

Search inevitably entails an element of risk, because costs must be incurred without any assurance that the search will prove fruitful. A rational consumer can minimize this risk by concentrating the search efforts on goods for which the variation in price or quality is relatively high and on those for which the cost of the search is relatively low.

■ 11.3 ASYMMETRIC INFORMATION

In Examples 11.1 to 11.5, the problem of incomplete information could be at least somewhat reduced by investing more effort in the search for information. However, the problem of incomplete information is fundamentally different if you cannot trust the only person who has the ability to provide you with the information you need.

One of the most common information problems occurs when the participants in a potential exchange are not equally well informed about the product or service that is offered for sale. For instance, the owner of a used car may know that the car is in excellent mechanical condition, but potential buyers cannot verify the car's condition merely by inspecting it or taking it for a test drive. Economists use the term **asymmetric information** to describe situations in which buyers and sellers are not equally well informed about the characteristics of products or services.

asymmetric information situations in which buyers and sellers are not equally well informed about the characteristics of goods and services for sale in the marketplace

In some markets, information is necessarily asymmetric because information is the commodity that is being sold. For example, when you go to the doctor, it is typically because you know you are sick but you do not know the exact nature of your illness. You have the symptoms and you want your physician to provide the diagnosis—you want the physician to supply information that you do not have because you believe she knows more about the causes of illness than you do. Information is necessarily asymmetric in such markets, because the whole transaction is based on the fact that the supplier knows more than the buyer.

In other cases, information may be asymmetric because of the incentives that market participants have to be less than honest. (Remember the lawyer who sold our young economist his first car?) Because everyone who sells a good has an incentive to *say* that it is of high quality, potential buyers may be unable to distinguish between those sellers whose claims are true and those whose claims are false. As a result, buyers will only be willing to pay a price that reflects the *chance* of getting a bad-quality product. In these situations, sellers are typically much better informed than buyers, but sometimes the reverse will be true.

As Example 11.6 illustrates, the problem of asymmetric information can easily prevent exchanges that would benefit both parties.

EXAMPLE 11.6

Will Jane sell her car to Tom?

Jane's 1995 Miata has 70 000 kilometres on the odometer, and most of these are highway kilometres driven during weekend trips to see her boyfriend in Toronto. (Highway driving causes less wear and tear on a car than city driving.) Moreover, Jane has maintained the car precisely according to the manufacturer's specifications. In short, she knows her car to be in excellent condition. Because she is about to start graduate school in Halifax, however, Jane wants to sell the car. Today, 1995 Miatas sell for an average price of $8000, but because Jane knows her car to be in excellent condition, her reservation price for it is $10 000.

Tom wants to buy a used Miata. He would be willing to pay $13 000 for one that is in excellent condition but only $9000 for one that is not in excellent condition. Tom has no way of telling whether Jane's Miata is in excellent condition. (He could hire a mechanic to examine the car, but many problems cannot be detected even by a mechanic.) Will Tom buy Jane's car? Will the outcome be efficient?

Because Tom cannot verify that Jane's car is in excellent condition, he will not pay $10 000 for it. After all, for only $8000, he can buy some other 1995 Miata that is in just as good condition, as far as he can tell. Tom therefore will buy someone else's Miata, and Jane's will go unsold. This outcome is not efficient. If Tom had bought Jane's Miata for, say, $11 000, his surplus would have been $2000 and Jane's another $1000. Instead, Tom ends up buying a Miata that is in average condition (or worse), and his surplus is only $1000. Jane gets no economic surplus at all.

THE LEMONS MODEL

We cannot be sure, of course, that the Miata Tom ends up buying will be in worse condition than Jane's—since *someone* might have a car in perfect condition that must be sold even if the owner cannot get what it is really worth. Even so, the economic incentives created by asymmetric information suggest that most used cars that are put up for sale will be of lower-than-average quality. One reason is that people who mistreat their cars, or whose cars were never very good to begin with, are more likely than others to want to sell them. Buyers know from experience that cars for sale on the used car market are more likely to be "lemons" than cars that are not for sale. This realization causes them to lower their reservation prices for a used car.

But that's not the end of the story. Once used car prices have fallen, the owners of cars that are in good condition have an even stronger incentive to hold onto them. That causes the average quality of the cars offered for sale on the used car market to decline still further. Berkeley economist George Akerlof was the first to explain the logic behind this downward spiral.[1] Economists use the term **lemons model** to describe Akerlof's explanation of how asymmetric information affects the average quality of the used goods offered for sale.

As Example 11.7 suggests, the lemons model has important practical implications for consumer choice.

lemons model George Akerlof's explanation of how asymmetric information tends to reduce the average quality of goods offered for sale

[1]George Akerlof, "The Market for Lemons," *Quarterly Journal of Economics,* 84:488–500, 1970.

EXAMPLE 11.7

Should you buy your aunt's car?

You want to buy a used Honda Accord. Your Aunt Germaine buys a new car every four years, and she has a four-year-old Accord that she is about to trade in. You believe her report that the car is in good condition, and she is willing to sell it to you for $10 000, which is the current red book value for four-year-old Accords. (The red book value of a car is the average price for which cars of that age and model sell in the used car market in Canada.) Should you buy your aunt's Honda?

Akerlof's lemons model tells us that cars for sale in the used car market will be of lower average quality than cars of the same vintage that are not for sale. If you believe your aunt's claim that her car is in good condition, then being able to buy it for its red book value is definitely a good deal for you, since the red book price is the equilibrium price for a car that is (on average) of lower quality than your aunt's.

Examples 11.8 and 11.9 illustrate the conditions under which asymmetric information about product quality results in a market in which *only* lemons are offered for sale.

EXAMPLE 11.8

What price will a used car fetch?

Consider a world with only two kinds of cars, good ones and lemons. An owner knows with certainty which type of car she has, but potential buyers cannot distinguish between the two types. Ten percent of all new cars produced are lemons. Good used cars are worth $10 000 to their owners, but lemons are worth only $6000. Consider a naive consumer who believes that the used cars currently for sale have the same quality distribution as new cars (i.e., 90 percent good, 10 percent lemons). If this consumer is risk-neutral, how much would he be willing to pay for a used car?

Buying a car of unknown quality is a gamble, but a risk-neutral buyer would be willing to take the gamble provided it were fair. If the buyer cannot tell the difference between a good car and a lemon, the probability that he will end up with a lemon is simply the proportion of lemons among the cars from which he chooses. The buyer believes he has a 90 percent chance of getting a good car and a 10 percent chance of getting a lemon. Given the prices he is willing to pay for the two types of car, his expected value of the car he buys will thus be 0.90($10 000) + 0.10($6000) = $9600. And since he is risk-neutral, that is his reservation price for a used car.

EXERCISE 11.4

How would your answer to the question posed in Example 11.8 differ if the proportion of new cars that are lemons had been not 10 percent but 20 percent?

EXAMPLE 11.9

Who will sell a used car for what the naive buyer is willing to pay?

Refer to Example 11.8. If you were the owner of a good used car, what would it be worth to you? Would you sell it to a naive buyer? What if you owned a lemon?

Since you know your car is good, it is worth $10 000 to you, by assumption. But since a naive buyer would be willing to pay only $9600, neither you nor any other owner of a good car would be willing to sell to that buyer. If you had a lemon, of course, you would be happy to sell it to a naive buyer, since the $9600 the buyer is willing to pay is $3600 more than the lemon would be worth to you. So the only used cars for sale will be lemons. In time, buyers will revise their naively optimistic beliefs about the quality of the cars for sale on the used car market. In the end, all used cars will sell for a price of $6000, and all will be lemons.

In practice, of course, the mere fact that a car is for sale does not guarantee that it is a lemon, because the owner of a good car will sometimes be forced to sell it, even at a price that does not reflect its condition. The logic of the lemons model explains this owner's frustration. The first thing sellers in this situation want a prospective buyer to know is the reason they are selling their cars. For example, classified ads often announce, "Just had a baby, must sell my 1999 Corvette" or "Transferred to Germany, must sell my 2000 Toyota Camry." Any time you pay the red book price for a used car that is for sale for some reason unrelated to its condition, you are beating the market.

THE CREDIBILITY PROBLEM IN TRADING

Why can someone with a high-quality used car not simply *tell* the buyer about the car's condition? The difficulty is that buyers' and sellers' interests tend to conflict. Sellers of used cars, for example, have an economic incentive to overstate the quality of their products. Buyers, for their part, have an incentive to understate the amount they are willing to pay for used cars (and other) products. Potential employees may be tempted to overstate their qualifications for a job. And people searching for mates have been known to engage in deception.

That is not to say that most people *consciously* misrepresent the truth in communicating with their potential trading partners. But people do tend to interpret ambiguous information in ways that promote their own interests. Thus, 92 percent of factory employees surveyed in one study rated themselves as more productive than the average factory worker. Psychologists call this phenomenon the "Lake Wobegon effect," after Garrison Keillor's mythical Minnesota homestead, where "all the children are above average."

Notwithstanding the natural tendency to exaggerate, the parties to a potential exchange can often gain if they can find some means to communicate their knowledge truthfully. In general, however, mere statements of relevant information will not suffice. People have long since learned to discount the used car salesman's inflated claims about the cars he is trying to unload. But as the next example illustrates, though communication between potential adversaries may be difficult, it is not impossible.

Why do new cars lose a significant fraction of their value as soon as they are driven from the showroom?

EXAMPLE 11.10

How can a used car seller signal high quality credibly?

Jane knows her Miata is in excellent condition, and Tom would be willing to pay considerably more than her reservation price if he could be confident of getting such a car. What kind of signal about the car's quality would Tom find credible?

Again, the potential conflict between Tom's and Jane's interests suggests that mere statements about the car's quality may not be persuasive. But suppose Jane offers a warranty, under which she agrees to remedy any defects the car develops over the next six months. Jane can afford to extend such an offer because she knows her car is unlikely to need expensive repairs. In contrast, the person who knows his car has a cracked engine block would never extend such an offer. The warranty is a credible signal that the car is in good condition. It enables Tom to buy the car with confidence, to both his and Jane's benefit.

THE COSTLY-TO-FAKE PRINCIPLE

costly-to-fake principle
to communicate information credibly to a potential rival, a signal must be costly or difficult to fake

The preceding examples illustrate the **costly-to-fake principle,** which holds that if parties whose interests potentially conflict are to communicate credibly with one another, the signals they send must be costly or difficult to fake. If the seller of a defective car could offer an extensive warranty just as easily as the seller of a good car, a warranty offer would communicate nothing about the car's quality. But warranties entail costs that are significantly higher for defective cars than for good cars—hence their credibility as a signal of product quality.

CONSPICUOUS CONSUMPTION AS A SIGNAL OF ABILITY

COST–
BENEFIT

Some individuals of high ability are not highly paid. (Remember the best elementary-school teacher you ever had.) And some people, such as the multibillionaire investor Warren Buffett, earn a lot, yet spend very little. But such cases run counter to general tendencies. As the following example suggests, these tendencies may lead us to infer a person's ability from the amount and quality of the goods consumed.

🍁 11.2   ECONOMIC NATURALIST

Why do many clients seem to prefer lawyers who wear expensive suits?

You have been unjustly accused of a serious crime and are looking for an attorney. Your choice is between two lawyers who appear identical in all respects except for the things they buy. One of them wears a cheap polyester suit and arrives at the courthouse in a 10-year-old rust-eaten Dodge Colt. The other wears an impeccably tailored suit and drives a new BMW 740i. If this were the *only* information available to you at the time you chose, which lawyer would you hire?

The correlation between salary and ability is particularly strong in the legal profession. A lawyer who usually prevails in court will be much more in demand than one who generally loses, and his fees will reflect the difference. The fact that one of the lawyers consumes much more than the other does not *prove* that he is the better lawyer, but if that is the only information you have, you can ill afford to ignore it.

If the less able lawyer loses business because of the suits he wears and the car he drives, why does he not simply buy better suits and a more expensive car? His choice is between saving for retirement or spending more on his car and clothing. In one sense, he cannot afford to buy a more expensive car, but in another sense, he cannot afford *not* to. If his current car is discouraging potential clients from hiring him, buying a better one may simply be a prudent investment. But because *all* lawyers have an incentive to make such investments, their effects tend to be mutually offsetting.

When all is said and done, the things people consume will continue to convey relevant information about their respective abilities. The costly-to-fake principle tells us that the BMW 740i is an effective signal precisely because the lawyer of low ability cannot afford one, no matter how little he saves for retirement. Yet from a social perspective, the resulting spending pattern is inefficient, for the same reason that other positional arms races are inefficient (see Chapter 10). Society would be better off if everyone spent less and saved more for retirement.

The problem of conspicuous consumption as a signal of ability does not arise with equal force in every environment. In small towns, where people tend to know one another well, a lawyer who tries to impress people by spending beyond her means is likely to succeed only in demonstrating how foolish she is. Thus the wardrobe a professional person "needs" in towns like Yarmouth, Nova Scotia, or Charlottetown, PEI, might well cost less than half as much as the wardrobe the same person would need in Vancouver or Calgary.

The previous two examples are cases in which signals transmit information from one participant in a market to another. When the Nobel Committee named Michael Spence (who once lived in Toronto) as one of three Nobel Laureates for 2001, it cited his work on market signalling.

STATISTICAL DISCRIMINATION

In a competitive market with perfect information, the buyer of a service would pay the seller's cost of providing the service. In many markets, however—the market for fire insurance is one example—the seller does not know the exact cost of serving each individual buyer.

In such cases, the missing information has an economic value. If the seller can come up with even a rough estimate of the missing information, she can improve her position. As the following examples illustrate, firms often do so by imputing characteristics to individuals based on the groups to which they belong.

 11.3   ECONOMIC NATURALIST

Why do males under 25 years of age pay more than other drivers for auto insurance?

Gerald is 23 years old and is an extremely careful and competent driver. He has never had an accident or even a moving traffic violation. His twin sister Geraldine has had two accidents, one of them serious, in the past three years and has accumulated three speeding tickets during that same period. Why does Gerald pay twice as much per year for auto insurance?

The expected cost to an insurance company of insuring any given driver depends on the probability that the driver will be involved in an accident. No one knows what that probability is for any given driver, but insurance companies can estimate rather precisely the proportion of drivers in specific groups who will be involved in an accident in any given year. Because males under 25 are much more likely than older males and females of any age to become involved in auto accidents, Gerald pays more than his sister. Even if, for example, it is true that Gerald never speeds, the insurance company is unlikely to believe him if he says so. The company knows that all young drivers have an incentive to *say* they never speed, but (on average) young male drivers tend to drive significantly faster than older drivers or young female drivers. Data gathered and analyzed over many years tell the insurance industry that even accident-free males under 25 are more likely to have an accident than females the same age who have had several accidents. An insurer cannot verify Gerald's claim that he is a safer driver than the average accident-free male driver who is Gerald's age. Since Gerald cannot distinguish his (truthful) claim from the bogus claims of other similar young male drivers, he will be lumped in with other "observationally equivalent" insurance purchasers. Gerald will pay more for his insurance than his twin sister pays.

Of course, females who have had two accidents and accumulated several tickets in the past three years are more likely to have an accident than a female with a spotless driving record. The insurance company knows that and

has increased Geraldine's premium accordingly. Yet it is still less than her brother's premium. That does not mean that Gerald is more likely to have an accident than Geraldine. Indeed, given the twins' respective driving skills, Geraldine clearly poses the higher risk. But because insurance companies lack such detailed information, they are forced to set rates according to the information they possess.

To remain in business, an insurance company must collect enough money from premiums to cover the cost of the claims it pays out, plus whatever administrative expenses it incurs. Consider an insurance company that charges lower rates for young males with clean driving records than for females with blemished ones. Given that the former group is more likely to have accidents than the latter, the company will suffer losses unless it charges females more, and males less, than the respective costs of insuring them. But if it does so, rival insurance companies will have a competitive advantage. They can offer females slightly lower rates and lure them away from the first company. In addition, young males will be attracted to the first company by its lower rates. The first company will end up insuring only young male policyholders and thus will suffer an economic loss at the low rates it charges. That is why, in equilibrium, young males with clean driving records pay higher insurance rates than young females with blemished records.

Gerald has no choice about buying insurance. If he wants to drive, the law requires him to purchase liability insurance, regardless of the price he must pay. This law is, in fact, a practical example of how a law can deal with an external cost, as discussed in Chapter 10. A driver who causes an accident involving someone else imposes a cost on that person. When the law requires liability insurance, it is providing a way of dealing with an external cost by requiring a driver to have the means of compensating other persons for any injury he may cause them.

statistical discrimination the practice of making judgments about the quality of people, goods, or services based on the characteristics of the groups to which they belong

The insurance industry's policy of charging high rates to young male drivers is an example of **statistical discrimination.** Other examples include the common practice of paying higher salaries to people with degrees than to people without them and the policy of favouring applicants for medical school who have high MCAT scores. Statistical discrimination occurs whenever people or products are judged based on the groups to which they belong.

Even though everyone *knows* that the characteristics of specific individuals can differ markedly from those of the group to which they belong, competition promotes statistical discrimination. For example, insurance companies know perfectly well that *some* young males are careful and competent drivers. But unless they can identify *which* males are the better drivers, competitive pressure forces them to act on their knowledge that as a group, young males are more likely than others to generate insurance claims.

Similarly, employers know that many people with only a high-school diploma are more productive than the average university graduate. But because employers usually cannot tell in advance who those people are, competitive pressure leads them to offer higher wages to university graduates, who are more productive, on average, than high-school graduates. Medical schools, too, realize that some applicants with lower MCAT scores will make better physicians than applicants with high scores. But if two applicants look equally promising except for their MCAT scores, competition forces universities to favour the applicant with higher scores since, on average, that applicant will perform better than the other.

Statistical discrimination is the *result* of observable differences in group characteristics, not the cause of those differences. Young males, for example, do not generate more insurance claims because of statistical discrimination. Rather, statistical discrimination occurs because insurance companies know that young males generate more claims. Nor does statistical discrimination cause young males to pay insurance rates that are high in relation to the claims they generate. Among any group of young male drivers, some are careful and competent, and others are not. Statistical discrimination means the more able males will pay high rates relative to the volume of claims they generate, but it also means the less able male drivers will pay low rates relative to the claims they generate. On average, the group's rates will be appropriate to the claims its members generate.

Still, these observations do little to ease the frustration of the young male who knows himself to be a careful and competent driver, or the high-school graduate who knows herself to be a highly productive employee. Competitive forces provide firms an incentive to identify such individuals and treat them more favourably whenever practical. When firms succeed in this effort, however, they have often discovered some other relevant information on group differences. For example, many insurance companies offer lower rates to young males who take a recognized driver's education program. Members of this group generate fewer claims, on average, than other young males. But even this group includes risky drivers, and the fact that companies offer discounts to its members means that that all other young males must pay higher rates.

Indeed, as Chapter 12 will discuss, the problem of statistical discrimination can go much further, and helps to explain why some groups of workers (e.g., women) may get lower wages in the labour market.

ADVERSE SELECTION

adverse selection the pattern that occurs when, at any given cost of insurance, people with a greater expectation of loss buy insurance while people with a lower expected value of claims choose not to buy insurance

Although insurance companies routinely practise statistical discrimination, each individual within a group pays the same rate, even though individuals within the group often differ sharply in terms of their likelihood of filing claims. Within each group, buying insurance is thus most attractive to those individuals with the highest likelihood of filing claims. As a result, high-risk individuals are more likely to buy insurance than low-risk individuals, a pattern known as **adverse selection.**

Adverse selection forces insurance companies to raise their premiums, which makes buying insurance even less attractive to low-risk individuals, which raises still further the average risk level of those who remain insured. In some cases, only those individuals faced with extreme risks may continue to find insurance an attractive purchase. In Chapter 14, we will discuss how adverse selection can affect health insurance, since private health care insurers must recognize that the people with the greatest incentive to purchase insurance, at any given premium rate, are the relatively unhealthy (those who have the greatest likelihood of making claims). Joseph Stiglitz's insights about insurance markets and adverse selection are among the contributions that caused him to be selected as a Nobel Laureate in 2001.

RECAP **ASYMMETRIC INFORMATION**

Asymmetric information describes situations in which not all parties to a potential exchange are equally well informed. In the typical case, the seller of a product will know more about its quality than the potential buyers. Such asymmetries often stand in the way of mutually beneficial exchange in the markets for high-quality goods, because buyers' inability to identify high quality makes them unwilling to pay a commensurate price.

Information asymmetries and other communication problems between potential exchange partners can often be solved through the use of signals that are costly or difficult to fake. Product warranties are such a signal, because the seller of a low-quality product would find them too costly to offer.

Buyers and sellers also respond to asymmetric information by attempting to judge the qualities of products and people on the basis of the groups to which they belong. A young male may know he is a good driver, but auto insurance companies must nonetheless charge him high rates because they know only that he is a member of a group that is frequently involved in accidents.

SUMMARY

- **11.1** Virtually every market exchange takes place based on less than complete information. Incomplete information is of two types: (1) the *uncertainty* that can be reduced if more effort or resources are *invested* in acquiring information; (2) the *asymmetry* of information between buyers and sellers that cannot be eliminated, because of the nature of the market or the inherent incentives that some agents have to not disclose true information.

- **11.1** More information is beneficial both to buyers and to sellers, but information is costly to acquire. The rational individual therefore acquires information only up to the point at which its marginal benefit equals its marginal cost. Beyond that point it is rational to remain ignorant.

- **11.2** Retailers and other sales agents are important sources of information. To the extent that they enable consumers to find the right products and services, they add economic value. In that sense they are no less productive than the workers who manufacture goods or perform services directly. Unfortunately, the free-rider problem often prevents firms from offering useful product information.

- **11.2** Several principles govern the rational search for information. Searching more intensively makes sense when the cost of a search is low, when quality is highly variable, or when prices vary widely. Further search is always a gamble. A risk-neutral person will search whenever the expected gains outweigh the expected costs. A rational search will always terminate before all possible options have been investigated. Thus, in a search for a partner in an ongoing bilateral relationship, there is always the possibility that a better partner will turn up after the search is over. In most contexts, people deal with this problem by entering into contracts that commit them to their partners once they have mutually agreed to terminate the search.

- **11.3** Many potentially beneficial transactions are prevented from taking place by asymmetric information—the fact that one party lacks information that the other has. For example, the owner of a used car knows if it is in good condition, but potential buyers do not. Even though a buyer may be willing to pay more for a good car than the owner of such a car would require, the fact that the buyer cannot be sure he is getting a good car often discourages the sale. More generally, asymmetric information often prevents sellers from supplying the same quality level that consumers would be willing to pay for.

- **11.3** Both buyers and sellers can often gain by finding ways of communicating what they know to one another. But because of the potential conflict between the interests of buyers and sellers, mere statements about the relevant information may not be credible. For a signal between potential trading partners to be credible, it must be costly to fake. For instance, the owner of a high-quality used car can credibly signal the car's quality by offering a warranty—an offer that the seller of a low-quality car could not afford to make.

- **11.3** Firms and consumers often try to estimate missing information by making use of what they know about the groups to which people or things belong. For example, insurance firms estimate the risk of insuring individual young male drivers based on the accident rates for young males as a group. This practice is known as statistical discrimination. Other examples include paying university graduates more than high-school graduates and charging higher life insurance rates to 60-year-olds than to 20-year-olds.

◼ KEY TERMS

adverse selection (318)
asymmetric information (312)
better-than-fair gamble (310)
costly-to-fake principle (316)

expected value of a gamble (310)
fair gamble (310)
free-rider problem (308)
lemons model (313)

risk-averse person (310)
risk-neutral person (310)
statistical discrimination (318)

◼ REVIEW QUESTIONS

1. Can it be rational for a consumer to buy a Chevrolet without having first taken test drives in competing models built by Ford, Chrysler, Honda, Toyota, and others?

2. Explain why a gallery owner who sells a painting might actually create more economic surplus than the artist who painted it.

3. Explain why used cars offered for sale are different, on average, from used cars not offered for sale.

4. Explain why the used-car market would be likely to function more efficiently in a community in which moral norms of honesty are strong than in a community in which such norms are weak.

5. Why might leasing a new Porsche be a good investment for an aspiring Hollywood film producer, even though he can't easily afford the monthly payments?

◼ PROBLEMS

1. State whether the following are true or false, and briefly explain why:
   a. Depreciation is the sole factor that causes the market value of a two-year-old car to be much lower than it was when the car was in the showroom.
   b. You may not get the optimal level of advice from a retail shop when you go in to buy a lamp for your bike because of the free-rider problem.
   c. If you need a lawyer, and all your legal expenses are covered by insurance, you should *always* choose the best-dressed lawyer with the most expensive car and the most ostentatiously furnished office.
   d. The benefit of searching for a spouse is affected by the size of the community you live in.

2. Consumers know that some fraction x of all new cars produced and sold in the market are defective. The defective ones cannot be identified except by those who own them. Cars do not depreciate with use. Consumers are risk-neutral and value non-defective cars at \$10 000 each. New cars sell for \$5000 and used ones for \$2500. What is the fraction x?

3. Carlos is risk-neutral and has an ancient farmhouse with great character for sale near Kingston. His reservation price for the house is \$130 000. The only possible local buyer is Whitney, whose reservation price for the house is \$150 000. The only other houses on the market are modern ranch houses that sell for \$125 000, which is exactly equal to each potential buyer's reservation price for such a house. Suppose that if Carlos does not hire a realtor, Whitney will learn from her neighbour that Carlos's house is for sale, and will buy it for \$140 000. However, if Carlos hires a realtor, he knows that the realtor will put him in touch with an enthusiast for old farmhouses who is willing to pay up to \$300 000 for the house. Carlos also knows that if he and this person negotiate, they will agree on a price of \$250 000. If realtors charge a commission of 5 percent of the selling price and all realtors have opportunity costs of \$2000 for negotiating a sale, will Carlos hire a realtor? If so, how will total economic surplus be affected?

4. Ann and Barbara are computer programmers in Winnipeg who are planning to move to Ottawa. Each owns a house that has just been appraised for \$100 000. But whereas Ann's house is one of hundreds of highly similar houses in a large, well-known suburban development, Barbara's is the only one that was built from her architect's design. Who will benefit more by hiring a realtor to assist in selling her house, Ann or Barbara?

5. For each pair of occupations listed, identify the one for which the kind of car a person drives is more likely to be a good indication of how good she is at her job.
   a. Elementary-school teacher, real estate agent
   b. Dentist, municipal government administrator
   c. Engineer in the private sector, engineer in the military

6. Brokers who sell stocks over the Internet can serve many more customers than those who transact business by mail or over the phone. How will the expansion of Internet access affect the average incomes of stockbrokers who continue to do business in the traditional way?

7. Whose income do you predict will be more affected by the expansion of Internet access:
   a. Stockbrokers or lawyers?
   b. Doctors or pharmacists?
   c. Bookstore owners or the owners of galleries that sell original oil paintings?

8. How will growing Internet access affect the number of film actors and musicians who have active fan clubs?

9. Fred, a retired accountant, and Jim, a government manager, are 63-year-old identical twins who collect antique pottery. Each has an annual income of \$100 000 (Fred's from a pension, Jim's from salary). One buys most of his pottery at local auctions, and the other buys most of his from a local dealer. Which brother is more likely to buy at an auction, and does he pay more or less than his brother who buys from the local dealer?

■ ANSWERS TO IN-CHAPTER EXERCISES

11.1 Internet search is a cheap way to acquire information about many goods and services, so the effect of increased Internet access will be an increase in the supply of information. In equilibrium, people will acquire more information, and the goods and services they buy will more closely resemble those they would have chosen in an ideal world with perfect information. These effects will cause total economic surplus to grow. Some of these gains, however, will be offset if the Internet makes the free-rider problem more serious.

11.2 The probability of getting heads is 0.5, the same as the probability of getting tails. Thus, the expected value of this gamble is $(0.5)(\$4) + (0.5)(-\$2) = \$1$. Since the gamble is better than fair, a risk-neutral person would accept it.

11.3 Since you still have a 20 percent chance of finding a cheaper apartment if you make another visit, the expected outcome of the gamble is again $2, and, being risk-neutral, you will search again. The bad outcome of any previous search is a sunk cost, and therefore it is irrelevant to your decision about whether to search again.

11.4 The expected value of a new car will now be $0.8(\$10\,000) + 0.2(\$6000) = \$9200$. Any risk-neutral consumer who believed that the quality distribution of used cars for sale was the same as the quality distribution of new cars off the assembly line would be willing to pay $9200 for a used car.

Labour Markets and the Public Sector

■

The market imperfections discussed in Part 3 help explain why no country leaves all important economic decisions entirely in the hands of market forces. In a mixed economy, government decisions affect both the equity and efficiency of economic outcomes. Thus, in Chapter 12 we will explore why some people earn so much more than others. We will discuss the human capital model, which emphasizes the importance of differences in personal characteristics. But we will also discuss why people with similar personal characteristics often earn sharply different incomes.

In Chapter 13 we will explore examples in which careful application of basic economic principles can help society design policies that mitigate the market imperfections discussed in Part 3. The thread uniting these examples is the problem of scarcity. In each case we will explore how intelligent application of the cost–benefit principle can help resolve the resulting trade-offs in ways that expand the economic pie.

In Chapter 14 we will tackle such questions as how large government should be, what sorts of goods and services it should provide, and how it should raise the revenue to pay for them. We will also explore why rational citizens might empower government to constrain their behaviour in various ways and how such powers should be apportioned among levels of government.

Finally, in Chapter 15 we will investigate why poverty and income inequality have become issues of concern to all democratically elected governments. Because government programs to redistribute income have costs as well as benefits, policymakers must compare an imperfect status quo with the practical consequences of imperfect governmental remedies.

LABOUR MARKETS

By only the slimmest of margins, Mary Lou Retton won the individual all-around gold medal in women's gymnastics at the Los Angeles Summer Olympic Games in 1984. In the years since, she has remained in the spotlight, continuing to earn millions of dollars from product endorsements and motivational speeches. In contrast, the silver medalist from 1984 has dropped completely from view. Can you name her? She is Ecaterina Szabo, one of the most talented Romanian gymnasts of her era, and although she came within a hairsbreadth of beating Retton, wealth and international recognition were not to be hers.

Many physicians in Szabo's homeland are likewise every bit as talented and hardworking as physicians in North America. But although Canadian physicians earn an average annual income of more than $100 000, Romanian physicians earn so little that some of them supplement their incomes by cleaning the Bucharest apartments of expatriates for just $10 a day.

Why do some people earn so much more than others? Citizenship, of course, is neither necessary nor sufficient for receiving high income. Many of the wealthiest people in the world come from extremely poor countries, and thousands of Canadians are homeless and malnourished.

Our aim in this chapter is to employ simple economic principles in an attempt to explain why different people earn different salaries. We'll discuss the human capital model, which emphasizes the importance of differences in personal characteristics. But our focus will be on why people with similar personal characteristics often earn sharply different incomes. Among the factors that we will consider are labour unions, winner-take-all labour markets, discrimination, and the effect of nonwage conditions of employment.

■ 12.1 WAGE AND SALARY DETERMINATION IN COMPETITIVE LABOUR MARKETS

In some respects, the sale of human labour is profoundly different from the sale of other goods and services. For example, although someone may legally relinquish all future rights to the use of her television set by selling it, the law does not permit people to sell themselves into slavery. The law does, however, permit us to "rent out" our services to employers. And in some key ways the rental market for labour services functions much like the market for most other goods and services. Supply and demand together determine both the equilibrium wage and the equilibrium quantity of employment for each category of labour.

What is more, shifts in demand and supply produce changes analogous to those produced by shifts in the demand and supply of labour for other goods and services. For example, an increase in the demand for a specific category of labour will generally increase both the equilibrium wage and the equilibrium quantity of employment in that category. By the same token, an increase in the supply of labour to a given occupation will tend to increase equilibrium employment and lower the equilibrium wage rate in that occupation.

As in our discussions of other markets, we will investigate the labour market by using a series of examples that shed light on different parts of the picture. In the first example, we focus on how the equilibrium principle helps us to understand how wages will differ among workers with different levels of productive ability.

Why do small differences in performance sometimes translate into enormous differences in pay?

EQUILIBRIUM

How much will the potters earn?   EXAMPLE 12.1

Mackintosh Pottery Works is one of numerous identical companies that hire potters who mould clay into pots. These companies sell the pots for $1.10 each to a finishing company that glazes and fires them and then sells them in the retail marketplace. Rennie and Laura are currently the only two potters who work for Mackintosh, whose costs, other than potters' salaries, are 10 cents for clay and all other inputs for each pot it delivers to the finisher. If we assume that this 10 cents completely accounts for the firm's costs of operation (including a "normal profit" sufficient to cover the opportunity cost of the owner's time), then $1.00 is the "net price" the firm gets from each pot produced. If all workers in this industry are known to have the same productivity (for example, 100 pots per week), competition among firms will produce an equilibrium wage of $100 per week for all workers. If Mackintosh were paying less than this amount (say $90), it could expect to lose Rennie and Laura to the competition, since a competing firm could make extra profits by hiring more workers, as long as the wage paid is anything less than $100 weekly. The competition of firms for workers in the labour market would bid up wages until the firm earned only a normal rate of profit, in equilibrium.

However, suppose that we change the example slightly and assume that Rennie delivers 100 pots/week and Laura delivers 120. If the labour market for potters is perfectly competitive, how much will each now be paid?

In this example, we assume that Rennie and Laura have decided to work full-time as potters, so our focus is not on how many hours they will work but on how much they will be paid. After taking costs into account, the value of the pots that Rennie delivers is $100/week, and that is the maximum amount Mackintosh is willing to pay him. If Mackintosh paid Rennie less (say, $90) and *if* other firms know that Rennie delivers $100 in output every week, then a rival firm could profit by paying Rennie just a bit more (say, $91) and hiring him away from Mackintosh. So, if Rennie's individual abilities are known to all rival firms, Mackintosh will have difficulty keeping Rennie if it pays him less than $100/week. And the company would suffer an economic loss if it paid him more than $100/week. Similarly, the value of the pots delivered each week by Laura is $120, and this will be her competitive equilibrium wage, if her output is similarly known to all firms.

marginal (physical) product of labour (MP) the additional output a firm gets by employing one additional unit of labour

value of marginal product of labour (VMP) the dollar value of the additional output a firm gets by employing one additional unit of labour

In Example 12.1, the number of pots each potter delivered each week is that potter's **marginal physical product,** or **marginal product** *(MP)* for short. More generally, a worker's marginal product is the extra output the firm gets as a result of hiring that worker. When we multiply a worker's marginal product by the net price for which each unit of the product sells, we get that worker's **value of marginal product,** or *VMP.* (In Example 12.1 the "net price" of each pot is $1.00—the difference between the $1.10 sale price and the $0.10 in non-labour costs.) The general rule in competitive labour markets where individual output is observable is that *a worker's pay in long-run equilibrium will be equal to his or her VMP—the net contribution he or she makes to the employer's revenue.* Employers would be delighted to pay workers less than their respective *VMPs,* to be sure. But if labour markets are truly competitive and fully informed, employers cannot do so for long.

However, as we discussed in Chapter 11, imperfect information is a fact of life. In this particular example, one should ask: "Just how does a rival firm get to know how many pots Laura and Rennie are producing?" It is not in the interest of Mackintosh Pottery Works to broadcast this information (or at least it is not in the interest of the firm to broadcast true information); Mackintosh would prefer that rival firms not try to bid away its best workers. And even if Laura and Rennie were to tell people how many pots they make, it is clear that they have an incentive to exaggerate their own output, so they are not credible sources.

Laura might expect employers to be willing to pay her more than Rennie if she could (somehow) signal that she produces more pots per week than he does, but how can she credibly do that? Rennie would also like to get higher wages, and he will have an incentive to pretend that he produces as many pots per week as she does. He is therefore likely to mimic anything that Laura does.

Labour markets sometimes function in the same way as other markets, but often there are important differences. Because people differ in their skills and abilities, and because those skills and abilities change over time, an individual worker's *quality* cannot be graded in the same easy, unambiguous way that commodities (such as coal or apples) can be graded. Information about a worker's output is crucial, but that information is highly imperfect. The true output of individuals is often difficult to observe directly—particularly if they work as part of a team. Furthermore, firms and workers often have incentives of their own not to reveal true information.

Imperfect information about a worker's true output, and the incentives that firms and workers have to misrepresent that output, are two pervasive problems in the labour market. In some cases (e.g., the scoring statistics of NHL hockey players or the batting averages of professional baseball players) it is possible for all potential employers to know what a worker is really producing. However, this situation is relatively rare. Usually, other firms cannot know, and workers cannot credibly signal, exactly how much they personally add to total output.

As a result, firms have to try to predict what workers of a particular *type* (i.e., of a particular age, work experience, education, etc.) will produce. Firms end up paying a wage that reflects what they expect a "typical" worker's level of output to be, *given* those observable characteristics. In some respects, labour markets function much like the insurance example that we considered in Chapter 11. Recall that insurance companies charge the same premium to all young male drivers with the same observable driving history because no company can directly observe which drivers are reckless and which are careful—so the insurers have to estimate what the average person of a particular type will do. If one firm underpays its workers who have a given set of observable characteristics, it faces the threat that other firms may hire them away. It risks losing a particular type of worker because other firms are paying them more. For example, if one firm systematically pays less than other firms for experienced workers with technical training, it can expect such workers to be lured away by offers from competing firms.

In Example 12.1, each worker's *VMP* was independent of the number of other workers employed by the firm. In such cases, we cannot predict how many workers a firm will hire. Mackintosh could make a normal profit with two potters, with 10, or even with 1000 or more. In many other situations, however, we can predict exactly how many workers a firm will hire. Consider Example 12.2.

How many workers will Adirondack hire? (Part I)

EXAMPLE 12.2

The Adirondack Woodworking Company hires workers in a competitive labour market at a wage of $350/week to make kitchen cutting boards. If the boards sell for $20 each and the company's weekly output varies with the number of workers hired as shown in Table 12.1, how many workers will Adirondack hire?

TABLE 12.1

Employment and Productivity in a Woodworking Company (When Cutting Boards Sell for $20 Each)

Number of workers	Total number of cutting boards/week	MP (extra cutting boards/week)	VMP ($/week)
0	0		
		30	600
1	30		
		25	500
2	55		
		21	420
3	76		
		18	360
4	94		
		14	280
5	108		

In Example 12.1 our focus was on wage differences for employees whose productive abilities differed. In contrast, we assume here that all workers are of the same type; that is, they are **observationally equivalent**. Although workers may actually differ in productive ability, there is no feasible way for this firm or its competitors to tell those workers apart, so they all get the same wage in the labour market. Hence, the firm faces a fixed market wage for each worker. The fact that the marginal product of labour declines with the number of workers hired is a consequence of the law of diminishing returns. (As discussed in Chapter 5, the law of diminishing marginal returns says that when technology, a firm's capital, and other productive inputs are held fixed in the short run, adding workers beyond some point results in ever-smaller increases in output.) The third column of Table 12.1 reports the marginal product for each additional worker, and the last column reports the value of each successive worker's marginal product—the number of cutting boards added times the selling price of $20. As a profit-maximizing firm, Adirondack will keep hiring as long as the next worker's expected *VMP* is at least $350/week (the market wage). The first four workers have *VMPs* larger than $350, so Adirondack will hire them. But since hiring the fifth worker would add only $280 to weekly revenue, Adirondack will not hire that worker.

observationally equivalent workers workers of the same "type," that is, with the same generally known personal characteristics (such as age, education, gender, work experience, race, ethnicity, etc.)

Note the similarity between the perfectly competitive firm's decision about how many workers to hire and the perfectly competitive firm's output decision, which we considered in Chapter 5. When labour is the only variable factor of production, the two decisions are essentially the same. Because of the unique correspondence between the firm's total output and the total number of workers it hires, deciding how many workers to hire is the same as deciding how much output to supply. Therefore, we can say that the firm's demand for labour is a *derived demand*, which depends entirely on how much the firm decides to produce. As we will see when we look at the total demand for labour in the economy as a whole, the demand for labour depends on the output decisions of firms, which always depend on the sales they expect to make.

As Example 12.3 illustrates, the worker's attractiveness for the employer depends not only on how many cutting boards she produces but also on the price of cutting boards.

EXAMPLE 12.3

How many workers will Adirondack hire? (Part 2)

Refer to Example 12.2. Suppose that the selling price of cutting boards rises from $20 to $30. If the wage rate and marginal physical products are as before, how many workers will Adirondack hire?

As shown in the last column of Table 12.2, the 14 cutting boards produced by the fifth worker now add (14)($30) = $420 to weekly revenue, and since her wage is only $350, the company will hire her.

TABLE 12.2
The Effect of a Price Increase on Employment

Number of workers	Total number of cutting boards/week	MP (extra cutting boards/week)	VMP ($/week)
0	0		
		30	900
1	30		
		25	750
2	55		
		21	630
3	76		
		18	540
4	94		
		14	420
5	108		

EXERCISE 12.1

In Example 12.3, what is the lowest cutting board price at which Adirondack will hire two workers?

EXAMPLE 12.4

How many workers will Adirondack hire? (Part 3)

Now suppose that cutting boards again sell for their original price of $20 but that the wage rate of workers is not $350/week but $370. If the company's weekly output of cutting boards again varies with the number of workers as shown in Table 12.1, how many workers will it hire?

This time note that although the fourth worker was an attractive hire at a wage of $350/week, she will not be worth hiring at a wage of $370. Her *VMP* is now smaller than her wage, so the company will hire only three workers.

In Example 12.4, how many workers would Adirondack hire if the wage rate were $275/week?

EXERCISE 12.2

RECAP	**WAGE AND SALARY DETERMINATION IN COMPETITIVE LABOUR MARKETS**

In competitive labour markets, employers face pressure to pay the typical worker the expected value of his or her marginal product. When a firm can hire as many workers as it wants at a given market wage, it will increase employment as long as the value of marginal product of labour exceeds the market wage.

12.2 MONOPSONY: THE LONE EMPLOYER IN A LABOUR MARKET

In perfectly competitive product markets, sellers have no control over product prices. Market supply and demand curves intersect, and firms take the resulting prices as given. Similarly, in perfectly competitive labour markets, firms have no control over wage rates. The wage in each market is determined by supply and demand. In Examples 12.2 to 12.4, Adirondack Woodworking was a buyer in a perfectly competitive labour market and viewed the market wage accordingly. The supply curve of labour facing such an employer is perfectly elastic—a horizontal line at the market wage.

But now suppose that Adirondack is a **monopsony**—the only buyer of labour services in its local labour market. The labour supply curve facing the company is now the labour supply curve for the market as a whole. There is no market wage per se. Workers are paid whatever Adirondack chooses to offer. But Adirondack is not free to offer just any wage, for if its offer is extremely low, workers may decide to relocate, or they may stop working. Even so, Adirondack now has some discretion about the wage it pays. In general, the more workers the company wants to hire, the more it will have to pay each worker. How much will it pay its workers?

monopsony a market with only a single buyer

In many ways, the problem facing the monopsonist (the only buyer) is similar to the one facing a monopolist (the only seller) in the market for a product. Because the monopolist's demand curve is the same as the demand curve for the market as a whole, the only way the monopolist can increase its sales is by reducing price. Similarly, because the supply curve of labour confronting the monopsonist is the supply curve for the labour market as a whole, the only way the monopsonist can hire additional workers is by offering higher wages. But raising the wage for an additional worker generally means also having to raise the wage for the workers hired earlier. And as Example 12.5 illustrates, the monopsonist has an incentive to limit employment, much as the monopolist has an incentive to limit output.

How many workers will Bluenose hire? (Part 4)

EXAMPLE 12.5

The Bluenose Woodworking Company is the only employer in a small town in rural Nova Scotia. It sells kitchen cutting boards for $20 each, and its weekly output again varies with the number of workers in exactly the same way as for Adirondack, as shown in Table 12.1. If there are five workers in town whom Bluenose might hire,

TABLE 12.3
Reservation Wages for the Monopsonist's Potential Employees

Worker	Reservation wage ($/week)
Alisha	200
Bertram	250
Carrie	300
Donna	350
Ernesto	400

with reservation wages as shown in Table 12.3, and if Bluenose must pay each worker the same wage, how many will it hire? (An individual's reservation wage for a job is the smallest payment for which she would accept the job.)

For the monopolist in the product market, recall that the decision rule is to sell another unit if marginal revenue (the amount by which its total revenue increases when it sells an extra unit) exceeds marginal cost. For the monopsonist in the labour market, the corresponding rule is to hire another worker if that worker's *VMP* exceeds **marginal labour cost**—the amount by which the monopsonist's total wage bill would increase if it hired the extra worker. Marginal labour cost in this example is shown in the last column of Table 12.4. (Again, we assume that the monopsonist does not know each worker's reservation wage and must therefore pay each worker the same wage.)

marginal labour cost
the amount by which a monopsonist's total wage bill goes up if it hires an extra worker

TABLE 12.4
Calculating Marginal Labour Cost for the Monopsonist

Worker	Reservation wage ($/week)	Total labour cost ($/week)	Marginal labour cost ($/week)
Alisha	200	200	200
Bertram	250	500	300
Carrie	300	900	400
Donna	350	1400	500
Ernesto	400	2000	600

If Bluenose offers a wage of $200, the only worker it will attract is Alisha. If the company also wants to hire a second worker (Bertram), it must not only pay him $50/week more than it is currently paying Alisha, but it must also raise Alisha's pay to $250/week. (Note again the importance of information. Each person knows his or her own reservation wage, but the firm does not—and individual workers like Alisha have no incentive to tell firms truthfully what the minimum wage they would accept really is.) Because as Table 12.4 shows, the company's total labour cost will go from $200 to $500/week in the process, the marginal labour cost of hiring Bertram is $300/week. But since Bertram's *VMP* is $500/week, hiring him is clearly in Bluenose's interest. Carrie, too, is a worthwhile hire because her marginal labour cost of $400/week is less than her *VMP* of $420. But Donna's marginal labour cost of $500/week is considerably more than her $360 *VMP*. So even though Donna's reservation wage of $350 is less than her *VMP,* the cost–benefit principle tells us that Bluenose will do better by not hiring her. Thus, the company will hire only three workers—Alisha, Bertram, and Carrie—and will pay each a wage of $300/week.

COST–
BENEFIT

EXERCISE 12.3

In Example 12.5, how many workers will Bluenose hire if cutting boards sold not for $20 but for $30?

In Chapter 8, we saw that a monopolist produces too little output because price exceeds marginal revenue. A similar inefficiency occurs with a monopsonist in the labour market. In Example 12.5, note that Bluenose, the monopsonist, has the same *VMP* schedule as its perfectly competitive counterpart, Adirondack, in Example 12.2 (Table 12.1). In both cases, the company *could* hire four workers at a wage of $350/week. Yet the monopsonist hires one less worker than its perfectly competitive counterpart in Example 12.2. With only three workers on the monopsonist's payroll, the *social* cost of adding another worker is just the fourth worker's reservation wage, namely, $350. Because the fourth worker would add 18 cutting boards at $20 each to the weekly production total, the gain in total revenue is $360. Therefore, society would gain output worth $10 more than the social cost of hiring the fourth worker. Yet the monopsonist will not hire a fourth worker, because the private cost (marginal labour cost) of doing so is $500.

The monopsonist produces too little because the private cost of an additional hire is greater than the social cost of that hire. The reason for the discrepancy is that the new hire necessitates paying existing workers more, which the monopsonist understandably views as a real cost, but which from society's perspective is merely a transfer from the monopsonist to the existing workers.

Monopsony was probably more common in the past than it is today. One reason for its decline is that a much greater proportion of workers now live in cities and can provide their own transportation, giving them a broad choice of employers within commuting distance of their homes.

RECAP | **MONOPSONY**

Unlike the perfectly competitive employer, which can hire as much labour as it wants at the market wage, the monopsonist can expand employment only by offering higher wages. And unlike the perfectly competitive employer, which continues hiring only until *VMP* equals the market wage, the monopsonist continues hiring until *VMP* equals marginal labour cost, which exceeds the market wage. The profit-maximizing employment level for the monopsonist is lower than the level that would maximize total economic surplus.

■ 12.3 THE DEMAND SIDE OF THE LABOUR MARKET

An employer's reservation price for a worker is the most the employer could pay without suffering a decline in profit. As discussed, this reservation price for the employer in a perfectly competitive labour market is simply *VMP*, the value of the worker's marginal product. Because of the law of diminishing marginal returns, the marginal product of labour, and hence *VMP*, declines in the short run as the quantity of labour employed rises. The individual employer's demand curve for labour in any particular occupation—say, computer programmers—may thus be shown, as in Figure 12.1(a), as a downward-sloping function of the wage rate. When several firms are in the same labour market, we can add up the number of workers each would like to hire at any given wage to get the total demand for labour. For example, if firm 1 [panel (a)] and firm 2 [panel (b)] are two firms that employ programmers in a given community, the demand for programmers in that community will then be the horizontal sum of the individual firms' demands [panel (c)].

FIGURE 12.1

The Occupational Demand for Labour

If firm 1 and firm 2 are two firms that employ labour in a given occupation, we generate the demand curve for labour in that occupation by adding the individual demand curves horizontally.

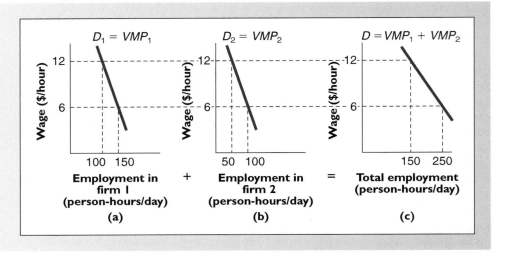

12.4 THE SUPPLY SIDE OF THE LABOUR MARKET

So far, we have only looked at the demand side of labour markets—how many workers each firm would like to employ, at any given wage. But whenever we observe somebody working, we necessarily observe the joint outcome of *two* decisions—(1) the firm decided to offer a job and (2) the person decided to accept the job. If we want to understand labour market outcomes, we always have to look at both decisions—i.e., *both* the demand for labour by firms and the supply of labour by individuals.

For the labour market as a whole, the "supply curve" is the total number of hours that workers want to work, at any given wage. It is often useful to think of this at various levels of aggregation—e.g., the total number of hours that workers would like to work, for a particular wage, in a given country, **or** in a specific city, **or** at a particular firm **or** in a particular occupation. We also need to specify the unit of time over which work hours are supplied—e.g., hours per week, hours per year, or lifetime hours of work. One fundamental question is: Will more labour be offered at high wage rates than at low wage rates? If we look at labour supply on a weekly basis, the average hours of work per week of individual workers has not changed much in Canada in the past 30 years, although it had been declining in the decades before then.

However, we get a different angle on trends if we look at labour supply from a lifetime point of view. Over time, the big trends for Canadian males have been a tendency to stay in school longer and retire earlier. Added together, the result is a decrease in their lifetime supply of paid labour. Canadian women now supply many more hours to the paid labour market over their lifetimes than previously. Until the 1950s most women withdrew from paid employment after marriage. Today, this is rare. Women's participation in the labour market rose dramatically between the 1960s and the 1990s in Canada and is increasingly similar to the labour force participation rate of men.

Overall, the labour force participation rate in Canada has increased because the increase in female labour supply has been greater than the decline in male labour supply. Furthermore, the decline in male labour supply has been concentrated in the under-25 and over-54 age groups. From a family perspective, that implies that middle-aged Canadian families—many of whom have young children—are now generally supplying the labour of two people to the paid labour market, while still having to do the unpaid household tasks that have always been there. This combination of greater paid labour supply by families, and continuing unpaid household labour, generates the time crunch that so many families feel.

The supply of labour *to any particular occupation* is almost surely upward sloping, because wage differences among occupations influence occupational choice. It is no accident, for example, that many more people are choosing jobs as computer programmers now than in 1970. Wages of programmers have risen during the past several decades, which has led people to forsake other career paths in favour of programming.

■ 12.5 EQUILIBRIUM—SUPPLY AND DEMAND

If we make the assumption that wages in other potential occupations are fixed, then we can draw the supply curve of labour to a particular occupation, such as computer programming. Higher wages can be expected to induce more people to want to work in programming, so the supply curve will slope up, to the left—but the actual wage at any point in time will depend on the intersection of demand and supply.

Curve S in Figure 12.2 represents the supply curve of computer programmers. As more tasks have become computerized in recent decades, the demand for programmers has grown, as shown by the shift from D_1 to D_2 in Figure 12.2. Equilibrium in the market for computer programmers occurs at the intersection of the relevant supply and demand curves. The increase in demand has led to an increase in the equilibrium level of programmers from L_1 to L_2 and a rise in the equilibrium wage from W_1 to W_2.

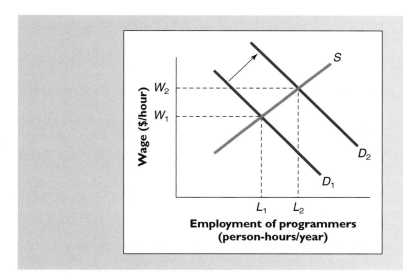

FIGURE 12.2

The Effect of an Increase in the Demand for Computer Programmers
An increase in the demand for programmers from D_1 to D_2 results in an increase in the equilibrium level of employment (from L_1 to L_2) and an increase in the equilibrium wage (from W_1 to W_2).

As discussed in Chapter 7, markets for some types of assets reaches equilibrium very quickly in the wake of shifts in the underlying supply and demand curves. Labour markets are often much slower to adjust. It takes quite a while to learn the skills required to be a good cabinetmaker or computer programmer or geologist. When the demand for workers in a given profession increases, shortages may remain for months or even years, depending on how long it takes people to recognize this and to acquire the skills and training needed to enter the profession. By contrast, it does not take very long to train people how to operate the cash register in a grocery store or how to flip hamburgers. Low-skill labour markets therefore tend to adjust more quickly than specialized labour markets. As our economy shifts toward more specialized and more highly skilled occupations, the problem of adjustment time increases in importance.

RECAP	**EQUILIBRIUM IN THE LABOUR MARKET**

The demand for labour in a perfectly competitive labour market is the horizontal sum of each employer's *VMP* curve. The supply curve of labour for an individual labour market is upward sloping. In each labour market, the demand and supply curves intersect to determine the equilibrium wage and level of employment.

12.6 EXPLAINING DIFFERENCES IN EARNINGS

We often see large salary differences even between people who appear equally talented and hardworking. Why, for example, do lawyers earn so much more than plumbers who are just as smart and work just as hard? And why do surgeons earn so much more than general practitioners?

HUMAN CAPITAL THEORY

human capital theory a theory of pay determination that says a worker's wage will be proportional to his or her stock of human capital

human capital the skills produced by education, training, and experience that affect a worker's marginal product

Answers to these questions are suggested by the **human capital theory,** which holds that an individual's *VMP* is proportional to his or her stock of **human capital** —the skills produced by education, experience, and training that affect a worker's marginal product. According to this theory, some occupations pay better than others because they require larger stocks of human capital. For example, a general practitioner could become a surgeon, but only by extending her formal education by several more years. And more years of education are required to become a lawyer than to become a secretary.

In general, a decision to invest in human capital, like decisions to invest in other assets, requires comparing costs incurred in the present with benefits received in the future. As Example 12.6 illustrates, intelligent decisions of this sort require us to determine the present value of any payments received or expenditures made in the future.

EXAMPLE 12.6	**Should Manon get an MA?**

Manon is 22 and has just graduated with a BA in economics. She now has a job as a local manager for a major corporation. However, she knows that her opportunities for promotion are limited and that if she were to go back to school and get an MA in economics, she would be eligible for a better paying job as a financial analyst. Let us assume that she would get the same level of job satisfaction from that job as from her current job, but her earnings would increase. Also, Manon is certain she can graduate. If she goes back to school, she will have to pay $5000 per year for tuition and books. She will also have to pay rent for an apartment and buy groceries, but she would have to do this whether she goes back to school or not. Because these costs are the same, regardless of her decision, they cannot be counted as a cost of the MA. Out-of-pocket costs of the MA are therefore $5000 per year for two years. In addition, she would have to forego her current earnings while in school.[1] Foregone earnings are a classic example of *opportunity cost*, since Manon cannot both go back to school full time and keep receiving her current paycheque.

Since she has to pay the costs of tuition and books right away, and has to forego salary, this is an expensive decision. She knows that it will take a while for her earnings as a financial analyst to recoup this investment. The question is: do the future benefits repay the early costs? Is the investment in an MA worth it?

DISCOUNTING AND PRESENT VALUE

Because Manon wants to compare the value of amounts of money that are received or paid at different times in the future, she needs to make these payments comparable by calculating their value at a single point in time. Manon is impatient—to be specific, she figures that a dollar received a year from now is worth about the same as 90 cents available right now. Similarly, a dollar received two years from now is only worth about 81 cents to her today, because that involves a wait of a year, followed by another wait of another year and $0.81 = (0.9)(0.9)$. A dollar received three years from now is worth even less to Manon—only 72.9 cents $[= (0.9)(0.9)(0.9)]$—since she has to wait three years to use that dollar. Since the return from an MA is spread over many years, Manon wants to know how much each future payment or receipt would be worth today (after discounting for the delay in receiving it). To get the total value of her investment in an MA, Manon has to add up all her costs and benefits over the near future to get a total *net present value*. If she does not calculate net present value, she cannot know the value of her investment.

Manon can make this calculation a little easier by constructing a table such as Table 12.5. To keep things simple, this table only goes up to age 30. A more realistic version of Table 12.5 would profile earnings through Manon's entire working

TABLE 12.5
Manon's Choice: MA or Not?

		Cash Flow			
Age	As local manager ($) (a)	As financial analyst ($) (b)	Net difference ($) (b) − (a)	Discount factor ($) (d)	Present value ($) (e)
22	25 000	−5000	−30 000	1.00	−30 000.00
23	25 000	−5000	−30 000	0.90	−27 000.00
24	30 000	30 000	0	0.81	0.00
25	30 000	40 000	10 000	0.73	7290.00
26	35 000	45 000	10 000	0.66	6561.00
27	35 000	50 000	15 000	0.59	8857.35
28	35 000	60 000	25 000	0.53	13 286.03
29	35 000	65 000	30 000	0.48	14 348.91
30	35 000	70 000	35 000	0.43	15 066.35
				Total	8409.64

[1]To keep this example simple, we assume Manon is not eligible for any scholarships nor does she get any assistance from her family. In reality, both are important since most universities offer scholarships to some of their MA students and parents often provide financial assistance for education, over and above other gifts to their children.

life. However, with a discount rate as high as Manon's, earnings differences later in life will make little difference to the calculation.

In Table 12.5, column (a) reports the after-tax earnings Manon expects if she sticks with her current job. She can expect her salary to go up a little, but then stall at $35 000. Column (b) is her after-tax cash flow if she chooses the MA option—note that it involves two years of cash deficit (−$5000), followed by rapid increases. The next column reports (b) − (a) or the *net* cost or benefit, in that year, of choosing the MA option. For the first two years, the net cost of an MA is the cost of tuition and books, *plus* the opportunity cost of her time—the earnings Manon has forgone because of her decision to return to school. In year three, earnings are the same in either option, so the net gain is zero. After that, her earnings as a financial analyst rise much more rapidly than if she had not chosen to do an MA in economics, so the net benefit of choosing the MA option increases over time. (The *net* advantages of choosing the MA option are the earnings Manon gets as a financial analyst *minus the opportunity cost of her time*.)

12.1 ECONOMIC NATURALIST

What is the present value of *your* financial return from attending university?

Table 12.5 presents a hypothetical example of a fictitious choice by an imaginary person—but you could use the same format to analyze the real choice (to attend university) of a real person (you). If you fill in column (a) with your best estimate of the earnings that you could have expected if you had not gone to university, and fill in column (b) with your best estimate of your earnings after university, it is straightforward to calculate the net difference in cash flow, as in column (c). The calculation of present value is especially easy if you use a spreadsheet program like Excel—with the added advantage that it becomes very easy to change your assumptions and to see how much any such changes in your estimates of future earnings actually matter. (Spreadsheet programs like Excel also contain pre-written functions to calculate present value, at whatever rate of interest you think is appropriate. If you experiment with different rates of discount, you can see to what degree your conclusion about the net present value of university education is sensitive to the choice of discount rate.) Why not give it a try?

Figures 12.3(a) and (b) present graphs that make the same points visually by plotting the first three columns of Table 12.5. In panel (a) Manon's cash flow as a BA graduate is the blue line and her cash flow from the MA option (the out of pocket costs of returning to school and subsequent earnings as a financial analyst) is the red line. Since the first two years of her MA involve a cash deficit, the red line is in negative territory until she is 23—but as panel (a) illustrates, we should focus on the difference between earnings streams. Panel (b) therefore plots the third column from Table 12.5 to show how a period of initial costs is followed by long-term benefits. But the question still remains: Is the investment in education worth it? Are the benefits greater than the costs?

To keep things simple, we'll assume that all receipts and payments in a year are made at the start of the year. Nevertheless, Manon still incurs the costs now and gets the benefits later. How should she adjust the value of payments several years in the future to account for the delay in getting them? The discount factor (column d) considers that. As already noted, Manon considers a dollar a year from now to be worth about 90 cents today. Generally, from her perspective a payment made or received a year from now is worth about 90 percent of its dollar value, if it happened today, and a payment two years in the future is worth about 90 percent of that. Column (d) of Table 12.5 calculates the implications of Manon's approximately 11 percent discount rate for payments made two, three, four, and more years into the future.

Column (e) of Table 12.5 pulls things together. It multiplies the current dollar cost or benefit of choosing the MA option in each future year [column (c)] by the

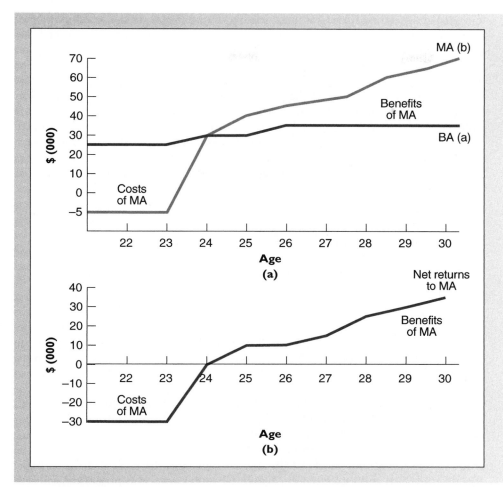

FIGURE 12.3
The Returns of an MA in Economics
Costs are incurred during the period an MA is being acquired. Once acquired, the MA provides benefits.

discount factor [column (d)] to get the *present value* of the costs or benefits of the MA option in that particular year. Remember that Manon values a dollar received in the present at more than a dollar received in the future. Therefore, as far as she is concerned, the **present value** of one dollar either received or paid in the future is less than one dollar. When Manon says that $1 received a year from now is, in her view, worth 90 cents received today, [i.e., she is indifferent between $1 in one year and 90 cents now] the discount (10 cents), as a fraction of today's value (90 cents) is approximately 11% [= 10/90].[2] Economists call this Manon's **discount rate** (i.e., the annual rate at which Manon discounts the future). If we know the discount rate, (let's call it "r"), we can compute the **discount factor** (let's call it "D") necessary to calculate the present value of a payment at some particular number (t) of years in the future.

If she gets an MA, Manon can make twice as much at age 30 as a senior analyst than as a local manager ($70 000 compared with $35 000). However, she also recognizes that she has to wait quite a while for that payoff and that she should only count the *net* benefits of her choice. How much are the added earnings of

present value The current value of an amount paid or received in the future. If people prefer current consumption to future consumption, a payment or receipt that occurs in the future will be discounted to a present value

discount factor a coefficient used to discount a payment or receipt that occurs in the future to a present value

[2]The discount factors given in Table 12.5 are approximations. The actual formula for calculating a discount factor is:

$$D = \frac{1}{1 + r^t}$$

where D is the discount factor, r is an annual interest rate, and t is number of years in the future. The appendix to this chapter provides an algebraic treatment of present values.

$35 000 at age 30 worth to her today? If her discount rate on the future is 11 percent per year and she has to wait eight years, the additional earnings she will get at 30 have a present value to Manon of $15 066 at age 22.

Of course, earnings at age 30 are only part of the story. Manon also has to consider the net costs and net benefits of choosing the MA option in each intervening year. She has to add up the present value of all future years [column (e)] to find out whether her investment in a MA is worthwhile financially. The total is called the *net present value* of her investment—which in this case is +$8410. Since a positive net present value means that the benefits of the investment outweigh the costs, Manon concludes on the basis of a single number that emerges from her calculations that it is financially worthwhile to get an MA—but she also recognizes that three things drive her calculations:

1. Costs = opportunity cost (forgone earnings) + out-of-pocket cost (how much she gives up by choosing to invest in education)
2. Benefits = the additional salary Manon forecasts that she will get from her MA choice (and when she gets it)
3. Discount rate = how impatient she is in waiting for future returns

In the human capital perspective, the supply of skills is, in the long run, driven by many millions of people making calculations such as Manon's. If there is a substantial net return to more education (in the sense of a positive net present value, adding up over all future years), the human capital approach forecasts that the supply of more highly educated labour will increase, because high-school graduates will decide to go to university, and university graduates will decide to go to graduate school, and so on.

If the supply of postsecondary graduates increases because high-school graduates stay in school, there will be fewer people who only have a high-school education. Hence, the supply of high-school graduates to the labour market will fall. As more people decide to continue in school, the supply curve of postsecondary graduates to the labour market shifts to the right and the supply curve of high-school graduates shifts to the left. Figure 12.4 illustrates the process. Assuming the demand curve for both types of labour does not shift, the wage of high-school graduates will tend to go up and the wage of postsecondary graduates will tend to go down. Both tendencies will narrow the differential between postsecondary and high-school wages, and the differential will continue to narrow as increasingly more people go on to higher education. These narrowing differentials will decrease the incentive for people to continue their educations, but as long as there is a positive net present value from the decision, people will invest in more education.

FIGURE 12.4

Wage Effects of an Increase in Postsecondary Enrolment

An increase in the supply of postsecondary graduates reduces the wage gap between high-school and postsecondary graduates.

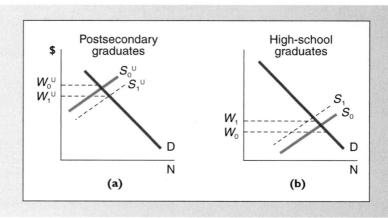

The final equilibrium is where the wage advantage of university graduates is just sufficient to repay the total costs of their investment in skills.

In this final equilibrium, the average level of earnings is higher because more people now earn the higher wages associated with postsecondary education. There still is a difference in pay between postsecondary and high-school graduates, but the inequality of annual earnings is now less than previously, because that differential is smaller.

The policy implication is that if governments can increase the supply of skills, Canadians will have both higher average income and less inequality. Because individuals will respond to changes in the costs as well as in the benefits of further education or training, there are a number of different ways governments can do this, but the most obvious way is to keep increases in the out-of-pocket cost of postsecondary education (like tuition) to a minimum.

**www.statcan.ca
Statistics Canada**

EXERCISE 12.4

Refer to Example 12.6. If Manon had been indifferent between getting an MA or not at an interest rate of 10 percent, which option will she choose if the interest rate is 12 percent?

Changes in demand can result in some kinds of human capital being more valuable than others. Consider again the increase in demand for computer programmers that has been occurring for the past several decades. During that same period, the demand for the services of tax accountants has fallen as more and more taxpayers use tax-preparation software in lieu of hiring accountants to help them with their taxes. Both occupations require demanding technical training, but the training received by computer programmers now yields a higher return in the labour market.

LABOUR UNIONS

Two workers with the same amount of human capital may earn different wages if one of them belongs to a **labour union** and the other does not. A labour union is an organization through which workers attempt to bargain collectively with employers for better wages and working conditions.

A union can be analyzed by using the simple model of monopoly developed in Chapter 8. However, by focusing solely on the reduced quantity of labour and higher wage rate that the simple monopoly model would imply, too much is left unexplained. Even though unionized firms pay their employees more, unionized and nonunionized firms often manage to compete directly for extended periods of time. If their costs are significantly higher, how do the unionized firms manage to survive?

Wages paid to workers in a unionized firm are sometimes 50 percent or more above the wages paid to their nonunionized counterparts. But this difference actually overstates the difference between the labour costs of the two types of firms. Because the higher union wage attracts an excess supply of workers, unionized employers can adopt more stringent hiring requirements than their nonunionized counterparts. As a result, unionized workers tend to be more experienced and skilled than nonunionized workers. Studies estimate that the union wage premium for workers with the same amount of human capital is only about 10 percent.

Unions also may actually boost the productivity of workers with any given amount of human capital, perhaps by improving communication between management and workers. Similarly, the implementation of formal grievance procedures, in combination with higher pay, may boost morale among unionized workers, leading to higher productivity. Labour turnover is also significantly lower in unionized firms, which reduces hiring and training costs. Studies suggest that union productivity may be sufficiently high to compensate for the premium in

labour union a group of workers who bargain collectively with employers for better wages and working conditions

union wages. So even though wages are higher in unionized firms, these firms may not have significantly higher labour costs per unit of output than their nonunionized counterparts.[3]

WINNER-TAKE-ALL MARKETS

Differences in human capital do much to explain observed differences in earnings. Yet earnings differentials have also grown sharply in many occupations within which the distribution of human capital among workers seems essentially unchanged. Consider the following example.

❦ 12.2   ECONOMIC NATURALIST

Why does Céline Dion earn millions more than singers of only slightly lesser ability?

Although the best singers have always earned more than others with slightly lesser talents, the earnings gap is sharply larger now than it was in the last century. Today, top singers like Céline Dion earn millions of dollars per year, hundreds or even thousands of times what singers only marginally less talented earn. Given that listeners in blind hearings often have difficulty identifying the most highly paid singers, why is this earnings differential so large?

The answer lies in a fundamental change in the way we consume most of our music. In the nineteenth century, virtually all professional musicians delivered their services in concert halls in front of live audiences. (In 1900, Iowa had more than 1300 concert halls!) Audiences of that day would have been delighted to listen to the world's best singers, but no one singer could hope to perform in more than a tiny fraction of the world's concert halls. Today, in contrast, most of the music we hear comes in recorded form, which enables the best singer to be literally everywhere at once. As soon as the master recording has been made, Céline Dion's performance can be burned onto compact discs at the same low cost as for a slightly less talented singer's performance.

Tens of millions of buyers worldwide are willing to pay a few dollars extra to hear the most talented performers. Recording companies would be delighted to hire those singers at modest salaries, for by so doing they would earn an enormous economic profit. But that would unleash bidding by rival recording companies for the best singers. Such bidding ensures that the top singers will earn multimillion-dollar annual salaries (most of which constitute economic rents, as discussed in Chapter 7). Slightly less talented singers earn much less, because the recording industry simply does not need those singers.

---

winner-take-all labour market a market in which small differences in human capital translate into large differences in pay

The market for singers is an example of a **winner-take-all labour market,** one in which small differences in ability or other dimensions of human capital translate into large differences in pay. Long familiar in entertainment and professional sports, this reward pattern is becoming more common in other professions, as technology enables the most talented individuals to serve broader markets. A winner-take-all market does not mean a market with literally only one winner. Indeed, hundreds of professional musicians earn multimillion-dollar annual salaries. Yet tens of thousands of others, many of them nearly as good, struggle to pay their bills.

One consequence of the spread of winner-take-all markets has been the sharp increase in the pay of top earners relative to others. Compensation of the chief executives of the largest companies, for example, is now more than 400 times the salary of the average production worker, up from 42 times the salary in 1980. These executives now average roughly $4 million/year, and the highest paid among them earn considerably more.

A similar earnings explosion has taken place in publishing, where six-figure advances for works of hardcover fiction were rare just two decades ago. For authors, the watershed event was the $5 million paid in 1985 by William Morrow for the rights to James Clavell's novel *Whirlwind*. Five years later, NAL/Viking paid Stephen King $40 million for the rights to his next four novels, and Dell/Delacourt paid Danielle Steel $60 million for her next five books.

---

[3]A classic study is R. Freeman and J. Medoff, *What do Unions Do?* New York: Basic Books, 1984.

Big winners have also become increasingly common in show business and professional sports. Both Mel Gibson and Adam Sandler now command approximately $25 million per film. In his final year of play for the Chicago Bulls, Michael Jordan was paid about $30 million, and he earned a considerably larger sum for his various product endorsements.

The fact that small differences in ability often give rise to extremely large differences in pay might seem to contradict human capital theory. Note, however, that the winner-take-all reward pattern is completely consistent with the competitive labour market theory's claim that individuals are paid in accordance with the contributions they make to the employer's net revenue. The leverage of technology can amplify small performance differentials into very large ones.

COMPENSATING WAGE DIFFERENTIALS

Why do garbage collectors earn more than daycare workers? Picking up the trash is important, to be sure, but is it more valuable than caring for young children? As the next examples illustrate, the wage for a particular job depends not only on the value of what workers produce but also on how attractive they find its working conditions.

 12.3   ECONOMIC NATURALIST

Why do garbage collectors earn more than lifeguards?

There are two summer jobs open to the 20 undergraduates who live in a small Ontario city: lifeguards at the local beach (10 positions) and garbage collectors for the municipal sanitation department (10 positions). All 20 summer job seekers possess the requisite skills for each job, and all view the lifeguard job as the more desirable of the two. What will happen if the city posts the same wage rate for the two jobs?

Because lifeguarding is generally regarded as pleasant work and garbage collecting is generally regarded as unpleasant, we may expect 20 applicants for the lifeguard job and none for the garbage job. If city employment directors respond to this imbalance in supply and demand, they will raise the wage of garbage collectors and lower the wage for lifeguards until both labour markets reach equilibrium.

Other things being equal, jobs with attractive working conditions will pay less than jobs with less attractive conditions. Wage differences associated with differences in working conditions are known as **compensating wage differentials.** Economists have identified compensating differentials for a host of different specific working conditions. Studies have found, for example, that safe jobs tend to pay less than otherwise similar jobs that entail greater risks to health and safety.[4] Studies have also found that wages vary in accordance with the attractiveness of the work schedule. For instance, working night shifts commands a wage premium.

As the next example illustrates, we see compensating wage differentials even for such hard-to-measure characteristics as the autonomy associated with different jobs.

Your economics professor, it is safe to say, could have gone into an MBA program and gone on to a life as a business executive, rather than as an academic. The marks required for entry into MBA programs have always been somewhat lower than the marks required for entry into Ph.D. programs of comparable status, and MBA programs are typically shorter (two years) than Ph.D. programs (four years or more). As noted earlier, the salaries of top business executives have grown quickly in the past 20 years, but even before then it was always clear that salaries in business are significantly higher than in universities.

compensating wage differential a difference in the wage rate—negative or positive—that reflects the attractiveness of a job's working conditions

[4]W. Kip Viscusi, "The Value of Risks to Life and Health," *Journal of Economic Literature*, v. 31 (December 1993), pp. 1912–1946.

So why did your economics professor not make the same calculation as Manon? If a higher salary is obtained after an MBA, and an MBA requires less investment, isn't this an easy choice?

The short answer is that there is more to life than money. A crucial part of the example of "Manon" is that we assumed that she would get the same job satisfaction in either job. If the *only* way in which two jobs differ is in terms of the salary, it makes sense to use income as the basis for choice. However, jobs typically differ in many more ways than that, and life as a business executive is quite different from life as a professor.

One of the key ways in which a professor's job differs from that of a business executive is in personal autonomy. To see this in a superficial way, look at how some of your professors dress. Ask yourself honestly, could they get away with dressing that way in the head office of a major corporation? The phrase "get away with it" is revealing, because it indicates the social pressures to adhere to a dress code that are part of the business world. On a more substantive level, Canadian professors, to a remarkable extent, make their own decisions about how they do their jobs: what their research priorities are, what issues to emphasize in class, and so on.

The job descriptions of "professor" and "business executive" differ in other ways as well, but the bottom line is that despite lower salaries in academia, some people continue to enrol in Ph.D. programs, because they prefer the lifestyle and the type of work. Of course, the presence of compensating differentials does not eliminate the importance of wages. If academic salaries get too low, fewer people will be willing to pay the price in lower salaries for the difference in job satisfactions they will experience. Canadian universities can expect a wave of retirements in the next few years as professors who were hired in the 1960s and 1970s hit 65. Currently, few graduate students in Canada are training to replace them, so salaries will have to rise to entice people to go to graduate school and fill these vacancies.

Not everybody likes the academic lifestyle to the same degree. When tastes as to job attributes differ, *the size and the sign* of the compensating differential depend on relative supply *and* demand. Some people clearly prize personal autonomy more strongly, while others prefer to be team players. Similarly, tastes differ for other job characteristics. Some people like to work outdoors, while others prefer to be indoors. When tastes differ, the crucial issue is how many jobs there are that have a particular characteristic *relative to* the number of people who like it. For example, if there are many outdoor jobs and only a few people who like being outdoors, then firms will have to pay higher wages for outdoor jobs to lure some indoor-lovers outside. However, if the number of people who like being outdoors is greater than the number of outdoor jobs, then outdoor jobs will pay less than indoor jobs. Economics has no way of knowing how many people will have particular tastes, so it is often hard to predict if "compensating differentials" will produce higher or lower wages in a particular occupation.

RECAP   **EXPLAINING DIFFERENCES IN EARNINGS**

Earnings differ among people in part because of differences in their human capital. Two people with the same amount of human capital may earn different wages if one belongs to a labour union and the other does not. Their earnings may also differ because a given amount of human capital has greater leverage in some contexts than others. The world's most talented singer is far more valuable, for example, if people can listen to her music not just in live performances but on compact discs as well. Earnings may also differ between equally productive individuals because of compensating wage differentials—positive or negative wage differentials attributable to differences in working conditions.

■ 12.7 DISCRIMINATION IN THE LABOUR MARKET

Women and minorities continue to receive lower wage rates, on average, than white males with similar education and years of experience. This pattern poses a profound challenge to standard theories of competitive labour markets, which hold that competitive pressures will eliminate wage differentials not based on differences in productivity. Defenders of standard theories attribute the wage gap to unmeasured differences in human capital. Critics of these theories, who reject the idea that labour markets are effectively competitive, attribute the gap to various forms of discrimination.

DISCRIMINATION BY EMPLOYERS

Employer discrimination is the term used to describe wage differentials that arise from an arbitrary preference by the employer for one group of workers over another. An example occurs if two labour force groups, such as males and females, are known to be equally productive, on average. If we think back to the example of Mackintosh Pottery Works at the start of the chapter, some employers ("discriminators") in the industry may prefer to hire males and may be willing to pay higher wages to do so.

employer discrimination an arbitrary preference by the employer for one group of workers over another

If male workers have higher wages than female workers of the same productivity, what will happen to wages and employment in long-run equilibrium? Most consumers are not willing to pay more for a good pot produced by males than for an identical one produced by females (if indeed they even *know* which type of worker produced the pot). If product price is unaffected by the composition of the workforce that produces the product, a firm's profit will be smaller the more males it employs, because males cost more yet are no more productive. Thus, the most profitable firms will be ones that employ only females.

Arbitrary wage gaps are an apparent violation of the equilibrium principle. The initial wage differential provides an opportunity for employers who hire mostly females to grow at the expense of their rivals. Because such firms make an economic profit on the sale of each clay pot, their incentive is to expand as rapidly as they possibly can. And to do that, they would naturally want to continue hiring only the less expensive female workers.

EQUILIBRIUM

But as profit-seeking firms continue to pursue this strategy, the supply of females at the lower wage rate will run out. The short-run solution is to offer females a slightly higher wage. But if other firms also start offering a higher wage, females' wages will be bid up. The only stable outcome will occur when the wage of females reaches parity with the wage of males. The wage for both males and females will thus settle at the common value of their *VMP*.

Any employer who wants to voice a preference for hiring males must now do so by paying males a wage in excess of their *VMP*. Employers can discriminate against females if they wish, but only if they are willing to pay premium wages to males out of their own profits.

Why then has study after study found an unexplained gap in the pay of men and women, even after accounting for the influence of all the measurable characteristics (such as education, experience, or industry of employment) that economists can think of? Why didn't this gap disappear long ago? Why have similar "unexplained" wage gaps also been found for different minority groups (such as Aboriginal Canadians)?

To understand this, we have to remember the limitations of the above example. We will stick with the example of male and female wage differentials, but the argument is more general and applies to wage differentials between other groups as well. The clay pot example assumed that (1) the consumers of a good did not know or care who actually produced the good they purchased, (2) although employers knew that men and women were of equal inherent productivity, they still preferred males, and (3) nondiscriminatory firms could easily obtain access to the capital and distribution networks that they need to expand production.

The assumption that consumers do not know or care who produced the product is only reasonable in part of the economy. More than 75 percent of the labour force is in the service sector. Far more Canadians work in offices, restaurants, and department stores than in pottery works or car factories (and the same is true in all the other developed countries). Although it is reasonable to assume that the purchasers of clay pots or automobiles have no real way of knowing whether assembly line workers in the plant were male or female, the diners in a restaurant are certainly aware of whether a waiter or a waitress served them.

Much of the service sector is characterized by personal contact of the service provider and the service consumer. In the service sector, the *quality* of the product is often hard to define precisely; indeed, it is often said that "good quality is whatever the customer thinks it is." This combination of characteristics means that customer attitudes can matter a great deal. If, for example, some investors have the idea that men are wise, dispassionate, and good with numbers, while women are not, such investors may prefer to purchase the services of male investment brokers and financial analysts, rather than trust their money with female advisers. If such people are numerous enough, it will not be worthwhile for financial services firms to hire women, or to pay them the same amount of money. And since financial analysts signal their success in delivering financial advice by their own prosperity, it will not do female financial analysts much good to try to compete by offering to accept lower pay. Saying that "I'll advise you financially for less pay" is likely to be interpreted as "My advice is worth less."

The structural problem is that if women are faced with barriers to advancement in some areas, such as the financial services sector, then it is reasonable for them to look elsewhere for a career. The combination of barriers to advancement and the supply response to those barriers then produces occupational segregation, which remains a characteristic of the Canadian labour market (and of the labour market of the United States, United Kingdom, and other developed countries). As Statistics Canada has noted: "In 1999, 70% of all employed women were working in teaching, nursing, and related health occupations, clerical or other administrative positions, and sales and service occupations."[5]

Occupational segregation interacts with the second assumption—that employers know men and women to be of equal productivity, yet prefer men. It is rare for people in Canada today to express such openly discriminatory attitudes, even to themselves, but it not quite so rare to find stereotyped thinking about the capabilities of different types of employees. Stereotyped thinking then produces the type of discrimination that comes from the assumption that a particular type of person "just couldn't do the job." Stereotyped thinking about job performance may not be universally negative. Women, for example, may be assigned the stereotyped virtue of compassionate empathy even as they are denied the stereotyped capability for tough decision making. Stereotypes may also be particularly strong where they reinforce traditional roles in family life. The net result is that people are assumed to only have the ability for some of the jobs in the labour market.

Recall our discussion of statistical discrimination in Chapter 11. Potential employers typically cannot directly know what an individual is actually producing, or capable of producing, at another firm, so firms therefore have to pay the same wage to particular "types" of observationally equivalent workers. If firms only use information that is truly relevant to productivity (such as years of education or job experience), then no problem exists. But the only way that incorrect assumptions about productivity are weeded out is with experience. And, of course,

---

[5]Statistics Canada. (2000). Reproduced from the Statistics Canada publication *Women in Canada 2000: A Gender Based Statistical Report*. Cat No. 89-503-XPE, p. 107. Ottawa: Statistics Canada. Statistics Canada information is used with the permission of the Minister of Industry, as Minister responsible for Statistics Canada. Information on the availability of the wide range of data from Statistics Canada can be obtained from Statistics Canada's Regional Offices, its World Wide Web site at http://www.statcan.ca, and its toll-free access number 1-800-263-1136.

an employer who acts on a prejudiced assumption and never hires a member of the discriminated against group is never proven wrong, because he or she never gets to observe whether that person could have done the job.

Furthermore, industry norms may make it costly for an individual employer to innovate. If a stereotype is widely held, individual employers who have different attitudes will be seen as odd. Firms that deviate from industry norms will have to prove that their policies actually work, and until they demonstrate that, those firms are risky for others to deal with. If they depend on other firms—for bank credit, for the supply of inputs, or to gain access to markets—they may find that other firms are uncooperative or demand more for their cooperation. Comparing the added costs of doing business with the wage savings from hiring a member of the discriminated-against group, it may just not be worth the bother.

Incorrect stereotypes, like any misconception about quality, are a cost to the economy. If, for example, the Canadian building industry believed pine to be a much stronger lumber than spruce, house prices in Canada would be higher than they need to be. If contractors were not using an equally good type of lumber and were bidding up the price of pine unnecessarily, the output of the industry would be unnecessarily expensive. Similarly, prejudice and misinformation are the source of both inequity (to the people who are denied access to employment) and inefficiency (for the economy as a whole).

The public policy issue at the root of this discussion is how to eliminate prejudice in a reasonably short time. It may be that the market will, itself, eventually weed out misconceptions. However, this will take time and it is reasonable for public policy to aim at speeding the process along a little. In particular, two major emphases of Canadian public policy have been antidiscrimination legislation and employment equity programs. By helping women and minorities get into nontraditional jobs, it becomes possible to show, by experience, how incorrect traditional misconceptions actually are.

RECAP   **DISCRIMINATION IN THE LABOUR MARKET**

Critics of the theory of competitive labour markets have offered a variety of theories of discrimination to explain why women and minorities continue to receive lower wages than would be predicted by standard human capital models. The theory of employer discrimination holds that part of the observed wage gaps are the result of continued stereotypes of employee productivity on the part of employers.

▪ SUMMARY

- **12.1** The long-run equilibrium pay in a competitive labour market will be equal to the value of the marginal product (VMP)—the market value of whatever goods and services that type of worker on average produces for an employer. The law of diminishing marginal returns says that when a firm's capital and other productive inputs are held fixed in the short run, adding workers beyond some point results in ever-smaller increases in output. Firms that purchase labour in competitive labour markets face a constant wage, and they will hire labour up to the point at which VMP equals the market wage.

- **12.6** Human capital theory says that an individual's VMP is proportional to his stock of human capital: education, experience, training, and other factors that influence productivity. According to this theory, some occupations pay better than others simply because they require larger stocks of human capital.

• **12.7** Wages often differ between individuals whose stocks of human capital appear nearly the same, as when one belongs to a labour union and the other does not. Technologies that allow the most productive individuals to serve broader markets can translate even small differences in performance into enormous differences in pay. Such technologies give rise to winner-take-all labour markets, which have long been common in sports and entertainment, and which are becoming common in other professions.

• **12.7** Compensating wage differentials—wage differences associated with differences in working conditions—are

another important explanation for why some earn more than others. They help to explain why garbage collectors earn more than lifeguards and, more generally, why individuals with a given stock of human capital tend to earn more in jobs that have less attractive working conditions.

• **12.8** Many firms pay members of certain groups—notably minority groups and females—less than they pay white males with similar personal characteristics. If such wage gaps are the result of employer discrimination, their existence implies profit opportunities for firms that do not discriminate. Several other factors, including the prevalence of stereotypes and discrimination by institutions other than firms, may explain at least part of the observed wage gaps.

■ KEY TERMS

compensating wage differential (341)
discount factor (337)
employer discrimination (343)
human capital (334)
human capital theory (334)
labour union (339)

marginal labour cost (330)
marginal (physical) product of labour (326)
monopsony (329)
observationally equivalent workers (327)

present value (337)
value of marginal product of labour (*VMP*) (326)
winner-take-all labour market (340)

■ REVIEW QUESTIONS

1. Suppose that you are the premier of a province and your government was elected on a pledge of increasing the earnings of daycare workers, most of whom are employed by nongovernmental organizations and private firms. What would be the most efficient way of accomplishing that objective?

2. Why is the supply curve of labour for any specific occupation likely to be upward sloping, even if, for the economy as a whole, people work fewer hours when wage rates increase?

3. True or false: If the human capital possessed by two workers is nearly the same, their wage rates will be nearly the same. Explain.

4. The U.S. Congress periodically holds hearings to examine the effects of smoking on health. The witnesses who testify at those hearings under the sponsorship of the Tobacco Institute (a cigarette industry organization) are generally thought to have weaker scientific reputations than the witnesses who testify under the sponsorship of the American Cancer Society. Why, then, do the former witnesses get paid much more than the latter?

5. True or false: Economic surplus would be larger if a profit-maximizing monopsonist in the labour market were required to hire one more worker than it otherwise would have chosen to. Explain.

■ PROBLEMS

1. Kevin Capitalist is thinking of going into hydroponics. He knows that he can get $20 per gram for high-value herbs and that any legal problems that he might personally have in connection with herb production can be solved with a payment of $5 per gram to the appropriate legal authorities. The cost of electricity, fertilizer, rental space, and other inputs is $3 per gram. Each plant he grows produces 10 grams of herbs and takes 60 days to grow to maturity. Sasha and Bobbi are willing to work for him, but Kevin knows that Sasha can tend 25 plants while Bobbi can only take care of 20 plants. What is the maximum amount that Kevin can pay each worker per day and still make a profit?

2. Stone, Inc., owns a clothing factory and hires workers in a competitive labour market to cut and sew denim fabric into jeans. The fabric required to make each pair of jeans costs $5. The company's weekly output of finished jeans varies with the number of workers hired, as shown in the following table:

Number of workers	Jeans (pairs/week)
0	0
1	25
2	45
3	60
4	72
5	80
6	85

   a. If the jeans sell for $35/pair, and the wage that other firms are offering workers is $250/week, how many workers should Stone hire? How many pairs of jeans will the company produce each week?

   b. Suppose the market wage other firms are willing to pay changes to $230/week. How does that change in the wages that other firms are willing to pay affect Stone's decision about how many workers to hire?

   c. If the market wage had changed to $400/week, how would this affect Stone's decision about how many workers to hire?

   d. If Stone again faces a market wage of $250/week, but the price of jeans rises to $45/week, how many workers will the company now hire?

   e. If the reason why Stone Inc. has to change its wage rate were different (e.g., if the wage rate changed because of union action or government regulation) would that change your answer to parts (b) to (d) above?

3. The Jiffy-Fast Stone Carving Company is the only employer in a small town on Baffin Island. After paying transportation costs, its net receipts per carving are $5 each, and its weekly output of carvings varies with the number of workers, as shown in the following table:

Number of workers	Carvings/week
0	0
1	50
2	90
3	120
4	140
5	150
6	155

There are six people in town potentially available to work at Jiffy-Fast. The six people, together with their reservation wages, are shown in the following table:

Worker	Reservation wage ($/week)
Jon	75
Joe	80
Jenny	85
Jeff	90
Jessica	100
Luke	150

    a. If Jiffy-Fast must pay the same wage to all workers, how many workers will the firm hire? What wage will it pay?

    b. What is the socially optimal number of workers to hire?

    c. If Jiffy-Fast could pay each worker exactly his or her reservation wage, how many workers would the company hire?

4. Acme, Inc., supplies rocket ships to the retail market and hires workers to assemble the components. A rocket ship sells for $30 000, and Acme can buy the components for each rocket ship for $25 000. Wiley and Sam are two workers for Acme. Sam can assemble one-fifth of a rocket ship per month, and Wiley can assemble one-tenth. If the labour market is perfectly competitive, and if every other firm knows that Sam is twice as productive as Wiley, and rocket components are Acme's only other cost, how much will Sam and Wiley be paid?

5. Carolyn owns a soda factory and hires workers in a competitive labour market to bottle the soda. Her company's weekly output of bottled soda varies with the number of workers hired, as shown in the following table:

Number of workers	Cases/week
0	0
1	200
2	360
3	480
4	560
5	600

    a. If each case sells for $10 more than the cost of the materials used in producing it and the competitive market wage is $1000/week, how many workers will Carolyn hire? How many cases will be produced per week?

    b. Suppose the Soda Bottlers Union now sets a weekly minimum acceptable wage of $1500/week. All the workers Carolyn hires belong to the union. How does the minimum wage affect Carolyn's decision about how many workers to hire?

    c. If the wage is again $1000/week but the price of soda rises to $15 more than the cost of materials per case, how many workers will Carolyn now hire?

    d. Suppose that a big automobile assembly plant opens up in town and because of the general increase in local demand for labour, the going wage rises from $1000 to $1500 per week. Suppose further that workers at the soda factory are not in a union and that soda sells for $10 more than the cost of the materials used in producing it. How many workers will Carolyn hire?

6. Laura has a nursing degree and 2 years of experience working at Women's College Hospital. If she continues along her present career path, the present value of her lifetime earnings will be $200 000. If she takes 2 years off and completes a midwifery degree, the present value of her lifetime earnings will be $221 000. She has a scholarship that will cover the cost of books and incidental expenses. However, she must make two tuition payments for the midwifery course, one now and one a year from now, both of $10 500. Apart from her salary, Laura is indifferent between nursing and midwifery. If the interest rate is 5 percent, is Laura better off if she goes to midwifery college? Explain.

7. Stefano is thinking about getting a law degree. If he continues along his present career path, the present value of his lifetime earnings will be $500 000. If instead he takes 3 years off and gets the law degree, the present value of his lifetime earnings will be $550 000. He has a scholarship that will cover the costs of books and incidental expenses. However, he must make annual tuition payments of $20 000 at the beginning of each academic year. If the interest rate is 20 percent, will Stefano be better off financially if he goes to law school? Explain. If we observe Stefano going to law school, even after making all these calculations, what does that say about his preferences for his current occupation, compared to being a lawyer?

8. A simple economy has two labour markets for carpenters: one for residential houses, the other for commercial buildings. The demand for residential carpenters is given by $W_R = 40 - 10L_R$, where W_R is the wage of residential carpenters in dollars per hour and L_R is the number of residential carpenters in hundreds per day. The demand for commercial carpenters is given by $W_C = 40 - 5L_C$, where W_C is the wage of commercial carpenters in dollars per hour and L_C is the number of commercial carpenters in hundreds per day. The economy has 300 carpenters, each of whom has the skills required to be either a residential or a commercial carpenter, and each of whom wants to work full-time in whichever type of carpentry pays best. What will be the equilibrium wage and employment level for each type? (*Hint:* To find the total demand curve for carpenters, first graph the two demand curves side by side and then add them horizontally.)

9. In Problem 8, suppose commercial carpenters form a union and announce that they will not work for less than $30/hour. Any union member who cannot find work in the commercial market will work in the residential market. How many carpenters work in each market, and what is the wage in the residential market? Are carpenters as a group better off or worse off?

10. Refer to Problem 9. By how much does the formation of the commercial carpenters' union reduce the total value of carpenters' services provided each hour?

ANSWERS TO IN-CHAPTER EXERCISES

12.1 Adirondack will hire a second worker only if the *VMP* with two workers is at least 300. Since $VMP = (P)(MP)$, and since the marginal product of the second worker is 25 cutting boards, the lowest P for which the company will hire two workers is found by solving $(P)(25) = 350$ to obtain $P = 14$.

12.2 Since the *VMP* of each worker exceeds $275, Bluenose will now hire five workers.

12.3 As shown in the following table, *VMP* for each of the first four workers now exceeds marginal labour cost, so Bluenose will now hire four workers.

Number of workers	Total number of cutting boards/week	MP (extra cutting boards/week)	VMP ($/week)	Marginal labour cost
0	0			
		30	900	200
1	30			
		25	750	300
2	55			
		21	632	400
3	76			
		18	540	500
4	94			
		14	420	600
5	108			

12.4 A higher interest rate reduces the present value of both the cost of an MA degree and the resulting higher earnings. But the cost of getting an MA occurs during the next two years, while the salary increase is spread out over many years. The higher interest rate will therefore reduce the present value of the benefit of the degree by more than it will reduce the present value of its cost. Since Manon was indifferent at an interest rate of 10 percent, she will choose not to get the degree if the interest rate is 12 percent.

CALCULATING THE PRESENT VALUE OF FUTURE COSTS AND BENEFITS

In Chapter 12, calculations of present value are made in the context of human capital theory. However, the calculation of present values is a general problem that occurs in many contexts. For example, someone who is trying to estimate how much a business is worth must take into account that earnings received in the future are less valuable than earnings received today. Consider a company whose only accounting profit, $14 400, will occur exactly two years from now. At all other times its accounting profit will be exactly zero. How much is ownership of this company worth today?

Our goal is to calculate what economists call the present value of $14 400 to be received two years in the future. To make this calculation, we must employ the concept of the *time value of money*, which we first encountered in Chapter 1. The time value of money is closely related to the growth of an initial amount at compound interest.

To start, suppose we deposit $10 000 in a bank account. Let the annual interest rate be 20 percent. At the end of one year, the value of the deposit will grow to the principal amount ($10 000) plus interest earned. If M_1 represents the value reached at the end of year one, we can write:

$$M_1 = \$10\ 000 + 0.2(\$10\ 000) = \$10\ 000 + \$2000 = \$12\ 000$$

If $12 000 remains in the bank account for another year, its value will grow to $12 000 plus interest earned. If M_2 is the value reached at the end of year two, we can write:

$$M_2 = \$12\ 000 + 0.2(\$12\ 000) = \$12\ 000 + \$2400 = \$14\ 400$$

At the end of two years, $10 000 deposited at an interest rate of 20 percent per year grows to $14 400—growth has been compounded over two years at an annual rate of 20 percent.

The calculation of M_1 can be written in more general notation:

$$M_1 = PV + r(PV) = PV(1 + r) \qquad (12A.1)$$

where PV is the amount deposited now, r is the annual interest rate expressed as a decimal fraction, and M_1 is as defined previously. Similarly, the expression for M_2 is:

$$M_2 = M_1 + r(M_1) = M_1(1 + r). \qquad (12A.2)$$

If equation 12A.1 is substituted into 12A.2, then:

$$M_2 = PV(1 + r)(1 + r)$$
$$M_2 = PV(1 + r)^2 \qquad (12A.3)$$

Equation 12A.3 can be generalized to:

$$M_T = PV(1 + r)^T \qquad (12A.4)$$

where T is the number of years over which an initial amount PV grows, M is the value reached after T years, and other terms remain as defined previously. For example, if PV is \$10 000, the annual interest rate is 20 percent, and T is 2 years, equation 12A.4 can be used to calculate M_T:

$$M_T = PV(1 + r)^T = \$10\,000(1 + 0.2)^2 = \$10\,000(1.44) = \$14\,400$$

Notice that the higher is the interest rate or the longer the time over which the initial amount remains on deposit, the greater is the value of M_T.

Equation 12A.4 gives the value that an initial deposit reaches over a given period of time. However, suppose we do not know the initial amount, but we do know the amount that will be reached after a specified interval of time has elapsed—we know the future value, but we do not know the present value. For example, suppose we know that two years in the future, we will have \$14 400. What is the present value of \$14 400?

To answer this question, divide equation 12A.4 by $(1 + r)^T$ to solve for PV, which represents present value:

$$PV = \frac{M_T}{(1 + r)^T} = \frac{1}{(1 + r)^T} M_T = DM_T \qquad (12A.5)$$

Notice that the term $\frac{1}{(1 + r)^T}$ has been factored out in equation 12A.5. This term is known as the **discount factor**. It is a coefficient used to discount a payment or receipt that occurs in the future to a present value. In equation 12A.5, D represents the discount factor.

We know M_T is \$14 400 and that T is 2. Again, we will let the annual interest rate be 20 percent. When these values are placed in equation 12A.5, the result is:

$$PV = \frac{\$14\,400}{(1 + 0.2)^2} = \frac{\$14\,400}{1.44} = \frac{1}{(1 + 0.2)^2}\,\$14\,400 = \frac{1}{1.44}(\$14\,400) = \$10\,000$$

Given an annual interest rate of 20 percent, the present value of \$14 400 received two years from now is to \$10 000. More generally, given an annual interest rate r, the **present value (PV)** of a payment M received T years in the future is the amount that must be deposited today if a balance M is to be reached after T years. Equation 12A.5 provides a convenient shorthand statement of this definition.

discount factor a coefficient, D used to discount a payment or receipt that occurs in the future to a present value. A discount factor can be defined algebraically as:

$$D = \frac{1}{(1 + r)^T}$$

where r = annual interest rate and T = number of years that will elapse before the payment is received.

present value when the annual interest rate is r, the present value (PV) of a payment M to be received T years from now is the amount that would have to be deposited today at an annual interest rate r to generate a balance of M after T years:

$$PV = \frac{M_T}{(1 + r)^T} = DM_T$$

Notice two things about the calculation of present value. First, it is the algebraic reciprocal of calculating the value reached by an initial amount deposited at compound interest. The calculation of present value is mathematically consistent with the calculation of values reached at compound interest. Second, as equation 12A.4 shows, the higher the rate of interest or the longer the interval of time that elapses, the greater will be the value reached by an amount deposited at compound interest. Therefore, as equation 12A.5 shows, the reciprocal must follow: the higher is the rate of interest or the longer is the interval of time that elapses, the lower will be the present value of an amount received in the future.

Up to this point, we have calculated the present value of a single amount that will be received at a point in the future. However, it is easy to modify equation 12A.5 to calculate the present value of a stream of payments. Suppose we receive payment M_1 one year in the future, M_2 two years in the future, and M_3 three years in the future. The present value of this stream of payments is calculated as

$$PV = \frac{1}{(1 + r)^1}M_1 + \frac{1}{(1 + r)^2}M_2 + \frac{1}{(1 + r)^3}M_3 \qquad (12A.6)$$

where the exponents indicate the number of years in the future each payment will be received and all other terms are as previously defined. Equation 12A.6 can be rewritten as

$$PV = \sum_{t=1}^{3}\frac{1}{(1 + r)^t}M_t = \sum_{t=1}^{3}D_tM_t \qquad (12A.7)$$

where Σ is a summation operator and t is an index that states the point in time at which a payment is received. Equation 12A.7 can be generalized to

$$PV = \sum_{t=1}^{T}\frac{1}{(1 + r)^t}M_T = \sum_{t=1}^{T}D_TM_T \qquad (12A.8)$$

where T indicates the point in time at which the last payment is received, and all other terms remain as previously defined.

EXERCISE 12A.1

What is the present value of a payment of $1728 to be received 3 years from now if the annual interest rate is 20 percent?

◼ PROBLEMS

1. Suppose you are the winner of a lottery. As your prize, you will receive a payment of $10 000 today, when you present your winning ticket to the Lottery Commission. You will also receive $10 000 one year from now, $10 000 two years from now, and a final payment of $20 000 three years from now.
    a. The Lottery Commission wants to encourage people to buy lottery tickets, so it advertises that you, the lucky winner, have won a prize worth $50 000. Do you agree with this statement? Why or why not?
    b. Suppose the prevailing interest rate is 5 percent. Calculate the present value of your prize.

   c. Suppose the prevailing interest rate is 2.5 percent. Calculate the present value of your prize.

   d. Suppose your prize can be sold to anyone who is willing to buy it. If the prevailing interest rate is 2.5 percent, what is the maximum price someone would be willing to pay for your prize today? Why?

2. You are shopping for a car. You have found a dealer who will sell you a car for $12 000. If you purchase from him, you must make a down payment of $2000. The dealer will arrange for you to borrow the remaining $10 000 at an annual interest rate of 1 percent, and the loan will be payable in full one year from now.

   a. If you take the loan the dealer is offering to arrange, what is the amount you must pay at the end of one year? What is the present value of this payment given an interest rate of 1 percent per year?

   b. Suppose you have sufficient cash to purchase the car outright for $12 000. You also have an opportunity to deposit this cash at an interest rate of 6 percent per year. What is the opportunity cost of using your cash to pay for the car instead of depositing it with interest? (For simplicity, ignore depreciation of the car and income tax.) What is the present value of your opportunity cost, given an interest rate of 6 percent?

   c. If you borrow $10 000 under the terms offered by the dealer, and deposit $10 000 of cash at 6 percent per year, what is the net amount of interest you will earn? From your point of view, what is the size of the discount from a price of $12 000 that the dealer is offering to you when he offers the $10 000 loan at an annual interest rate of 1 percent?

   d. Suppose the dealer can also deposit any cash he has at 6 percent per year. Given the terms of the loan he has offered, do you think the dealer would be interested if you offered to buy the car for less than $12 000, provided you offer to pay cash? How much less? Why?

■ ANSWER TO APPENDIX EXERCISE

12A.1 Present value = $1728/(1.2)^3 = 1000$

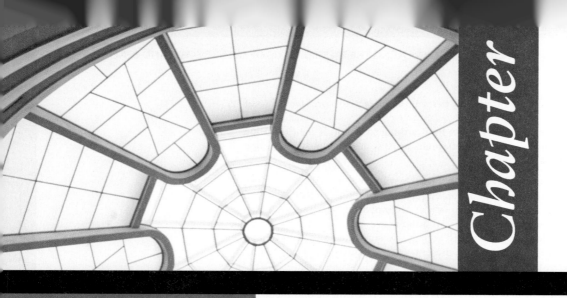

THE ECONOMICS OF PUBLIC POLICY

I n 1979, just after the second major oil price shock disrupted international oil markets, the newly elected Progressive Conservative government of Joe Clark tabled its first budget. A key part of the budget was its proposal for an increase in the gasoline tax. With the slogan of "Short-term pain for long-term gain," the finance minister urged the adoption of this tax increase, as a way of discouraging the consumption of nonrenewable energy resources and decreasing the federal deficit.

Proponents of the gasoline tax argued that in addition to reducing the nation's dependence on foreign oil, the tax would reduce air pollution and ease highway congestion. But critics ridiculed the proposal, charging that the quantity of gasoline demanded would remain essentially the same, because people would just pay more taxes, on top of the increase in world prices, and would still have to drive the same number of kilometres in the same cars.

The proposed gasoline tax was never implemented. The Clark government did not have a majority in the House of Commons, and they had not consulted with a small group of Creditiste Members of Parliament from rural Quebec, whose support they lost. As a result, the budget was defeated in the House of Commons. Clark went on to lose the subsequent general election and acquire the distinction of having led the briefest federal government in Canadian history (nine months). Nevertheless, the price of oil increased under the subsequent Liberal government. (See Chapter 6.)

In retrospect, the Clark government's proposals were not so bad. Early reduction of the federal deficit would have prevented an accumulation of federal debt and a good deal of later pain. The proposal of a tax that will discourage energy consumption and benefit the environment is an issue that Canada (and much of the rest of the world) has not yet grappled with. Furthermore, the argument that the tax would not affect consumption because people would still have to go to the same places in the same cars is only true in the very short run.

COST–BENEFIT

As we saw in Chapter 4, the cost–benefit principle could lead consumers to change their behaviour to escape the effects of a steep rise in the after-tax price of gasoline, by switching to cars with smaller, more fuel-efficient engines, forming carpools, and so on. Such changes free up money to spend on other goods and services, which become relatively more attractive because they are not taxed as heavily.

No society can hope to formulate and implement intelligent economic policies unless its citizens and leaders share an understanding of basic economic principles, but knowledge of economics is not enough. Basic economic principles help us to understand how markets work and the choices available to us, but economic principles alone cannot tell us what we *should* do.

In Scandinavia there is a saying: "The market is a good servant, but a bad master." We cannot expect the market to tell us what our social values should be. The market mechanism is simply not able to say how much attention Canadians *should* pay to social issues such as poverty, or the degradation of the environment. However, *given* our social values and the political processes that try to define a set of social priorities, market mechanisms can often be a useful tool for realizing social objectives.

As well, understanding how to use the market to help achieve more efficient and equitable economic outcomes is not necessarily straightforward. Economics would be a dull (but much easier) discipline if all markets were the same. It is *because* different areas of the economy have different characteristics that economic policy has to be designed somewhat differently to suit the different reality of different sectors. The complexity, and the fascination, of economic analysis was nicely expressed in 1933 by the great English economist John Maynard Keynes in his book *Essays in Biography*, while writing about another great economist, Alfred Marshall:

www.socserv.mcmaster.ca/
econ/ugcm/3113/marshall/
prin/index.html

> The study of economics does not seem to require any specialised gifts of an unusually high order. Is it not, intellectually regarded, a very easy subject compared with the higher branches of philosophy and pure science? Yet good, or even competent, economists are the rarest of birds. An easy subject, at which very few excel! The paradox finds its explanation, perhaps, in that the master-economist must possess a rare *combination* of gifts. He must reach a high standard in several different directions and must combine talents not often found together. He must be mathematician, historian, statesman, philosopher—in some degree. He must understand symbols and speak in words. He must contemplate the particular in terms of the general, and touch abstract and concrete in the same flight of thought. He must study the present in the light of the past for the purposes of the future. No part of a man's nature or his institutions must lie entirely outside his regard. He must be purposeful and disinterested in a simultaneous mood; as aloof and incorruptible as an artist, yet sometimes as near the earth as a politician. Much, but not all, of this ideal many-sidedness Marshall possessed. But chiefly his mixed training and divided nature furnished him with the most essential and fundamental of the economist's necessary gifts—he was conspicuously historian and mathematician, a dealer in the particular and the general, the temporal and the eternal, at the same time.[1]

Our aim in this chapter is to explore how careful application of economic principles can help us design policies that both expand the economic pie and make everyone's slice larger. We will begin with a discussion of government policy toward natural monopoly, and then we will explore a seemingly unrelated collection of policy issues, including the pricing of public services, health care delivery, environmental regulation, and public policy toward addictive goods and services. The thread unifying these issues is the problem of *scarcity*. In each case, we will explore how the cost–benefit principle can help to resolve the resulting trade-offs, and how differences in market structure shape the appropriate public policy response.

[1]John Maynard Keynes, *Essays in Biography*, 2nd ed. Edited by Geoffrey Keynes. New York: W.W. Norton & Company, 1951, p. 141. Printed with permission of Macmillan Ltd.

■ 13.1 PUBLIC POLICY TOWARD MONOPOLY

Monopoly is problematic not only because of the loss in efficiency of resource allocation associated with restricted output but also because the monopolist earns an economic profit at the buyer's expense. For these reasons, voters in many societies have empowered government to adopt policies aimed at controlling natural monopolists.

There are several ways to achieve this aim. A government may assume ownership and control of a natural monopoly, or it may merely attempt to regulate the prices it charges. In some cases government solicits competitive bids from private firms to produce natural monopoly services. In still other cases, governments attempt to dissolve natural monopolies into smaller entities that compete with one another. But many of these policies create economic problems of their own. In each case, the practical challenge is to come up with the solution that yields the greatest surplus of benefits over costs. Natural monopoly may be inefficient and unfair, but the alternatives to natural monopoly are far from perfect.

STATE OWNERSHIP AND MANAGEMENT

Recall from Chapter 8 that an unregulated natural monopoly is inefficient because the monopolist's profit-maximizing price is greater than its marginal cost. But even if the natural monopolist *wanted* to set price equal to marginal cost, it could not do so and hope to remain in business without subsidy. After all, the defining feature of a natural monopoly is economies of scale in production, which means that marginal cost will always be less than average cost. Setting price equal to marginal cost would fail to cover average production cost, which implies an economic loss.

Consider the case of a local cable television company. Once an area has been wired for cable television, the marginal cost of adding another subscriber is very low. If the company's pricing is economically efficient, all subscribers will pay a price equal to that marginal cost. Yet a cable company that priced in this manner would never be able to recover the fixed cost of setting up the network. This same problem applies not just to cable television companies but to all other natural monopolies. Even if such firms wanted to set price equal to marginal cost (which, of course, they do not, since they will earn more by setting marginal revenue equal to marginal cost), they cannot do so without suffering an economic loss.

Figure 13.1 represents the natural monopoly case where a monopoly firm has substantial fixed costs and the marginal cost of production is constant. Demand for the monopolist's product is represented by D, and marginal revenue is represented by MR. In the cable television example, the firm's fixed cost is the expense of putting in the poles and wiring to service the whole neighbourhood and its marginal cost is the expense of connecting a particular house to the network. When marginal cost is constant, marginal cost is equal to average variable cost, so the MC curve (= AVC curve) in Figure 13.1 is a horizontal line. As the number of customers increases, fixed costs can be averaged over more units, so average fixed costs decline. Average total cost (ATC) is equal to average variable cost (AVC) plus average fixed cost (AFC). As the red line in Figure 13.1 indicates, average total cost declines as sales increase.

As noted in Chapter 8, if we leave this market to a private monopoly, profit maximization implies that the monopolist charges the price P_0 and sets output at Q_0 (where marginal revenue equals marginal cost). Average total cost is AC_0. The monopolist makes a per-unit profit equal to the difference between price and average total cost $[P_0 - AC_0]$, so total monopoly profits are equal to $Q_0[P_0 - AC_0]$, which is represented by the grey box in Figure 13.1.

When the monopolist charges a price of P_0, and only produces Q_0 units, the allocation of resources in the economy is inefficient because producing one more

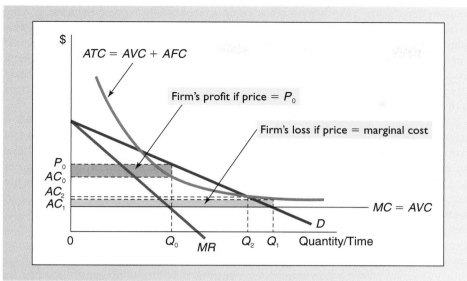

FIGURE 13.1

Demand, Costs, and Revenues for a Natural Monopolist
If a natural monopolist maximizes its profit, total economic surplus is reduced below its potential value. If price is set equal to marginal cost in order to maximize total economic surplus, the natural monopolist incurs a loss.

unit costs less than the price that consumers would be willing to pay for it. An additional unit produced would only add MC to production costs, while consumers would be willing to pay P_0, so the difference $[P_0 - MC]$ is the consumer surplus that would be gained if the additional unit were produced. Total economic surplus is maximized if price is set equal to marginal cost at output level Q_1 in Figure 13.1. However, because marginal cost is less than average total cost, the firm incurs a loss. On average, the loss per unit is equal to the difference between average total cost and price $[AC_1 - P_1 = AC_1 - MC]$, so the firm's total financial loss can be represented by the pink box in Figure 13.1 (whose area is $Q_1[AC_1 - P_1]$, i.e., the total loss of the firm).

What to do?

One way to attack the efficiency and fairness problems is for the government to take over the industry, set price equal to marginal cost, and then absorb the resulting losses out of general tax revenues.

As we saw in Chapter 8, a necessary condition for economic (or Pareto) efficiency in allocation is that market price be equal to marginal cost. If this condition is violated, resources are not allocated efficiently, because by reallocating resources it will then be possible to make at least one person better off without harming anyone else. However, when economists use the word "efficiency" in this way, they do not quite mean what most people usually think of as "efficiency." The ordinary person's idea of efficiency is "avoiding unnecessary waste." Economists call it **technical efficiency in production**, which occurs when the least possible amount of inputs is used to produce a given level of output. Critics of government often charge that the public sector does not achieve technical efficiency in production. Although the public sector may be able to set price equal to marginal cost, is the public sector's marginal cost curve "too high" compared with what the private sector could accomplish? If it is, the public sector is not achieving technical efficiency in production. (On the other hand, if a private sector monopolist does not have to worry about competition, might one not expect technical inefficiencies to creep into private sector monopolies, too?)

Granted, the state-owned natural monopoly is free to charge marginal cost, while the private natural monopoly is not. Yet private natural monopolies may face incentives to cut costs that are different from their government-owned counterparts.

An economist would predict that the decisions of managers within organizations will reflect the incentive structure that those managers personally face. If a manager's own salary and probability of promotion are based on his success in cutting costs within his production unit, then we would expect cost cutting to be

technical efficiency in production occurs when the least possible amount of inputs is used to produce a given level of output

his personal priority. Both privately owned and publicly owned enterprises may set cost cutting as an objective and structure incentives accordingly. If so, the decisions of publicly and privately owned firms are likely to be very similar. Furthermore, if the organization is a large one, junior managers will compete with each other for promotions, and senior managers can easily compare their subordinates' success in cutting costs. The organization thus is likely to be technically efficient in production (whatever its pricing decisions are).

The issue of assessing relative efficiency becomes more difficult when managers are asked to achieve other social objectives—such as environmental preservation or job creation or integrating disadvantaged groups into the labour market—as well as cost minimization. At least in the past, public sector managers have more frequently been asked to balance a multiplicity of such objectives than private sector managers. Although private sector firms may also espouse such goals in public relations rhetoric, in practice their objectives are usually one-dimensional, which may not produce better social outcomes, but which have the administrative advantage for the firm of providing a clearer criterion for the evaluation of managerial performance. The picture of managerial performance is necessarily more blurred when multiple objectives beyond profit maximization are being considered, leaving more room for managers to conceal their own mistakes.

The public policy dilemma is that if a public sector firm is asked to focus solely on cost minimization, its managers will generally behave in much the same way as private sector managers who are tasked with cost minimization, but other social objectives will not be achieved. If, however, managers are asked to balance multiple objectives, it will be more difficult to evaluate and reward their performance.

STATE REGULATION OF PRIVATE MONOPOLIES

The most common method of curbing monopoly profits is for government merely to regulate the natural monopoly rather than own it. Most provinces, for example, take this approach with electric utilities and natural gas providers. The standard procedure in these cases is called **cost-plus regulation**: Government regulators gather data on the monopolist's explicit costs of production and then permit the monopolist to set prices that cover those costs, plus a markup to ensure a normal return on the firm's investment. In terms of Figure 13.1, price is set equal to average total cost and output is Q_2. This is less than the socially optimal output level Q_1, but represents a big improvement on the monopoly output level Q_0 (and there is no need to find a way to cover the firm's financial losses from taxes, unlike the situation at Q_1).

cost-plus regulation a method of regulation under which the regulated firm is permitted to charge a price equal to its explicit costs of production plus a markup to cover the opportunity cost of resources provided by the firm's owners

Although it may sound reasonable, cost-plus regulation has several pitfalls. First, it generates costly administrative proceedings in which regulators and firms quarrel over which of the firm's expenditures can properly be included in the costs it is allowed to recover.

Traditionally, telephone service in North America was provided by privately owned monopolies, subject to government regulation. (In Europe and Australia, the policy choice was to provide telephone service through the public sector, typically by expanding the post office into a publicly owned post and telecommunications company.) This interference with the market was seen as justifiable—telephones were seen as the classic natural monopoly, since the cost of hooking up one more person to a telephone line that is already serving the neighbours is much less than the average cost of putting up the telephone pole and lines in the first place. Furthermore, the benefits of having a telephone increase with the number of other people whom each person can call; each subscriber is better off when other people also decide to have telephone service. For decades, charges on long distance calls were set much higher than cost to cross-subsidize residential telephone service—a practice encouraged by regulators, who wanted to ensure that access to local telephone service was within everyone's financial reach.

With rapidly accelerating technological change in the 1980s and 1990s, however, it became technically possible to have many long distance service providers, some of whom could provide much lower cost service, using new technologies like fibre optics or satellite transmission. Telephone companies also developed technology to provide new types of services (such as burglar alarms and call forwarding) through the telephone line. How can regulators continue to ensure that basic telephone service is provided at a reasonable cost? This question is difficult to answer even in theory. If local telephone service is subject to cost-plus regulation but other products and services provided by the same company are unregulated, many employees, from the president on down, are involved in both regulated and unregulated activities. How should their salaries be allocated between the two? The company has a strong incentive to argue for greater allocation to the regulated activities, which allows it to capture more revenue from captive customers in the local telephone market.

A second problem with cost-plus regulation is that it blunts the firm's incentive to adopt cost-saving innovations. If it does cut costs, regulators will require the firm to cut its rates. The firm gets to keep its cost savings in the current period, which is a stronger incentive to cut costs than the one facing a government-owned monopoly. But the incentive to cut costs would be stronger still if the firm could retain its cost savings indefinitely. Furthermore, in cases in which regulators set rates by allowing the monopolist to add a fixed markup to costs incurred, the regulated monopolist may actually have an incentive to *increase* costs rather than reduce them. Why not install gold-plated faucets in the company restrooms or allow selected employees to attend conferences in desirable vacation spots? Under cost-plus regulation, price will be marked up by the same percentage over costs regardless of whether or not costs are inflated. Outrageous though the thought may be, the monopolist may earn a higher profit by installing those gold-plated faucets.

Finally, cost-plus regulation does not solve the natural monopolist's basic problem, the inability to set price equal to marginal cost without losing money. Although these are all serious problems, governments seem to be in no hurry to abandon cost-plus regulation.

EXCLUSIVE CONTRACTING FOR NATURAL MONOPOLY

One possibility for dealing with natural monopoly is for the government to invite private firms to bid for the natural monopolist's market. The government could specify in detail the service it wants—cable television, fire protection, garbage collection—and have firms submit bids describing how much they will charge for the service. The low bidder wins the contract.

The firm's incentive to cut costs under such an arrangement is every bit as powerful as that facing ordinary competitive firms, but it does depend on there being competition among bidders to ensure that profits will not be abnormally high. If the government is willing to provide a cash subsidy to the winning bidder, exclusive contracting even allows the monopolist to set price equal to marginal cost.

Contracting out has been employed with good results for some services (e.g., garbage collection). Despite its attractive features, however, exclusive contracting is not without problems, especially when the service to be provided is complex or requires a large fixed investment in capital equipment. In such cases, contract specifications may be so detailed and complicated that they become tantamount to regulating the firm directly. And in cases involving a large fixed investment—electric power generation and distribution or service centre franchises on a freeway, for example—officials face the question of how to transfer the assets if a new firm wins the contract. The winning firm naturally wants to acquire the assets as cheaply as possible, but the retiring firm is entitled to a fair price for them. What, in such cases, is a fair price?

Garbage collection is a simple enough service that the costs of contracting out this function are not prohibitive. But in other cases, such costs might easily outweigh any savings made possible by exclusive contracting.

VIGOROUS ENFORCEMENT OF COMPETITION LEGISLATION

When the Soviet Union disintegrated in the early 1990s, many economists initially predicted that a surge in economic growth would accompany the abolition of communist central planning. Eastern Europe and the new nations of the former USSR had a well-educated populace and had made large investments in capital stock and infrastructure, so the factors of production (labour, human capital, and physical capital) were there. Instead, these countries experienced substantial declines in output and income. In fact, national income in the nations of the old Soviet Union fell continuously for 6½ years, to a level 50 percent below that of 1989. Even 11 years later, GDP was still 37 percent below its 1989 level.[2] Part of the reason is that much of the capital stock turned out to be of poor quality and design, but it has also become apparent that these countries lack the social and legal framework (the "social capital") that sustains a productive market system.

The importance of the social and legal framework can be illustrated by posing a hypothetical question. If you are running a factory that produces shoes and you discover that you are losing sales to a competitor, will you make the effort to improve designs, streamline the production process, cut costs, and deliver a better product at a lower price to win back market share? Or is it easier and quicker to hire an arsonist to destroy your competitor's factory? Or can you accomplish the same objective by spreading rumours about the diseases carried by your competitor's product?

Many observers note that in the absence of a generally accepted and enforced system of law—particularly competition law—*gangster capitalism* has become entrenched in much of the former Soviet Union. If laws about what is acceptable as a competitive strategy do not restrain some types of strategies, competition may become socially destructive. A well-designed legal framework will channel competitive behaviour into types of competition that are economically productive. Society as a whole has an interest in setting up a system of law that ensures that firms compete by innovating and cutting costs, and not by hiring better arsonists and more vicious rumour mongerers.

Destroying your competitor's factory is an extreme example of an obviously illegal (but very effective) strategy that can improve a firm's competitive position in the marketplace. However, society as a whole has a strong interest in making wasteful strategies (such as arson) illegal—thereby encouraging firms to try more socially productive methods (like product innovation). For that reason, arson and other crimes are suppressed by the judicial system, and the judicial system is supported by a common consensus that such "criminal" activity is unacceptable. In Canada, competition law and its administration and enforcement revolve around issues much more subtle than arson. For example, during 2000, the long struggle between Canadian Airlines (initially owned by Canadian Pacific) and Air Canada (initially a Crown corporation, but privatized in the 1990s) was resolved with the absorption of Canadian by Air Canada. The domestic air travel market in Canada became one dominated by a single carrier, and a large airline has significant advantages over its competitors (e.g., the ability to schedule frequent connecting flights).

Once it was established as the dominant carrier, Air Canada's shares initially rose rapidly in value, as the stock markets anticipated healthy dividends for Air Canada stockholders resulting from the carrier's ability to charge high fares (particularly for business travellers: the same-day return fare from Halifax to Ottawa was, for example, approximately $1200). However, those high prices also pre-

www.aircanada.ca
Air Canada

[2]Table 1.1 on Page 5 of Part 1. The World Bank, *Transition—The First Ten Years: Analysis and Lessons for Eastern Europe and the Former Soviet Union*, Washington, D.C.: The International Bank for Reconstruction and Development/The World Bank, 2002.

sented opportunities for new firms to enter the market. CanJet Airlines, for example, was quick to offer a fare of $77 one way ($154 return, any day with no weekend stayover required) on the Halifax–Ottawa route.

Where natural monopoly is not present, the prospect of monopoly profits can lead firms to undertake actions that limit competition. Under Canadian competition law, *predatory pricing* is illegal, but competitive pricing is perfectly legitimate. Dominant firms are not allowed to set an artificially low price below their cost of production for the express purpose of squeezing competitors out of the market. Laws against predatory pricing are necessary to maintain competition because otherwise a dominant firm could scare off rivals by threatening potential competitors with a devastating price war should they challenge its position. A dominant firm that is willing to take temporary losses in a price war can, in the long run, continue to charge excessively high prices by deterring potential competitors.

However, firms are allowed—indeed, are encouraged—to match the market and to pass on cost savings. If a large carrier can offer lower fares because it has lower costs, the public interest demands that it be allowed to do so. When Air Canada cut its prices drastically on those routes and times that CanJet serviced at the same time as CanJet opened for business, CanJet protested that this was predatory pricing (Air Canada argued that it was just being competitive).

Distinguishing between activities that restrain competition or encourage competition is a never-ending and subtle endeavour. Air Canada lost this particular case, and discount carriers have since dramatically increased their share of the Canadian air travel market. By 2003, Air Canada shares had collapsed as it filed for bankruptcy protection. Air Canada has laid off thousands of employees and contracted out services as it struggles to match the prices of its discount competitors. Consumers who live in Canada's major cities have benefitted from the remarkably low airfares generated by cutthroat competition, but the residents of outlying communities (where the traffic cannot support alternative carriers) now face high fares and reduced services. The general problem—ensuring that the competitive process is healthy and is channelled in socially constructive directions—remains.

RECAP | **PUBLIC POLICY TOWARD MONOPOLY**

The unregulated natural monopolist sets price above marginal cost, resulting in too little output from society's point of view (the efficiency problem). The unregulated natural monopolist may also earn an economic profit at the buyers' expense (the fairness problem). Policies for dealing with the efficiency and fairness problems of natural monopoly include government ownership and management, government regulation, and exclusive contracting. Vigorous enforcement of competition laws can thwart anticompetitive practices. Each of these remedies entails problems of its own.

13.2 MARGINAL COST PRICING OF PUBLIC SERVICES

Suppose the government decides to become the provider of a natural monopoly good or service. How much should it charge its customers? The theory of competitive supply, normally applied to perfectly competitive firms that can sell any quantity they choose at a constant market price (see Chapter 5), helps to answer this question. Consider Example 13.1, in which a local government supplies water to its residents.

EXAMPLE 13.1

What is the marginal cost of water in Red Bay?

Suppose that the municipal water supply company in Red Bay, Labrador, has three potential sources of water: an underground spring, a nearby lake, and the Atlantic Ocean. The spring can supply up to 1 million litres/day at a cost of 0.2 cents/litre. The lake can supply an additional 2 million litres/day at a cost of 0.8 cents/litre. Additional water must be distilled from the ocean at a cost of 4.0 cents/litre. Draw the marginal cost curve for water in Red Bay.

To minimize cost, the town will use the cheapest source of water first (the spring). Only when the quantity demanded exceeds the spring's capacity will the city turn to the next least expensive source, the lake; and only when the lake's capacity is exceeded will the city supply water from the ocean. The marginal cost curve will thus be as shown in Figure 13.2.

FIGURE 13.2

The Marginal Cost Curve for Water

The current marginal cost of water is the cost of producing an extra litre by means of the most expensive production source currently in use.

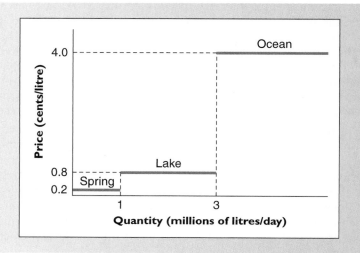

EXAMPLE 13.2

How much should the government charge for water?

In Example 13.1, suppose that if the price of water were 4.0 cents/litre, citizens of Red Bay would consume 4 million litres/day. Given the marginal cost curve shown in Figure 13.1, how much should the city charge a citizen whose water comes from the underground spring? How much should it charge someone whose water comes from the lake?

The citizens of Red Bay will enjoy the largest possible economic surplus if the price they pay for water exactly equals the marginal cost of providing it. Since the total amount of water demanded at 4.0 cents/litre exceeds 3 million litres/day, the city will have to supply at least some households with water distilled from the Atlantic Ocean, at a cost of 4.0 cents/litre. At 4 million litres/day, the marginal cost of water is thus 4.0 cents/litre, and *that is true no matter where the water comes from.*

This statement might seem to contradict the claim that water drawn from the spring costs only 0.2 cents/litre, water drawn from the lake, only 0.8 cents/litre. But there is no contradiction. To see why, ask yourself how much the city would save if a family that currently gets its water from the spring were to reduce its consumption by one litre/day. The cutback would enable the city to divert that litre of spring water to some other household that currently gets its water from the ocean, and that in turn would reduce consumption of ocean water by one litre. So if a family currently served by the spring were to reduce its daily consumption by one litre, the cost savings would be 4.0 cents. That, by definition, is the marginal cost of water.

To encourage the efficient use of water, the city should charge every household 4.0 cents/litre for all the water it consumes. Charging any household less than that would encourage households to use water whose marginal benefit is less than its marginal cost. For example, suppose the city charged households who get their water from the spring only 0.2 cents/litre. Those households would then expand their use of water until the benefit they received from the last litre used equalled 0.2 cents. Because that litre could have been used to serve someone who is currently using water distilled from the ocean, for whom the value of the marginal litre is 4 cents, its use would entail a loss in economic surplus of 3.8 cents.

EXERCISE 13.1

Suppose that at a price of 0.8 cents/litre the citizens of Red Bay would consume a total of only 2 million litres/day. How much should the city charge for water? Should that same charge apply to people who get their water from the spring?

The general rule is that a public utility maximizes economic surplus by charging its customers the marginal cost of the goods or services it provides. Example 13.3 provides another illustration of this principle.

EXAMPLE 13.3

How should electricity rates charged by an Ontario utility vary by season?

A government-owned electric utility in Ontario has two sources of power, a nuclear generator and a coal-burning steam generator. Electricity from the nuclear facility can be delivered to households at a cost of 2 cents/kilowatthour for any amount up to 4 million kilowatthours/day. Additional electricity can be produced in unlimited quantities by the steam generator, at a cost of 6 cents/kilowatthour. The company's daily demand curve for electricity during the summer months is $P = 4 - 2Q$, where P is the price in cents per kilowatthour and Q is the quantity demanded, in millions of kilowatthours per day. The demand curve for electricity in the winter months is $P = 12 - Q$. How much should this utility charge for electricity during the summer months? during the winter months? Should a family that receives its power directly from the nuclear generator during the winter months pay less than a family that receives its power from the steam generator?

As before, the efficient pricing rule is to set price equal to marginal cost, which depends on how much energy the utility produces each day. As shown in Figure 13.3, marginal cost *(MC)* is 2 cents/kilowatthour when production is between 0 and 4 million kilowatthours/day and 6 cents/kilowatthour when production

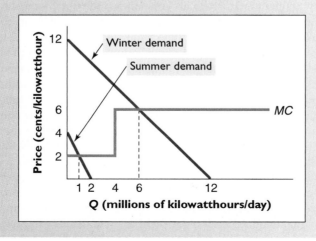

FIGURE 13.3
Seasonal Differences in Electricity Rates
The efficient price in each season is the one that equates marginal cost with seasonal demand. Given the two seasonal demand curves shown, the utility should charge 2 cents/kilowatthour in the summer months and 6 cents/kilowatthour in the winter months.

levels exceed 4 million kilowatthours/day. To sell power efficiently, the utility should view this marginal cost curve as its supply curve and charge the market-clearing price for each season. During the winter months, demand intersects marginal cost at a price of 6 cents/kilowatthour, so that is the price the utility should charge in the winter. During the summer months, demand intersects marginal cost at a price of 2 cents/kilowatthour, so that is the optimal price during the summer months.

Note that the optimal price during the winter months is 6 cents/kilowatthour for *all* families, even those whose electricity is supplied by the nuclear generator. If you were the public relations spokesperson for this utility, how would you respond to a family that complained it was being overcharged for the power it received from the nuclear generator in the winter? You might begin by pointing out how much the utility would save if it no longer had to supply power to this family. It could allocate the nuclear capacity this family used to some other family that would otherwise have been served by the steam generator, for a savings of 6 cents/kilowatthour. Whenever the utility has to supply more electricity than it can produce with the nuclear generator, the marginal cost of serving every user is 6 cents/kilowatthour.

EXERCISE 13.2

How would your answer to the question posed in Example 13.3 have differed if the winter demand curve had been $P = 8 - 2Q$?

RECAP	**MARGINAL COST PRICING OF PUBLIC SERVICES**

For a good or service—private or public—to be allocated efficiently, its price must equal its marginal cost of production. This principle tells us that when a public utility supplies water or electricity from several different sources, each with different costs, economic efficiency requires *all* users to pay a price equal to marginal cost. Marginal cost is determined by the highest-cost source in current use.

■ 13.3 WHY THE GOVERNMENT IS INVOLVED IN THE HEALTH CARE SECTOR

As we have said earlier, *scarcity* is the core problem of economics. The objectives of public policy on economic issues are efficiency and equity—to enable society to maximize the economic surplus that individuals can obtain from the production and consumption of scarce commodities, and to ensure the equitable distribution of that surplus. As we discussed in Chapter 7, in perfectly competitive markets the "invisible hand" of private sector competition can produce efficiency in the allocation of resources, with government's role limited to the protection of property rights. However, Chapters 8 and 9 also discussed the problems created by monopoly and imperfect competition, so the present chapter has considered some of the practical difficulties imperfect competition presents for public policy. And in Chapter 11, we considered imperfect information, which also has important public policy implications—the health care sector provides an example.

In Canada, as in almost all other developed countries, the government is heavily involved in the health care system (the United States is only a partial exception, since their Medicaid program provides health care insurance for many senior citizens and social assistance recipients).

Why do almost all societies treat the health care sector somewhat differently from the way they treat the construction industry? We let market forces organize most of our economic life because in many sectors the competition between alternative suppliers creates continual pressure for decreased costs and improved quality. When buying or selling a commodity of known characteristics—such as lumber of a particular grade—both buyer and seller can make their decisions based solely on price and can shop around for the best price. As we have argued in Chapter 7, a decentralized market process will, in these circumstances, usually converge to an equilibrium in which production costs are minimized. Total output will then be determined by the relative utility that consumers derive from one commodity compared to others.

The health care sector, however, is different. People buy lumber to build things they enjoy and they go to cinemas and restaurants because they derive utility from those activities, but they typically do not go to doctors because they enjoy it. Rather, people consult physicians because something unpleasant has happened to their health, and they want a diagnosis of the cause and some guidance as to the cure. Health care is dominated by **informational asymmetry** between consumer and producer; it is inherent in the doctor–patient relationship that the patient needs the physician because the doctor has knowledge that the patient lacks. Although the patient experiences the symptoms, the physician provides the diagnosis and suggests the remedy. If the patient knew enough to accurately assess the validity of the doctor's diagnosis and proposed remedy, the patient could self-medicate, and the physician's services would be unnecessary. Unlike markets for commodities whose characteristics are known by both buyer and seller, the market for health services exists because the purchaser of health care does not have the same level of knowledge as the seller. As well, insurers typically pay the bills for health care, even if it is individual consumers who get the benefits.

informational asymmetry occurs when two parties in a relationship do not have the same level of knowledge of product quality

HOW INFORMATION AFFECTS MARKETS

As we discussed in Chapter 11, markets work very differently when information is asymmetric. In the health care sector, the supplier of health care services (the physician) diagnoses the problem and prescribes the remedy while health care insurers pay most of the bills. The health economics literature has therefore long recognized the potential importance of the problem of supplier-induced demand and adverse selection in this sector of the economy.

The idea of "supplier-induced demand" refers to the ability of health care service providers to influence the level of demand for their services. When a doctor tells a patient that their ailment might be serious, and tells the patient to come back again next week for another examination, most people comply. As a result, *unlike other markets, in health care supply and demand are not independent.* For example, the best predictor of the number of surgical procedures of a particular type done in an area, even controlling for the general health of the local population, is the number of surgeons in the area who are qualified to do the procedure. Supplier-induced demand is only partly due to the economic motivation physicians have to recommend an operation for which they will be paid. We must also emphasize the professional uncertainty surrounding diagnosis; as the old saying goes, "If the only tool you have is a hammer, pretty soon every problem starts looking like a nail." Physicians diagnose the types of problems they were trained to solve in medical school.

In the Canadian health care system, physicians are the gatekeepers to specialists, prescription drugs, and hospital services, all of which can only be obtained on the recommendation of a doctor. As a result, physicians initiate more than 90 percent of the costs of the health care sector, leaving relatively little room for the possible impact of consumer choice by patients.

In one episode of the TV series "The Simpsons," Homer thinks he needs a heart transplant and, when he sees an advertisement of a "Special Sale Price" for heart transplants of $179.95, he signs up for this bargain. (Fortunately for Homer, on the day of the operation, Lisa is able to read up on what should be done and finishes the job.) When the "quality" of a service is important but hard for the consumer to judge before purchasing, the price charged may become a signal of quality. Because the information available in the health care sector is so different from the information available in markets for standardized commodities, these markets function differently. In the market for lumber, the grading standards of the industry ensure that everyone knows the quality of each piece of lumber, so the price charged serves as a rationing device to allocate that lumber to its most productive use. In the market for physicians' services, the price signal plays two roles. The price charged by individual health care providers serves both as a signal of their relative quality *and* as a mechanism for rationing access to their services. Thus, even when consumers know what medical procedure they want, those who want "the best" will often choose the highest-priced physician because they take high price to be an indicator of high quality. As a result, consumer choice cannot possibly produce the same pressures for cost minimization as in normal commodity markets.

In short, because of the informational structure inherent in the health care sector, the rational pursuit of perceived self-interest by individuals would generate a very different market equilibrium than it does in the market for lumber. But health care is also expensive. Given the potential cost of medical services, rational individuals will generally want to insure themselves against the risk of catastrophic health expenses, but the private market for individual health insurance also faces the informational problem of adverse selection.

adverse selection the pattern that occurs when, at any given cost of insurance, people with a greater expectation of loss buy insurance while people with a lower expected value of claims choose not to buy insurance

Adverse selection is just another example of the self-interest principle at work. It refers to the tendency, in insurance markets, for people who expect to make claims to sign up for insurance and for people who do not expect to claim not to sign up (and therefore not pay premiums). In the health care insurance industry, insurance companies make money on the healthy people they sign up and lose money on their sickly policyholders. Hence, their profitability depends on whether enough healthy people (who do not make many insurance claims) will pay the insurance premium.

In Chapter 11, we saw that car insurance companies have to charge the same premium to both careful and reckless drivers when they are "observationally equivalent"—i.e., when the insurance firm cannot tell them apart. Here again, the health sector is bedevilled by the problem of asymmetric information. Individuals may not know exactly what is wrong with them (they need the physician for that) but they do have some idea of their general state of health. However, they have no incentive to reveal all that they know to insurers, so the insurance company must charge the same premium to the pooled population.

At any given level of premiums for individual health care insurance, the relatively healthy will therefore tend not to purchase insurance. Although better information about their own health may mean that people are less vulnerable to "supplier-induced demand," better informed consumers are also better able to calculate their expected costs and benefits of private purchase of health care insurance—so adverse selection increases in importance. Those who expect to have large medical bills have an incentive to buy insurance, so the relatively ill will find it worthwhile to purchase a health care insurance policy. This self-selection of insurance purchasers means that if people buy individual policies, the purchasers of health insurance will tend to be a high-risk group. However, insurance companies that raise their premiums to cover their losses will simply drive away their lower-risk clients (i.e., the profitable ones).

The only way that private markets for health care insurance can work effectively is if low-risk and high-risk individuals are pooled together by some criterion unrelated to health, such as the fact that they all work for the same employer. Because of the problem of adverse selection for individual insurance, and because there are administrative savings involved in group health plans, it is cheaper for firms than for individuals to buy health care insurance. (As well, in both Canada and the United States, health insurance premiums are tax deductible.)

As a result, employers have an incentive to pay part of their employees' wages as an untaxed in-kind benefit, in the form of prepaid health insurance. Unlike normal commodities, whose purchase is decided on and paid for by the consumer, in both public and private health care, the service provider usually decides the level of services and also a third party usually pays the bills.

COST SAVINGS

Insurance companies are, of course, vitally interested in whether their company, or some other, has to pay a particular bill. Even if the employer provides health insurance to new employees, if their ailment already existed at the time of their hire, the costs of treatment might not be covered. Private insurance companies are also vitally concerned with underwriting—assessing the health care costs of each particular group of employees. Consequently, a multi-payer market-driven health care system contains significant incentives for firms to do a lot of detailed financial analysis and record keeping.

If health care is viewed as a basic right of citizenship and is financed from tax revenue, there is little point in detailed underwriting analysis and record keeping. As a result, a fundamental difference between the Canadian and American health care systems is that in Canada, the health care sector employs a much smaller ratio of clerical and financial workers. The differential in administrative and record keeping costs between the Canadian and U.S. health care systems is substantial. In 1999, health administration costs in the U.S. totalled $294.3 billion or $1059 (U.S.) per capita, compared with $307 (U.S.) per capita in Canada. This gap of $752 per person would add up to about $23.3 billion (U.S.) for Canada as a whole.[3]

These differences in administrative overhead are easily explicable by economic theory. The self-interest of each insurance corporation is to maximize its premium income and minimize its claims expense. Multiple-payer systems are therefore dominated by the attempts of individual insurers to offload health care risk, either to other firms or to individuals. Such strategies as denying coverage for preexisting ailments, screening of new clients, and experience rating of individual firms are privately profitable for firms, but these efforts to shuffle costs to another payer in a multi-payer system absorb administrative resources and do not effectively control aggregate expenditures.

Private sector health insurance may also have efficiency costs for the labour market and the broader economy. When preexisting ailments are not covered by a new employer's health plan, labour market mobility may decrease, since changing jobs might expose a family to long-term liability for uncovered health care costs. When quitting your job and setting up your own business involves sacrificing health care coverage for yourself and your family, many may think twice. In Canada, the availability of Medicare means that the decision to start a new business is not affected by health care insurance (and the percentage of the Canadian labour force that is self-employed is roughly twice as high as in the United States).

On average, Canadians have better health outcomes than Americans. Life expectancy at birth in Canada was 79.2 years in 2002, 1.2 years longer than the 78.0 year life expectancy of the United States. Life expectancy for a baby girl

---

[3]See S. Woolhandler, T. Campbell and D. Himmelstein "Costs of Health Care Administration in the United States and Canada," *New England Journal of Medicine*, Vol. 349, pp. 768–776, Aug. 21, 2003.

is somewhat higher, for a baby boy somewhat lower, than 79.2 years.) Out of one thousand male 15 year olds, 101 can expect to die before reaching the age of 60 in Canada, but 141 will die before 60 in the United States. For women, the adult mortality rate in 2002 was 57 out of 1000 in Canada, compared with 80 in the United States.

In Canada, total health care expenditure (public plus private) was about 9.5 percent of GDP in 2001, well below the 13.9 percent of GDP spent in the United States. Since the United States is spending a greater percentage of a higher average income on health care, the cost ratio in absolute dollars is even greater. Expressed in current U.S. dollars, the United States spent $4887 per person in 2001, or about twice as much as Canada (U.S.$2163). Interestingly, the burden on United States taxpayers of their fragmented system is in fact comparable to the burden on Canadian taxpayers. In the United States, public health expenditures by all levels of government were about 6.2 percent of GDP in 2001, compared with 6.8 percent in Canada.[4] Despite this expenditure, 17.3 percent of the non-elderly American population—43.3 million people—had no health insurance coverage in 2002.

As well, if the well-being of society depends on the level of inequality and insecurity faced by its citizens, the Canadian system has distinct advantages. Canadians do not have to worry about the chance of losing health care coverage, or about being ground down financially by deductibles and co-pay provisions during a long illness. Although the very affluent in the United States can purchase the very best of health care, others do without. Such inequality in care is inconsistent with the United Nations' Universal Declaration of Human Rights, which stated in 1948 that medical care is a basic human right.

However, Medicare in Canada is undeniably under pressure. Provincial treasurers face huge pressures to reduce public sector expenditures. Alberta has been particularly clear in advocating a shift to a more market driven health care model, but other provinces have also reduced the comprehensiveness of the Medicare system by decreasing coverage or tolerating the extension of clinics, facility fees, and other forms of co-payment. However, Canadian health economists such as Evans, Barer, and Stoddart[5] have argued that it is both a snare and a delusion to think that increased co-payment will assist the control of aggregate health care costs.

To the extent that the reduction of effective coverage under the public Medicare system makes an appreciable dent in public expenditures, a corresponding increase in the financial risks borne by individuals will necessarily occur. Those dependent on transfer payments and those without supplementary health insurance may have to do without health care. Others will use private insurance to guard against the increased risks of health care costs. Employer-paid group health plans are an advantageous way to purchase such supplementary insurance, especially since part of the cost is borne indirectly by government through the tax deductibility of health insurance premiums. Each small cut to direct public expenditure on Medicare is therefore matched by a corresponding small expansion of supplementary private health insurance coverage, indirectly financed by the ero-

---

[4]All figures are drawn from the World Bank website http://devdata.worldbank.org/dataonline/ (July 13, 2004).

[5]Stoddart, G.L., M.L. Barer, R.G. Evans, and V. Bhatia, *Why Not User Changes: The Real Issues* (Toronto: The Premier's Council on Health, Well Being and Social Justice, 1993); Evans, R.G., M.L. Barer, G.L. Stoddart, and V. Bhatia, *It's Not the Money, It's the Principle: Why User Charges for Some Services and Not Others?* (Toronto: Premier's Council on Health, Well Being and Social Justice, 1994); Evans, R.G., M.L. Barer, and G.L. Stoddart, *Charging Peter to Pay Paul: Accounting for the Financial Effects of User Charges.* (Toronto: The Premier's Council on Health, Well Being and Social Justice, 1994); Evans, R.G., M.L. Barer, G.L. Stoddart, and V. Bhatia, *Who Are the Zombie Masters and What Do They Want?* (Toronto: The Premier's Council on Health, Well Being and Social Justice, 1994); Stoddart, G.L., M.L. Barer, and R.G. Evans, *User Charges, Snares and Delusions: Another Look at the Literature* (Toronto: The Premier's Council on Health, Well Being and Social Justice, 1994).

sion of the income tax base. As the private insurance industry expands its role, the system as a whole drifts toward the U.S. model.

The tragedy in all this is that there is no incentive for individual insurers to ask, "In general, what is making people sick?" As long as they can get the same premium income, insurers *are* interested in improving the claims history of their own policyholders, but insurers are not interested in paying for some benefit that they would get anyway. Where, for example, seat belt laws exist, all health care insurance companies will have fewer claims from car accidents, but there is no way that an individual company could institute such a law. A private company has little incentive to incur significant expenses in promoting a general public health measure. General improvements in the health of the population as a whole will reduce the claims cost of the industry as a whole but will not give any particular company a competitive advantage.

Some of the biggest gains in public health can come from improvements in such things as early childhood care and nutrition, but the returns from such programs are far in the future and are too diffused in the general population to help the bottom line of any particular private insurance company. A better level of general health of the population will mean lower claims for insurance companies *in general*, but competition will also imply lower premiums. Since no individual private insurer can expect to see the benefits in higher profits of a higher *general* level of health, a health care system dominated by private insurers has a systematic tendency to underinvest in preventative public health. In essence, this is another illustration of the free rider problem discussed in Chapter 11. By contrast, a public system has the incentive to recognize interdependencies among the determinants of health and to invest in the general health of the population. But if our health care system becomes more fragmented, the opportunity for structural reform that provides the improvements to health care that Canadians want is lost.

❦ 13.1 ECONOMIC NATURALIST

Why do many states have laws requiring students to be vaccinated against childhood illnesses?

Even in a country with predominantly "free market" approach to health care such as the U.S., the state is heavily involved. For example, proof of immunization against diphtheria, measles, poliomyelitis, and rubella is now universally required for entry into American public schools. Most states also require immunization against tetanus (49 states), pertussis (44 states), mumps (43 states), and hepatitis B (26 states). Why these requirements?

Being vaccinated against a childhood illness entails a small but potentially serious risk. The vaccine against pertussis (whooping cough), for example, is believed to cause some form of permanent brain damage in 1 out of every 110 000 children vaccinated. Contracting the disease itself also poses serious health risks, and in an environment in which infections were sufficiently likely to occur, individuals would have a compelling reason to bear the risk of being vaccinated in order to reduce the even larger risk from infection. The problem is that in an environment in which most children were vaccinated, infection rates would be low, making the risk of vaccination loom large in the eyes of individual families. There is abundant empirical evidence that

when risks are quite small, many people react more strongly to the fact that *any* risk is mentioned, rather than to the quantitative importance of that risk—for example, many people would treat 1 chance in 100 000, 1 000 000 or 10 000 000 as all indicating *some* risk, without distinguishing the *level* of risk involved. However, the risk from infection still has to be balanced against the risk from vaccination. The problem is that as long as there is *any* risk from vaccination, each individual will rationally prefer that "everyone else" should get vaccinated, because the ideal situation from the perspective of any individual family is to remain unvaccinated in an environment in which all other families are vaccinated. However, as more and more families decide to forego vaccination, infection rates would mount. Furthermore, a decision to remain unvaccinated poses a risk not just to the individual decision maker, but also to others who have decided to become vaccinated (since no vaccine affords 100 percent protection against infection).

Relegating the vaccination decision to individuals results in a suboptimally low vaccination rate, because individual decision makers fail to take adequate account of the cost that their becoming infected will impose on others. It is for this reason that most states require vaccinations against specific childhood illnesses.

Even these laws, however, allow parents to apply for exemptions on religious or philosophical grounds. Communities vary in the extent to which parents avail themselves of these exemptions. In Colorado, for example, Boulder County heads the list of parents who opt to exempt their children from taking the pertussis vaccine (with an exemption rate of 8.4 percent, more than four times the rate statewide). Not surprisingly, the incidence of whooping cough is much higher in Boulder (34.7 cases per year per 100 000 people) than in the state as a whole (9.4 cases per year per 100 000 people).[6]

■ 13.4 ENVIRONMENTAL REGULATION

As we saw in Chapter 10, goods whose production generates negative externalities, such as atmospheric pollution, tend to be overproduced whenever negotiation among private parties is costly. Suppose we decide, as a society, that the best attainable outcome would be to have half as much pollution as would occur under completely unregulated conditions. In that case, how should the cleanup effort be distributed among those firms that currently discharge pollution into the environment?

The most efficient—and hence best—distribution of effort is the one for which each polluter's marginal cost of abatement is the same. To see why, imagine that under current arrangements, the cost to one firm of removing a metric ton of pollution from the air is larger than the cost to another firm. Society could then achieve the same total reduction in pollution at lower cost by having the first firm discharge one metric ton more into the air and the second firm one metric ton less.

Unfortunately, government regulators seldom have detailed information on how the cost of reducing pollution varies from one firm to another. Many pollution laws therefore require all polluters simply to cut back their emissions by the same proportion, or to meet the same absolute emissions standards. If different polluters have different marginal costs of pollution abatement, however, those approaches will not be efficient.

TAXING POLLUTION

Fortunately, alternative policies can distribute the cleanup more efficiently, even if the government does not know firms' costs. One method is to tax pollution and allow firms to decide for themselves how much pollution to emit. The logic of this approach is illustrated in Example 13.4.

EXAMPLE 13.4

What is the least costly way to cut pollution by half?

Two firms, Sludge Oil and Northwest Lumber, have access to five production processes, each of which has a different cost and produces a different amount of pollution. For this example, assume that changes in their costs of production and prices are sufficiently small that they can stay in business for all the pollution control options under consideration. The daily costs of the processes and the number of metric tons of pollution emitted are shown in Table 13.1. Pollution is currently unregulated, and negotiation between the firms and those who are harmed by pollution is impossible, which means that each firm uses process *A*, the least costly of the five. Each firm emits four metric tons of pollution/day, for a total of eight metric tons of pollution/day.

---

[6]Colorado Department of Public Health and Environment, *Vaccine Preventable Diseases in Colorado* http://www.cdphe.state.co.us/dc/Epidemiology/vaccinepreventable2000.pdf Figures are updated annually.

TABLE 13.1

Costs and Emissions for Different Production Processes

Process (metric tons of pollutant)	A (4 metric tons/day)	B (3 metric tons/day)	C (2 metric tons/day)	D (1 metric ton/day)	E (0 metric tons/day)
Cost to Sludge Oil ($/day)	100	200	600	1300	2300
Cost to Northwest Lumber ($/day)	300	320	380	480	700

The government is considering two options for reducing total emissions by four metric tons—i.e., by half. One is to require each firm to curtail its emissions by half. The other is to set a tax of $T on each metric ton emitted each day. How large must T be to curtail emissions by half? What would be the total cost to society under each alternative?

If each firm is required to cut pollution by half, each must switch from process A to process C. The result will be two metric tons/day of pollution for each firm. The increase in cost due to the switch for Sludge Oil will be $600/day − $100/day = $500/day. The increase in cost to Northwest Lumber will be $380/day − $300/day = $80/day. Requiring both firms to cut pollution by the same amount therefore has a total cost of $580/day.

Consider now how each firm would react to a tax of $T/metric ton of pollution. If a firm can cut pollution by one metric ton/day, it will save $T/day in tax payments. Whenever the cost of cutting a metric ton of pollution is less than $T, then each firm has an incentive to switch to a cleaner process. For example, if the tax were set at $40/metric ton, Sludge Oil would continue to use process A, because switching to process B would cost an additional $100/day but would save only $40/day in taxes. Northwest Lumber, however, would switch to process B, because the $40 saving in taxes would be more than enough to cover the $20 cost of switching.

The problem is that a $40/day tax on each metric ton of pollution results in a reduction of only one metric ton/day, three metric tons short of the four-metric-ton target. Suppose instead that the government imposed a tax of $101/metric ton. Sludge Oil would then adopt process B, because the $100 daily cost of doing so would be less than the $101 saved in taxes. Northwest Lumber would adopt process D, because for every process up to and including D, the cost of switching to the next process would be less than the resulting tax saving.

Overall, then, a tax of $101/metric ton would result in the desired pollution reduction of four metric tons/day. The total cost of the reduction would be only $280/day ($100/day for Sludge Oil and $180/day for Northwest Lumber), or $300/day less than when each firm was required to cut its pollution by half. (The taxes paid by the firms do not constitute a social cost of pollution reduction, because the money can be used to reduce whatever other taxes would otherwise need to be levied on citizens.)

The tax approach has the advantage of concentrating pollution reduction in the hands of the firms that can accomplish it at least cost. Requiring each firm to cut emissions by the same proportion ignores the fact that some firms can reduce pollution much more cheaply than others. Note that under the tax approach, the cost of the last metric ton of pollution removed is the same for each firm, so the efficiency condition is satisfied.

One problem with the tax approach is that unless the government has detailed knowledge about each firm's cost of reducing pollution, it cannot know how high to set the pollution tax. A tax that is too low will result in too much pollution, while a tax that is too high will result in too little. Of course, the government could start by setting a low tax rate and gradually increase the rate until pollution is reduced to the target level. But because firms often incur substantial sunk costs when they switch from one process to another, that approach might be even more wasteful than requiring all firms to cut their emissions by the same proportion.

AUCTIONING POLLUTION PERMITS

Another alternative is to establish a target level for pollution and then auction off permits to emit that level of pollution. The virtues of this approach will become clear in Example 13.5.

EXAMPLE 13.5

What will be the price of pollution permits?

Suppose the same two firms, Sludge Oil and Northwest Lumber, have access to the same five production processes described in Example 13.4. The government's goal is to cut the current level of pollution, eight metric tons/day, by half. To do so, the government auctions off four permits, each one of which entitles the bearer to emit one metric ton of pollutants/day. No pollution may be emitted without a permit. What price will the pollution permits fetch at auction, how many permits will each firm buy, and what will be the total cost of the resulting pollution reduction?

If Sludge Oil has no permits, it must use process *E*, which costs $2300/day to operate. If it had one permit it could use process *D*, which would save it $1000/day. Thus, the most Sludge Oil would be willing to pay for a single one-metric-ton pollution permit is $1000/day. With a second permit, Sludge Oil could switch to process *C* and save another $700/day; with a third permit, it could switch to process *B* and save another $400; and with a fourth permit, it could switch to process *A* and save another $100. Using similar reasoning, we can see that Northwest Lumber would pay up to $220 for one permit, up to $100 for a second, up to $60 for a third, and up to $20 for a fourth.

Suppose the auction starts at $90. Sludge Oil will then demand four permits and Northwest Lumber will demand two, for a total demand of six permits. Since only four permits are available, the price must increase until the two firms together demand a total of only four permits. Once the price reaches $101, Sludge Oil will demand three permits and Northwest Lumber will demand only one, for a total demand of four permits. Compared to the unregulated alternative, in which each firm used process *A*, the daily cost of the auction solution is $280: Sludge Oil spends $100 switching from process *A* to process *B*, and Northwest Lumber spends $180 switching from *A* to *D*. This total is $300 less than the cost of the original alternative, requiring each firm to reduce its emissions by half. (Again, the permit fees paid by the firms do not constitute a social cost of cleanup, because the money can be used to reduce taxes that would otherwise have to be collected.)

The auction method has the same virtue as the tax method—namely, that of concentrating pollution reduction in the hands of those firms that can accomplish it at the lowest cost. But the auction method also has other attractive features that the tax approach does not. First, it does not induce firms to commit themselves to costly investments that they will have to abandon if the cleanup falls short of the target level. Second, it allows private citizens a direct voice in determining where the emission level will be set. For example, any group that believes the pollution target is too lenient could raise money to buy permits at auction. By keeping those permits, while not exercising their right to emit pollution, the group could ensure that they will not be used to emit pollution.

Several decades ago, when economists first proposed the auctioning of pollution permits, reactions of outrage were widely reported in the press. Most of those reactions amounted to the charge that the proposal would "permit rich firms to pollute to their hearts' content." Such an assertion betrays a misunderstanding of the forces that generate pollution. Firms pollute not because they *want* to pollute, but because dirty production processes are cheaper than clean ones. Society's interest is in keeping the *total* amount of pollution from becoming excessive, not in *who* actually does the polluting. And in any event, the firms that do most of the polluting under an auction system will not be rich firms but those for whom pollution reduction is most costly. The U.S. acid rain program provides perhaps the best known example of trading in pollution permits, and there is growing interest in the approach in other countries.[7]

Of course, the auction of pollution permits is not a panacea. Essentially, a system of pollution permits uses the price mechanism to help solve a social problem. The key insight is that by setting up property rights and selling the right to emit a certain volume of pollutants, the government creates a situation in which those firms that have the lowest cost of reducing pollution are guided by their knowledge of their own technological options and their self-interest to reduce pollution the most. However, this model is not always feasible. A system of property rights typically has to have some mechanism of enforcement.

How successful would a system of pollution permits be in reducing pollution if firms just ignored their quotas? If firms actually emit more pollutants than their permit entitles them to, or if other firms and individuals pollute the atmosphere without having purchased permits, they are ignoring the law and essentially acting as if property rights in pollution do not exist. Similarly, if people who dine in restaurants leave without paying, they are ignoring the law—the restaurant owner will probably call the police. However, proving in a court of law that someone left a restaurant without paying is much easier than proving how much pollution a firm has produced over a period of time. Monitoring emission levels can be costly and uncertain, and takes resources to do properly. If the permit is for a certain amount of pollution per year, observation of pollution on any given day will not be enough, since excess pollution on one day could, in principle, be balanced by less pollution on other days (indeed, this could be a more efficient way for the firm to comply with regulations). Thus, taking offenders to court is costly and the outcome is often uncertain. Since enforcement is an activity that takes resources, the costs of that enforcement have to be compared with the efficiency gains to be had from enabling firms and individuals to trade pollution rights.

In practice, pollution permits work most effectively in situations where large amounts of pollution come from point sources (e.g., an oil refinery or a cement plant). However, a good deal of our air pollution comes from multi-point sources, such as private automobiles. A policy of tradable pollution permits is not really a feasible way of dealing with many small pollution sources. If all car owners had to buy pollution permits to cover their total emissions, the gains to be obtained from reallocating pollution among individual motorists would be relatively small and the costs of enforcement would be high. Since total emissions vary with the distance and speed of travel, each car would have to be monitored and policed, as well as inspected for its rate of emissions. Consequently, the environmental policy for private automobiles adopted in almost all countries is to require all cars to meet a specified target level of emissions and to periodically inspect the pollution control devices that keep emissions at that rate. It is recognized that the policy is not perfect, since people who drive more and faster are thereby allowed to pollute

[7]Peter Cramton, "A Review of Markets for Clean Air—The U.S. Acid Rain Program," by A. Denny Ellerman, Paul L. Joskow, Richard Shmalensee, Juan Pablo Montero, and Elizabeth M. Bailey, *Journal of Economic Literature XXXVIII*, pp. 627–633, September 2000.

more and since some gain might be realized from reallocating pollution rights among individuals, but the costs of implementing a more technically efficient pollution control policy are greater than the probable benefits.

COST–
BENEFIT

Generally, the cost–benefit principle applies to the choice of policies by government, as well as to the choice of production techniques by firms. If the administration costs of policy A are so much greater than the administration costs of policy B that they outweigh the improvement in outcomes associated with policy A, then policy B is the better choice. In environmental affairs this implies that a mix of policies—both standard setting (as in automobile emissions standards) and pollution permit auctions—are part of the package.

RECAP | **ENVIRONMENTAL REGULATION**

An efficient program for reducing pollution is one for which the marginal cost of abatement is the same for all polluters. Taxing pollution has this desirable property, as does the auction of pollution permits. The auction method has the advantage that regulators can achieve a desired abatement target without having detailed knowledge of the abatement technologies available to polluters.

13.5 LEGALIZED GAMBLING AND OTHER ADDICTIONS

In this chapter, we have noted that the desirability of public intervention depends on how well the market mechanism could otherwise be expected to allocate resources, and that often depends on the information structure of particular markets. In the pollution control case, if government knew what the pollution control costs of each firm were, it could simply allocate to each firm the pollution control target that is most efficient. However, in reality there are too many firms and technology is too complex for government to be expected to have such knowledge. Hence, creating a new market (in tradable pollution permits) can sometimes be an efficient way of solving the government's problem of lack of information. In this case, the market mechanism is a way of getting each individual firm to use their own knowledge of pollution costs, and their desire to maximize profits, to produce a socially efficient reduction in pollution.

In markets for health care services and insurance, however, the problem of information is different. Informational asymmetries are pervasive, and these markets cannot work in the same way as other commodity markets do when both buyers and sellers of a commodity know what they are buying and selling. Most nations have therefore decided that public provision must be a large part of a more efficient and equitable solution.

Two common elements in these examples are information and choice. The perspective of most economists is, in general, to let people choose for themselves, since they are likely to be the best judges of their own self-interest. However, in the case of health care, "consumer sovereignty" is impaired because information is imperfect in the sense that consumers cannot really know what they are getting. Without a medical education and years of experience, the patient cannot really know how good the physician's diagnosis and prescription are. Similarly, in workplace safety, the scientific complexity of many workplace hazards often makes risk assessment difficult. However, people themselves know what they want (to be healthy and uninjured), and they have good reason to want it.

Some other public policy issues pose deeper ethical and economic questions. What should public policy be when some people want something that is harmful to themselves and others but cannot anticipate that harm or cannot stop themselves from consuming? Should government intervene in markets when those markets are selling addictive goods or activities? If so, should governments attempt to stop such addiction or to profit from it?

Currently, governments in Canada and other nations prohibit the sale or possession of drugs like cocaine and heroin. Market transactions in these commodities are illegal, with heavy penalties for those convicted of trafficking. To prevent market transactions between willing buyers and sellers, governments spend billions on interdiction efforts and prisons, and the scarcity value of these drugs generates huge profit margins for those who are willing to run the risks of the trade. These opportunities for profit, in turn, fuel major criminal organizations whose turf wars for market area have cost many lives (e.g., the "biker wars" in Quebec) and corrupted the administration of justice in the nations where drugs originate.

In contrast, governments profit from the sale of tobacco and alcohol, which are also addictive. Taxes from alcohol and tobacco sales are a significant revenue source for all provincial governments, and in all provinces except Alberta, government-owned liquor stores have a monopoly on retail sales of alcohol, except wine.

Public attitudes toward markets in these commodities have changed. Although the U.S. attempt at stopping alcohol sales during the Prohibition Era of the 1920s is more famous, several Canadian provinces also experimented with partial or complete bans on alcohol around the same time. During the 1920s, the opportunity to export alcohol to the United States at artificially high prices also laid the foundations for the fortunes of several of Canada's now-respectable billionaire families. Attitudes to smoking have also changed dramatically in the past decade, as bans on smoking in public places attest. However, a particularly clear example of changing public policy is government's attitude to gambling.

Lotteries used to be illegal in every province. Recent years, however, have witnessed the steady proliferation of legalized gambling. Proponents of legalization call gambling a victimless crime. They argue that since neither bettors nor casino operators can be *forced* to gamble, any gambling that occurs must be a voluntary exchange that benefits all parties. In this view, gambling is just like any other form of entertainment; prohibiting it is like prohibiting the sale of basketball tickets.

Why, then, did most Canadian provinces and U.S. states originally enact laws to prohibit gambling? The apparent explanation is similar to the one for bans on the sale of heroin, cocaine, and other mood-altering drugs. Although many people—perhaps most people—appear to be capable of gambling in moderation, for a small minority gambling is a highly addictive activity. When the opportunity to gamble is freely available, many of these people will gamble to excess, jeopardizing their psychological health and, more important from the state's point of view, their ability to support and care for their families.

Before 1970, although gambling was officially against the law, the authorities made little attempt to prosecute people who gambled discreetly. At that time, virtually all gambling occurred surreptitiously. People who really wanted to gamble could find ways to do it, but those who wanted to avoid the temptation could easily steer clear. As legalized gambling has proliferated, however, problem gamblers have experienced more difficulty staying out of trouble. Casinos advertise heavily, and states and provinces themselves often promote their lotteries with sophisticated multimillion-dollar advertising campaigns, for example, television commercials portraying people's fantasies about winning the lottery ("I'd buy the company and fire my boss!").

Gambling is a potentially addictive activity that has gone from being clandestine and hard to locate to being widely available and actively promoted. Since people are now being urged to gamble with the most sophisticated marketing tools that modern advertising agencies can devise, we have to expect that more will start and be unable to stop and that the incidence of addiction will increase.

Addiction is a hard problem for economists to analyze, because economists generally analyze markets using the assumption that the tastes of consumers remain unchanged and that individuals are the best judges of their own self-interest. However, the process of addiction changes addicts in many ways and certainly changes the desire for the addictive substance or activity. Once addicted, they may recognize that they are destroying their own life and hurting all those whom they hold dear but be unable to stop. Before their addiction, they could not anticipate what it would do to them, or they would never have started, but the essence of addiction is that they cannot stop once they start. It is hard to say that addicts are acting "in their own best self-interest."

Over the past decade, tax revenue from casino gambling and lotteries has become an increasingly important part of provincial government revenues in Canada (amounting, for example, in Nova Scotia to 5.9 percent of own-source revenues in 2000–01). However, the lucrative nature of gambling as a revenue source is simply the flipside of the fact that gambling is a bad bet for those who participate; only about half the revenue from lottery ticket sales, for example, is paid out in prizes. Since it is often the relatively poor, who can least afford to lose, who are repeatedly drawn into the dream of a payoff that will change their lives, some analysts worry about the regressive nature of this revenue.

Should gambling be outlawed again? Should government make potentially addictive activities illegal, because *some* people suffer harm? Should government leave it to individuals to decide what they want to do, *knowing* that if it is left to market forces, some people will not be able to control their addictions? Should those people who are not addicted profit indirectly from the addictions of their fellow citizens? These questions raise fundamental moral issues, which go well beyond economics. However, economic analysis would predict that any province that attempted to outlaw gambling on its own would have serious difficulty. Residents of a province that did not sponsor a lottery or casino could still patronize lotteries in neighbouring provinces. The lottery-free province would then lose much of its tax revenue yet fail to re-create a nongambling environment. Each province confronts a decision to ban gambling much like the prisoner's dilemma discussed in Chapter 9. As we said at the beginning of this chapter, economics is useful because it can often help us to analyze the implications of our choices—but economics cannot tell us what our values *should be*.

■ SUMMARY

- **13.1** Our aim in this chapter was to apply basic microeconomic principles to a variety of government policy questions. We began by looking at the various policies governments employ to mitigate concerns about fairness and efficiency losses arising from natural monopolies. Such policies include government ownership and management of natural monopolies, government regulation, private contracting, and vigorous enforcement of antitrust laws. Each of these remedies entails costs as well as benefits. In some cases, a combination of policies will produce a better outcome than simply allowing natural monopolists to do as they please. But in other cases, a hands-off policy may be the best available option.

- **13.2** Basic economic principles can help to determine the optimal pricing policy when government is the direct provider of a service. We saw that the total economic surplus from the provision of a service will be largest if each user is charged the marginal cost of providing the service. In the case of public utilities, such a policy often entails charging different rates for similar services provided at different times.

- **13.3** Economic principles can also help to show how different methods of paying for health care affect the efficiency with which medical services are delivered. In the case of health care, the basic asymmetries of information in health care and insurance make a private multi-payer system both inefficient and inequitable.

- **13.3** A perennially controversial topic is the application of the cost–benefit principle to policies involving health. Many critics feel that the use of cost–benefit analysis in this domain is not morally legitimate, because it involves putting a monetary price on human life. Yet the fundamental problem of scarcity applies to health and safety, just as it does to other issues. Spending more on health and safety necessarily means spending less on other things of value. Failure to weigh the relevant costs and benefits, means that society will be less likely to achieve its stated goals in law enforcement, health care, workplace safety, and pollution abatement.

- **13.4** An understanding of the forces that give rise to environmental pollution can help to identify those policy measures that will achieve a desired reduction in pollution at the lowest possible cost. Both the taxing of pollution and the sale of transferable pollution permits promote this goal. Each distributes the environmental cleanup effort so that the marginal cost of pollution abatement is the same for all polluters.

- **13.5** Until the 1960s Canada had laws against gambling but did not vigorously enforce them. The implicit aim of those laws may have been to shield potentially vulnerable citizens from the temptation to gamble excessively, without preventing gambling entirely. In recent decades most provinces have actively promoted the sale of tickets in province-sponsored lotteries. One result has been a steep increase in compulsive gambling, which has led to renewed calls to declare gambling illegal. But the decision to ban gambling confronts provinces with a prisoner's dilemma. Any province that unilaterally outlawed it would lose substantial tax revenue without reducing gambling, for many citizens would simply patronize lotteries in neighbouring provinces.

KEY TERMS

adverse selection (366)
cost-plus regulation (358)

informational asymmetry (365)

technical efficiency in production (357)

REVIEW QUESTIONS

1. Since natural monopolists tend to produce less than the socially optimal level of output, does this mean that we should always try to break up natural monopolists into several smaller firms?

2. Why might pollution taxes and effluent permits be a more efficient way to curb pollution than laws mandating across-the-board cutbacks?

3. Does it make sense to require more sophisticated and expensive safety equipment in large commercial passenger jets than in small private planes?

PROBLEMS

1. In Ontario, citizens can get their electric power from two sources: a hydroelectric generator and a coal-fired steam generator. The hydroelectric generator can supply up to 100 units of power/day at a constant marginal cost of 1 cent/unit. The steam generator can supply any additional power that is needed at a constant marginal cost of 10 cents/unit. When electricity costs 10 cents/unit, residents of Ontario demand 200 units/day.
   a. Draw the marginal cost curve of electric power production in Ontario.
   b. How much should the city charge for electric power? Explain. Should it charge the same price for a family whose power comes from the hydroelectric generator as it does for a family whose power comes from the steam generator?

2. The municipal waterworks of Cortland draws water from two sources, an underground spring and a nearby lake. Water from the spring costs 2 cents/100 litres to deliver, and the spring has a capacity of 1 million litres/day. Water from the lake costs 4 cents/100 litres to deliver and is available in unlimited quantities. The demand for water in the summer months in Cortland is $P = 20 - 0.001Q$, where P is the price of water in cents per hundred litres and Q is quantity demanded in hundreds of litres per day. The demand curve for water in the winter months is $P = 10 - 0.001Q$. If the waterworks wants to encourage efficient water use, how much will it charge for water in the summer months? In the winter months?

3. Refer to Problem 2. By how much would daily total economic surplus go down if, in response to complaints from summer residents, the Cortland city council passed a law requiring all water to be sold at 3 cents/100 litres throughout the year.

4. Two firms, Sludge Oil and Northwest Lumber, have access to five production processes, each one of which has a different cost and gives off a different amount of pollution. The daily costs of the processes and the corresponding number of metric tons of smoke emitted are as shown in the following table.

Process (smoke)	A (4 metric tons/day)	B (3 metric tons/day)	C (2 metric tons/day)	D (1 metric ton/day)	E (0 metric tons/day)
Cost to Sludge Oil ($/day)	50	70	120	200	500
Cost to Northwest Lumber ($/day)	100	180	500	1000	2000

  a. If pollution is unregulated, which process will each firm use, and what will be the daily pollution emission?
  b. The city council wants to curb pollution emissions by 50 percent. To accomplish this, it requires each firm to curb its emissions by 50 percent. What will be the total cost to society of this policy?

5. The city council in Problem 4 again wants to curb emissions by half. This time, it sets a tax of T on each metric ton of pollution emitted per day. How large will T have to be to effect the desired reduction? What is the total cost to society of this policy?

6. Refer to Problem 5. Instead of taxing pollution, the city council decides to auction off four permits, each of which entitles the bearer to emit 1 ton of pollution/day. No pollution may be emitted without a permit. Suppose the government conducts the auction by starting at $1 and asking how many permits each firm wants to buy at that price. If the total is more than four, it then raises the price by $1, and asks again, and so on, until the total quantity of permits demanded falls to four. How much will each permit sell for in this auction? How many permits will each firm buy? What will be the total cost to society of this reduction in pollution?

7. Tom and Al are the only two members of a household. Each gets satisfaction from three things: his income, his safety at work, and his income relative to his roommate's income. Suppose Tom and Al must each choose between two jobs: a safe job that pays $100/week and a risky job that pays $130/week. The value of safety to each is $40/week. Each person evaluates relative income as follows: Having more income than his roommate provides the equivalent of $30/week worth of satisfaction, having less implies a reduction of $30/week worth of satisfaction, and earning the same income as his roommate means no change in satisfaction. Will Tom and Al choose optimally between the two jobs?

8. Refer to Problem 7. If Tom and Al could negotiate binding agreements with one another at no cost, which job would they choose? Suppose that negotiation is impractical and that the only way Tom and Al can achieve greater workplace safety is for the government to adopt safety regulations. If enforcement of the regulations costs $25/week, would Tom and Al favour their adoption?

■ ANSWERS TO IN-CHAPTER EXERCISES

13.1 At a consumption level of 2 million litres/day, the marginal source of water is the lake, which has a marginal cost of 0.8 cents/litre. The city should charge everyone 0.8 cents/litre, including those who get their water from the spring.

13.2 If winter demand were $P = 8 - 2Q$, all winter power could be provided by the nuclear generator, and the marginal cost of producing electricity would be 2 cents/kilowatthour during both the winter and summer months.

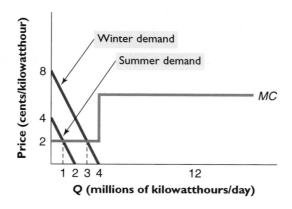

PUBLIC GOODS AND TAXATION

Up to now in this text, we have concentrated our attention on the supply and demand for goods in private markets. In private markets, individual consumers decide how much of each commodity to buy—and personally pay for—while profit-maximizing firms decide how much to supply. However, when governments decide how much of a good or service is to be produced, and when the cost is paid from taxes, that model clearly does not apply. For example, Canadian university students attend institutions that receive much of their funding from government. To get to class, they travel on roads provided by governments, sometimes in buses whose costs are subsidized by government. If they have an accident and are injured en route, they expect to be taken to a public hospital, but they also hope that this is unlikely—in part because they know that the police are directing traffic and keeping dangerous drivers off the road.

Schools, roads, hospitals, and police services are some examples of the many goods and services that we consume every day that are provided by government and paid for by taxes. In all these instances, we face the basic economic problem of scarcity. We would like to have smaller class sizes in universities, better roads, and less waiting time for hospitals but we cannot really expect to get more public services for free (i.e., without paying something more in taxes). We also cannot expect to get the same level of public services if we are not willing to pay the taxes necessary to finance them. We thus face a fundamental trade-off—higher taxes would enable the provision of more public services, but they would also imply less after-tax income available for private consumption.

Although there may be a broad consensus in contemporary politics that some government is necessary (and a general realization that this implies that some taxes are also necessary), debate rages over the appropriate size and functions of government.

How big, exactly, should government be? What goods and services should it provide? How should it raise the revenue to pay for them? What other powers should it have to constrain the behaviour of its citizens? And how should the various powers we assign to government be apportioned among local, provincial, and federal levels? Our goal in this chapter will be to employ the principles of microeconomics in an attempt to answer these pragmatic questions.

■ 14.1 GOVERNMENT PROVISION OF PUBLIC GOODS

One of the primary tasks of government is to provide what economists call **public goods**, such as national defence and the criminal justice system.

public good a good or service that, to at least some degree, is both nonrival and nonexcludable

PUBLIC GOODS VERSUS PRIVATE GOODS

Public goods are those goods or services that are, in varying degrees, **nonrival** and **nonexcludable**. A nonrival good is one whose consumption by one person does not diminish its availability for others. For example, if the military prevents a hostile nation from invading your city, your enjoyment of that protection does not diminish its value to your neighbours. A good is nonexcludable if it is difficult to exclude nonpayers from consuming it. For instance, even if your neighbours do not pay their share of the cost of maintaining an army, they will still enjoy its protection.

nonrival good a good whose consumption by one person does not diminish its availability for others

When the City of Toronto puts on a fireworks display to celebrate Canada Day, it is difficult to charge admission, because the display can be viewed from so many different locations in the city. And the fact that additional persons view the display does not in any way diminish its value to other potential viewers.

nonexcludable good a good that is difficult, or costly, to exclude nonpayers from consuming

In contrast, the typical private good is diminished one-for-one by any individual's consumption of it. For instance, when you eat a cheeseburger, it is no longer available for anyone else. Moreover, people can be easily prevented from consuming cheeseburgers they don't pay for.

EXERCISE 14.1

Which of the following, if any, is nonrival?
a. The Web site of Statistics Canada at 3 A.M.
b. The World Cup Soccer championship game watched in person.
c. The World Cup Soccer championship game watched on television.

Goods that are both highly nonexcludable and nonrival are often called public goods. Two reasons favour government provision of such goods. First, for-profit private companies would have obvious difficulty recovering their cost of production. Many people might be willing to pay enough to cover the cost of producing the good, but if it is nonexcludable, the company cannot easily charge for it (an example of the free-rider problem discussed in Chapter 11). Second, if the marginal cost of serving additional users is zero once the good has been produced, then charging for the good would be inefficient, even if there were some practical way to do so. This inefficiency often characterizes the provision of **collective goods** —nonrival goods for which it is possible to exclude nonpayers. Pay-per-view cable television is an example. People who do not pay cannot watch, a restriction that excludes many viewers who would have benefited from watching. Since the marginal cost to society of their tuning in is literally zero, excluding these viewers is wasteful. The waste is increased if it takes real resources to administer the pricing system, such as technicians to connect and disconnect subscribers.

collective good a good or service that, to at least some degree, is nonrival but excludable

A **private good** is one from which nonpayers can easily be excluded and for which each unit consumed by one person means one fewer unit is available for others. The theory of perfectly competitive supply developed in Chapter 5 applies to private goods, of which basic agricultural products are good examples. A **commons good** is a rival good that is also nonexcludable, so called because goods with this combination of properties almost always result in a tragedy of the commons (see Chapter 10). Fish in ocean waters are an example.

private good one for which nonpayers can easily be excluded and for which each unit consumed by one person means one fewer unit is available for others

The classification scheme defined by the nonrival and nonexcludable properties is summarized in Table 14.1. The columns of the table indicate the extent to which one person's consumption of a good fails to diminish its availability for others. Goods in the right column are nonrival, and those in the left column are

commons good one for which nonpayers cannot easily be excluded and for which each unit consumed by one person means one fewer unit is available for others

TABLE 14.1
Private, Public, and Hybrid Goods

	Rival	Nonrival
Nonexcludable	Commons good (fish in the ocean)	Public good (national defence)
Excludable	Private good (wheat)	Collective good (pay-per-view TV)

not. The rows of the table indicate the difficulty of excluding nonpayers from consuming the good. Goods in the top row are nonexcludable, those in the bottom row, excludable. Private goods (lower left cell) are rival and excludable. Public goods (upper right cell) are nonrival and nonexcludable. The two hybrid categories are commons goods (upper left cell), which are rival but nonexcludable, and collective goods (lower right cell), which are excludable but nonrival.

Collective goods are sometimes provided by government, sometimes by private companies. Most public goods are provided by government, but even private companies can sometimes find profitable ways of producing goods that are both nonrival *and* nonexcludable. An example is broadcast radio and television, which covers its costs by selling airtime to advertisers.

The mere fact that a good is a public good does not necessarily mean that government ought to provide it. On the contrary, the only public goods the government should even *consider* providing are those whose benefits exceed their costs. The cost of a public good is simply the sum of all explicit and implicit costs incurred to provide it. The benefit of a public good is measured by how much people would be willing to pay for it. Although that sounds similar to the way we measure the benefit of a private good, an important distinction exists. The benefit of an additional unit of a private good, such as a cheeseburger, is the highest sum that any individual buyer would be willing to pay for it. In contrast, the benefit of an additional unit of a public good, such as an additional broadcast episode of *This Hour Has 22 Minutes,* is the sum of the reservation prices of all people who will watch that episode.

www.cbc.ca
CBC

Even if the amount that all beneficiaries of a public good would be willing to pay exceeds its cost, that only implies that government should provide the public good in question. It is useful to distinguish between *provision* by government and *production* by government. For example, whereas city governments often pay for fireworks displays, they almost invariably hire private companies to put on these events. In fact, a mix of public servants and private sector employees produce many of the services provided by the public sector. For example, although defence is a public good provided by the state, from which all citizens benefit, that does not imply that all military jobs have to be done by government employees. The military often subcontracts aircraft or building maintenance to private firms.

Similarly, the operation of the criminal justice system is a public responsibility, but the government uses a mix of public and private employees. In choosing how much use to make of the private sector, there are many complex issues to balance. Although it is efficient to subcontract courthouse cleaning to private firms, some positions (such as judges) are hard to contract out, and other functions (such as the operation of prisons) are currently under strenuous debate. The proponents of increased subcontracting often argue that it can enable the public sector to use competition among private sector firms to restrain costs. Suppose competitive bidding by private sector firms is used to determine which private firm will win a contract to produce a service that is supplied by government (for example, the operation of a prison). If the private sector bidders want to maximize profits, they have a strong incentive to restrain costs. Opponents typically question the size of financial savings and point to other social costs. Governments often use the threat of subcontracting as a way of limiting public sector wage demands.

Generally, however, it is important to distinguish between *provision* and *production* by the public sector because even if we agree that the public sector should be responsible for the *provision* of a service, the optimal method of *production* of that service will often include private firms. This section focuses on the issue of whether the public sector should *provide* a service. The basic rule is that if the benefit of a public good does not exceed its cost, we are better off without it.

PAYING FOR PUBLIC GOODS

Not everyone benefits equally from the provision of a given public good. For example, some people find fireworks displays highly entertaining, but others simply don't care about them, and still others actively dislike them. Ideally, it might seem that the most equitable method of financing a given public good would be to tax people in proportion to their willingness to pay for the good. To illustrate this approach, suppose Chen values a public good at $100, Smith values the same good at $200, and the cost of the good is $240. Chen would then be taxed $80, and Smith would be taxed $160. The good would be provided, and each taxpayer in this example would reap a surplus equal to 25 percent of his tax payment: $20 for Chen, $40 for Smith.

In practice, however, government officials usually lack the information they would need to tax people in proportion to their willingness to pay for specific public goods. (Think about it: If you were asked how much you would be willing to pay to have a new hospital and you knew you would be taxed in proportion to the amount you responded, wouldn't you have an incentive to give a low number in order to pay low taxes, and let the cost be borne by those who say they are willing to pay?) Examples 14.1 to 14.3 illustrate some of the problems that arise in financing public goods and suggest possible solutions to these problems.

Will Prentice and Wilson buy a water filter?   **EXAMPLE 14.1**

Prentice and Wilson own adjacent summer cottages along an isolated stretch of shoreline on Lake Huron. Because of a recent invasion of zebra mussels, each must add chlorine to his water intake valve each week to prevent it from becoming clogged by the tiny mollusks. A manufacturer has introduced a new filtration device that eliminates the nuisance of weekly chlorination. The cost of the device, which has the capacity to serve both houses, is $1000. Both owners feel equally strongly about having the filter. But because Wilson earns twice as much as Prentice, Wilson is willing to pay up to $800 to have the filter, whereas its value to Prentice, a retired schoolteacher, is only $400. Would either person be willing to purchase the device individually? Is it efficient for them to share its purchase?

Neither will purchase the filter individually because each has a reservation price that is below its selling price. But because the two together value the filter at $1200, sharing its use would be socially efficient. If they were to do so, total economic surplus would be $200 higher than if they did not buy the filter.

Since sharing the filter is the efficient outcome, we might expect that Prentice and Wilson would quickly reach agreement to purchase it. However, if Wilson proposes that they just split the cost of the filter equally, it will yield a net benefit to him of $300 (= $800 benefit − $500 cost) but Prentice will turn the idea down because he would incur a net cost of $100 (= $400 benefit − $500 cost). Without some agreement on the sharing of costs, the joint purchase and sharing of facilities

is often easier proposed than accomplished. An additional hurdle is that people must incur costs merely to get together to discuss joint purchases. With only two people involved, those costs might not be significant. But if hundreds or thousands of people were involved, communication costs could be prohibitive.

With large numbers of people, the free-rider problem also emerges (see Chapter 11). After all, if there are thousands of people involved, the contribution of any one person is only a tiny percentage of the cost, so the project can go ahead without them. Thus, everyone knows that the project will either succeed or fail independently of any one person's contribution to it. Everyone thus has an incentive to withhold contributions—i.e., get a free ride—in the hope that others will pay.

Even when only a few people are involved, reaching agreement on a fair sharing of the total expense may be difficult. For example, Prentice and Wilson might be reluctant to disclose their true reservation prices to one another. Suppose Prentice can keep his own reservation price secret while getting Wilson to reveal that he would be willing to pay up to $800 for the filter. Prentice could then announce that he is willing to pay $205. He knows that the filter will be installed because Wilson will be better off paying $795 than with no deal at all. If Prentice can follow this strategy successfully, he will be better off by $195, and Wilson will be better off by $5, compared to the "no deal" option. In total, the consumer surplus of installing the filter is $200, and since Prentice pays much less than he would really have been willing to pay, he gets almost all of it.

Of course, as soon as Wilson figures this out, he will understate his true willingness to pay. Since both Prentice and Wilson have an incentive to play games with each other and to understate their personal benefits, the filter may never be installed at all.

These practical concerns may lead us to empower government to buy public goods on our behalf. But as Example 14.2 makes clear, this approach does not eliminate the need to reach political agreement on how public purchases are to be financed.

| **EXAMPLE 14.2** | **Will the government buy the water filter if there is an "equal tax" rule?** |

Suppose Prentice and Wilson from Example 14.1 could ask the government to help broker the water filter purchase. And suppose that the government's tax policy must follow a "nondiscrimination" rule that prohibits charging any citizen more than his or her neighbour for a public good. Another rule is that public goods can be provided only if a majority of citizens approve of them. Will a government bound by these rules provide the filter that Prentice and Wilson want?

A tax that collects the same amount from every citizen is called a **head tax**. If the government must rely on a head tax, it must raise $500 from Prentice and $500 from Wilson. But since the device is worth only $400 to Prentice, he will vote against the project, thus denying it a majority. So a democratic government would not provide the water filter if it must rely on a head tax.

head tax a tax that collects the same amount from every taxpayer

A head tax is an example of a **regressive tax** on income, one for which the proportion of a taxpayer's income that is paid in taxes declines as the taxpayer's income rises.

regressive tax a tax under which the proportion of income paid in taxes declines as income rises

The point illustrated by Example 14.2 is not confined to the specific public good considered. It applies whenever taxpayers place significantly different valuations on public goods, as will almost always happen whenever people earn significantly different incomes. An equal tax rule under these circumstances will almost invariably rule out the provision of many worthwhile public goods.

As Example 14.3 suggests, one solution to this problem is to allow taxes to vary by income.

Will the government buy the filter if there is a proportional tax on income?

EXAMPLE 14.3

Suppose that Prentice proposes that the government raise revenue by imposing a proportional tax on income to finance the provision of the water filter described in Example 14.1. Will Wilson, who earns twice as much as Prentice, support this proposal?

A **proportional income tax** is one under which all taxpayers pay the same percentage of their incomes in taxes. Under such a tax, Wilson would support Prentice's proposal, because if he didn't, each would fail to enjoy a public good whose benefit exceeds his share of its cost. Under the proportional tax on income, Prentice would contribute $333 toward the $1000 purchase price of the filter and Wilson would contribute $667. The government would buy the filter, resulting in additional surpluses of $67 for Prentice and $133 for Wilson.

proportional income tax a tax under which all taxpayers pay the same proportion of their incomes in taxes

The water filter in the previous example is not a pure public good. In this case, excludability is not a problem, since either Prentice or Wilson could buy the filter and not share its use. However, since the capacity of the filter is more than enough for both of them, not using it would be inefficient—their consumption is nonrivalrous. The water filter is thus best seen as a collective good, at the level of the neighbourhood.

In general, there are often aspects of "publicness" to many goods, the degree of which depends on the level of analysis. Housing is, for example, a private good for each household since it is both rival and excludable. However, although within families it is normal for bedrooms to be private, other rooms are typically common space. Furthermore, each house has some common attributes: for example, its location determines the travel times of all inhabitants and (unless each room has a separate thermostat) all the inhabitants enjoy (or tolerate) the same temperature, whatever that is. Thus, the common space, heating, location, and other aspects of the house can be seen as a "local public good" *for family members*. We can therefore see, at the family level, some of the problems of public goods provision and financing that are also present at the societal level. Just as equal contributions are often a poor way to pay for public goods, they are also often a poor way to share expenses within the household.

ECONOMIC NATURALIST   14.1

Why do spouses not contribute equally to joint purchases?

Suppose Frances earns $2 000 000 per year while Marcel earns only $20 000. Given that level of income, Frances as an individual would want to spend much more than Marcel would on housing, travel, entertainment, education for their children, and the many other items they consume jointly. What will happen if the couple adopts a rule that each must contribute an equal amount toward the purchase of such items?

This rule would constrain the couple to live in a small house, take only inexpensive vacations, and skimp on entertainment, dining out, and their children's education. It is therefore easy to see why Frances might find it attractive to pay considerably more than 50 percent for jointly consumed goods, because doing so would enable *both* of them to consume in the manner their combined income permits.

Public goods and jointly consumed private goods are different from individually consumed private goods in the following important way: *Different individuals are free to consume whatever quantity and quality of most private goods they choose to buy, but jointly consumed goods must be provided in the same quantity and quality for all persons.*

As in the case of private goods, people's willingness to pay for public goods normally increases with income. Wealthy individuals tend to assign greater value to public goods than low-income people do, not necessarily because the wealthy have different tastes but because they have more money. A head tax would result in high-income persons getting smaller amounts of public goods than they want. By increasing the total economic surplus available for all to share, a tax system that assigns a larger share of the tax burden to people with higher incomes makes possible a better outcome for both rich and poor alike. Indeed, virtually all industrialized nations have tax systems that are at least mildly **progressive**, which means that the proportion of income that is taxed actually rises with a family's income.

progressive tax a tax in which the proportion of income paid in taxes rises as income rises

Progressive taxation and even proportional taxation of income have often been criticized as being unfair to the wealthy, who are forced to pay more than others for public goods that all consume in common. The irony in this charge, however, is that exclusive reliance on head taxes, or even proportional taxes, would curtail the provision of public goods and services that are of greatest value to high-income families. Studies have shown, for example, that the income elasticity of demand for public goods such as parks and recreation facilities, clean air and water, public safety, uncongested roads, and aesthetically pleasing public spaces is substantially greater than one. Failure to rely on progressive taxation would result in gross underprovision of such public goods and services.

TABLE 14.2
A Summary of Different Types of Income Taxes

Head Tax	*Same dollar amount* paid by all taxpayers, regardless of income
Regressive Tax	Low-income taxpayers pay *higher percentage* of their income in tax than high income taxpayers
Proportional Tax	*Same percentage* of income paid by all taxpayers, regardless of income
Progressive Tax	Low-income taxpayers pay *lower percentage* of income in tax than high-income taxpayers

| RECAP | PUBLIC GOODS |

A public good is both nonrival and nonexcludable. Private firms typically cannot recover the costs of producing such goods because they cannot exclude nonpayers from consuming them. Nor would charging for a public good promote efficiency, since one person's consumption of the good does not diminish its availability for others.

Both obstacles can be overcome by creating a government with the power to levy taxes. Even high-income citizens often favour progressive taxes, because proportional or regressive taxes may generate insufficient revenue to pay for the public goods those taxpayers favour.

■ 14.2 THE OPTIMAL QUANTITY OF A PUBLIC GOOD

In the examples considered thus far, the question was whether to provide a particular public good and, if so, how to pay for it. In practice, we often confront additional questions about what level and quantity of a public good to provide.

Standard cost–benefit logic also applies to these questions. For example, according to the cost–benefit principle, Toronto will add another rocket to its Canada Day fireworks display if and only if the amount citizens would collectively be willing to pay to see the rocket is at least as great as its cost.

THE DEMAND CURVE FOR A PUBLIC GOOD

To calculate the socially optimal quantity of a public good, we must first construct the demand curve for that public good. The process for doing so differs in an important way from the one we use to generate the market demand curve for a private good.

For a private good, all buyers face the same price and each chooses the quantity they want to purchase at that price. Recall that to construct the demand curve for a private good from the demand curves for individual consumers, we place the individual demand curves side by side and add them horizontally. That is, for each of a series of fixed prices, we add the resulting quantities demanded on the individual demand curves. In Figure 14.1, for example, we add the individual demand curves for a private good, D_1 and D_2 [panels (a) and (b)], horizontally to obtain the market demand curve for the good D [panel (c)].

For a public good, all buyers necessarily consume the same quantity, although each may differ in terms of willingness to pay for additional units of the good.

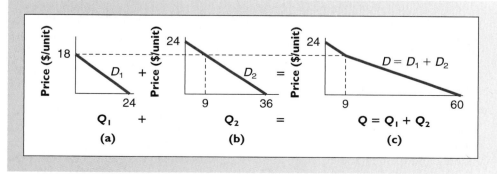

FIGURE 14.1

Generating the Market Demand Curve for a Private Good

To construct the market demand curve for a private good [panel (c)], we add the individual demand curves [panels (a) and (b)] *horizontally*.

Constructing the demand curve for a public good thus entails not horizontal summation of the individual demand curves but vertical summation. That is, for each of a series of quantity values, we must add the prices that individuals are willing to pay for an additional unit of the good. The curves D_1 and D_2 in Figure 14.2 panels (a) and (b) show individual demand curves for a public good by two different people. At each quantity, these curves tell how much the individual would be willing to pay for an additional unit of the public good. If we add D_1 and D_2 vertically, we obtain the total demand curve D for the public good [panel (c)].

FIGURE 14.2

Generating the Demand Curve for a Public Good

To construct the demand curve for a public good [panel (c)], we add the individual demand curves [panels (a) and (b)] *vertically*.

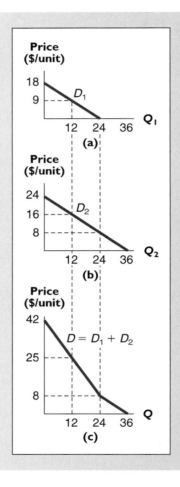

EXERCISE 14.2

Bill and Tom are the only demanders of a public good. If Bill's demand curve is $P_B = 6 - 0.5Q$ and Tom's is $P_T = 12 - Q$, construct the demand curve for this public good.

In Example 14.4, we see how the demand curve for a public good might be used in conjunction with information about costs to determine the optimal level of parkland in a city.

EXAMPLE 14.4

What is the optimal quantity of urban parkland?

The city government of a new planned community must decide how much parkland to provide. The marginal cost curve and the public demand curve for urban parkland are as shown in Figure 14.3. Why is the marginal cost curve upward sloping and the demand curve downward sloping? Given these curves, what is the optimal quantity of parkland?

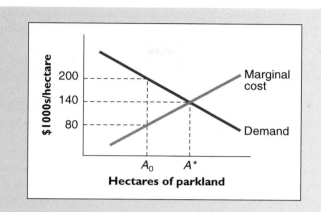

FIGURE 14.3
The Optimal Quantity of Parkland
The optimal number of hectares of urban parkland is A^*, the quantity at which the public's willingness to pay for additional parkland is equal to the marginal cost of parkland.

The marginal cost schedule for urban parkland is upward sloping because the city acquires the cheapest parcels of land first, and only then turns to more expensive parcels. Likewise, the marginal willingness-to-pay curve is downward sloping because of the law of diminishing marginal utility. Just as people are generally willing to pay less for their fifth hot dog than for their first, they are also willing to pay less for the 101st hectare of parkland than for the 100th hectare. Given these curves, A^* is the optimal quantity of parkland. For any quantity less than A^*, the benefit of additional parkland exceeds its cost, which means that total economic surplus can be made larger by expanding the amount of parkland. For example, at A_0, the community would be willing to pay \$200 000 for an additional hectare of urban parkland, but its cost is only \$80 000. Similarly, for any quantity of parkland in excess of A^*, the community would gain more than it would lose by selling off some parkland.

INCREASING
OPPORTUNITY
COST

PRIVATE PROVISION OF PUBLIC GOODS

One advantage of using the government to provide public goods is that once a tax collection agency has been established to finance a single public good, it can be expanded at relatively low cost to generate revenue for additional public goods. Another advantage is that because government has the power to tax, it can summarily assign responsibility for the cost of a public good without endless haggling over who bears what share of the burden. And in the case of goods for which nonpayers cannot be excluded, the government may be the only feasible provider.

However, governments are not the exclusive providers of public goods in any society. Indeed, many public goods are routinely provided through private channels. The challenge, in each case, is to devise a scheme for raising the required revenues.

Funding by Donation   In 2002 Canadians gave \$5.8 billion (about 0.5 percent of GDP) to private charities, many of which provide public goods to their communities. People also volunteer their time on behalf of organizations that provide public goods. As well, when you paint your house, mow your lawn, or plant a flower garden, you are enhancing the quality of life in your neighbourhood, and in that sense you are voluntarily providing a public good to your neighbours.

Furthermore, many Canadians voluntarily donate their time, as well as their money, to activities that benefit their community, rather than themselves personally. In everything from coaching youth soccer to providing meals on wheels to housebound seniors, Canadians depend heavily on the voluntary motivation of concerned citizens.

Why do people voluntarily provide their time and money to worthy causes? If we think of individuals as utility maximizing, the answer will be that the individuals who coach soccer or provide meals on wheels get some satisfaction from the idea that these social needs are being met. The problem, however, with relying entirely on the warm glow that volunteers get from their voluntary donations for these activities is the fact that others will also derive benefits. (For example, when volunteers coach youth soccer, the players benefit, and so do the other parents who like the fact their children enjoy soccer but who are too busy to coach.) Volunteers who maximize only their own utility will not take into account these benefits to other people. In consequence, under purely voluntary provision these services will be undersupplied.

Undersupply is a general problem with relying on private donations to provide public goods. For example, if road maintenance were to depend on voluntary effort to fill potholes, we can be sure that some people would voluntarily contribute their own time and resources to help solve the pothole problem. However, others would reason that since their own efforts cannot reverse the deterioration of the road system, they might as well just buy a sport utility vehicle with stronger suspension and more road clearance. Similarly, some people now devote their own time and resources to community recreation projects that divert youth from crime, while others try to protect themselves from robbery.

Development of New Technology In general, the boundary line between public and private goods depends partially on the available technology. If excludability is a criterion of whether or not something is a public good, then we must face the fact that the difficulty of excluding those who have not paid for a service depends on the available technology.

For decades, lighthouses have been used in economics texts as a classic example of a public good. Once a lighthouse is built, all boaters in the area can see its signal of the location of dangerous rocks (nonrivalrous consumption) and no vessel can be prevented from profiting from that information (nonexcludability). For centuries, lighthouses were the most practical way of warning ships about the proximity of hazards to navigation, and since the time of the Egyptian pharaohs, governments have generally paid for their construction.

In the 1990s, with the advent of global positioning satellite systems (GPS), a new technology became available to tell navigators how close they are to hazards. The launching of satellites is expensive, but once they are in place and broadcasting signals, the information they provide is still nonrivalrous in consumption. However, in principle, the signal could be scrambled, and a charge made for the sale of each receiver equipped with a decoder (i.e., location information would no longer be nonexcludable). This has not happened, and GPS signals are presently provided free to the world (courtesy of the U.S. military), but in principle, a charge could be made.

Similarly, TV and radio broadcast signals were classic public goods during the era when this was the only way that such signals could be sent and received. However, broadcast television stations now have the ability to scramble their signals, making them available only to those consumers who purchase or rent descrambling devices.

Private Contracting Some Canadians now live in gated private communities—private homeowners' associations which wall off contiguous properties and provide various services to residents. Many of these associations provide security services, schools, and fire protection and in other ways function much like ordinary local governments. Recognizing that individual incentives may not be strong enough to ensure socially optimal levels of maintenance and landscaping, these associations often bill homeowners for those services directly. Many of the rules imposed by these associations are even more restrictive than those imposed by local governments, a distinction that is defended on the grounds that people are always free to choose some other neighbourhood if they don't like the rules of any particular homeowners' association. Many people would be reluctant to tolerate a municipal ordinance that prevents people from painting their houses purple, yet such restrictions are common in the bylaws of homeowners' associations.

Sale of By-Products Some public goods are financed by the sale of rights or services that are generated as by-products of the public goods. For instance, as noted earlier, radio and television programming is a public good that is paid for in many cases by the sale of advertising messages. Internet services are also underwritten in part by commercial messages that appear in the headers or margins of Web pages.

Given the quintessentially voluntary nature of privately provided public goods, it might seem that reliance on private provision might be preferred whenever it proves feasible. But as the following example makes clear, private provision often entails problems of its own.

14.2 ECONOMIC NATURALIST

Why do television networks favour "Jerry Springer" over "Masterpiece Theater"?

In a given time slot, a television network faces the alternative of broadcasting either the "Jerry Springer Show" or "Masterpiece Theater." If it chooses "Springer," it will win 20 percent of the viewing audience, but only 18 percent if it chooses "Masterpiece Theater." Suppose those who would choose "Springer" would collectively be willing to pay $10 million for the right to see that program, while those who choose "Masterpiece Theater" would be willing to pay $30 million. And suppose, finally, that the time slot is to be financed by a detergent company. Which program will the network choose? Which program would be socially optimal?

A detergent maker cares primarily about the number of people who will see its advertisements and will thus choose the program that will attract the largest audience—here, the "Springer Show." The fact that those who prefer "Masterpiece Theater" would be willing to pay a lot more to see it is of little concern to the advertiser. But to identify the optimal result from society's point of view, we must take this difference into account. Because the people who prefer "Masterpiece Theater" could pay the "Springer" viewers more than enough to compensate them for relinquishing the time slot, "Masterpiece Theater" is the efficient outcome. But unless its supporters happen to buy more soap in total than the "Springer" viewers, the latter will prevail. In short, reliance on advertising and other indirect mechanisms for financing public goods provides no assurance that the goods chosen will maximize economic surplus.

Of course, the fact that the programs that best suit advertisers' needs may not be socially optimal does not mean that government decisions would necessarily be better.

One way to avoid the inefficiency that arises when advertisers choose programming is to employ pay-per-view methods of paying for television programming. These methods allow viewers to register not just which programs they prefer but also the strength of their preferences, as measured by how much they are willing to pay.

But although pay-per-view TV is more likely to select the programs the public most values, it is also less efficient than broadcast TV in one important respect. As noted earlier, charging each household a fee for viewing discourages some households from tuning in. And since the marginal social cost of serving an additional household is exactly zero, limiting the audience in this way is inefficient. Which of the two inefficiencies is more important—free TV's inefficiency in choosing among programs or pay TV's inefficiency in excluding potential beneficiaries—is an empirical question.

In any event, the mix between private and public provision of public goods and services differs substantially from society to society and from arena to arena within any given society. These differences depend on the nature of available technologies for delivering and paying for public goods, and also on people's preferences.

Why do detergent companies care more about audience size than about how much people would be willing to pay to see the programs they sponsor?

EXAMPLE 14.5

By how much is economic surplus reduced by a pay-per-view charge?

If "Mystery Theater" is shown on pay-per-view television at 10 P.M. on Thursdays, the demand curve for each episode is given by $P = 20 - Q$, where P is the price per household in dollars and Q is the number of households who choose to watch the program (in millions). If the regulated pay-per-view charge is $10 per household, by how much would economic surplus rise if the same episode were shown instead on "free" broadcast public TV?

With a fee of $10 per episode, 10 million households will watch (see Figure 14.4). But if the same episode were shown instead on broadcast public TV, 20 million households would watch. The additional economic surplus reaped by the extra 10 million households is the area of the blue triangle, which is $50 million. The marginal cost of permitting these additional households to watch the episode is zero, so the total gain in surplus is $50 million.

FIGURE 14.4

The Loss in Surplus from a Pay-per-View Fee
Twice as many households would watch the program if its price were zero instead of $10. The additional economic surplus is the area of the blue triangle, or $50 million.

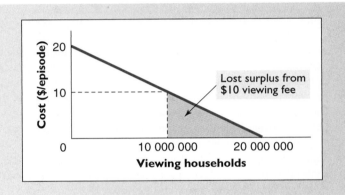

A similar situation arises when government departments charge fees for services that do not cost any extra resources to provide. For example, Statistics Canada, unlike its U.S. counterpart, charges substantial user fees for access to its data, well in excess of the cost of storing that data on its computers. As a result, Canadian citizens who cannot afford these user fees are prevented from getting data. Regardless of whether those data might have helped them to make better economic decisions or to represent themselves more effectively in public policy debates, a loss in economic surplus results from that less informed decision-making. And as this example illustrates, the loss in economic surplus from charging a price in excess of marginal cost is *not* an issue that depends on whether the provider of the service in question is a private firm or a government department. There is a loss in consumer surplus whenever a price is charged but consumption is nonrivalrous. If letting one more person consume a service has zero real resource cost, charging a price just prevents potential consumers from deriving a real benefit, while transferring revenue to the agency or firm.

In general, charging a positive price for a good whose marginal cost is zero will result in a loss in surplus. As we saw in Chapter 6, the size of the loss that results when price is set above marginal cost depends on the price elasticity of demand. When demand is more elastic, the loss in surplus is greater. Exercise 14.3 provides an opportunity to see that principle at work.

EXERCISE 14.3

How would your answer to Example 14.5 have been different if the demand curve had been given instead by $P = 15 - 2Q$?

HUMAN RIGHTS AS PUBLIC GOODS

In part, greater economic efficiency explains why Canadian governments are now involved in education and health. As we noted in Chapter 13, the Canadian system of public single-payer health insurance absorbs considerably fewer resources, but produces better average health outcomes, than the mix of public sector, individual, and private insurance company provision and payment extant in the United States. Similarly, the public sector provides schooling because it is inefficient for a society not to make use of the potential abilities of all its citizens. If parents have to pay for all the education that their children get, some parents will not be able to pay and some will not want to pay, even if they could. Historically, the argument for a system of high-quality public education was only partly driven by the high-minded ideal of equality of opportunity. Support for public schooling has always been partly based on a pragmatic concern that talent not be wasted. However, education and health care can also be seen as human rights issues.

Canadians like to feel that their society is a fair one, in which basic human rights are observed. And to a greater or lesser degree, they (like other nationalities) take pride in the accomplishments of their country or feel shame at its failures. Not only is there a vicarious enjoyment of the moments of triumph when Canadian athletes win medals or Canadian scientists win international prizes, but Canadians also care about Canada's human rights reputation. Since the human rights record and fairness of Canadian society is a source of utility that is freely available to all Canadians (i.e., nonrivalrous and nonexcludable in consumption), it can be seen as a public good.

Human rights are partly an economic issue, because making sure that rights are provided is often expensive. Guaranteeing the legal rights of the accused in the criminal justice system is, for example, costly. It is more expensive for governments to pay for judges and legal aid lawyers than it would be to assume that the police never make mistakes and just lock up whomever they arrest. It is rational for Canadians to spend money on maintaining human rights—both because individuals know that they personally may some day benefit from the protection of their personal rights and because of the utility that they get from knowing they live in a fair society.

Furthermore, when it comes to education and health care, a perception of fairness is important in part because it enables the affluent to conclude that their own advantages in life were justly acquired. *Equality of opportunity* is an important component of most conceptions of a fair society (indeed, it is explicitly recognized as an objective of Canadian governments in Article 36 (1) of the Constitution Act of 1982), but it is hard to see how a society where poor children were condemned to illiteracy and poor health could claim to offer meaningful equality of opportunity.

More specifically, the Universal Declaration of Human Rights of 1948 clearly identified health care and education as basic human rights:

> Article 25. Everyone has the right to a standard of living adequate for the health and well-being of himself and of his family, including food, clothing, housing and medical care and necessary social services, and the right to security in the event of unemployment, sickness, disability, widowhood, old age or other lack of livelihood in circumstances beyond his control....
>
> Article 26. Everyone has the right to education. Education shall be free, at least in the elementary and fundamental stages. Elementary education shall be compulsory. Technical and professional education shall be made generally available and higher education shall be equally accessible to all on the basis of merit.

Since somewhat similar wording is contained in the International Covenant on Economic, Social and Cultural Rights (1966) and other human rights treaties ratified by Canada, spending on health care and education can be seen as necessary to abide by Canada's international obligations to protect basic human rights. In economic terms, this produces the pure public good of Canada's record in human rights observance, which is valued to different degrees by different people.

ENVIRONMENTAL PUBLIC GOODS

Canadians also value the quality of the natural environment in which they live. Since no one has figured out how to charge for the consumption of clean air, and since each of us breathes an infinitesimal fraction of the air available, clean air is both nonrivalrous and nonexcludable—a classic public good. Consequently, regulation of pollution is another function of government. In Chapter 13 we discussed how economic principles can be used to control pollution in the most efficient manner possible. However, the problem of pollution is difficult to solve when the various sources of pollution are not subject to regulatory control by a single government. Much of the acid rain experienced in Canada, for example, is the result of sulphur dioxide emissions from industrial sources in the upper midwest of the United States. These emissions are beyond the reach of Canadian environmental regulations. In many instances, as with the discharge of greenhouse gases, not even a coalition of all the governments in North, Central, and South America would have the power to take effective action. Carbon dioxide emitted anywhere on the planet disperses to uniform concentrations around the globe in a matter of months.

The choice between different levels of government, then, often confronts us with difficult trade-offs. Ceding the power of taxation to a federal government often entails painful compromises for voters in individual provinces. But the loss of political autonomy is an even less attractive option. Similarly, nations are understandably reluctant to cede any of their sovereign powers to a higher authority, but failure to take such steps may entail unacceptable environmental costs in the long run.

RECAP   **THE OPTIMAL QUANTITY OF A PUBLIC GOOD**

A public good is nonrival and nonexclusive. Therefore, the quantity of a public good must be the same for every consumer, the total demand curve for a public good is constructed by adding individual demand curves vertically. Optimal production of a public good occurs at the quantity for which the demand curve intersects the marginal cost curve for the public good.

14.3 EXTERNALITIES AND GOVERNMENT

The provision of public goods is not the only or even the most important, rationale for the existence of government. Government also creates and enforces the rules without which the efficient production of private goods would not be possible.

As we saw in Chapter 10, for example, externalities often stand in the way of socially optimal resource allocation. We saw, too, that optimal allocations are unlikely to result whenever property rights are poorly defined (for example, the tragedy of the commons). These observations suggest the existence of two additional important roles for government: namely, the regulation of activities that generate externalities and the definition and enforcement of property rights.

These rationales for government action explain why most governments regulate activities that generate pollution, control access to fishing waters and public timber lands, and enforce zoning laws. Most laws, in fact, represent attempts to define property rights or to control externalities. The law requiring motorists to drive on the right, for example, is an attempt to prevent the activities of one motorist from causing harm to others.

However, the mere fact that an externality exists does not necessarily mean that the best outcome is for the government to regulate it. As we will see, regulation entails costs of its own. The ultimate question is therefore a practical one: Will government regulation of the externality in question do more good than harm?

RECAP	**EXTERNALITIES AND GOVERNMENT**

Government creates economic surplus not only by providing public goods but also by regulating activities that generate externalities and by defining and enforcing property rights. These rationales explain why most governments regulate pollution, control access to fishing waters and public timber lands, and enforce zoning laws.

14.4 RENT-SEEKING

A source of inefficiency in the public sphere occurs when the gains from a government decision are concentrated in the hands of a few beneficiaries, while the costs are spread among many. This means that beneficiaries often have a powerful incentive to organize and lobby in favour. Individual taxpayers, by contrast, have little at stake and therefore have little incentive to incur the cost of mobilizing themselves in opposition.

The Canadian pharmaceutical industry is one example. In the 1980s, local firms in Canada began manufacturing generic drugs under licence. These drugs did the same thing as the drugs made by multinational drug companies, but retailed at far lower prices. When the Mulroney government extended Canada's patent laws to restrict this, critics charged that there was a net loss to Canada since all Canadians paid higher drug prices while the profits flowed out of the country. However, since the industry promised to locate high-profile research facilities in Montreal, Members of Parliament from that area lobbied strongly for the change.

Still other sources of inefficiency arise in the case of projects whose benefits exceed their costs. Several years ago, for example, the federal government considered building a high-energy physics research facility (the "TRIUMF Facility"), which ignited an intense competition to be chosen as the site for this facility. Millions of dollars were spent on proposal preparation, consultants' fees, and various other lobbying activities. When such investments are mutually offsetting, they are known as **rent-seeking**, and they tend to be inefficient for the same reason that investments by contestants in other positional arms races are inefficient (see Chapter 10).

rent-seeking the socially unproductive efforts of people or firms to win a prize

RECAP	**RENT-SEEKING**

Government does much to help the economy function more efficiently, but it can also be a source of waste. Rent-seeking occurs when individuals or firms use real resources in an effort to win favours from the regulator.

■ 14.5 LOCAL, PROVINCIAL, OR FEDERAL?

Thus far in this chapter we have discussed government in the abstract, without being at all specific about which level of government is being considered. However, as a practical matter, in all countries public services are delivered by a variety of government agencies operating at several levels: national, regional, and local. In some countries, such as Sweden, the United Kingdom, and France, all these levels of government are created by acts of the national legislature. This type of government is called a *unitary* system, since the legislation that establishes regional and local government authorities can be amended by the national legislature at its discretion, and the national government can therefore decide how much power it wants to delegate to local authorities.

The Canadian system is different. Like many other countries (such as the United States, Australia, and Germany), Canada has a federal system of government and a constitution that establishes the jurisdiction and the powers of both the federal and provincial levels of government. Consequently, changes in the jurisdiction of the provinces and the federal government can only come about by mutual agreement or amendment of the constitution. These two levels of government must therefore constantly negotiate how to avoid duplication or conflict in overlapping areas of tax and program jurisdiction. Moreover, when there are multiple levels of government, politicians at each level are always exposed to the temptation of trying to claim credit for all successes while shifting the blame for all failures. Local politicians are also often tempted to divert discontent by protesting that their jurisdiction has somehow been unfairly treated in taxes or services or both. As the daily newspapers attest, many provincial and federal politicians in Canada are unable to resist these temptations.

Given the stresses and strains of federalism, why do we bother? Why not do away with continual negotiation and posturing for political advantage? Why not just have a single government that provides all public services?

The primary reason for having multiple levels of government is to better enable government to differentiate its delivery of services to meet the differing preferences and needs of local communities. For example, in Canada it has always been recognized that the majority of the residents of Quebec want to be educated in French, while in other provinces the majority prefer education to be delivered in English. As long as Quebec was a separate colony, its francophone majority could protect their desires for French-language education, but if a wider union, in which francophones were a minority, was to be established, there had to be some guarantee that education in French would not be at risk. The British North America Act of 1867 therefore assigned to the provinces exclusive control over education (and other social services). Ever since, the Government of Quebec has insisted on protecting the constitutional right to provincial jurisdiction over education, because it sees provincial control as essential to the continued existence of a distinct francophone culture in North America.

Language preference is just one aspect of the ways in which local communities may differ. Some communities may prefer to have soccer fields for youth sports while baseball may be more popular elsewhere. In some places, the preservation of historic buildings may be considered more important than speeding up traffic flow by widening roads, but other places may prefer to avoid traffic jams. The devolution of decision making on these and many other practical matters to the local level enables government to have a better chance of matching local decisions to local preferences.

However, although many useful activities of government are best designed at the local level, some others are most efficiently done at regional or national levels. It is, for example, extremely useful for businesses to have reliable and timely statistics on total sales (both in the economy as a whole and in their own industry), as a way of guiding their planning and investment decisions. However, it would be very inefficient for each municipality in Canada to design and administer its own survey of local business conditions, both because of the waste of duplicated design effort and because it would be impossible for survey results to be added up or compared, if each local jurisdiction asked slightly different questions in a different way.

There are, therefore, efficiency advantages to devolving some public activities to local or provincial levels while centralizing others. Although, in every federal country, the constitution establishes an initial division of jurisdiction and powers, these are not carved in stone. The courts can interpret the constitution to favour one level of government or the other and governments can agree to transfer power and responsibility (as, for example, in the 1990s when the federal government offered provinces control and funding of labour market training programs). In Canada, the balance between provincial and federal governments has changed over time, as economic conditions and policies have changed.

However, since the federal government has more sources of tax revenue available to it than the provinces do, some of the revenue raised by the central government has always been transferred to the provinces for their use. In fact, federal–provincial transfer payments were, initially, a much larger fraction of provincial revenues than they are today. At the time of Confederation, import tariffs and duties were the major revenue source for governments. However, if the separate colonies were to realize the economic benefits of free trade in a wider economic union, it was essential for them to give up their power to levy import taxes to the new Dominion of Canada—but for that to happen, the federal government had to agree to replace their lost revenues.

Over time the provincial governments developed new sources of taxation to meet the needs of a growing population for roads, wharves, and other public works. However, during the Great Depression of the 1930s, the provinces (particularly Alberta and Saskatchewan) found that although the need for relief payments grew dramatically, their capacity to raise revenue fell with depressed business conditions. The result was a crisis in provincial public finances, which the Rowell-Sirois Commission was appointed to examine. Before it could deliver its report (which recommended a major expansion of the federal government's role in maintaining national standards in education, health care, and public assistance), World War II created a massive surge of defence expenditure by the federal government.

For about 50 years after the war, total federal program spending fluctuated in a narrow range of about 15 percent to 16 percent of GDP, but since 1994, it has been significantly cut. Federal spending on programs was forecast at 11.5 percent of GDP in 2002–03.[1] However, that figure includes transfers to the provinces. If we look at federal expenditures on goods, services, and direct transfers to individuals, there has been an even sharper decline, to 8.3 percent of GDP in 2002–03, down considerably from 11.7 percent of GDP in 1989–90 (and substantially less than the 10.3 percent of 1949–50). As the Federal Budget of 2000 noted: "federal government spending, as percentage of GDP, is at its lowest level in 50 years." Since the government is committed to freezing government spending in real per capita terms at the same time as the economy is growing, federal government expenditure will continue to shrink as a percentage of Canada's economy.

By contrast, in the past 55 years provincial government expenditures have grown significantly. Although in 1949–50, direct federal spending dwarfed provincial government spending (10.3 percent compared to 5.8 percent of GDP), by 1969–70 the provinces and the federal government were close to a balance, and by 1989–90, federal expenditures were only about 70 percent of provincial government spending. For the last quarter of the twentieth century, the federal government was, in expenditure terms, the "junior order of government," and the disparity in size has increased with time.

---

[1] All figures from *Fiscal Reference Tables*, available online at www.fin.gc.ca/purl/frt-e.html.

This growth in provincial spending arose because the constitution assigned to the provinces jurisdiction over health care, education, and social spending, and these public services have grown in importance over time. The three main budget items of provincial governments are health care, education, and social assistance—as well as the financing costs of past debt. Added together, in 2003 they amounted to an average 71 percent of total provincial spending, leaving just 29 percent of spending to pay for all other services (roads, police and courts, parks, agricultural services, environmental regulation, etc.).

However, although public spending on health care (at 7.1 percent of GDP in 2002 to 2003) and education (5.6 percent of GDP) are the two biggest items of government expenditure in Canada,[2] neither is a pure public good from the point of view of the individual consumer. In neither case is it difficult to exclude people who have not paid from consumption of the services. In both health care and education, consumption is rival as well as excludable, since the space used for one patient or student is not available for another. Both these goods are therefore better analyzed as "publicly provided private goods," rather than "public goods" in the strict sense in which economists use the term. Indeed, during the nineteenth century and before, to the extent that health care and education were provided at all, private suppliers did most of the job.

■ 14.6 WHAT SHOULD WE TAX?

Although the primary purpose of the tax system is to generate the revenue needed to fund public goods and other government expenditures, taxes also have many other consequences, some intended, others not. For example, taxes alter the relative costs and benefits of engaging in different activities. They also affect the distribution of real purchasing power in the economy. The best tax system is one that raises the needed revenues while at the same time has the most beneficial, or least deleterious, side effects.

What impact do taxes have on incentives? As discussed in Chapter 6, taxes will hold production and consumption below socially optimal levels in markets where private costs and benefits are identical to social costs and benefits. Suppose, for example, that the long-run private marginal cost of producing cars is $10,000/unit and that the demand curve for cars is as shown in Figure 14.5. Equilibrium quantity and price will be 6 000/month and $10,000, respectively. If no externalities accompany the production or consumption of cars, these will be the socially optimal levels for quantity and price. But if we now add a tax of $2,000/car, the new equilibrium price and quantity will be $12,000 and 4 000, respectively. The loss in economic surplus will be equal to the area of the blue triangle ($2 million/month), which is the cumulative sum of the differences between what excluded buyers would have been willing to pay for extra cars and the marginal cost of producing those cars.

The loss in surplus caused by taxes like the one shown in Figure 14.5 is the basis of the argument that the economy would perform better if taxes were lower and total government expenditures were smaller.

However, as discussed in Chapter 6, even if a tax in a market like the one shown in Figure 14.5 did produce a loss in surplus for participants in that market, it might nonetheless be justified if it led to an even larger gain in surplus from the public expenditures it financed. We also saw in Chapter 6 that the deadweight loss from taxing a good (or activity) will be smaller the smaller the elasticity of demand or supply for the good. This principle suggests that deadweight losses could be minimized by concentrating taxes on goods with highly inelastic supply or demand curves. Thus, the prevalence of taxes on alcohol, tobacco, and gasoline, all of which have highly inelastic demands.

[2]see CANSIM TABLE 385-0001 (http://cansim2.statcan.ca/cgi-win/cnsmcgi.exe?Lang=E&RootDir=CII/&ResultTemplate=CII/CII_pick&Array_Pick=1&ArrayId=385-0001)

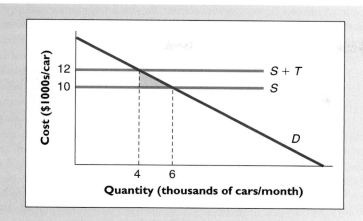

FIGURE 14.5

The Loss in Surplus from a Tax on Cars
If the supply and demand curves for cars embody all relevant cost benefits of producing and consuming cars, then placing a tax on cars will lead to under-production of them and a corresponding reduction in economic surplus.

In some instances taxes need not cause any loss in surplus at all, even in the markets in which they are directly applied. Suppose, for example, that in the market for cars considered earlier, private marginal cost is again $10,000 but the production and use of cars now generates air pollution and congestion, external costs that sum to $2,000/car each month. The socially optimal quantity of cars would then be not 6,000/month but only 4,000 (see Figure 14.5). Without a tax on cars, the market would reach equilibrium at a price of $10,000 and a quantity of 6,000/month. But with a tax of $2,000/car, the equilibrium quantity would shrink to 4,000/month, precisely the socially optimal number. Here, the effect of the tax is not only not to reduce total economic surplus but actually to augment it by $2 million/month. To that amount we would then add the additional monthly surplus made possible by the additional $8 million worth of public goods financed by the tax.

There are numerous other examples of taxes that might reduce external costs. For instance, when another car enters a congested freeway or downtown core, it creates additional delays for the motorists already there. As the example of the city of London illustrates (Economic Naturalist 10.4), it is possible to levy road-use taxes that reflect these congestion externalities. Each time fossil fuels are burned, they emit greenhouse gases into the atmosphere, which will accelerate the trend toward global warming. A tax on carbon would increase economic surplus by causing decision makers to take this external cost into account. Taxes on other forms of air and water pollution would have similarly benign effects on resource allocation. Recent experience with refundable taxes on food and beverage containers demonstrates that taxes like these can also raise needed revenue while at the same time contributing to a cleaner environment. Although it is unlikely that such taxes can ever more than partially replace those taxes that do cause a reduction in economic surplus, it is also true that their potential is far from being fully realized.

■ SUMMARY

- **14.1** Our aim in this chapter was to apply principles of microeconomics to the study of the government's role in modern society. One of government's principal tasks is to provide public goods, such as national defence and the criminal justice system. Such goods are, in varying degrees, nonrival and nonexcludable. The first property describes goods for which one person's consumption does not diminish the amount available for others, while the second refers to the difficulty of preventing nonpayers from consuming certain goods.

- **14.1** Goods that are both highly nonexcludable and non-rival are often called public goods. A collective good—such as pay-per-view cable television—is nonrival but excludable. Commons goods are goods that are rival but nonexcludable.

- **14.1** Because not everyone benefits equally from the provision of any given public good, charging all taxpayers equal amounts for the provision of public goods will generally not be either feasible or desirable. As in the case of private goods, people's willingness and ability to pay for public goods generally increases with income, and most governments therefore levy higher taxes on the rich than on the poor. Tax systems with this property have been criticized on the grounds that they are unfair to the wealthy, but this criticism ignores the fact that alternative tax schemes generally lead to worse outcomes for both rich and poor alike.

- **14.2** The economic criterion for providing the optimal quantity or quality of a public good is to keep increasing quantity or quality as long as the marginal benefit of doing so exceeds the marginal cost. One advantage of using the government to provide public goods is that once a tax collection agency has been established to finance a single public good, it can be expanded at relatively low cost to generate revenue to finance additional public goods. A second advantage is that because government has the power to tax, it can easily assign responsibility for the cost of a public good. And in the case of goods for which non-payers simply cannot be excluded, the government may be the only feasible provider.

- **14.2** One disadvantage to exclusive reliance on government for public goods provision is the element of coercion inherent in the tax system, which makes some people pay for public goods they don't want, while others do without public goods they do want. Some public goods are provided through private channels, with the necessary funding provided by donations, sale of by-products, by development of new means to exclude nonpayers, and in many cases by private contract. A loss in surplus results, however, whenever monetary charges are levied for the consumption of a nonrival good. In addition, reliance on purely voluntary provision will usually result in the undersupply of public goods.

- **14.3** In addition to providing public goods, government serves two other important roles: the regulation of activities that generate externalities and the definition and enforcement of property rights. Despite a general view that government is more responsive the shorter the distance between citizens and their elected representatives, factors such as economies of scale in the provision of public goods and externalities with broad reach often dictate the assignment of important functions to provincial or national governments.

- **14.6** To finance public goods and services, governments at all levels must tax. But a tax on any activity not only generates revenue, it also creates an incentive to reduce the activity. If the activity would have been pursued at the optimal level in the absence of a tax, taxing it will result in too little of the activity. This observation has led many critics to denounce all taxes as harmful to the economy. Yet the negative effects of taxes on incentives must be weighed against the benefits of the public goods and services financed by tax revenue. Furthermore, taxes on inelastically supplied or demanded activities may generate only small deadweight losses, while taxes on activities that create negative externalities may actually increase economic efficiency.

■ KEY TERMS

collective good (381)	nonrival good (381)	public good (381)
commons good (381)	progressive tax (386)	regressive tax (385)
head tax (385)	proportional income tax (385)	rent-seeking (395)
nonexcludable good (381)	private good (381)	

■ REVIEW QUESTIONS

1. a. Which of the following goods are nonrival?
    - (i)   Apples
    - (ii) Stephen King novels
    - (iii) Street lighting on campus
    - (iv) CBC radio broadcasts
    b. Which of these goods are nonexcludable?

2. Give examples of goods that are, for the most part:
    a. Rival but nonexcludable
    b. Nonrival but excludable
    c. Both nonrival and nonexcludable

3. Why might even a wealthy person prefer a proportional income tax to a head tax?

4. True or false: A tax on an activity that generates external costs will improve resource allocation in the private sector and also generate revenue that could be used to pay for useful public goods. Explain.

5. Consider a good that would be provided optimally by private market forces. Why is the direct loss in surplus that would result from a tax on this good an overstatement of the loss in surplus caused by the tax?

■ PROBLEMS

1. Jack and Jill are the only two residents in a neighbourhood, and they would like to hire a security guard. The value of a security guard is $50/month to Jack and $150/month to Jill. Irrespective of who pays the guard, the guard will protect the entire neighbourhood.
   a. What is the most a guard can charge per month and still be assured of being hired by at least one of them?
   b. Suppose the competitive wage for a security guard is $120/month. The local government proposes a plan whereby Jack and Jill each pay 50 percent of this monthly fee, and asks them to vote on this plan. Will the plan be voted in? Would economic surplus be higher if the neighbourhood had a guard?

2. Refer to Problem 1. Suppose Jack earns $1000/month and Jill earns $11 000/month.
   a. Suggest a proportional tax on income that would be accepted by majority vote and would pay for the security guard.
   b. Suppose instead that Jack proposes a tax scheme under which Jack and Jill would each receive the same net benefit from hiring the guard. How much would Jack and Jill pay now? Would Jill agree to this scheme?
   c. What is the practical problem that prevents ideas like the one in part (b) from working in real-life situations?

3. The following table shows all the marginal benefits for each voter in a small town whose town council is considering a new swimming pool with capacity for at least three citizens. The cost of the pool would be $18 per week and would not depend on the number of people who actually used it. The interest rate is 1 percent per week.

Voter	Marginal benefit ($/week)
A	12
B	5
C	2

   a. If the pool must be financed by a weekly head tax levied on all voters, will the pool be approved by majority vote? Is this outcome socially efficient? Explain.
   b. The town council instead decides to auction a franchise off to a private monopoly to build and maintain the pool. If it cannot find such a firm willing to operate the pool, then the pool project will be scrapped. If all such monopolies are constrained by law to charge a single price to users, will the franchise be sold, and if so, how much will it sell for? Is this outcome socially efficient? Explain.

4. Refer to Problem 3. Suppose now that all such monopolies can perfectly price-discriminate.
   a. Will the franchise be sold, and if so, how much will it sell for? Is this outcome socially efficient? Explain.
   b. The town council decides that, rather than auction off the franchise, it will give it away to the firm that spends the most money lobbying council members. If there are four identical firms in the bidding and they cannot collude, what will happen?

5. Two consumers, Smith and Jones, have the following demand curves for Podunk Public Radio broadcasts of recorded opera on Saturdays:

Smith: $P_S = 12 - Q$
Jones: $P_J = 12 - 2Q$,

where P_S and P_J represent marginal willingness to pay values for Smith and Jones, respectively, and Q represents the number of hours of opera broadcast each Saturday.
   a. If Smith and Jones are the only public radio listeners in Podunk, construct the demand curve for opera broadcasts.
   b. If the marginal cost of opera broadcasts is $15 per hour, what is the socially optimal number of hours of broadcast opera?

6. Suppose the demand curves for hour-long episodes of the "Jerry Springer Show" and "Masterpiece Theater" are as shown in the following diagram. A television network is considering whether to add one or both programs to its upcoming fall lineup. The only two time slots remaining are purchased by Colgate, which is under contract to pay the network 10 cents for each viewer who watches the program, out of which the network will have to cover its production costs of $400 000 per episode. (Viewership can be estimated accurately with telephone surveys.) Any time slot the network does not fill with "Springer" or "Masterpiece Theater" will be filled by infomercials for a weight-loss program, for which the network incurs no production costs and for which it receives a fee of $500 000. Viewers will receive $5 million in economic surplus from watching each installment of the infomercial.

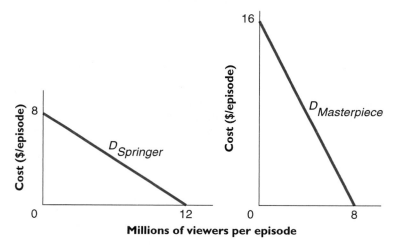

a. How will the network fill the two remaining slots in its fall lineup?
b. Is this outcome socially efficient?

7. Refer to Problem 6. By how much would total economic surplus be higher if each episode of "Masterpiece Theater" were shown on TVO free of charge than if it were shown by a profit-maximizing pay-per-view network?

8. When a TV company chooses a pay-per-view scheme to pay for programming, which of the following statements is true? Explain.
   a. The outcome is socially efficient.
   b. The programs selected will maximize advertising revenue.
   c. The marginal cost to an additional viewer of watching the programs is lower than when advertising is used to finance programming.
   d. The outcome is always more socially efficient than when advertising is used to finance programming.
   e. The variety of programs provided is likely to rise.

9. When a group of people must decide whether to buy a shared public good or service, the free-rider problem frequently occurs because:
   a. People have an incentive to understate how much the facility is really worth to them if they have to pay taxes to finance it.
   b. Each individual's needed contribution is an insignificant amount of the total required.
   c. People have an incentive to overstate how much the facility is worth to them if they don't have to pay taxes to finance it.
   d. People hope that others will value the facility enough to pay for it entirely.
   e. Only one of the above statements is not a reason for the existence of the free-rider problem.

10. The town of Smallsville is considering building a museum. The interest on the money Smallsville will have to borrow to build the museum will be $1000 per year. Each citizen's marginal benefit from the museum is shown in the following table, and this marginal benefit schedule is public information.

Citizen	Marginal benefit from museum ($/year)
Anita	340
Brandon	290
Carlena	240
Dallas	190
Emiko	140

   a. Assuming each citizen voted his or her private interests, would a referendum pass to build the museum and raise each citizen's annual taxes by $200?
   b. A citizen proposes that the city let a private company build the museum and charge the citizens a lump-sum fee each year to view it as much as they like. Only citizens who paid the fee would be allowed to view the museum. If the private company were allowed to set a single fee, would any company offer to build the museum?
   c. A second citizen proposes allowing the private company to charge different prices to different citizens and auctioning the right to build the museum to the highest bidding company. Again, only the citizens who pay the fee may view the museum. What is the highest bid a private company would make to supply the museum to Smallsville?

■ ANSWERS TO IN-CHAPTER EXERCISES

14.1 a. The Statistics Canada Web site at 3 in the morning is nonrival. It has the capacity to serve far more users than it attracts, so an additional user calling up the site does not prevent some other user from doing so. Other Web sites, however do not show the nonrival property, at least during certain hours, because they attract more users than their servers can accommodate.
   b. The stadium at the championship game is always full, so anyone who watches the game in person prevents someone else from doing so. It is rival.
   c. Additional people can watch the game on television without diminishing the availability of the telecast for others, making it nonrival.

14.2 To construct the demand curve [panel (c)], we first graph Bill's demand curve [panel (a)] and Tom's demand curve [panel (b)] and then add the two individual demand curves vertically. The equation for the demand curve is $P = 18 - 1.5Q$.

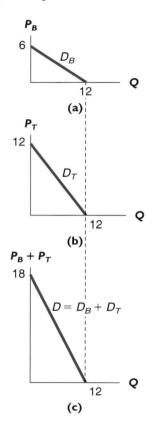

(a)

(b)

(c)

14.3 Whereas elasticity of demand was 1 at a price of $10 on the original demand curve, it is 1.5 on the new demand curve. As a result, the $10 fee now excludes 20 million viewers, and the resulting loss in surplus (again the area of the blue triangle) is now $100 million.

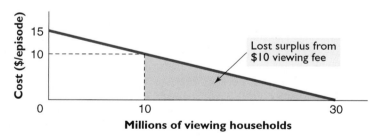

INCOME DISTRIBUTION

Some Canadians wake up in the morning in the opulent splendour of monster homes, where they can enjoy a quick dip in their indoor pool before a leisurely breakfast in the cathedral-ceilinged dining room. Every day they have economic decisions to make—investment decisions about the allocation of their stock portfolio, for example, or consumption decisions such as choosing whether to take the Porsche, the Mercedes, or the BMW when they go shopping.

On the same morning, other Canadians wake up on the sidewalk, trying to find a bit of privacy amid the street cleaners and pedestrians. The homeless also start their day looking for breakfast, but the first economic problem of their day is whether they can get enough change together for a coffee and a doughnut.

The vast majority of Canadians are somewhere in between—some wake up each morning in cramped apartments, some in small row houses, and some in larger single-family dwellings. All of them face the economic problem of allocating their income among the many competing possible expenditures available to Canadian consumers, but the income constraints that each faces differ enormously from the most affluent to the poorest.

Some degree of income inequality is present in all societies, but the extent of inequality varies quite a lot between nations, and has differed over time within Canada and other countries. All the economic policy issues that we have discussed in this text affect both the total output of society and the distribution of income. Thus, when economists discuss the objectives of economic policy, they routinely specify *"efficiency <u>and</u> equity"*—because good economic policy helps enable society to maximize the economic surplus that individuals can obtain from the production and consumption of scarce commodities, and also helps ensure the equitable distribution of that surplus.

But how "fair" is the distribution of income in Canada?

What (if anything) should we do about it?

If we are to answer these questions in a reasonable way, we need to know: (1) how much inequality and poverty there is in Canada now, (2) what criteria might help us to judge how much inequality would be "fair" and (3) what the costs and benefits of specific policies to reduce inequality and poverty might be. The objective of this chapter is to introduce some of the essential conceptual tools, and some of the basic data on trends and quantities, needed for analysis. Ultimately, though, each of us will have to come to a personal decision about "equity"—opinions clearly differ on this basic issue, and probably always will.

COST–BENEFIT

▇ 15.1 RECENT TRENDS IN INCOME INEQUALITY

In 2001, 6.5 percent of Canadian households received more than $100 000 in total income—coincidentally, the number who received less than $10 000 was about the same—6.2 percent. Those in the top end of the income distribution have a huge range of affluence, from salaried professionals to the billionaires who control much of Canadian media and industry. At the bottom, there is less room for differences among people who share a common reality of deprivation and an unrelenting inadequacy of income. The inequality in economic rewards that is at the heart of a capitalist system raises fundamental questions of equity and social policy—but is it true that the rich get richer while the poor get poorer?

In some countries, the answer has clearly been "yes." Since the early 1980s, some countries—particularly the United Kingdom and the United States—have seen a strong trend toward increased inequality in the distribution of income. In the United States, between 1978 and 1998, the incomes of the bottom 20 percent of Americans actually declined by more than 4 percent, while the incomes of the top 20 percent rose by more than 40 percent, and the incomes of the top 5 percent jumped by a dramatic 68 percent. The United Kingdom has witnessed similar trends. However, different countries make different choices in economic and social policy, and income distribution trends in Canada have not been quite the same.

Table 15.1 summarizes the long-term picture of income distribution in Canada. If we lined up all the families and unattached individuals in Canada in order of their income, and divided the line into five equal parts (or **quintiles**), we could ask: "What is the share of total money income (before tax) received by the poorest fifth? How much does the next 20 percent get? What share do the middle 20 percent get? the 20 percent who are second from the top? the top 20 percent?" Table 15.1 presents the answers.

**www.statcan.ca
Statistics Canada**

quintile that portion of a group of individuals that contains one-fifth of the total

---

TABLE 15.1

Share of Aggregate Incomes Received by Each Quintile of Families and Unattached Individuals

	1951	1961	1971	1981	1991	1996	2001
	(Percentages)						
Bottom 20% (poorest)	4.4	4.2	3.6	4.6	4.7	4.4	4.2
Second 20%	11.2	11.9	10.6	10.9	10.3	10.0	9.9
Middle 20%	18.3	18.3	17.6	17.6	16.6	16.3	16.0
Fourth 20%	23.3	24.5	24.9	25.2	24.7	24.7	24.1
Top 20 % (richest)	42.8	41.1	43.3	41.8	43.8	44.6	45.8

Sources: Adapted from the Statistics Canada publications *Incomes of Canadians*, Catalogue 99-544, 1968, *Income Distribution by Size in Canada*, 1997, Catalogue 13-207, April 14, 1999 and from Statistics Canada CANSIM database http://cansim2.statcan.ca Table 202-0701.

THE LORENZ CURVE

The problem with Table 15.1 is that it contains a lot of numbers that may not provide a clear answer to the question of whether inequality has decreased or increased. Fortunately, we can use Table 15.1 to construct a measure of overall inequality in any given year. If all Canadian households were lined up in order of income, from poorest to richest, and if we went part way down this line asking people their incomes, we could ask, at each point in the line, "How much of national income is, in total, received by all the people up to this point in the income distribution?"

If we have data on each individual family's income, we can get the answer exactly, but even if we do not have complete data, we can get a close approximation if we have a table like Table 15.1, which reports the income received by each 20 percent of the income distribution. We can also use a graph to present the answer visually. Using Table 15.1, we can easily plot the percentage of income received by the bottom 20 percent (4.2 percent in 2001) as point *A* in Figure 15.1. If we go a little further up the income distribution and ask how much of the nation's total income was received by the poorest 40 percent, we can find the answer by adding the top two entries from the last column of Table 15.1 (4.2 percent + 9.9 percent = 14.1 percent) and plotting it as point *B*. The total share of the poorest 60 percent can be calculated in the same way (4.2 percent + 9.9 percent + 16.0 percent = 30.1 percent) and plotted as point *C*. To get the share of the poorest 80 percent of families we just add 24.1 percent from Table 15.1 and plot the answer as point *D*. Connecting points *A*, *B*, *C*, and *D*, we get the solid line in Figure 15.1, which graphs the relationship between the cumulative percentage of income received on the horizontal axis, and the cumulative percentage of population on the vertical axis. (This line is called a **Lorenz curve**, in honour of the first person to draw the relationship in this way.)

Lorenz curve a graph that orders the members of a population from poorest to richest. The *Lorenz curve* plots on the *x* axis the percentage of the population below a given income, and on the *y* axis the cumulative percentage of total income received by them

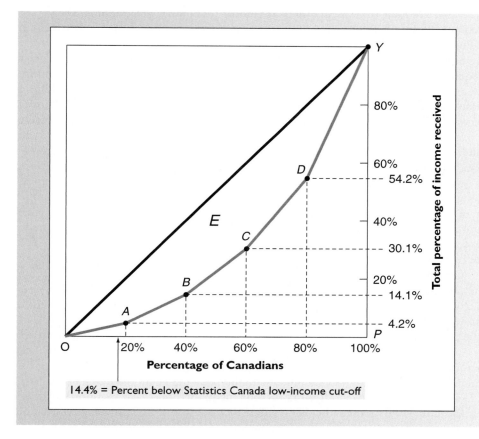

FIGURE 15.1

Canada's Income Distribution before Taxes, 2001

A Lorenz Curve

14.4% = Percent below Statistics Canada low-income cut-off

Since Table 15.1 presents data only on each fifth of the population, Figure 15.1 has straight segments and sharp corners, but if more data were available, the Lorenz curve would be smoother. If, for example, we had data available on the share of total income received by each 10th of the population, we could have drawn a Lorenz curve with ten flat segments rather than five, which would look much smoother; if we had data on individual families—what economists call *micro data*—the curve would be nicely rounded.

However, the main message of Figure 15.1 does not depend on its smoothness. Its main use is to compare the actual degree of inequality in different societies or at different points in time. To see this, suppose that everyone in society had the same income (perfect equality). In this case each 20 percent of families would get 20 percent of income. Since the bottom 20 percent would get 20 percent of income, while the bottom 40 percent would get 40 percent, and the bottom 60 percent would get 60 percent, and so on, the Lorenz curve would be the straight line OY of Figure 15.1. Alternately, if one person in society had all the income and the rest had nothing (perfect inequality), then the income share of the bottom 99.99 percent of the population would be zero. In this case the Lorenz curve would lie along the horizontal axis for almost all its length (line OPY).

THE GINI INDEX OF INEQUALITY

To summarize the extent of inequality, an Italian economist of the late nineteenth century—Corrado Gini—proposed a measure of inequality that has been used since. He realized that the area between the Lorenz curve and the line of perfect equality (area E in Figure 15.1) is zero if everyone has the same income (perfect equality). He also saw that if there is perfect inequality (one person has all the income) the area between the Lorenz curve and the line of perfect equality (area E in Figure 15.1) and the triangle OPY are the same, so their ratio will be one.

Since actual societies are somewhere between perfect equality and perfect inequality, Gini proposed that the *degree* of inequality in a society can be summarized by calculating the *ratio* of the area between the Lorenz curve and the line of perfect equality (area E in Figure 15.1) to the area of the triangle OPY. This is known as the **Gini coefficient.** When the Lorenz curve for one country lies entirely above the Lorenz curve for another, inequality comparisons are unambiguous. The country with the higher Lorenz curve has a lower degree of inequality. In this case, whether we want to look at the poorest 20 percent, the poorest 40 percent, or some other point in the income distribution, a larger share of total income is going to the less well off and it is straightforward to say that there is less inequality. (Notice that Table 15.1 can be used to compare the income shares of each quintile of households in 1996 and 2001. The income shares of the poorest 80 percent of the population were, in every instance, lower in 2001 than in 1996—so the trend to greater inequality in Canada is unambiguous.)

Over the past two decades, the Gini coefficient of total income in Canada has increased. Starting from 0.380 in 1982, it rose to 0.394 in 1991 and 0.417 in 2001. Of course, to get a better picture of inequality, we have to look more carefully at the data underlying Table 15.1. If we want an accurate idea of how much families can potentially consume, we should subtract the income tax they pay and compute the inequality in *disposable* income. Inequality in after-tax income is lower—it was essentially constant during the 1980s and early 1990s (the Gini index for after-tax income inequality was 0.351 in 1982 compared with 0.354 in 1994). However, after-tax income inequality increased substantially during the late 1990s, when the Gini index increased to 0.382 in 2001. Since the average family in Canada is now significantly smaller than it was 20 years ago, comparisons of *family* income over time will be misleading if we do not adjust family income to reflect the number of people who have to share a given family income. Since there are also significant differences across countries in average family size, international comparisons also have to be adjusted for family size. After making these adjustments for family size and direct taxes paid, we find that for Canada, the Gini index in the mid-1990s was about .084 less than the Gini index in the United States, while northern European countries like Norway and Finland had Gini indices that were about .065 less than those in Canada. In short,

Gini Coefficient an index, which ranges between zero and one, of the amount of inequality in a population. When all persons have the same income (perfect equality) it equals zero. When only one person has all the income (perfect inequality) it equals one. Graphically, it can be represented as the ratio of area between the *Lorenz Curve* and the line of perfect equality to the area of the triangle below the line of perfect equality.

Canada had less inequality than the United States, but more inequality than northern European nations.[1]

POVERTY

So far, we have considered the extent of *inequality* among all families in Canada, but *poverty* is a slightly different issue. Figure 15.1 also marks, on the horizontal axis, the proportion of the Canadian population that is considered poor. The most commonly used criterion for poverty in Canada is the "low-income cut-off" (LICO) of Statistics Canada. In 2001 some 14.4 percent of Canadians had incomes below that level. As can be seen from the vertical axis, in aggregate the people whose incomes were below the LICO received a little under 4 percent of the total income of Canadian households.

The LICO is not the only published poverty line in Canada and debate exists about exactly where the poverty line should be drawn.[2] However, all poverty lines imply that only a minority of the population are poor. (In fact, using the LICO one could equally well say that 14.4 percent of the population is poor or that 85.6 percent is not poor.) Since most members of the population are not poor, inequality among them is highly important. Families making $40 000 are above the poverty line, but they still have a lot more money pressures and a much lower living standard than the family of a bank president making $4 000 000. Inequality among the middle class, and inequality between the middle class and the very affluent, necessarily dominates inequality in the income distribution as a whole because, as Figure 15.1 illustrates, most of the Lorenz curve is drawn for the 85.6 percent of the population whose incomes are above the poverty line.

In describing trends in poverty, the most common statistic used in the popular press is the *poverty rate:* the percentage of the population whose incomes fall below the poverty line. However, the number of people who are poor is only one dimension of the problem. The seriousness of the poverty problem also depends on whether most poor people are mildly deprived, with incomes just below the poverty line, or very deprived, with incomes far below the poverty line. If we look just at the poverty rate, we will have no way of knowing how far below the poverty line the poor are, on average. Many analysts therefore also emphasize another dimension to the issue, the *average poverty gap,* which is the average shortfall between the actual incomes of poor people and the poverty line, as a percentage of the poverty line. Putting these two elements together provides a good index of poverty called *poverty intensity*, which is the product of both terms:

$$\text{poverty intensity} = (\text{poverty rate}) \times (\text{average poverty gap})$$

Poverty intensity is an indicator of poverty that can pick up shifts in the economy that the poverty rate would miss. If, for example, government were to cut social assistance payments, this would decrease the incomes of the most deprived. However, *when people who are already poor get poorer, the poverty rate does not change*. Since people on social assistance are already well below the poverty line, a cut to social assistance payments would not show up in the poverty rate. How-

**www.worldbank.org
World Bank**

---

[1]For further data see "International Comparisons of Poverty Intensity: Index Decomposition and Bootstrap Inference," L. Osberg with Kuan Xu, *Journal of Human Resources 35*(1), Winter 2000, pp. 51–81; errata corrected vol. 35, no. 3, Summer 2000.

[2]In 2002, a family of four living in a city with a population of half a million or more would be counted as "low income" if the total after-tax income for all family members was below $30,576. The LICO is revised each year to reflect any increase in consumer prices.

ever, poverty is worse, since the average poverty gap and inequality among the poor have both increased. Hence, a measure like poverty intensity is to be preferred, since it will increase when the depth of poverty increases.

THE POVERTY BOX

Poverty intensity is proportional to the area of the *poverty box*. The *poverty box* is a rectangle whose base is the *poverty rate* and whose height is the average *poverty gap*.

Figure 15.2 presents the "Poverty Box" in the year 2000 for Canada, Norway, and the United States, which are three of the world's most affluent nations. To compare poverty across countries, it uses the commonly recognized international standard that the poverty line in affluent countries should be set at one half the median household income (adjusted for household size). Since, in Canadian data, this calculation produces a poverty line that is in fact a bit lower than the Low Income Cut Off (LICO) of Statistics Canada, it suggests that the poverty rate in Canada in 2000 was a bit lower (11.2 percent) than the LICO would indicate (14.4 percent). However, the advantage of using this poverty line is that incomes can be compared with local norms of consumption.

FIGURE 15.2
Poverty Rate and Relative Poverty Gap   Canada, Norway, and The United States 2000

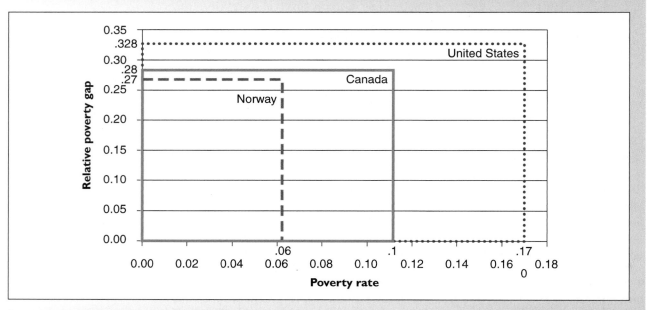

Source: Authors' calculations using the Luxembourg Income Study. Poverty Line = 1/2 Median equivalent household disposable income (After-Tax and After-Transfer Income).

Figure 15.2 indicates that these three countries are quite different in the fraction of the population that is poor—ranging from 6.3 percent in Norway to almost twice that in Canada and almost three times as high a poverty rate in the U.S. (17 percent). However, the three countries are much more similar in average depth of poverty (27 percent in Norway, 28.5 percent in Canada and 32.8 percent in the U.S.), for those people who are poor. In all three countries, both the poverty rate and the average poverty gap would be considerably higher if households had to depend solely on their labour market earnings and capital income (i.e., their "market income"). Figure 15.2 reflects "disposable income" (i.e., disposable income = market income − direct taxes + transfer payments), thus poverty intensity falls substantially. Although there is quite a bit of variation across states within the U.S., transfer payments tend to be somewhat lower there than in Canada, while Norwegian transfers are more generous. As we will discuss in more depth below, transfer payments (Canada Pension Plan, Old Age Security, and the Guaranteed Income Supplement) are particularly important in keeping Canadians over the age of 65 out of poverty—indeed, over the last forty years, the major success story of Canadian social policy has been a huge reduction in the poverty of Canadian senior citizens.

INEQUALITY AT THE TOP

In Canada, there has been a trend toward increased inequality of earned income but until 1994–95 this was largely offset by redistribution through taxes and transfers. Since then, inequality has increased sharply. In the United States, trends to greater inequality have been going on longer.

Executives' total annual pay packets in the United States have inflated more than in most other countries, but they have started to set a standard that corporate leaders in other countries envy. In Canada, John Roth and Clarence Chandran of Nortel topped the executive compensation rankings in 2000, with total pay packets of $70.8 million and $59.3 million, respectively. Both shareholders and employees of Nortel were a little unhappy with these numbers, since the next year saw a collapse of Nortel's stock price and the layoff of a third of the company's workforce. Frank Stronach of Magna International came third on the pay list in 2000, with a package worth $48.5 million. Overall, there has been a substantial increase in the share of total income received by the top 1 percent of Canadian taxpayers—almost doubling from about 7.5 percent in the late 1970s to 13.5 percent in 2000.[3]

▪ 15.2 WEALTH INEQUALITY

Strictly speaking, when we say that somebody is "rich," we mean that they have a lot of *wealth*. To calculate a person's wealth, we add up the value of all their assets (e.g., real estate, bank balances, stock holdings, etc.) and subtract the total amount of their liabilities (e.g., mortgages, personal debts).

Recent decades have witnessed dramatic growth and increased concentration of personal wealth. Wealth, of course, is a *stock* while income is a *flow*. Although the two are linked, they are not the same. To see the difference, think of your bathtub. The level of water in the bathtub is the *stock* of water you have available to bathe in at any given point in time, much like your *stock* of assets is the amount you could potentially consume at any given point in time. The *flow* of water into the tub from the tap is, like your income, the rate at which the stock tends to increase. But you will find that the more water you splash out of the tub (or the more you spend on consumption) the slower is the rate at which the stock increases. Thus, income and wealth are not the same, but they are always related by the following identity:

$$\text{income} - \text{consumption} = \text{change in wealth}.$$

[3]The Evolution of High Incomes in Canada, 1920-2000, Emmanuel Saez and Michael R. Veall, Working Paper 9607, http://www.nber.org/papers/w9607, National Bureau of Economic Research, April 2003

For some people, the distinction between income and wealth is very important. Seniors, for example, may have significant assets saved, but their current income from pensions and interest payments may be quite modest. Alternatively, someone with a high current income (such as a hockey player who has just made it to the NHL) may not have had much time to accumulate many assets. Nonetheless, wealth does produce income. People from a rich family will be wealthy because they will inherit assets from their parents; although they may never earn a particularly high income on their own, they receive interest and dividend payments from their assets.

Because large, unearned incomes strike many people as being unfair and because many believe in the social value of "equality of opportunity," most countries collect taxes on large inheritances to limit the concentration of wealth across generations. Canada is one of the few developed countries that has no estate or inheritance tax at present.

Reliable Canadian surveys of the distribution of wealth are infrequent; Statistics Canada did one in 1984 and another in 1999. Since the billionaires of this world are so few in number and likely to refuse to answer surveys, the wealth of the very rich is often missed in these surveys (and they do have a lot of wealth). Nevertheless, the available data clearly indicate that wealth inequality has increased in Canada. Figure 15.3 shows the wealth shares, and the change in wealth shares between 1984 and 1999, from the bottom to the top ten percent of households. The poorest fifty percent of households had, in total, 3.9 percent of net wealth in 1999—by coincidence, the *increase* in wealth share of the top ten percent of households (from 51.8 percent in 1984 to 55.7 percent in 1999) was also 3.9 percent.[4] The top 10 percent in 1999 had an average net worth of $980 804, which was an increase of 47 percent ($313 232) over 1984.[5]

FIGURE 15.3

Wealth Shares of Canadian Households

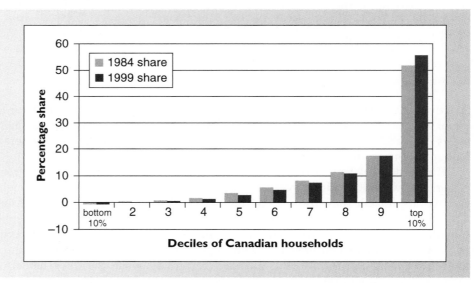

In general, there is more inequality in the wealth distribution than in the distribution of annual income—and the rich and poor differ in the type of assets they own as well as in the amount of assets. In 1999, as in previous years, the basic picture is 30-60-10. The poorest 30 percent of the population have essentially no assets (except perhaps automobiles, which are the most equally distributed type of

[4]*Source*: Table 5 "The Evolution of Wealth Inequality in Canada, 1984-1999" by René Morissette, Xuelin Zhang, and Marie Drolet. No. 187 Business and Labour Market Analysis, Statistics Canada 2003.
[5]Adapted from the Statistics Canada publication *The Assets and Debts of Canadians: An Overview of the Results of the Survey of Financial Security*, 1999, Catalogue Number 13-595, March 15, 2001.

asset but one that unfortunately depreciates) and that changes little over their lifetimes. For the 60 percent who are "middle class," the key asset is the family home. When someone can buy a house, and gradually pay off the mortgage, their net worth increases and they gradually work their way up the distribution of wealth. As they age, many people also acquire more consumer durables, and often an RRSP—but those who experience a divorce, major illness, or long spell of unemployment can sometimes be forced to liquidate their financial assets or home equity.

Although there has been some increase in the percentage of the population who own financial assets such as stocks, bonds, and mutual funds outside their RRSPs, this is still a distinct minority. Among Canadian family units aged 45 to 54 in 1999, for example, only 14 percent reported owning stocks and only 16 percent had mutual funds outside their RRSPs. Furthermore, most of these holdings are relatively small—only a few people have major money in the markets. Most financial assets are owned by the top 10 percent of households, who in total owned almost 56 percent of total net worth in 1999, up significantly from 1984.

The United States provides better data on wealth distribution and those data indicate an even bigger increase in wealth inequality. Wealth holdings for the richest 1 percent of Americans have roughly doubled since 1980. The combined wealth of the richest 1 percent of Americans now exceeds the combined wealth of the bottom 95 percent of Americans. The Forbes 400—the celebrated list of the 400 richest people in America—included 243 billionaires in 1998, up from 170 just a year earlier. In 1982 the list contained just 13 billionaires—five of them children of Texas oil tycoon H. L. Hunt. Together the Forbes 400 are worth more than U.S.$1 trillion, which is more than the national income of Canada, and more than the national income of China, a country of more than 1.3 billion people.

www.forbes.com
Forbes 400

To say that recent changes in the distributions of income and wealth have produced a fundamental shift in the North American economic landscape is hardly an exaggeration. People who had a lot of money to begin with have considerably more now, and many more people have a lot more money now than in the past.

In purely economic terms, those near the top of the income ladder are prospering as never before. In contrast, those farther down the ladder have seen their living standards grow much more slowly, or even decline.

RECAP	**RECENT TRENDS IN INEQUALITY**

Over the past 20 years, some countries—particularly the United States and United Kingdom—have seen very significant increases in economic inequality. In Canada, the increase in the income share of the top 20 percent has been smaller. There is a trend to greater inequality of labour market earnings, but transfer payments have been an offsetting influence. The Canada/Quebec Pension Plan and the Guaranteed Income Supplement have been particularly important in reducing the poverty of senior citizens in Canada. However, poverty among those under 65—and particularly the poverty of children—is a growing concern, and it is clear that the top 10 percent has received most of the gains in wealth of the past 15 years.

■ 15.3 HOW MUCH INEQUALITY WOULD BE "EQUITABLE"?

Thus far, we have described the inequality of outcomes, but we have not discussed why income and wealth are unequally distributed. To some extent, inequality of opportunity shapes the actual degree of inequality we observe. On entering the world, some people are born into penniless families while others can expect to inherit millions of dollars; some face discrimination while others do not; and some are born with disabilities while others are naturally talented. These differences in initial conditions may be accentuated, or diminished, over time by chance events (e.g., there is some chance that even the most naturally gifted person can get hit by a bus and be unable to work afterwards) and by personal and family choices (such as the decision to continue in school). As well, all societies make choices which affect economic inequality—such as whether or not to pass anti-discrimination legislation, to provide remedial education for the disabled, or how much to give in transfers or take in taxes from households at any given income level.

The degree of inequality of outcome that we observe in any society therefore depends on both the inequality in initial conditions and the extent to which inequalities of opportunity are accentuated, or diminished, over time by chance events and by personal and social choices. Since all societies have to make some set of decisions on taxes, transfers, and the distribution of government services (like education), it is inescapable that all societies will affect, to some degree, the distribution of income—but what criteria should guide these social decisions? What degree of redistribution of income is appropriate? Does redistribution blunt incentives to work and exercise initiative and, if so, is the effect large or small? To what extent should taxes or transfers depend on the process that generates income (e.g., is redistribution to the poor equally appropriate for both those able to work and the disabled? Should the origin of disability matter when disability can be caused by reckless driving or by a workplace accident?) Questions such as these raise both normative and positive economic issues. The three perspectives that follow have been particularly influential in economics.

"JUSTICE AS FAIRNESS"

John Rawls, a moral philosopher at Harvard University, has constructed a theory of ethics based heavily on the economic theory of choice itself.[6] In thinking about what constitutes a just distribution of income, Rawls asks us to imagine ourselves meeting to choose the rules for distributing income. The meeting takes place behind a "veil of ignorance," which conceals from participants any knowledge of what talents and abilities each has. Because no individual knows whether he or she is smart or dull, strong or weak, fast or slow, no one knows which rules of distribution would work to his or her own advantage. One way to understand the thought-experiment that Rawls proposes is to ask yourself these questions:

- If you did not know whether you would be born male or female, black or white, Aboriginal or non-Aboriginal, would you think it fair that women or black people or Aboriginals receive lower incomes than others? If so, how much lower?
- If you did not know whether you would be born with a disabilities, would you think it fair that people with disability receive lower incomes than others? If so, how much lower?
- If you did not know whether you would dive off a wharf just before graduation from university and be paralyzed for the rest of your life, would you think it fair that paraplegics receive lower incomes than others? If so, how much lower?
- If you did not know whether, in the end, all your investments for your retirement would turn out badly and you would end up penniless in your old age, would you think it fair that society should expect seniors to finance their own retirement years? If not, would you suggest there be any assistance for penniless seniors and if there were assistance, how much?

[6] John Rawls, *A Theory of Justice*, Cambridge, Mass.: Harvard University Press, 1971.

Rawls argues that we think of a game as fair if its rules do not confer an advantage on any particular participant. In reality, we all actually know whether we were born black or white, rich or poor, with or without a disability. However, if we try to think of what the rules of society *should* be like, we would think of life as fair if those rules were not tilted in favour of particular people (including ourselves). The idea of asking what we would freely and rationally agree on as the rules of the game *if we had to choose those rules from behind "the veil of ignorance"* asks us to accept the chance that we might personally have the characteristics that would put us at the bottom of the socioeconomic heap, and to think about how badly off we might be, in that event.

Rawls' concept of "the rules of the game" is very broad and encompasses both the mechanisms by which life's rewards are allocated and the size of those rewards. He argues that even if we all chose from behind the veil of ignorance, free and rational individuals would probably not choose to equalize incomes entirely—some inequalities are likely to be necessary to provide incentives for labour supply, savings, and effort. However, if there were a chance that we personally would get the lowest prize in life's lottery, it would be rational for us to want that prize to be as high as possible. Rawls therefore argues that the fairness of social arrangements depends on how they affect the least well off members of society. Economists often refer to this as the idea of "maxi-min," since it means that a society should try to *maxi*mize the *min*imum income in that society.

Rawls argues that the rules people would choose in such a state of ignorance would necessarily be fair, and if the rules are fair, the income distribution to which they give rise will also be fair.

In a country without rewards for hard work and risk taking, national income would be dramatically smaller than in a country with such rewards. Of course, material rewards for effort and risk taking necessarily lead to inequality. Rawls argues, however, that people would be willing to accept a certain degree of inequality as long as these rewards produced a sufficiently large increase in the total amount of output available for distribution.

But how much inequality would people accept? Much less than the amount produced by purely competitive markets, Rawls argues. The idea is that behind the veil of ignorance, each person would fear being put in a disadvantaged position, so each would choose rules that would produce a more equal distribution of income than exists under the marginal productivity system. And since such choices *define* the just distribution of income, he argues, fairness requires at least some attempt to reduce the inequality produced by the market system.

THE UTILITARIAN ARGUMENT

The branch of moral philosophy called **utilitarianism** holds that the right course of action is the one that results in the highest total level of utility. Utilitarians argue against income inequality on the grounds that the marginal utility of income is typically smaller for a wealthy person than for a poor person. In their view, transferring $1000 of income from a rich person to a poor person is justified because the extra happiness experienced when the poor person receives the money would far outweigh the decline in happiness when the rich person gives it up.

The argument is based on the concept of diminishing marginal utility presented in Chapter 4. To understand it, it is useful to review the example presented in Table 4.2. That example refers to the utility two people gain from eating four ice cream cones. For each person, the utility derived from eating the first ice cream cone is 100, while the second cone eaten yields additional utility of 50, the third cone consumed provides 25 additional utils, and the fourth cone has a benefit of 12 utils. This example captures the idea of diminishing marginal utility because each person gets more utility from consuming more ice cream; it is just that the first cones eaten are *so* much more enjoyable than the last few consumed.

utilitarianism a moral theory in which the right course of action is the one that results in the highest total utility

Let us suppose there are two people of identical tastes, Jim and Angelo. If Jim eats four ice cream cones (with a total utility of $187 = 100 + 50 + 25 + 12$) while Angelo consumes zero, then total utility is 187.

The transfer of one ice cream cone from Jim to Angelo would give Angelo 100 utils while Jim now has 175 utils, producing total utility of 275 for a net gain in total utility of 88 (Jim loses 12 utils while Angelo gets 100 utils). If we were to go further and transfer another ice cream cone to Angelo (so they now have two each) then total utility rises to 300 ($= 150 + 150$). Total utility is maximized when consumption is equalized, if both individuals have identical tastes.

This argument for greater equality based on diminishing marginal utility has been an influential one, but notice that the example of Jim and Angelo illustrates two levels of equalizing transfers, moving from a (4,0) division of extreme inequality to a (3,1) division of moderate inequality, and then moving from moderate inequality to total equality (2,2). Notice that the move from high to moderate inequality produces a large gain (88) in total utility, while the move from moderate inequality to total equality produces a much smaller gain in total utility (25). The principle of diminishing marginal utility implies that total utility increases in both cases, and it also implies that the closer a society is to absolute equality, the smaller is the size of the gains in total utility of *further* reductions in inequality.

The principle of diminishing marginal utility applies to both incomes in general and ice cream cones in particular. However, in real life we cannot measure utility and we know that different people have different tastes. People may also differ in their general ability to derive pleasure from their incomes. Unfortunately for the utilitarians, we generally have no way of getting inside people's heads and knowing how much utility different people get from the same bundle of goods. Hence, we cannot actually add the utility of different people and use the criterion of maximizing total utility as a guide to public policy. Furthermore, the issue of how to divide a given amount of goods (as in the example of four ice cream cones and two people) ignores the problem of how to establish incentives for people to produce goods. Hence, although most people accept the claim that an extra dollar generally meets more pressing demands for a poor person than for a rich person, even utilitarians do not argue for complete equalization on these grounds. With Rawls, they recognize that a regime of complete equality would so weaken incentives that it would not, in fact, produce the greatest utility for all.

POVERTY AND HUMAN RIGHTS

Many modern disciples of Adam Smith appear reluctant to introduce concerns about inequality into discussions of economic policy. Yet as Smith himself recognized, such concerns are a basic component of human nature. Writing more than two centuries ago, he introduced the important idea that local consumption standards influence the goods and services that people consider essential for life (or "necessaries," as Smith called them):

> By necessaries I understand not only the commodities which are indispensably necessary for the support of life, but whatever the custom of the country renders it indecent for creditable people, even of the lowest order, to be without. A linen shirt, for example, is, strictly speaking, not a necessary of life. The Greeks and Romans lived, I suppose, very comfortably though they had no linen. But in the present times, through the greater part of Europe, a creditable day-labourer would be ashamed to appear in public without a linen shirt, the want of which would be supposed to denote that disgraceful degree of poverty which, it is presumed, no body can well fall into without extreme bad conduct. Custom, in the same manner, has

rendered leather shoes a necessary of life in England. The poorest creditable person of either sex would be ashamed to appear in public without them.[7]

The absolute standard of living in Canada today is vastly higher than it was in Adam Smith's eighteenth-century Scotland. Yet Smith's observations apply with equal force to contemporary industrial societies.

The general level of income crucially affects contemporary standards as to what is "decent" or "acceptable" in every aspect of life. A century ago it was, for example, considered entirely normal for most families in Canada to use an outdoor toilet. Today, a home without indoor plumbing would be considered substandard, and probably would be demolished.

Rising living standards have altered both the availability of commodities and the frame of reference that defines an acceptable standard of living.

But, poverty in terms of money income is only part of the story. Nobel Prize winner Amartya Sen has argued that "poverty must be seen as the deprivation of basic capabilities rather than merely as lowness of income."[8] His focus is on the "substantive freedoms—the capabilities—to choose a life one has reason to value" that individuals actually possess, and he argues that individuals are not really "free" unless they possess "capabilities." For example, one capability Sen considers basic is the capability to appear in public without shame—as Adam Smith remarked more than two hundred years ago, this requires "decent" clothing, by the standards of the society in which a person lives. A second basic capability is the ability to visit friends or go to work—which requires a means of transportation. Another example is the capability to understand the world around us, which requires some level of literacy and education. A fourth is the ability to function without pain (healthiness is a very general capability, which requires some level of medical care). Sen's point is that it is substantive freedoms, not formal legal guarantees, that actually matter in people's lives and that people who do not have basic capabilities do not actually have much freedom.

Sen's work is also a reminder that public services in health care, education, and the urban environment (e.g., mass transit) are even more important to the poor than to the affluent, since the poor do not have the money to purchase private market substitutes. In Europe, these services are often referred to as the "social wage," since they are available to all citizens. However, whether individuals get public services or pay privately, the more general point is that if individuals are to have substantive freedoms, they need access to economic resources.

In drawing the link among poverty, capabilities, and freedom, Sen is echoing a long tradition in the human rights literature. The actual exercise of human rights typically requires a basic level of economic resources. For example, Article 12 of the UN Universal Declaration of Human Rights asserts a right to privacy, and so does the Canadian Bill of Rights. However, what "right to privacy" do the homeless actually possess? Privacy requires control over a definable personal space, which, in a market economy, generally requires the ownership of property or the income with which to rent property. The lack of income to rent housing (or the lack of public housing for those who have no income) means that people have no choice but to live on the street. Once this happens, their privacy rights are nothing but hollow words. The lack of income, or compensating public services, can therefore be seen as a human rights issue.

[7]Adam Smith, *The Wealth of Nations,* with introductions by Max Lerner and Edwin Cannan. Edited by Edwin Cannan. New York: Random House, Inc., 1965 (1776), Book V, Chapter II, Article 4th, pp. 821–822.
[8]Sen, A.K. (1999), *Development as Freedom.* New York: A.A. Knopf Publishers.

> **RECAP** **MORAL CONCERNS RAISED BY INCOME INEQUALITY**
>
> High levels of income inequality have drawn moral objections on several grounds. John Rawls has argued that the degree of inequality typical of unregulated market systems is unfair because people would favour substantially less inequality if they chose distributional rules from behind a veil of ignorance. Utilitarians favour reducing inequality because the marginal utility of income is smaller for wealthy persons than for poor persons. Poverty can also be seen as a human rights issue, since the actual attainment of effective functioning, or the actual exercise of freedoms, often requires access to goods and services.

■ 15.4 PRACTICAL CONCERNS RAISED BY POVERTY AND INCOME INEQUALITY

Even if we set moral concerns completely aside, compelling practical reasons to limit poverty and inequality remain. Clearly, poverty affects many (about 3.5 million) Canadians. In a turbulent labour market where people are often laid off and may find it difficult to claim Employment Insurance, many more people have occasional years of poverty—about 7.9 million Canadians were, for example, poor in at least one year between 1992 and 1996. As a result, the probability and depth of potential poverty affects the sense of economic insecurity with which many people contemplate the future—even if they are not poor right now.

However, although poverty has been discussed for centuries, very little of the discourse on poverty was actually written by the poor or near poor. So why have the affluent cared about poverty? In 1683, Sir Matthew Hale, Lord Chief Justice of Kings Bench, gave three reasons:

> A due care for the relief of the poor is an act,
>
> 1, of great Piety towards Almighty God, who requires it of us:...
>
> 2. It is an act of greatest Humanity among men. Mercy and Benignity is due to the very Beasts that serve us, much more to those that are partakers of the same common nature with us.
>
> 3. it is an Act of great Civil Prudence and Political Wisdom: for Poverty in it self is apt to Emasculate the minds of men, or at least it makes men tumultuous and unquiet. Where there are many very poor, the Rich cannot long or safely continue such.[9]

A strong moralistic element has always existed in the poverty debate—just remember Adam Smith's comment that poor clothing indicates "extreme bad conduct." This moralism is surely part of the reason why some people now focus on the poverty of children, whose clear lack of power to affect their situation presumptively identifies them as "deserving poor." However, part of the concern of the affluent with child poverty also undoubtedly stems from an enlightened self-interest motivation. Today's economists would likely say that "poverty causes suboptimal investment in human capital," rather than use the more colourful phrasing of 1683 that poverty "is apt to Emasculate the minds of men"—but the underlying idea is really much the same. Furthermore, today's economist would now likely

---

[9]*A Discourse Touching Provision for the Poor.* Written by Sir Matthew Hale, late Lord Chief Justice of the Kings-Bench. London, Printed for William Shrowsbery, at the Bible in Duke-Lane, 1683. Accessed online at <www.ecn.bris.ac.uk/het/hale/poor>, August 17, 2004.

add that the long-run economic growth rate would be higher if the children of the poor could acquire the skills and education to become productive employees.

Concern with child poverty as a denial of equality of opportunity may also have blended motivations. For some people, such concern is ethically motivated. Earlier in this chapter we emphasized Rawls's argument that justice as fairness entails maximizing the well-being of the least advantaged. However, this ethical perspective motivates a concern with the long-term poverty of all persons, not just children. An equally important criterion for Rawls is that any opportunities to hold offices and positions are "open to all under conditions of fair equality of opportunity," which does mandate special consideration for the life chances of poor children.

Equality of opportunity may also appeal to the enlightened self-interest of the affluent. Politically, a perception of fairness is probably essential for long-term political legitimacy. Back in 1683, English clergy often told their parishioners that the positions of the King and the nobility were ordained by God—but not nearly as many people now go to church, and when they do, few ministers say that any more. In our secular age, the capitalist system cannot depend on the sort of divine will rationales for inequality that feudalism could rely on, so maintaining belief in "equality of opportunity" is important for political legitimacy. And since children live in families, it is not possible to address child poverty independently of the poverty of their parents.

RECAP	PRACTICAL CONCERNS RAISED BY POVERTY AND INCOME INEQUALITY

Apart from moral concerns about income inequality, practical reasons would argue for limiting the gap between the rich and poor. One is that poverty imposes costs on the nonpoor. High-income persons benefit from having highly skilled people to work with, and poverty often limits the extent to which people can develop their skills.

15.5 METHODS OF INCOME REDISTRIBUTION

Do we *want* to reduce poverty and inequality in Canada? The answer depends partly on how much inequality and poverty there is in Canada and partly on the criteria by which we judge whether a given amount of inequality and poverty is equitable (or not). But even if one decides that "something should be done," the next question is: "what is the best way to do it?" There are costs and benefits to each possible public policy to alter the distribution of income—so economic analysis can be useful in deciding both *whether* and *how* we might want to change inequality and poverty.

MINIMUM WAGES

Canada and many other industrialized countries have sought to ease the burden of the working poor by enacting minimum wage legislation—laws that prohibit employers from paying workers less than a specified hourly wage.

How does a minimum wage affect the market for low-wage labour? In Figure 15.4, note that when the law prevents employers from paying less than W_{min}, employers hire fewer workers (a decline from L_0 to L_1). Unemployment is the result. The L_1 workers who keep their jobs earn more than before, but the $L_0 - L_1$ workers who lose their jobs earn nothing. Whether workers together earn more or less than before thus depends on the elasticity of demand for labour. If elasticity of demand is less than one, workers as a group will earn more than before. If it is more than one, workers as a group will earn less.

FIGURE 15.4
The Effect of Minimum Wages

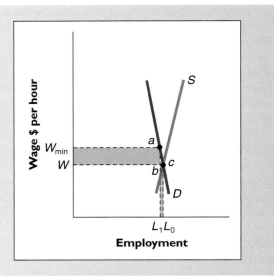

In Figure 15.4, the amount of wage income lost by those workers who lose their jobs is represented by the thin blue rectangle. The amount of income gained by those who remain employed is represented by the green rectangle. When employment falls from L_1 to L_0, the total loss in wages is the number of jobs lost $(L_1 - L_0)$ multiplied by the wage rate (W); graphically this is the blue rectangle cbL_1L_0. Since the wages of those who retain employment rise from W to W_{min}, the total increase in their incomes is given by the increase in wages $(W_{min} - W)$ multiplied by the number of workers who keep their jobs (L_1); graphically this is the green rectangle $abWW_{min}$ (it will be larger in area than the blue rectangle cbL_1L_0 when the elasticity of demand is less than one). In other words, when the elasticity of demand for low wage labour is less than one, the income gains of those who keep their jobs is larger than the income losses of job losers, and the total earnings of low wage workers increases.

As Figure 15.4 illustrates, the demand curve for labour should be drawn with a steep slope, since a large body of research has estimated its wage elasticity to be in the range of 0.1 or less. Estimates of the wage elasticity of the supply curve of labour are often somewhat greater for women than for men, but are also typically close to 0.1. Some influential recent studies argue that we should draw the demand curve for low-wage labour as essentially vertical because minimum wages may have a positive impact on labour productivity (perhaps because workers are less likely to quit if wages are higher, which increases the average experience of the workforce and reduces the cost to the employer of training replacements).

At one point, economists were almost unanimous in their opposition to minimum wage laws, arguing that those laws reduce total economic surplus, much like other regulations that prevent markets from reaching equilibrium. In recent years, however, some economists have softened their opposition to minimum wage laws, citing studies that have failed to show significant reductions in employment following increases in minimum wage levels. These studies imply that as a group low-income workers are better off with minimum wage laws than without them. Of course, we must remember that these studies demonstrate the impact—or lack of impact—of minimum wages on employment *over the range of minimum wages that have actually been implemented*. As always, data from the past illustrate what we can learn from experience, and we have to be very cautious in extrapolating outside that experience. If minimum wages are raised too much above the historically observed range, any possible positive impacts of minimum wages on productivity will have to be balanced against the rising cost of labour—and theory does predict very clearly that *too large* an increase in the minimum wage will have an adverse effect on employment.

As Canadian governments have cut back on expenditures on social assistance and unemployment insurance, the political pressure to make the private sector pay for the reduction of poverty by raising the minimum wage increases. However, there is a fundamental problem with relying on an increase in low wages as an anti-poverty strategy. *Individuals get wages, but it is families that are poor.* Market forces (and human rights legislation) imply that employers will pay the same wage to all the workers who do the same type of job, regardless of their family circumstances. However, some minimum wage workers—like teenagers working in the fast-food sector who have rich parents—are members of affluent households. Some low-wage workers have only themselves to support, while others have large families. The very poorest families are those without anyone who can work at all. Consequently, an increase in the minimum wage will benefit some people who were never poor, but will often not be enough to raise families out of poverty and will miss entirely the very poorest households.

In the first half of the twentieth century, social policy was much simpler. Before 1960, most families only had one wage earner, so the basic issue for them was whether the household head could earn a living wage, that is, whether one full-time, full-year job could support a family. This model always had problems, since large families always found it harder to make ends meet and any spell of unemployment could mean deprivation. However, if all families had one earner, and if that person could hold a full-time job, the combination of a decent minimum wage for employed people and adequate employment insurance benefits during periods of unemployment could perhaps prevent poverty.

In the past 40 years, however, the world has become much more complex. In many Canadian families both parents work full-time, and single parents head an increasing number of families. Some so-called traditional one-earner/two-parent households exist, but social policy now has to recognize a multiplicity of family types. As a result, the living wage model of the single-earner household has become increasingly unable to cope—partly also because work arrangements have also become increasingly fluid and changeable.

For people under 65, social assistance and Employment Insurance have been the most important transfer programs affecting poverty, but there have been many changes in recent years. Until 1996, the program we know as Employment Insurance (EI) was known as Unemployment Insurance. Although a package of changes in 1971 increased the duration and level of benefits, since then a series of reforms has cut it back to about the level of generosity of the 1950s. In some regions of Canada (particularly where only seasonal employment is available) EI has historically been important in maintaining family incomes; however, EI is much less important now than it was 20 years ago—considerably less than 40 percent of unemployed people now receive EI benefits.

SOCIAL ASSISTANCE

If Canadians have no other way to get income, they must turn to their provincial government for Social Assistance. During the recession of the early 1990s, as many as 3.1 million Canadians depended on social assistance, but declining unemployment rates in the latter part of the decade reduced the total to about 1.8 million in 2002.[10] To receive social assistance, individuals have to pass a needs test—that is, they must have no source of income and have spent down their assets. (Since social assistance regulations are set by the provinces, they differ across the country in level of benefits, asset exemptions, and so on, but in Ontario or Manitoba, a single employable person in 2002 could not have any liquid assets, while in Saskatchewan or Alberta they could keep $1500.)

[10]Source: *Welfare Incomes: 2002* National Council of Welfare, Ottawa 2003.

As an anti-poverty policy, the major advantage of social assistance is that it recognizes that families of different sizes, in different circumstances, have different income needs. Wages are the same for single people and those who have families, and therefore take no account of financial need, but social assistance payments vary by family status and family size. However, these support levels are well below the poverty line. For example, even when we add together all federal tax credits and maximum provincial social assistance, in 2002 a single employable person in Ontario received $6833 yearly (which was only about 35 percent of the low-income cut-off), while a single parent with one child got $13 871 (about 58 percent of the LICO), and a couple with two children got $18 400 (which was 51 percent of the LICO). Furthermore, social assistance payments are much lower in the poorer provinces—single employables in New Brunswick received only $3378 per year in 2002, or about 20 percent of the LICO.

Many economists have also noted that people on social assistance face disincentives to work. Although the details differ by province, social assistance recipients typically face a very high penalty in reduced benefits if they start to earn much money. Typically, they are allowed to keep only a small amount before benefits are reduced (in Ontario, a single employable in 2002 could keep the first $143 of a month's earnings, while Quebec allowed $200). After that, benefits are reduced substantially—in most provinces by 75 percent of any further earnings. In effect, this means that social assistance clients face a marginal tax rate of 75 percent—well above any other segment of society. Since social assistance clients may also lose some other benefits (such as access to public housing) if their incomes rise, some analysts have labelled these very high tax rates the Welfare Trap.

Measured in constant 2002 dollars, social assistance support levels have fallen dramatically in Canada in recent years. For example, in Alberta in 1986, a single employable recipient would have received $9238 in provincial social assistance, while in 2002, the same person would get $4824 (both measured in 2002 dollars)—a decline of 47.8 percent. On average, from 1986 to 2002, the provinces cut the real value of social assistance benefits by 30.5 percent for single employable individuals and by 21.5 percent for a couple with two children. The least well-off members of Canadian society have become substantially worse off over the last 15 years.

THE NEGATIVE INCOME TAX

negative income tax a system under which the government would grant every citizen a cash payment each year, financed by an additional tax on earned income

Nobel Laureate Milton Friedman has proposed that current welfare programs be replaced by a single program called the **negative income tax** (**NIT**). Under the NIT, every man, woman, and child—rich or poor—receives a substantial income tax credit. The NIT is thus just like the earned-income tax credit except that it also applies to people who are not employed and hence have no earned income. A person who earns no income would receive the credit in cash. People who earn income would be taxed at some rate less than 100 percent.

breakeven income level under a negative income tax, the level of before-tax income at which a family's tax liability exactly offsets its initial tax credit

Under a negative income tax, the initial credit and the tax rate would combine to determine a **breakeven income level** at which a person's tax liability exactly offsets the initial tax credit. People earning below that level would receive a net benefit payment from the government; people earning above it would make a net tax payment. Example 15.1 illustrates how the breakeven income level would be calculated.

| EXAMPLE 15.1 | **What is the breakeven level of earned income in an NIT program?** |

Consider a negative income tax program with a tax credit of $6000/year and a tax rate of 50 percent. At what income level would an individual in this program neither pay a tax nor receive a benefit? How large a net benefit would a person earning $6000/year receive? How large a net tax payment would a person earning $18 000/year owe?

The horizontal axis of Figure 15.5 shows an individual's before-tax income, while the vertical axis measures after-tax income. With the credit payment set at $6000/year, someone with a before-tax income of $0 would end up with an after-tax income of $6000/year. From that point, his net income would rise by 50 cents for each dollar earned, as shown by the red line labelled "After-tax income," until at some point it equalled his before-tax income. The 45° line shows all the points at which after-tax income equals before-tax income. In this program, the break-even level of income is the before-tax income level at which the two lines intersect, which is $12000/year. A person who earned $6000/year would receive an after-tax income of $9000, which implies that the government would send that person a check for $3000. A person who earned $18000/year would receive an after-tax income of $15000, which implies that he would pay $3000 in taxes.

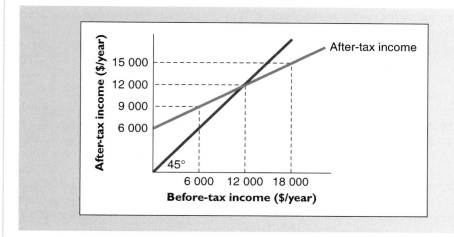

FIGURE 15.5

A Hypothetical Negative Income Tax Program
Under this negative income tax program, each person starts with a cash grant of $6000/year, which is reduced at the rate of 50 cents for each dollar of income earned during the year. The breakeven income level is $12 000/year.

In Example 15.1, what would the breakeven income level be if the tax credit were $4000/year?

EXERCISE 15.1

The negative income tax would do much less than current programs to weaken work incentives, because unlike current programs, it would ensure that someone who earned an extra dollar would keep more of it. And because the program would be administered by the existing income tax system, administrative costs would be lower than under the current welfare system.

Despite these advantages, however, the negative income tax is by no means a perfect solution to the income-transfer problem. The core problem is that of maintaining adequacy of benefits for those who cannot work, while preserving incentives to work for those who can. Anybody who looks carefully at the poverty problem in Canada soon realizes that the reason some people are poor is crucial. Most Canadians, after all, get their family incomes from work in the paid labour market, and the vast majority of Canadians are not poor. Thus, the issue is, why are some Canadians not similarly able to get enough income from the labour market?

Of course, a substantial number of Canadians are not expected to work because they are past the normal age of retirement (about 12 percent of the population is 65 or older). For them, the issue is whether they have been able to save enough from their working years to finance their retirement and whether they have an adequate pension. In Canada, private pensions are not a solution to the problem of poverty among senior citizens—less than half the labour force is covered by a private pension plan; people with pension coverage tend to have higher-income jobs; workers often lose coverage when they change jobs; and the number of seniors covered by private pensions has been shrinking over time. Therefore, as a practical matter the universal coverage and portability of the Canada/Quebec Pension Plan are extremely important.

As we have already seen, transfer payments from government reduce poverty among senior citizens very substantially. Indeed, poverty reduction among senior citizens is a Canadian success story. In 2002, the poverty rate among Canadians over 65 was 6.9 percent. In 1961 (before the introduction of the CPP/QPP and the OAS/GIS system), almost half of families with a head of household over 65, and over two-thirds of single senior citizens, fell below the poverty line.[11] Public pensions are particularly important.

In a mandatory public pension plan, such as CPP or QPP, premiums are paid during an individual's working life as a percentage of earnings (up to a contribution ceiling) and benefits are similarly related to earnings. In both plans, the fact that benefits are tied to previous earnings means that people who had very low (or no) earnings while they were younger tend to get little (or no) pension when they are old. However, although CPP/QPP was not introduced until 1967, it was accompanied by the introduction of the Guaranteed Income Supplement (GIS), which has much the same structure as a negative income tax.

In 1999, 1.4 million Canadians (about 37 percent of seniors) received payments under the GIS. For a single person, GIS provided benefits of $491.65 per month (just under $6000 per year), which were reduced by 50 cents for every dollar of other income received. Hence, the GIS (at least for single Canadian senior citizens) is very much the same as the hypothetical negative income tax system described in Example 15.1 and Figure 15.5.

However, in addition, Canadian seniors received $415 per month in Old Age Security cheques, as a universal, but taxable, benefit to all persons aged 65 or more. In total, a senior citizen living alone with no other income received $10884 per year from OAS and GIS (indexed for inflation). It is the combination of a floor on incomes set by OAS and GIS for those seniors who had little earnings of their own (especially women who took some time out of the paid workforce to raise children) and CPP/QPP benefits for people without private pensions that enables Canada to pull so many senior citizens' incomes above the poverty line.

Fifty years ago, many seniors had no real choice but to keep on working as long as they could, but today people over 65 are not expected to be in the workforce. Perhaps for that reason, policymakers have not been particularly worried about undermining the work ethic among seniors; transfer payments have been made available to deal with the poverty problem among senior citizens. For people under 65, however, there has always been a concern among policymakers that if transfer payments are made "too generous," the work ethic may be undermined.

However, whether or not people *want* to work, are they *able* to work? In the 1990s, about 2.3 million Canadians between the ages of 15 and 64 reported that they have a long-term disability that limits their normal activities in some way. Clearly, people with disabilities face a range of limitations on their ability to work and in many cases a barrier in one dimension may preclude some types of jobs but be no impediment to productivity in another line of work (e.g., people who are visually impaired cannot expect to fly airplanes for a living, but they can do many other jobs just as well as people with full sight).

All the same, it is equally clear that some people have very severe disabilities (which can be physical, mental, or emotional) or have multiple disabilities. Even with all the will in the world, some people face *enormous* barriers to finding productive employment. Furthermore, employers may have to make investments to enable some people with disabilities to be hired (e.g., workplaces must be wheelchair accessible) and they may be reluctant to do so. Although society benefits in many

---

[11]L. Osberg, "Poverty Among Senior Citizens—a Canadian Success Story," *The State of Economics in Canada Festschrift in Honour of David Slater*. Patrick Grady and Andrew Sharpe (ed) John Deutsch Institute for the Study of Economic Policy, Queen's University, Kingston, 2001, Pp. 151-182

noneconomic ways when people with disabilities can participate in the workforce, there is no way around the fact that many people with disabilities are very likely to have low (or no) individual earnings in the labour market. As a result, many people with disabilities have to depend on social assistance. In 2002, a disabled person on social assistance got $11 763 per year in Ontario, $9784 in British Columbia, but only $6906 in New Brunswick. In addition, social assistance administrators may, in some provinces, be able to make supplementary payments to cover some of the direct costs of disabilities (wheelchairs are, for example, quite expensive).

Single parents of young children are another group that faces a significant barrier to full participation in the labour market. Adequate daycare is an essential prerequisite if they are to work. If they are poorly educated or live in a depressed local labour market, low wages may mean that they have to work long hours to make enough income to stay above the poverty line—but small children cannot be left unattended. In 2002, a single parent with one child on social assistance got $13 800 per year in Quebec, $11 634 in Alberta, and $13 706 in British Columbia.

In all this discussion, of course, we have so far assumed that jobs are available for those that want them. Sometimes this is a reasonable assumption, but when the economy moves into recession, firms stop hiring and start firing, and there are few jobs of any kind to be had. As well, in a country as big as Canada, the available jobs may be far away from the people who need them. When vacancies are scarce, employers tend to demand better credentials, even for entry-level jobs. The people who find themselves at the end of the queue for jobs are those with relatively few years of schooling, little work experience, or a "negative" credential (such as a criminal record or unstable work history). At times when jobs are hard to find, these people may look in vain for work—and in some parts of the country there is a chronic shortage of paid employment at any time.

The issue of incentives to work is therefore only part of the story—we must also consider the individual's ability to work and the availability of work. Nevertheless, the debate on the design and level of social assistance support has focused heavily on the issue of work incentives.

Remember that all of these social assistance support levels fall well short of reasonable definitions of the poverty line. Statistics Canada's LICO differs by family size and the size of area of residence to reflect, at least in part, the differences in cost of living that families face. However, across Canadian provinces, the total income of a four-person family on social assistance in 1999 was typically about half the LICO. And, when someone doesn't have much, it doesn't take much to make a big difference in their lives. Whether it is a cut in social assistance levels or an increase, a thousand dollars per year more or less is very important to, for example, a person with a disability in Alberta whose social assistance payments were $7061 in 1999. For someone making $100 000 at the top end of the income distribution, the same amount of money would be much less noticeable.

Although the incentive problem would be less severe under a negative income tax than under current welfare programs, it would remain a serious difficulty. And, note that if the negative income tax were the *sole* means of insulating people against poverty, the payment to people with no earned income would need to be at least as large as the poverty threshold.

RECAP | **METHODS OF INCOME REDISTRIBUTION**

Minimum wage laws may help to increase the earnings of the working poor, but they do nothing to assist jobless individuals. Furthermore, even full-year, full-time work at current levels of the minimum wage produce incomes that are well below the poverty line for families. Minimum wage laws provide no benefits for those who are not employed.

> For those aged 65 and over, Old Age Security, the Guaranteed Income Supplement, and CPP/QPP have succeeded in pulling the incomes of many seniors above the LICO. For those under 65 years of age, social assistance payments are the major instrument in the battle against poverty. Because benefits under this program are means-tested, beneficiaries often experience only a small increase in net income when they accept paid employment while receiving assistance.
>
> The negative income tax is a universal program that pays a basic, guaranteed income to all people. Payments are reduced in proportion to other income, so that above a *breakeven income*, people pay net taxes. The Guaranteed Income Supplement in Canada is essentially a negative income tax for seniors.

■ 15.6 PAYING FOR INCOME-SUPPORT PROGRAMS: EQUITY VERSUS EFFICIENCY?

Policymakers must choose not only which policies to employ in the effort to reduce poverty and income inequality but also how to pay for them. A common proposal is to make the federal income tax more progressive. Proponents contend that such a change would not only finance additional transfers to low-income families but would also reduce the gap between the after-tax incomes of wealthy and middle-class families. Opponents of this proposal worry about the unintended side effects of increasing top tax rates.

ADVERSE EFFECTS ON INCENTIVES

Most liberals, and even many conservatives, have always considered a more progressive tax structure to be desirable on the grounds of equity. Yet many fear that steeply progressive taxes might kill the proverbial goose that lays the golden egg. Thus, as John Rawls emphasized, sufficiently high tax rates on top earners could weaken their incentive to work hard and take risks. But most empirical evidence suggests that modest increases from current tax rates would not seriously undermine the incentive to work. If tax rates at the top rose slightly, the 40 vice presidents in a large corporation who aspire to become CEO probably would not start taking Fridays off to play golf.

Another concern is that raising top marginal tax rates might compromise economic efficiency by channelling talent and effort from productive work into tax avoidance (legal) and tax evasion (illegal).

Without doubt, the payoff from a dollar invested in tax avoidance is higher when tax rates are high than when they are low. But if rational tax avoiders know about a legal deduction or exemption, they will almost surely claim it whether their tax rate is 40 percent or 60 percent. They may spend a little more effort searching out exemptions when the tax rate is higher, but their tax consultants are unlikely to advise them differently in the two cases.

At the very top of the income pyramid, where the CEOs of major corporations receive multi-million dollar compensation packages, one encounters the "problem" of how to spend it all. How exactly could one spend four or five million dollars in useful ways, without being ostentatious—or is it possible that ostentatious consumption is the whole point? If one takes "monster homes," which are becoming ever bigger and more grandiose, as an example, the "Grand

Halls" and "Big Room" do serve to impress one's guests, even if their owners find that they actually make little personal use of most of their space. As Thorstein Veblen noted over a century ago, the whole point of ostentatious consumption is to display one's ability to consume wastefully, thereby deriving *relative* status, compared with those who cannot afford to consume as much. At the very top of the income pyramid, income may be the competitive score-card, and ostentatious consumption may be the way one shows who is "winning," but the underlying issue is comparison: "Am I a bigger 'success' than everybody else?"

As an article in *The Globe and Mail* commented:

> What does a successful financier do when Porsches become passé, and the bank account has more zeroes than ever seemed possible way back when studying for that MBA, three decades ago? How does one stay motivated when bank buyouts, tech scores and leveraged co-investment wins have given a small-town kid the ability to buy a small town?
>
> Simple. It's time to move the goalposts farther down the field. Got to get the "jet."[12]

However, the crucial part of "competitive consumption" is relative rank—having more and bigger goodies *compared with* almost everybody else, however much everyone else actually has. But a person's *relative rank* is not affected if everyone at the top pays the same tax rate—an annual pre-tax income of two million dollars, compared with a one million dollar pre-tax income, will generate more after-tax dollars (and bigger consumption expenditure) whether the tax rate at the top is 35 percent, 40 percent or 60 percent. Since higher tax rates for *everyone* do not affect the *relative* ranking of individuals, they do not affect the incentive that each senior executive has to try to get ahead of everyone else. Thus, as the international evidence indicates,[13] although there are large differences across countries in the tax rates that people at the top end of the income distribution pay, top executives work hard everywhere—so there are relatively small international differences in the weekly hours of work that they supply.

RECAP	PAYING FOR INCOME-SUPPORT PROGRAMS: EQUITY VERSUS EFFICIENCY?

Poverty is more effectively attacked by transferring additional income to the poor than by trying to regulate prices and wages. Yet many fear that the higher taxes on top earners needed to pay for such transfers will reduce effort and investment and stimulate wasteful tax avoidance. Tax avoidance can be curtailed by making the tax code simpler, and moderate increases in current top tax rates probably would not cause significant reductions in effort.

Higher tax rates on top earners have positive effects on efficiency as well as negative ones. Individuals with the highest earnings are often the winning contestants in labour markets with limited numbers of positions at the top.

[12]In 2004, the up-front cost of a 1/16th share in a basic Learjet 40 was $515,000, with annual operating costs estimated at $145,000. "Getting the jet's the big dream on Bay St." Andrew Willis, *The Globe and Mail*, Wed. June 16, 2004. Reprinted with permission from *The Globe and Mail*.
[13]L. Osberg (2003) "Understanding Growth and Inequality Trends: The Role of Labour Supply in the U.S.A. and Germany," *Canadian Public Policy* Vol. XXIX, Supplement January 2003, Pp. S163–S184.

■ SUMMARY

- **15.1** Although incomes grew at almost 3 percent a year for all income classes during the three decades following World War II, income growth in the years since has been concentrated among top earners.

- **15.4** Many fear that the higher taxes needed to finance social programs could curtail economic growth. The benefits of anti-poverty policy in reducing illness and creating a more productive labour force can, however, be expected to encourage economic growth.

- **15.5** Policies and programs for reducing poverty include minimum wage laws and social assistance. Minimum wage laws can increase the net income going to low-wage workers, but they provide no benefit to the very poorest families—those without any employed household mem-

ber—and are likely to be insufficient for the needs of large families. If raised too high, they may also adversely affect employment. Social assistance payments vary with family size and characteristics, but in Canada they are set well below the poverty line.

- **15.5** The negative income tax works much like the Guaranteed Income Supplement for seniors, except that it includes people of all ages.

- **15.6** Poverty is more effectively attacked by transferring additional income to the poor than by regulating prices and wages. Tax avoidance that is motivated by high tax rates can be reduced by simplifying the tax code. Available data suggest that moderately higher tax rates on high incomes would not significantly reduce effort.

■ KEY TERMS

breakeven income level (422)
Gini coefficient (408)

Lorenz curve (407)
negative income tax (NIT) (422)

quintile (406)
utilitarianism (415)

■ REVIEW QUESTIONS

1. What costs does greater concentration of income among top earners impose on middle-class families?

2. Why does John Rawls believe that policies to redistribute income would command unanimous support behind a veil of ignorance?

3. Mention two self-interested reasons that a top earner might favour policies to redistribute income.

4. Why is exclusive reliance on the negative income tax unlikely to constitute a long-term solution to the poverty problem?

■ PROBLEMS

1. Suppose the demand for unskilled labour in the Chilliwack labour market is given by $W = 20 - 0.001L$, where W is the wage rate in dollars per hour and L is the quantity of labour demanded in person-hours per day. If the supply curve of unskilled labour in Corvallis is given by $W = 0.001L$, by how much will the imposition of a minimum wage at \$12/hour reduce total economic surplus? Calculate the amounts by which employer surplus and worker surplus change as a result of the minimum wage.

2. What is the breakeven level of before-tax earned income in a negative income tax program with a tax credit of \$5000/year and a tax rate of 40 percent? How large a net benefit would be received by a person earning \$6000/year? How large a net tax would be paid by someone earning \$15 000/year?

3. Enfield is a small economy consisting of five identical people who can earn a living in either of two ways: by acting or by growing corn. A corn farmer can earn \$10 000 (corn farmers can earn more, but this suits our example), and the best actor in Enfield will be chosen for a film contract that pays in accordance with the performer's acting ability. The only audition requirement is to be filmed working as an unpaid actor in a theatre in Montreal, which means being unable to work as a farmer. From among the filmed performances, a winner is chosen and paid. All contestants perceive the same

likelihood of being chosen, and the payment to the winner increases with the number of contestants in the manner shown in the following table.

Number of contestants	Expected payment to the winner ($1000s)	Expected payoff per contestant ($1000s)
1	21.0	21.0
2	34.0	17.0
3	45.0	15.0
4	50.0	12.5
5	55.0	11.0

    a. If all villagers have the same tastes and are risk-neutral, how many will compete to become an actor? What will be the total income of the residents of Enfield?

    b. What is the socially optimal number of villagers to enter the competition? How much would village income be if only the optimal number entered?

4. Refer to Problem 3. What is the smallest lump-sum tax on the winner's earnings that would ensure that the optimal number of villagers entered the competition?

■ ANSWERS TO IN-CHAPTER EXERCISES

15.1 The breakeven level falls from $12 000/year to $8000.

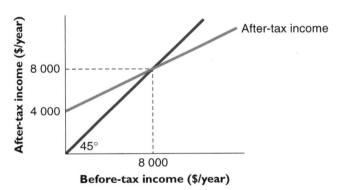

Glossary

A

Absolute advantage. One person has an absolute advantage over another if he or she takes fewer hours to perform a task than the other person.

Accounting profit. The difference between a firm's total revenue and its explicit costs.

Adverse selection. The pattern that occurs when, at any given cost of insurance, people with a greater expectation of loss buy insurance while people with a lower expected value of claims choose not to buy insurance.

Allocative function of price. Directs resources away from overcrowded markets and toward markets that are underserved.

Arc elasticity of demand. Elasticity calculated between the endpoints of a segment of a demand curve.

Asymmetric information. Situations in which buyers and sellers are not equally well informed about the characteristics of goods and services for sale in the marketplace.

Attainable point. Any combination of goods that can be produced using currently available resources.

Average benefit. Total benefit of undertaking n units of an activity divided by n.

Average cost. Total cost of undertaking n units of an activity divided by n.

Average product. Total output divided by total units of the variable factor of production.

B

Barrier to entry. Any force that prevents firms from entering a new market.

Basic elements of a game. The players, the strategies available to each player, and the payoffs each player receives for each possible combination of strategies.

Better-than-fair gamble. A gamble whose expected value is positive.

Breakeven income level. Under a negative income tax, the level of before-tax income at which a family's tax liability exactly offsets its initial tax credit.

Buyer's reservation price. See **Demander's reservation price.**

C

Capital. Any durable inputs to the production process, such as tools, machinery, and buildings.

Cartel. A coalition of firms that agree to restrict output for the purpose of earning an economic profit.

Change in demand. A shift of the entire demand curve.

Change in supply. A shift of the entire supply curve.

Change in the quantity demanded. A movement along the demand curve that occurs in response to a change in price.

Change in the quantity supplied. A movement along the supply curve that occurs in response to a change in price.

Coase theorem. If at no cost people can negotiate the purchase and sale of the right to perform activities that cause externalities, they can always arrive at efficient solutions to the problems caused by externalities.

Collective good. A good or service that, to at least some degree, is nonrival but excludable.

Commitment device. A way of changing incentives so as to make otherwise empty threats or promises credible.

Commitment problem. A situation in which people cannot achieve their goals because of an inability to make credible threats or promises.

Commons good. One for which nonpayers cannot easily be excluded and for which each unit consumed by one person means one less unit is available for others.

Comparative advantage. One person has a comparative advantage over another if his or her opportunity cost of performing a task is lower than the other person's opportunity cost.

Compensating wage differential. A difference in the wage rate—negative or positive—that reflects the attractiveness of a job's working conditions.

Complements. Two goods are complements in consumption if an increase in the price of one causes a leftward shift in the demand curve for the other.

Constant or **parameter.** A quantity that is fixed in value.

Constant returns to scale. A situation in which long-run average cost does not change as scale changes.

Consumer surplus. The economic gain of the buyers of a product, as measured by the cumulative difference between their respective reservation prices and the price they actually paid.

Costly-to-fake principle. To communicate information credibly to a potential rival, a signal must be costly or difficult to fake.

Cost-plus regulation. A method of regulation under which the regulated firm is permitted to charge a price equal to its explicit costs of production plus a markup to cover the opportunity cost of resources provided by the firm's owners.

Credible promise. A promise to take an action that is in the promiser's interest to keep.

Credible threat. A threat to take an action that is in the threatener's interest to carry out.

Cross-price elasticity of demand for two goods. The percentage change in the quantity demanded of one good in response to a 1 percent change in the price of a second good.

D

Deadweight loss. The deadweight loss caused by a policy is the reduction in economic surplus that results from adoption of that policy.

Decision tree (or game tree). A diagram that describes the possible moves in a game in sequence and lists the payoffs that correspond to each possible combination of moves.

Demand curve. A curve or schedule showing the total quantity of a good that buyers want to buy at each price.

Demander's (or buyer's) reservation price. The highest price a demander will offer in order to obtain a good or service.

Dependent variable. A variable in an equation whose value is determined by the value taken by another variable in the equation.

Discount factor. A coefficient used to discount a payment or receipt that occurs in the future to a present value (Chapter 12); a coefficient, D_1, used to discount a payment or receipt that occurs in the future to a present value. A discount factor can be defined algebraically as:

$$D = \frac{1}{(1 + r)^T}$$

where r = annual interest rate and T = number of years that will elapse before the payment is received. (Chapter 12 Appendix 12A).

Diseconomies of scale. A situation in which long-run average cost increases as a firm's output increases.

Dominant strategy. One that yields a higher payoff no matter what the other players in a game choose.

Dominated strategy. Any other strategy available to a player who has a dominant strategy.

E

Economic efficiency. Condition that occurs when all goods and services are produced and consumed at their respective socially optimal levels.

Economic loss. An economic profit that is less than zero.

Economic or excess profit. The difference between a firm's total revenue and the sum of its explicit and implicit costs.

Economic rent. That part of the payment for a factor of production that exceeds the owner's reservation price, the price below which the owner would not supply the factor.

Economic surplus. The benefit of taking any action minus its cost.

Economics. The study of how people make choices under conditions of scarcity and of the results of those choices for society.

Economies of scale. A situation in which long-run average cost decreases as a firm's output increases.

Efficient (or Pareto-efficient). A situation is efficient if no change is possible that will help some people without harming others.

Efficient point. Any combination of goods for which currently available resources do not allow an increase in the production of one good without a reduction in the production of the other.

Efficient quantity. The efficient quantity of a good is the quantity that results in the maximum possible economic surplus from producing and consuming the good.

Elastic. The demand for a good is elastic with respect to price if its price elasticity of demand is greater than one.

Elastic supply. Supply is elastic if price elasticity of supply is greater than one.

Employer discrimination. An arbitrary preference by the employer for one group of workers over another.

Equation. A mathematical expression that describes the relationship between two or more variables.

Equilibrium. A stable, balanced, or unchanging situation in which all forces at work within a system are cancelled by others.

Equilibrium price and equilibrium quantity. The price and quantity of a good at the intersection of the supply and demand curves for the good.

Excess demand, or shortage. The difference between the quantity supplied and the quantity demanded when the price of a good lies below the equilibrium price; buyers are dissatisfied when there is excess demand.

Excess profit. See **Economic profit**.

Excess supply, or surplus. The difference between the quantity supplied and the quantity demanded when the price of a good exceeds the equilibrium price; sellers are dissatisfied when there is excess supply.

Expected value of a gamble. The sum of the possible outcomes of the gamble multiplied by their respective probabilities.

Explicit costs. The actual payments a firm makes to its factors of production and other suppliers.

External benefit (or positive externality). A benefit received by others that arises from an activity undertaken by an individual, firm, or other economic agent for which the agent is not compensated in the market price paid for the good or service involved.

External cost (or negative externality). A cost that arises from an activity undertaken by an individual, firm, or other economic agent and that is borne by others because the cost is not incorporated in market prices the agent pays.

Externality. An external cost or benefit of an activity.

F

Factor of production. An input used in the production of a good or service.

Fair gamble. A gamble whose expected value is zero.

Firm. An organization that combines factors of production to produce a good or service or some combination of goods and services; a perfectly competitive firm produces one good of uniform quality.

Fixed cost. A cost that does not vary with the level of an activity.

Fixed factor of production. An input whose quantity cannot be altered in the short run.

Foreign exchange rate. The price of one unit of a country's currency in terms of another country's currency. Foreign exchange rates are determined in foreign exchange markets.

Free-rider problem. An incentive problem in which too little of a good or service is produced because nonpayers cannot be excluded from using it.

G

Game tree. See **Decision tree**.

Gini Coefficient. An index, which ranges between zero and one, of the amount of inequality in a population. When all persons have the same income (perfect equality) it equals zero. When only one person has all the income (perfect inequality) it equals one. Graphically, it can be represented as the ratio of the area between the *Lorenz Curve* and the line of perfect equality to the area of the triangle below the line of perfect equality.

H

Head tax. A tax that collects the same amount from every taxpayer.

Human capital. The skills produced by education, training, and experience that affect a worker's marginal product.

Human capital theory. A theory of pay determination that says a worker's wage will be proportional to his or her stock of human capital.

Hurdle method of price discrimination. The practice by which a seller offers a discount to all buyers who overcome some obstacle.

I

Imperfectly competitive firm (or price setter). A firm that has at least some control over the market price of its product.

Implicit costs. All the firm's opportunity costs of the resources supplied by the firm's owners and for which the owners do not make an explicit charge.

Income effect. The change in quantity demanded of a good that occurs because a change in the price of the good changes the real income of the person who purchases it.

Income elasticity of demand. The percentage change in the quantity demanded of a good in response to a 1 percent change in income.

Independent variable. A variable in an equation whose value determines the value taken by another variable in the equation.

Indivisible cost. The cost of an indivisible factor of production.

Indivisible factor of production. A factor of production that must be available in some minimum amount if a productive activity, even of minimal size, is to occur at all.

Inefficient point. Any combination of goods for which currently available resources enable an increase in the production of one good without a reduction in the production of the other.

Inelastic. The demand for a good is inelastic with respect to price if its price elasticity of demand is less than one.

Inelastic supply. Supply is inelastic if price elasticity of supply is less than one.

Inferior good. A good whose demand curve shifts leftward when the incomes of buyers increase.

Informational asymmetry. Occurs when two parties in a relationship do not have the same level of knowledge of product quality.

Invisible hand theory. A theory stating that under carefully specified circumstances, the actions of independent, self-interested buyers and sellers will often result in the most efficient allocation of resources.

L

Labour union. A group of workers who bargain collectively with employers for better wages and working conditions.

Law of demand. Other things remaining equal, people will purchase a smaller quantity of the goods or services they want as the cost of purchasing one more unit of them increases.

Law of diminishing marginal returns. A property of the relationship between the amount of a good or service produced and the amount of a variable factor required to produce it; the law says that when technology and at least one factor of production is fixed, beyond some point marginal product of the variable input diminishes.

Law of diminishing marginal utility. As consumption of a good increases beyond some point, the additional utility gained from an additional unit of the goods tends to decline.

Lemons model. George Akerlof's explanation of how asymmetric information tends to reduce the average quality of goods offered for sale.

Long run. A period of time of sufficient length that all the firm's factors of production are variable.

Long-run average cost. The lowest cost per unit that can be achieved for a given level of output when all factors of production, all costs, and the size of the firm are variable, but technology is constant.

Lorenz curve. When the members of a population are ordered from poorest to richest, the *Lorenz curve* is a graph which plots on the x axis the percentage of the population below a given income, and on the y axis the cumulative percentage of total income received by them.

M

Macroeconomics. The study of the performance of national economies and the policies that governments use to try to improve that performance.

Marginal benefit. The increase in total benefit that results from carrying out one more unit of the activity.

Marginal cost. The increase in total cost that results from carrying out one additional unit of an activity (Chapter 1); the increase in total cost incurred by producing one more unit of output (Chapter 5).

Marginal labour cost. The amount by which a monopsonist's total wage bill goes up if it hires an extra worker.

Marginal product. The increase in total output caused by an increase of one unit in the variable factor of production, holding technology and all other inputs constant.

Marginal (physical) product of labour (MP). The additional output a firm gets by employing one additional unit of labour.

Marginal revenue. The increase in total revenue obtained by producing and selling one more unit of output.

Marginal utility. The additional utility gained from consuming an additional unit of a good.

Market. The market for any good consists of all potential buyers and sellers of that good.

Market equilibrium. Occurs when all buyers and sellers are satisfied with their respective quantities at the market price.

Market power. A firm's ability to raise the price of a good without losing all its sales.

Microeconomics. The study of individual choice under scarcity and its implications for the behaviour of prices and quantities in individual markets.

Minimum efficient quantity. The smallest quantity of output that will achieve minimum long-run average cost.

Monopolistic competition. A market structure in which a large number of firms sell slightly differentiated products that are reasonably close substitutes for one another.

Monopolistically competitive firm. One of a large number of firms that produce slightly differentiated products that are reasonably close substitutes for one another.

Monopoly. A market with a single seller of a good or service for which there are no close substitutes.

Monopsony. A market with only a single buyer.

N

Nash equilibrium. Any combination of strategies in which each player's strategy is his or her best choice, given the other players' strategies.

Natural monopoly. A monopoly that results from economies of scale.

Negative externality. See **External cost.**

Negative income tax. A system under which the government would grant every citizen a cash payment each year, financed by an additional tax on earned income.

Nominal price. Absolute price of a good in dollar terms.

Nonexcludable good. A good that is difficult, or costly, to exclude nonpayers from consuming.

Nonrival good. A good whose consumption by one person does not diminish its availability for others.

Normal good. A good whose demand curve shifts rightward when the incomes of buyers increase.

Normal profit. The opportunity cost of the resources supplied by the firm's owners; normal profit = accounting profit − economic profit.

Normative economics. Economic statements that reflect subjective value judgments and are based on ethical positions.

O

Observationally equivalent workers. Workers of the same "type," that is, with the same generally known personal characteristics (such as age, education, gender, work experience, race, ethnicity, etc.).

Oligopoly. A market in which there are only a few rival sellers (each of which is called an *oligopolist*).

Opportunity cost. The value of the next-best alternative that must be foregone in order to undertake the activity.

Optimal combination of goods. The affordable combination that yields the highest total utility.

P

Parameter. See **Constant.**

Pareto-efficient. See **Efficient.**

Payoff matrix. A table that describes the payoffs in a game for each possible combination of strategies.

Perfect hurdle. One that completely segregates buyers whose reservation prices lie above some threshold from others whose reservation prices lie below it, imposing no cost on those who jump the hurdle.

Perfectly competitive firm. See **Price taker.**

Perfectly competitive market. A market in which no individual supplier has significant influence on the market price of the product.

Perfectly discriminating monopolist. A firm that charges each buyer exactly his or her reservation price.

Perfectly elastic. The demand for a good is perfectly elastic with respect to price if its price elasticity of demand is infinite.

Perfectly elastic supply curve. A supply curve whose elasticity with respect to price is infinite.

Perfectly inelastic. The demand for a good is perfectly inelastic with respect to price if its price elasticity of demand is zero.

Perfectly inelastic supply curve. A supply curve whose elasticity with respect to price is zero.

Point elasticity of demand. Elasticity calculated at a specific point on a demand curve.

Positional arms control agreement. An agreement in which contestants attempt to limit mutually offsetting investments in performance enhancement.

Positional arms race. A series of mutually offsetting investments in performance enhancement that is stimulated by a positional externality.

Positional externality. Occurs when an increase in one person's performance reduces the expected reward of another's in situations in which reward depends on relative performance.

Positive economics. Economic analysis that offers cause-and-effect explanations of economic relationships; the propositions, or hypotheses, that emerge from positive economics can, in principle, be confirmed or refuted by data; in principle, data can also be used to measure the magnitude of effects predicted by positive economics.

Positive externality. See **External benefit.**

Present value. The current value of an amount paid or received in the future. If people prefer current consumption to future consumption, a payment or receipt that occurs in the future will be discounted to a present value; when the annual interest rate is r, the present value (PV) of a payment M to be received T years from now is the amount that would have to be deposited today at an annual interest rate r to generate a balance of M after T years:

$$PV = \frac{M_T}{(1 + r)^T}.$$

Price ceiling. A maximum allowable price, specified by law.

Price discrimination. The practice of charging different buyers different prices for essentially the same good or service.

Price elasticity of demand. The percentage change in the quantity demanded of a good that results from a 1 percent change in its price.

Price elasticity of supply. The change in quantity supplied arising from a 1 percent change in price.

Price floor. A minimum allowable price, specified by law.

Price setter or imperfectly competitive firm. A firm with at least some latitude to set its own price.

Price taker (perfectly competitive firm). A firm that can exert no perceptible influence over the price of the product it sells.

Prisoner's dilemma. A game in which each player has a dominant strategy, and when each plays it, the resulting payoffs are smaller than if each had played a dominated strategy.

Private good. One for which nonpayers can easily be excluded and for which each unit consumed by one person means one fewer unit is available for others.

Producer surplus. The economic gain of the sellers of a product as measured by the cumulative difference between the price received and their respective reservation prices.

Production function. A technological relationship between inputs and outputs.

Production possibilities curve. A graph that describes the maximum amount of one good that can be produced for every possible level of production of the other good.

Productivity. Units of output per hour divided by units of input per hour.

Profit. The total revenue a firm receives from the sale of its product minus all costs—explicit and implicit—incurred in producing it. See **Economic profit**.

Profit-maximizing firm. A firm whose primary goal is to maximize the difference between its total revenues and total costs.

Progressive tax. A tax in which the proportion of income paid in taxes rises as income rises.

Proportional income tax. A tax under which all taxpayers pay the same proportion of their incomes in taxes.

Public good. A good or service that, to at least some degree, is both nonrival and nonexcludable.

Q

Quintile. That portion of a group of individuals that contains one-fifth of the total.

R

Rational person. Someone with well-defined goals who tries to fulfill those goals as best he or she can.

Rational spending rule. The rule that in order to maximize the total utility a consumer can derive from a fixed budget, spending must be allocated across goods so that marginal utility per dollar is the same for each good.

Rationing function of price. Distributes scarce goods to those consumers who value them most highly.

Real price. Dollar price of a good relative to the average dollar price of all other goods and services.

Regressive tax. A tax under which the proportion of income paid in taxes declines as income rises.

Rent-seeking. The socially unproductive efforts of people or firms to win a prize.

Reservation price. See **Demander's reservation price** and **Seller's reservation price**.

Rise. In a straight line, the vertical distance the straight line travels between any two points that corresponds to the horizontal distance (run). See **Slope**.

Risk-averse person. Someone who would refuse any fair gamble.

Risk-neutral person. Someone who would accept any gamble that is fair or better than fair.

Run. In a straight line, the horizontal distance that corresponds to the vertical distance the straight line travels between any two points (rise). See **Slope**.

S

Scale. The size of a firm relative to other possible sizes of firms serving a particular market.

Seller's reservation price. The lowest price a supplier will accept in return for providing a good or service.

Shortage. See **Excess demand**.

Short run. A period of time sufficiently short that at least one of the firm's factors of production cannot be varied.

Short-run cost-minimizing quantity of output. The quantity of output at which a factory reaches minimum average total cost.

Short-run shutdown point. A firm's minimum average variable cost; if price drops below minimum average variable cost, the firm will minimize its losses by shutting down.

Side payment. A payment made from one party to another in compensation for an external cost or benefit.

Slope. In a straight line, the ratio of the vertical distance the straight line travels between any two points (*rise*) to the corresponding horizontal distance (*run*).

Statistical discrimination. The practice of making judgments about the quality of people, goods, or services based on the characteristics of the groups to which they belong.

Stock. A claim to partial ownership of a firm; also called equity.

Substitutes. Two goods are substitutes in consumption if an increase in the price of one causes a rightward shift in the demand curve for the other.

Substitution effect. The change in quantity demanded of a good whose relative price has changed that occurs when a consumer's real income is held constant.

Sunk cost. A cost that is beyond recovery at the moment a decision must be made.

Supplier's reservation price. See **Seller's reservation price**.

Supply curve. A curve or schedule showing the total quantity of a good that sellers want to sell at each price.

Surplus. See **Excess supply**.

T

Technical efficiency in production. A condition that occurrs when the least possible amount of inputs is used to produce a given level of output.

Time value of money. The fact that a given dollar amount today is equivalent to a larger dollar amount in the future, because the money can be invested in an interest-bearing account in the meantime.

Total economic surplus. The total economic surplus in a market is the sum of all the individual economic surpluses gained by buyers and sellers who participate in the market.

Total expenditure = total revenue. The dollar amount consumers spend on a product is equal to the dollar amount sellers receive.

Tragedy of the commons. The tendency for a resource that has no price to be used until its marginal benefit falls to zero.

U

Ultimatum bargaining game. One in which the first player has the power to confront the second player with a take-it-or-leave-it offer.

Unattainable point. Any combination of goods that cannot be produced using currently available resources.

Unit elastic. The demand for a good is unit elastic with respect to price if its price elasticity of demand is equal to one.

Utilitarianism. A moral theory in which the right course of action is the one that results in the highest total utility.

V

Value of marginal product of labour (*VMP*). The dollar value of the additional output a firm gets by employing one additional unit of labour.

Variable. A quantity that is free to take a range of different values.

Variable cost. A cost that varies with the level of an activity; any cost that changes as the firm changes its output.

Variable factor of production. An input whose quantity can be altered in the short run.

Vertical intercept. In a straight line, the value taken by the dependent variable when the independent variable equals zero.

W

Winner-take-all labour market. A market in which small differences in human capital translate into large differences in pay.

Index